OBLIGATIONS OF CITIZENSHIP
AND DEMANDS OF FAITH

OBLIGATIONS OF
CITIZENSHIP
AND DEMANDS OF FAITH

RELIGIOUS ACCOMMODATION IN
PLURALIST DEMOCRACIES

Edited by Nancy L. Rosenblum

PRINCETON UNIVERSITY PRESS

PRINCETON, NEW JERSEY

LIBRARY OF CONGRESS CATALOGING-IN-PUBLICATION DATA

OBLIGATIONS OF CITIZENSHIP AND DEMANDS

OF FAITH : RELIGIOUS ACCOMMODATION IN PLURALIST

DEMOCRACIES / EDITED BY NANCY ROSENBLUM.

P. CM.

INCLUDES BIBLIOGRAPHICAL REFERENCES AND INDEX.

ISBN 0-691-00707-1 (CLOTH : ALK. PAPER) —

ISBN 0-691-00708-X (PBK. : ALK. PAPER)

1. RELIGION AND POLITICS.   2. DEMOCRACY—RELIGIOUS ASPECTS.

I. ROSENBLUM, NANCY L., 1947–

BL65.P7 O36 2000   322′.1—DC21   99-04917

THIS BOOK HAS BEEN COMPOSED IN GALLIARD

THE PAPER USED IN THIS PUBLICATION MEETS THE

MINIMUM REQUIREMENTS OF ANSI/NISO Z39.48-1992

(R1997) (*PERMANENCE OF PAPER*)

WWW.PUP.PRINCETON.EDU

PRINTED IN THE UNITED STATES OF AMERICA

1   3   5   7   9   10   8   6   4   2

1   3   5   7   9   10   8   6   4   2

(Pbk.)

CONTENTS

102609

ACKNOWLEDGMENTS

THIS VOLUME grew out of a conference entitled "Law and Religion: the Obligations of Citizenship and the Demands of Faith" held at Brown University in April 1998. I would like to thank the Brown University Lectureship Committee and the Departments of Political Science, Philosophy, and Religious Studies for supporting this meeting. Lucas Swaine helped with the organization and brought his dissertation research and expertise to bear on the proceedings. I am also grateful to my undergraduate students in courses in political theory and constitutional law for their engagement in these issues, provocative questions, and faithful attendance at this event. Their enthusiasm is inspiring. Ann Wald shepherded the manuscript through the review process with her usual wisdom and efficiency.

Chapter 1 is adapted from "Quiet Faith," from *One Nation, After All*, by Alan Wolfe, copyright © 1998 by Alan Wolfe. Used by permission of Viking Penguin, a division of Penguin Putnam Inc.

Chapter 12 is adapted from "The Role of Religion," from *Women and Human Development: The Capabilities Approach*, by Martha Nussbaum, copyright © 2000 by Cambridge University Press. Reprinted with the permission of Cambridge Univeristy Press.

OBLIGATIONS OF CITIZENSHIP
AND DEMANDS OF FAITH

INTRODUCTION

PLURALISM, INTEGRALISM, AND POLITICAL THEORIES
OF RELIGIOUS ACCOMMODATION

Nancy L. Rosenblum

THIS BOOK is about religion and law in contemporary democracies and in democratic theory. A chronicle of successive challenges to liberal democracy in this century suggests that religious challenges are the most pervasive and powerful today, supplanting Marxism and other political ideologies. Worldwide, religious beliefs provide perspectives for diagnosing democratic ills and touchstones for constitutional reform and public policy. Religious challenges are brought by minority ethnic communities claiming some dimension of autonomy from the decisions of democratic majorities. They are brought by majority faiths, asserting themselves against what they see as a hostile or indifferent secular order. Challenges also arise from more diffuse conflicts of values, or "culture wars."

Militant secularists fight to keep religion out of political arenas and public coffers, and believers fight back, both sides firing accusations and threats and both sides claiming not victory but vulnerability. Some believers charge that secular democracy demonizes faith or offensively relegates it to the margins, demoting them to "second class citizens." They insist that dominant public norms amount to a civic religion, constituting nothing less than an official Establishment. They argue for exemptions from general laws, for other forms of accommodation, and for varying degree of autonomy and jurisdiction over the affairs of their members. For their part, some advocates of strong democracy see secular citizenship under siege. They prescribe stern measures to assert the priority of democratic values in public life and to enhance civic identity, among other things by limiting accommodation of religious groups or requiring that the internal organization and activities of religious associations conform to public principles of justice. Mutual feelings of vulnerability and self-defensiveness are only exacerbated when both religious and political groups are fluid and have difficulty keeping a firm hold on their members. In the United States, every side sees itself as fragile, the object of hostility, and politically disadvantaged—logically so, since when it comes to religion (and irreligion) minority status is universal.

One of the tasks of political theory is to refuse to take at face value alarmist proclamations of either religious or democratic decline, and to think soberly about the conditions that actually threaten the viability of particular religious communities on the one hand and the stability and legitimacy of particular democratic governments on the other. This is the prelude to the difficult normative task of drawing the proper bounds of democracy and religion, and justifying accommodation.

Ideally, of course, a happy congruence obtains between religious and political mandates. Ideally, civic and religious opinions and the laws of civil and religious polities are reciprocally supportive. Then, citizens enjoy a "reflective equilibrium" between their religious beliefs and democratic values, and political principles rooted in religious doctrine and history are expressed in public life in a form that strengthens common ground. In fact, the view that citizenship and faith are mutually reinforcing is more common than the current temper sometimes suggests. That is why political theorists reflect not only on tensions between obligations of citizenship and demands of faith but also on the ways in which religion complements and supports democratic citizenship, or compensates for acknowledged limitations of democratic government and civic identity.

The authors of these essays advocate different ways of carving out and justifying the proper bounds of "church and state" in religiously pluralist democracies. The contributors are often in sharp disagreement with one another. But they all write from within democratic theory. They recognize the painfulness of conflict between obligations of citizenship and demands of faith for men and women, personally and individually. They all oppose absolute separation between religion and public life. They share the aim of democratic accommodation of religion, carefully attending to national differences in the role religion plays in particular democratic societies and political institutions. The authors also reject strong versions of "integralist" claims about the religious basis of moral and civic virtue and strong versions of the "integralist" goal of a uniform and seamless identity between citizenship and faith. An overview of these essays, accenting the themes that tie them together, is the subject of the final section below.

My main objective in this introduction is to consider the changed conditions that are at work today unsettling democratic accommodations of religion and inspiring contemporary reflection on this enduring theme. The contemporary context is marked by three changes: an explosion of religious pluralism; an increase in government activism effecting religious associations—both coercive regulations and subsidies, benefits, and inducements; and the prominence of "integralism," or the push for a "religiously integrated existence." Before turning to these developments, I want to emphasize a distinctive feature of the essays in this volume: the authors' attention to the rich array of legal norms and jurisdictions, civil and religious, and to the crucial part legal pluralism plays in shaping this subject.

Legal Pluralism

As we would expect, many of the essays address constitutional questions of religious free exercise and autonomy for religious groups; they focus on key legal cases in both American and comparative law. But constitutional law is only one element of legal pluralism. The proliferation of religious beliefs and practices and of civic obligations that impinge on them are rooted in a variety of systems of law—municipal and international law, constitutional law and the internal laws of religious communities. We see that "higher law" exists both "above" and "below" state constitutions and legislation. In the absence of either an agreed on hierarchy or a stable nesting arrangement, tension between obligations of citizenship and demands of faith often takes the form of competing authorities, jurisdictions, and conflicts of rights, and results periodically in "warring sovereignties."[1] Moreover, "the force of law and the empire of opinion" (to truncate a familiar line from Rousseau) remind us that both the obligations of citizenship and the demands of faith are experienced as imperatives that operate through law and authoritative commands as well as through other forms of cultural expression. Plainly, political theory misses an essential dimension of the subject if it disregards the layers of law within which tensions between democracy and religion arise and resolution must take place.

Consider four dimensions of legal pluralism.

Whether or not democracies embrace official religious establishments, they promise toleration and a reasonable degree of impartiality among faiths, guaranteed by *constitutional law*. Both the exemption of religious groups from uniform public obligations and the distribution of public benefits to religion raise constitutional issues. Within these constitutional bounds, however, a broad field for democratic decision making exists, and *national legislation* impinges on religion both directly and indirectly, as governments go about their normal business of imposing regulations and meting out benefits. Legislatures often have considerable authority to accommodate religion (or not)—to exempt them from the requirements of antidiscrimination law, for example. Indeed, the competing authority of the force of law as interpreted by courts and the empire of public opinion as expressed in political arenas is an important part of this subject. One current example is the U.S. Congress's response to the Supreme Court's decision in *Employment Division v. Smith*, the Religious Freedom Restoration Act, and the Court's decision in *City of Boerne v. Flores* that the Act was unconstitutional. This scenario provides a window onto alternative views of the extent to which democracy should accommodate faith, and onto vying accounts of the authority and relative institutional competence of courts and legislatures to oversee these settlements.[2]

Constitutional and municipal law do not exhaust the elements of legal pluralism. For their part, *religious associations are juris generative*. They advance the general principle of religious self-government over their communal arrangements. (At the limit they claim exclusive authority over believers, insisting that government deal only with the religious community, not with its individual members directly.) They claim authority to decide for themselves free from state interference not only matters of worship and doctrine but also the structure of religious authority, ownership and control of property, decisions to appoint, fire, and defrock clergy, and to admit and discipline members. One aspect of the claim of religious autonomy is freedom to designate which activities are properly religious rather than secular (hiring nonclerical employees, for example, or a business enterprise run as a mission) and therefore deserving of democratic deference to the laws of the "religious polity." Religious laws based on sacred texts, traditions, codes, and the directives of religious authorities are often taken as commands, sometimes unquestioningly. They may be congruent with public principles of justice or sanction practices adverse to norms of equality or due process. In some cases they give rise to overt resistance to civic obligations. It is also clear that religious laws are not necessarily restricted to subcommunities or associations; religious authorities may have a transhistorical and transnational character that reaches across borders in a way that political authority does not.

In some democracies *religious law supplements or serves in place of uniform civil law*. Governments afford religion legal jurisdiction and enforce (or allow ecclesiastical courts to enforce) doctrine in areas like the personal law of marriage and divorce, property rights, education, even civil status. One common result is religiously based subordination of vulnerable members, typically women. Particularly when religion is tied to organized national minorities, this dictates a system of "differential citizenship" based on ascriptive belonging. Governments may also allocate public funds and public offices on the basis of faith. The challenge for democracy is to see that religious law does not altogether replace civil law, even for members, so that religious groups do not have exclusive control over property settlements, say. The challenge is to ensure that citizens who resist the bonds of religious affiliation have the opportunity to switch affiliations or exit religious groups altogether so that their civil rights and daily conduct are not under the jurisdiction of clerical authority they do not recognize as binding.[3]

Finally, *international law* in the form of human rights covenants issued by the United Nations or conventions like those of the European Community provide universal higher law standards that identify rights governments are expected to enforce within their borders: collective rights like the right of national minorities to practice their religions, and individual rights such as gender equality. The effectiveness of international law owes less to the threat of sanctions if violations are not reformed from within than to the gradual incorporation of international norms into domestic law. Incorporation owes in part to appeals to international standards by religious groups against governments and to appeals by members of religious groups to their governments for protection against the edicts of religious authorities. Clearly, one difficulty in incorporating international norms into municipal law is the divergence between intergroup and intragroup justice: the fact that claims of justice among religious groups may be coincident with injustice within them. International law is an impetus to guarantees for religious liberty and some degree of autonomy for religious groups vis-à-vis government, including varieties of legal jurisdiction over members. At the same time, international law is an impetus to limiting the jurisdiction of religious law and restricting accommodation when communal practices frustrate the extension of basic civil and political liberties to all citizens. The problem is difficult because the political stability and legitimacy of democratic governments may depend on arrangements that grant considerable autonomy and legal jurisdiction to these groups.

Complicating the plurality of legal systems is the inevitability of divergent interpretations of civil law and of religious texts and doctrines. In the United States, for example, constitutional interpretation of the First Amendment religion clauses is ceaselessly contested both on the Supreme Court and within and among lower federal and state courts. Disagreement reigns over what sort of exemptions from general laws are mandated by the Free Exercise clause, when accommodation is permissible but not required, and when concessions to religious groups constitute an impermissible establishment of religion. Discretionary accommodations by the political branches are challenged by secularists who see them as preferences for religious groups over other voluntary associations and for religious conscience over other moral claimants. Similar interpretive differences are evident in the rulings of high courts in other democracies.

Interpretive pluralism is also evident when it comes to religious law and the demands of faith. If it is true, as Locke observed, that every sect is orthodox to itself, still, *within* groups orthodoxy is contested. There is radical disagreement over doctrine and practice among orthodox, conservative, and reform Jews regarding the authority of rabbinic courts and their relation to civil law in Israel, for example; among Catholics over papal directives that bishops may not issue binding statements that diverge from Vatican views on matters of doctrine or public policy, with consequences for church authority and for the everyday conduct of believers. In the United States, which is the most religiously pluralist democracy, schism and the continuous formation of independent religious groups is graphic evidence of ever-changing theology and authority.

Fissures also exist, though they are harder to discern, where officially recognized religious communities are represented by presumptively authoritative clerical voices pronouncing the demands of faith. There may be no ecclesiastical order for interpreting and administering religious law, or, there may be no institutional mechanisms for challenging acknowledged religious spokesmen. In any case, there are always divergent interpretations of religious law, as there are of constitutional and statutory law, and varying degrees of commitment to the dictates of religious authorities, from militant to passive to rebellious. Internal reinterpretation of religious traditions, among them readings of sacred texts and legal canons by women, is ongoing. Within every religious tradition and community there are always dissenters, including dissident clerics. Ferment and adversarial relations within, not just among, religious factions is as normal a part of living faith as the evolution of theology, or as divisions of partisan political opinion among active citizens.

Democratic theorists are divided about the priority of obligations of citizenship and its implications for accommodating the demands of faith. Believers are divided about the priority of the demands of faith and its implications for a public role for religion. These divisions are perennial. Nonetheless, we can identify two classic elements of democratic accommodation: voluntarism and separationism. We can also identify the particular changed conditions that unsettle democratic accommodations, raise new practical and theoretical challenges, and provide the context for these essays.

Voluntarism and Separationism:
The Traditional Elements of Democratic Accommodation

Tensions between the obligations of citizenship and demands of faith are as old as politics. They have shaped the course of modern democracy. Emerging from wars of religion, liberal democracy is defined by a commitment to enlarging the domain of personal freedom, which begins with religious toleration: "The cruelties of the religious wars had the effect of turning Christians away from the public policies of the churches to a morality that saw toleration as Christian charity."[4] Toleration refers to both an official policy of limited government and a moral disposition; the specific form toleration takes depends in part on the value attributed to it and ranges from pragmatic acceptance to principled respect to genuine enthusiasm for religious diversity. Modern democratic regimes cannot boast a continuous history of religious liberty or impartiality among faiths. Still, creating conditions that encourage mutual toleration among religious groups is a defining liberal democratic aspiration. So is progressive cooperation and respect between government and religion—whether that is facilitated in a particular state by the privatization of religion, partial establishment, or designated spheres of autonomy for religious communities.

Political theorists can draw on a canon of liberal democratic thought on the relation between religious conscience and community and civic obligation. Locke and Madison, Montesquieu and Tocqueville from the continental tradition are the authorities most often cited, along with theologians and locally important political and legal theorists less familiar to American scholars. As these names suggest, there is no unified democratic theory on religious accommodation. These theorists also remind us that religious settlements are the original and model for relations between government and civil society generally. Of course, the great historical lessons of liberal democratic regimes are as much pragmatic as principled. Political theorists can draw on this history with its armory of well-grounded, finely contextual reasons for accommodating conscience and communities of faith, and its arsenal of justifications for setting limits to accommodation as well. Theory and practice converge on two key elements: voluntarism and separationism.

· · · · ·

It would be wrong to identify religious voluntarism with the "protestantized" formula that prescribes how people come to have "beliefs that save," which is one basis for Locke's argument in *A Letter Concerning Toleration*. Membership in religious groups may not be best described as consensual and a matter of unfettered individual choice, either; it may be ascriptive or characterized as an imperative. Voluntarism means, instead, that membership is not determined by public law, and that religious associations are constrained from exercising coercive political authority over their members and outsiders. The internal laws of groups may be powerful, command obedience, and regulate members' lives in minute ways, but they are not legally coercive.[5] Whatever jurisdiction they have, it is not political authority. Religious groups cannot make their demarcations of who belongs obligatory; they cannot require those they claim as their own to affirm or maintain membership. The critical guarantee of voluntarism is that important civil and political rights are not conditional on professing a particular set of beliefs, or any belief.

That is why voluntarism requires a minimum of separationism. Separationism is never absolute, of course; the "wall" between church and state is permeable and moveable; it shifts all the time (though religious groups sometimes subscribe to a rigid doctrine of separate spheres and seek detachment in their own perfectionist community). For the most part, separationism simply says that government and religion need mutual protection from certain kinds and degrees of intervention and control. The general purpose of some separation of spheres is clear. It secures religion from attempts by government to dictate doctrines and practices and to interfere with or inhibit religious self-government. It secures government from domination by religious believers who would systematically shape policy in accord with particular tenets of faith or use public office to promote intolerance and enhance clerical authority.

The broad outlines of these arrangements in the United States are well known. Membership in religious communities is viewed as voluntary association—not surprising, where there is open and aggressive competition for believers and where shifting religious affiliation is commonplace. Faith is "privatized." Contrary to what opponents of privatization imply, this does not mean that religion is trivialized, that "God is a hobby."[6] Nor does it mean that religious exercises are closeted and banished from "the public square"; rituals, practices, and religious missions have always been a prominent part of organized social life. Churches are the original corporations of civil society, after all, and religion is a staple in democratic politics. Out of ignorance or sheer polemics, liberal democracy is often charged with mistaking religious experience as a "wholly private matter" for the solitary individual.[7] If the political history of toleration and accommodation of religious communities does not correct this misrepresentation, then insight into the protections afforded religious self-government should. Properly speaking, "privatization" means that religions must go without official recognition and imprimatur in the form of guaranteed representation or access to government power, legal jurisdiction over members, or authority over their civil status. Relative to other democracies, separation of church and state is severe in the United States; jurisdictions are strictly delineated and government aid to advance religion is prohibited. Official expressions of religion survive from an earlier era, but normally so diluted that they have been described as "ceremonial deism."

Comparative politics and comparative constitutionalism bring the distinctiveness of this American settlement into sharp relief. All democracies are characterized by some form of voluntarism and separationism, but they do not all aim at privatization. Democratic states may extend legal recognition and public support to a plurality of religions. They may subsidize religious activities in areas such as education and cede jurisdiction to religious authorities in the domain of personal law. They do not always insist on government neutrality among faiths or between religion and irreligion, either; a single established religion is often at the core of public ceremonies and recognized in national history. The range of justifications for these settlements is broader than those we find in American legal and political thought.

The last several decades have seen key aspects of voluntarism and separationism challenged everywhere. Settlements between religion and democracy have been disturbed by internal and external forces, sometimes international forces, for greater secularization and democratization of civil law on the one hand and by religious advocates of what I call "integralism" on the other. Classic defenses of separation of church and state and commitment to voluntary religious membership provide groundwork and inspiration for political theorists addressing these challenges, but they cannot simply be cranked up to meet the new demands of faith and the heightened obligations of citizenship. One contribution of this volume is to assess where standard elements of liberal democratic theory provide a sure guide, where they are taxed, and what alternative resources are available. The authors reaffirm voluntarism and separationism, but only after reconsideration, and they leave them in altered states.

I want to turn now to the changed conditions that unsettle accommodations between democracy and religion and provide the impetus to fresh theorizing.

Religious Pluralism and State Activism

Two changed conditions are best confronted in tandem. Religious pluralism and state activism have increased together. They jointly account for the many new kinds and occasions for tension between the obligations of citizenship and the demands of faith.

Consider first the explosion of radical religious pluralism. Since the Enlightenment, thinking about religion in western democracies has been guided by the experience of Catholic authority and Protestant dissent. These faiths no longer hold exclusive sway. In the United States, for example, the proliferation of faiths—through schism, invention of new religions ("American originals" like the Mormons and Jehovah's Witnesses), and importation of nonwestern religions—is ceaseless. Today there are literally hundreds of religious sects. Alongside mainstream churches, Christian and non-Christian, are traditionalist communities ("traditional traditionalists" and newly formed "functionally traditionalist" groups), "first generation religions," and charismatic groups whose apocalyptic revelations are live and present, not safely in the past. Rajneesh Meditation Centers, the Society for Krishna Consciousness, the Nation of Islam, and Jews for Jesus can appear positively familiar beside Satanic cults, devotees of New Age spirituality, and groups in the thrall of psychotic prophets. Democracy must accommodate not only established religious associations with stable structures and institutionalized authorities ("organized religion") but also small, independent religious fellowships loosely congregated around self-declared leaders.

Religious pluralism taxes toleration, meaning the disposition as well as public policy, particularly when religious groups are territorially dispersed and people come up against faiths and practices they find alien and sometimes abhorrent in their daily lives. People confronted with myriad religious groups in their own figurative neighborhoods are required to exercise self-restraint, to suppress their fear and abomination, but too often religious pluralism provokes enmity and discrimination. Religious pluralism is inescapable because religious activities are not purely spiritual, circumscribed by associational life and restricted to believers. They are exhibited in virtually every social sphere from prayer in the workplace to rituals in the street to the host of affiliated charities and hospitals, business enterprises, family-counseling centers, broadcasting networks, and legal-aid clinics that seek to strengthen the commitment of supporters and win converts.

In short, contemporary demands of faith deviate from the modest Christian duties Locke described: "charity, meekness, and toleration." More and more they are removed from inward-looking matters of doctrine, worship, ritual, and authority. Ministries expand outward. Except for rare, genuinely closed and separatist groups, the idea that faith is relegated to the private lives of individuals ("privatization" misconceived) is plainly misleading.

·   ·   ·   ·   ·

By itself, the proliferation of faiths imposing a multiplicity of obligations on followers enlarges the domain of free exercise claims beyond the known boundaries. It increases the number and kind of government actions that can be said to impose a burden on religion. At the same time that religious pluralism increases, so do the obligations of citizenship. In the course of enacting general laws for legitimate secular purposes, governments impose obligations in their sovereign capacity as lawmakers and regulators. These regulations inevitably touch on some exercise of faith and on the sphere of some clerical authority. Governments also impact religion indirectly in their expanding capacities as patrons, sponsors, proprietors, educators, and participants in the marketplace. Governments at every level pursue religious groups with regulations and entice them with subsidies and partnerships, once again making comfortable "privatization" of religion impossible even for groups that would retreat from public life if they could.

The result of hyper-interaction between a plurality of religious groups and active government is that believers develop new accounts of burdens on religion and feel compelled to defend new and expansive parameters of religious freedom. Claims for religious exceptions to general laws arise in every area, from zoning to exemption from the nondiscrimination requirements of federal and state employment law. Until recently free exercise claims in the United States were brought mainly by "marginal" religious groups—Old Order Amish, Jehovah's Witnesses, Seventh Day Adventists, Orthodox Jews, Muslims, and Native American churches. With the expansion of government regulation, few groups are immune, and political alliances across faiths are common. Religious groups assert the necessity of exemptions if their communities are to survive and flourish. They resist government interference with activities that are only tangentially related to religious belief, ritual, or authority *on principle*, in terms of a general right to autonomy. The combination of religious pluralism and government activism spurred Justice Scalia of the U.S. Supreme Court to take a strong stand against what he portrayed as an avalanche of religious opt-outs from civic obligations and a slippery slope into ungovernability

A further development pushes the bounds of accommodation. Government activism extends beyond coercive regulation to providing groups of all kinds with benefits and subsidies, patronage and inducements. Religious associations want not only exemption from certain obligations but also a share of public benefits, and courts and legislatures are forced to articulate the grounds on which they extend or deny public funding for the activities of religious groups in specific areas. In the United States, strictures have ruled out direct government aid for the advancement of religion, or proselytizing. When does public support constitute impermissible establishment? One consideration is whether public funds remain under government control or are under the sole control of religious authorities. Another is whether the conditions accompanying government benefits threaten religious autonomy. Yet another is whether support causes government to be identified with one or any religion and seen as endorsing one or any faith. But no general theory of separationism and no single standard of impermissible government "entanglement" with religion guides thinking about whether and under what conditions aid amounts to an establishment of religion.

The deeper challenge posed by advocates of public support for religion comes from the claim, often explicit today, that democracy has a positive responsibility for religion that goes beyond toleration and free exercise. The state's care for religion is not restricted to care for religious freedom, in this view. Rather, government is responsible for insuring the conditions for religious flourishing. We are familiar with the charge that sometimes wittingly, sometimes not, sometimes covertly under the guise of neutrality, sometimes as a secular creed promulgated in public schools and rituals, public policy undermines religion. At a minimum, the argument continues, government must refrain from policies that have the effect of weakening religion and threatening the viability of faith-based groups. Nothing is more difficult than actually assessing whether public measures cause religious decline. (Nothing, that is, except deciding what government activities are justifiable regardless of their effects on faith.) But some advocates today go even further and would have government actively support either a single faith or vigorous religious pluralism.

It is not hard to see why democracies ought to disclaim responsibility for relieving religion of *all* publicly imposed burdens and from the deleterious effects of obligations, however general and indirect. Clearer still, democratic governments ought to disclaim responsibility for the viability of communities of faith, much less for religious flourishing. It would be a taxing public obligation, given the proliferation of groups and individuals that would sincerely claim to be religious and solicit official recognition and support. It would aggravate conflict among religious groups and between them and secular associations, a point to which I will return. It would require democracy to support groups whose tenets and practices are incongruent with public norms and principles of justice, including some overtly opposed to liberal democracy. Above all, the viability of religion minimally entails a sustaining number of willing members; for democracy to seek to preserve any or every religious association, that is, to support proselytizing and authority, crosses the line of separationism.

The current tendency to cast government as the guardian of religion and to urge democratic responsibility for the flourishing of religious associations is remarkable. It takes a certain historical myopia and lack of healthy liberal mistrust of the state to contemplate tying religious flourishing to secular political authority and public policy. This is plain to believers committed to strong separationism as the best protection for religious autonomy and as a necessary safeguard against the corruption of faith. What accounts for the forceful advocacy of democratic solicitude for religion today? The explanation lies in a third changed condition, this one ideological.

"Integralism"

Perhaps the most significant development of recent decades is the emergence of a set of challenges to democratic government in the name of faith that I will call "integralism." Its defining characteristic is a push for a "religiously integrated existence."[8] At its heart is a sense of alienation, or a falling off from unity, which comes from being "forced" to live what is described as the divided life of believer and citizen. Integralists want to be able to conduct themselves according to the injunctions of religious law and authority in every sphere of everyday life, and to see their faith mirrored in public life.

The best-known and most severe integralist challenges are posed by fundamentalists—Protestant, Islamic, or Jewish. They are rooted in theology, religious law, and the injunctions of clerical authorities who may insist that religious commands are the supreme law, cover every aspect of life, and are binding on everyone in society. We associate these demands of faith with desecularization, antimodernism, or pervasive rejection of the profane world, and with the characterization of secular democracy as atheistic and nihilist. Integralism in its strongest forms conflates discipleship and citizenship. It entails an outright rejection of voluntarism and separationism. But in the United States and other democracies, versions of integralism are advanced by well-established, "mainstream" religious groups, evangelicals, and adherents of "new religions." By attending only to fundamentalism we are liable to miss the pervasiveness of integralist claims.

The striking thing about the array of integralist challenges to democratic accommodation today is that they are not justified in strictly theological terms or in terms of religious doctrine and law. Believers seldom advocate the political rule of clergy or the subordination of secular to religious authority. They are not theocrats. Religious challengers do not necessarily see themselves as antidemocratic. On the contrary, they insist that fragmentation and the falling off of unity affects all citizens, and that faith redounds to the benefit of nonbelievers as well as believers by reinforcing democracy. The warrant for integralism is as much civil as religious.

A common feature of the integralist challenge, then, is preoccupation with repairing fragmentation and restoring personal moral and political wholeness. Believers testify to the psychological stress that comes from living a divided life, feeling that they must split off an important part of their personality. They point to the political disadvantage they suffer, arguing that constitutional obstacles to public support for religious institutions makes them "second class citizens." Integralists in the United States move from the observation that "for vast numbers of American men and women, religion is . . . inseparable from the rest of social life" to the demand for changes in constitutional settlements and public policy.[9] They challenge one or another aspect of separationism and sometimes separationism *tout court*. They want some form of public endorsement of religion: either public recognition of the dominant national faith or, more ecumenically, an active regime of religious pluralism. That is why integralists may urge government to endorse not one particular religion but religion in general, or religious practice in general, or spirituality. For some, the truth of particular religious teachings is less at issue than the social value of belief and practice. Integralists see changes in accommodation as the condition for a unified, affective identity—believer-citizen—and for reinvigorated democracy.

A simple typology of contemporary integralist prescriptions for altering democratic accommodation of religion may be helpful.

The most common integralist position promises general *moral regeneration* through faith. Believers do not always insist that morality is impossible without religion, but they do insist that religious belief and association strengthen moral conduct and compensate for the failures of secular values, institutions, and authorities. "Silence religion, and the debasement represented by private and group egoism will follow."[10] The idea is to supplant social relations that are presumably based on rational calculations of individual self-interest with moral relations. For religion to provide meaning and moral guidance, the sphere of religious authority over adherents must be broadened, and religious community and identity must be strengthened. Integralists want society to recognize individuals' moral dependence on God. What does this imply for government?

The proposition that "the moral structure of religious community should be treated as an island of autonomy" is intended to protect religious associations from democratic policies that undermine their authority over members, not to recommend isolation, precisely so that religious groups can effectively cultivate moral dispositions that advance the public welfare.[11] That requires government deference to the religious task of correcting individual and collective moral failings. It begins with exemption from general laws and varying degrees of communal autonomy in hiring and education. It means that the Leviathan state should not aggregate to itself, destroy, or absorb functions that these groups naturally perform with greater moral authority, vitality, and legitimacy. At the same time, religious groups campaign for "a new deal for religion": government support for everything from parochial schools to religious missions. They seek assistance in pursuing their strategies "from below," building faith-based institutions and creating networks of social services, schools, businesses, and media focused on individual commitment and redemption.[12]

The integralist position on public support is distinctive because it does not argue only for religions' share of the neutral distribution of subsidies to all groups providing specified public goods—tax exemptions for all charitable groups, for example, or support for all private schools, secular as well as parochial. Rather, integralists commend public support qua religious groups. The moral effectiveness of religious associations is said to depend on their uninhibited religious identity, precisely because they offer prayer along with job training, drug rehabilitation, schooling, and counseling. Briefly, this type of integralist challenge to separationism is justified by a mix of arguments about the intrinsic value of religion and utilitarian claims. Religion is vital to the solution of problems ranging from teen pregnancy to crime. Religious tenets are represented as improvements on secular business management practices. Shared faith and work as a "calling" are motivating factors that produce better performance in everything from sales to a victorious football offense. Koran study groups at Boeing improve quality. The whole point is not to water down faith-based practices but to encourage them. The emphasis is on religious exceptionalism rather than functional equivalence to other social groups.

In making the case for religion as a force for moral regeneration, integralists willingly trespass across two separationist boundaries that are more strictly patrolled in the United States than in other democracies. One is the denial of public support to religious activities aimed principally at advancing the faith. The other is granting public funds for programs that are under the control of religious authorities.

Advocates of a publicly endorsed moralizing role for religion assume a felicitous congruence between religious and democratic values. They also assume that government recognition and support for religious pluralism will increase political harmony. This is doubtful. When religious associations shift from the classic self-protective, separationist aim of exemption from burdensome public obligations and aim instead at public subsidy, ecumenical cooperation is likely to be replaced by sectarian division. Groups allied in support of a generous interpretation of religious free exercise and autonomy are more likely to collide when it comes to carving up public funds. After all, government support is ultimately inseparable from endorsement of the value, if not the truth, of religious tenets and practices. Citizens, believers and nonbelievers, are not likely to approve public subsidy for schools and social missions sponsored by the Nation of Islam, the Church of Scientology, or a just-formed charismatic "cult."

The emphasis of the first type of integralism is on the moral quality of social relations, rather than political roles and institutions. A second type of integralist challenge asserts a distinctively *civic role* for religion. In this view, religious groups promote the priority of responsibility over rights and entitlements. Religious associations are also cast as "public spaces" and sources of "social capital." They teach organizational skills and generate civic participation in ways that offset inequality of resources. They help citizens overcome the sense of intimidation that inhibits public involvement; they oppose political passivity. This integralist claim for public recognition and support has less to do with morality generally than with civic virtue in particular, which is why believers object to the perceived marginalization of religious associations as schools of citizenship. They "welcome the return of religion to the naked public square."[13]

In this spirit, integralists commend government support for religious schools specifically as a way of reinforcing democratic values. Of course, nothing in the argument for publicly funded religious education per se is integralist. The reasons invoked include parental rights, free exercise claims (secular or theologically based), and civil egalitarian grounds. The integralist strain emerges with the claim that families who believe that all of life should be understood in an integrated fashion "as subject to the sovereignty of God," for whom secular education is fragmenting, should be awarded funding for parochial education, that is, when avoiding personal division is key. Integralism emerges more forcefully still when the focus is on the civic value of religiously integrated education. Public support reduces alienation, in this view, and draws believers firmly into the democratic community rather than fueling detachment. A still stronger version has it that publicly supported religiously integrated education is actually a more reliable and effective form of *democratic education* than secular education offered in public schools. Because public education generally shies away from controversial comprehensive values of any kind, its civic education is "thin." By contrast, religious groups bring their own stories and sacred histories to bear in support of democracy, endorsing civic virtues and democratic institutions from their own points of view, and thickening the grounds of commitment to democracy.[14]

Arguing that religion enriches not only democratic education but also democratic discourse, civic integralists encourage political engagement, often via religious associations, on religious terms. By itself, nothing in political participation by religious groups challenges separationism or implies integralist aims. The necessity for boundaries between church and state has never put democratic politics off limits to religion. Religious groups have interests and opinions to add to the Madisonian mix, on issues ranging from abortion to education to immigration law. They may or may not adhere to the strict norms of theorists of deliberative democracy for whom political beliefs rooted in religious doctrine should be expressed in ways that advance "ecumenical political dialogue" and proceeds from common political principles.[15] (Of course, secular groups, too, decline to exercise the self-restraint of offering only strict "public reasons.") In practice, commentators see a steady course of assimilation when it comes to the political methods employed by religious participants in the United States. "Religious groups in America seem forced to choose . . . between adopting the techniques of secular . . . interest groups or else having no influence . . . on American public life."[16] Religious groups form or support political parties, direct the faithful to vote for specific candidates, wield mass media on referenda issues or matters facing legislators, and forge pragmatic alliances across faiths for lobbying and litigation. Evangelical groups join secular environmentalists in preserving the Endangered Species Act as "the Noah's ark of our day," and a broad range of groups made common cause in passing the Religious Freedom Restoration Act. Most importantly, religious groups perform classic liberal democratic functions when they enter political arenas self-defensively to insure toleration, publicize and resist oppression, protect the weak against powerful elites, curb careless and arbitrary exercises of power. They have always been vital checks on government.

That said, there is little assurance that in their self-appointed role as schools of civic virtue and players in democratic decision making religious groups will be benign. Insofar as religion is linked to civic as well as moral virtue, it matters what kind of religion claims a public role. In many democracies, appeals to particular religious identities and to enmity among religious groups is a part of electoral politics. Religious hate speech within religious institutions has political consequences. In the United States, armed "citizen militias"—self-styled patriots and minutemen—combine anti-Semitism and white racism with the strange theol-

ogy of the Christian Identity Church, to name just one. American ideologies of inequality and hate are almost always steeped in religion. The
appeal of these churches is precisely their ability to eliminate the disjunc-
ture between daily immersion in racism and conspiracism on the one
side and typical Sunday services preaching unity on the other: "it was
tearing them apart."[17] These faiths, too, promise integralism.

The severest integralist challenges, then, assert an exclusive connection between *particular* religious beliefs and national identity or civic
virtue. They argue that because of its truths, religion is the sole carrier
of value.

These elements mark the third type of integralist challenge, which demands public acknowledgment of *the sacred foundation of secular values,
law, and political authority.* From this standpoint, the Protestant or
Christian or Judeo-Christian (or Hindu or Islamic) foundation of democratic freedom should be officially asserted. Separationism is anathema
because of the need to imbue laws with the force of faith. The point is
not simply for religious groups to bring their moral considerations (and
collective interests) to bear in political decision making; integralist aims
extend beyond specific public policies that conform to religious imperatives (prayer in schools, tax incentives for particular marriage arrangements, outlawing abortion, and so on). The goal is a political awakening
to the religious foundations of democracy. This form of integralism encourages (though it does not entail) establishment. In any case, it sees
democracy as a religious commitment and religion as its sole guarantor,
whether democracy is conceived as a religious regime guided by a particular faith or by religiosity in general.

The first two types of integralism, moral and civic integralism, aim at
rejuvenating virtue through direct impact on individuals by building up
networks of faith and social works from below. By contrast, foundation-
alist integralism uses means calculated to get a share of political as well
as social power; its goal is to give religion a controlling place in public
arenas and public law. Toward this end, the faithful are urged to form
religious parties, support candidates who promise to rule with divine
guidance, justify postures in theological terms, and aim at political
power qua believers—in short, to alter the foundations of democratic
public life from above.

Foundational integralist challenges to democracy are less severe in the
United States than in democracies where religious communities are territorially based, religious affiliation is tied to socially and economically
differentiated groups, and religious courts have jurisdiction over areas of
personal and civil law. Moreover, in some democracies religious groups
use public resources to organize and finance political activities that
strengthen their religious and political offices; their aim is to make or-

thodoxy irreversible. At the extreme, integralism leads to attempts by insurgent groups to seize political power by revolutionary means.

Not all demands of faith are compatible with the obligations of democratic citizenship, even if they claim to be. Religious groups are not always committed to toleration. They are not always averse to conspiracy and violence as a way of exerting political influence. They may be millennialist, indifferent to the consequences of their actions, or desirous of martyrdom. The question for them is not accommodation between democracy and faith but the compatibility of democracy with faith. Where integralist challenges pose clear dangers to political stability and legitimacy, democracies will struggle to justify limiting the autonomy of religious groups. Governments may justify constricting the heart of free exercise by regulating religious speech and association as well as specific practices.

An Overview of *Obligations of Citizenship and Demands of Faith*

Today, these challenges, and the disturbance of democratic settlements with religion they entail, threaten to outpace political theory. Political and legal theorists are playing catch-up with religious pluralism, state activism, and integralist challenges. I don't mean to suggest that the subject of religion is foreign to democratic theory. There is ongoing commentary on the history of liberal democratic thought on the subject of religious liberty, discussions in contemporary theories of justice of how religion fits into the "basic structure" of a well ordered democracy, and evolving interest in religion on the part of communitarians, multiculturalists, and political theorists of "identity" and "difference." That said, there has been little sustained work, and fewer broad-based collections of work on democracy and religion.

One exception is the much discussed proposition in political philosophy that "public reasons" should guide democratic deliberation and that religious reasons should be excluded. The idea is that men and women should be ready and able to show that their views can be supported by secular "public reasons" because this is how citizens indicate their cooperation, their intention not to coerce others for reasons they cannot reasonably endorse, in short, their mutual respect. Through deliberation on the basis of "public reasons," citizens contribute to society's political capital. Political philosophers who oppose bracketing religion and advocate inclusive political discussion base their arguments on similar grounds. For them, expansive and inclusive dialogue is the key to reasoned respect. In this literature on democratic deliberation and religious belief, political theorists write in predominantly Rawlsian or critical theory idioms, and the status of religious beliefs is just one element of a general theory of how to justify democratic decisions.[18]

The essays in this volume cover a much wider terrain, and the authors come to the subject of democracy and religion from a wider variety of academic and ideological perspectives. The volume brings together political philosophers, legal scholars, theologians, and social scientists. These essays occupy a middle ground between ideal theory and empirical cases in politics and law. The authors are attentive to political circumstances and to national differences in democratic theory and practice. They take account of the particularities of constitutional and legal systems and of differences among and within religious groups. The contributors' overarching purpose is to explore whether and how democracies can justifiably accommodate the changing obligations of citizenship to the current demands of faith.

An overview of the individual essays provides a guide for readers and an opportunity to highlight the volume's themes.

The titles of the two opening essays—"Civil Religion Revisited: Quiet Faith in Middle-Class America" and "Public Religion: Bane or Blessing for Democracy"—forecast the authors' intention to reconsider strict "privatization," or exclusion of religion from public life. Both Alan Wolfe and Ronald F. Thiemann caution against alarmism about the decline of either democracy or faith. Both authors are sanguine that there is strong, reciprocal support between democratic attitudes and religious beliefs in the United States.

Alan Wolfe explains the results of his in-depth study of American middle class attitudes toward religion and public life and morals in "Civil Religion Revisited." The compelling question, in his view, is not whether religion is good for us—nearly all Americans think it is—but whether they think it is good for others. Wolfe reports that Americans are moderates; they exhibit humility and affirm modest virtues. They overwhelmingly reject absolutist beliefs that lead to excluding those who don't share their own religious commitments. They are disturbed about passing judgments on others' religious beliefs. They oppose the politicization of religion, and turn away from religious fanaticism and excessive zeal. The exception to this picture of tolerance and moderation is the issue of homosexuality and gay rights. Public opinion opposes not only gay and lesbian marriage but also teaching civil respect for gays and lesbians in schools. Nonetheless, Wolfe concludes, the commitment to tolerance among faiths and to separation of church and state prevails so that we can say the United States has a civil religion in the sociologist's sense—"the use of religious imagination to uphold and reinforce national traditions and institutions."

Ronald F. Thiemann writes about religion's meliorating role as a force for moral renewal, and gives an affirmative answer to the question, "Public Religion: Bane or Blessing for Democracy?" "Religious groups," he argues, "can provide a sense of individual motivation and communal involvement often lacking in purely secular government programs." Inquiring what makes public religion a positive force in pluralist democracies, Thiemann writes as a theologian and in a personal voice. (Although he reflects on religious truth from within his own Christian faith, he suggests that other traditions provide similar resources.) He argues that because ultimate loyalty and absolute love belong to God, other commitments do not fully define identity. The public realm of persuasion and power is not the final one, and Thiemann represents democratic engagement as "pilgrim citizenship." At the same time, because religious truth is not absolutist regarding earthly commitments, religious convictions do not determine choices in the public realm. The chief task of people of faith in democracy is to be "committed critics," to appeal to transcendent ideals to elevate our understanding of democratic values.

Wolfe and Thiemann offer correctives to preoccupation solely with tensions between obligations of citizenship and demands of faith; they find deep mutual support, which encourages them to avow the benefits of "civil" and "public" religion. The nature and scope of political accommodation of religion and the legal frameworks for accommodation are outside their purview. Essays by Michael W. McConnell, Graham Walker, Amy Gutmann, as well as my own, contribute to both constitutional interpretation and democratic theory by taking up the proper bounds of accommodation for the United States.

Michael W. McConnell represents a moderate version of what I have called the integralist challenge to democracy in "Believers as Equal Citizens." Under current law, he argues, American believers are unequal citizens, deprived of important public benefits by a restrictive interpretation of the Constitution's Establishment Clause. More important, with "one foot in the city that God has prepared for them," they experience divided allegiances and "citizenship ambiguity." This gives an advantage to citizens whose commitment to secular democratic norms is undiluted. McConnell indicates the gravity of the problem religious convictions pose for those who experience conflict between spiritual and temporal authorities, warns that a happy coincidence between religious and civic principles is just that, and proposes a political ideal that does the least possible violence to religious convictions. Although fragmentation is inescapable for men and women of faith, it is made particularly painful and unjust by the legal and political commitment to separationism. Instead of defining democracy as a secular state that enforces civic obligations as paramount (and grants exemptions as a matter of democratic discretion rather than right), McConnell would redefine democracy as a regime of religious pluralism, so that in his words, "to the Protestant it is a Protestant country, to the Catholic a Catholic country, to the Jew a Jewish country." McConnell concedes that "every citizen his own country" will weaken the common core of American identity, but he insists that the compensatory benefits to equal citizenship outweigh it. McConnell does not expand on the political contours of this settlement here, but he does indicate some implications of his model of democracy for constitutional interpretation. It requires a general right of exemption for religious groups from civil laws as mandated by an expansive interpretation of the Free Exercise Clause. It also requires interpreting the Establishment Clause to prohibit government policies that increase religious uniformity and to permit public commitment to religious flourishing, so long as it is pluralistic.

Graham Walker shares McConnell's view that secular democracy disadvantages believers. Secularism amounts to a pervasive establishment made more inescapable because it is unacknowledged and molds consciousness covertly. In "Illusory Pluralism, Inexorable Establishment," Walker analyzes McConnell's model of an all-inclusive regime of religious pluralism. On the one hand, the logic of McConnell's argument pushes in the direction of autonomy for religious groups, toward balkanization and anarchy. It is insufficiently attuned to the requirements of political cohesion. On the other hand, and contrary to McConnell's intent, the regime of religious pluralism has the opposite failing: it reproduces pretended liberal neutrality in another guise. McConnell's regime would require abandoning the professed goal of religious inclusiveness, Walker argues. Because democracy can only provide public support to communities committed to constitutional democracy and mutual toleration, it cannot be neutral among faiths. Indeed, Walker thinks that McConnell's regime of religious pluralism would likely mature into a regime of de facto Protestant establishment. Walker prefers overt establishment, be it secularism as "official public theology" or the establishment of a dominant faith, and he would amend the Constitution to eliminate the Establishment Clause altogether. So long as democracy constitutionally guarantees religious freedom for subordinate faiths, establishment is more respectful of difference than secular neutralism. A majority religious order may even invigorate groups that stand outside the establishment, strengthening their religious identities.

In "Religion and State in the United States: A Defense of Two-Way Protection" Amy Gutmann argues the other side: in support of separationism and a strong Establishment Clause for the United States. In contrast to theorists who are solely concerned with maximizing religious freedom, she advocates "two-way protection": for the state from religion as well as of religion from the state. So long as government acts for legitimate public purposes and laws are not intended to burden religion (though they may have that effect), the state need not have a "compelling interest" in order to restrict exemptions from laws on free exercise grounds. Gutmann would set severe limits on exemption and accommodation: neither religious nor nonreligious citizens should be permitted to override or disobey democratically enacted laws that serve legitimate public purposes. Without Establishment Clause restrictions, free exercise exemptions would result either in runaway precedents undermining democratic authority or in discriminatory precedents—granting exemptions to one religion over another or favoring the claims of religious conscience over the claims of citizens whose dissent from laws is based on a functionally similar set of moral convictions. Gutmann finds historical support for her constitutional reading; focusing on Madison, she argues that there was no original intent to grant a general right of exemption from civil laws. She also finds justification in the fact that a strong Establishment Clause, which guarantees that laws and programs serve public purposes and are not controlled by religious authorities, protects not only the religious freedom of nonbelievers but also the political freedom of the group's own members, who may not want to follow clerical authority on political matters.

My essay concerns the proper bounds of accommodation. In "*Amos*: Religious Autonomy and the Moral Uses of Pluralism" I take as my template Congress's decision to exempt all the activities of religious associations, secular as well as religious, from the antidiscrimination requirements of Title VII employment law. This is an important test of accommodation: it is a discretionary exemption for religion, decided by the political branch and aimed exclusively at religious groups rather than at a broad range of charitable or voluntary associations. It forces us to look beyond constitutional interpretation of exemptions required by the Free Exercise Clause or prohibited by the Establishment Clause (the focus of the next set of essays) and draws attention to the wide field of permissible accommodation to be decided on by democratic majorities. I consider first the Supreme Court's reason for upholding this broad exemption of religious employers from antidiscrimination law in hiring. The Court's account of a valid secular purpose is insupportable—solicitude for religious "self-definition" and the "viability" of religion—are too elastic to justify blanket deference to religious groups; they should be required to show a nexus between employment discrimination and some aspect of doctrine, practice, or authority. I go on to criticize arguments in support of nearly unconditional religious autonomy put forward by "pluralist" theorists as well as arguments by theorists of strong democracy who support legally enforced congruence between the internal practices of religious associations and democratic norms, "all the way down." I conclude by pointing to three considerations that ought to be decisive in justifying accommodations of this kind but are missing from political theory and judicial opinions: the effect of the economic leverage of religious employers on the free exercise rights of employees, the question of economic opportunity, and what I call "the moral uses of pluralism"—the singular importance of workplaces as schools of civic virtue. Both too much and too little autonomy for religious association can subvert the moral uses of pluralism.

The next group of essays continue the theme of democratic accommodation of religion but concentrate more closely on U.S. constitutional law and judicial reasoning.

Kent Greenawalt addresses the paradox at the heart of the religion clauses of the First Amendment: the guarantees demand that someone identify what counts as religion, yet if officials must define religion and assess the sincerity of people making religious claims, they are liable to favor some religions over others. "Five Questions about Religion Judges Are Afraid to Ask" is a critical examination of the judicial role. When it comes to determining religious truth or whether religious claimants are faithful to a religious tradition, the idea that courts should not make determinations is firmly entrenched, and Greenawalt indicates the importance of this restraint in a pluralist democracy. Harder to decide are questions about the sincerity of a religious claim (in cases involving conscientious objection or fraud, for example). Harder still is determining the centrality or importance of a particular practice to a religion and the allied question of whether a government action substantially burdens religion. Greenawalt rejects as too stringent a test of whether a government action creates an absolute conflict of obligations between practices compelled by religious and civil law. He rejects as too lenient reliance on the perspective of the individual believer. He defends an intermediate position and affirms the competence of judges to formulate a reasonable standard. On the key matter of defining religion for legal purposes, Greenawalt surveys alternative approaches beginning with single factor approaches; he indicates why each factor taken alone is untenable; and he proposes an alternative "definition by analogy," which has the advantage of allowing for flexible outcomes depending on the legal issue.

Aviam Soifer takes exception to Supreme Court rulings that have reduced free exercise protections for religion except in cases of overt discrimination among faiths. In "The Fullness of Time" he criticizes the Court for advocating a "New Formalism" that emphasizes jurisdictional grounds of separation of powers and the federal balance and demonstrates the justices' unwillingness to comprehend the perspectives of those who resist majoritarianism and invoke the Court's protection. The Court's latest decisions do two things. They limit constitutionally required exemptions and assign questions of religious accommodation to politics, thereby making religious liberty vulnerable to majoritarianism. At the same time, they forbid Congress from intruding onto the Court's turf as it did with the Religious Freedom Restoration Act, which would have required every level of government to show a compelling interest before denying free exercise exemptions to laws that substantially burden religion. The Court compounds its error, Soifer goes on to argue, by misreading the history of the Free Exercise Clause. Soifer's historical reconstruction diverges from Gutmann's. He examines Madison's proposed guarantee of "full and equal rights of conscience" as well as other appearances of the notion of "full liberty" and "free and full" conscience. The import of these phrases, in his view, is that religious liberty was considered absolute, limited only by manifest danger to the state. Soifer does not insist that the Framers' intentions should determine constitutional outcomes. Rather, he uses these propositions as touchstones to propose a unitary approach to the Religion Clauses. Soifer reads Madison's guarantee of "full" rights of conscience in the Free Exercise Clause and "equal rights" in the guarantee against establishment.

In "Let Them Eat Incidentals: RFRA, the Rehnquist Court, and Freedom of Religion," H. N. Hirsch joins Soifer in criticizing recent Supreme Court decisions. He joins Greenawalt in arguing that it is the Court's responsibility and within its competence to decide what constitutes an impermissible burden on religious exercise. For Hirsch, the *Smith* decision, which obviated the need for weighing burdens by ruling that the Free Exercise Clause did not shield believers from the "incidental effect" of "a generally applicable and otherwise valid provision," represented a dramatic departure from the proper standard. Thinking about what considerations the Court should employ in determining whether exemptions are constitutionally (and morally) required, Hirsch invokes its role as defender of vulnerable minorities. Although he agrees with the Court that Congress's attempt to direct constitutional interpretation through the Religious Freedom Restoration Act went too far, the Court's flawed reasons for striking down the effort to protect religion demonstrate why Congress thought it had to act. The Court contrasted the "notorious" discrimination against racial minorities that justified the Voting Rights Act with the burden on religious liberty Congress used to justify RFRA, characterizing the burden on religion as "incidental" and supported only by "anecdotal evidence." For Hirsch, this is a disregard for "social facts" that downplays the persistence of religious animus and hostility and glosses over the consequences for believers of carelessness and indifference on the part of political decision makers.

The set of essays by Gary Jeffrey Jacobsohn, Yael Tamir, Martha C. Nussbaum, and Carol Weisbrod continue the themes of the proper role of religion in public life and the parameters of accommodation. But they shift the discussion from the United States to comparative democratic theory and constitutional law.

Gary Jeffrey Jacobsohn's "'By the Light of Reason': Corruption, Religious Speech, and Constitutional Essentials" is a comparative study of the place of religious speech in public forums. Jacobsohn explores why offensive and controversial rhetoric about religion in the context of election campaigns, which is protected under U.S. law, may be found to constitute an illegal "corrupt practice" in India. A case decided by the Indian Supreme Court upheld a law prohibiting candidates from appealing to religion, race, caste, community, or language and from promoting feelings of enmity between classes of citizens on these grounds. In their ruling, the judges invoked a model of procedurally correct democratic deliberation based on "public reason" that excludes religious-based considerations. Jacobsohn proposes a better justification for this restriction on political speech grounded in the particulars of the Indian experience with secular constitutionalism. "Corrupt practices" entails a notion of corruption of the identifying principles of a particular regime. In India, Jacobsohn argues, the constitutional essential is principled regulation of social and economic inequality. Because a rigidly hierarchical social order is correlated with religion, and because deep structural inequalities threaten Indian democracy, inequalities are reasonably addressed through policies that limit religious freedom in ways that would not pass scrutiny in the United States. India's egalitarian aspiration is a constitutional essential, a "compelling state interest"that justifies constraint on religious speech.

Yael Tamir, too, explores restrictions on religious speech in "Remember Amalek: Religious Hate Speech." Liberal democratic assumptions about the benign character of religious speech assume that modern faiths have lost their authoritative, salvational, and expansionist dimensions and that they accept mutual toleration. In Israel, Tamir argues, this liberal optimism is unwarranted, and the question "Can one censor the Bible?" cannot be answered simply by invoking freedom of religion and freedom of speech. Should protection be afforded speech by religious leaders that uses religious texts to identify religious enemies and excite hatred? Tamir focuses on three cases before the Israeli Supreme Court dealing with religious hate speech by Jewish rabbis aimed at Palestinians. The Court agreed that the nature and interpretation of sacred texts were beyond its ken, but that the intention to incite made the religious teachings punishable. Tamir argues that the decision was justified. Religious hate speech should not receive more protection than other kinds of hate speech, or speech that incites violence. Indeed, she gives reasons why religious hate speech is more likely to produce harm than nonreligious speech in secular contexts and should therefore be supervised more closely. In small, closed, authoritarian religious communities the ideas and rulings of religious teachers have the status of commands that must be obeyed. In addition, words in a religious setting create a new reality: defining something or someone as sacred or profane is to make that person sacred or profane. Finally, the other-worldly aspect of some religions allows leaders to offer followers benefits and punishments of incomparable magnitude. Tamir concludes that tighter supervision and restriction of religious hate speech is justifiable not only in the public realm but also within religious institutions. Her essay makes the need to realistically balance concerns for democratic peace and stability against religious liberty vivid.

In "Religion and Women's Equality," Martha C. Nussbaum studies the tension between democratic commitment to religious liberty and the fact that autonomous religious communities often deny basic liberties to classes of people on the basis of race, caste, or sex. Her focus is India, whose constitution guarantees religious liberty, nondiscrimination on the basis of religion, and equality of the sexes. At the same time, religiously based personal laws of marriage, conjugal rights, divorce, and property create differential civil rights for Christian, Muslim, and Hindu citizens, and inequality for women. She points to the concurrent problems of intergroup and intragroup inequality. Nussbaum organizes her essay around three cases involving inheritance, polygamy, and divorce and maintenance. She considers the limitations of both secular humanist feminist and traditionalist feminist approaches to the problem and goes on to propose an alternative way of thinking about justifiable limits on religious autonomy. Nussbaum brings two principles to bear. The principle of "individual capability" says that a good for the group is unacceptable if it does not do good for each and every member. The principle of the "moral core" says that all major religions embody an idea of compassion for suffering—a principle that commends skepticism toward any religious claim that involves harm or patent cruelty and injustice, especially when it infringes on basic capabilities. Drawing on a standard from U.S. constitutional law, Nussbaum proposes that government may interfere with religion if it can show a compelling interest, and that protection of the central capabilities of citizens constitutes a compelling interest. Thus, singling women out for differential treatment in a central area of human functioning or in a way that stigmatizes and humiliates them gives rise to a compelling state interest in eradicating that discrimination. Nussbaum argues for a uniform civil code and for free egress from one religious tradition into another, for guarantees of sex equality within religious systems and parity among them. These requirements are not an assault on religious freedom, she concludes, but a deeper defense of its basic principle.

Carol Weisbrod brings us full circle to the opening theme of this introduction: legal pluralism. "Women and International Human Rights: Some Issues under the Bridge" begins with a dialogue between two kinds of lawgivers, Rex and Pontifex. For one, law is about universals and serves as a bridge between a main culture (or international regime) and a subordinate one. For the other, the world is filled with normative communities and sanctions and the question posed by legal pluralism is not hierarchy and subordination or settling conflicts of sovereignty but living together. "The central difference . . . is that Rex, who limits the word 'law' to those rules emanating from the state, has . . . little regard for what might be thought of as a group claim to be a lawmaker." Weisbrod fleshes out the sides in this exchange by demonstrating how each would address challenges to international norms guaranteeing women's rights that are couched as defenses of religious liberty. Her affinities are with Pontifex, that is, with appreciation of complexity, rejection of the view that international human rights imperatives must be invariable and nonwaivable, and refusal to minimize the difficulties of dealing with traditional practices. She urges practical provisional accommodation, and in a section that serves as a review of problems taken up by other contributors she surveys issues involving women's equality. Weisbrod concludes with an exhortation to see human rights, and civil law in general, as a bridge from reality to imagined alternatives. She cautions that progress is not only slow but also reversible: "If we are moving cautiously in relation to this issue, that seems only right."

Notes

1. Various Catholic and Protestant political theories form the historical background to this subject: from doctrines of sovereign spheres to subsidiarity to versions of federalism and pluralism. The British pluralist tradition is particularly relevant here, in particular the view that the state is a "community of communities" that must share sovereignty with all the self-governing sources of law within it. John Neville Figgis, "Churches in the Modern State," in *The Pluralist Theory of the State*, ed. Paul Q. Hirst (London: Routledge, 1989), p. 121.

2. 494 US 872 (1990) and 117 S. Ct. 2157 (1997). In *Smith*, the Supreme Court assigned "accommodation" of religion—constitutionally permissible but not constitutionally required—to federal and state legislatures. In *Boerne*, the Court ruled that with RFRA, Congress had overstepped its bounds. The chapters herein by Gutmann, Hirsch, and Soifer deal with the pivotal *Smith* case at length.

3. See Ayelet Shachar, "Group Identity and Women's Rights in Family Law: The Perils of Multicultural Accommodation," *Journal of Political Philosophy* 6, no. 3 (September 1998): 285–305.

4. Judith Shklar, "The Liberalism of Fear," in *Liberalism and the Moral Life*, ed. Nancy L. Rosenblum (Cambridge: Harvard University Press, 1989), p. 23.

5. This is not to discount the often powerful material and psychological means that groups have to hold members.

6. Stephen L. Carter, *The Culture of Disbelief: How American Law and Politics Trivialize Religious Devotion* (New York: Basic Books, 1992), pp. 22–23.

7. For an example of this misrepresentation, see Mary Ann Glendon and Raul F. Yanes, "Structural Free Exercise," 90 *Michigan Law Review* 477 (1991): "The individual rights/separationist/antimajoritarian approach prevailed even through the Burger Era," at 479.

8. Nicholas Wolterstorff, "Why We Should Reject What Liberalism Tells Us," in *Religion and Contemporary Liberalism*, ed. Paul J. Weithman (Notre Dame, Ind.: Notre Dame University Press, 1997), p. 177.

9. Glendon and Yanes, "Structural Free Exercise," 516.

10. Wolterstoff, "Why We Should Reject What Liberalism Tells Us," p. 178.

11. Richard Posner and Michael McConnell, "An Economic Approach to Issues of Religoius Freedom," 56 *University of Chicago Law Review* 1, 49 (Winter 1989). Some religious communities are truly rejectionist, like the Amish in the United States. Others are separationist only circumstantially: the Lubavitcher are separationists in the United States but challenge secular democracy in political arenas in Israel. Integralist demands, by contrast, are for inclusion and stronger bonds with political community as a whole.

12. The distinction between strategies from above and from below is Gilles Kepel's in *The Revenge of God* (University Park, Pa.: Pennsylvania State University Press, 1994).

13. Jose Casanova, *Public Religions in the Modern World* (Chicago: University of Chicago Press, 1994), p. 205.

14. Michael McConnell, "Education Disestablishment: Why Democratic Values are Ill-Served by Democratic Control of Schooling" (paper presented at meeting of American Society for Political and Legal Philosophy, Washington, D.C., December 1998).

15. The idea is widespread in political and legal theory; it has been worked out by Michael J. Perry among others in *Love and Power: The Role of Religion and Morality in American Politics* (Oxford: Oxford University Press, 1991).

16. Michael McConnell, "Religious Freedom at a Crossroads," in *The Bill of Rights in the Modern State*, ed. Geoffrey Stone, Richard Epstein, and Cass Sunstein (Chicago: University of Chicago Press, 1992), p. 139.

17. Pastor Pete Peters, cited in Morris Dees and James Corcoran, *The Gathering Storm* (New York: Harper Collins, 1996), p. 2.

18. See the essays in Weithman, *Religion and Contemporary Liberalism*.

1

CIVIL RELIGION REVISITED:

QUIET FAITH IN MIDDLE-CLASS AMERICA

Alan Wolfe

A SIGNIFICANT revival of moral inquiry has taken place in American academic life, especially among philosophers, theologians, and social scientists. At the same time, politicians and policymakers have either written best-sellers pronouncing on the moral state of Americans or introduced legislation designed to address it. Yet missing in all this attention is some sense of what ordinary Americans themselves think about major moral controversies.

In an effort to shed light on this question, I carried out the Middle-Class Morality Project. Two hundred middle-class Americans were interviewed in the Boston, Tulsa, Atlanta, and Georgia suburbs. I talked with them about God, country, family, the work ethic, civil society, welfare, immigration, race, affirmative action, the left, and the right. In this chapter, I will provide an overview of how middle-class Americans think about the role that religion ought to play in American public life.

Let me begin with Jesse O'Donnell, a navy wife living in Eastlake, California. "I usually don't have religious discussions with people," she told us when we asked her whether those who are not religious can still be good people. Mrs. O'Donnell is a Methodist and a Republican. As she sat in a coffee shop one evening not far from the stucco condominium in which she lived with her husband and two young children, still wearing the dark blue business suit she had put on for her job placing temporary workers, she reflected on how she was brought up in the 1960s. "We were always taught that you don't discuss religion," she said, before pausing to add, "No politics or religion."

Mrs. O'Donnell's upbringing, if we consult what sociologists and historians say about American religious belief in the years after World War II, was anything but unusual. From the moment suburbanization began to expand exponentially in the 1950s and 1960s, critics wondered whether strong religious commitments could be sustained in middle-class America.[1] All religions are different, and, despite ascetic origins, nearly all of them have made their accommodations with material things, but across the religious fault lines which divided America in the 1950s, one could hear the ubiquitous lament that suburbanization might not be good for the soul.[2] For Will Herberg, the leading writer on these questions at that time, people's willingness to go to church was not due to their inner convictions but to what their neighbors might think if they did not: "The vogue of Van Gogh and Renoir reproductions in the suburban home and the rising church affiliation of the suburban community may not be totally unconnected," he wrote. "Both may . . . be interpreted, in part at least, as the consequence of the craving for adjustment and conformity involved in other-direction."[3]

Each of America's major religions pondered the question of suburbanization in its own way. Protestant concerns, like Protestantism itself, were split: liberal Protestants such as Chicago Divinity School theologian Gibson Winter worried that suburban middle-class status would disconnect individuals from a larger social conscience,[4] while more conservative Protestants—one thinks of the eminent sociologist Peter Berger—simply could not image how suburban churches, given over to primarily social tasks, could wrestle with the deep theological concerns which lay at the heart of religious traditions.[5] Jews, the most upwardly mobile of America's ethnic groups in the years after World War II, moved from the city to the suburbs—or the "frontier" as it was called—in ever increasing numbers, but not without questioning whether the effect, especially among the young, would be to encourage intermarriage, always a threat to minority religion.[6] For the first generation or two after they arrived in this country as immigrants, Catholics tended to live in tightly bound city parishes; heavy investments in the creation of those parishes slowed Catholic out-migration from cities, resulting in substantial conflict with African Americans moving into northern cities from the South.[7] But suburbanization eventually did come to American Catholicism. While there may not have been a direct cause and effect, the fact that the period of suburbanization was also a period when the rates of those leaving the church doubled,[8] the number of men entering the priesthood declined, and parochial schools lost large numbers of both teachers and students indicated just how much suburbanization, in the words of historian Jay Dolan, constituted a "mighty challenge" for the Church.[9]

Fears that suburbanization would produce a religious decline were confirmed by the fact that church membership reached its peak in 1958 before beginning a steady decline until the 1970s, a trend that was particularly true of Catholics.[10] In retrospect we know that the decline did eventually stabilize. What was more important for the period of rapid suburbanization in the twenty years after World War II was not how many people would attend church, but what kind of churches they would attend.

The kind of religion that turned out to be most compatible with suburban growth was very much like Jesse O'Donnell's religion. Making religion a private matter to be discussed only reluctantly with others seemed to be appropriate for the way people wanted to live in these new communities outside the city. Suburban housing developments, no matter how vigorously they tried to attract people of the same faith, simply could not be organized with the same sharp religious boundaries as were the urban neighborhoods people were leaving. Children were finding the more orthodox religious views of their parents a hindrance to their acceptability in school and with friends. Commuting to the city during the day, men were available to their church only on weekends, reinforcing trends by which religious activity during the week was increasingly feminized. In such a world, one didn't talk about religion for exactly the same reason one did not talk about politics: there were too many diverse views that might lead to conflict, and conflict, in turn, would interfere with the imperative of building a new life in the suburbs.

Like Mrs. O'Donnell's family, the U.S. Supreme Court, in the decades after World War II, also fashioned an understanding that held that the American belief in belief was essentially private:[11] in your home, with your coreligionists, and in matters involving your own children, you were free to believe anything you wanted, but once you entered into public institutions, you accepted that such institutions would be neutral between religions—indeed, in later manifestations of the understanding, that they would be neutral between religion and nonreligion. No longer did Supreme Court justices claim, as Mr. Justice David Brewer did in a 1904 speech, that America was a Christian nation;[12] "Judeo-Christian," soon after he spoke, became the term of art, and even that one would come to seem exclusionary when significant numbers of immigrants who were neither Christians nor Jews began to arrive in America in the 1970s. Unlike other countries, in which religion and politics were blended, we would uphold the principle of separation of church and state and maintain our belief in tolerance among faiths. These tenets were compatible with the broad contours of what sociologists called "civil religion," the use of the religious imagination to uphold and reinforce national traditions and institutions.[13]

By the 1990s, however, when the Middle-Class Morality Project went out to talk with suburban Americans about the role religion played in their moral understanding of the world, this solution of relegating religion to the realm of private life seemed to be breaking down—both in the views of people themselves and in the decisions handed down by courts. America, in most accounts, was experiencing a return to tradition; one no longer content to accept that questions of faith were best kept out of the public realm. Not all Jews followed what had once been seen as an all but inevitable path from Conservative to Reform to Unitarian; orthodox, even ultra-orthodox movements blossomed, some of them in the very suburbs that were only recently believed to be hostile to such expressions of faith.[14] In the years after Vatican II, Catholics surpassed Protestants in both educational attainment and socioeconomic status,[15] with the consequence that "white Catholics are now very much a part of the established American middle class and upper-middle class life," as sociologists Barry Kosmin and Seymour Lachman wrote.[16] But even as third- and fourth-generation Catholics intermarried and became more secular, religion in the suburbs was revitalized by the presence of Hispanics, many of whom, arriving as immigrants, skipped over the city and moved directly to the outskirts.[17] The most public manifestation of the return to religion, however, was the huge growth in conservative Protestant sects that took place not only in the South but throughout America.[18] As the religious schism became not the one between Protestants, Catholics, and Jews but the one between the orthodox of all faiths and the reformers of all faiths, what most marked the differences between the two sides was the insistence by strong religious believers that unless religion became a more public force in American life, the country would slide into moral anarchy.[19]

While all this was happening, the Supreme Court began to tinker with earlier versions of its privatistic formulation, allowing the formation and funding of religious groups at public universities, for example, as some justices made fairly explicit their desire to seek new constitutional understandings on this question.[20] No sharp line between politics and religion could be found anymore: the Christian Coalition was formed to influence American politics primarily by gaining influence within the Republican Party,[21] with the predictable consequence of leading some on the left also to claim religious backing for their political ideals.[22] Nor was it possible to draw a sharp distinction between tolerant and secular America on the one hand and a religiously charged Third World on the other, as immigrants from the latter bring their faith with them to the former. At the start of the twentieth century, America's first culture war—which involved such issues as whether Catholic schools could be supported by government funds or whether communities could pass blue laws that prevented Jewish shops from opening on Sunday—was fought *over* religion.[23] In the new culture war that observers found brewing in America, the battle seemed to be taking place *with* religion, as each side mobilized (or questioned) God in support of its positions on poverty, pornography, and school prayers.

Once it may have been enough for the faithful to have had their own niches: Mormons had Utah, deeply devout Protestants the South and parts of the Midwest, and Jews and Catholics New York City (the secular elite had Cambridge and Berkeley). But questions about religious faith have become nationalized: the Supreme Court, in making sweeping rulings on such controversial matters as abortion, which applied to everyone everywhere, opened the door to a response seeking public affirmations of faith for everyone everywhere.[24] No wonder that the ways in which social scientists and social critics discuss religion at century's end are quite different from the terms used to characterize the emergence of suburban middle-class America a generation or two earlier. Worried that religion was losing its texture, critics now began to fear that people would take the word of God too literally. Accused just a few decades ago of excessive privatization, religion now was seen as invading the public sphere. Sectarianism replaced ecumenicalism as a dominant concern. A people who had trouble finding the time to pray now seemed to want prayer in schools. It is as if the social critics of the 1950s finally got middle-class Americans to take something seriously only to discover that when they did they took it far too seriously for the critics' comfort.

As a result of these changes, Jesse O'Donnell is not the only middle-class American talking about religion and politics in ways quite different than those taught by her upbringing. Religion has once again become a public issue in America. And because this country is a democracy, the public will, one way or another, have the final say on how public that issue should be.

Quiet Faith

Compared to other prosperous liberal democracies, Americans stand out for the depth of their religious belief;[25] a 1991 study by Andrew Greeley found that 94 percent of Americans said they believed in God, in contrast to 70 percent of Britons and 67 percent of West Germans. Indeed, polling data regularly yield results that suggest that Americans are among the most faithful people in the world:[26] 82 percent believe that the Bible is the actual word of God (although only 35 percent say that the Bible should be taken literally), 80 percent believe in the after life, 70 percent believe in the existence of heaven (compared to 57 percent who believe in the existence of hell), 79 percent say that God guided them in making decisions or that prayer is very important in their lives, and 63 percent think that religion can answer all or most of today's problems. When they respond to questions about their religious activities, twice as many Americans say that they go to church regularly

TABLE 1.1
Distribution of Religious Belief

	Strong Believer	*Believer*	*Nonbeliever*	*Insufficient Information*
Brookline	2	12	4	7
Medford	4	15	3	3
Broken Arrow	7	14	0	4
Sand Springs	4	18	1	2
DeKalb	7	14	0	4
Cobb	2	17	2	4
Eastlake	2	13	3	7
Rancho Bernardo	5	10	9	1
Total	33	113	22	32

as those who say they do not, 51 percent claim to pray every day, and 45 percent watch or listen to religious programming on television or radio. Even if we accept the well-established point that more Americans tell pollsters they attend church than they actually do[27]—and that televangelists claim more viewers than they can possibly have—there can be no doubt that church attendance is higher in America than it is in, say, Great Britain.[28]

The Middle-Class Morality Project, in keeping with its focus on public rather than private morality, was reluctant to probe too deeply into people's personal views, but we did ask people to tell us about their religious beliefs, so long as they were comfortable doing so. I then coded their answers depending on how strong those beliefs were. One coding category was relatively easy to establish: those who considered themselves religious nonbelievers.

One hundred sixty-eight of the 200 people interviewed in the Middle-Class Morality Project talked about their religious beliefs, and only 22 of those were prepared to use terms like "agnostic" or "atheistic" in describing themselves. (See table 1.1.) "I don't think anyone would accuse me of being religious," said one of the respondents in Rancho Bernardo (where, perhaps reflecting something about California, close to half the nonbelievers lived), but he was the exception. More often, people who talked about their lack of belief in God did so hesitantly, even defensively, rather than as self-proclamation. Ian Dodson, also of Rancho Bernardo said, "We're not particularly religious in this house . . . we're atheists probably," at which point his wife broke in, "Oh Ian, . . . good grief, I am not." The Drakes, who live nearby, call themselves atheists—"most of the things that people believe in, like the supreme being and the power and all that, I never see any real example of it," as

TABLE 1.2
"America has become far too atheistic and needs a return to
strong religious belief."

	Strongly Agree	Agree	No Opinion	Disagree	Strongly Disagree
Brookline	2	5	2	11	5
Medford	2	7	2	12	2
Broken Arrow	7	7	5	4	2
Sand Springs	5	12	4	3	1
DeKalb	4	13	2	6	0
Cobb	6	7	1	11	0
Eastlake	2	10	1	11	1
Rancho Bernardo	1	10	4	8	2
Total	29	71	21	66	13

Mr. Drake put it—before adding that "we believe that the Ten Commandments make pretty good sense." Militant atheists—those who insist that reason and rationality constitute the only sensible guides by which to live—are very hard to find in America.

But what about the other end of the spectrum: people who take their faith in God extremely seriously? In the way they respond to survey questions about heaven, God's existence, or the importance of church and prayer, Americans give every indication of being deeply religious. Comparative survey data reported by the political scientist Ronald Inglehart bear this out.[29] Asked whether morality was absolute or relative to specific circumstances, more people in Britain, France, West Germany, Italy, Sweden, and Canada said circumstantial rather than absolute; only in America was there a higher percentage for absolute (50 percent) rather than circumstantial (45 percent). Results such as those were confirmed by our survey, taken after we completed our more in-depth interviews with each of the people with whom we spoke; half of them, the same percentage as Inglehart's believers in absolute morality, agreed or strongly agreed with the statement that America has become too atheistic. (See table 1.2.)

One of the questions that we hoped the Middle-Class Morality Project would be able to answer is whether the United States is experiencing a deep religious revival equivalent to the earlier "awakenings" that have been so much a part of American history. If such a revival is indeed taking place, then the solution worked out in the years after World War II of privatizing religious belief should no longer have strong support in middle-class America. The fact that there are so few nonbelievers among our sample—and that so many insist on the need for strong belief—

suggests that this question should be answered in the affirmative. Yet just because people think that faith is important does not necessarily mean that they think the United States has slipped into the hands of secular humanists and requires more public affirmations of religious belief. The compelling question is not whether they think religion is good for them—nearly everyone thinks that it is—but whether they think it is good for others.

It should come as no surprise to discover that, in a country which prides itself on its religious heritage, there are Americans who believe that God provides an absolute sense of right and wrong binding on all people. The McLaughlins of Broken Arrow, Oklahoma, are among them. Jim McLaughlin thinks that a nation which believes in humanism—"the religion of academia," he calls it—will be in serious trouble. As the country gets "further and farther away from God, then we replace it with whoever's morals are in force at the time, and God is out of the picture. Then you have no absolute laws, you have nothing but relativism." Mr. McLaughlin uses a metaphor from golf to explain his point. If you slice your drive, it will continue to fade farther and farther off course. America is also off course, moving inexorably away from its proper target. "This nation was not formed by Buddhist framers of the Constitution; it was formed by Christians," he continues. That is important to him because "our whole nation was founded on the principles of God and God's principles are absolute not relative." Mr. McLaughlin wanted to bring prayer and the Bible back into the schools, "not just as literature," he emphasized, "but as a way of study." One of the problems with education today, he said respectfully but firmly to Maria, my research assistant, is that schools teach more sociology than religion. "If you went into the field of sociology," he asked her, "how much training have you had in religion? I don't really think that you've got a good foundation in that if you've gone through the typical educational process in sociology."

The Middle-Class Morality Project purposely selected the Tulsa area in which to conduct interviews because we wanted to hear from people whose ideas resonated with the revival of conservative Protestantism that has, in recent years, driven American politics, especially the Republican Party. In one sense, we were not disappointed; people in the Tulsa suburbs talk about their faith with more certainty than, say, people in Brookline, Massachusetts. But in another sense we were quite surprised, for as religious as the residents of Tulsa may have been, they were not as comfortable as Jim McLaughlin in expressing themselves in the language of absolutes. Being born again was important to at least one of them (although she also said that she did not regularly attend church). Another felt that groups like the Moral Majority had done some good for America. Yet very few of them—indeed very few of the two hundred people to whom we talked around the country—used words like sin, moral rot, decay, or Satan, terms that, whether fairly or unfairly, are usually identified with revivalist preachers, talk show hosts, and conservative Christians.

How many? Although it was relatively easy to code the category of nonbelievers, it was more difficult to make distinctions between different degrees of belief: clearly some people take their belief in God more seriously than others, and the coding principle involves finding the appropriate criterion which separates one from the other. In trying to determine how many of our respondents were as devout as Jim McLaughlin, my first inclination was to identify as a strong religious believer anyone for whom, like him, religion provided answers to questions of right and wrong so certain that anyone who did not share those convictions would have to be considered wrong, sinful, or unsaved. But that criterion turned out to be too strict to be very meaningful: only five, maybe six, of the people with whom we spoke would be considered strong believers if we had used it.

Such a coding principle would have eliminated from the category of strong believers Julie Skinner, a devout Mormon mother of six living in Medford, for Mrs. Skinner, like most of those with whom we spoke, did not think that there was only one way to God. "Most religions share the same basic values," she told us. "I don't feel good about one church coming out and saying, 'You're all wrong, and you're all bad.' . . . I don't believe in telling everyone else that they're wrong." It seemed more in accord with the way middle-class Americans understood their religious commitments to broaden the category of strong believers to include people like Mrs. Skinner—those who talked enthusiastically and with deep conviction about their specific faith and how it served as a guideline for their moral conduct, even if they did not think that anyone who did not share their convictions was immoral.

Based on that definition, religious belief in middle-class America bears a certain similarity, at least with respect to its distribution, to political belief: Americans are instinctive moderates who tend to seek the center on any important issue. Answers to questions about political belief often take the form of a bell-shaped distribution curve, with roughly equal small groups at either extreme and the large majority in the middle. This is true of religious belief as well: our responses, as table 1.1 shows, indicate twenty-two nonbelievers at one end and, even by the relatively loose definition I have adopted, only thirty-three strong believers at the other. Given that so many Americans do believe in God—after all, 146 of the 168 who indicated something of their beliefs are religious in one way or another—the question that concerned me is why more middle-class Americans are not like Jim McLaughlin. What is it that makes so many middle-class Americans say that, no matter how religious they are, they are still unwilling to think of religious commandments as so absolute that all people, and not just they themselves, must be guided by them?[30]

One reason became clear in the interview conducted immediately after the one with the McLaughlins. Barbara Tompkins, a retired piano and organ teacher, is the daughter of a Southern Baptist preacher who ultimately became a district supervisor responsible for thirty-six churches. If Jim McLaughlin spoke for that part of Oklahoma which holds to strong faith, Mrs. Tompkins spoke to that part which is still frontier country dominated by an ethic of individualism. Without mentioning any names, Maria told Mrs. Tompkins about her interview with Mr. McLaughlin the previous evening, especially about what he had had to say about homosexuality not being merely an alternative lifestyle. "That's his right to his belief," she responded, "but he cannot make a broad statement that that's wrong. . . . Why is it wrong for them? I mean, do we all have to have the same color hair?" People who insist that there is only one way to morality, in her opinion, have "stopped preaching and gone on to meddling." Well, Maria continued, his point was that we had to have absolutes. Yes, Mrs. Tompkins agreed, we do. But "people don't [have to] choose the absolutes." For her, insistence on the priority of absolutes for everyone violates people's freedom. "Tend to their business," she says, "I'll tend to mine. . . . Where their nose starts is where my fist should end."

Mrs. Tompkins views herself as a religious person. "I think everyone inside has their own persona of God," she comments. "You don't have to accept anybody's dogma whole. Live with the concept of God as you perceive it." The difference between the way Mrs. Tompkins thinks about the relationship between religion and public morality and the way Mr. McLaughlin does is important to emphasize. For Mr. McLaughlin, if something is right and true for one person, it ought to be right and true for all; as he put it in our interview with him, "There's only one spirit," which for him means that if you don't believe in God, or even if you believe in a God other than the Christian one, "you're gonna be reading out of the wrong book." In his view, then, a virtuous person is one who does what his God commands him to do.

Mrs. Tompkins, by contrast, would also claim to be a virtuous person, but one who thinks about virtue in a different way. Her outlook on the world illustrates what I propose to call "modest virtues." Because she is religious, Mrs. Tompkins believes that there are right ways and wrong ways to act. But because she is modest in her beliefs, she also believes that however strongly one applies principles of right and wrong to oneself, one ought to hesitate before applying them to others. Modesty, as she understands the idea, follows from a belief in individual freedom; if we proclaim our religious ideas too publicly, we run the risk of interfering with the rights of others to believe in God as they want to.

There is a further argument on behalf of modest virtues, and it was made by another resident of Broken Arrow, Joyce Umber, a Baptist. Her point involved humility: Something about religious absolutism strikes Mrs. Umber as presuming too much, not only about others, and not only about ourselves, but also about God. Mrs. Umber certainly does not like the secular drift she sees in America, and she hopes that a return to church will correct it. She also worries about her own commitments: "You know, everyday you have to seek God's guidance. . . . You drift away from God once in a while and you don't stay close to him. You know, you can be caught up in another world if you stray." Surely as religious as Jim McLaughlin, she would, however, be put off by his certainty; for her, we need God's forgiveness because we are imperfect. And because we are, how can we be certain that there is only one true way? To condemn others for lacking the proper way to God is to substitute one's own evaluation for God's.

For those who adhere to modest virtues, softer is better. In his study of the way Americans think about the moral dimensions of their lives, the Princeton sociologist Robert Wuthnow quoted a respondent who said, "I tend to be quietly religious."[31] Kenneth Easterbrook, a black software consultant living in Cobb County, told us the same thing in nearly identical words: "I would say that we choose to practice our religion quietly in the sense that I don't go to others and try . . . to convince them that my religion, my approach to life, is best for them. It's an awareness you have to reach on your own. You cannot mandate religion." Religion is one thing, people like Mr. Easterbrook believe, but loud and ostentatious religion is another.

For the overwhelming majority of middle-class Americans with whom we spoke, the sticking point, the aspect of absolutist religious belief that bothers them most, is the idea of excluding others who may not share one's particular religious commitments. Are Jews immoral because they do not accept Jesus as the one true way? we asked people. Buddhists or Moslems? Well, responded one African American woman in Georgia, yes, there is only one answer to our problem: Jesus. Pausing as she said this, she looked at me with dawning self-revelation and said, "Now I don't know if you are Jewish," before recovering to add, "but if you are, hopefully you will be a Messianic Jew." Her response stood out for its uniqueness. Overwhelmingly, again and again, and in every region of the country, middle-class Americans believe that people of religious faiths other than their own are moral people. "I mean, gosh, I have all kinds of friends," we were told by Anne Harding of Sand Springs, "and they have all kinds of beliefs. I think that they're all good people." "I know an awful lot of people who are not Christian, and I respect the hell out of them," added Nancy Elliott of DeKalb. The important thing for both of them is that people believe in something.

And nonbelievers? Here again a reluctance to exclude turns out to be as powerful, if not more powerful, a moral force than a requirement to believe. It is not the beliefs of others we ought to respect, some of our respondents felt, but the person who holds those beliefs. Like so many others in Tulsa, Fred Jones, a jet engine mechanic and the man who believes in God, family, and country, in that order, thinks that we made a mistake in turning away from God: "I think the reason we are in the shape we're in today is that we have excluded God instead of including God in our lifestyles," he told us. But precisely because of his religious beliefs, "I would kill my own testimony by putting someone else down." Mr. Jones works with different kinds of people every day: "I take the individual and respect him for who he is and for his beliefs." Two of his best friends never go to church. "I think they're both good, spiritual, moral people, but they do not honor God by coming to his House. I respect them. I like them." Americans understand that their belief in God does not foreclose the possibility of a belief in human beings. Their deeply held and strongly expressed faith in people prevents them from a disposition to accept the proposition that a large number of their fellow Americans are godless sinners—even when they do not believe in God.

To exclude, to condemn, is to judge, and middle-class Americans are reluctant to pass judgment on how other people act and think. Peter Strong, a white man living in a primarily black section of DeKalb County, was one of the most conservative people to whom we talked, an enthusiastic supporter of Newt Gingrich and someone not afraid to express politically incorrect views. A Baptist, Mr. Strong believes that "the church does a lot of good," and that the country's decline can be attributed to people's lack of faith, but at the same time, he said, "I don't go around preaching to people." His opinion was widely shared. A. C. Stewart, a retired football coach in Oklahoma, quit going to church because of "the self-judgment, the 'I'm right, you're wrong'" attitude. Talking about religious leaders who would presume to judge others, Patricia Bates of DeKalb County pointed out, "The Bible also says you cannot judge. . . . The Scripture says 'Only my father can judge which is heaven.'"

> So all of you are playing God here. I think we need to step outside that. Step outside of self. Look at self. Get a mirror. Are you that great? Don't throw rocks at my house because it might shatter. . . . If everybody would

step back and look at themselves, take a mirrored view of themselves, and then ask "What is my purpose? Where do I fit this puzzle?," then we'd be much better off.

Middle-class Americans have added an Eleventh Commandment, best formulated by Dolores Wales of Sand Springs, Oklahoma: "Thou shalt not judge."

Our respondents can name what disturbs them about passing judgment on others' religious convictions: such a move politicizes religion, taking it out of the private realm where it belongs and placing it in politics—a realm of human activity for which people have relatively little respect. For Tommy Fasano, a Jehovah's Witness living in Rancho Bernardo, and one of those we classified as a strong religious believer (but not by the original stricter definition), judgmentalism leads to politicians like Patrick Buchanan, whom he considers an extremist. Mr. Fasano illustrates his point with the question of abortion: "Abortion is a moral issue. It has nothing to do with politics. You don't like it, don't get one. I am not a proponent of it. [But] I'm not about to tell you, 'Hey, you're a sinner, because you're getting one.' That's not me. I am not here to judge anyone." Many would not object, and some would be quite pleased, if a pastor or rabbi advised a woman, in private, that abortion was wrong. To so do in public, and in a way not directed toward a particular person but as a general moral injunction to all whatever their circumstances—that strikes them as poking your nose into other people's business. "I would be the first one to go down with my church and stand in front of an abortion clinic. This is something that I've evolved into believing that I think is wrong," said Trent Tartt of Broken Arrow. "But," he continued, "I also wouldn't be the one to stand up and say it's wrong in every single case. Because my church would say 'Well, you haven't grown to that point,' but I would say 'That's maybe what you call it, but I don't think it's right that if a woman was raped, she shouldn't have a choice.'"

From the interviews we conducted, an answer to the question of whether a new religious awakening is taken place in the United States can be given. Clearly most middle-class Americans take their religion seriously. But very few of them take it so seriously that they believe that religion should be the sole, or even the most important, guide for establishing rules about how *other* people should live. And some, if even fewer, also would distrust such rules for providing guidelines about how they personally should live. Despite the attention that conservative Christians have commanded in the political realm, in other words, there is not much support out there in middle-class America, at least among our respondents, for the notion that religion can play an official and didactic role in guiding public morality.

Standing in the way of a religious revival that would undermine the privatistic solutions that have governed American approaches to religious obligations since World War II is a strongly held belief in modest virtues. People who adhere to modest virtues think the best way to think about our obligations to others is not by lecturing them about right and wrong, but rather by personal example. They do not believe in absolutes but in balancing what is right with what is practical. They distrust extremes, even those whose views they considered correct but are asserted with too much finality. And they feel that one has to do one's best to understand, even when one does not agree with, those who think otherwise. Modest virtues, in their opinion, do not make headlines or win medals. They tend to get drowned out by the brash blaring of the media, the self-interest of groups and organizations, the certainties of ideologists, the indifference of social scientists, and, when it comes to religion in particular, the rantings of fanatics.

Our interviews were conducted at a time when questions of fanaticism, religious or otherwise, were very much in the news: a number of those to whom we spoke brought up the incident in which federal agents raided the headquarters of David Koresh in Waco, Texas, and killed him and a large number of his followers; they mentioned it not as an example of oppressive government but to illustrate the dangers of religious fanaticism. Fanaticism, moreover, was not some distant phenomenon for them: for the Brookliners with whom we talked, John Salvi, who shot and killed two people at an abortion clinic in their suburb before taking his own life in prison, represented everything that could go wrong with literal absolutism. And our interviews in Oklahoma, conducted shortly after the largest act of domestic terrorism in American history, were certainly influenced by that event. Still, the degree to which middle-class Americans expressed a distrust of religious extremism is worth emphasizing.

So deep is this distrust that it extends well beyond violence-prone extremists to include revivalist preachers. During the 1980s, as a result of the televangelist scandals of 1987 and 1988, the proportion of Americans who believed that television evangelists could be trusted with money went from 41 percent to 16 percent, those who believed they were honest decreased from 53 percent to 23 percent, with roughly similar declines among those who believed that they cared for people or had a special relationship with God.[32] Our interviews indicate that little had changed by 1995. Broken Arrow disc jockey Jim Stone, a deeply conservative man with a proclivity to conspiracy theories, certainly had little respect for them: "Oral Roberts has been ready for the butterfly net since he discovered television," he told us, before going on to make sarcastic remarks about Jimmy Swaggert—"he can't keep his pants up"—

and Jim Bakker. Preachers who meddle too much in public affairs are, simply put, too loud: the very public character of their utterances is what leads people to distrust them. Political religion is to be found in other countries, especially the Middle East, not here, we were frequently told. Indeed among the most moving thoughts on the subject we heard came from an Iranian woman living in Broken Arrow for whom religious fundamentalism represents everything from which she fled—and for whom American religious tolerance represents freedom in a very palpable sense.

A consistent theme running through the large majority of our interviews was that religion is too important, too much a matter of personal identity, to be forced on people. Jamie Willis believes that "religion is the backbone of your morals and values and it teaches you a great deal of yourself," but, she added, "I've never tried to force religion on anyone." Religion is fine, said James Alexander of Brookline, but "don't push it in someone's face." Bob Cameron of Sand Springs has backed off from his once strict religious views, since he now realizes that "you can't force religion on people." "I don't like the extremism on either side of the thing," said George Slade of Cobb County, referring to the debate over the role of religion in American life. "I have good morals. I'm not hurting anybody. . . . I'm not doing things that are wrong. I don't like the trend toward 'if you're not a Christian, or their definition of a Christian, then you're just not worth it.'"

As Mr. Slade's comments illustrate, efforts by organizations like the Moral Majority and the Christian Coalition to mobilize Christians around specific political positions were not very well received by those middle-class Americans with whom we spoke. A case could be made that this distrust is not merely the result of revivalist preachers being arrested for sexual and financial peccadilloes: politicized Christianity is everything that an inclusive, nonabsolutist, modest, and nonjudgmental religious mentality is not. Jake and Molly Sandford, a semiretired couple in Sand Springs worry about the decline of religion in America, but they worry even more that, as Mr. Sandford put it, "the fanatics took over. They drove away people like us." "The God I believe in," he continued, "is a God of love." But the kinds of people attracted to the Seven Hundred Club [a television program on Pat Robertson's Christian Broadcasting Network]—"them's the meanest people. They talk mean." Sociologists believe that levels of education are the most important determining feature in accounting for the fact that some Americans hold to very conservative theological notions while others tend to be liberal.[33] Because our sample was middle class and relatively well educated, we have no way of testing this hypothesis. But examples like that of the Sandfords—and there were many of them—illustrate that in places like

Sand Springs, where many of our respondents did not attend college, there are just as many people who fear a linking of religion and politics as in places like Brookline.

Listening to so many people expressing a distaste for efforts to politicize religion, I was at first convinced that there must be something unrepresentative about my sample. The year of our interviews in Oklahoma and Georgia, 1995, witnessed triumphant attempts by the Republican Party to pass its Contract with America. Nearly all political commentators believed that the election of the previous year was a watershed event, one that marked a long-term transition to a conservative majority in America. The Christian Coalition had played a major role in that triumph, symbolized by Patrick Buchanan's speech at the 1992 Republican convention proclaiming the existence of a culture war in America and carried forward by the Republican electoral victory in 1994. As I watched the Republican Congress begin to carry out its agenda, even to the point of shutting down the government, I began to think that they had to be right and my data had to be wrong: after all, they could afford surveys of far greater depth and technological sophistication than my two hundred conversations.

Events since 1995, however, have shed a very different light on the matter. More popular within the Republican Party than Patrick Buchanan was Colin Powell, a man who symbolizes moderation in everything he does or says. Even more important, the Christian Coalition struck a new note in its political presentation of self. Under the leadership of Pat Robertson, the organization had developed an extremist public image; one 1996 survey gave Robertson an approval rating of 29 percent compared to a 45 percent favorable rating for the Christian Coalition,[34] while another showed that Robertson's name evoked roughly the same percentage of negative reactions as Oliver North's (and more than Jesse Jackson's).[35] With Ralph Reed, a politically savvy leader, in charge, the Christian Coalition began to present a softer face to the general public, realizing something about American political sentiment: while it is undoubtedly true that the number of Evangelical Christians is increasing,[36] and while it is also true that white Evangelicals tend to support Republicans, and while it is even the case that the percentage of Americans who think that religion does have a role to play in politics has gone up, none of that translates into automatic support for those who might, in their excessive zeal, violate deeply held beliefs about fair play, second chances, and tolerance. There are more conservative Christians in America, but among them there is anything but consensus.[37] America is, simply put, not poised on the brink of a religious counterrevolution; more Americans disagree with the statement that the federal government is hostile to religion, for example, than agree with it.[38]

Further evidence to the effect that conservative Christian leaders realize how badly a harsh version of their message is generally received was provided by an incident that took place while we were in Georgia. In Atlanta, I wanted to attend services at a primarily African American church, and I was directed by one of our respondents to the Cathedral at Chapel Hill in suburban Decatur.[39] Its preacher, Bishop Earl Paulk, I was told, although white, has great rapport with his primarily black congregation. When we arrived, we discovered that he was not to give the sermon that day; it would be offered instead by the Reverend Jim Bakker, the very evangelist, and former prison inmate, about whom so many of our respondents had negative feelings.

"I don't deliver sermons anymore," Bakker began. His "message," as he called it, would be based on Proverbs 17:17—"A friend loveth at all times"—and would be devoted to the theme of forgiveness. At first cynical—he has a lot to be forgiven for, I thought—I was unprepared for the degree to which Bakker's thoughts resonated with the nonjudgmental, inclusive way most of our respondents talked about their relationship with God. Denouncing preachers who wanted to fill up the jails and throw away the keys, Bakker told his audience, "Those people in prison are just as real as you are—you just didn't get caught, that's all." Being in prison had taught him, he said, that his former approach to preaching was wrong. (One year after we heard his message, Bakker would publish a book called *I Was Wrong*).[40] "Many of the churches today, they leave you when you have a divorce or take drugs, if you go to prison, or if you had an abortion. They abandon you in your moment of crisis," he told his audience. A church that walks away from young women who have children out of wedlock or those suffering from AIDS is not a church of mercy, and Bakker, like Jesus, would rather have mercy than religion. To thunderous amens, Bakker's talk seemed little different from one President Clinton might have delivered to the same group, except that Clinton, when he did address a black congregation in the South, was more willing to pass judgment on self-destructive behavior than Bakker. Perhaps Jim Bakker was converted to a new worldview while in jail; perhaps his message was always directed at reaching as large an audience as possible; more likely, he, like other Christian preachers, realizes that a language of meanness wins few hearts in America. When even Jim Bakker, however boastfully, becomes a convert to the modest virtues, they must be very powerful in America indeed.

By softening their tone, conservative Christians are trying to undo the damage of their original intransigence. If our interviews are any indication, they have their work cut out for them. The now disbanded Moral Majority left a bad taste in the mouth of middle-class America, one that a chastened Christian Coalition may never be able to neutralize. "I personally think that when the world comes to an end, there will be people that have lived well, that have tried to be good to each other," said Cathy Peterson, a Cobb County housewife.

> I feel like there will be all religions there. I feel like there will be Buddhists there—if they believe that in their heart and soul and that's the way they're taught and they live a good life. I feel like there'd be all different religions there. . . . No, I don't think those people are bad, if you say they don't go to church. It's a personal thing for me.

Real Diversity

The United States has become a far more religiously diverse society than anyone could have anticipated in the decades when suburban expansion took off. The trend began when more and more Americans found themselves marrying outside their faith.[41] It picked up as Americans began to choose for themselves the faith that fit them best rather than relying on the religion of their upbringing.[42] Then immigration brought with it a large number of old religions, which, in characteristic American fashion, were called "new" ones, eventually reaching into the very heartland of the country.[43] That was accompanied by multiculturalism, and, with it, an effort to teach about all the different roads to God, including the faiths of Native American peoples. Comparative religion, an exotic subject when I went to college in the early 1960s, has become something of a staple of public school curricula throughout the country.

According to the survey we took at the end of our interviews, middle-class Americans have accommodated themselves rather easily to America's religious diversity. A very small number of our respondents—19 out of 200—disagreed with the statement "There are many different religious truths and we ought to be tolerant of all of them," while quite a large number—167—agreed or strongly agreed with it. (See table 1.3.) Considering how many lives have been lost in the religious wars that have characterized Western history—as well as how much violence remains associated with conflicts over religious beliefs in today's world—this tolerance is quite remarkable. As much as they admire religion, it would seem, middle-class Americans dislike doctrinal strife and sectarian conflict more.

By downplaying denominational sectarianism in favor of tolerant acceptance, middle-class Americans redefine religion to make it more suited to their tastes. For religious diversity to work, all religions, even public ones, many of them believe, have to transform themselves into

TABLE 1.3

"There are many different religious truths and we ought to be tolerant of all of them."

	Strongly Agree	Agree	No Opinion	Disagree	Strongly Disagree
Brookline	10	13	2	0	0
Medford	13	9	0	3	0
Broken Arrow	3	15	3	1	3
Sand Springs	7	13	3	2	0
DeKalb	9	11	0	1	4
Cobb	10	10	4	1	0
Eastlake	11	10	1	2	1
Rancho Bernardo	12	11	1	0	1
Total	75	92	14	10	9

private ones, for if you permit Christianity to be the "official" religion of the United States, what are you going to do about the others? "My wife has a fit because they can't hold Christmas programs up here in school," Stephen Jackman of Sand Springs informed us. To which he responded, "Well, what if they demanded that they observe Rosh Hashanah? How are you going to feel then?" Religious tolerance in America bears a distinct resemblance to laissez-faire economics: you can do what you want so long as you let me do what I want. This is especially true now that there are others here besides Christian and Jews. "If you are a Hindu and you grew up being a Hindu, keep it to yourself," said Jody Fields, an unemployed social worker in DeKalb County. "Don't impose your religion, and don't make me feel bad because I do this and you do that." You come here and practice your faith, Americans implicitly tell those outside the Judeo-Christian tradition, but you cannot practice your faith the way it is done in theocracies abroad.

This message that everyone should leave everyone else alone might strike a strong believer as odd, since many religions have contained an obligation to convert nonbelievers. Most of our respondents have a way to deal with that history as well: they simply ignore religious sectarianism. "All religions have basically the same common good things," we were told by Joti Mehta, a substitute teacher in Rancho Bernardo who emigrated from India. "Whether it's the Koran or the Bible or Gita or whatever, they have these ten commandments or eighteen commandments or twenty commandments. . . . All these things are there, you know, brotherhood and all, that's everywhere." Carmen Tosca of Eastlake is aware that in the Middle East people kill each other over questions of faith, but, because they do, people over there cannot be truly religious; "I don't think any religion really teaches you to hate others and to be mean to others," she argues. "I think most religions really teach you to be spiritual and to be compassionate and all that, and I think religion is good, or almost any religion is good." Aaron Feldman, a physician in Cobb County, spoke to us the day after his office celebrated its "holiday" party. Although all the doctors in his office are Jewish, nearly all the staff are not, a situation that led everyone to agree that the party would celebrate neither Christmas nor Hanukkah. One could interpret responses like these as involving a form of deep denial: eternally optimistic, middle-class Americans are reluctant to acknowledge the tragic dimension to religious strife. On the other hand, perhaps these people know that life in America will have a bigger impact on people of orthodox faith than people of orthodox faith will have on life in America. If so, then the way they think about religious accommodation, while insufficiently appreciative of religious conflict today, may foreshadow a period of increasing religious pluralism tomorrow.

Although laissez-faire religious norms are widely shared in middle-class America, they are not shared by all. For the most devout among our respondents, those who believe that religion's commandments are absolute and binding on everyone in our society, confining religion to the private realm itself violates a core belief: that one should proudly proclaim one's faith and help others seek the truth. Because those who hold to this view argue that privatizing religion does not permit them to be true to the commandments of their religious faith as they understand them, their insistence that religion be given more of a public role in America upsets liberals, such as members of the American Civil Liberties Union, who hold strongly to the principle that church and state should be as separate as possible. Devout religious believers have forced Americans to deal with a question that, for most of the post–World War II period, has been kept somewhat underground: can we still find ways to get along if we not only hold deep beliefs about the nature of morality but also think that those beliefs should be operative for society as a whole?

One answer to this question has been offered by the political theorists Amy Gutmann and Dennis Thompson in their book *Democracy and Disagreement*.[44] They argue that citizens in a democracy have an obligation to reason their way to mutually acceptable decisions on controversial matters—a process they call deliberative democracy. Not only is such an ideal desirable, they claim, it is also possible. On questions such as welfare and affirmative action, positions exist that can respect the views of deeply divided antagonists.

A possible objection to deliberative democracy is that it is the kind of solution that academics, who like to deliberate, would prefer, but that would have little relevance for people at large. Yet we found that a small but nonetheless eloquent number of suburbanites believed that religious diversity was valuable in precisely the way Gutmann and Thompson suggest: to enable those of different beliefs to argue out their differences in public. Consider what Rachel Benjamin, a Brookline dentist, had to say on these themes. Like so many others in her community, she was appalled when two women working in an abortion clinic were killed by someone claiming to be carrying out the will of God. Yet despite her distaste for John Salvi, she nonetheless realized that the entire conflict over abortion "really highlighted the fact that people are allowed to have different views." The only way to live with such conflict is "to talk out these issues," since "people need to understand that we see things in different ways." Her views were seconded by Bea Cohen of Cobb County. Religious diversity, she said, is a good thing "because there is no one right and no one wrong and the greater the exposure you have to different ideas . . . more tolerance, I would think, grows out of that." Mrs. Duncan, a white woman in a primarily black section of DeKalb County, put the same point this way: "Even if you disagree with someone's politics, it doesn't hurt to communicate. 'Don't you see my point? Can't you see my point a little bit?'"

What one hears being expressed here is something more than laissez-faire. Rather than emphasizing a negative—no one should interfere with anyone else's beliefs—this way of thinking seeks a positive: how can another's beliefs strengthen and broaden my own? The more views we have, the more resources on which we have to draw. The resulting common morality may be thinner than the religious beliefs of one particular church, but it will also, in Dr. Benjamin's terms, constitute a set of "civilization morals" around which people of many different faiths can agree. That's why Paul Kemp, a minister in Medford, can say that religious diversity is a "blessing for this country. . . . I think people will recognize that there is value and truth in Hinduism, in Buddhism, in Judaism, in Catholicism, in Protestantism. There is a kernel of something in each of them that I think contributes to a wider vision of reality and how we need to relate to one another."

Yet deliberative democracy is not just a process that can be used to evaluate ends: it is also an end in itself. Just as there are Americans for whom communication is important, there are others for whom faith lies beyond deliberation or argument of any kind. To ask them to enter into a dialogue with skeptics is to ensure that the skeptics win by default. What to liberals seems like a perfectly reasonable way to argue about difference seems to a person of faith like a way of taking the liberal position against the conservative one. Their reasoning can be illustrated by examples involving such charged issues as prayer in the schools or the constitutionality of allowing public displays of faith in America. For the deeply devout to whom we spoke, there is no escaping the iron-clad logic of either/or: if, in the interests of fairness, prayer is not allowed in school or crosses in public places, the rights of atheists have simply trumped those of believers. On issues such as these, they believe, there simply is not much to discuss.

Yet it would be wrong to conclude that people who think this way are necessarily illiberal or undemocratic. A script exists for debates over religion in the public square,[45] and each side in the debate is expected to recite its lines. Those who want prayer in school or crosses in public places are said by their opponents to be engaged in an effort to impose their religion, the majority religion, on the beliefs of minorities. Those who favor banning all religion from the public sphere are held by their opponents to be atheists intent on having the world run their way. There is, however, something amiss in both positions. People who believe in public displays of religion often fail to recognize that not all those who support religious neutrality are atheists; some are sincerely devout people protecting minority religions against majority ones. But adherents of strict neutrality misunderstand the points made by deeply religious believers as well, for the latter see themselves as most definitely not trying to impose their Christian beliefs on an increasingly diverse society. However wide the gap between the secular and the orthodox sides in debates of this sort, those who want religious symbols to be allowed in public do so in support of the very religious tolerance and diversity praised by many who do not. That may be why, for all the rhetoric generated on the issue by the American Civil Liberties Union on the one hand and the Christian Coalition on the other, at the local level, in places such as Springfield, Massachusetts, most such controversies are settled relatively peacefully by informal agreements among all the groups involved.[46]

If once in America the question of religious toleration was raised in defense of nonbelievers who dissented from religious orthodoxy, today it is raised by believers who feel excluded from a predominantly secular public world. Jen Morgan of Cobb County, like Jim McLaughlin, is a strong believer and is one of the many Catholics in this country attracted to the ideas of the Christian Coalition. "Our country was founded with Christian principles in mind," she pointed out, "and when the public school system started, they were allowed to pray. . . . A Christian teacher could teach from her Christian perspective to the kids, because that was what society was like. Now, our society is atheistic or agnostic . . . and the Christians are being pushed aside." Mrs. Morgan elaborated her beliefs in ways indicating how long and hard she had thought about the issue:

> The separation of church and state was put into our laws because the people that came here from Europe wanted to be allowed to have religious freedom. . . . Now it's been twisted around to use it to suppress religious freedom. . . . They probably never foresaw that was going to happen. It was actually put in so that you would free to profess your faith without the government interfering. Now the government is intervening and not allowing us to profess our faith.

For a significant group in the San Diego area, Mrs. Morgan's concerns were shared in the context of a real-life example. Our interviews in Eastlake and Rancho Bernardo took place when local residents were debating whether a cross that had long stood on top of a local mountain should be taken down because the land in which it stood was public property. A few of our respondents were indifferent on the question. The others who talked about it did so with a tone of bewilderment. Don't Christians have rights too? they wanted to know. Karen Calingo, born and raised in the Philippines, feels, like Jen Morgan, that the atheists are winning all the battles over the public square. "They are catering to these people," she says of the atheists. "They are winning. . . . We don't say Merry Christmas anymore in the public school. We say Happy Holiday because Christmas denotes God, denotes Jesus. There are a lot of Roman Catholics in the schools. There are a lot of Protestants. They still believe in God. . . . But here comes along people who are atheists and who are only a certain portion of the population, and they are the ones being heard."

Because they see themselves as a victimized minority, people such as Mrs. Calingo and Mrs. Morgan believe they have more in common with dissenting and minority religions than they do with establishment, monopolistic ones. Like many Christians to whom we talked, Mrs. Calingo would much prefer to have more devout Muslims and Buddhists in the country than agnostics who may have been born Christian. (As one respondent in Oklahoma put it, "Any religion is probably better than no religion at all."). And even Mrs. Morgan, who strongly believes that America was born as a Christian country, when pressed on her views about religious diversity, said that "there's ways to talk about God that wouldn't offend Moslems and Buddhists. . . . There's common ground in all of the faiths that you could talk about God and do some prayer without it offending anyone except the people who don't believe in God." In the wake of a Supreme Court ruling allowing the state of Oregon to prohibit the use of peyote in religious ceremonies, constitutional scholars have begun to question whether the Court is sufficiently protective of the free exercise rights of minority religious believers.[47] Although they do not use legal language, Mrs. Calingo and Mrs. Morgan were essentially arguing that the Free Exercise clause of the First Amendment, which says that everyone has the right to practice their religious beliefs as they see fit, contradicts the Establishment clause, which prohibits government from naming one church as the state's official religion. For them, a constitutional prohibition on the establishment of a religious symbol in a public space violates their First Amendment freedom to put into practice their religious beliefs.

With their arguments rooted in notions of free exercise and support for diversity, these advocates of a more public recognition of faith understand themselves as trying to be accommodating to all faiths, not seeking to impose one of them. There was a time when Protestantism was the dominant religion in America, and people of other faiths needed the protection of the Constitution to carve out space for their own religious practices, most of our devout respondents recognize. But this condition, they argue, no longer applies. For them public displays of religious symbols or prayer in school, even if rooted in Christianity, are meant to stand for all religions, which is why they should be as broad and inclusive as possible (without, of course, losing their religious character). If Christians were out to convert everyone to the cross, such a broad symbolic meaning would not be possible. But, they claim, they are not out to make everyone Christians; they want public symbols of religion to encourage everyone from every religion to believe whatever they prefer to believe. Although many of those who want to see more public displays of religion believe in absolutes, their arguments on behalf of their position are contextual, based on an understanding that what may have been true at the time when America was overwhelmingly a Christian nation needs to be rethought at a time when the country has become so religiously diverse.

In a diverse religious climate, the proper way to treat conflicts between one religion and another is to give space to them all, or so many of our believers argued. "Everybody ought to have a turn," said Sand Springs fireman John Pollan. "It doesn't take very long to say a prayer for anybody. And you could have a Muslim prayer, a Hindu prayer, and a Catholic prayer, and a Baptist prayer. You know, you could have all four of those in the span of five minutes and then go on about the day's chores." "When I heard all of this nonsense about how we can't have Christmas carols in the schools because the Muslims will be upset," added Cathy Ryan of Brookline, "well, excuse me, let's teach Muslim songs too. . . . Don't wipe out all the culture, add to it. . . . Do Hanukkah songs. Let's find out what a dreidel represents. Let's find out what Muslims do." In a fashion not fully appreciated by their opponents, this way of thinking puts people like these on the side of practitioners of minority religions. One need not accept their point that atheism has become the new established religion to accept their point that deep believers are a kind of dissenter in an increasingly secular American culture.

But if religious conservatives have accepted the principle that the state should be neutral between religions, they do not accept the proposition that it should be neutral between religion and nonreligion. No neutrality between believers and atheists is possible, they argue, and as a result the only proper choice in a democracy is to side with the majority, which happens to be people of faith (all faiths, let us recall, not just one). This, of course, is exactly the kind of reasoning that leads liberals to argue for the need to protect minorities even at the cost of sacrificing a democratic principle such as majority rule. Perhaps I should make clear that, on this question, I am on the liberal side: as I listened to conservative Christians make their arguments, I could not help but feel that this country remains sufficiently religious—and sufficiently Christian—that one needs to worry about the rights of nonbelievers. Yet I heard something else in their views as well: conservative Christians are often more willing to acknowledge the degree to which America has changed since the battles over fundamentalism earlier in this century than are those adherents to the American Civil Liberties Union who act as if religious intolerance, rather than nonjudgmentalism, is still the dominant tone of the country's religiosity.

Just as conservative Christians believe that the question of religious establishment is a different question under conditions of religious diversity than of religious monopoly, they also feel that minority rights look different when adherents to a religious point of view no longer practice the kind of violence and intimidation once used to reinforce their dominance. The most striking aspect of our interviews on this subject is what they lacked: no one at any time, not even the strongest believers, used the word "infidel." In a way similar to the general acceptance by whites that racism against blacks is wrong, Protestants no longer argue that Catholics and Jews serve the interests of Satan. A people as nonjudgmental as middle-class Americans cannot be intolerant. Whether this means that we can override the rights of atheists is another matter. But the Middle-Class Morality Project does suggest that middle-class Americans are not ready to replay the Scopes trial. The conflict between believers and nonbelievers is as deep as it ever has been in America, but it is no longer a conflict between know-nothings and an enlightened elite. Those who want prayer in schools or crosses on mountains are anything but know-nothings: they have arguments on their side and, even more important, those arguments are lodged not in blind acceptance but in a liberal language of inclusion and accommodation.

For the American middle class, religious diversity is here to stay; as Barbara Odessa of Cobb County put it, "We've just got a more diverse society, so we're gonna get more diverse religions." Diversity being a fact of life, one might as well make the best of it. When we consider how many people have died in the name of religion over the years, the acceptance of so many different kinds of belief in America is remarkable. One is tempted to call it real diversity, not because the idea of diversity is inappropriate to race, gender, or sexual orientation, but because religion claims to speak to what really and truly matters in life. I confess that at some level I did not fully understand the nonjudgmentalism of middle-class Americans. I wondered why, if people were so libertarian, they were as religious as they claimed to be and why, if they were so religious, they were so unwilling to speak of sin and Satan. But those who have qualms about nonjudgmentalism ought at least to recognize what comes along with it: a strong commitment to the principle that a wide variety of religious views ought to be allowed to flourish.

The Ultimate Test

Moderation and tolerance—an appreciation of the modest virtues—are the bedrock moral principles of the American middle class: on most controversial issues, Americans instinctively try to find the centrist position between two extremes *and* attempt to carve out private spaces in which people can do what they want so long as others do what they want. But these two principles can contradict each other. If one believes in tolerance for everyone under all conditions, one is hardly moderate. And if one prizes moderation, one should look for a position that combines respect for privacy with the need to adhere to common public principles that can occasionally overrule not only private rights but also the tolerance that goes along with them. How are middle-class Americans likely to react when their two "default" moral positions come into conflict?

No issue taps into such a potential conflict more than the issue of homosexuality. The question of gay rights is important to a discussion of religious toleration, for it is over this question that the more liberal and more conservative religious believers have had their most persistent clashes. From specific congregations to whole denominations such as the Episcopalian Church, which recently experienced a formal trial over heresy involving a decision to ordain a gay minister, a seemingly unbridgeable gulf has opened between those who believe that the Bible's condemnation of homosexuality as an abomination must be taken as a moral injunction versus those who believe that Christianity requires love for and acceptance of everyone.[48] Secular America has also been transformed by this clash: controversies involving gay rights in Colorado, President Clinton's response to the conflict between the military and gay advocacy groups, the frequent denunciation of homosexuality by adherents to the Christian Coalition, and highly publicized efforts to teach about homosexuals in New York City public schools demonstrate the degree to which issues involving gays have begun to dominate American politics. For conservatives, here, more than anyplace else, is where the line should be drawn: if Americans are unwilling to condemn sodomy, they would presumably be unwilling to condemn anything. For liberals, the test is the same but the results different: tolerance means little until it includes what the majority dislikes the most. The question is easily posed: are middle-class Americans so nonjudgmental that public recognition of homosexuality is fine with them or so religious that they still believe that what the Bible condemns must remain a sin?

The debate about gay rights taking place among intellectuals and academics often focuses on whether homosexuality is a choice or is determined by the biological, neurological, or genetic makeup of an individual. Americans are divided on this point; according to the Post-Modernity Project's poll, 38 percent agree that "a person is born either a homosexual or a heterosexual, and there is little they can do to change that" compared to 47 percent who disagree.[49] Although the middle-class Americans to whom we spoke think differently than the cultural elite on many issues, on the question of gay rights they pose the issue in much the same way. Those who believed that homosexuality is a choice were more likely also to believe it was a sin; "I just don't think people are born that way," said Mavis Wright, a Jehovah's Witness in DeKalb County. "So I wouldn't want that taught to my child." On the other hand, those who believed homosexuality to be a condition would apply the same reasoning to gays that they would to any other group born different. Included in the latter group is Karen Calingo, the devout Christian from the Philippines who believes that atheists have too much power. "I think it is something we have to accept because it's part of their nature," she says about gay people. "It's not to their own making that their genes are like that." When we followed up by asking her explicitly if she is saying that homosexuality is not a sin, Mrs. Calingo emphasized that it was not. What are we going to do, she asked sarcastically, get into "gene alteration"?

For the American public as a whole, Mrs. Wright's position has more support than Mrs. Calingo's. According to the General Social Survey, roughly 70 percent of the American people believe that sexual relations between members of the same sex are wrong.[50] But it is one thing to believe that homosexuality is wrong and another to believe that people should not be allowed to do whatever they want in the privacy of their own homes. There will always be those who treat the question of gay rights in the same laissez-faire way they would treat any other issue involving matters of privacy.[51] "I don't care what you look like, what you're wearing, what your hair color is, what sexual preference you have," said Katherine Mullins, a Broken Arrow businesswoman with decidedly libertarian views on most questions of the day. Others are willing to show respect to gays and lesbians because, they believe, nonjudgmentalism implies that one should show respect to everyone. "You know, there are a lot of people out there that I totally disagree with, I disagree with their lifestyles," said Anne Harding of Sand Springs. "I disagree with their viewpoints, but I respect them as an individual, as a human being. I think that needs to be taught. You know, you can't judge another person. . . . You need to be fair to everybody no matter how you feel about that person." And then there are those who, making use of the same distinction between public and private which applies to religious belief, argued in favor of the right of gays to do "whatever they wanted behind closed doors in the privacy of their homes," as one resident of Broken Arrow put it, but not to bring "it out in public, like if you're in a restaurant and I have my little small children and then two men are sitting there kissing each other."

In making sense of this issue, it is important to distinguish between respect for privacy and respect for what takes place in private. The question is whether people would be willing to go beyond expressions of "negative" liberty to the "positive" position that homosexuals are deserving of public respect as homosexuals. This is not the same issue as whether homosexuals should be permitted to teach in colleges and universities; it is clear from General Social Survey data that Americans not only think they should but that the percentage who think this way has increased since 1973 from 50.1 percent to 73.2 percent.[52] That support can be explained on the grounds of respect for rights; in endorsing the right of homosexuals to teach, people are not necessarily endorsing homosexuality. To get at the more positive issue of acceptance of gays in general, we asked instead whether people would support teaching respect for homosexuality in public schools. We cannot report distribution of opinion on this issue across our entire sample, because our question was not in our original interview schedule; it evolved out of the responses we were getting to questions about teaching values in public schools. Had we included it, especially in Brookline, our national data might well have shown the same kind of bell-curve distribution we have seen on most issues. Still, the curve would surely have had a different shape. For in the rest of the country outside of Massachusetts, particularly but not exclusively in Oklahoma, the tilt of opinion, compared to middle-class tolerance on other issues, leans firmly against the idea of teaching respect for homosexuality in public schools.

The coding scheme I developed to classify opinion on questions involving homosexuality was designed to distinguish between "positive" and "negative" tolerance. Easiest to classify were those who believed that, because homosexuality was a sin or was unnatural, schools should avoid teaching about homosexuality entirely; such condemnatory attitudes usually were expressed unambiguously. Somewhat harder to classify were those who did believe that schools had an obligation to teach about homosexuality but who differed in their reasoning. Nonetheless, two relatively distinct ways of arguing in favor of teaching about gays in the schools emerged from our interviews. Some have already made clear, on the "negative" grounds of toleration, that they were not necessarily condoning homosexuality but felt that we ought to teach respect for gay people because all people deserve respect. Others argued on more "positive" grounds. On the one hand, gay people have experienced discrimination so that we should go out of our way to treat them with dignity; on the other, they may, because they have had experiences different from most of us, have something important to say to which we need to listen.

Once our respondents were divided into these three categories, the middle category—tolerance without condoning—was, as is true of all bell-curve distributions, larger than those who condemned gays on the one hand and those who sought their positive acceptance on the other. But in this case, the distribution of opinion on the ends of the bell-curve are not even close to being equal: nearly three times as many respondents condemned homosexuality as accepted it. (See table 1.4.) For those who admire tolerance, the good news in these data is the still relatively large number of people who take a nonjudgmental position on homosexuality. But for those who believe that right and wrong still exist—and that homosexuality is wrong—there is also good news. The best that can be said is that support for public acceptance of homosexuality is negative rather than positive, rooted more in a libertarian appreciation of privacy than in active acceptance of homosexuality per se.

Not only is the shape of the bell curve different on this issue, but, just as significantly, the intensity of opinion on this question was quite different than it was toward most other subjects we discussed: those who opposed teaching about homosexuality expressed their views in a very determined manner. Many were clearly made uncomfortable by the topic and did not want to speak about it; one flat-out refused to discuss the subject, while others responded with nervous laughter, confusion, or expressions of pity. A large number of our respondents, while reluctant to condemn people of a different faith or even atheists, had little trouble condemning gays. Among the characterizations of homosexual-

TABLE 1.4
Positions on Teaching Respect for Homosexuals

	Teach Positively	Tolerate	Condemn	Insufficient Information
Broken Arrow	0	10	13	2
Sand Springs	3	12	6	4
DeKalb	6	14	5	0
Cobb	3	18	4	0
Eastlake	2	14	2	7
Rancho Bernardo	1	10	12	2
Total	15	78	42	15

ity that popped up in our interviews were: abnormal, immoral, sinful, unacceptable, sick, unhealthy, untrustworthy, mentally ill, wrong, perverted, and mentally deficient. Both the size of the group willing to condemn homosexuality, and the vehemence with which they do so, indicate that here is indeed the ultimate test of American tolerance: the line separating gay America from straight America is a line that an unusually large number of middle-class Americans are unwilling to cross.

If so many people feel so strongly about the issue, how do they reconcile their rejection of homosexuality with their otherwise strong support for moral individualism? Our follow-up questions to the issue of teaching respect for homosexuality in public school shed some light on this question. Because homosexuality is viewed by its opponents as a choice, it is, some of them believe, possible to reject the choice without rejecting the person who made it. "I hate homosexuality," said Herbert Almond, a black minister in Georgia, but "I love a homosexual. I don't hate him, I hate what he's doing." "God didn't ever say to hate people," added Jen Morgan, the conservative Christian from Cobb County. "He said to love everyone, so you love everyone but hate what they're doing. You can hate the sin but love the person." Gays, for whom sexual preference defines precisely that aspect of their identity that makes them different, would view such comments as hypocritical at best and would doubt the genuineness of the love being offered them. Would they be correct to do so? Yes, I think, they would; the tone and body language of many who spoke this way convinced me that it was intolerance, not love, I was hearing. One might be tempted to admire those middle-class Americans who have not become so taken with inclusive tolerance that they are willing to pronounce definitive judgment on what others do, but one cannot also deny that, when they do so, they are, in effect, condemning the person and not just how he or she acts.

A second prominently asserted reason to oppose teaching respect for gay lifestyles in the schools had to do with the meaning of the word respect. "You earn respect, you just don't get it," said Luis Garcia, a hairdresser in Eastlake. "You don't just get it because you're a homosexual. . . . I don't get it because I am a Mexican." For Winston Cobb in Rancho Bernardo, respect is reciprocal: you are entitled to get it if you are willing to give it, but homosexuals, by their very nature, do not give respect to the majority's sensibilities. George Slade of Cobb County believes that everyone should be treated with respect, but, he continues, gays are divisively asking for special rights: "I see it as the type of thing where . . . you're trying to force something on people rather than some other way of educating people." Just as he would oppose forcing people to believe in one religion—Mr. Slade is among those who dislikes the Christian Coalition—he would also oppose forcing anyone to show respect for a lifestyle of which they would otherwise disapprove. While arguments such as these were hardly models of tolerance, they at least represent an attempt to find a theoretical, primarily secular justification for the position they are supporting. In that sense, they are open to counterargument, which is not true for those who claim to love the person but not the sin.

A third way of justifying opposition to public school teaching of respect for homosexuals involves making a distinction between personal rejection of same-sex orientations and an equally heartfelt rejection of extremism in defense of heterosexuality. Trent Tartt of Broken Arrow, who said he would protest in front of an abortion clinic but would never apply an absolutist moral reasoning that condemned abortion under any and all circumstances, does not want his children exposed in school to ideas about gay people, but he is also afraid that such an attitude could lead to gay bashing, the thought of which appalls him. Reflecting on his dilemma, he admits that he might be narrow as well as wrong; maybe, he muses, he ought to explain such things to his children. "But," he continues, "I don't think morally I am obligated to do that. What I am obligated to do is to teach them what the Bible teaches: 'A man and a woman will become as one and create God's gift.'"

In explaining the different rationales by which a number of middle-class Americans try to reconcile their belief in freedom with their condemnation of homosexuality, I am not suggesting that they share enough underlying moral precepts to imagine possible agreement. It is true that some of those who believe that homosexuality is a sin, like Mr. Tartt, say so, in the spirit of their moral sensibility, modestly, as if too vehement a condemnation of homosexuality would stigmatize too severely. But there is no doubting the matter: the question of homosexuality reveals two genuinely different moral camps in America, ones that disagree profoundly about the fundamental nature of what they are contesting.

At the opposite end of the spectrum from those who condemn homosexuality unambiguously are those who argued in favor of teaching respect for homosexuals in public school. Many of the reasons they offered were practical, based on the simple grounds that homosexuality is a fact of human life that cannot be ignored. As Mrs. Behzadi, the Iranian woman living in Broken Arrow, put it: "I mean, I'm not approving or disapproving any kind of lifestyle, but if I know my kid is going to be taught that . . . there is this fact, there are homosexuals, there are bisexuals, they don't go away by not knowing about them." Others cited the existence of AIDS, which demands, if for no other reasons than self-interest, that young people learn about how diseases are transmitted; large majorities in America support the idea of using sex education classes in schools to teach children how to avoid getting AIDS.[53] In fact, according to polls, far more were in favor of teaching about AIDS than supported prohibiting children with AIDS from attending school or quarantining people with AIDS at home. For a small number of those with whom we talked, such support spilled over into teaching respect for those most at risk for getting the disease.

Because they tend to be deeply devout, African Americans in Georgia ought not to be especially tolerant of gays, both because southern blacks are more likely to believe that homosexuality is wrong than southern whites (by 92 percent compared to 82 percent according to one poll)[54] and because there has long existed a history of condemnation of homosexuality by black preachers. That is not what I found. The middle-class blacks to whom we talked overwhelmingly understood gays as a group that, having suffered discrimination like them, was owed respect. "Black people are more sensitive to everybody because we know how it feels," Laurie Shepard said. "If you're going to teach heterosexual behavior, why not teach homosexual behavior?" added Anna Stevens's husband Gerald. "I'm not homophobic at all," said Vaughn Hyde. "Schools are supposed to prepare. If that's the world we live in, prepare your children." "If you're gonna respect someone or disrespect someone because of their sexual orientation," asked Todd Smith, "where does it end? Next you can disrespect someone because of the color of their skin or the way they walk." The strongest statement—and the most surprising, given that he is a Baptist minister—came from Martin Wolcott:

> Well. I'm a preacher. My wife's a teacher. So we've taught our children to respect other people. Of course if a person is a homosexual, it doesn't mean you have to be a homosexual, but you owe it to show respect to that person. . . . I've had some very close friends that were homosexuals. I cherish their friendship. I know they're homosexuals. . . . I don't preach to them about it.

Not all the African Americans in Atlanta were quite as accepting of homosexuality, but only very few were condemning. Their views were remarkably like two other groups in America especially sensitive to discrimination: Hispanics in Eastlake, who, despite a culture presumably stressing machismo, nonetheless found parallels between discrimination they have experienced and discrimination gays have experienced; and Jews who also tended to support gay rights on the grounds of past discrimination.

Views such as these represent something of a minority position on the question of homosexuality, but they do exist. The question is whether they will remain a minority position. At the present time, Americans strongly oppose the right of gays to marry. Sixty-five percent are against it to one degree or another, while only 28 percent support the idea.[55] Yet one could imagine a situation in which, like the once controversial issue of miscegenation, such opposition will also wane over time on the grounds that any marriage is better than no marriage at all. On the other hand, it could also turn out to be the case that the line drawn over homosexuality will be dug even deeper; fed up with cultural relativism, Americans may well conclude that if the distinction between right and wrong is to be applied anywhere, it should be applied here. Some differences cannot be talked out. This may well be one of them.

Capacious Individualism

When it comes to matters of religious faith, a libertarian stand in American thought is likely to guarantee that strong believers like Jim McLaughlin will be keeping his beliefs to himself and will not have much success insisting that they apply as well to others. But if America avoids the problem of coercing belief, does it open itself up to the problem of believing nothing, or at least nothing worthwhile?

It certainly has not escaped the attention of conservative writers that although Americans say they are religious, they tend not to be religious in a deeply devout way.[56] American religion, in their view, has lost all the important things religion can offer: a sense of the tragic, wonder in the face of powers higher than human beings, necessary constraints on hedonism. Faced with a choice between submission to a power outside (and greater than) themselves and a focus on their own particular needs, American individualism guarantees that the former will rarely triumph over the latter. In one sense such critics are correct: middle-class Americans are very individualistic in outlook. When we talked to her in the Eastlake coffee shop, Jesse O'Donnell gave us a reason for discomfort with public discussions of religion. For her, religion is ultimately an individual experience. To be sure, faith in God "gives you a guideline, you know a foundation to start off with," she said. But it is not God who tells us what is right and wrong, but we ourselves. "It's just right to do certain things," Mrs. O'Donnell affirms. "You know in your gut that something is wrong, so you have to listen to what's inside."

So deep-rooted is religious individualism in America that it led a number of our respondents to make sharp distinctions between their religion and their morality. When I included a question in our interviews about the relationship between morality and religion, I assumed that most people would equate the two. To my surprise, I found that a significant number did not. "I consider myself a moral person. I don't consider myself religious," said Marion Kates of Eastlake. "Having morals can exist without believing in God," was the way Maria Kowalski of Brookline made the same point. "One doesn't need a religious structure in order to have morality," as Joseph Palumbo of Medford put it. "There are loads of behavior which are mutually beneficial which we would call moral. It is not good if we go around murdering each other over cutting each other off at a red light or something like that." "I think morality is a kind of personal decency you have about you," added Ms. Sinclair of Sand Springs. "I think it's kind of more personal as to whether you can respect yourself." Americans are not comfortable being told what to do, even if, perhaps especially if, the teller is a supernatural force whose words are meant as commands.

It is this strong strain of individualism that helps explain why, as religious as Americans are, they also distrust organized religion: in 1990, as few as 23 percent of the American population expressed a great deal of confidence in religious institutions.[57] The notion that Americans would be more comfortable living next to blacks than to religious sectarians is not just an apocryphal story; a 1987 Gallup poll discovered that 44 percent of Americans were hostile to the idea of a religious sectarian living next door compared to 13 percent who said blacks.[58] We found similar sentiments; one of our survey questions stated, "There is such a thing as being too religious," (see table 1.5), and we found, again to my surprise, overwhelming support for that proposition. A situation in which every individual finds his or her own way to God is one that a large number of Americans find more comfortable than one in which highly organized institutions fight with each other both for members and for truth.

Americans, it has been said, like marriage so much that they constantly get divorced so that they can do it again. Much the same applies to their attitudes toward churches: they appreciate them to the point of constantly quitting one and joining another. "In today's society," Adam Grant of Sand Springs told us, "you know, you can go shopping; you can find anything you want out there. You can find anything that fits

TABLE 1.5
"There is such a thing as being too religious."

	Strongly Agree	Agree	No Opinion	Disagree	Strongly Disagree
Brookline	6	13	0	4	2
Medford	8	15	0	2	0
Broken Arrow	2	19	1	3	0
Sand Springs	7	17	1	0	0
DeKalb	3	13	0	8	1
Cobb	2	16	2	1	4
Eastlake	5	15	2	2	1
Rancho Bernardo	4	15	4	2	0
Total	37	123	10	22	8

your beliefs and how you've come to interpret certain things." What's your religious affiliation, we asked Iris Schneider of nearby Broken Arrow? "We've gone to Catholic churches, Lutheran churches—my husband went to a Methodist church. Went to a Church of Christ in St. Louis which is nothing like the Church of Christ down here. And we know a lot of Baptist people, a lot of Jewish people." No wonder that Rhema, the megachurch in Broken Arrow that dominated the area in which we conducted our interview with her, provides such wonderful day care centers and soccer leagues; without them, it might lose competition for parishioners. As a sociologist, I am not a great fan of "rational choice theory," the notion that human beings make decisions based on calculations of self-interest. As middle-class Americans talked, not about their faith but about their churches as institutions, I came to believe that rational choice theory was a good way of understanding which ones they joined and which ones they left. Americans are free-agent churchgoers. As they do with marriages and with jobs, they leave situations they find uncomfortable for ones that promise more happiness. When it comes to religious affiliations, short-term contracts are better.

One reason why religion is seen by so many people in individual terms has to do with personal experiences of religious sectarianism. While dating his wife, Pedro Govea, a Catholic, went to a Baptist meeting with her only to hear it turn into an attack on Catholicism. Joanna Cage, an accountant in Broken Arrow, attended a number of different churches and was repelled by their sectarianism before finding one that made her and her husband comfortable. Rancho Bernardo's Henry Carter grew up as an active Methodist, joined the army, discovered how sectarian Protestants could be, and doesn't consider himself very religious any longer. A common *rite de passage* among middle-class Americans brought up Catholic is to relate a story about how the strictness of the Church eventually caused them to leave it, or at least to tone down their allegiance. There is a widespread feeling in middle-class America that religious belief, which is personal, is more important than religious affiliation, which is organizational. Churches and sects, not people, cause discord. By getting around the churches in the middle, individuals and God can come to know each other better. But before concluding that Americans are so committed to individualism that they lack genuine faith, it is important to understand what they remain faithful to.

A generation ago Will Herberg wrote that Americans put their faith in faith.[59] Now it would be more correct to say that they put their faith in people. A deep-seated belief in people's goodness enables middle-class Americans to accept the principle that people should be free to choose their God, or even not to choose God at all, without worrying that the consequence will be anarchy, for good people will always make the right kinds of choices. Americans are not dissatisfied with the moral fiber of their fellow Americans. Is this country becoming Godless? we asked our respondents, and they overwhelmingly replied that it was not. Relatively few Americans think the world is filled with evil and sin compared to those who believe that, as the General Social Survey phrases one of its questions, "There is much goodness in the world which hints at God's greatness."[60] America, its citizens believe, is too good a place, and the people who live here too good a people, for jeremiads to have all that much credibility.

"Religion is a big, binding thing," we were told by Samina Hoque, a physicist in Medford from Bangladesh. "Good religions, you know, not the cult thing. Good religions teach you how to care for each other, how to have faith in life, faith in things, . . . and be happy with what you have." If people are reasonable, the existence of many competing religions need not be an obstacle to finding a common morality, many of those with whom we spoke believe, and can even be an advantage. "I don't think we're all gonna read out of the same Bible," says Joyce Umber of Broken Arrow, "and I don't think we're all gonna read the same things if we did. I think there's good people and I think we are all striving for the same place. And I'm not gonna say that their religion is wrong because they might hate my religion." Compared to religious absolutists like Jim McLaughlin, who fears that without one true faith moral anarchy is inevitable, believers in the modest virtues are convinced that liberal democracies must make room for people of faith but must also ensure that such room is never so confining that it excludes people of different faiths.

If the American belief in individualism were focused only on the self, there would be reason to fear that the separation of religion from one

God, and then the separation of morality from religion, would lead to a situation of moral anarchy. But when Americans talk about their faith, their individualism is meant not only for themselves but also for others; the individualism that guides their beliefs is a capacious one meant to apply to all. Religious individualism as they understand it is a compromise position between immoral selfishness and coercive conformity; a selfish person cannot be religious, while a believer in religious absolutism cannot be individualistic. That is why it can even include people who have no religious beliefs, so long as all of them share the same faith that others can be trusted to do the right thing.

"The way I like to picture things," Judy Dropkin of Eastlake, a volunteer coordinator, summed up, "is that God is at the top of a mountain and there's a whole lot of sides to him and the easiest way for you to get there is the easiest way for you to get there and there are a whole lot of roads to the top. I think we all struggle to get there, and you got to find your own way." Bostonians use a different metaphor; one compared religious diversity to a rotary—everyone else in America calls them traffic circles—that different drivers enter and leave at different points. The fact that so many Americans, when searching for metaphors to discuss religion and morality, turn to transportation—wheels, highways, roads up a mountain, traffic circles—suggests that, like good liberals, they are always going somewhere but also that, like good communitarians, they expect to arrive at a destination.

In the years after World War II, critics worried that Americans were not religious enough. Then, convinced that a new religious revival was taking place in America, other critics began to believe that Americans were becoming too religious, suppressing, in turn, the rights of non-Christians and nonbelievers. And critics from all sides of the debate understand that there will always be conflicts between the liberal-democratic commitments that govern public life and the need for faith that enriches private life. None of the questions raised by any of these critics are easy to answer. But because the first person cited in this chapter shall be the last, let me once again offer the views of Jesse O'Donnell:

> My general belief is that people are inherently good and they can make the right decisions based on what's right and what's wrong, not necessarily because that's what their religion taught them. If you don't have religion, there's still right and wrong. I think religion gives you the hope that no matter how bad things get, something is always there to make it better and that there's a reason for things. I think you almost have to believe that there's a higher [power].

As the country tries to negotiate its way through the question of the right public role for religion, people like Mrs. O'Donnell, who organize their thoughts around the modest virtues, are likely to help us find, if not the right answers in some ultimate sense, then answers we can live with for the here and now.

Notes

1. James Hudnut-Beumler, *Looking for God in the Suburbs: The Religion of the American Dream and Its Critics, 1945–1965* (New Brunswick, N.J.: Rutgers University Press, 1994).

2. R. Laurence Moore, *Selling God: American Religion in the Marketplace of Culture* (New York: Oxford University Press, 1994).

3. Will Herberg, *Protestant-Catholic-Jew: An Essay in American Religious Sociology*, rev. ed. (Garden City, N.Y.: Anchor Books, 1960), 59.

4. Gibson Winter, *The Suburban Captivity of the Churches: An Analysis of Protestant Responsibility in the Expanding Metropolis* (Garden City, N.Y.: Doubleday, 1961).

5. Peter L. Berger, *The Noise of Solemn Assemblies: Christian Commitment and the Religious Establishment in America* (Garden City, N.Y.: Doubleday, 1961).

6. Hillel Levine and Lawrence Harmon, *The Death of an American Jewish Community: The Tragedy of Good Intentions* (New York: Free Press, 1992); Albert J. Gordon, *Jews in Suburbia* (Boston: Beacon Press, 1959), 244–45; Marshall Shklare and Joseph Greenbaum, *Jewish Identity on the Suburban Frontier: A Study of Group Survival in Society* (New York: Basic Books, 1987), 306–7.

7. Allen Ehrenhalt, *The Lost City: Discovering the Forgotten Virtues of Community* (New York: Basic Books, 1995); John T. McGreevy, *Parish Boundaries: The Catholic Encounter with Race in the Twentieth Century Urban North* (Chicago: University of Chicago Press, 1996).

8. Joseph J. Casino, "From Sanctuary to Involvement: A History of the Catholic Parish in the Northeast," in *The American Catholic Parish: A History*, Vol. 1, ed. Jay P. Dolan (New York: Paulist Press, 1987), 91–92.

9. Jay P. Dolan, *The American Catholic Experience: A History from Colonial Times to the Present* (Garden City, N.Y.: Doubleday, 1985), 358.

10. Robert Wuthnow, *The Restructuring of American Religion: Society and Faith Since World War II* (Princeton, N.J.: Princeton University Press, 1988), 159.

11. Ronald F. Thiemann, *Religion in Public Life: A Dilemma for Democracy* (Washington, D.C.: Georgetown University Press, 1996).

12. Cited in Kenneth Karst, *Law's Promise, Law's Expression: Visions of Power in the Politics of Race, Gender, and Religion* (New Haven, Conn.: Yale University Press. 1993), 6.

13. Robert N. Bellah, *The Broken Covenant: American Civil Religion in a Time of Trial* (New York: Seabury Press, 1975), 3.

14. Herbert M. Danzger, *Returning to Tradition: The Contemporary Revival*

of Orthodox Judaism (New Haven, Conn.: Yale University Press, 1989); Lynn Davidman, *Tradition in a Rootless World: Women Turn to Orthodox Judaism* (Berkeley and Los Angeles: University of California Press, 1991). In the New York suburbs, areas of Rockland County, particularly around New City, became the locus of Orthodox Jewish suburbanization.

15. McGreevy, *Parish Boundaries*, 80; Gene Burns, *The Frontiers of Catholicism: The Politics of Ideology in a Liberal World* (Berkeley and Los Angeles: University of California Press, 1992), 99.

16. Barry A. Kosmin and Seymour P. Lachman, *One Nation under God: Religion in Contemporary American Society* (New York: Harmony Books, 1993), 256.

17. Mirta Ojito, "Immigrants' New Road Leads to Suburbia," *New York Times*, September 30, 1996, B1.

18. Dean M. Kelley, *Why Conservative Churches Are Growing* (New York: Harper, 1977).

19. Wuthnow, *The Restructuring of American Religion*, 132–72; James Davison Hunter, *Culture Wars: The Struggle to Define America* (New York: Basic Books, 1991).

20. *Rosenberger v Rector and Visitors of the University of Virginia et al.* 115 S.Ct. 2510. The Court had clearly been influenced by Michael McConnell, "Accommodation of Religion," in *The Supreme Court Review, 1995*, ed. Philip B. Kurland (Chicago: University of Chicago Press, 1988), 1–60, and "Religious Freedom at the Crossroads," in *The Bill of Rights*, ed. Geoffrey Stone (Chicago: University of Chicago Press, 1992), 115–94.

21. Ralph Reed, *Active Faith: How Christians Are Changing the Soul of American Politics* (New York: Free Press, 1996).

22. Jim Wallis, *Who Speaks for God? An Alternative to the Religious Right* (New York: Delacorte, 1996).

23. Robert T. Handy, *Undermined Establishment: Church-State Relations in America, 1880–1920* (Princeton, N.J.: Princeton University Press, 1991); Isaac Kramnick and R. Laurence Moore, *The Godless Constitution: The Case against Religious Correctness* (New York: Norton, 1996).

24. Elizabeth Mensch and Alan Freeman, *The Politics of Virtue: Is Abortion Debatable?* (Durham, N.C.: Duke University Press, 1993).

25. Andrew Greeley, *Religion around the World: A Preliminary Report* (Chicago: National Opinion Research Center, 1991), 39, cited in Seymour Martin Lipset, *American Exceptionalism: A Double-Edged Sword* (New York: Norton, 1996), 61.

26. The Pew Research Center for the People and the Press, "The Diminishing Divide: American Churches, American Politics," 25 June 1996, 10–11; *The American Enterprise* 5 (September/October 1994): 90; Tom W. Smith, "The Polls: Religious Beliefs and Behaviors and the Televangelist Scandals of 1987–88," *Public Opinion Quarterly* 56 (Fall 1992): 367–71. Data from the General Social Survey (hereafter GSS) were downloaded from the home page of the Inter-University Consortium for Political and Social Research: http://www.icpsr.umich.edu/gss. The suggested reference is James Allen Davis and Tom W. Smith, *General Social Surveys, 1972–1994* [machine-readable data file]

(Chicago: National Opinion Research Center, 1994) See GSS, Trends, AT-TEND. Similar findings are reported in the National Election Study: 13 percent said that "[t]he Bible is a book written by men and is not the word of God," compared to 38 percent who indicated that "[t]he Bible is the word of God and is to be taken literally, word for word," and 45.6 percent who said that "[t]he Bible is the word of God, but not everything in it should be taken literally, word for word." The National Election Study (hereafter NES) was also downloaded from the home page of the Inter-University Consortium for Political Research at the University of Michigan. The formal citation is Stephen J. Rosenstone, Donald R. Kinder, Warren E. Miller, and the National Elections Studies, *American National Election Study 1994: Post-Election Survey* [enhanced with 1992 and 1993 data] [computer file] (Ann Arbor, Mich.: Inter-University Consortium for Political Research, 1995). See NES, VAR 1047.

27. C. Kirk Hadaway, Penny L. Marler, and Mark Chaves, "What the Polls Don't Show: A Closer Look at U.S. Church Attendance," *American Sociological Review* 58 (December 1993): 741; Jeffery Haddon and C. E. Swann, *Prime-Time Preachers: The Rising Power of Televangelism* (Reading, Mass.: Addison-Wesley, 1981).

28. Steve Bruce, *Religion in the Modern World: From Cathedrals to Cults* (Oxford: Oxford University Press, 1996), 129.

29. Ronald Inglehart, *1990 World Values Survey* (Ann Arbor, Mich.: Institute for Social Research, 1990), cited in Lipset, *American Exceptionalism*, 64.

30. For a similar finding, see Theodore Caplow, Howard M. Bahr, and Bruce A. Chadwick, *All Faithful People: Change and Continuity in Middletown's Religion* (Minneapolis: University of Minnesota Press, 1983), 98.

31. Robert Wuthnow, *Poor Richard's Principle: Rediscovering the American Dream through the Moral Dimension of Work, Business, and Money* (Princeton, N.J.: Princeton University Press, 1996), 312.

32. T. Smith, "The Polls: Religious Beliefs," 364–65.

33. Wuthnow, *The Restructuring of American Religion*, 169.

34. Pew Research Center, "The Diminishing Divide," 7.

35. James Davison Hunter and Carl Bowman, *The State of Disunion: 1996 Survey of American Political Culture* (Ivy, Va.: In Medias Res Educational Foundation, 1996), tables 15.A–15.P

36. Pew Research Center, "The Diminishing Divide," 1–6.

37. Nancy J. Davis and Robert V. Robinson, "Religious Orthodoxy in American Society. The Myth of a Monolithic Camp," *Journal for the Scientific Study of Religion* 35 (September 1996): 229–45.

38. Hunter and Bowman, *The State of Disunion*, table 16.M.

39. This church is the subject of a doctoral dissertation. See Scott L. Thumma, "The Kingdom, the Power, the Glory: The Megachurch in Modern American Society" (Ph.D. diss., Candler School of Theology, Emory University, 1996).

40. Jim Bakker, *I Was Wrong* (Nashville: Thomas Nelson, 1996).

41. Egon Mayer, *Love and Tradition: Marriage between Christians and Jews* (New York: Plenum Press, 1985).

42. This tendency of Americans to pick their own religious faith led to the

development of rational choice approaches to religion. See Roger Finke and Rodney Stark, *The Churching of America 1576–1990: Winners and Losers in Our Religious Economy* (New Brunswick, N.J.: Rutgers University Press, 1992).

43. R. Stephen Warner, "Work in Progress toward a New Paradigm for the Sociological Study of Religion in the United States," *American Journal of Sociology* 98 (March 1993): 1044–93, and the essays in R. Stephen Warner and Judith G. Wittner, eds., *Gatherings in Diaspora: Religious Communities and the New Immigration* (Philadelphia: Temple University Press, 1998).

44. Amy Gutmann and Dennis Thompson, *Democracy and Disagreement* (Cambridge: Harvard University Press, Belknap Press, 1996).

45. Richard John Neuhaus, *The Naked Public Square* (Grand Rapids, Mich.: Eerdmans, 1984).

46. N. J. Demerath III and Rhys H. Williams, *A Bridging of Faiths: Religion and Politics in a New England City* (Princeton, N.J.: Princeton University Press, 1992), 100.

47. Jesse Choper, *Securing Religious Liberty: Principles for Judicial Interpretation of the Religious Clauses* (Chicago: University of Chicago Press, 1995), and Stephen D. Smith, *Foreordained Failure: The Quest for a Constitutional Principle of Religious Freedom* (New York: Oxford University Press, 1995).

48. Keith Hartman, *Congregations in Conflict: The Battle over Homosexuality* (New Brunswick, N.J.: Rutgers University Press, 1996).

49. Hunter and Bowman, *The State of Disunion*, table 42.A.

50. GSS, statistical data, HOMOSEX1. See also Tom W. Smith, "The Polls: The Sexual Revolution," *Public Opinion Quarterly* 54 (Fall 1990): 424. For similar results, see *Public Opinion* 10 (July/August 1987): 27.

51. Americans are more likely to allow homosexuals to speak or to permit gay books in libraries than not; GSS, statistics, SPKHOMO, LIBHOMO. In 1987, slightly more Americans thought that homosexual relations between consenting adults in the privacy of their own homes should be legal than believed it should be illegal. T. Smith, "The Polls: The Sexual Revolution," 424.

52. GSS, Trends, COLHOMO.

53. Theresa F. Rogers, Eleanor Singer, and Jennifer Imperio, "The Polls: AIDS, an Update," *Public Opinion Quarterly* 57 (Spring 1993): 109, 111–12.

54. *Public Opinion* 10 (January/February 1988): 31.

55. Pew Research Center, "The Diminishing Divide," 65. See also Hunter and Bowman, *The State of Disunion*, table 42.B, for roughly similar results. A 1988 GSS question showed 77.6 percent disagreeing and 12.5 percent agreeing that gays should have the right to marry. GSS, statistics, MARHOMO.

56. Thomas C. Reeves, "Not So Christian America," in *The Empty Church: The Suicide of Liberal Christianity* (New York: Free Press, 1996).

57. T. Smith, "The Polls: Religious Beliefs," 367.

58. *Public Opinion* 10 (July August 1987): 23

59. Herberg, *Protestant, Catholic, Jew*, 89.

60. GSS, WORLD1.

2

PUBLIC RELIGION:

BANE OR BLESSING FOR DEMOCRACY?

Ronald F. Thiemann

AMERICAN democracy is under severe scrutiny today. At the center of the current debate about democracy's future lies the recognition that American citizens are increasingly disaffected from the large bureaucratized organizations that determine their political and economic welfare. Recent polling data collected by the Postmodernity Project at the University of Virginia reveal that while Americans remain firmly committed to the ideals of democracy—individual liberty, equal opportunity, social justice, toleration of differences—they are deeply suspicious of government's ability to realize these ideals in their daily lives.[1] Moreover, many citizens experience growing anxiety about the decline of those moral communities that provide the virtues necessary for democratic citizenship: families, communities of faith, civic associations of all kinds.[2] These two interlocking concerns about the demise of effective government and the decay of those communities of virtue that constitute civil society conspire to create serious misgivings about the health of American democratic institutions.

Given the prominence of communities of faith among the associations within civil society, it is not surprising that some politicians have urged a more active role for churches, synagogues, mosques, and temples in providing government-supported but faith-based delivery of social services.[3] Such proposals come, of course, at precisely the time when the government has dramatically slashed the budgets of federal social service agencies. Officials of Catholic Charities USA estimate that each of the nation's 258,000 local communities of faith would have to donate at least $225,000 a year to make up for the congressionally approved cuts in the current federal budget. Since, however, the average budget of American congregations is around $100,000, the shortfall in funding remains a key unresolved issue. Still, the dramatic successes of faith-based programs like Chicago's One Child, One Church adoption program[4] or Boston's "Ten Point Coalition" against drugs and gang violence[5] or the many spiritually oriented twelve-step programs suggest that religious institutions can be effective agents for social healing and reconciliation. Religious groups can provide a sense of individual motivation and communal involvement often lacking in purely secular governmental programs. If the crisis in today's cities is, as Cornel West has argued, a spiritual crisis, that is, "a loss of hope and absence of meaning,"[6] then the involvement of faith-based agencies in the amelioration of that crisis would seem salutary.

Despite the positive results achieved by faith-based social programs, many still remain skeptical of granting religious groups the authority to deliver services to diverse populations. Should public funding go to groups that have a specific proselytizing mission? Should the Joy of Jesus organization, an evangelical job-training program in Detroit, be allowed to require daily Bible readings and prayers of all its clients if it receives government funds? The state of Michigan answered no, whereupon the placement rate of the program dropped from over 60 percent to near zero in just over a year.[7] The tendency of some religious groups toward discrimination, intolerance, and fanaticism lends further support to those who would ban public funds from faith-based social agencies. The fact that so many of our fundamental moral disagreements in matters like abortion, homosexuality, physician assisted suicide, and the like are grounded in seemingly irresolvable religious disputes leads many to claim that religion should be severely limited in the public realm. Sociologist James Davison Hunter has offered a grim view of the role of religion in such cultural disagreements.

> In the final analysis, each side of the cultural divide can only talk past the other. . . . This is true because what both sides bring to the public debate in non-negotiable. . . . What is ultimately at issue are deeply rooted and fundamentally different understandings of being and purpose . . . [i.e.], different conceptions of the sacred. . . . Communities cannot and will not tolerate the desecration of the sacred. The problem is this: not only does each side of the cultural divide operate with a different conception of the sacred, but the mere existence of the one represents a certain desecration of the other.[8]

Must religion lead inevitably to cultural contention, discord, and warfare? Is religious belief inherently intolerant? When religion enters public life will it always serve to fragment and divide democratic citizens? Certainly the Enlightenment ethos out of which the founders of the American republic emerged was suspicious of religion's public role. The European advocates of Enlightenment philosophy and politics had witnessed the devastating effect of the post-Reformation religious wars upon continental culture and were determined to restrict religious fervor to the private realm. Contemporary defenders of the Enlightenment position continue to advocate that democratic government must be rigorously secular and neutral. That argument has recently been restated for a popular readership by Isaac Kramnick and R. Laurence Moore in their book *The Godless Constitution*. Appealing to the Jeffersonian tradition of the "wall of separation between church and state," the authors argue that the founders advocated both a "godless Constitution and . . . a godless politics." In brief, this position recognizes that the nation's founders, both in writing the Constitution and in defending it in the ratification debates, sought to separate the operations of government from any claim that human beings can know and follow divine direction in reaching policy decisions."[9] Moreover, "the founders left the business of teaching morality to private concerns. . . . It follows from this formulation that if the United States at the end of the twentieth century has lost its moral way, many of our voluntary institutions, including our megachurches and our television ministries, have badly let us down."[10]

This position, which I like to call "classical liberalism," has recently been subjected to criticism by a group of progressive thinkers who want to break with classical liberalism's assertion that democratic public life must be scrupulously neutral and secular. These "new liberals" also sense that public religion may have an important role in addressing the moral crisis that currently grips our nation. Rather than assuming that public religion will ignite cultural warfare, these scholars—rather tentatively at times—offer the hope that religion might help us to deal more effectively with the pluralism of contemporary democratic life. The neo-Marxist and pragmatist philosopher Richard Bernstein has argued that there are "still the vestiges of community life and community bonds in religious life" that might enable it to "play a role in the vitalization of public life."[11] Pointing to his own personal experience in the civil rights movement, Bernstein notes, "The fact that there was *already* a preexisting sense of communal religious bonds provided many individuals with the courage, hope, and conviction to join together in public action. It illustrates what I think is becoming increasingly evident in our time— that if there is to be a renewal of public life, a communal basis for individuals coming together, it is to be found outside those great impersonal abstractions of society and state."[12] In a remarkably similar mode, Adam Michnik, the Polish intellectual and Solidarity activist, highlighted the essential role of religion in providing counter–public spaces for those who opposed the tyranny of the Eastern European communist states. "In East Germany, Czechoslovakia, Hungary, as well as in Poland, the recovery of freedom, the revival of civil society, and the public presence of the churches were closely connected. . . . An active, public role for religion, therefore, would seem to be one of the preconditions of a vibrant democratic life."[13] Finally, in his new book *Democracy's*

Discontent, Harvard political philosopher Michael Sandel notes that the work of the Industrial Areas Foundation (IAF), a network of community-based organizations devoted to teaching the poor the skills of political involvement, increasingly rely upon communities of faith as their organization focal points. "In recent decades . . . most traditional bases of civic activity in inner cities have eroded, leaving religious congregations the only vital institutions in many communities. As a result . . . the IAF [has] organized primarily around congregations, especially Catholic and Protestant churches. . . . [These] parishes [provide] not only a stable source of funds, participants, and leaders but also a shared moral language as a starting point for political discourse."[14]

Public religion: bane or blessing? Public religion: source of cultural warfare or political vitality? Public religion: threat to democracy or its last best hope? The fact that cultural analysts can have such diametrically opposed evaluations of the role of religion in our public life is one indication of our deep confusion concerning public religion. We can never hope to reach cultural consensus concerning religion's proper role in public life until we gain clarity regarding three key issues: (1) Should religion be relegated solely to the private realm, or can it have a role in our common public life as well? (2) Does the First Amendment of the Constitution mandate the "separation between church and state" thereby prohibiting the mixing of religion and politics? (3) How might public religion become a force for moral renewal in our religiously diverse society? I will treat each of these issues in turn and then conclude by offering some proposals about reforms I believe are needed within churches and other communities of faith if religion is to play a positive role in the future of American democracy.

1. Should religion be relegated solely to the private realm or can it have a role in our common public life as well? During much of the twentieth century theories of secularization dominated the intellectual landscape of most academic disciplines. Secularization theories argued that as capitalist economics and democratic politics expanded worldwide we would witness a withering away of religion's public role. The social differentiation of modern societies, so the common wisdom went, creates discreet spheres of human activity, each with its own internal rationality. The increased division of labor characteristic of the modern world requires specialized modes of reasoning, knowledge, and skills or competence within each sphere. While there may be some intersection of the forms of knowledge required by fields such as engineering, organizational management, heart surgery, and agriculture, clearly no single way of knowing and reasoning could encompass every field, discipline, and profession. Consequently, overarching religious and metaphysical worldviews can no longer play the role of providing the common discourse or moral orientation for all persons in modern society. Each sphere of activity will inevitably develop the standards of rationality and behavior appropriate to competence or success in that field. The complexity of modern differentiated societies makes the totalizing aims of religion and metaphysics irrelevant to the modern world.[15]

Just as importantly, secularization theories continued, the expansion of democratic forms of government and capitalist economies created major spheres of activity within which religious beliefs are not only irrelevant but dangerous. Given the "pluralization of life-worlds," i.e., the diversity of ways of believing and acting in the modern world, the dominance of any single religious view would lead to suppressions of freedom contradictory to the aims of democracy. Moreover, the attempt to introduce religious controls in the economic sphere can only spell disaster for the play of free market forces essential to the world of business and commerce. Freedom and self-determination are the hallmarks of modern democratic and capitalist societies, and religious beliefs, grounded as they are in authority and tradition, must give way, so the secularization theorists argued, to the inexorable forward movement of modernity. Religion in the modern world can no longer play a public role, i.e., a role that provides common ground and shared principles for belief and action. If religion were to survive modernity, it must do so in the private lives of individual citizens. Religion, like other commodities in the smorgasbord of democratic capitalism, is something you are free to choose or reject as personal preference dictated. Religion in modernity is "the kind of thing you like, if you like that kind of thing."

The withering away of public religion—or of religion altogether—seemed to many a reliable prophecy until at least the mid-1970s. The advanced democratic societies of northern Europe, particularly the Scandinavian countries, provided the ideal laboratories for secularization theories. As freedom and prosperity grew in these nations, church attendance and professed religious belief declined accordingly. Sweden and Denmark became the dream societies of secularization theorists. Then, seemingly out of nowhere, came the Shiite revolution in Iran, and the world-altering power of public religion became apparent. Still, secularization theory could accommodate the Iranian revolution, since Islamic fundamentalism is itself a pre- or antimodern phenomenon. Indeed, advocates for secularization theory pointed to Iran as evidence for the intolerant and fanatical character of public religion in the modern world. Thus the theories continued to hold sway—despite ample evidence to the contrary in Africa, Asia, and South America—until the more recent revolutions in the communist nations of Eastern Europe. In almost every case religion played a decisive role in providing counter–

public space for citizens to organize and protest against the ruling communist regimes. In East Germany citizen rallies were held every Sunday evening following vesper services at St. Thomas Kirche in Leipzig. At the conclusion of worship, these citizens would light candles and march around the walls of the old city singing the songs of the American civil rights movement in highly accented English. And, sure enough, soon the wall came a-tumblin' down. In Romania the violent coup began with protests of the arrest of the Reverend Lazlo Tokes, a Protestant minister who had spoken out against the suppression of the Hungarian minority in Romania. So, too, the revolutions in Poland and Czechoslovakia were fomented in part by the roles of the Catholic worker union Solidarity and the spiritual humanism of Vaclav Havel. Clearly, religion was not the sole factor in this dramatic shift of political power, but classical secularization theory would never have predicted this remarkable outburst of public religion. At the same time, as the tragic events in the former Yugoslavia have shown, public religion continues to play a role in igniting the flames of ethnic hatred worldwide. Nonetheless, the forecasted withering away of public religion—or its consignment to the private realm—seems to have been premature, to say the least.

Let me be clear about my argument. I am not disputing the notion that pluralistic societies can no longer be organized around the religious beliefs of a single faith or tradition. Cultural, religious, and moral diversity is a fact of modern democratic life. I am only disputing the conclusion that this pluralism inevitably leads to the disappearance of religion or to its banishment to the private sphere. Public religion remains a potent force—for good and ill—in the modern world. The question is, What role should public religion properly play in pluralistic democratic societies? Can public religion provide any common ground for our increasingly diverse and contentious societies? Does the success of public religion in organizing the protests within the nations of Eastern Europe give us reason for hope in our own situation? Before we can address that question, we must look briefly at the special situation that exists within the constitutional democracy of the United States.

2. Does the First Amendment to the American Constitution mandate "the separation of church and state," thereby prohibiting the mixing of religion and politics? For many reasons the situation within the United States is unique among the postindustrial democratic capitalist nations of the world. In contrast to the European nations, which provided the raw data for modern secularization theory, American society has always had, in the words of William James, "a buzzin' bloomin' confusion" of religion. Recent polling information indicates that fully 93 percent of American identify themselves as "professing" religious persons, and nearly 77 percent of the population characterize themselves as "practicing" some form of organized religion. Among practicing American Christians more than half report they are "regular" in their church attendance. While Christianity remains, by some considerable margin, the majority religion in the United States, the last two decades have witnessed a sharp increase in genuine religious diversity within the American populace.

While statistical information on religious practice outside of Christianity and Judaism is notoriously difficult to gather, the best analyses indicate that growth patterns among Muslims, Buddhists, and Hindus are particularly striking. While the Jewish population has remained relatively stable during the past twenty years (approximately 3.2 percent of the population), the number of Muslims has more than quadrupled during the same period. It is now estimated that there are more than 3 million practicing Muslims in the United States; in 1970 there were fewer than 800,000. There are currently more Muslims than Episcopalians or Presbyterians in the United States, and, if growth trends continue, early in the twenty-first century there will be more Muslims than Jews.[16]

Not only is religious practice alive and well in the United States, the signs of public religion are also apparent in American life today. The Moral Majority and its successor organization the Christian Coalition have had an enormous impact on American politics, particularly within the Republican Party. African American religion has always seen a continuity between the spiritual and the political, as witnessed in the careers of clergymen like Martin Luther King, Jr., Adam Clayton Powell, and Jesse Jackson. The Roman Catholic bishops have become increasingly influential in debates about public policy issues as diverse as abortion, nuclear arms, human rights, and welfare policy. Yet many people wonder how this political activity can be permitted in a democracy with a mandated "separation between church and state." How does our official policy of "separation" square with the fact of congressional and military chaplains paid from public funds; of tax exemptions for churches, synagogues, and their auxiliary institutions; of currencies inscribed with the motto "In God We Trust"? Why is state-sponsored prayer permitted in the Supreme Court and the U.S. Congress but not in American public schools? (Perhaps, former Chief Justice Burger once surmised, because prayer is more needed in the Supreme Court and the U.S. Congress!)

Does the First Amendment of the American Constitution mandate the "separation of church and state"? Most Americans would without hesitation answer yes to that question; indeed, many believe that those very words appear in the Constitution. Of course, they do not. The religion clauses of the First Amendment read, "Congress shall make no law respecting an establishment of religion or prohibiting the free exercise thereof." For the first 150 years of judicial interpretation of the First

Amendment the phrase "the wall of separation between church and state" played virtually no role in Religion Clause jurisprudence. The phrase entered the court's lexicon for the first time in 1947 in Justice Hugo Black's decision in *Everson v. Board of Education.* It is derived from a metaphor first used by Roger Williams, founder of the Rhode Island colony, in a letter to John Cotton and then borrowed by Thomas Jefferson in a letter to the Baptist Association of Danbury, Connecticut. (I am convinced that an enterprising law clerk, seeking a memorable phrase for Justice Black's decision, discovered the Jefferson letter and suggested its use in *Everson*, thereby altering Religion Clause interpretation forever.)

"The First Amendment has erected a wall [of separation] between church and state. That wall must be kept high and impregnable. We could not approve the slightest breach."[17] The day Justice Black penned those fateful words, the U.S. Supreme Court was convened with the invocation, "God save this honorable court." A few hundred yards across the Mall from the Supreme Court building, the two houses of Congress opened their sessions with prayers offered by chaplains supported by public funds and paid with currency inscribed with the motto "In God We Trust." Some months later President Harry S. Truman would follow the custom of nearly every president since the founding of the republic by issuing a proclamation declaring a national day of thanksgiving and urging Americans to engage in prayer of thanks to the Creator for his manifold gifts to the nation.

In light of these apparently contradictory sentiments about the role of religion in American public life, it should not surprise you to learn that the decision that introduced the phrase "wall of separation" into the Court's lexicon actually *upheld* a New Jersey state statute that provided public funding for transportation of children attending Roman Catholic schools. Justice Black, having affirmed that the wall of separation must not be breached, then offered the puzzling opinion that "New Jersey has not breached it here," even though the state used public tax funds to support the busing of Roman Catholic schoolchildren.

Space does not permit full treatment of the Supreme Court's confusing and contradictory record of religion clause adjudication since the *Everson* decision. Suffice it to say that the judgments of critics characterizing the Court's decision making in this area as "bizarre," "fatuous," "a hodgepodge . . . derived from *Alice's Adventures in Wonderland*" seem no overstatement. In a recent establishment case, for example, the Court ruled by a 5–4 margin, with divided and often conflicting arguments, that a crèche erected on Allegheny County property violated the First Amendment but a menorah did not.[18] Why? Because the menorah is, in the Court's judgment, a secular symbol—an opinion that will come as a surprise to many practicing Jews. A much more serious trend in the Court's adjudication, however, has been the tendency to restrict defendants' appeal to the protection of the free exercise clause.

On June 25, 1997, the Supreme Court in a 6–3 decision (*City of Boerne v. Flores, Archbishop of San Antonio*) overturned the Religious Freedom Restoration Act enacted by Congress in 1993.[19] This act (RFRA) prohibited government from "substantially burdening" a person's exercise of religion even if the burden results from a law generally applicable to the entire population. Drawing on earlier Supreme Court decisions, especially *Sherbert v. Verner*, Congress declared that free exercise of religion could be constrained only on grounds of "a compelling governmental interest" and that government must use "the least restrictive means of furthering that . . . interest."[20] The Supreme Court ruled that this act was unconstitutional because Congress overstepped its constitutionally mandated bounds by "altering the meaning" of the Free Exercise clause. The doctrine of the separation of powers grants the sole right of constitutional interpretation to the Judiciary, and Congress in mandating the "compelling governmental interest" criterion engaged in improper Constitutional interpretation.[21]

Justice Sandra Day O'Connor in her dissenting opinion did not disagree with the Court's interpretation of the separation of powers doctrine but pleaded that the Court reverse its earlier flawed reasoning in free exercise cases and specifically asked the Court to overturn its decision in the landmark case *Employment Division v. Smith*.[22] "I remain of the view that Smith was wrongly decided, and I would use this case to reexamine the Court's holding there. . . . If the Court were to correct the misinterpretation of the Free Exercise Clause set forth in Smith, it would simultaneously put our First Amendment jurisprudence back on course and allay the legitimate concerns of a majority in Congress who believed that Smith improperly restricted religious liberty."[23]

I am in complete agreement with Justice O'Connor. Whatever the merits of the Court's finding regarding separation of powers, the substantive question of the meaning and application of the Free Exercise Clause remains the primary issue. Two cases decided in the last decade demonstrate the Court's increasing tendency to restrict the free exercise of religion, particularly of minority religious traditions.

In 1986, the Supreme Court upheld a lower court decision prohibiting Captain Simcha Goldman, an Orthodox Jew, from wearing a yarmulke while on duty in a health clinic in which he served. In writing for the majority, Justice Rehnquist stated that the standard military uniform encourages "the subordination of the desires and interests of the individual to the needs of the service." In this characterization the wearing of the yarmulke is identified not as an aspect of required religious practice but of mere individual desire and interest. Consequently, the religious dimension of the case was simply sidestepped, and the Court rendered its opinion by supporting the need of the military for a uniform dress code. The irony is that the Court thus avoided altogether the religious question and refused to treat this case as one of free exercise.

Had they taken more seriously the wearing of the yarmulke as a matter of required Orthodox religious practice the case would undoubtedly have been decided otherwise. Had the question of religious obligation been considered, it is difficult to imagine that the Court could have sustained a judgment that the state had a compelling governmental interest. Surely the wearing of a yarmulke is a significant religious practice and deserved the protection of the First Amendment guarantee of freedom of religion. The fact that minority religious practice received this discriminatory ruling is of particular concern.

The free exercise case that occasioned the RFRA is *Employment Division v. Smith*, 1990. In this case, the Supreme Court upheld Oregon's denial of unemployment compensation sought when two employees were dismissed from their jobs for using a controlled substance, peyote, in a native American religious ritual. By refusing to include this ritual under the protection of the Free Exercise Clause, the Court struck right at the heart of the First Amendment protections. As James Madison so often argued during the ratification debates, the First Amendment clauses are especially designed to protect the practices of minority religions from the "tyranny of the majority" whether political or ecclesiastical. It is important to remember that when alcohol was officially a "controlled substance" during the Prohibition era, the sacramental use of wine was specifically exempted from the ordinance. Had Congress not taken action, it is inconceivable to imagine that the Court would not have acted to exempt a practice so central to the faith of the majority religion. Why should a minority faith not be similarly protected?

I have argued at length in my book *Religion in Public Life: A Dilemma for Democracy* that the Court's confusion about the Religion Clauses stems directly from the introduction of the notion of separation into the Court's adjudication. The only sense in which religious communities and the modern welfare state are to remain "separate" is that neither should exercise final authority over the values, beliefs, and practices of the other. But "separation" is surely an odd word to use to make that important point. Independence of authority is necessary precisely because religion and government are so deeply intertwined in so many ways. My own strong conviction is that the phrase "wall of separation between church and state" should be jettisoned from the Court's lexicon. The Court needs to sit again at the feet of James Madison and so rediscover the fundamental constitutional values of liberty, equality, and tolerance. Those concepts alone will provide ample guidance to the Court's interpretation of the religion clauses. More important, they will provide new clarity for the larger question of public religion's proper place in our pluralistic democracy. And so we turn, at last, to our final question.

3. How can public religion become a force for moral renewal in pluralistic democratic societies? If it is, indeed, the case that religion is not constitutionally prohibited from our public life, we need to ask whether communities of faith in America today can meet the expectations of those secular observers who believe that religion can make a positive contribution to the renewal of our common life. The presence of religion in public debate in no way guarantees the elevation of discourse concerning the moral purposes of democracy. Michael Sandel has posed the crucial question about religion's public role. "Is religion among the forms of identity likely to generate a fuller citizenship and a more vital public life? Or does it depend on the religion; might some religious convictions erode rather than enhance the civic virtues required of citizens in a pluralistic society?"[24] By way of conclusion, I want to offer a view of religion that, I believe, provides an apt model for public religion in a pluralistic democracy. While I will draw on the resources of my own tradition, Christianity, I hope that adherents of other religious communities will be able to offer similar arguments from within their own traditions.

The greatest challenge facing American democracy today is to develop "pluralist citizens," people capable of living in a variety of different and sometimes conflicting worlds of meaning while still maintaining a robust sense of personal and communal identity. Many people fear an encounter with those who are different, because they suspect that these "others" will hold opposing fundamental beliefs about the world and human behavior. If the beliefs of these "others" are in conflict with my own, and I hold my own beliefs to be true, then it seems to follow necessarily that the beliefs of these "others" are an offense to me. And, as sociologist James Davison Hunter has pointed out, when I take my own beliefs to define the nature of the sacred, then the beliefs of the "others" are not just false or offensive but sacrilegious.

It is clear that many theologians and practitioners of religion accept the absolutist understanding of truth I have just described. Faith requires, many believe, not only the affirmation of one's own religion's truth but the claim to its absolute superiority.[25] Such claims imply that those who disagree with one's own religious beliefs stand outside of or in opposition to the sacred. Such opposing beliefs are not only false; they are also sacrilegious, i.e., an assault on all that I hold sacred. Therefore not only can I not tolerate those beliefs; I cannot tolerate those who hold them. That is why practitioners of other religious beliefs are often characterized as infidels, blasphemers, apostates, or heretics. That is also why the history of religion is filled with so much violence and bloodshed.

Despite the widespread acceptance of religious claims to absoluteness, I want to argue that such claims are neither essential to most religious traditions nor the best interpretation of those traditions' claims to truth. In making this argument I will draw upon the resources of my own faith, Christianity, but I am confident that similar arguments are available in other traditions as well. If people of faith are committed to claims of absoluteness, then they will not be capable of helping to shape faithful disciples who are also good citizens in a diverse society. If, however, there is an alternate, theologically sound view of religious truth, then it may be possible for churches and other communities of faith to serve as "schools of virtue" for pluralistic democracies.

"For here we have no lasting city, but we seek the city which is to come" (Hebrews 13:14). If pluralism creates a situation in which people have conflicting commitments and divided loyalties, then it should hardly be a novel experience for people of faith. Faith in God demands of religious believers their ultimate loyalty. Indeed, the sin of idolatry is defined as the transfer of the commitment owed solely to God to any other object or person in the world. That one owes ultimate loyalty to God does not mean, however, that other lesser loyalties cannot lay claim to one's commitment. These other loyalties—to spouse, children, job, or, in this case, nation—are serious and important, but they should never become the commitments that fully define one's identity. Absolute love of spouse, children, job, or nation can easily become jealous, obsessive, or fanatical. The challenge to the person of faith is to see all the goods of this life as gifts from the hand of a gracious and loving Creator. Loved ones claim deep and abiding loyalties from us, but when a parent or spouse faces death, faith reminds the believer that the beloved is returning to the care of the One from whom all good gifts come. So it is also with the commitment to community or nation; these, too, demand our serious loyalties—occasionally even our loves—but they dare never substitute for the loyalty and love owed to God.

The engagement of the religious citizen with democratic regimes is, then, perhaps captured under the notion of "pilgrim citizenship." Recognizing the penultimate character of the public realm, believers will not seek their final resting place in this sphere of power and persuasion. Nonetheless, people of faith will sometimes find the public realm to be a place of genuine fulfillment and bracing engagement, a place in which their own deepest convictions and beliefs are tested, criticized, confirmed, and reformed. Precisely because a pluralistic society requires conversation and exchange with those who are "different," public space provides a context within which faith seeks understanding in dialogue with persons holding diverse commitments. Conversation makes a crucial contribution to understanding in the public realm because people of faith do not enter that realm with a divinely authorized program of policy prescriptions. Religious persons bring a set of fundamental convictions and orienting principles to public debate, but the application of the resources of faith can only be determined in each particular situation. Religious convictions and principles may provide a basic framework within which policy reflection takes place for the believer, but those resources do not determine choices in the public realm.

People of faith, then, should function in a democratic society as "connected critics,"[26] persons committed to the fundamental ideals of democracy yet able to see the shortcomings of any particular democratic regime. Because connected critics care so deeply about the values inherent in a particular venture, their critique serves to call a community back to its better nature. Because people of faith share the fundamental values of democratic societies, they remain connected to public life even as they engage in criticism; because their commitment to democracy remains penultimate, however, they can appeal to transcendent ideals to critique current practice and to elevate the understanding of democratic values themselves. Two of America's greatest "public theologians," Abraham Lincoln and Martin Luther King, Jr., appealed to religious ideas to criticize the practices of slavery and segregation, and in so doing redefined the very meaning of freedom and equality for American citizens. People of faith—pilgrim citizens and connected critics—can help churches and other communities of faith serve as "schools of virtue" for a pluralistic democracy, places where the critical consciousness of an informed citizenry can be nurtured.

But, still, some would ask, doesn't engagement in the give and take of pluralist democratic conversation deny the ultimate or absolute character of one's religious commitment? Isn't pluralism in fact the great *threat* to religious commitment today? Hasn't our society drifted into such a state of relativism that no commitment, not even that of faith, makes a final and ultimate claim on peoples' lives?

If my argument is to be understood, it is essential that pluralism, that is, the openness to the voices of others, not be confused with moral or ethical relativism, that is, the belief that there are no definitive standards for belief or action, that moral choice is simply the expression of personal preference. Communities of faith must come to recognize the compatibility between deep and abiding commitment to the truth claims of one's tradition and an openness to and respect for the claims of another tradition. Truth claiming and an acceptance of pluralism are not inconsistent. Nicholas Rescher has stated the issue well:

> Pluralism holds that it is rationally intelligible and acceptable that others can hold positions at variance with one's own. But it does not maintain that a given individual need endorse a plurality of positions—that the fact that others hold a certain position somehow constitutes a reason for doing so oneself. . . . Pluralism is a feature of the collective group; it turns on the fact that different experiences engender different views. But from the standpoint of the individual this cuts no ice. We have no alternative to proceeding as best we can on the basis of what is available to us. That others agree with us is not proof of correctness; that they disagree, no sign of error.[27]

Moreover, it is important to recognize that my argument in favor of pluralism is motivated not by some desperate concern that religious folk be given a hearing in an increasingly secular world but by my own deepest religious and theological commitments. And with an account of those commitments I want to conclude my defense of a pluralist understanding of religious truth.

"Faith is the assurance of things hoped for, the conviction of things not seen" (Hebrews 11:1). For believers, religious faith is the most deeply felt and most broadly encompassing conviction a person can have. And yet it would be a profound theological mistake to equate the confidence of faith with apodictic or absolute certainty. For the Christian tradition, faith is our finite, sinful grasping of the saving grace of a transcendent God, offered as a gift through the person and work of Jesus Christ. God's grace reorients the believer's life and inaugurates a lifelong journey of discipleship. That life of discipleship is a process of "faith seeking understanding." Since Christians confess God to be the transcendent mystery who lovingly shares himself with us, our knowledge and grasp of God's mysterious nature will always be partial and inadequate. Consequently, all religious and theological statements must be uttered with a genuine sense of both gratitude and humility.

Moreover, the biblical narratives through which the identity of God is displayed to the reader reach their climax in a remarkable sequence whereby Jesus undergoes death at the hands of the Romans and yet "on the third day" is raised to life by God. At the heart of the Christian Gospel lies the mystery of God's redemptive suffering, whereby God brings life out of death itself. No rational account can justify the belief that life can emerge from the despairing depths of the grave, and yet that affirmation constitutes the core of the Christian Gospel. There is no inevitability that those who read the Gospel texts will accept the belief that

Jesus, the crucified now lives, but those who do commit themselves to a life of faith and discipleship. This mysterious movement from unbelief to faith lies beyond the competence of reason to grasp. Whether God's promise of new life is reliable, whether the path of discipleship leads to its promised end, we cannot know with certainty now, for "we see through a glass darkly." Still believers follow on in hope and the power of the Spirit, awaiting that day when we may "see face to face." For now we have only faith, the demands of discipleship, and the beckoning presence of the one who bids us come and follow. And for some, that is enough.

The God whom Christians confess and worship is thus a God of transcendent mystery, redemptive suffering, and sustaining hope. Christian discipleship is shaped by the theological virtues of faith, hope, and love. At the same time, Christians recognize with gratitude and humility the surprising and unexpected character of the Christian Gospel. If God's unsurpassing love is found in a community of sinners and outcasts and epitomized by the symbol of criminal's death, then Christians can hardly be surprised if the voices of God's promptings are to be found in the insights of those who are fellow travelers on the journey of discipleship, particularly those who are different from ourselves. Grounded in the confidence of faith, the sustenance of hope, and the renewing power of love Christians seek to make their way, like all others, in a world that both confirms and undermines their deepest convictions. Precisely because they must always live in more than one world of meaning, people of faith have insights to offer to those who struggle to maintain commitment in the midst of the confusing diversity of a pluralistic world. If people of faith can learn to share those insights in a manner that contributes to our nation's common good, then religion might become not bane but blessing for our fragile but beloved democracy.

Notes

1. The Postmodernity Project, *The State of Disunion* (Charlottesville: University Press of Virginia, 1996).

2. See Robert D. Putnam, "Bowling Alone: America's Declining Social Capital," *Journal of Democracy* (January 1995), and "The Strange Disappearance of Civil Society," *The American Prospect* (Winter 1996): 34–48.

3. See, for example, the "Faith and Families" project of the state of Mississippi, Amy L. Sherman, "A New Path Out of Poverty?" *The American Enterprise* 7, no. 4, 43–47, or the partnerships between government and faith communities in the state of Michigan, Amy L. Sherman, "Cross Purposes: Will Conservative Welfare Reform Corrupt Religious Charities?" *Policy Review* 74 (Fall 1995): 58–63. Such programs are likely to proliferate since the new welfare reform law

includes a provision called "charitable choice," which allows communities of faith to solicit government funds directly rather than set up charitable subsidiaries. These issues will be discussed in detail in a volume forthcoming from Harvard Divinity School's Center for the Study of Values in Public Life. Among the authors contributing to *Who Provides? Religion, Civil Society, and the Welfare State* are Mary Jo Bane, David Ellwood, Bryan Hehir, Martha Minow, Theda Skocpol, Ronald Thiemann, Cornel West, and William Julius Wilson.

4. See *The Chicago Tribune*, March 23, 1981, and July 28, 1981.

5. Eugene F. Rivers, "Take Your Inheritance," *Sojourners* (February-March 1994): 12–14.

6. Cornel West, *Race Matters* (Boston: Beacon Press, 1993), p. 15

7. "The Faith Factor: Can Churches Cure America's Social Ills?" *U.S. News & World Report* (September 9, 1996), and "Feeding the Flock," *Time* (August 15, 1997).

8. James Davison Hunter, *Culture Wars* (New York: Basic Books, 1991), p. 131.

9. Isaac Kramnick and R. Laurence Moore, *The Godless Constitution* (New York: W. W. Norton, 1996), p. 12.

10. Ibid., p. 151. The authors have taken a more moderate view on the question of government's relation to faith-based social service institutions. See Kramnick and Moore, "Can the Churches Save the Cities? Faith-Based Services and the Constitution," *The American Prospect* (November–December 1997): 47–53.

11. Robin Lovin, ed., *Religion and American Public Life* (New York: Paulist Press, 1986), p. 46.

12. Ibid.

13. "Towards a Civil Society: Hopes for Polish Democracy," interview with Adam Michnik, *Times Literary Supplement*, February 19–25, 1988, 887.

14. Michael Sandel, *Democracy's Discontent* (Cambridge: Harvard University Press, 1996), pp. 336–37.

15. Among the many important statements of this issue, see especially Peter L. Berger, *The Sacred Canopy: Elements of a Sociological Theory of Religion* (Garden City, N.Y.: Doubleday, 1967), and Peter L. Berger and Thomas Luckman, *The Social Construction of Reality: A Treatise in Sociology of Knowledge* (Garden City, N.Y.: Doubleday, 1967).

16. The Pluralism Project at Harvard University under the direction of Professor Diana Eck is attempting to profile the new religious diversity in the United States; see Diana Eck, ed., *On Common Ground: World Religions in America* (New York: Columbia University Press, 1997).

17. *Everson v Board of Education*, 330 U.S. 1, 16 (February 10, 1947).

18. *Allegheny County v Greater Pittsburgh ACLU*, 109 S. Ct. 493 (1988). See my treatment of this case in Ronald F. Thiemann, *Religion in American Public Life: A Dilemma for Democracy* (Washington, D.C.: Georgetown University Press, 1996), pp. 45–55.

19. 177 S. Ct. 762 (1997). For an insightful treatment of the significance of this act see, Angela C. Carmella, "The Religious Freedom Restoration Act: New

Roles for Congress, the President, and the Supreme Court in Protecting Religion," *Religion & Values in Public Life* 3, no. 2 (Winter 1995): 1–4.

20. 374 U.S. 398 (1963).

21. As this volume goes to press the U.S. Congress is preparing to pass new legislation, the Religious Liberty Protection Act (RLPA), which avoids the separation of powers problem. The RLPA, like the previous act, seeks to protect religious expression in cases in which it conflicts with other government regulations. As with the Religious Freedom Restoration Act, RLPA mandates that government show a "compelling reason" for interfering with religious liberty and that government use the "least restrictive manner" to infringe upon religious practices or beliefs. Backing for RLPA includes the leadership of both House and Senate as well as widespread support from members of Congress in both parties and from all ideological and political perspectives. Representatives from more than eighty religious organizations also support the measure.

22. 494 U.S. 890 (1990).

23. 177 S. Ct. 762 (1997) at 64–65.

24. Michael Sandel, "Freedom of Conscience or Freedom of Choice?" in *Articles of Faith, Articles of Peace*, ed. Os Guinness (Washington, D.C.: Brookings Institution, 1990), p. 76.

25. The classic treatment of this issue is Ernst Troeltsch, *The Absoluteness of Christianity and the History of Religions* (Richmond, Va.: John Knox Press, 1971).

26. I gratefully borrow this phrase from Michael Walzer, *Interpretation and Social Criticism* (Cambridge: Harvard University Press, 1987).

27. Nicholas Rescher, *Pluralism: Against the Demand for Consensus* (Oxford: The Clarendon Press, 1993), p. 89.

3

BELIEVERS AS EQUAL CITIZENS

Michael W. McConnell

Every citizen here is in his own country. To the protestant it is a
protestant country; to the catholic, a catholic country; and the
jew, if he pleases, may establish in it his New Jerusalem.
(Oral argument of Attorney William Sampson in
People v. Philips *[Court of General Sessions, City of New York, 1813])*

Be a man in the streets and a Jew at home.
(Poet Yehuda Leib Gordon, paraphrasing the philosophy
of Moses Mendelssohn)

But our citizenship is in heaven.
(Philippians 3:20 [NIV])

UNTIL THE modern period, citizenship was inextricably tied to
religion. The legitimacy of government was based in large part
on claims of divine sanction, and those who disputed that
sanction could not be trusted. Dissenters could be dealt with tolerantly
or harshly, but they could not be full and equal citizens. Throughout
most of Europe, Jews, the quintessential dissenters, constituted virtually
a state within a state. Subjects of the king but not citizens of the realm,
Jews were vulnerable to special exactions and—at the mercy of the sovereign—to violence, insult, and expulsion. At the same time, they typically enjoyed a kind of home rule, running their own schools, courts,
hospitals, and social services. Ostracism and indignity were coupled with
a kind of communal autonomy.[1] In England, where the Glorious Revolution was predicated on the Protestant succession and the victory over
Catholic tyranny, adherence to Catholicism was associated with Jacobit-
ism and hence with treason, and radical Protestants might bring about
a return to the Commonwealth and civil war. Under such circumstances, it seemed prudent to confine public offices to adherents of the
Church of England.

With the rise of liberal constitutionalism, especially at the American founding and the French Revolution, an attempt was made to sever the connection between citizenship and religion by divorcing the state from its sacred foundations and identification with an established religion and opening the doors of citizenship to all inhabitants, without regard to their religion. No special privileges for adherents of a favored denomination, no special disabilities for anyone else. That individuals of all religious faiths can be full and equal citizens became a fundamental and uncontroversial premise of liberal constitutional order. As stated in the Virginia Bill for Establishing Religious Freedom, "our civil rights have no dependence on our religious opinions; any more than our opinions in physics or geometry."

The problem with this formulation is that it makes it sound too easy. Religion is not like physics and geometry. Religion is connected to conscience and character and loyalty, in a way physics and geometry are not. If we do not grasp why religious convictions pose a problem for citizenship, we may become careless in our interpretation of what it means to treat religious believers, of all faiths, as full and equal citizens. The purpose of this chapter is to recall the nature and seriousness of the problem. The first section will describe the problem, as it has been seen by several noted philosophers and statesmen. The second section will describe two broad approaches to the problem adopted by liberal democracies, and their implications for constitutional questions of church and state.

The Problem

The essential problem is that religious believers have an allegiance to an authority outside the commonwealth. To be sure, the demands of faith do not necessarily (or even frequently) conflict with the laws of the civil society; often they are mutually reinforcing. Much depends on the nature of the religion and of the state. Religions that place few nonspiritual demands on their adherents, or whose cultural and moral commitments are more or less congruent with the wider community, will create relatively few conflicts. Governments that confine themselves to the few essential functions necessary to peace and good order will generate fewer conflicts than governments active in the educational, cultural, and moral lives of their citizens. But in principle, so long as church and state are separate, there is always the possibility of conflict between spiritual and temporal authorities. Believers inevitably face two sets of loyalties and two sets of obligations. In this respect, they resemble resident aliens, or, at best, persons with dual citizenship. This conflict of loyalties and obligations I will call the problem of "citizenship ambiguity."

The problem of citizenship ambiguity was articulated with characteristic bluntness by Rousseau. He wrote in *The Social Contract* that adherents of certain religions (including Catholic Christianity) cannot be "at the same time both churchmen and citizens." Under Christianity, "men have never known whether they ought to obey the civil ruler or the priest." Christianity gave men "two legislative orders, two rulers, two homelands," and it put them under "two contradictory obligations." This situation is "so manifestly bad," he said, that the "pleasure of demonstrating its badness would be a waste of time."[2] If this sounds overly hostile to Christianity, it is well to remember that Christians have said it of themselves. Paul's *Letter to the Philippians* affirms that "our citizenship is in heaven."[3] Those who live the life of faith, according to the writer of *Hebrews*, are "aliens and strangers on earth." They are "longing for a better country—a heavenly one." "God . . . has prepared a city for them."[4] If believers have one foot in the city that God has prepared for them, the potential for conflict with the city in which they temporarily find themselves is inevitable. How can believers insist upon enjoying the status of equal citizens if they admit that their true citizenship—their ultimate loyalty and allegiance—lies elsewhere?

Citizenship ambiguity is not an oddity of Christian doctrine; it will be present in any religion that recognizes a divine or transcendent normative authority higher than that of earthly institutions. Only if the religion contains no teaching relevant to civil life, or if it is either subordinate to or dominant over the civil regime, will there be no possibility of conflict.

Nor is the diagnosis of the problem an oddity of Rousseau, or of the Old World. In the single most influential document expounding the American theory of relations between religion and government, Madison's *Memorial and Remonstrance Against Religious Assessments*, Madison presupposes a relation between religion and government remarkably similar to Rousseau's. Like Rousseau, he recognizes the potential for conflict between the "claims of Civil Society" and the duty of "every man" to render homage to the Creator. Unlike Rousseau, however, Madison avers that the latter duty "is precedent both in order of time and degree of obligation" to the former.

> Before any man can be considered as a member of Civil Society, he must be considered as a subject of the Governor of the Universe: And if a member of Civil Society, who enters into any subordinate Association, must always do it with a reservation of his duty to the general authority; much more must every man who becomes a member of any particular Civil Society, do it with a saving of his allegiance to the Universal Sovereign.[5]

Madison's terminology draws attention to the question of citizenship: believers are "subjects" of the "Universal Sovereign," to whom they owe "allegiance." In effect, Madison is saying, much like Rousseau, that the problem of church and state is the problem of citizenship ambiguity: How can we deal with the fact that religious believers are both subjects of God and citizens of earthly commonwealths?

The difference between Rousseau and Madison is that Rousseau deplored this "conflict of jurisdiction," while Madison deduced from it the "unalienable right" to worship God in accordance with the dictates of conscience. Rousseau maintained that a properly ordered civil society required suppression of religion as it then existed and substitution of a mandatory civil religion that preaches "the sanctity of the social contract and the law." Rousseau thus created his own new "civil religion," no less intolerant and no less tied to government than the religions and governments of yore. Madison argued, by contrast, that government may not tamper with the dictates of conscience, and he created a new form of government that would protect the believer's dual allegiance. Rousseau thought it essential that loyalty to the state supersede religious faith; Madison maintained that religious obligation takes precedence, "both in order of time and degree of obligation," since allegiance to God is primary and civil society is a "subordinate" form of association. Different solutions, different constitutions—but essentially the same understanding of the underlying problem.

Admittedly, not everyone has agreed with Rousseau and Madison that religious conviction and civil obligation are in conflict. There have been important attempts to understand religion and citizenship in such a way as to minimize or eliminate the problem of citizenship ambiguity.

One such attempt may be found in the device of separation between church and state. The philosophical foundation of church-state separationism was laid by John Locke in his *Essay on Toleration*. So long as civil and religious sources of authority are clearly distinguished and given separate jurisdictions, according to Locke, the problem of citizenship ambiguity can be eliminated. The problem is not inherent in the situation of religious people in secular communities, but is a result of either government, or religion, or both, overstepping their proper bounds. If religion and government would stick to their own proper spheres, a believer could be a citizen of both sacred and secular realms—he could enjoy dual citizenship—with no conflict of obligations. That is why Locke "esteem[ed] it above all things necessary to distinguish exactly the business of civil government from that of religion and to settle the just bounds that lie between the one and the other."[6] The religious citizen would obey God within God's proper jurisdiction, and would obey the magistrate within the magistrate's proper jurisdiction. Eliminate the jurisdictional overlap—get the magistrate out of God's business and God out of the magistrate's business—and there would be no further difficulty.

Locke's vision found adherents on this side of the Atlantic. In his noted *Letter to the Danbury Baptists*, Jefferson wrote that he

> contemplate[d] with solemn reverence that act of the whole American people which declared that their legislature should "make no law respecting an establishment of religion, or prohibiting the free exercise thereof," thus building a wall of separation between Church and State. Adhering to this expression of the supreme will of the nation in behalf of the rights of conscience, I shall see with sincere satisfaction the progress of those sentiments which tend to restore to man all his natural rights, convinced he has no natural right in opposition to his social duties.[7]

The Lockean character of this profession can be seen not only in the famous metaphor of the "wall of separation," but in Jefferson's faith that man "has no natural right"—presumably including obligations of conscience—"in opposition to his social duties." This obviously presupposes that the realms of conscience and social duty are sufficiently distinct that conflict between them will not legitimately arise.

The flaw in Locke's prescription is not with its desirability but with its congruence to reality. To the extent that church and state *can* be separated, without violence to the just and proper jurisdiction of either, they should be separated. The less overlap there is between sacred and secular authority, the less serious the problem of citizenship ambiguity will be. If it were possible to "distinguish exactly the business of civil government from that of religion," the field of church-state law would be easy, and religious freedom would be secure.

Alas, it is not so. Even conceding, with Locke, that "the care of souls is not committed to the civil magistrate," there remain numerous and inevitable potential conflicts between the demands of civil society and the demands of faith. Indeed, the very boundary between sacred and secular is a point of contention on which persons of various religious and secular persuasions will inevitably disagree. How should children be raised? Parents may wish to pass on the truths and joys of their religious tradition through inculcation of the faith, but the state may think that children are better off with exposure to a multiplicity of views, coupled with science, modernist philosophy, and sex education. Which is overstepping its bounds? What should be the relations between the races? In 1908, a religious college in Kentucky was criminally prosecuted for its insistence on educating black and white students together,[8] and in 1983 the tax-exempt status of a religious college was revoked for forbidding its students to engage in interracial dating.[9] Which should prevail, church or state? What mind-altering substances may be used as a sacrament in worship?[10] What headcovering may be worn by a Jewish officer in the military?[11] Should there be chaplains in public hospitals? Prisons?[12] Legislatures?[13] Military installations?[14] Who should pay for them? Can religious radio stations get free access to the broadcast spectrum? Can they get discretionary construction grants?[15] Should commercial rock climbing be halted on Devil's Tower, sacred to the Sioux, during the month of their holy celebrations there?[16] Can the government prevent the church in Boerne, Texas, from remodeling its sanctuary?[17] Can it force the Bishop of Newark to allow parochial school teachers to unionize?[18] Can it apply discrimination laws to a congregation's choice of clergy?[19] Can believers opposed to alcohol keep their counties dry?[20] Whose side of the "wall of separation" are these questions on?

What happens when civil law does conflict with religious conscience? According to Locke, this "will seldom happen." But if it does, the believer should suffer the punishment. "For the private judgement of any person concerning a law enacted in political matters, for the public good, does not take away the obligation of that law, nor deserve a dispensation."[21] Only if the magistrate has overstepped the bounds of his proper authority is the believer properly entitled to disobey. And since "there is no judge upon earth between the supreme magistrate and the people,"[22] in cases of conflict between religious conscience and the exercise of civil authority, civil authority always prevails, no matter which party to the dispute—believer or magistrate—has overstepped the proper bounds.[23] Moreover, the teachings of some religions—atheism and Roman Catholicism—seemed to Locke to be so inimical to public order that they should be denied toleration altogether. It is not obvious that this is much of an improvement over Rousseau.

The disagreement—if there is a disagreement—is not over what is desirable, but over social reality. Locke and Jefferson profess to believe that religion is essentially irrelevant to the affairs of this world, while Rousseau insists that the opposite is true. In the end, however, their response to conflict is the same. Whether common or rare, conflicts must be resolved in favor of the state.

The greater gulf is between Rousseau and Madison, who, while agreeing about the reality of citizenship ambiguity, respond in different ways to it. Madison does not dwell upon the practical consequences of treating religious obligations as superior to civil obligations, except to say (in another place) that religion should prevail "in every case where it does not trespass on private rights or the public peace."[24] Evidently, Madison is willing to sacrifice some degree of social control (on matters not related to private rights or the public peace) in exchange for liberty of conscience. Indeed, it is possible that Madison viewed citizenship ambiguity as a strength rather than a weakness. Perhaps religion, as an authority independent of the state, would serve much the same function as federalism and separation of powers: to minimize the dangers of tyranny by dividing power. The difference between Madison and Rousseau may have been that the latter had more ambitious plans for government.

With all respect to Locke and Jefferson, it would be naive to assume that civil society is unaffected by the moral and even the theological teachings of its major religions. Locke was well aware that his unorthodox understanding of the afterlife—Locke believed in a future state of rewards but not of punishments—could be expected to have earthly consequences: the divine sanction against evildoers would be weakened, to the detriment of civil order. Today, feminists have no doubt that the patriarchal character of many major religions (in their eyes) has earthly consequences, and they often do not hesitate in asking the civil magistrate to intervene in the internal affairs of churches to solve this problem. Environmentalists are not oblivious to the earthly consequences of the "stewardship" and "dominion" models of man's relation to Creation. Welfare reformers have noticed that ministries preaching spiritual regeneration are markedly more successful in changing the lives of their clients than secular programs that dole out money. Jefferson's comment that "it does me no injury for my neighbor to say that there are twenty gods, or no god. It neither picks my pocket nor breaks my leg" seems oblivious to the fact that religion affects character and character affects conduct.[25] Edmund Burke appears much more realistic when he says that "it is the right of government to attend much to opinions; because, as opinions soon combine with passions, even when they do not produce them, they have much influence on actions."[26]

Jefferson may ultimately have been right (I think he was) in saying that "it is time enough for the rightful purposes of civil government for its officers to interfere when principles break out into overt acts against peace and good order."[27] But he was not right because religious opinions are irrelevant to the common good. If he was right, it is because liberty of conscience is precious enough to sacrifice other public goods for its attainment, and because government is not to be trusted in judging which opinions are likely to be injurious to the public good. The danger in Jefferson's "pick my pocket or break my leg" reasoning is that, whenever my neighbor's religion *does* have secular consequences, it will seem appropriate to intervene. Locke's exclusion of atheists and Catholics from toleration cannot be dismissed as a quaint exception to his beneficent liberalism; it follows logically from the ground on which his argument for toleration rested. If religious freedom means nothing more than that religion should be free so long as it is irrelevant to the state, it does not mean very much.

A second response to the problem of citizenship ambiguity is to agree that religion is relevant to citizenship, but to maintain that the teachings of religion, taken as a whole, tend to foster the virtues on which a democratic republic depends. In his Farewell Address, Washington stated that "[o]f all the dispositions and habits which lead to political prosperity, religion and morality are indispensable supports." Religion, in this view, does not undermine good citizenship; rather, religion and morality are the "firmest props of the duties of men and citizens." In "religion," Washington was not using a code word for the dominant religion. His formal letters to the Jewish congregations of Newport, Philadelphia, New York, Richmond, Charleston, and Savannah make clear that his regard extended to them,[28] and he gave instructions to American troops in Canada to respect the rights of conscience of the Catholic French Canadians. Nor was Washington unaware that religious convictions could produce confls with civil duties. In writing to "the religious society called Quakers," Washington noted that except in "their declining to share with others the burden of common defense," there was "no denomination among us, who are more exemplary and useful citizens." He insisted that "in my opinion the conscientious scruples of all men should be treated with great delicacy and tenderness: and it is my wish and desire, that the laws may always be as extensively accommodated to them, as a due regard for the protection and essential interests of the nation may justify and permit."[29] In contrast to Locke (as well as Rousseau), Washington thus maintained that conflicts should be minimized by accommodating the laws to religious convictions (where it is possible to do so without excessive injury to the essential interests of the nation), rather than by insisting that in all matters religious citizens conform to the law of the state.

The difference between Washington and Madison was more one of tone than of substance, but the difference in tone is significant. Washington tended to address the situation of minority religions from a posture of toleration by the society toward the dissenter, while Madison tended to see believers of all religions as occupying a similar position in relation to the secular state. Perhaps more strikingly, Madison spoke in more emphatic terms of "unalienable rights," whereas Washington spoke in terms of treating religious conscience with "great delicacy and tenderness"—language of forebearance rather than right. Finally, while Washington and Madison both expressed concern about conscience, Madison placed the rights of conscience at the fore while Washington placed greater emphasis on the contributions of religion to virtue and hence to republican citizenship.

It does not, and did not, follow from the Washingtonian view that government has the authority to use its power directly for the inculcation of religion. The founders of the American regime believed not only that government should not, but also that it cannot, advance the cause of genuine religion by use of state power. A genuine religion is a matter between each believer and his God. "[A]ll attempts to influence it by temporal punishments or burdens, or by civil incapacitations, tend only to beget habits of hypocrisy and meanness."[30] Experience showed that government support for religion produced only "pride and indolence in the Clergy" and "ignorance and servility in the laity."[31] The only effectual support government could give to religion was to guarantee its freedom.

Washington thus combined a favorable posture toward religion as a political matter with a commitment to religious freedom and respect for the "conscientious scruples" of religious minorities.[32] His position is neither separationist nor majoritarian. The central theme is his belief that religion—all religion—is a salutary prop for democratic citizenship, and therefore that the religious commitments of all citizens should be treated with "great delicacy and tenderness." It is important to see the deep congruence between this view and Rousseau's: neither believes that religion is irrelevant to citizenship; neither believes that the spheres of government and religion can be so separated that the state can be indifferent to the influence of religion. But what accounts for the equally profound difference: that Washington sees religion as salutary while Rousseau sees religion as disruptive? One answer may be that Rousseau envisioned a society of much deeper and thicker solidarity, making difference of religion—or even deep commitment to religion as a locus of truth and loyalty—a threat. Washington, by contrast, desired only enough virtue to allow republican institutions to work. This idea was later developed by Tocqueville, who wrote that "all Americans" think that religion is "necessary to the maintenance of republican institutions."[33] "Despotism may be able to do without faith," Tocqueville wrote, "but freedom cannot. Religion is much more needed in the republic they [French revolutionaries] advocate than in the monarchy they attack, and in democratic republics most of all. How could society escape destruction if, when political ties are relaxed, moral ties are not tightened?"[34] The characteristic vice of the liberal republic is its tendency toward selfish individualism; all republicans of the founding era agreed that republics required a virtuous citizenry, where "virtue" was understood to mean public spiritedness. Religion was thus especially needful to a republic, because, as Tocqueville pointed out, "[e]very religion also imposes on each man some obligations toward mankind, to be performed in common with the rest of mankind, and so draws him away, from time to time, from thinking about himself."[35]

A second reason for the difference is that in France, the dominant religious faith was associated with the *ancien régime*, and hostile to the republican future Rousseau envisioned, while the churches of America were in the forefront of this nation's struggle for independence. When Rousseau thought of religion, he thought principally of Catholicism, whose organization was hierarchical, autocratic, and nonegalitarian. As Tocqueville points out, the situation in America was the reverse: the American colonists had "brought to the New World a Christianity which I can only describe as democratic and republican; this fact singularly favored the establishment of a temporal republic and democracy."[36] American republicans thus never shared the anticlericalism of their republican counterparts in France. In America, unlike France, the dominant Protestant religion reinforced the essential philosophical presuppositions of the republic, and the religious minorities—whatever the details of their doctrine—as a practical matter favored the liberalism of the new regime.[37]

Washington's happy accommodationism must therefore be seen, in significant part, as contingent: contingent both on the principles of the regime and on the principles of religion. Washington saw no conflict between religion and citizenship because the dominant religion of America—Protestant Christianity—preached ideals consistent with the principles of the republic. It was therefore safe to allow religion to be free, and therefore strong. What would happen if, as in France, the ideals espoused by religion were inimical to the principles of the regime? To make matters concrete, but at the risk of exaggerating our current situation, what if the regime were based on such principles as radical feminism, acceptance of homosexuality, and the superiority of modernist philosophy, and if the most prominent and visible religions were opposed to these trends? Far from being the most democratic and egalitarian of citizens, as in Washington and Tocqueville's day, religious individuals might come to be seen as the most retrograde. The happy coincidence of freedom and good citizenship would be broken. It would then be necessary to choose. And which would we choose? Religious freedom, or other ideals closer to the heart of the modern polity? That is the issue raised by modern feminist scholarship critical of religious freedom.[38]

This brings us back to Rousseau, and to the potential for conflict between being a good citizen and being a person of faith. Rousseau proposed one solution: to crush religion that does not reinforce the dogmas of the state. Madison proposed another: to recognize the duty to God as an unalienable right, precedent to the demands of civil society. The easy answer of separationism will only go so far, and the easy answer that religion is good for citizenship is to some degree contingent on historical circumstance. None of the answers will satisfy all legitimate demands; all come at a price.

Two Models of Equal Citizenship

For the most part, we no longer argue about whether believers should be equal citizens. But we are still far from agreement about how to achieve this objective. According to Rousseau, it is impossible for adherents of traditional religions (such as Catholicism) to be proper citizens. Your citizenship can be in heaven or in France, but not in both. For obvious reasons, that cannot be the answer in a liberal republic. It is not possible for a liberal republic to grant or withhold the privileges or immunities of citizenship on the basis of adherence to one or another religion. Instead, liberal regimes have developed a range of answers to the problem of citizenship ambiguity. Here, I will describe two models of religious citizenship that cast light on the problem: one characterized by insistence on the secular character of the state, the other by the idea of religious pluralism. Both of these have a pedigree in the practice and theory of liberal constitutionalism, but I would contend that the pluralist model best achieves the ideal of full equality of all citizens.

The first model is that of the secular state, sometimes called "strict separation" between church and state. In this model, the public sphere is strictly secular in nature: laws are based on secular premises, government programs and activities are strictly secular in nature, and religion is deemed to be irrelevant to determination of the citizens' civil obligations. Public schools are the favored form of education and should be used to inculcate ideals of democratic citizenship, untainted by sectarian teaching or dogma. Religious exercise is protected, so long as it is confined to the private sphere of home and church. The approach is captured by the saying: "Be a man in the streets and a Jew at home"—with the understanding that the same is true of adherents of every faith.

The assumption underlying this model is that the secular public philosophy of the society is "neutral" toward religion. The approach is generally associated with the idea that politics should be conducted on the basis of public reason, which is accessible to all citizens, and not on the basis of sectarian dogma. One modern exponent of this view has explained: "The establishment clause should be viewed as a reflection of the secular, relativist political values of the Enlightenment, which are incompatible with the fundamental nature of religious faith. As an embodiment of these Enlightenment values, the establishment clause requires that the political influence of religion be substantially diminished."[39] The effect is to force all citizens to put aside their sectarian loyalties and convictions in their capacities as citizen, but to allow everyone complete freedom to practice religion in private. Don't ask, don't tell.

This approach tends to be animated by fear of religious divisiveness, religious warfare, sectarianism, and intolerance. The hope is to domesticate religion by privatizing it. For some, disestablishmentarianism and privatization are the first steps toward reducing attachments to sectarian religion and fostering assimilation and secularization. If religion is understood as largely superstitious, propped up by the force of the state, then disestablishment of religion and the spread of enlightened reason should cause religion to wither away, without the need for coercion. Even the most liberal of gentile supporters of Jewish emancipation in France expected the Jewish religion to disappear as a distinctive group once Jews were given their civil rights.[40] In a similar vein, Jefferson predicted that, with the advent of religious freedom, sectarian religion would decline and within a generation all would become Unitarians.[41]

This model of religious liberty repudiated the enforced difference of the *ancien régime* and substituted an enforced denial of difference. Under the *ancien régime*, religious minorities were treated by the state as radically different and apart from the citizenry, whether they liked it or not. Under emancipation, they were admitted to membership in the citizenry—but at the price of forgoing their distinctiveness: "Jews, according to the terms of emancipation, were expected to divest themselves entirely of their national character—they were to give up the civil aspects of Talmudic law; disavow the political implications of Jewish messianism; abandon the use of Yiddish; and, most importantly, relinquish their semi-autonomous communal institutions. They were to become like other Frenchmen in every respect, save religion."[42] One prominent French legislator explained that no one could be his fellow citizen "who does not wish to drink or eat with me, who cannot give me his daughter in marriage, whose son cannot become my son-in-law, and who, by the religion he professes is separated from all other men. Only when Jews do what other men do," he said, "what the constitution and law requires of us all, will we welcome them as citizens."[43]

This view has not disappeared. An excellent example is the recent controversy in France over whether Muslim girls may wear the traditional head scarf in public school. This touched a nerve, or more precisely, two nerves, in French public opinion. First was the offense against secularity, or what the French call *laicité*. In a public school, all must put aside forms of dress or conduct that set them apart from others. That was the deal: religious minorities would be full and equal citizens so long as they acted "French" in the public sphere. Second was the offense against modern feminist sensibilities, which reject the notion that

Muslim girls must cover their heads. That certain religious traditions are at odds with the feminist ideal in this regard was all the more reason to insist on conformity in school; by this means, children would be encouraged to challenge, and perhaps depart from, the oppressive traditions of their families.

Nor is this attitude toward religious difference confined to France. Although it is unlikely that Muslim head scarves would be prohibited in the freewheeling sartorial atmosphere of American public schools, there have been incidents in which evangelical students were reprimanded for wearing T-shirts with religious slogans, or for engaging in other expression that is deemed inconsistent with the secular character of public schools.

The American version of *laïcité* is to insist that religious believers bend their religious conscience to the law, rather than asking government to accommodate the law to religious conscience. It is not uncommon to hear the argument, in various forms, that any exception to generally applicable laws would be a form of "preference" for religious believers.[44] As Justice Felix Frankfurter wrote in his dissenting opinion in *West Virginia Board of Education* v. *Barnette*, "[t]he constitutional protection of religious freedom terminated disabilities, it did not create new privileges. It gave religious equality, not civil immunity. Its essence is freedom from conformity to religious dogma, not freedom from conformity to law because of religious dogma."[45] According to Isaac Kramnick and R. Laurence Moore in their book *The Godless Constitution*, religion should have "the same rights in the public sphere as General Motors, no more and no less."[46] Since General Motors is subject to extensive regulation in almost every aspect of its operations, short of expropriating its property, this suggests that the authority of the state to regulate or restrain the exercise of religion is substantial, and that free exercise rights are minimal.

While never fully embraced by the Supreme Court, this position has obvious connections to the constitutional doctrine of the past few decades, though less so in recent years. If the state must be strictly secular, then laws based on religious justifications are unconstitutional. This idea is reflected in the first part of the Supreme Court's test for an establishment of religion: that government action must have a "secular purpose."[47] In theory, legislation predicated on religious views (such as religious condemnation of abortion or gambling) could be held to be unconstitutional, even though legislation predicated on competing worldviews (feminism or libertarianism, for example) would pose no constitutional problem. Moreover, if all publicly funded activities must be strictly secular, there can be no public subsidies of religious schools, universities, or social welfare programs—at least, if those programs are identifiably religious in nature. Thus, for many years, the Supreme Court held that public funds could not be provided to any activity that is "specifically religious," or even to secular activities conducted by "pervasively religious" organizations.[48] Finally, the Free Exercise Clause must not be interpreted to require accommodation of religious dissenters.[49] As Suzanna Sherry argues, "the constitutional protection of religion—found primarily in the Free Exercise Clause—is a limited aberration in a secular state, and thus best interpreted narrowly."[50] Indeed—although the Supreme Court has never gone so far—it would seem to follow that the Establishment Clause should forbid religious accommodations as a form of preference for religion.

The alternative to this idea of the secular state is the religiously pluralistic state. The animating purpose of this constitutional position is to enable people of all religious persuasions to be citizens of the commonwealth with the least possible violence to their religious convictions. The Jew can be a Jew not just in his house but in the public square as well. So can the Muslim and the Christian. If this requires accommodation—a relaxation of the general rules of society—it is worth the price. Perhaps the most eloquent statement of the pluralist view came from the Irish lawyer William Sampson in a case in New York in 1813.[51] The question before the court was whether a Roman Catholic priest could be forced to testify to information learned in the confessional.[52] This, it turned out, would be the first recorded decision by any court in the United States that Free Exercise protects believers from laws that would require them to violate their religious conscience. In his argument before the court, Sampson expressed a broad vision of religious liberty in America: "Every citizen here is in his own country," Sampson argued. "To the protestant it is a protestant country; to the catholic, a catholic country; and the jew, if he pleases, may establish in it his New Jerusalem."[53] No talk here of a "secular state," as if only secular individuals can fully be citizens, or as if one had to leave religion behind when entering the public sphere of citizenship. To the Protestant it is a Protestant country, to the Catholic a Catholic country, to the Jew a Jewish country. By accommodating the laws to every citizen, this approach aspires to eliminate citizenship ambiguity: to make everyone at home.

The difference between the secular and pluralist approaches came to the fore in the first recorded case in the United States involving a claim of freedom of religion. In this case, in Pennsylvania in 1793, a Jewish witness, Jonas Phillips, resisted a subpoena to testify in court in a civil case on Saturday, his day of sabbath. Phillips was a leader of the Philadelphia Jewish community and active in the struggle against religious tests for office. It is likely that it was a test case, closely watched by members of the small Jewish community of America, curious to find out what freedom of religion would mean in this new liberal regime. The news was not good: Phillips was fined £10 for refusing to appear in court on Saturday. But the case never was finally resolved, because the party on whose behalf the subpoena was issued excused the fine before an appellate court could review the matter.[54] This may appear to be a minor case, but the implications of Jonas Phillips's position were profound. In effect, he was asking that the civil court system adjust its schedule to the Jewish law. He was asking that civic obligations be accommodated to religious faith. He was, in effect, embracing the pluralist vision of religious citizenship, for he wished to be *both* an American citizen *and* a faithful Jew—even in his public role as a witness in court.

The pluralist model rejects the assumptions that the polity is based on "secular, relativist" Enlightenment values, or that secularism is a "neutral" position. Indeed, what passes for "neutrality," according to pluralist thinkers, is actually a deeply embedded ideological preference for some modes of reasoning and ways of life over others—rationalism and choice over tradition and conscience.[55] No specific law or policy can be "neutral"; all are based on ideological or philosophical positions. "Neutrality," therefore, cannot be achieved by scrutinizing each individual law. Rather, the overall constitutional framework must leave the choice among competing worldviews and perspectives to the people, privileging neither religious nor secular values. This means that religious citizens, like everyone else, are entitled to advocate laws that reflect their best judgment of what will promote the public good, even if their premises derive from religious teachings. The resulting system is "neutral" toward religion not because the laws are based on nonsectarian "reason," but because all citizens are equally free to adopt or reject arguments without any limitation arising from their metaphysical, philosophical, epistemological, or theological foundations. To tell religious citizens that their conceptions of justice or the common good must be "bracketed" is to treat them as second-class citizens.

The claim that religious or theological arguments have no place in democratic politics is especially odd when we consider the unbroken record of religious participation in social and political controversy throughout American history. From the struggle for Independence, abolition, and the Civil War, through women's suffrage and prohibition, to the modern controversies over civil rights, the Vietnam War, and abortion, religious voices and religious arguments have been among the most prominent. It is hard to sympathize with a position that implies that Sam Adams, William Lloyd Garrison, Dorothea Dix, and Martin Luther King were bad citizens, or that someone should have delivered them a lecture on the separation of church and state. Even the Religion Clauses themselves were justified, in large part, on the basis of theological principle. The Virginia Bill for Establishing Religious Freedom begins with the theological assertion that "Almighty God hath made the mind free"; Madison argued against the establishment on the ground that man's duties to the Creator are superior to positive law, and the political muscle for religious freedom came from Baptists and other evangelical Protestants who derived their love of liberty and equality from the sectarian Protestant dogmas of the priesthood of all believers and unmediated access of the soul to the love and grace of God. Advocates of the secular state claim that laws based on religious reasoning demean the status of nonbelievers as equal citizens. The pluralist would respond that no citizen is demeaned by laws that he disagrees with, so long as he has an equal right both to advocate for laws he deems just and to disagree with arguments he does not find persuasive. The pluralist state thus affirms the equality of all citizens by allowing all to participate in public affairs without privileging any particular ideology or mode of persuasion.

By the same token, the pluralist approach encourages communities of conscience to preserve the institutions necessary to perpetuate their distinctive ways of life and to pass these on to future generations. Our long-standing tradition of broad-based tax exemptions and tax-deductible contributions for nonprofit religious and charitable groups is a practical means by which government can support these institutions without government involvement in the selection of worthy recipients or control over their operations. Where government-funded programs duplicate or compete with religious institutions that perform public functions (such as hospitals, universities, schools, or soup kitchens), the pluralist view suggests that, where possible, it should allow a range of choice so that those who wish to educate their children, receive their medical care, or participate in public programs in a manner consistent with their faith can do so. In the past, any financial support of religious institutions was constitutionally suspect, unless it could be shown convincingly that the funded activity had no religious component.[56] The recent trend, however, is to uphold government assistance so long as it is provided to a broad array of beneficiaries, secular as well as religious, on the basis of objective secular criteria.[57] The most difficult problem is how to ensure that the assistance is given in such a way that it does not destroy the autonomy of the institutions. Some thoughtful pluralists think that religious institutions are better off if they continue to be excluded from government assistance, because the threat of regulation and control is more dangerous than the deprivation of resources.

None of this is to deny that pluralism comes at a cost: it dilutes the concept of "citizen," making it difficult to identify what being an "American" is all about. If there is to be a common core of tradition and affection, it must emerge *indirectly*, from what Rawls might call the "overlapping consensus" of different traditions, rather than through conscious inculcation of a public ideology or civil religion. It is for this reason that many thoughtful Americans fear that the pluralist approach will exacerbate an already dangerous balkanization of American public life.

The key battleground between these two approaches to religious freedom has been over the question of education. Advocates of the secular state, following in the tradition of Horace Mann and John Dewey, hold that the government's control over education should be used to inculcate a common set of democratic ideals in keeping with the principles of the regime. In the United States, this usually means commitment to toleration, equality, critical rationality, and liberal democracy. Pluralists, by contrast, think it is better to permit families and subgroups to educate their children in the principles of their own tradition, so long as they satisfy basic educational standards. Strangely, although the United States tends to be the most pluralist of the western liberal democracies, it is alone among these countries in its insistence that government schools enjoy a monopoly over public funding. England, France, Germany, Holland, Belgium, and Canada all permit families to choose among nonreligious and religious schools, of different denominations, without forfeiting their right to a share of public educational funding.[58]

The pluralist idea, especially in education, came under sharp attack during the last half of the nineteenth century and first quarter of the twentieth century, when Protestant, anti-immigrant, and educational reform advocates combined for different reasons to produce the common school and "Americanization" movements.[59] This movement sought to inculcate democratic, supposedly nonsectarian values among the (often Catholic or Jewish) immigrant classes through a combination of control over the public school curriculum and an attack on private education. One prominent educational reformer stated: "The children of this country, of whatever parentage, should . . . be *educated together*,—not as Baptists, or Methodists, or Episcopalians, or Presbyterians; not as Roman Catholics or Protestants, still less as foreigners in language or spirit, but as Americans, as made of one blood and citizens of the same free country,—educated to be one harmonious people."[60]

The most extreme manifestation of this movement—the attempt to mandate public schooling and outlaw private alternatives—was rebuffed by the Supreme Court in *Pierce v. Society of Sisters*, in 1925.[61] "The fundamental theory of liberty upon which all governments in this Union repose," according to the Court, "excludes any general power of the State to standardize its children by forcing them to accept instruction from public teachers only."[62] But while overt coercion was prevented, the power of the purse was used to make it difficult and costly for children from disadvantaged familes to take advantage of this constitutional freedom. Whether we will continue this attempt to use control over public resources to induce the families of America to accept instruction from government employees only is one of the most hotly contested constitutional questions of our day.

· · · · ·

The great public feast given in 1789 in Philadelphia, then the nation's capital, to celebrate ratification of the Constitution included a fitting symbol of this new pluralistic philosophy: the feast included a special table where the food conformed to Jewish dietary laws.[63] This was a fitting symbol because it included Jewish Americans in the celebration without requiring that they sacrifice their distinctiveness as Jews. In France, by contrast, Napoleon summoned the leaders of the Jewish community to a "Great Sanhedrin," where he insisted that the Jewish law be modified to enable the Jewish people to be integrated into the French nation.[64] In a gesture no less revealing than the kosher table in Philadephia, Napoleon's minister of the interior scheduled the first session to be held on Saturday. Here we see the three alternatives. Under the *ancien régime*, Jews would be excluded from the celebration, for they could not be citizens. Under the secular state, Jews would be welcome to attend, but they would be expected to eat the same food that other citizens eat. If they want to keep kosher, they should do it at home, in private, at their own expense. Under the pluralist vision, multiple tables are provided to ensure that for Protestants, it is a Protestant country, for Catholics a Catholic country, and the Jew, if he pleases, may establish in it his New Jerusalem.

Notes

1. See Paul Johnson, *A History of the Jews* (New York: Harper and Row, 1987), 280.

2. Jean-Jacques Rousseau, *The Social Contract*, trans. Maurice Cranston (Penguin, 1968), 179, 181. In this analysis, Rousseau was anticipated by Hobbes.

3. Philippians 3:20 (NIV).

4. Hebrews 11:13–16 (NIV).

5. James Madison, *Memorial and Remonstrance Against Religious Assessments*, ¶ 1, vol. 2 of *The Writings of James Madison*, ed. G. Hunt (New York: G. P. Putman's Sons, 1901), 183.

6. John Locke, *Essay on Toleration*, in vol. 6 of *The Works of John Locke* (Locke 1823; photo reprint, 1963), 1, 9.

7. Thomas Jefferson to the Danbury Baptist Association, 1 January 1802, *The Founders' Constitution*, ed. P. Kurland and R. Lerner (Chicago: University of Chicago Press, 1987) 5:96.

8. *Berea College v Kentucky*, 211 U.S. 45 (1908).

9. *Bob Jones University v United States*, 461 U.S. 574 (1983).

10. *Employment Division v Smith*, 494 U.S. 872 (1990); *People v Woody*, 61 Cal. 2d 716, 394 P.2d 813 (1964).

11. *Goldman v Weinberger*, 475 U.S. 503 (1986).

12. *Cruz v Beto*, 405 U.S. 319 (1972).

13. *Marsh v Chambers*, 463 U.S. 783 (1983).

14. *Katcoff v Marsh*, 755 F.2d 223 (1985).

15. *Fordham Univ. v Brown*, 856 F. Supp. 684 (D. D.C. 1994).

16. *U.S. v Means*, 858 F.2d 404 (8th Cir. 1988), cert. denied, 492 U.S. 910 (1989).

17. *City of Boerne v Flores*, 117 S. Ct. 2157 (1997).

18. *South Jersey Catholic School Teachers Org. v St. Teresa of the Infant Jesus Church Elementary School*, 150 N.J. 575, 696 A.2d 709 (1997).

19. *Rayburn v General Conference of Seventh-Day Adventists*, 772 F.2d 1164 (4th Cir. 1985), cert. denied, 478 U.S. 1020 (1986).

20. See Christopher Smith, "Booze Fight Looks Like It Will Go to Trial; Still No Rum at the Inn: Lodge Owner's Fight to Sell Liquor in 'Mormon Country' Appears Headed for a Trial," *Salt Lake Tribune*, 7 February 1997, sec. B.

21. *Works of John Locke*, 6:43.

22. Ibid.

23. For additional discussion of this point in Locke, see Michael W. McConnell, *Freedom from Persecution or Protection of the Rights of Conscience?: A Critique of Justice Scalia's Historical Arguments in City of Boerne v. Flores*, 39 Wm. and Mary L. Rev. 819 (1998).

24. *Writings of James Madison*, 98–100 .

25. Thomas Jefferson, *Notes on the State of Virginia* (Chapel Hill: University of North Carolina Press, 1955), 159.

26. Edmund Burke, Speech on the Petition of the Unitarians (11 May 1792), in vol. 7 of *Works of the Right Honorable Edmund Burke* (Little, Brown, 1889), 44. For further discussion of Burke's views on this subject, see Michael W. McConnell, *Establishment and Toleration in Edmund Burke's "Constitution of Freedom,"* 1995 Sup. Ct. Rev. 393.

27. Thomas Jefferson, A Bill for Establishing Religious Freedom (12 June 1779), reprinted in *The Founders' Constitution*, 5:77.

28. Joseph Blau and Salo Baron, eds., *The Jews of the United States 1790–1840: A Documentary History* (New York: Columbia University Press, 1963), 1:9–11.

29. George Washington to the Religious Society Called Quakers (October 1789), in *George Washington on Religious Liberty and Mutual Understanding*, ed. E. Humphrey (Washington D.C., 1932), 11.

30. *Founders' Constitution*, 5:77.

31. *Writings of James Madison*, 2:185.

32. Washington's views about the theological truth of religion are harder to determine and are irrelevant to his constitutional position.

33. Alexis de Tocqueville, *Democracy in America*, ed. J. P. Mayer, vol. 1, pt. 2, ch. 9 (Garden City, N.Y.: Doubleday, 1969), 293.

34. Ibid., 294.

35. de Tocqueville, *Democracy in America*, vol. 2, pt. 1, ch. 5, 444–45.

36. Ibid., 287.

37. Tocqueville explains why, under the social conditions of America, Catholics make good democratic citizens. Ibid., 289. ("Most of the Catholics are poor, and unless all citizens govern, they will never attain to the government themselves. The Catholics are in a minority, and it is important for them that all rights should be respected so that they can be sure to enjoy their own in freedom.")

38. See, for example, Jane Rutherford, *Equality as the Primary Constitutional Value: The Case for Applying Employment Discrimination Laws to Religion*, 81 Cornell L. Rev. 1049 (1996); Mary Becker, *The Politics of Women's Wrongs and the Bill of "Rights": A Bicentennial Perspective*, in *The Bill of Rights in the Modern State*, ed. Geoffrey R. Stone, Richard A. Epstein, and Cass R. Sunstein (Chicago: University of Chicago Press, 1992), 453.

39. Stephen G. Gey, *Why Is Religion Special? Reconsidering the Accommodation of Religion under the Religion Clauses of the First Amendment*, 52 U. Pitt. L. Rev. 75, 79 (1990). To similar effect, see Suzanna Sherry, *Enlightening the Religion Clauses*, 7 J. of Contemp. Legal Issues 473, 483 (1996): "It is historically uncontroversial [!] that the Enlightenment, with its emphasis on rationalism and empiricism and its rejection of religious faith and mysticism, was the primary epistemology of the founding generation. Most scholars consider the Constitution itself to be a product of the Enlightenment." From this premise, Sherry concludes that "our Constitution does—as a matter of history—and ought to—as a matter of policy—privilege reason over faith." Ibid., 477.

40. See generally Arthur Hertzberg, *The French Enlightenment and the Jews* (New York: Columbia University Press, 1968).

41. Thomas Jefferson to Dr. Benjamin Waterhouse (22 June 1822), in *The Works of Thomas Jefferson*, ed. P. Ford (New York: G. P. Putnam's Sons, 1905), 241–3; Thomas Jefferson to James Smith (3 December 1822), in *The Life and Selected Writings of Thomas Jefferson*, ed. A. Koch and W. Peden (New York: Random House, 1944), 703–4.

42. Vicki Caron, "French-Jewish Assimilation Reassessed: A Review of the Recent Literature," *Judaica* 42 (Spring 1993): 134, 138, summarizing Simon Schwarzfuchs, *Du Juif à l'Israélite: Histoire d'une mutation*, 1770–1879 (Paris: Fayard, 1989).

43. Frances Malino, *A Jew in the French Revolution: The Life of Zalkind Hourwitz* (Oxford: Blackwell, 1996), 145, quoting *Le Patriote Français*, 4 Prairial, An VI (24 May 1798).

44. See *City of Boerne v Flores*, 117 S. Ct. 2157, 2172 (1997) (Stevens, J., concurring).

45. 319 U.S. 624, 653 (1943).

46. Isaac Kramnick and R. Laurence Moore, *The Godless Constitution: The Case against Religious Correctness* (New York: Norton, 1996), 15.

47. *Lemon v Kurtzman*, 403 U.S. 602, 612 (1971). The Court has not relied on this test in recent years, but has refrained from overruling it.

48. *Hunt v McNair*, 413 U.S. 734, 743 (1973); *Roemer v Board of Public Works*, 426 U.S. 736, 752 (1976).

49. *Employment Division v Smith*, 494 U.S. 872 (1990); see also *City of Boerne v Flores*, 117 S. Ct. 2157 (1997).

50. Sherry, *Enlightening the Religion Clauses*, 477.

51. For details about Sampson, and about the case, see Walter J. Walsh, *Religion, Ethnicity and History: Clues to the Cultural Construction of Law*, in *The New York Irish*, ed. R. Baylor and T. Meagher (Baltimore: Johns Hopkins University Press, 1996), 48:53–61.

52. *People v Philips*, New York City Court of General Sessions (1813), published in W. Sampson, *The Catholic Question in America* (New York: Edward Gillespy, 1813; photo reprint, New York: Da Capo Press, 1974).

53. Ibid., 85.

54. *Stansbury v Marks*, 2 Dall. 213 (Pa. 1793).

55. See Alasdair MacIntyre, *Three Rival Versions of Moral Enquiry* (Notre Dame, Ind.: University of Notre Dame Press, 1990).

56. See *Lemon v Kurtzman*, 403 U.S. 602 (1971); *Committee for Public Education & Religious Liberty v Nyquist*, 413 U.S. 756 (1973).

57. See *Rosenberger v Rector & Visitors of the University of Virginia*, 515 U.S. 819 (1995); *Witters v Washington Dept. of Services*, 474 U.S. 481 (1986).

58. Charles L. Glenn, *Choice of Schools in Six Nations* (Washington, D.C.: Government Printing Office, 1989).

59. See Charles Glenn, *The Myth of the Common School* (Amherst: University of Massachusetts Press, 1987); Diane Ravitch, *The Great School Wars, New York City 1805–1973: A History of the Public Schools as Battlefield of Social Change* (New York: Basic Books, 1974); Michael McConnell, *Multiculturalism, Majoritarianism, and Educational Choice: What Does Our Constitutional Tradition Have To Say?* 1991 U. Chi. Leg. For. 123, 134–39.

60. W. S. Dutton, "The Proposed Substitution of Sectarian for Public Schools," *Common School Journal* (1 June 1848), 166–68, quoted in Glenn, *Myth*, 223.

61. 268 U.S. 510 (1925).

62. Ibid., 535.

63. Johnson, *History of the Jews*, 303.

64. See Simon Schwarzfuchs, *Napoleon, the Jews and the Sanhedrin* (London: Routledge and Kegan Paul, 1979), 54.

4

ILLUSORY PLURALISM,

INEXORABLE ESTABLISHMENT

Graham Walker

DURING THE last decade or so, Michael McConnell has unfailingly provided the most farseeing accounts of the legal and philosophical questions surrounding religious faith and American public life. His accounts have also been, almost without exception, the most sympathetic (among serious academic commentators) to the public claims of traditional revealed religion.[1] McConnell has increasingly made "religious pluralism" the central theme of his argument, which has become, in effect, a liberal argument for the robust public presence of religion in a liberal regime. I will argue here that McConnell's latest efforts at this argument help to reveal what he never intended: that liberal religious pluralism is a mirage, that some form of religious establishment is inexorable, and that the conceptual repertoire of liberalism is—at least with respect to religion—largely exhausted.

According to McConnell's analysis, especially as distilled in this book, liberal democracy admits of two basic approaches to the place of religion: secular neutralism and religious pluralism.[2] He exposes the flaws of the former. He praises the latter, both as the best rendition of the First Amendment to the U.S. Constitution and as the best arrangement intrinsically. His praise of religious pluralism would in effect raise the animating premise of the 1984 Equal Access Act to the level of constitutional principle of the highest rank.[3]

McConnell's diagnosis of secular neutralism echoes a growing company of thinkers who dispute the possibility of neutrality, either in principle or in practice or both. He does the job with more verve than many. Whatever its original intent, the effect of secular neutralism, he says in the present volume, is "to force all citizens to put aside their sectarian loyalties and convictions in their capacities as citizens, but to allow everyone complete freedom to practice religion in private. Don't ask, don't tell." Secular neutralism requires Jews, for instance, to practice an adage derived from Moses Mendelssohn: "Be a man in the street and a Jew at home." Not only does this force religious citizens to truncate their identities, but it gives a special public advantage to those who embrace in their persons the principle of the polity, that is, to secularists. While a Jew can be a Jew at home but not in the street, a secularist can be a secularist at home and a secularist in the street. More than anyone else, the person with a secularist religious outlook feels perfectly at home in, and is psychologically and rhetorically equipped for success in, the constitutional regime of secular neutralism.

It is only rephrasing McConnell's point to observe that secular neutralism is, in practice, secularistic neutralism. Secular neutralism has many of the same features and problems of what we normally might call a religious establishment—but with a major difference. Unlike ordinary religious establishments, this one is covert and unacknowledged; indeed its very premises require it to be so, and render it almost invisible *qua* establishment. By its very nature it is especially invisible to its most ardent advocates. The fact that this covertness is unintended exculpates guilt but does not change the effect. A covert and unacknowledged religious establishment is more powerful and harder to resist than any previously known establishment. The effects of secular neutralism as a religious establishment are to be found most directly in cultural matters—education, family law, social policy; that is, in any dimension of public life that is bound up with the articulation and transmission of meaning.

American judges committed to this approach often mention the impressionability of young children as one of the natural facts that necessitate a secular neutralist approach, especially in education; consequently, for instance, classroom prayers mandated by local or state school boards are judged improper. Such judges act, they say, on behalf of impressionable children, whose liberty of conscience must be protected from the powerful pressure of politically-sanctioned religion. But such judges—and the legal theorists whose ideas support them—are strangely oblivious to the reverse implication of impressionability.[4] Children are indeed impressionable, but for that reason they are deeply susceptible to the politically sanctioned absence of God, to the state-sponsored refusal to recognize, in public or common life, God's relevance and His claims. What habits of mind does this induce in impressionable children (who grow up to be adults)? It induces either a discomfort with talk of God, as something unfamiliar, or else it induces a tendency among religious believers to regard their beliefs as true in only a private sense: "It's true for me, but not necessarily for you," as Americans are now pervasively inclined to say.[5] Despite the prevailing jurisprudential rationale for religious neutralism, the facts of impressionability suggest that, when it comes to education and culture, there is no default, neutral position that state authority can assume toward religion.

Secularist establishments are worse than overt religious establishments because they get their force—at least as practiced in recent decades in the United States—by denial and by indirection. They are almost impossible for most people to see, much less to resist, and their consequences are pervasive for culture. As Stephen Macedo acknowledges, the "mechanisms and practices" of secular liberalism "have the effect of shaping our commitments and habits very deeply, without exactly announcing that purpose on their face." He celebrates this effect, however, rather than lamenting it. After all, he reminds us, "The operation of these institutional tendencies and biases is also *gentle* rather than oppressive, influencing the deeply held beliefs of vast numbers of people without coercion or force."[6] Yet if this influence operates invisibly and covertly, does it really operate without coercion? The invisible nature of the process—which Macedo admits—necessarily moots consent to the process; it also moots resistance to the process, for all but the most self-conscious and intransigent dissenters. By contrast, remaining silent during an official classroom prayer in pre-1962 America was a straightforward and easily intelligible act of resistance (which deserved, and typically enjoyed, legal protection).

The culturally transformative power of American secular liberalism was borne home to me recently in conversations with neighbors from overseas, visiting scholars from many countries living together in an international academic community in Princeton, New Jersey. One neighbor had been exposed to the American observance of Easter through the local public schools. Truly puzzled, she asked us what "Easter" was, since she was unfamiliar with any holidays centered around rabbits. When we explained that Easter commemorated the resurrection of Jesus, she understood immediately; she knew it by another name, and without rabbits, in her own language. We had to explain that for legal reasons American public schools are skittish about any mention of God in connection with holidays and special observances. Consequently, there is little or no transmission of communal memory about such things. Scrupulous about maintaining the constitutionally mandated posture of neutrality, public school teachers, even though they are permitted to do so, are uncomfortable talking about the religious content of Christmas, Easter, Passover, and Yom Kippur; consequently, such days lose their religious content in the minds of impressionable children. Or where teachers choose pluralism instead of silence, and give each religious holiday equal time and equal respect, children (who do not cease being impressionable under this policy) learn not indifference but equivalence: the public, and therefore respectable, attitude accords equal truth value to the claims of all. Under this scheme, children imbibe either the notion that all religions are ultimately pursuing the same vision, or else the notion that competing religious truth claims cannot be navigated by reason. Whatever the mechanism, the effect is that of a religious establishment: the state promotes a preferred religious message, whether of indifference, equivalence, or incommensurability. And children—and their parents—are induced to acquiesce to this establishment message because it is presented as the absence of establishment.

Such consequences are pervasive and inescapable, but not because of the duplicity of liberal judges and schoolteachers (who are, truth to tell, usually even more unknowingly in the thrall of their establishment than their classroom charges). Rather, such consequences are pervasive for a deeper structural reason. This reason can be stated abstractly: a political society's constitution of religion forms consciousness. Interestingly, on this point the traditional Western revealed religions (Judaism, Christianity, and Islam) seem to be in accord with contemporary postmodern doctrine. They agree, that is, that consciousness, the operative arena of rationality, is "socially constructed," as postmodernists like to say. Unlike postmodernists, however, traditional religionists insist that there are proper or improper, healthy or deformed, true or false ways to construct consciousness.[7]

In keeping with this account, we discover that the fundamentalist parents in Tennessee who objected to secularist textbooks[8] had the same basic complaint about modern liberalism as have current feminist critics of liberalism, and as current Third World theorists hostile to liberal "westernization" of their societies by liberal capitalism. The common complaint is that liberalism—in this case liberal secularism with reference to religion—handles difference dishonestly and imperialistically. Liberalism tends to trivialize difference; it displaces and co-opts differences in the name of tolerating them. This is especially true of profound differences—differences rooted in alternative truth claims, alternative claims about the nature of reality. We are most familiar with such arguments coming from the "left"—for instance in the work of Iris Marion Young, Edward Said or Uday Mehta.[9] They also appear in almost identical form on the "right," for instance as articulated by Alain de Benoist, who complains about liberalism's "inclusive racism."[10] De Benoist shares with his ideological opposites a certain hostility to traditional western Christianity, which de Benoist identifies as the source of liberalism's key concepts and its universalizing pretensions. But for all that, a strikingly similar complaint is raised by the Reverend Richard John Neuhaus and other American Christian traditionalists who complain about the "naked public square."[11]

Such criticisms of liberalism far exceed Michael McConnell's critique of secular neutrality on religious matters. But they indicate that McConnell's criticism places him in good, or at least in diverse, com-

pany, and that his skepticism about liberal neutralism is either warranted, or widely shared, or both. The same cannot be said for his enthusiasm about pluralism as the constitutional antidote to the errors of
neutralism.

McConnell's solution to the quandaries of religion and law is "religious pluralism." The calling card of this solution is its inclusivity: Who
could object to a pluralism that encompasses all and excludes none? If
such a pluralism were possible, it may be that no one would object to it.
Since it is not possible, objections arise, and they sound familiar. For in
the final analysis, McConnell's religious pluralism is apt to replicate the
errors of secular neutralism, because it operates on the same principles as
secular neutralism. It is, in fact, merely secular neutralism writ large. Political authority is still secular and ostensibly neutral, only its neutrality
extends to groups rather than to individuals. It emphasizes the autonomy of institutions (or of "communities of conscience") rather than
only the autonomy of individuals. More precisely, McConnell's religious
pluralism is a secular neutral pluralism, and will inevitably pull either toward its secular, neutralist pole or toward its pluralist pole. It will either
secularize and eviscerate (and thus homogenize) religious differences at
only a slightly slower rate than secular neutralism, or, precisely insofar as
it does not do that, it will ultimately pluralize political society to an untenable degree.

McConnell acknowledges this latter difficulty. He admits that, as applied in America, a constitutional policy of religious pluralism would
tend to eliminate a "common core" of American identity. His admission
is more than warranted, since all the arguments about the limits of pluralism in an effective polity apply with equal force to a polity constituted
by McConnell's pluralism. It is of course the ostensibly all-inclusive
quality of McConnell's religious pluralism that would tend in the direction of fragmentation. Yet it is also this all-inclusive quality that gives it
its appeal, or more accurately, its liberal appeal.

If the desirability of all-inclusive pluralism is doubtful (to anyone but
anarchists), its likelihood is more doubtful still. Simple logic precludes
it in the strict sense. Where there are religions that are the negation
of one another and also require their adherents to persecute or subju-
gate nonadherents, simultaneity of public inclusion would be, shall we
say, risky. More significantly, where there are antithetical religions
whose tenets require adherents to seek a civil religious establishment in
their favor (as some religions apparently do), simultaneity of inclusion
would be similarly impossible. Any attempt at all-inclusive religious pluralism would therefore seem only capable of including those religions
whose tenets demand benignity and benevolence, whose doctrines require minimal public validation, and whose view of religion is more

individualistic than communal. In other words, all-inclusive religious pluralism—like the constitutional policy of all-inclusive free exercise and nonestablishment of religion, of which it is an extension—will have a tendency to include all those religions that are on the Protestant model, or those willing to divest themselves of enough of their non-Protestant features to make inclusion possible.[12] This is no charge of dishonesty against either McConnell's pluralism or against the aspiration to the "free exercise of religion." It is simply to take seriously the logical and, even more, the inescapable human limitations on their application.

If McConnell's religious pluralism cannot be allowed to become a de facto Protestant establishment—which is clearly not his intention—then it must be kept deeply rather than viably pluralist. But this will make it careen toward the Balkanization or fragmentation I mentioned above. Authentic pluralism ushers in authentic war.[13] Most people agree that anything—even institutional disingenuousness—is better than war. Thus, if religious pluralism is to be kept from maturing into either anarchy on the one hand or Protestant privilege on the other, then its secular, neutralist premises are likely to gain ascendancy. It must become a subspecies of the secular neutralism it was supposed to replace. Because the overarching, architectonic principle of McConnell's pluralism is political neutrality (equal treatment), the principle of neutrality must prevail in the long run over the subordinate principle of pluralism.

We are obviously here not so much in the domain of law as of political theory. After all, a polity, to succeed, must hold itself together. All successful polities generate their proper virtues and reinforce a common identity to some degree—that is to say, to a degree sufficient for political cohesion. This makes the stakes of political order—very much including liberal political order—higher than many of us would like them to be. We may lament this feature of political existence, but we cannot overcome it.[14] It simply cannot be, and nowhere has ever been the case, that citizens of a polity find their common identity in differing with one another over fundamental questions. The attempt to foster such a condition must be seen for what it really is: the attempt to propagate a common sentiment—namely, the feeling that becoming indifferent to our differences is our greatest and noblest common bond. And so we come to value our toleration of difference more than we value the things over which we differ. And eventually we stop feeling so strongly about those things that once seemed worth differing over. Consequently, we stay together, because we find that we agree with one another about the most fundamental question. Man is a political animal, and if he is denied unity in the common affirmation of truth, he will find unity in the common denial of it.

The conclusion thus far may be stated simply: if McConnell's religious pluralism is not a morass of fragmentation, it is really another version of liberal, secular neutralism. But precisely for that reason it must ultimately fall prey to the critique of secular neutralism that McConnell himself, and others, have offered.

But this is not the end of the road. To McConnell, to traditional religious believers, to difference feminists, to postmodernists and to non-Western theorists, neutralist liberalism entails inconsistencies and harms that seem decisive. If they are right, then it would seem that what is needed is not a more liberal version of liberalism, not a more neutral version of neutralism or a more plural version of pluralism. Rather what is needed is something *other* than liberalism, or at least a mixed system that tempers liberalism with something other than itself. A brief consideration of how questions of religious pluralism and religious establishment are treated in Canada and Israel may shed light on such a possibility.

Canada has been attempting something like McConnell's pluralism in recent decades, and especially since the patriation of the Constitution in 1982. This pluralism embraces religion in a broader sweep of plurality by which the country seeks to organize itself. In Canada religion is treated in a way that is more or less consistent with McConnell's proposal; so also, by the same logic, are nationality, language, and culture more generally. The modern Canadian scheme involves, in McConnell's terms, the autonomy of groups rather than of individuals, or more accurately of both individuals and groups.[15] The federation is neutral among individuals, but also among provinces, languages, religions and original peoples. Most Canadian provinces provide public support for religiously organized schools on a fairly inclusive basis. The greatest consequence of this policy of pluralism is that Canadian national identity has become for most Canadians a non sequitur, and the country seems in danger of literally splitting up, not exactly along religious lines, to be sure, but along analogous ethnic/linguistic lines.[16]

The state of Israel, by contrast, was not constituted, and has never imagined itself to be constituted, by an ultimate principle of pluralism. The modern state of Israel is an unabashedly Jewish state. Yet it embodies an equivocal mix of constitutive principles that cannot easily be resolved in favor of either its liberal or illiberal elements. The 1948 Declaration of Independence that proclaimed Israel a Jewish state also announced protection for the rights of all, regardless of religion or ethnicity. Jewish values and symbols and the Hebrew language are paramount, and Jews (returning from diaspora) have entitlements under the Law of Return that are available to them by accident of birth and are *not* available to Christians, Muslims, Buddhists, or Gaians. Yet non-Jewish citizens of Israel enjoy legal protection for their voting, speech, and religious rights. Indeed, Israel bends over backward, in a way that more consistently liberal polities do not, to accommodate its minority religious subcommunities: the Jewish state funds their schools and allows them exclusive authority (for their members) over laws of personal status (e.g., there is no civil marriage, only marriage formalized by the respective religious authorities). One can hardly deny that the Jewish state fails its *non*citizen residents—the refugees—in many regrettable ways; nevertheless, it supports a relatively decent public order that inhibits the arbitrary use of power, and gives non-Jewish citizens protections that are far from trivial. And it does this in considerable defiance of liberal norms.[17]

The real alternative to secularist liberalism, then, is not simply religious establishment—at least for the reason that secularist liberalism itself possesses the functional attributes of a comprehensive religious establishment. And the problems of comprehensive religious establishments are well known. They were undesirable in the days of the divine right of kings, and they have turned out to be almost as undesirable in the day of the divine right of individualists. The real alternative is some form of constitutionally limited religious establishment. To say the same thing differently, the real alternative is a form of mixed constitution, reminiscent of Aristotle and Polybius, in which alternative justice principles are deliberately incorporated and juxtaposed in one constitutional structure.[18] Such a mixed system assumes the possibility of a principled middle position between strict privatization of religion on the one hand and inquisitorial religious hegemony on the other. A general principle to govern the concrete features of such a mixed constitution might go something like this: explicit constitutional preference for a nonliberal communal religious value should be constructed so as to deter the legal or political abolition of dissenting alternatives, except in the case of dissenters whose value systems exalt murder, rape, genocide, torture, theft, and slavery. After all, and aside from such cases, surely a state can favor one side of a value polarity without having to go so far as to outlaw the other. Moreover, a state can *promote* a given religious orientation without having to go so far as to *require* it; indeed, even while it makes its official preferences plain it can scrupulously remind citizens of their prerogatives of individual nonconformity.[19]

This mixed constitution would in many ways resemble Michael McConnell's proposal in practice, but it would differ profoundly at the level of principle. In practice it would resemble McConnell's proposal because it would seek to incorporate various communities of conscience and nurture the institutions necessary to preserve their distinctive ways of life. In principle it would depart sharply, because a mixed constitution of this sort would not pivot on the liberal principle of neutrality or all-inclusiveness. In a mixed constitutional regime of this sort, political authority would overtly prefer one religion, or an explicitly finite set of religious options, while constitutionally binding itself to protect the prerogatives of constitutionally subordinate religious orientations.

This might be thought of as a constitutional policy of "partial establishments of religion," in a way forbidden (at least to the national government) by the First Amendment to the text of the U.S. Constitution. A partial establishment would be like a system with a "free exercise of religion" clause but without a "no-establishment" clause—or rather *with* an establishment clause. This is the Israeli model—non-Jewish citizens are free and even funded, but not equal in symbolic status to Jewish citizens.

It is worth noting that the mixed constitutional principle of "partial establishments" applies to the full range of identity issues whose relation to political authority is in dispute in many parts of the world—issues such as ethnicity, language, sexual orientation, and social ideology.[20] Where there is no preexisting constitutional obstacle like the American one, the logic of mixture could be embraced in partial establishments of particular cultural affirmations of meaning. If they fit into a pervasive logic of constitutional mixture that is principled rather than ad hoc, and if they are constructed so as to deter a collapse of the polity into either its liberal or nonliberal poles, then partial establishments can remain genuinely partial.

Does the notion of a constitutionally limited partial establishment of religion stand any chance of actually being adopted anywhere? Perhaps a more daunting question is whether the contemporary American version of secular neutralism stands a chance of actually being adopted anywhere else, since in every country where religion is a major factor in public life, strict secularism seems to enjoy little public support.

With respect to partial establishments, it is worth watching developments in Poland. Poland's overwhelmingly Roman Catholic identity has apparently made it impossible, despite the urgings of visiting American legal scholars, to adopt a postcommunist constitutional settlement in the mold of American religious neutrality. The recently ratified constitutional text addresses the question of religion in terms suggestive of partial or mixed establishment. In the place where American advisors hoped for a no-establishment clause, the relevant provision of the new constitution asserts the principle of "amicable cooperation of church and state for the common good." Remarkably (at least as seen from North America), the Catholic bishops of Poland publicly opposed the ratification of this constitution, partly for its insufficient embrace of

Catholic values. Shortly after disregarding the bishops' advice on the constitution, the Polish electorate returned the heavily Catholic Solidarity Party to a parliamentary majority, and it is the Solidarity community that will flesh out the terms of the new Polish configuration of religion and public life.

While contemporary American constitutional jurisprudence is light-years away from the new Polish approach, it may be worth remembering that American history provides evidence that the current American model has not always prevailed in America, even under the present constitutional text.[21] In this vein, Michael McConnell, in seeking to ground his argument for religious pluralism in American history, invokes George Washington's approach to the question of religion and public life. But even as McConnell presents him, Washington seems to be an advocate not of all-inclusive religious pluralism, but of a constitutionally limited religious establishment of the sort I have sketched here. Washington's benign tolerance was not the tolerance of a liberal, nor the tolerance of a religious pluralist in McConnell's sense. By McConnell's account of him, Washington's magnanimity was the magnanimity of one belonging to a majority religion with public standing toward dissenting minorities who were all within the pale (as opposed to beyond it). His was apparently the magnanimity of a self-confident Anglican, one accustomed to a limited religious establishment and certainly to the social equivalent thereof. Magnanimity and equanimity came easier to an Anglican, since Anglicanism long identified itself as the *via media* of Christendom, a mantle inherited in late eighteenth- and early nineteenth-century America by the Episcopalians and Methodists. If George Washington was an exemplar of pluralist tolerance, it was within the broad but decidedly finite boundaries of historical Protestant, Catholic and Jewish belief and practice. To mismate some phrases, Washington's finite religious pluralism constituted a partial establishment privileging the "people of the Book."

Let me conclude by anticipating some reactions to my proposal.

First, some defenders of liberal neutralism acknowledge its covert exclusions and injustices. Like Stephen Macedo, they may argue that liberalism's hegemony is legitimate because it is "gentle" rather than "oppressive."[22] Or like H. N. Hirsch in his widely read article "The Threnody of Liberalism," they may simply argue—persuasively—that liberalism's exclusions are historically less dangerous than those of non-liberal regimes based openly on a traditional religion.[23] But they conclude from this that the liberal solution ought to be wholly embraced and its alternatives wholly rejected. They obviously overconclude, even on their own terms. They neglect the possibility of a mixed constitution, of partial establishments, that would seem to be the more logical answer to the conflicting problems they acknowledge.

Second, some liberals say that the impartial mind should judge the options from the minority vantage point. Even here a partly illiberal mixed constitution wins. If I am a member of a minority religion, I certainly do not want to face a majority community that has politically arrogated to itself all the means of absolutizing its alien religious vision. At the same time, a minority dissenter also finds liberal establishments deeply troubling. Assuming I do not have the opportunity to get constitutional supremacy for my community's religion, only the mixed constitution has some appeal. After all, if I am in a minority position, I would rather possess my religious identity in the face of a majority religious order overtly at odds with me—so long as my subordinate existence is constitutionally ensured—than to stand in the midst of a scheme whose mask of neutrality will strip my identity from me—or from my children—without our even realizing it.

Such a minority vantage point illuminates a creative paradox in the notion of mixed constitution or partial establishment, for as the minority perspective implies, partial establishments of religion may actually be the necessary condition for the claims of both majority communities *and* those who differ with them on central affirmations of meaning. They may be the necessary condition, especially, for the perdurance and vigor of those communities who consider the content of the partial establishment to be deeply mistaken. Why? Because a mixed constitution comprising partial establishments respects difference more powerfully than either wholesale liberalism or illiberalism can ever manage. Unlike a liberal establishment, it does not colonize dissenters. Unlike an illiberal establishment, it does not extirpate dissenters. The most potent basis of difference or dissent is an alternative truth claim; a mixed constitution of partial establishments respects dissent because it values truth-seeking publicly. Unlike liberalism, it sanctions truth-seeking as potentially significant beyond idiosyncratically private preference; it does not insist in advance that truth-seekers can never find any truth deserving public validation—because in fact it partially validates some claims to truth (in "partial establishments"). Unlike illiberalism, it systemically deflects truth-seeking from hubris—that is, from prematurely calling a halt to the search in the name of a comprehensive possession of the truth. Its constitutional structure implies—and probably promotes—the belief that truth-seeking never secures more than a partial grasp of its object; and the belief that that partial grasp validates whatever deserves public validation, including the search itself.

I come now to a third objection. Some will object to my proposal quite differently, saying that liberal regimes have historically always had the mixed quality I admire. This is no doubt the truth. Actual "liberal regimes" have always brooked greater or lesser degrees of illiberal elements, the result of inadvertence or compromise. But a dominantly liberal regime does not constitutionally entrench its mixed qualities. Rather, as in the United States, it progressively purges itself of illiberal vestigial remnants (e.g., the prerogatives of subordinate jurisdictions, like local school boards, to promote reverence for God). The purging may take a long time, but the iron logic of liberalism determines the trajectory. The same logic of course characterizes the trajectory, in the opposite direction, of dominantly religious (or nationalist or ethnic or moralistic) regimes. The parallel nature of this problem is precisely what makes a *deliberately* mixed constitution so necessary. Mixture, at its best, is a principle, not merely a compromise, although it may be institutionalized via compromise. It is a principle that, in its own moderate way, exalts the virtue of moderation over against the immoderate compulsions of both liberal and illiberal political forms. Only the mixed constitution can effectively obstruct the twin absolutisms of liberalism and its opposites. And the obstruction of absolutism is the essential function and virtue of constitutionalism itself.

Astute liberals who have digested my argument may well propose not a final objection but a final version of my proposal. If secular liberalism is in essence the equivalent of a religious establishment, then my "partial establishment" could just as well be a partial or mixed establishment of secular liberalism as of some historical revealed religion. And they are right. There is nothing to prevent—indeed, on my terms there is everything to recommend—repackaging American "religious neutralism" as an overt rather than covert form of public religious establishment. There is everything to recommend it, that is, as a *partial* establishment, subject to the limitations and qualifications that any such establishment would need to stay healthy. As a theologically conservative believing Christian, I personally would rather live in a polity where state authority overtly acknowledged and preferred secular liberalism as the official public theology—so long as my dissenting prerogatives were constitutionally and institutionally protected—than in the present American scheme of unacknowledged secularist supremacy where a massive cultural transformation has been carried out by means of strict separationist sleight of hand. Such a constitutional settlement would be strikingly similar to what Stephen Macedo—one of the most honest of liberals—has recently advocated.[24] But honestly establishing the "moderate [religious] hegemony of liberalism" would require an explicit constitutional amendment. At least, it would require such an amendment if we are bound by the provisions laid out in the American constitutional text that explicitly govern such fundamental constitutional changes—and if we value the consent of the governed. Unfortunately, absent either consent or formal constitutional amendment, Americans now face the prospect of the immoderate hegemony of liberalism.

No doubt our anxieties vary. Some of us are more worried about the dangers of publicly established traditional religion, others about the dangers of publicly established secularism or religious indifference. If either of these anxieties predominates, we are probably quite serious about avoiding comprehensive establishments of any stripe. I have argued that, to do so, we need to go at least partly outside the conceptual apparatus of liberalism. Michael McConnell stays safely just inside the gate of the liberal compound. I invite him, and others worried about the impasses of law and religion, to venture a half-step outside.

Notes

1. Among McConnell's most important contributions to the subject are the following: Michael W. McConnell, "Religious Freedom at a Crossroads," *University of Chicago Law Review* 59 (1992): 115–94; "Freedom from Persecution or Protection of the Rights of Conscience: A Critique of Justice Scalia's Historical Arguments in City of Boerne v. Flores," *William and Mary Law Review* 39 (1998): 819–47; "Tradition and Constitutionalism before the Constitution," *University of Illinois Law Review* vol ? (1998): 173–98; "Establishment and Toleration in Edmund Burke's 'Constitution of Freedom,'" *Supreme Court Review* vol ?(1995): 393–462; "'God Is Dead and We Have Killed Him!' Freedom of Religion in the Postmodern Age," *Brigham Young University Law Review* (1993): 163–88; "Christ, Culture and Courts: A Niebuhrian Examination of First Amendment Jurisprudence," *DePaul Law Review* 42 (1992): 191–221; "Coercion: The Lost Element of Establishment," *William and Mary Law Review* 42 (1986): 933–41; "Accommodation of Religion," *Supreme Court Review* (1985): 1–59.

2. Michael W. McConnell, "Believers as Equal Citizens," chapter 3 in this book.

3. Equal Access Act, 20 USCS §§ 4071 et seq. (1984).

4. In *Engel v Vitale* (370 U.S. 421, striking down New York's nonsectarian theistic prayer in 1962) the U.S. Supreme Court asserted: "When the power, prestige, and financial support of government is placed behind a particular religious belief, the indirect coercive pressure upon religious minorities to conform to the prevailing officially approved religion is plain." (370 U.S. at 430–1). The Court failed to foresee the obvious: when the power and prestige of government are deployed to make classrooms God-free zones, the indirect coercive pressure to conform to the officially approved attitude is *not* plain. Instead it is hidden. Unlike New York's official classroom prayer policy, the new policy is an even more indirect form of coercion. Its effects are almost impossible to resist precisely because they are concealed even, or perhaps especially, from those who support the policy. See Shelley Burt's discussion of the problem of impressionability in "Religious Parents, Secular Schools: A Liberal Defense of an Illiberal Education," *The Review of Politics* 56 (1994): 51–70.

5. See Stephen Carter, *The Culture of Disbelief: How American Law and Politics Trivialize Religious Devotion* (New York: Basic Books, 1993). On the language habits of internalized relativism among the American middle classes, see Alan Wolfe, *One Nation After All: What Americans Really Think about God, Country, Family, Racism, Welfare, Immigration, Homosexuality, Work, the Right, the Left and Each Other* (New York: Viking Press, 1998).

6. Stephen Macedo, "Transformative Constitutionalism and the Case of Religion: Defending the Moderate Hegemony of Liberalism," *Political Theory* 26 (1998): 69–70 (emphasis in original).

7. In that respect, traditional revealed religion has more in common with old-fashioned Marxism than with new-fashioned postmodernism—except that supernaturalist religion has a more intelligible account than Marxism of how its special insights could be untainted by the generalized false consciousness otherwise afflicting mankind. Marx never claimed divine revelation, but he never explained how he possessed knowledge that was not itself merely an epiphenomenon of the material, economic processes that dialectically controlled history.

8. *Mozert, et al. v Hawkins County Public Schools*, 579 F.Supp. 1051 (1984), and *Mozert v Hawkins County Public Schools*, 582 F.Supp. 201 (1984).

9. Uday S. Mehta, "Liberal Strategies of Exclusion," *Politics and Society* 18 (1990):427–54; Edward W. Said, *Culture and Imperialism* (New York: Knopf, 1993); Iris Marion Young, "Polity and Group Difference: A Critique of the Ideal of Universal Citizenship," Ethics 99 (1989): 250–74; Iris Marion Young, *Justice and the Politics of Difference* (Princeton, N.J.: Princeton University Press, 1990); see also Tomislav Sunic, "Historical Dynamics of Liberalism: From Total Market to Total State?" *The Journal of Social, Political and Economic Studies* 13 (1988): 455–71; Cornel West, "The New Cultural Politics of Difference," in *Out There: Marginalization and Contemporary Cultures*, ed. Russell Ferguson, Martha Gever, Trinh T. Minhha, and Cornel West (New York and Cambridge: New Museum of Contemporary Art and the Massachusetts Institute of Technology Press, 1990).

10. Alain de Benoist, *Démocratie: le problème* (Paris: Le Labyrinthe, 1985); Alain de Benoist, *Europe, Tiers monde, même combat* (Paris: R. Laffont, 1986).

11. Richard J. Neuhaus, *The Naked Public Square*; J. Budziszewski, "The Illusion of Moral Neutrality," *First Things*, no. 35 (1993): 32–37; Mark C. Henrie, "Rethinking American Conservatism in the 1990's: The Struggle against Homogenization," *Intercollegiate Review* 28, no. 2 (1993): 8–16.

12. Come to think of it, a denatured Protestantism divested of its supernatural truth claims would fit this bill even better than actual, historic Protestantism. What could be better than a religion that insisted on tolerance, recoiled from any form of official religious establishment, and taught that ultimate truth is at base an individual and private affair? Such a religion would necessarily have pride of place in any regime of pluralism, since its metaphysical pluralism would be a perfect fit with the regime principle. Here we discover why neutral, inclusive premises initially favor Protestantism but ultimately foster an establishment of secularism, a mutated descendant of its Protestant progenitor.

13. McConnell's religious pluralism is far better suited to interpolity affairs than to intrapolity affairs—that is, to the United Nations or to a loose confeder-

ation, but not to a cohesive, viable political society. By all means let us have pluralism as the rule of international law.

14. Chantal Mouffe has recently given us an astute reminder that politics inevitably involves conflict and antagonism over issues of identity and meaning: Mouffe, *The Return of the Political* (London: Verso, 1993).

15. See Robert Justin Lipkin, "The Problem of Multicultural Constitutionalism in the Canadian Experience" (paper delivered at Fourth Biennial Georgetown Constitutional Law Discussion Group, December 1993). See also, Robert Justin Lipkin, "Liberalism and the Problem of Multicultural Constitutionalism: The Distinction Between Deliberative and Dedicated Cultures," *University of Richmond Law Review* 29 (1995): 1263–325.

16. Mark A. Noll, "The End of Canadian History," *First Things*, no. 22 (1992): 29–36.

17. For a portrayal of Israel's mixed constitutional practices, see Joav Peled, "Ethnic Democracy and the Legal Construction of Citizenship: Arab Citizens of the Jewish State," *American Political Science Review* 86 (1992): 432–43; also Gary J. Jacobsohn, *Apple of Gold: Constitutionalism in Israel and the United States* (Princeton, N.J.: Princeton University Press, 1993). For instance, out of respect for the sensibilities of its Christian subcommunity, Israel initially banned the showing of the blasphemous (to Christians) film *The Last Temptation of Christ*; most European states with state-established Christian churches, of course, did not.

18. See my development of this theme in Graham Walker, "The Mixed Constitution After Liberalism," *Cardozo Journal of International and Comparative Law* 4 (1996): 311–28.

19. After all, American liberal secularism does this all the time, without admitting it (and without always reminding dissenters of their prerogatives of resistance).

20. No doubt there are any number of other institutional arrangements expressive of a mixed constitutionalism, touching further on such matters as property and capital, ethnic privileges, public promotion of culture and the arts, and the character of public education. Since my primary task here is conceptual, I will not attempt to develop these examples further here. I think it is important, however, to draw attention to the ways in which social control of property can be constitutionally mixed with private prerogatives, breaking down both socialist and liberal absolutism and hearkening back to Aristotle. A discussion of the anomaly of the American welfare state fits in here. As Mary Ann Glendon points out, America opted for a mixed constitution of property at the New Deal, but in every other respect American law and political culture have increasingly centralized individual autonomy; privacy, for instance, is now treated in the absolutist way property was before the Supreme Court changed its mind about the New Deal. This does not necessarily weaken American commitment to the welfare state, but it does make it harder than ever to articulate its justification, and to explain why the mixed approach adopted in economics is inapplicable to other matters. Glendon, *Rights Talk: The Impoverishment of Political Discourse* (New York: Free Press, 1991).

21. I present this argument at some length in Graham Walker, "Virtue and

the Constitution: Augustinian Theology and the Frame of American Common sense," in *Vital Remnants: America's Founding and the Western Tradition*, ed. Gary L. Gregg (Wilmington, Del.: ISI Press, 1999).

22. Macedo, "Transformative Constitutionalism," 69.

23. H. N. Hirsch, "The Threnody of Liberalism: Constitutional Liberty and the Renewal of Community," *Political Theory* 14 (1986): 438 and 448 nn. 82, 83. See also Stephen Holmes, *The Anatomy of Antiliberalism* (Cambridge, Mass.: Harvard University Press, 1993).

24. Macedo, "Transformative Constitutionalism"; also Macedo, "Liberal Civic Education and Religious Fundamentalism: The Case of God v. John Rawls?" *Ethics* 105 (1995): 468–96.

5

RELIGION AND STATE IN THE

UNITED STATES: A DEFENSE OF

TWO-WAY PROTECTION

Amy Gutmann

THE BILL OF RIGHTS begins by calling upon Congress not to establish religion. "Congress shall make no law respecting an establishment of religion"—the Establishment Clause—is followed immediately by the Free Exercise Clause—"nor prohibiting the free exercise thereof." Prominent contemporary proponents of religious freedom, including Stephen Carter and Michael McConnell, suggest that the Establishment and Free Exercise Clauses serve a single important purpose: they protect the free exercise of religion. The two clauses, in Carter's words, "protect religion from the state, not the state from religion."[1] Their one overarching aim is "to permit maximum freedom to the religious."[2]

In this essay, I call the one-way (only) protection view into question as a matter of both political philosophy and constitutional interpretation. I focus on the United States (with a brief comparison to the Israeli context) and therefore leave open the question of how well the philosophical case for two-way protection applies within other social contexts. At least in the American context, the separation of church and state, supported by the Establishment Clause, serves valuable public purposes in addition to protecting the free exercise of religion: it protects citizens from the united power of church and state, and in so doing it helps secure space for the pursuit of public purposes that are justifiable to a wide range of religious, nonreligious, and antireligious citizens. The two religion clauses, taken together, help provide two-way protection: to some significant extent (although, I shall argue, in principle not absolutely), they protect religion from the state and the state from religion.

Neither protection is—or should be—absolute because each protection taken to the extreme denies the importance of the other. Religion includes religiously based beliefs, and religiously based beliefs per se should not be excluded from politics. To do so is to devalue a publicly defensible part of religious freedom. Two-way protection should focus on the separation of church and state rather than on the separation of religiously based beliefs and politics. To defend a general right of exemption for churches from otherwise legitimate laws is to devalue a publicly defensible part of political freedom. Because both religious and political freedoms are fundamental, controversies that involve issues of establishment as well as free exercise are often complex and difficult to resolve beyond reasonable disagreement. The nonabsolutist version of two-way protection that I defend certainly does not offer resolutions beyond reasonable disagreement. But it takes greater account of the competing values than does either one-way protection or an absolutist version of two-way protection.

One-way protection sees the Establishment Clause as serving the cause of maximizing religious freedom and therefore as redundant with free exercise. It defends guarding churches against state interference but often opposes guarding states against church interference. The entanglement of church and state permitted by one-way protection threatens the pursuit of public purposes by citizens and also threatens free exercise for many individuals by offering state protection to the dominant interpretations of religious doctrines offered by the most powerful members of a religious community.

An absolutist version of two-way protection reads the Establishment Clause as requiring the separation not only of church and state but also of religiously based beliefs (and sometimes even religious motivations) and politics.[3] Yet this absolutism also threatens the pursuit of public purposes by citizens. It narrows the legitimate grounds upon which citizens may pursue those purposes. Some religiously based beliefs applied to politics—such as the belief that all people are created equal in the eyes of God and therefore should be granted equal civil and political rights— serve a valuable public purpose. They are translatable into complementary, non–religiously based beliefs that can be accepted by citizens who are nonbelievers and that can therefore help to create or maintain an overlapping *moral* consensus in politics. (Legitimacy, like justice, demands not merely consensus, but a morally defensible consensus.)

This essay is divided into six parts. Section 1 evaluates the "originalist" argument (most forcefully made by Michael McConnell in this volume) that Madison—unlike Locke—defended a general right to exemption for religious believers by virtue of recognizing that religious duties take precedence over civil duties. Section 2 sets originalism aside and examines some implications of reading the Establishment Clause as redundant with free exercise. Section 3 offers reasons why the separation of church and state should not extend to the separation of religiously based beliefs and politics. Two-way protection can and should converge with one-way protection in not discriminating against religiously based beliefs in politics.[4]

The question of whether religious citizens have a general right to exemption from otherwise legitimate laws needs to be distinguished from the question of whether exemptions for religious convictions can ever be justified. Section 4 examines the important case of public schooling and argues that religious parents do not have a general free exercise right to exempt their children from (otherwise legitimate) laws that govern public schooling. Section 5 distinguishes the absence of such a general right from the defense of particular exemptions that do not create discriminatory or runaway precedents. I suggest that such exemptions are justifiable. Section 6 concludes with a defense of two-way protection as a means of protecting both the political freedom and the spiritual freedom of individuals from the united power of church and state.

1. Did Madison Advocate One-Way Protection?

One-way protection treats religious freedom as an exception to the rule that constitutional freedom is freedom within the limits of legitimate law. The exception arises from "the conflict between spiritual and temporal authorities." As McConnell succinctly puts it:

> Believers inevitably face two sets of loyalties and two sets of obligations. In this respect, they resemble resident aliens, or at best, persons with dual citizenship.[5]

Madison, according to McConnell, not only recognized this "conflict of jurisdiction" but also maintained that "religious obligation takes precedence," and he therefore defended a general right of religious exemption from (otherwise legitimate) civil laws.[6] In giving priority to religious convictions over civil laws, the Madisonian view would contrast sharply with the Lockean view, which, according to McConnell, imagines that believers "could enjoy dual citizenship—with no conflict of obligations."[7]

Are the Madisonian and Lockean views at odds with one another as McConnell argues? Comparing Locke's and Madison's writings on the subject shows no such sharp contrast. The positions of the two men on this subject are remarkably similar, and in both cases more complex than McConnell suggests. Locke, like Madison, recognizes that religious and civic obligations can conflict. A conflicting religious conviction per se is not sufficient grounds to exempt a citizen from obligation to the law, according to Locke, but neither does law always take precedence over religious conviction. In *A Letter Concerning Toleration*, Locke writes:

> [T]he private judgment of any person concerning a law enacted in political matters, for the public good, does not take away the obligation of that law, nor deserve a dispensation.[8]

Does Madison—by contrast to Locke—defend exemptions from legitimate laws for religious believers? McConnell cites as evidence Madison's claim in *The Memorial and Remonstrance against Religious Assessments* that every man's duty to pay homage to God "is precedent both in order of time and degree of obligation to the claims of civil society.[9] But this claim—that a person's highest obligation is to God—cannot be evidence that Madison differed from Locke in favoring exemptions for believers from legitimate laws, because *A Letter* supports the very same claim of the precedence of man's duty to God. As Locke writes:

> [T]he observance of these things [necessary to the obtaining of God's favor, and . . . prescribed by God to that end] is the highest obligation that lies upon mankind, and . . . our utmost care, application, and diligence ought to be exercised in the search and performance of them; because there is nothing in this world that is of any consideration in comparison with eternity.[10]

There is no textual evidence in Madison, nor is there a logical argument that would require a right to exemptions from laws for religious believers based on recognizing the precedence of man's duty to God. What Madison says about the precedence of man's duty to God is completely consistent with Locke's view that a law that is "enacted in political matters, for the public good" may legitimately be enforced even against citizens with conflicting religious convictions. On the other hand, laws that try to force a profession or practice of faith do not oblige because they overstep the legitimate jurisdiction of the civil magistrate.[11] As Locke writes:

> But if the law indeed be concerning things that lie not within the verge of the magistrate's authority (as, for example, that the people, or any party amongst them, should be compelled to embrace a strange religion and join in the worship and ceremonies of another church), men are not in these cases obliged by that law, against their consciences.[12]

Like Locke (and in all likelihood heavily influenced by him), Madison neither justifies the exemption of citizens from legitimate laws nor justifies laws that overstep the state's legitimate jurisdiction:

A just government . . . will be best supported by protecting every citizen in the enjoyment of his religion with the same equal hand which protects his person and his property; by neither invading the equal rights of any sect, nor suffering any sect to invade those of another.[13]

Madison's beliefs were consistent with Locke's on this issue.[14]

Locke, Madison, and Jefferson converge in understanding the free exercise of religion to be freedom within the limits of laws that serve public purposes and that are not intended to limit religious freedom.[15] Legitimate laws may have the *effect* of limiting religious freedom as an unintended byproduct. Although some exemptions from legitimate laws for believers may be constitutionally permissible or even required, no general right of exemption from legitimate laws for the sake of religious freedom was originally read into the First Amendment (nor, I argue, should it be on grounds of political morality).

The strongest historical evidence cited by McConnell for reading a general right of exemption into the Free Exercise Clause are the religion clauses of some state constitutions. Some state constitutions, such as New Hampshire's, contained caveats that recognized a person's right to free exercise "provided he doth not disturb the public peace."[16] Were it the case that disturbing the public peace was narrowly construed at the time to mean creating a civil disorder, then the caveat would suggest an early recognition of a broad right of exemption from civil laws. "Whereas McConnell assumes that a disturbance of the peace was simply nonpeaceful behavior," Hamburger documents that "eighteenth-century lawyers made clear that 'every breach of law is against the peace.'"[17] Original intent leaves little or no room for reading a general right of exemption from civil laws into the Free Exercise Clause, and therefore for weakening the Establishment Clause in the name of free exercise on originalist grounds.[18]

The many critics of the Court's decision in *Employment Division v. Smith*, Justice Scalia notes, have not found a single early case in which a major court overturned "a generally applicable statute because of its failure to make accommodation" for a citizen on free exercise grounds. This, as anyone who recognizes the moral limits of originalism (and as Scalia himself recognizes), does not in itself justify the Court's decision in either *Boerne* or *Smith*. But it does effectively undermine O'Connor's originalist critique of the Court's decisions in these cases and her defense of free exercise exemptions as consistent with the "early American tradition of religious free exercise" and "the original understanding of the Free Exercise Clause."

The closest any critic of the contemporary Court has come to finding evidence of an early refusal to enforce a generally applicable statute prior

to 1850 is (as Scalia notes in *Boerne*) the case of a New York City municipal court, which in 1813 held that "the New York Constitution of 1777
. . . required acknowledgement of a priest-penitent privilege, to protect
a Catholic priest from being compelled to testify as to the contents of a
confession." Scalia observes:

> Even this lone case is weak authority, not only because it comes from a
> minor court, but also because it did not involve a statute, and the same
> result might possibly have been achieved (without invoking constitutional
> entitlement) by the court's simply modifying the common-law rules of evi-
> dence to recognize such a privilege. On the other side of the ledger, more-
> over, there are two cases, from the Supreme Court of Pennsylvania, flatly
> rejecting the dissent's view.[19]

The lone case is *People v. Philips*, from which McConnell approvingly
cites the Attorney William Sampson as saying, "Every citizen here is in
his own country. To the protestant it is a protestant country; to the
catholic, a catholic country; and the jew, if he pleases, may establish in
it his New Jerusalem." Sampson's statement suggests a vision of the way
some religious believers may view this country that is worthy of serious
consideration and to which I therefore return, but the vision is certainly
not one that is representative of early American jurisprudence regarding
the free exercise of religion.

Summarizing his detailed examination of early American constitutional jurisprudence, Philip Hamburger concludes that, "In fact, late
eighteenth-century Americans tended to assume that the Free Exercise
Clause did not provide a constitutional right of religious exemption
from civil laws."[20] Hamburger's study shows that "the overwhelming
majority of dissenters sought, not a constitutional right of exemption,
but an end to establishments."[21] He writes, "For these Americans, the
possibility of a general right of exemption was, at most, a distraction
from the real issues at stake. . . . A right of exemption for the religiously
scrupulous could be considered a law respecting religion."[22] After considering McConnell's interpretation of Madison's writings as a defense
of exempting religious citizens from general laws, Hamburger concludes, "Similarly, the evidence does not support the position that Madison sought a general constitutional right of religious exemption."[23]

Defense of one-way protection and a redundant Establishment
Clause therefore cannot rest on the claim that the original understanding of the Establishment Clause rendered it subservient to the Free Exercise Clause. Quite the contrary: as far as historians can tell, the most
common understanding, which Madison and Jefferson also articulated,
was that a right to the free exercise of religion should not generally exempt religious dissenters from the legal obligation to obey general laws

that serve public purposes. As Hamburger puts it, "In eighteenth-century America, where varied Christian sects bickered with one another and thrived, a constitutional right to have different civil obligations on account of religious differences was precisely what dissenters did not demand."[24] And a nonredundant Establishment Clause is precisely what the Constitution offers to block a general right of exemption on religious grounds.

2. Should the Establishment Clause Be Read as Redundant?

Even if originalism does not support a redundant Establishment Clause, other arguments may be offered for a redundant Establishment Clause, as favored by one-way protection. In a context where minority religions are treated poorly, a state may take special measures to protect minority religions without limiting the freedom of members of other religious or nonreligious groups. When state entanglement with religion is in the interests of protecting a minority religion, the Establishment Clause may seem to be an obstacle rather than an aid to equity. The case for a redundant Establishment Clause seems stronger under such circumstances.

In a social context where a majority religion systematically wields political power in such a way as to harm the civil interests of the members of one or more minority religions, the most equitable alternative may be for the constitution to cede countervailing political power to minority religions. But one rationale of the religion clauses of the United States Constitution is to prevent majority religions from systematically wielding political power in this way (as, for example, may be the case in India).

A complementary rationale is to prevent the state from becoming so entangled with any religion—majority or minority—that religious and political power become united in some partial segment of society, rather than distributed as far as possible in accordance with the principle of free and equal citizenship. The uniting of political and religious power, even if well-intended to protect a minority religion, is unlikely to protect the religious freedom of dissenting members of the minority religion. When political authority is ceded to a religious group, it is wielded by the dominant members of that group. The combination of political and religious authority is so powerful as to be threatening to individual freedom, including religious freedom.

These are among the reasons that support two-way protection in general and the Supreme Court's decision in *Kiryas Joel v. Grumet* in

particular. The Court in *Kiryas Joel* struck down the creation of a school
district for a minority religious denomination.[25] The case helps illustrate
the rationale and implications of a nonredundant Establishment Clause,
which distinguishes two-way from one-way protection. Why did the
New York state legislature violate the establishment of religion when it
created the village of Kiryas Joel as a separate public school district? The
statute in question did not directly, either in purpose or effect, violate
freedom of religion. There was no threat to the religious freedom of
those residents of the Monroe-Woodbury School District who were not
residents of Kiryas Joel. The school district favored carving out Kiryas
Joel. "From all appearances," Thomas Berg writes, "this was a happy
instance in which the political and cultural majority protected the practices of an unconventional minority without imposing any costs on
other citizens."[26]

From the perspective of two-way protection, all appearances in this
case are not as happy as this scenario suggests. Kiryas Joel "uses covenants to maintain religiously segregated and impermeable borders,
[and] so the school district physically busses students into (and, in theory, out of) Kiryas Joel in order to maintain religiously segregated
schools."[27] Political dissent in the village is treated as religious heresy.
When a Satmar resident tried to run for the first (and only) school board
election without the Grand Rabbi's approval, "he was banished from the
congregation, his tires were slashed, his windows broken, and several
hundred people, including the Rabbi, marched outside his house chant-
ing, 'Death to Joseph Waldman!'" Religious and political dissidence
went together in *Kiryas Joel* precisely because religious and political authority were entangled by state action. Dissidents "faced showers of cold
water, heckling, removal of their yarmulkes, and signs proclaiming their
outcast status."[28] Some of these reactions are of course illegal and therefore give the dissenters legal recourse, whose ultimate outcome could be
to deter the perpetrators by legal sanction. It was illegal to hold the
school board elections in the synagogue, but they were held there nonetheless. Over one hundred dissident villagers voted by absentee ballots,
explaining that they were doing so because intimidation prevented them
from voting in the synagogue. They also filed a lawsuit to move the voting booths from the synagogue to a neutral site, but local lawmakers
were unresponsive.[29]

The dissidents in *Kiryas Joel* did not claim that their free exercise of
religion was being violated. But the distinction between religious freedom and political freedom under these circumstances becomes blurred.
By carving out a political jurisdiction for a religious group, the state of
New York delegated local governmental power "to an electorate defined
by common religious belief and practice."[30]

Kiryas Joel is a paradigmatic example of how protecting the state from religion also indirectly serves to protect religion from the state in a way that goes beyond preventing the state from coercing religious belief or practice. State-church entanglement entails the ceding of state power to religious leaders, religious power to state officials, or both. Had the Court not struck down the Kiryas Joel school district, the Satmar Grand Rabbi, whose power in the village was already unusually great by virtue of his religious authority, would have gained even more power to pressure his coreligionists to conform to his religious and political views. This power, moreover, would be publicly created.

Is it realistic to think that the public authority of religious-political leaders who wield not only religious power but also state power can be limited in a way that prevents the stifling of internal dissent? Under circumstances of church-state entanglement, effective regulation becomes all the more important at the same time that it becomes all but impossible. Dissenting citizens at the local level might look to public authorities at another level to regulate and restrain their local religious-political officials. But why would an Establishment Clause jurisprudence that permitted church-state entanglement at the local level not also permit it at the county and state level? The very need to regulate religious authorities because they are so entangled with state authority is an unfortunate development from the perspective of limiting state power to protect both the freedom of citizens and the relative autonomy of religious institutions. An important and often overlooked advantage of a nonredundant Establishment Clause is that it minimizes the state's need to regulate religious authorities precisely because they do not wield (or generally threaten to wield) political power.

Soon after invalidating the school district of Kiryas Joel, the Court shifted the wall of separation between church and state by permitting Title I teachers, who are government employees, to provide remedial instruction to disadvantaged children on the premises of religious schools.[31] The Court's decision in *Agostini v. Felton* is controversial, and the controversy is principled on both sides. A more absolutist version of two-way protection would side with the dissent in *Agostini*, fearing that *Agostini* simply re-creates the problem of church-state entanglement in another, similarly problematical guise as did the separate school district of *Kiryas Joel*. Now there is literally no wall of separation between public teachers and religious schools.

A nonabsolutist version of two-way protection can support *Agostini*. And in doing so, it can also respond to the critique that the refusal to carve out a special school district in *Kiryas Joel* comes at the cost of depriving children with special needs of an adequate education because their parents are members of a religious minority. *Agostini*, interpreted from the perspective of a nonabsolutist two-way protection, helps re-solve the problem of *Kiryas Joel* by making it unnecessary to create a religiously-segregated school system in order to provide adequate edu-cation for the Satmar Hasidic children who need remedial education. A nonabsolutist version of two-way protection can make a principled peace with a permeable wall. As long as publicly funded teachers are teaching nonreligious subjects from a nonreligious perspective, their presence in religious schools is consistent with two-way protection.

Nonabsolutism is not without its costs. None of the positions avail-able—one-way protection or either version of two-way protection—is without its costs. The argument of this essay is not that a nonabsolutist version of two-way protection brings about the best of everything. Once the wall of separation becomes permeable, the ease of illegitimate state regulation of religious functions increases while the ease of legitimate state oversight of public functions decreases, because they are taking place within religious institutions. It is harder for public educational au-thorities to be sure that publicly funded teachers are not teaching from a religious perspective when they are teaching behind the walls of a pri-vately controlled religious school.

The critical fact from the perspective of a nonabsolutist version of two-way protection is that *Agostini* does not cross the principled line of permitting public funds or programs *to come under the control of reli-gious authorities* as the New York legislature did when it created a school district along religious lines. Under *Agostini*, the teachers who admin-ister Title I programs in private schools must be hired and directed by public authorities and must carry out public purposes, not religious (or antireligious) purposes. In this case the public purpose is providing an adequate remedial education for all disadvantaged students. It is a moral advantage of the nonabsolutist over the absolutist version of one-way protection that it can fulfill this purpose, and it is a moral advantage of two-way over one-way protection that it fulfills this purpose without permitting religious authorities to control publicly funded education.

Had the Court in *Agostini* interpreted the Constitution as maximiz-ing religious freedom, the teachers administering Title I could have been hired or directed by the religious schools themselves. This implica-tion of making the Establishment Clause a servant to Free Exercise high-lights the problem with such a simple First Amendment jurisprudence. The institutional incentives for American citizens to pursue public pur-poses—rather than religious or antireligious purposes—would decrease. Under a regime of one-way protection, nonpublic authorities—whether religious or antireligious—would be ceded more power by the primary agency responsible for pursuing public purposes, government. More-over, the power ceded to religious and antireligious authorities would directly implicate the government, which is just what the Establishment Clause prohibition on church-state entanglement should avoid.

The Court in *Agostini* preserves two important barriers to the kind of church-state entanglement that most threatens the pursuit of public purposes: public control must remain over public resources that are employed within a religious (or antireligious) institution, and those resources must be used to serve public purposes, in this case, remedial nonreligious education to disadvantaged students whose parents choose for them to attend religious schools.

3. Should Separation Extend to Religiously Based Beliefs?

A common way of characterizing the Establishment Clause is to say that it requires a wall of separation between religion and politics. *Agostini* implicitly calls this characterization into question. Any nonabsolutist interpretation of two-way protection will support a permeable wall between religion and politics. The nonabsolutist version of two-way protection that I consider throughout this essay distinguishes between separating church and state on the one hand and religion and politics on the other. It does so because the basic reasons that two-way protection offers for separating the institutional power of church and state are consistent with admitting religiously based beliefs into politics on the same terms as any other beliefs, which is what one-way protection also recommends. The nonabsolutist version of two-way protection that we are considering here therefore economizes on moral disagreement while one-way protection as a more absolutist version of two-way protection does not.

Since religion includes religiously based beliefs, the wall of separation between religion and politics on an absolutist view of two-way protection would be impermeable (at least in principle). Religiously based beliefs—such as the idea that all human beings are created equal in the eyes of God—would be considered suspect in politics, even if the right of citizens to invoke these beliefs would still be protected by the right to free speech. On the absolutist view, public opposition to slavery in the nineteenth century should not have invoked religiously based ideas any more than should opposition to capital punishment today.

When Stephen Carter accuses contemporary liberals of not taking religion seriously, he has a point against liberals who defend an absolute separation of religion and politics. But the nonabsolute version of two-way protection defended in this essay does not disrespect religiously based beliefs in politics. It defends a wall of separation between the institutions of state and church, but it does not keep religiously based beliefs out of politics, nor does it delegitimize the use of religiously based beliefs in politics.

A recent Court case, *Rosenberger v. Rector of University of Virginia*, helps illustrate how important—and difficult—it is to determine when public institutions do in fact wall off religiously based beliefs in a way that discriminates against religion.[32] On the two-way protection view, a public institution may decide not to fund an entire subject matter—such as religious and antireligious speech—but it may not engage in viewpoint discriminating, for example, by funding antireligious speech but not religious speech, or by funding some religious perspectives but not others. In *Rosenberger*, the Court was divided over the question of whether the University of Virginia, a state institution, engaged in viewpoint discrimination, which is unconstitutional (and unjustified according to both one-way and two-way protection) or subject-matter discrimination, which is constitutional (and justified according to both one-way and two-way protection).

A five-person majority found viewpoint discrimination in the University's denial of funding—from its Student Activities Fund, supported by mandatory student fees—to *Wide Awake: A Christian Perspective at the University of Virginia*, published by a student religious group, Wide Awake Productions (WAP). The University had denied funding to *Wide Awake* because it is a primarily religious publication; it "primarily promotes or manifests a particular belief in or about a deity or an ultimate reality."[33] Justice Kennedy argued that the University's denial of funding to *Wide Awake* amounted to viewpoint discrimination, and the University's funding *Wide Awake* would not violate the Establishment Clause because no public funds "flow directly into WAP's coffers."[34] (The University pays the printers rather than the organizations themselves.)

Writing for a four-person minority, Justice Souter argued that the University's policy did not amount to viewpoint discrimination. Quite the contrary, Souter argued, the University established a subject matter distinction: it would not fund religious—or antireligious—speech. Funding speech on the basis of subject matter is constitutionally protected. In requiring the University to fund *Wide Awake*, despite the University's policy of not funding religious (or antireligious) speech, "the Court today, for the first time," Justice Souter wrote in dissent, "approves direct funding of core religious activities by an arm of the State."

If *Wide Awake* is committed to "nothing other than the preaching of the word," as Souter argues, then it is seriously misleading to say that the University's no funding policy amounts to viewpoint discrimination.

Funding "one position but not its competitors" constitutes viewpoint discrimination. But a policy of not funding *any* "hortatory speech that '*primarily* promotes or manifests' *any view* on the merits of religion" is completely different.[35] A state may legitimately fund publications only about arts or sports, or it may even (foolishly) decide to fund "no speech beyond the subjects of pasta and cookie preparation."

But if the University funded viewpoints that were antireligious or antagonistic to various religious beliefs, then to exclude *Wide Awake* from funding on the sole grounds that its viewpoint is religious constitutes viewpoint discrimination, as McConnell had argued as counsel of record in his brief for *Rosenberger*.[36] There was no dispute that *Wide Awake* was dedicated to expressing a Christian point of view, and that it spoke out on issues as far ranging as "racism, crisis pregnancy, eating disorders, market economics, music, education, and the fall of the Soviet Union." *Wide Awake* therefore did significantly more from a public perspective— in this case as a student publication at the University of Virginia—than preach the word. It had publicly relevant things to say about political issues. The fact that what it had to say was religiously based is not a legitimate basis for a refusal of funding unless the University's policy and practice is not to fund any student organizations that engage in religious or anti-religious speech.

An absolute separation of religiously based beliefs and politics would prohibit a state institution from funding any publication that "primarily promotes or manifests a particular belief in or about a deity or an ultimate reality."[37] By funding such publications, the state gets unnecessarily entangled in matters that are primarily religious. The entanglement is unnecessary because there is no evidence that primarily religious speech in this society will be suppressed without state support. In his dissenting opinion, Souter does not argue for such absolute separation. He argues that the majority has collapsed the distinction between viewpoint and subject matter. Whereas a state university is bound not to discriminate in its funding according to viewpoint, it may discriminate according to subject matter, and that is what Souter claims that the University of Virginia did in its policy and practice of not funding *Wide Awake* (or any other religious—or antireligious—speech by student organizations).

Two-way protection makes clear that the absence of state support for religious speech is discriminatory *when the state is supporting antireligious speech on the same publicly relevant issues.* It remains an open question whether and when the state should support *any* such speech. But a state university that supports political speech by nonreligious and antireligious groups discriminates against religion if it refuses to support political speech on the same subjects by religious groups on the sole grounds that the group is religious or the speech is religiously based.[38]

Arguments against viewpoint discrimination have special force when they concern politically relevant speech. At stake is fair consideration of all relevant perspectives that citizens bring to bear upon their politics, broadly understood. The fact that someone's political position on an issue is (or is not) religiously based should not be a cause for discrediting (or crediting) it in a public forum. Regardless of the pedigree of the position, the question remains to what extent the position and the reasons offered for it should be accepted by the people who would be bound by its practical implications. If the sole reason available in support of a religiously based belief is that "God commands it and therefore I am advocating it as law," the reason should be rejected by people who lack access to the divine command. (This is probably the paradigm case that defenders of absolute separation have in mind when they call for keeping religiously based beliefs out of politics.) Similarly unacceptable on moral grounds, however, are nonreligious beliefs that are backed solely by reasons of the sort "My self-interest—or my individual conscience—commands it and therefore I am advocating it as law." The principled question of public acceptability, as these examples suggest, is distinct from the question of the position's religious (nonreligious, or antireligious) pedigree. There are examples of positions with each kind of pedigree that are more and less publicly acceptable in principle. The ultimate source of a citizen's belief rarely exhausts the publicly acceptable reasons that are available to defend that belief.

Although it would be discriminatory for the University of Virginia to fund an antireligious publication but not a religious one, it would not be discriminatory for the University to fund nonreligious activities but not religious or antireligious ones. (This is not to say that the line between speech and activities is easy to draw, only that it is necessary to draw the line somewhere sensible in order to preserve two-way protection and separation of church and state.) When a publicly supported institution funds the building of sports stadiums and museums but refuses to fund the building of churches, synagogues, and mosques, it does not discriminate against religion.[39] Rather, it honors a principle of separating church and state that itself expresses public respect for religious institutions and practices insofar as they pursue their highly valued purposes without enlisting coercive state power (in this case, the power of taxation) on their behalf. By not relying on coercive state power to pursue their religious purposes, religious institutions are free to pursue a wide range of religious purposes that would otherwise not be exempt (either in principle or practice) from state interference. Citizens are also protected from the added power of direct governmental endorsement of religious institutions, and direct religious endorsement of government, for which there would be an enormous incentive created by the lure of direct public funding. Both governments and churches are protected from the potentially corrupting effects of the mutual entanglement of such historically great powers.

Justice Kennedy weakens the majority's case in *Rosenberger* by arguing that funding of *Wide Awake* is legitimate because it is indirect. It is literally true, as Kennedy claimed, that student funds for publishing *Wide Awake* would not "flow directly into WAP's coffers." The public agency paid the printer and therefore did not transfer any funds directly to the religious publication. But this is surely far less relevant, both morally and constitutionally, than establishing whether the university was engaging in viewpoint discrimination by not funding *Wide Awake*.

If a policy of funding *Wide Awake*—along with other religious and antireligious student publications—is legitimate, then its direct funding is not problematic. If such a policy is illegitimate, if the Court is forcing the University to fund religious and antireligious speech when it has consistently chosen not to do so, then the Court is crossing a principled line that it had not previously crossed. In *Rosenberger*, unlike *Agostini*, as Souter notes, "there is no third party standing between the government and the ultimate religious beneficiary to break the circuit of its independent discretion to put state money to religious use. The printer, of course . . . only gets the money because of its contract to print a message of religious evangelism at the direction of *Wide Awake*, and it will receive payment only for doing precisely that." The distinction between payment directly to a religious organization so that it can pay an approved bill and indirect payment of the approved bill to a third party is a formalistic distinction that does no moral or constitutional work. "If this indeed were a critical distinction," as Souter recognizes, "the Constitution would permit a State to pay all the bills of any religious institution; . . . the State could simply hand out credit cards to religious institutions and honor the monthly statements (so long as someone could devise an even handed umbrella to cover the whole scheme)."[40]

The *Rosenberger* decision is defensible if and only if it rests on protection of religious speech against viewpoint discrimination. (I cannot possibly establish the facts in this case, which are still hotly contested among legal scholars.) One-way protection and the nonabsolutist version of two-way protection converge on this common ground, whereas a more absolutist version of two-way protection would oppose funding even if the University's policy of funding religious and antireligious publications were evenhanded. But neither one-way nor two-way protection of any sort offers any ground for defending the part of the *Rosenberger* decision that suggests that state support for a religious activity can become legitimate (when it otherwise would not be) if the state transmits its financial support directly to a (nonreligious) third party who is paid only if it carries out a religious activity as determined by the religious party.

Two-way protection in its nonabsolutist version converges with one-way protection on permitting a nondiscriminatory policy of university funding of religious and antireligious speech. But two-way protection diverges from one-way protection in its general opposition to direct state support of religious activities. In the context of a welfare state that funds an extensive range of nonreligious activities, why should religious citizens value the separation of church and state, as two-way protection suggests, if it means forsaking direct funding of religious activities? Is it not unfair to permit a nonreligious majority but not a religious majority to pursue its purposes with public funding? Doesn't the asymmetry between religion and nonreligion effectively establish secularism as the official religion of American democracy? Establishing secularism is surely no more justifiable than establishing any other religion. Even if secularism is not a religion, the charge can be rephrased as an objection to the state establishing an equally controversial and comprehensive philosophy of life over and against religion.

To assess the claim that the nonabsolutist version of two-way protection (the version to which I am referring unless otherwise indicated) is biased in favor of secularism and against religion, we need to distinguish two competing uses of the term "secular." Critics of two-way protection typically use "secular" to mean "nonreligious" (or sometimes more narrowly to mean "antireligious"). By contrast, in many Court decisions and among many liberals, "secular" is used interchangeably with "public," so that secular reasons are by definition public reasons. (John Rawls is an important exception, and I follow him in distinguishing between the meaning of secular and public reasons.) To identify secular with public has the effect of establishing a presumption in favor of the secular over the religious. This is because public reasons must by definition satisfy some public standard: they must be accessible to all citizens or satisfy a standard of reciprocity. Both uses of secular (as nonreligious or as public) are understandable, and both will no doubt continue in common language. But for purposes of assessing the merits of one-way versus two-way protection, it is important to stipulate one or the other usage.

Like Rawls, I use the term "secular" to mean "nonreligious" rather than "public" for several reasons. The identification of secular reasons with public reasons leads to considerable confusion because it implies that all nonreligious reasons are public reasons. Were two-way protection to identify secular reasons with public reasons, it would beg the important question of whether religious or nonreligious reasons can also be publicly defensible reasons, and why. This question ought to be answered rather than begged, out of respect for the case made by defenders of one-way protection.

The identification of secular with nonreligious also has the great advantage of not presupposing as a matter of definition that all secular reasons, simply by virtue of being secular, are more publicly acceptable or accessible than all religious reasons, simply by virtue of being religious. This usage, moreover, lends itself to a more refined and relevant set of distinctions than does the identification of secular with public. Reasons can be religious or secular and still potentially be public reasons. In principle, both types of reasons can be broadly accessible and reciprocal, especially those that are readily translatable into the other (such as the religious idea that all people are created equal and the secular idea of the dignity of all human beings).[41] I cannot here pursue the question of whether any particular religious or secular reason actually has the status of a public reason. (This would depend in part on the social context.) The point is rather that whether a reason is religious or secular, it is an eligible candidate for being considered a public reason. In either case, we need to ask: is this reason, be it secular or religious, also a good public reason?[42]

We also need to ask whether denying state funding to religious institutions while funding nonreligious institutions is tantamount to establishing secularism as the state religion. There is something seriously wrong with two-way protection if in the name of defending disestablishment it ends up establishing another state dogma, the dogma of secularism. There is no reason why the dogma of secularism should be acceptable to a diverse, overwhelmingly religious citizenry. Surely secularism elevated to official state dogma in the United States cannot be justified to the people bound by it.

Liberal and deliberative democrats of all sorts should be opposed to establishing secularism as state dogma in the United State. But two-way protection does not establish secularism as state dogma. It opposes the establishment of secularism as an official religion by the state just as it opposes state establishment of any religion or all religions. A democratic state should not expect faith from its citizens, nor belief or disbelief in a transcendent being, nor belief or disbelief in any particular meaning of life.[43] Religious and secular citizens alike should feel free to criticize what the state says and does, and to criticize the state (and each other) from a secular or a religious perspective.

Two-way protection denies religious, antireligious, and nonreligious citizens alike a *general* right—based on conscientious objection—to disobey laws that serve legitimate public purposes. Were religious citizens—unlike nonreligious citizens—granted a general right to exemption because eternal salvation is at stake for them whereas something less important (such as moral integrity) is at stake for nonreligious citizens who similarly dissent from legal demands, religious beliefs would be privileged over non-religious ones. (A great civic premium—the *right* to be granted exemption from otherwise legitimate laws—would also be put on sincerely believing that what is at stake is eternal salvation, rather than religious righteousness.)

Two-way protection consistently can and should, I argue, still grant exemptions in some cases for religious citizens only, for example, when so doing does not discriminate against nonreligious citizens because no parallel exemption exists, as in the case of mandated ceremonial religious uses of wine or peyote. Two-way protection can also consistently grant exemptions for both religious and nonreligious citizens, as in the case of conscientious objection to war, when such exemptions do not create runaway precedents, which would effectively undermine the legitimate purpose of the law.

In keeping with its general defense of legitimate laws and public policies, two-way protection denies that religious citizens have a constitutional right to teach creationism alongside of evolution in biology classes of public schools. This denial does not establish secularism as official state doctrine. Public schools also refuse to teach atheism. Advocates of one-way protection sensibly do not claim that this refusal amounts to teaching deism. A constitutional prohibition on teaching creationism in public schools does not establish secularism as a state religion any more than a constitutional prohibition on teaching atheism in public schools, were a democratic majority to require its teaching, establishes deism as the state religion.

The separation of religion and public schooling has been conducive to religiosity. The vast majority of graduates of public schools in the United States have grown up, generation after generation, to be believers, much like their parents. An extensive, but not absolute, separation of church and state institutions supports a diversely religious citizenry, with beliefs that are not dependent on state orthodoxy or heterodoxy.

4. The Special Case of Public Schooling

Democratic governments in the United States are authorized to tax citizens to support public schooling that is neither religious nor antireligious, but nonreligious, and not, therefore, morally neutral. Mandatory schooling is special because, as the Court recognized in *Prince v. Massachusetts*: "The state's authority over children's activities is broader than over like actions of adults."[44] Mandatory schooling, as it applies to children, is justifiable to the extent that it serves public purposes and is democratically supported. Central among the purposes is providing all children with an education appropriate to exercising the rights and responsibilities of democratic citizenship. Courts have long upheld this purpose as legislatures try to put it into effect, with varying success.

Religious citizens who send their children to private religious schools must pay extra for them. This in itself is not unfair. It is generally not unfair to expect citizens to pay extra for something, such as religious (or antireligious) education, that the public is not obligated to supply. The unfairness of forcing parents to fund public schools if their children do not use them cannot be sustained as a moral or constitutional standard. The same argument impugns taxing citizens who are not parents, who also gain no private good from this use of their taxes. Taxation for public schooling does not and need not aim at subsidizing a private good for parents or nonparents.

It still seems unfair that some parents, through no fault of their own, cannot afford to pay to send their children to a private school while others can afford to do so. Similarly, some parents can afford private tutors, SAT review programs, and expensive universities for their children, while others cannot. There *is* a general problem of unfairness here rather than one that can be resolved by public subsidies for religious (or antireligious) schooling. Many Americans are unable to afford some highly valued goods and services that their fellow citizens can afford but that the government is not obligated to fund (because they are not basic opportunity goods) or in some cases not permitted to fund (because funding would entail an unjustifiable entanglement of church and state). The unfairness rests with the inadequate resources available to many Americans. A negative income tax for poor Americans who cannot work and an expanded earned income tax credit for those who can work coupled with a more progressive tax system for middle-class Americans would be an appropriate response to this problem.

Two-way protection recommends against public funding of religious schools in order to protect a public space for, among other things, schooling whose primary purpose is public, and neither religious nor antireligious. A central public purpose of schooling—preparing children for the rights and responsibilities of democratic citizenship—can be defended on many different grounds, including religious and secular grounds. Secularly based reasons are not favored over religiously based reasons (or vice versa) for pursuing public purposes. Some citizens may legitimately argue for public schooling based on the idea that all children are created equal in the eyes of God and deserve a public education for free and equal citizenship. Others may legitimately invoke the secular idea of human beings as ends in themselves, and still others may invoke reasons (such as free and equal citizenship) that have a pedigree that is more purely public.

From a moral and constitutional perspective, what needs to be judged is not whether the *reasons* have a religious or secular *basis*, but rather whether the *purposes* that they serve are *public*. If the purposes are public, then public education may legitimately be funded on constitutional grounds even against the religious or secular convictions of some parents. Other considerations matter as well from a moral and constitutional perspective, although they are rarely discussed because they are so taken for granted. Perhaps the most important consideration is that schooling for democratic citizenship is only part of a child's education, and schooling for citizenship also need be only a part of the purpose of mandatory schooling. Far more of a child's education occurs within the family, subject to parental, not public, authority.

Children are not only democratic citizens; they are also family members. And they are also, increasingly as they mature, their own persons. Mandatory schooling is only part of a child's education, but it's an important part. The Court has consistently argued that the purpose of educating children as democratic citizens is compelling. Regardless of whether a child's parents are religious or secular, a democratic government may require that the child be educated for democratic citizenship, but it may not restrict parents to educating their children only for democratic citizenship.

On what basis could the Court then exempt Amish children from two compulsory years of high school education, as it did in *Wisconsin v. Yoder*?[45] *Yoder* is an exceptional case, which two-way protection recognizes as such: one of the only cases concerning public education where the Court required an exception in the name of parental free exercise rights to an otherwise legitimate law governing public schooling that did not compel profession of belief.

In *Barnette v. Board of Education*,[46] a far more typical case, the Court mandates an exemption to requiring children to pledge allegiance to the flag in the name of forbidding the state to compel profession of belief against one's convictions, in this case by children of Jehovah's Witnesses.[47] The central issue in *Barnette*, as Justice Jackson emphasized, was freedom of expression, not freedom of religion. "The mere possession of religious convictions which contradict the relevant concerns of a political society," Justice Frankfurter had argued in an earlier flag salute case, "does not relieve the citizen from the discharge of political responsibilities."[48] In reversing the Court's conclusion in *Barnette*, Jackson does not contradict Frankfurter's general defense of two-way protection. Instead, Jackson paves a more consistent course of two-way protection by denying the legitimate power of the state to compel profession of belief in the first place. "It is not necessary to inquire whether non-conformist beliefs will exempt from the duty to salute," Jackson argues in *Barnette*, "unless we first find power to make the salute a legal duty." Consistently with two-way protection, *Barnette* limited the legitimacy of laws to those that do not "prescribe what shall be orthodox in politics, nationalism, religion, or other matters of opinion or force citizens to confess by word or act their faith therein."[49]

The Court's moral and constitutional reasoning in *Yoder* is far more strained than in *Barnette*. Justice Burger must go to great lengths to preserve two-way protection. He does so by carving out an almost unique exception for the Amish. Burger does not say that the Amish parents can override the public purposes of education with their own religious purposes. Rather, he declares that the education provided by the Amish parents—although it consists of no schooling beyond eighth grade—equally satisfies the state's public educational purposes.

Most striking about the *Yoder* decision is the emphasis placed by the Court on the unique set of attributes of the Amish community. The Amish community is described and apparently commended (on constitutional grounds) as a highly stable, traditional, law-abiding, self-sufficient, separatist, agrarian, and religious community whose religion dictates its entire way of life. To further emphasize the exception the Court is making to the rule of nonexemption from legitimate laws on grounds of religious freedom, Burger concludes the Court's opinion by noting, "Nothing we hold is intended to undermine the general applicability of the State's compulsory school-attendance statutes."[50]

In light of the fact that Amish children were exempted from two years of compulsory education, why should the children of the fundamentalist parents in *Mozert v. Hawkins County Board of Education* not be exempted from reading textbooks that their parents find offensive on religious grounds? In *Mozert*, the Sixth Circuit Court of Appeals denied a group of fundamentalist parents the constitutional right to exempt their children from the reading texts required by the Hawkins County Board of Education, texts to which their parents had sincere religious objections. The Supreme Court refused certiorari. On constitutional grounds, the *Mozert* Court upheld the decision of the Hawkins County school board to require all children to read from the same series. The school board could have accommodated the children without forcing any other children to read materials offensive to their parents' religion. Like the *Yoder* parents, the *Mozert* parents were not asking the board to change the curriculum for any other children. Yet the *Mozert* Court denied the parents' right to override the school board's decision in the name of those beliefs.

The *Mozert* case illustrates the importance of distinguishing between (1) denying citizens with religious (or secular) convictions special authority to override democratically authorized laws that serve legitimate public purposes, especially when those purposes are educational and therefore directly apply to children, and (2) devaluing the authority of citizens with religious convictions as compared to secular convictions (because their convictions are *religious*). The *Mozert* decision does not devalue the authority of any citizens because of the religious basis of their beliefs, but it does deny religious citizens special authority to override democratically authorized laws that serve the legitimate purposes of public education. *Yoder* remains an exception; *Mozert* reflects the rule.

Almost all rules have exceptions, but it is important to see how narrow an exception *Yoder* makes to this rule. Even in authorizing Amish parents to override a legitimate law concerning public education, the *Yoder* Court reaffirmed the state's authority to set requirements over public schooling, *except* in the case where parents are part of a traditional religious community that is unusual in the degree of self-sufficiency, separateness, law abidingness, and stability over time. In offering grounds for the exception, the *Yoder* Court almost exclusively identifies the Amish. Subsequent Court opinions reaffirm that religious convictions by themselves are insufficient to override facially neutral educational requirements that serve legitimate public purposes. Public purposes are broadly identified and include teaching skills, conveying knowledge, and cultivating dispositions that are conducive to democratic citizenship.

The *Mozert* parents had the right as equal citizens to try to convince the school board to provide their children with alternate texts that also served the civic purposes of the reading curriculum. The parents tried and failed to convince the school board. Secular parents with a different set of objections—based on their moral convictions—could have similarly tried and failed. Dissenting parents with religious convictions and those with secular convictions are similarly respected as free and equal citizens. Both are free to speak their minds and try to persuade their fellow citizens, but neither has special authority to exempt themselves (or their children) from democratically authorized policies that serve legitimate public purposes.

Democratic authority over education also has important limits, which permit religious and irreligious parents alike to send their children to private schools (accredited by the state) that may teach religion, atheism, or agnosticism in addition to the state requirements of civic education. Two-way protection supports the Court's decision in *Pierce v. Society of Sisters*, affirming the right "of parents to provide an equivalent education in a privately operated system."[51] The Court in *Pierce* ruled—

on the basis of substantive due process, not free exercise of religion—that in requiring all children to attend a public school, the state of Oregon went beyond its legitimate authority to run and regulate schools. In the absence of any "peculiar circumstances or present emergencies which demand extraordinary measures relative to primary education," states must allow parents the liberty to *supplement* state schooling requirements with additional and alternative schooling of their choice. The fundamental liberty at stake extends to religious and secular education alike. Parental authority over their children's education must be *alongside* democratic authority.

Pierce does not give parents a right to override an otherwise legitimate state educational requirement, even on the basis of a sincere religious belief. It rightly does not give parents exclusive or overriding authority in the area of education. It rightly recognizes parental authority as an important limit on democratic authority, just as democratic authority is an important limit on parental authority in the area of education. "The child is not the mere creature of the State," Justice McReynolds wrote for a unanimous Court. Neither are children the mere creatures of their parents, as *Pierce* and every other Court decision in the area of education also recognizes. The state has legitimate authority but not exclusive authority over publicly funded education.

Pierce offers no license to religious or secular parents to override democratic authority in the area of publicly funded education. It does not extend the free exercise of religion to include a parental right to exempt one's children from otherwise legitimate educational requirements. What *Pierce* establishes is consistent with two-way protection and is fair as between religious and secular citizens. Both religious citizens and secular citizens have the right to send their children to private schools (which satisfy the state's educational requirements but are free to teach far more than what the state requires). Neither religious nor irreligious citizens have a constitutional right to override democratic laws regulating their children's education, as long as those laws serve legitimate public purposes and do not require profession of belief by children. The exception for the Amish is truly exceptional; two-way protection helps explain why the exception should not become the rule.

5. Protecting Accommodation against Discriminatory and Runaway Precedents

Even the Amish exception, as Burger wrote in *Yoder*, presents "a most delicate question" of "what is a 'religious' belief or practice entitled to constitutional protection." Burger is apparently concerned that the precedent not be extended so as to undermine democratic authority over education or democratic authority more generally. "The very concept of ordered liberty," he notes, "precludes allowing every person to make his own standards on matters of conduct in which society as a whole has important interests." Does the very concept of nondiscrimination and the prohibition on the establishment of religion also preclude making exceptions to legitimate laws for religious citizens but not for nonreligious citizens whose objections are similarly conscientious?

Making exemptions to legitimate laws for believers presents a double-edged challenge: an exemption risks creating either a discriminatory precedent or a runaway precedent. A discriminatory precedent distinguishes between beliefs in cases where the beliefs are functionally equivalent; they occupy essentially the same place in a person's life as, for example, conscientious objection to war occupies in the life of a Quaker and a secular pacifist, yet they are treated differently by the law. This discrimination can be avoided by not distinguishing between such beliefs, but a Court (or other public authority) that denies the distinction may thereby risk a runaway precedent that undermines the effective aim of the law. Had the *Yoder* Court not distinguished between the Amish and Thoreau, for example, it could have made mandatory exemptions for school-age children on the basis of the conscientious dissent of parents the rule rather than a rare exception.

The *Yoder* Court answered the "delicate question" of what a religious belief is for the purposes of constitutional protection by claiming that religious beliefs by their very nature occupy a more central place in the lives of believers. Nonreligious beliefs, according to Burger, are based on "subjective evaluation" and are "philosophical and personal." By contrast, religious beliefs are nonphilosophical and impersonal, and based on objective evaluations. Thoreau is Burger's example of a nonreligious dissenter whose beliefs are presumed to be subjective and personal.

Is Burger's (quite common) distinction defensible? There is a sense in which Thoreau's beliefs are subjective and personal, the same sense in which the beliefs of religious citizens are also subjective and personal. Their beliefs manifest themselves internally rather than externally, and they are someone's, not everyone's, beliefs. In a far more substantial sense, however, Thoreau's moral convictions, against slavery for example, were no more subjective and personal than the antislavery convictions of religious believers. In both cases, citizens take themselves to be constrained by objective moral standards that are, strictly speaking, the opposite of personal preferences. In both cases, citizens personally believe in their standards, but in neither case does this make the standards subjective or purely personal, simply a matter of individual taste. As the Court has recognized in the case of conscientious objection, exceptions made for religious convictions call for similar exceptions made for moral convictions that are nonreligious but occupy a parallel place in a person's life, because a nonreligious conviction may be no less "objectively" binding or discretionary than a religious conviction.[52]

In a society where the vast majority of citizens are religious, democratically elected legislatures are more likely to risk discrimination against nonreligious believers than to risk runaway precedents, even though the risks of creating a runaway precedent may be low. Because so many Americans are religious, any exemption made for a member of a religious group runs a far greater risk of creating a runaway precedent. The *Yoder* court did not simply distinguish between religious and nonreligious convictions; it distinguished between the Amish religion (and religious community) and almost all other religions (and religious communities.) It was by *distinguishing among religions* that the *Yoder* Court avoided a runaway precedent. In the context of a society where the vast majority of citizens are religious, admitting an exemption on the basis of religious belief is at least as likely to risk a runaway precedent as extending exemptions from religious to non-religious citizens.

Two-way protection recognizes that making exemptions from otherwise legitimate laws runs the risk of creating discriminatory or runaway precedents. But it also recognizes the possibility of justifiable exemptions in particular cases on the very same grounds: nonexemption in some cases (from facially neutral laws) implicitly entails discrimination. *Employment Division of Oregon v. Smith* was probably such a case.[53] The Court's decision in *Smith* signaled a retreat from making any exceptions to facially neutral laws for religious believers. Rather than resolve the problems of discriminatory and runaway precedents, this judicial retreat sidesteps them. If no exception to Oregon's drug law is granted to members of the Native American Church, which has long prescribed peyote for sacramental use (only), a democratic state still risks discrimination, not between religious and secular citizens but between mainstream and nonmainstream religious believers. The Oregon state legislature would not have so burdened the practice of a mainstream religion as it burdened the practice of the Native American church by refusing to make an exception to its drug law for the sacramental use of peyote.

In defending the Court's refusal to require an exemption in the *Smith* case, Justice Scalia does not deny that exempting members of the Native American church would be fairer than not exempting them.[54] He admits that "leaving accommodation to the political process will place at a relative disadvantage those religious practices that are not widely engaged in." But he argues for judicial restraint in deference to democracy and in avoidance of anarchy. He concludes for the Court majority that "that unavoidable consequence of democratic government must be preferred to a system in which each conscience is a law unto itself or in which judges weigh the social importance of all laws against the centrality of all religious beliefs."[55]

A nonabsolutist version of two-way protection offers an alternative to Scalia's standard while similarly respecting democracy and the rule of law. Because of the twin risks of discriminatory and runaway precedents, the Court should not routinely override legislatures or defer to them in the case of a facially neutral law that disadvantages a religious minority by prohibiting a prescribed religious activity. Even when an exemption does not risk harm to others, the issue of discriminatory and runaway precedents remain. In light of these issues, the Court should not routinely require the state to show a compelling interest to defer to laws that differentially burden some religions. The Court should judge whether an exemption is constitutionally mandated by asking whether more mainstream religious beliefs or actions of a functionally equivalent sort (such as the ceremonial use of sacramental wine) would be exempted from facially neutral laws (such as liquor prohibitions for minors). This inquiry incorporates concern for the rule of law (therefore avoiding anarchy) without exaggerating the risk of anarchy when exemptions are made for ceremonial religious practices that have few if any harmful externalities and few if any secular analogues. The risk of a runaway precedent is therefore slight, and need for a nonmajoritarian institution to protect religious minorities against discrimination is great.

If the *Smith* decision showed too little willingness to make exemptions from facially neutral laws for free exercise, the Religious Freedom Restoration Act (RFRA), which Congress passed in reaction to *Smith*, showed too much. Two-way protection recognizes three serious risks posed by routine exemptions for religion from facially neutral laws: (1) public discrimination between moral convictions that are and those that are not religious; (2) state establishment of religion over nonreligion; and (3) a threat to ordered liberty when the state authorizes every person "to make [and act upon] his own standards on matters of conduct in which society as a whole has important interests."

RFRA set a standard for exempting religion from otherwise legitimate laws that posed all three of these problems. From this perspective, it was fortunate that RFRA was short-lived.[56] Under an RFRA regime, exemptions routinely would be required for religion from any law that "substantially burdens" religion but does not serve a "compelling" public interest. RFRA's discrimination in favor of religion was almost as broad as can be. The substantial burden that would bring exemption need not even have been a burden on religious conscience. It might be the substantial burden of taxation on funding one's religious practices or the substantial burden of zoning on expanding one's church. RFRA could have forced every municipality to exempt every church, synagogue, and mosque from zoning laws, even if the same zoning laws did not more generally exempt buildings of secular or nonreligious charitable associations. In *Boerne v. Flores*, the Court struck down RFRA.

A state's legitimate interest in regulating property must be exercised in a way that does not prefer religion over irreligion or one religion over another. RFRA gave preference to religious over nonreligious (and antireligious) associations. It represented an attempt to overturn an independently important Establishment Clause by reinterpreting the Free Exercise Clause to require a compelling state purpose to place a substantial burden on a religious association (but not a nonreligious or an antireligious one).[57] If a substantial burden on religion (but not nonreligion) becomes sufficient to override an otherwise legitimate law, then religion can be established over nonreligion.

To avoid discrimination against nonreligion, exemptions to all substantially burdensome laws would need to be extended to all conscientious dissenters. This evenhanded and general practice of conscientious exemptions would not threaten to establish religion, but it would threaten to disestablish democratic government by making the democratic pursuit of public purposes all but impossible. Standards for exemption need to be more limited. A nonabsolutist version of two-way protection justifies making exceptional exemptions—such as the one at issue in the *Smith* case—that are necessary to avoid discrimination (among believers) and are not runaway precedents. (Granting conscientious objector status to both religiously and nonreligiously based pacifists is another defensible exception to facially neutral draft laws.) These and other exceptions are consistent with the general rule of two-way protection: all religious and nonreligious citizens alike are legally bound by legitimate laws that serve public purposes, and none of us is legally bound by illegitimate laws. The public sphere serves in this way to unite rather than to divide citizens, as would be the case to the extent that exemptions for religious citizens became the rule rather than the exception.

6. Protecting Freedom to Pursue Public Purposes

Legitimate laws are not equally conducive to, or burdensome on, the varied moral convictions of citizens or their diverse ways of life. When the Court tests a law for its "neutrality"—a term that tends to generate more heat than light in political philosophy—it is not requiring neutrality of effect on people's lives (or compatibility with their deepest convictions), nor is it claiming that its test is morally neutral. The Court generally invokes neutrality as a test of the *purpose* of the law, not its *effect* or *value*. To pass constitutional muster, a law's purpose must not be to prefer or to promote religion over irreligion, irreligion over religion, or a particular religion over other religions. To say that the purpose of a law is neutral is therefore not to say that the law is morally neutral, or that the reason for requiring neutrality of purpose is morally neutral.

Consider the curricular policy of the Hawkins County school board that was sustained in the *Mozert* case. It was certainly not morally neutral. But neither did it establish secularism in the schools, as some critics suggest. The required readings of the Holt, Rinehart, and Winston series included many readings by and about religious believers. The pedagogy did not pressure any student to conform to the viewpoints expressed in the readings. But the school board's policy of exposing students to varied viewpoints, both religious and nonreligious, was not morally neutral. Nor did it claim to be. The curricular policy was neutral only in the very limited sense that its purpose was not to teach children to be religious or irreligious.

Imagine that the Hawkins County school board instituted a policy requiring atheism or its equivalent to be taught in public schools. The purpose of such a law would be antireligious and therefore would violate the Court's neutrality test and the Establishment Clause for the same reason that a law requiring equal time for creationism violates both. The primary purpose of the law is not public, but religious or antireligious.

Why should laws be constrained by Courts not to be primarily religious or antireligious in their purposes? The bloody history of bickering religious sects is certainly part of what inspired Locke and early American thinkers like Madison and Jefferson to defend the pursuit of public purposes by government rather than religious (or antireligious) purposes. Separation of church and state would not end the struggle among religions. But the bickering of religious sects outside of government need not be a matter of general concern for citizens or civil government provided that the bickering churches and sects are not vying for state power.

Two-way protection recognizes three reasons why democratic politics needs to be protected from churches competing for state power, even when their competition does not immediately or directly threaten the free exercise of any citizen. First, as long as religious stakes are believed to be as high as eternal salvation, such competition is likely to be particularly fierce and soon become downright bloody. The lives and basic liberties of many innocent people have been lost in religiously inspired battles for state power. Second, competition among churches for state power decreases the incentives for peaceful states to pursue public purposes and therefore decreases the chances of justifying laws to the people who are bound by them, regardless of their religion. Third, protecting democratic politics from the competition of churches makes it all the more possible and desirable to protect churches from the competition of democratic politics.

Defenders of one-way protection seem to imagine many churches competing for state power in much the same way that they now compete for membership among individuals. In competing for all the many goods that state power can bring, the churches would not threaten a peaceful civil order; they would not make it more difficult to pursue public purposes; and they would not appear to use state power in ways that manipulate the religious convictions of citizens. State power would be peacefully and fairly divided among many religions in the same way that religions shared power in civil society before any state existed. This counterfactual assumes a social baseline analogous to a state of nature, where religious institutions exist prior to political institutions. For the United States, it yields the null set of religious institutions because those we now know developed in a way that is inseparable from a political context of state power.

One-way protection asks us to imagine that peaceful competition among churches for state power, fairly constrained by courts, would result in some local townships being democratically controlled by particular churches, democratically pursuing the religious ends of that church with the aid of state power. No dissenting citizen would be coerced into practicing the majority religion or into living in a particular township. All citizens would be free to find the township that comes closest to pursuing their religion or nonreligion. Every township that is religiously pluralistic would democratically distribute tax revenues (for education, for example) among either parents or the competing religious and non-religious groups, who would then distribute the revenues to parents. If the democratic distribution were unfair, courts would intervene as the arbiters of fairness. The political pursuit of public purposes cutting across religious groups would be minimized in this society, and the political pursuit of particular religious purposes would be correspondingly maximized (assuming peaceful competition and coexistence among religious groups).

Perhaps it is a pluralistic vision of this sort that leads McConnell to imagine the United States as a society in which "every citizen . . . is in his own country."[58] Paraphrasing Attorney Sampson in the 1813 New York case, McConnell says that his pluralistic vision would ensure that "[t]o the Protestant it is a Protestant country, to the Catholic a Catholic country, to the Jew a Jewish country."[59] I say "perhaps" because this positive vision is very elusive, both theoretically and practically speaking.[60]

What it would mean for the United States to be simultaneously Protestant and Jewish? McConnell offers the example of state provision of a

special table with kosher food at the great public feast in 1789 in Philadelphia. "This was a fitting symbol," McConnell writes, "because it included Jewish Americans in the celebration without requiring that they
sacrifice their distinctiveness as Jews."[61] The example as McConnell describes it is ambiguous between two importantly different alternatives.
Kosher meals might be provided in a way that enables and encourages
Jewish Americans and non-Jewish Americans to sit together at the same
tables, or Jewish Americans might be served at a separate (kosher) table.
Both alternatives are better than not providing kosher food at all and
thereby excluding Orthodox Jewish Americans, but providing kosher
meals in a way that Jewish Americans can sit at any table would be more
consistent with a pluralism that values integration in public places rather
than either separation or assimilation. Neither of these alternatives,
however, is nearly adequate to McConnell's description of making the
United States a Jewish country to Jewish Americans.

What would make this country Jewish to Jewish Americans? Jews do
not agree on what Judaism requires of them individually, let alone
what Judaism requires or permits of a country that would be a Jewish
country to its Jews. Nor do coreligionists of any other major faith with
which I am familiar agree among themselves (or even necessarily agree
more among themselves than they do with some members of other religious groups).[62] Moreover, most Jewish Americans, I suspect, think it
better that the United States is not a Jewish country to Jewish Americans, just as many other American citizens morally approve of this country not being a Protestant, Catholic, Muslim, Buddhist, or atheist country to them.

Perhaps the two-way protection view is mistaken in suggesting that
the Constitution does not (or should not) support this country being a
Jewish, Protestant, Catholic, Muslim, Buddhist, or atheist country, as
the case may be, to each of us. But to see how two-way protection might
be mistaken, one-way protection must be clearer about how the United
States could be a Jewish country to its Jews, a Catholic country to its
Catholics, *and* an atheistic country to its atheists. (The United States
once was, roughly speaking, a Protestant country to its Protestant citizens, but this is largely no longer the case. Today the United States still
seems Protestant in some respects, but probably more so to me and
other non-Protestants than to its Protestant citizens.) I suspect that the
reason that one-way protection says so little about how the United
States could be all these various religions to various of its citizens is that
it cannot be.

Could the United States realize the vision of one-way protection, and
should a religiously diverse citizenry want it to? This is a question of
political morality that in a sense precedes the constitutional question.

Answering it lends support to two-way protection, which offers an interpretation of the Establishment Clause, but does not presuppose it or the written constitution of the United States.

Consider the case of a democratic state in which free exercise of religion reigns without the moral or constitutional constraint of separation of church and state. Unlike the United States, Israel is a Jewish country, religiously as well as culturally speaking, to many although by no means all of its Jewish citizens. There may be some advantages of its being so, especially in light of the history of persecution of Jews that preceded the creation of Israel (although the survival of Israel does not depend on its being a religiously Jewish state). There are certainly some obvious disadvantages from the perspective of its non-Jewish citizens. But there are also some less obvious but equally significant disadvantages from the perspective of Jewish citizens. I focus here on these disadvantages from the perspective of religious citizens because they call into question the core idea of recognizing one's religion in one's state.[63] Israeli Jews who speak in the name of their faith are themselves deeply divided over whether Israel is or should be a religiously Jewish state, and for at least two good reasons.

The first reason is that when the state speaks in the name of Judaism, it speaks in the name of a "state establishment" interpretation of Orthodox Judaism over and often against other interpretations of Judaism. Consider one (perhaps the most) significant way in which Israel is a religiously Jewish state to some of its Jewish citizens: Israeli Jews must be married by Orthodox rabbis for their marriages to be respected under the state marriage law as Jewish. If you are an Israeli Jew and a Reform or Conservative Jewish marriage is more in keeping with your faith, you must either agree to be married by an Orthodox rabbi or not have your marriage recognized as Jewish by the state. This entanglement of church and state encourages Jews who do not recognize the sanctity of Orthodox marriage to be married by Orthodox rabbis.

An eminent Israeli advocate of a strong separation of church and state, Yeshayahu Leibowitz, himself an Orthodox Jew, argues that Orthodox control over Jewish marriage in Israel violates a religious prohibition: "[T]he proscription of placing a stumbling block before the blind. Men and women are led into a far more serious halakhic transgression [violation of Jewish law] than that of living together without religious marriage."[64] Because church and state are not separated in this way, non-Orthodox Jews as well as Orthodox Jews like Leibowitz find their religious convictions devalued by the state, although not coerced by it.

This problem suggests a second reason that some Israeli Jews oppose any state establishment of religion, which cuts even closer to the core of one-way protection. Some Orthodox Jews, like Leibowitz, themselves take religious exception to the idea that state officials can be entrusted to determine what counts as the correct practice of Orthodox Judaism. Orthodox Israeli Jews can reasonably question the religious expertise of their state officials, even (or especially) when Orthodox rabbis serve as state officials for the purposes of setting religious standards for the state. A religious state, for these Orthodox Jews, is suspect not because it devalues the non-Orthodox but rather because it deforms Orthodoxy. As Leibowitz writes:

> At no time have the religious leaders [in Israel] ever offered a concrete program for operating the existing state in accordance with the Torah. . . . There can be no greater logical and moral incoherence . . . than the appearance on the political scene of a religious bloc of parties demanding "a state in accordance with the Torah," but lacking any concrete program for administering the state in accordance with halakhic norms. The result is mere clerical politics.

By "mere clerical politics," Leibowitz means a thoroughly hypocritical politics that "can only discredit religion, even in the eyes of religious Jews" because it depends on "the non-observance of Halakhah by those who run the state" and run it in the name of Orthodox Judaism! "Let other Jews keep electric current and water supply running on the Sabbath . . . so long as our group is exempted from that duty."[65] Let other Jews police the streets on the Sabbath. Let all men and women be required to engage in military service, but exempt all our Torah students and our daughters. And so on for a myriad of state functions that cannot be carried out in accordance with the laws of Orthodox Judaism yet are to be carried out—according to those who defend a religiously Jewish state—in the name of Orthodox Judaism. Leibowitz speaks in the name of two-way protection when he argues that political authorities are not and should not be religious experts, nor can religious experts be entrusted with interpreting religious doctrine when they become political authorities. Most religious matters, like a religiously sanctified marriage, are too important to entrust to the state.

Every state, however, has (and needs) a marriage policy. What counts as a legitimate marriage for public purposes such as taxation and child rearing is a political matter. Suppose that Israel changed its marriage policy so that any ordained rabbi could officially marry Israeli Jews and their marriages could then be recognized as Jewish by the state.[66] This would avoid the problem of devaluing non-Orthodox Judaism. But it would not necessarily make Israel more Jewish to its Jewish citizens, and the reason it would not reveals another problem with seeking endorsement of one's religious identity by the state. Many Orthodox Jews in

Israel could oppose liberalizing of the marriage laws on grounds that to do so would make Israel *less* Jewish to them. Some Jews believe that being Jewish requires being married by an Orthodox rabbi; other Jews believe that it does not.

As long as Jews disagree, which means as long as Jews survive, a Jewish state cannot be neutral on the question of what constitutes a truly Jewish marriage and still be a Jewish state to its Jews. This suggests yet another advantage of rejecting as a political ideal the notion of a one-to-one correspondence between one's religion and one's state. The moral advantages of not seeking such one-to-one correspondence are not unique to the relationship between one's religious identity and one's state. They also extend, for example, to recognizing the moral dangers of a diverse citizenry seeking one-to-one correspondences between their race, ethnicity, and even something as broad as their (necessarily diverse) culture and their state.

This is not to say, however, that politics can be morally neutral in its effects or influences on religious, racial, ethnic, or cultural identities. States, for example, need marriage policies, and no marriage policy can be morally neutral. But a state's marriage policy need not answer the question of what counts as a Jewish, Catholic, Protestant, or any other religious marriage. The United States does not and morally and constitutionally should not answer the question of what counts as a Jewish marriage. It should not answer this question because it should not try to be a Jewish state to Jews, or a Catholic state to Catholics, or a Protestant state to Protestants, or an atheistic state to atheists.

Two-way protection—of religion from the state and the state from religion—opposes a politics of religious recognition by which a state would strive to be a religious state to any or all denominations, and to be an antireligious state to its secular citizens. By permitting clergy of all churches to marry couples in the eyes of the law at the same time as they perform religious marriages, state governments in the United States do not take a position on what constitutes a true Jewish, Catholic, or Protestant marriage. Although state governments also authorize justices of the peace to marry couples, they do not therefore consider the citizens who are married in a town hall to be atheists. For all a state that practices two-way protection should know or care, the couples married by justices of the peace may or may not be religious.

It is important to recognize that the strongest argument for separating state power from church power is not based on the misleading notion that religious citizens can simply conform their convictions to the demands of democratic citizenship, whatever those demands may be. Separation protects religious citizens from being unduly pressured by churches to conform to their orthodoxies. The more state power churches can wield, the greater the pressure can be. Just as separation protects nonbelievers from the pressures to conform to a religion they reject, it also protects believers from the pressures to conform to an interpretation they reject of a religion they accept. Because every major religion lacks consensus among its members, separation helps guard against religious leaders becoming political demagogues.

Separation of church and state also protects churches from state regulation of their internal religious affairs. There is no corresponding prohibition on a democratic state's regulation of the internal affairs of corporations, unions, or many other (nonintimate) associations that are substantially less separated from state power.[67] The less the separation of church and state, the greater the political incentives and the moral arguments for making churches more democratically accountable. It is therefore fair to say that separation of church and state helps protect churches from state power, the state from church power, and the freedom of individuals from the united power of both.

Notes

1. Stephen L. Carter, *The Culture of Disbelief* (New York: Basic Books, 1993), pp. 105–106.

2. Ibid., p. 106.

3. For a strong case for absolute separationism, which also recommends separating religious motivations from politics, see Robert Audi, "Liberal Democracy and Religion in Politics," in Robert Audi and Nicholas Wolterstorff, *Religion in the Public Square* (Lanham, Md.: Rowman and Littlefield, 1997), esp. pp. 28–34. "The principle of secular motivation," Audi writes, "may be viewed as a *virtue principle*, whereas the principle of secular rationale is better viewed as a *justification principle* (and is the more important of the two for the ethics of citizenship)" (p. 33).

4. Finding points of principled convergence between otherwise opposed perspectives is part of a democratic practice of economizing on moral disagreement, which is defended in Amy Gutmann and Dennis Thompson, *Democracy and Disagreement* (Cambridge: Harvard University Press, 1996).

5. Michael W. McConnell, "Believers as Equal Citizens," chapter 3 in this volume.

6. Ibid.

7. Ibid.

8. John Locke, *A Letter Concerning Toleration* (Indianapolis: Library of Liberal Arts, 1955), p. 48.

9. James Madison, *The Memorial and Remonstrance against Religious Assessments*, in *The Annals of America* (Chicago: Encyclopedia Brittanica, 1968), 3:17.

10. Locke, *Letter*, p. 46.

11. In the face of diverse religious beliefs, there is yet another possibility to which Locke responds, in a way that is completely consistent with the rest of his argument. A legitimate civil law that does not force a profession or practice of faith may still be judged illegitimate by a dissenting believer who takes it to violate divine law (even though most other believers for good reason do not). The dissenting believer need not be exempted from this law, Locke argues, but the believer may still act consistently with the view that his highest allegiance is to obey divine, not civil, law. The believer, Locke writes, so long as he is a private person, "is to abstain from the action that he judges unlawful, and . . . undergo the punishment *which it is not unlawful for him to bear*" (*Letter*, p. 48, emphasis added). Locke therefore recognizes that even the most legitimate civil authority that a religiously diverse group of human beings is capable of instituting among themselves may leave conflicts of claims in the minds of some sincere believers.

12. Ibid., p. 46.

13. Madison, *Memorial and Remonstrance*, p. 18.

14. As Philip Hamburger demonstrates in a detailed examination of early American constitutional thinking, to which I return later in this essay, "even Madison did not believe that the right of free exercise included a right of religious exemption from civil laws." Philip A. Hamburger, "A Constitutional Right of Religious Exemption: An Historical Perspective," 60 *The George Washington Law Review*, 926 (April 1992).

15. For Jefferson's views, see for example his *Notes on the State of Virginia*, in *Thomas Jefferson: Writings*, ed. Merrill Peterson (New York: The Library of America, 1984), pp. 123–325, esp. 283–285; and *Virginia Statute of Religious Freedom*, in *Thomas Jefferson: Writings*, pp. 346–348; and "Letter to P. H. Wendover," March 13, 1815, in *The Writings of Thomas Jefferson*, ed. Thomas Jefferson Randolph, vol. 4 (Charlottesville, Va.: F. Carr and Co., 1829), pp. 252–255.

16. *New Hampshire Constitution of 1784*, pt. I, art. V, quoted in Hamburger, "Constitutional Right," 918.

17. Hamburger, "Constitutional Right," 918.

18. This is all the more apparent on originalist grounds when we consider that the First Amendment was originally intended to apply only to the federal government and not to the states, including those that had laws establishing religion, which did not exempt religious dissenters. For an excellent discussion of this issue, see Jed Rubenfeld, "Antidisestablishmentarianism: Why RFRA Really Was Unconstitutional," 95 *Michigan Law Review* 2347–2384 (August 1997).

19. *City of Boerne v P. F. Flores, Archbishop of San Antonio, and United States*, 138 L.Ed. 2d 624 at 653–654.

20. Hamburger, "Constitutional Right," 916.

21. Ibid., p. 946.

22. Ibid., p. 947.

23. Ibid., p. 948.

24. Ibid.

25. *Board of Education of Kiryas Joel Village School District v Louis Grumet*, 512 US 687, 129 L.Ed. 2d 546 (1994).

26. Thomas C. Berg, "Slouching Toward Secularism: A Comment *on Kiryas Joel School District v. Grumet*," 44 *Emory Law Journal* 433, 434 (1995).

27. Jeffrey Rosen, "*Kiryas Joel* and *Shaw v. Reno*: A Text-Bound Interpretivist Approach," 26 *Cumberland Law Review* 387, 392 (1996).

28. Ibid.

29. Ibid.

30. *Kiryas Joel*, 512 US 687 at 710, 129 L.Ed. 2d 546 at 565.

31. *Rachel Agostini, et al. v Betty-Louise Felton, et al.*, 65 LW 4524.

32. *Ronald W. Rosenberger, et al., v Rector and Visitors of University of Virginia, et al.*, 515 US 819 (June 29, 1995).

33. Ibid. at 822.

34. Ibid. at 842.

35. Ibid. at 896 (emphasis added).

36. For a more extensive argument to this effect, see Michael W. McConnell's "Brief for the Petitioners," *Rosenberger*, December 15, 1994. 1994 U.S. Briefs 329. McConnell was Counsel of Record for the petitioners in *Rosenberger*.

37. *Rosenberger* at 822.

38. See McConnell, "Brief for the Petitioners," 13.

39. There are hard cases even here. When the federal government (through FEMA) provided disaster relief to reconstruct buildings in Oklahoma City after the bombing, did it wrongly discriminate against religion by not funding the reconstruction of churches, synagogues, and mosques? Or should the government keep its distance from direct financial support of church institutions even in emergencies? Principled exceptions for "extreme emergencies" are common in moral argument. But even if federal aid to churches in emergencies and disasters is justifiable—or morally mandatory—it does not follow that such aid is justifiable under normal conditions. I owe this example to Sanford Levinson.

40. *Rosenberger* at 886–887.

41. Webster's definition of public as "accessible to or shared by all members of the community" comes close to expressing the aspiration of public reasoning. *Webster's Ninth New Collegiate Dictionary* (Springfield, Mass.: Webster, 1990), p. 952. For any reasoning actually to be shared by all members of a community may be impossible to achieve, but public reasoning expresses the aspiration of achieving that end by offering reasons that, to the extent possible, can be justified to all members of the community. The members of the community are in this way, as in other ways, considered to be free and equal beings with the capacity for a sense of justice and for pursuing their own conception of the good life.

42. By John Rawls's definitions, secular reasoning is also nonreligious, but not all nonreligious reasoning is secular. Rawls defines secular reasoning as "reasoning in terms of comprehensive nonreligious doctrines" (emphasis added). My usage is closer to ordinary usage in that secular reasoning need not be based on a comprehensive doctrine, although it may be. Nor need religious reasoning be based on a comprehensive doctrine, although it too may be. People may have secular or religious reasons to be for or against capital punishment, for example, without those reasons being based on a comprehensive secular or a comprehensive religious doctrine. These definitions leave open the question of

whether any particular line of religious or secular reasoning can also be public reasoning, justifiable to the people bound by them. In Rawls's conception, religious and secular reasoning cannot be public reasoning because both are by definition based on a comprehensive doctrine, whereas public reasoning "proceeds entirely within a political conception of justice." John Rawls, "The Idea of Public Reason Revisited," 64 *The University of Chicago Law Review* 775, 776 (Summer 1997).

43. For a related discussion of arguments concerning the need for faith in the Constituiton, see Sanford Levinson, *Constitutional Faith* (Princeton, N.J.: Princeton University Press, 1988).

44. 321 US 158 at 168 (1944).

45. *Wisconsin v Yoder*, 406 US 205 (1971).

46. *Board of Education v Barnette*, 319 US 624 (1943).

47. The Court in *Barnette* overturned Justice Frankfurter's earlier decision in *Minersville v. Gobitis*, which denied an exemption from the flag salute on grounds of religious freedom. See *Minersville School District v Gobitis*, 310 US 586 (1940).

48. *Minersville* at 594–595.

49. *Barnette* at 642.

50. *Wisconsin v Yoder* at 236.

51. Opinion of Mr. Chief Justice Burger citing *Pierce* in *Wisconsin v Yoder* at 213.

52. See *Welsh v United States*, 398 US 333 (1970).

53. I say "probably" because I would want to engage in a more extensive analysis than space permits here to support a more certain conclusion. *See Employment Div. Ore. Dept. of Human Resources v Smith*, 496 US 913, 110 S.Ct. 1595 (1990). There is an extensive and excellent literature on the *Smith* decision to which I cannot possibly do justice here. For an incisive critique of that decision, see Michael W. McConnell, "Free Exercise Revisionism and the Smith Decision," 57 *University of Chicago Law Review*, 1109–1153 (1990). And for an incisive defense, see William P. Marshall, "In Defense of *Smith* and Free Exercise Revisionism," 58 *University of Chicago Law Review*, 308–328 (1991). See also McConnell's response, "A Response to Professor Marshall," in the same issue.

54. Scalia writes, "[T]o say that a nondiscriminatory religious-practice exemption is permitted, or even that it is desirable, is not to say that it is constitutionally required, and that the appropriate occasions for its creation can be discerned by the courts." *Smith* at 1606.

55. Ibid.

56. There is another perspective—the legitimacy of Congress's claim of authority to interpret the Constitution in a way that contradicts the Supreme Court. This issue lies beyond the scope of this essay. Pursuing it here would lead us far afield from a discussion of the value of a strong Establishment Clause.

57. For an excellent historically grounded critique of RFRA, which converges on the same conclusion, see Jed Rubenfeld, "Antidisestablishmentarianism: Why RFRA Really Was Unconstitutional," 95 *Michigan Law Review* 2347–2384 (August 1997).

58. William Sampson, *People v Philips* [Court of General Sessions, City of New York 1813], excerpted in "Privileged Communications to Clergymen," 1 *Catholic Lawyer* 199 (1955).

59. McConnell, "Believers as Equal Citizens."

60. One can gather this positive vision not only from McConnell's contribution to this volume but also from his other writings on free exercise of religion. Note that Sampson's statement about the United States being a religious country is subtly and significantly different from McConnell's. Sampson says that the United States is "to protestant . . . a protestant country, to the catholic, a catholic country." But he does not say that to the Jew, it is a Jewish country. Rather, he says, "the jew, if he pleases, may establish in it his New Jerusalem." Establishing a New Jerusalem *in* this country can be consistent with two-way protection to the extent that its members do not depend on state power for maintaining or sustaining their religious community.

61. McConnell, "Believers as Equal Citizens."

62. I discuss the implications for political morality of diversity within cultural and religious groups in "The Challenge of Multiculturalism in Political Ethics," *Philosophy and Public Affairs* 22, no. 3 (Summer 1993): 171–206.

63. A large part of what makes Israel a Jewish state is cultural rather than religious, but I focus here on the religious part, which is tied to the institutionalized political power of the Orthodox Jewish rabbinate. For a superb synthetic account of the nature of the Israeli state in relation to the closely related issue of toleration, see Michael Walzer, *On Toleration* (New Haven, Conn.: Yale University Press, 1997), pp. 40–43.

64. Yeshayahu Leibowitz, *Judaism, Human Values, and the Jewish State* (Cambridge: Harvard University Press, 1992), p. 181.

65. Ibid., pp. 169–170.

66. The political fight would be seriously skewed against reform because of the political power now vested in the Orthodox rabbinate by virtue of state establishment of Orthodox Judaism and the concomitant power of the political parties that represent Orthodox Jews.

67. See *Roberts v Jaycees*, 468 US 609, 82 L.Ed. 2d 462 (1984).

6

AMOS: RELIGIOUS AUTONOMY

AND THE MORAL USES OF PLURALISM

Nancy L. Rosenblum

TITLE VII OF THE Civil Rights Act of 1964 prohibits discrimination in employment but provides an exemption for religious groups. The case I use as the foundation for this essay upholds this exception. *Corporation of Presiding Bishop of the Church of Jesus Christ of Latter-Day Saints v. Amos* is singular because for the first time Congress enacted and the Supreme Court sustained the constitutionality of a law that exempted only religious associations, not a broad class of groups, from an important general obligation.[1] The case holds political interest: in making this exception, Congress exercised its discretionary power to accommodate religion—an increasingly familiar response by the political branches to judicial action (or inaction), magnifed in the recent Religious Freedom Restoration Act, which the Court struck down in 1997.[2] The case is interesting doctrinally for its application of the controversial *Lemon* test for Establishment. Above all, *Amos* holds particular interest for political theory because it provides an entrée into the question of religious self-government.

What exceptions to legally enforceable public norms like nondiscriminatory workplaces are constitutionally required by the religion clauses? What discretionary exemptions are warranted? What can we learn from the reasons given by courts and political representatives, and why are these reasons inadequate? What alternative resources are there for thinking about accommodation?

I approach the subject of religious autonomy from the standpoint I call "the moral uses of pluralism."[3] My focus is whether and how the internal lives of associations cultivate or inhibit the practices and moral dispositions undergirding democratic public life in America. My question is whether government should respect associational autonomy or enforce congruence with public norms, making groups, including religious groups, "schools of virtue." Because workplaces are key arenas for inculcating liberal democratic norms (fairness, due process, nondiscrimination, and so on) as well as critical sources of social and economic opportunity, few exemptions from general public obligations are more significant than exceptions to antidiscrimination law in hiring, promotion, and firing. *Amos* underscores the fact that religious associations are not only membership groups but also actors in the social world and employers in the secular economy, whose practices effect nonmembers directly.

Particularly in the United States, assurances of congruence between religious and civic values are commonplace. They are typically stated at a high level of generality and divorced from the institutional features of faith. "A taste for the infinite," Tocqueville wrote, can "purify, control, and restrain the excessive and exclusive taste for well-being."[4] Michael McConnell echoes this view: religion "helps to overcome the aggressive individualism that so threatens civil order."[5] It is one thing to speak of "religion" or "religiosity" complementing liberal democracy, however, and another to look concretely at religious associations as formative settings.

Religious *associations*, not spiritual inclinations, habituate members to forms of authority, to altruism and reciprocity among members and between members and outsiders (or not), to race and gender segregation or integration and equality, to expectations of fairness and due process or to clerical discretion or personal authority. Religious *associations* encourage or discourage dispositions of tolerance and nondiscrimination through tenets of faith, but also through practices such as admitting and excluding members, educating children, managing internal affairs, and relating to outsiders in the course of proseletyzing or hiring. Because the *internal life* of associations is the heart of the moral uses of pluralism, self-government for religious associations commands attention.

Religious groups claim "a spirit of freedom . . . an independence from secular control or manipulation—in short, power to decide for themselves, free from state interference, matters of church government as well as those of faith and doctrine."[6] The question is, "power to decide for themselves" in what areas?

Strong advocates of religious autonomy have proposed a categorical right to self-determination—inspired sometimes by deference to the intrinsic value of religion and sometimes on grounds that "religious groups are a locus for certain of the constitutive, foundational activities by which Americans define and determine who and what they are, both individually and communally."[7] I will assess this position shortly. For now, suffice to say that absolute autonomy is neither practicable nor justifiable. The "sovereignty" of associations advocated by the British pluralist tradition has had little resonance in the United States, for good reasons. Given the tradition of freedom of association and the proliferation of voluntary associations, there is no need for a political theory designed to counter Hobbesian hostility to associations as "worms in the entrails of a natural man," for one thing. For another, the First Amendment is interposed between government and religious groups; balancing religious freedom against legitimate state interests is an ineliminable feature of legislative and judicial decisions.

On the other hand, looking to religious groups to preach civic values and transform members into good democrats and ensuring that they serve as "bootcamps for citizenship" by enforcing congruence between their internal lives and public norms is not justifiable either, even as a regulative ideal. Constitutional protections aside, this is a violation of fundamental liberty and disregards the many vital moral uses of membership in democracy that have little to do with specifically civic virtues.

I want to consider first the general push for accommodation by religious groups, the broad exemption to antidiscrimination law Congress granted by amending Title VII, and the divergent lower court and Supreme Court opinions regarding this new kind of accommodation—a discretionary statutory exemption from an important general law exclusively for religious associations.

Exemption and Accommodation: Title VII

It is rare today to find legislation that interferes with worship directly or discriminates among religions on its face, though the local ordinance outlawing animal sacrifice overturned in 1993 in *Church of the Lukumi Babalu Aye v. City of Hialeah* appears to have been aimed at the Santeria faith. For the most part, religious exercise and self-government are burdened as a consequence of government enacting general laws for valid secular purposes—imposing regulations, meting out benefits like unemployment insurance, and acting in its capacities as proprietor, employer, educator, and patron. At the same time that faith-based groups proliferate and become ubiquitous, engaged in every aspect of social life, so do the ways liberal democracy impinges on them. As a result, constitutional claims for mandatory exemptions and political demands for statutory accommodation mark every area of law from zoning and taxes to legislation that directly implicates liberal democratic practices and dispositions—antidiscrimination law, employment law, and the demands of due process.[8] For advocates of expansive freedom for religious groups, the constitutional agenda is to carve out "a zone of permissible accommodation." Without it, "where government advanced, religion must retreat."[9]

Spurred by an appreciation of the plurality of religious groups and theological notions of religion, the Supreme Court's *definition* of religion is capacious and government is normally loathe to define, interpret, or enforce forms of worship and tenets of faith.[10] So we might expect to find a bright line separating solicitude for religious authority in matters of doctrine, worship, and church government from authority over non-religious activities and dealings with nonmembers. In fact, discriminating between religious and nonreligious associations and assessing the nexus between a group's activities and faith for purposes of judging the burden on faith and grounds for accommodation is unavoidable. It gives rise to the "Five Questions about Religion Judges Are Afraid to Ask" and to the strategies of avoidance Kent Greenawalt outlines in his essay in this volume.

"Divining the good faith and legitimacy of religious grounds asserted as a defense" against having to conform to general laws is plainly difficult.[11] As Christian theologians witnessed and Hegel philosophized, the paralyzing question of a pure heart can never be resolved, even for oneself. The difficulty is compounded when the question is the sincerity of an association rather than an individual. Take the example of the New Testament Baptist Church, which excluded black children from its school and claimed a free exercise exemption from federal antidiscrimination law. Citing a directive from the church's board forbidding commingling of whites and blacks, the circuit court in *Brown v. Dade Christian Schools* denied that segregation was based on a "sincerely held religious belief that socialization would lead to [the sin of] racial intermarriage." Instead, it characterized this discriminatory exclusion as "a recent policy" designed to circumvent the law, and ruled against the exemption on this ground.[12] As this example suggests, ascertaining whether a group's practices are sincere or central implicates the very questions of faith and authority that government is supposed to avoid.[13] The inquiry can be daunting: having to decide whether an employee was fired for adultery (which Title VII permits, in view of the Adventist tenet that adultery is a sin) or for becoming pregnant out of wedlock (which is impermissible under Title VII because it is not an article of Adventist faith).[14]

Nonetheless, as ministries expand beyond charities and schools and as church-state partnerships multiply, so do efforts at categorization: conduct required by doctrine or individual conscience from exercises of religion that are not required; denominational hospitals that are an integral part of a church's religious mission and "infused with religious purpose" from "affiliated institutions" that are not "pervasively sectarian" (and are therefore eligible to receive federal and state grants, contracts, and reimbursements for social welfare services); church-owned businesses run in "intrinsically religious ways" from those formed for a "purely business purpose." Local zoning regulations often exempt religious groups, and in evaluating applications for special permits communities ask whether or not a particular activity—a soup kitchen or homeless shelter—is a "customary accessory use of church property."[15]

Title VII of the 1964 Civil Rights Act highlights these issues. The law prohibits discrimination with respect to hiring, discharging, compensation, terms, conditions, or privileges of employment on account of race, color, religion, sex, and national origin. It covers standard cases of religious discrimination by secular employers and imposes an affirmative duty on employers to accommodate workers' religious needs unless they can show "undue [economic] hardship." It also protects employees against private employers who want to create a work environment dedicated to the glory of God and run as a discipleship, by requiring workers to attend Bible study meetings, say, and making employment decisions on the basis of beliefs about sex or marital status.[16] But Section 702 of the act does permit religious associations to discriminate in favor of coreligionists:

> This subchapter shall not apply . . . to a religious corporation, association, educational institution or society with respect to the employment of individuals *of a particular religion* to perform work connected with the carrying on by such corporation . . . of its activities."[17]

Although this language refers to employment of individuals "of a particular religion," it has been interpreted to allow religious associations to discriminate on the basis of race and sex in matters of "purely ecclesiastical cognizance" such as the selection of ministers (including commissioned officers in the Salvation Army) or seminary teachers. Thus, a civil court declined to hear the case of a deposed minister who claimed he was fired because of his wife's race: "who will preach from the pulpit of a church and who will occupy the parsonage" is a purely ecclesiastical question.[18]

Apart from "purely ecclesiastical" matters, federal courts are split on the scope and standards for exemption when it comes to discrimination on the basis of race and sex. One approach utilizes the distinction between religious and nonreligous activities (though disagreement remains about whether the necessary religious nexus is to the specific job performed—secretarial or janitorial work, say—or to the activity of the association overall—a gym or manufacturer of sacred garments). Another approach looks at whether the discriminatory employment practice can be justified on the basis of tenets of faith. Thus, a church successfully defended discharging its homosexual organist in a suit brought under a local gay rights ordinance, on grounds of belief that homosexuality is a sin.[19] In a case involving wage and benefit disparities in a religious publishing house, Seventh Day Adventists were found guilty of discrimination against a female employee. Title VII permits the church to hire only members in good standing, the court ruled in *EEOC v. Pacific Press*, but not to discriminate on the basis of sex or marital status: "preventing [sex] discrimination can have no significant impact upon the exercise of Adventist beliefs because the Church proclaims that it does not believe in discriminating against women . . . its policy is to pay wages without discrimination on the basis of race, religion, sex, age, or national origin."[20]

Today, religious associations that discriminate on the basis of sex and race are regularly challenged to show the religious nature of the activity or basis of the practice. But Section 702, the 1972 Amendment to Title VII, foreclosed this question in cases of discrimination in favor of coreligionists. The original language of Title VII had allowed religious corporations to discriminate on the basis of religion in relation to their "religious activities" only. The legislative record shows that those who favored broadening the exception by dropping the qualifier "religious" were motivated by concern for educational institutions affiliated with religious groups.[21] As Senator Allen pointed out, under the original formulation "there would be nothing to prevent an atheist being forced upon a religious school to teach some subject other than theology." Senator Ervin seized the occasion to wage an all-out attack on *any* regulation of the employment practices of religious groups: "For the life of me, I cannot comprehend why the EEOC and why those who are championing this cause are so greedy for power that they want to lay the political hands of Caesar on the employment practices of churches of God," he intoned, and he proposed amendments that would have removed religious associations from EEOC jurisdiction altogether. On the other side, there was resistance to broadening the existing Title VII exemption at all; Senator Williams: "I do not believe that the religious integrity of these institutions would be compromised by providing equal job opportunities for employees in positions unrelated to the religious activities of such institutions."[22] In what amounted to a compromise in this context, Congress amended the act to permit religious associations to discriminate in employment on grounds of religion regardless of the nature of the enterprise.

We can understand the impetus to continue to enforce democratic norms of nondiscrimination when employment practices do not have a religious basis. We can also appreciate the difficulty of judging when activities are sufficiently close to matters of faith to mandate a constitutional exemption or warrant a statutory exemption. But what is the thinking behind relieving religious associations of Title VII obligations even with respect to secular jobs and enterprises? How did Congress and the Court justify eliminating any obligation on the part of religious associations *to make the case* that their discriminatory practices have a basis in faith? I will argue that the original Title VII exemption struck the balance correctly, and that even if the law as extended is constitutionally permissible, as the Supreme Court ruled, it is unjustifiable.

Amos

A janitor employed for sixteen years at a nonprofit Mormon-run gymnasium open to the public was fired for not complying with the eligibility test for attendance at Mormon temples (the standards include church attendance, tithing, and abstinence from coffee, tea, alcohol, and tobacco). Arthur Mayson filed suit on behalf of a class of employees, present and future.[23]

The district court failed to find a sufficiently close connection between the work performed and tenets of faith to say that government regulation would burden religion. Nothing in Mayson's duties was "even tangentially related to any conceivable religious belief or ritual of the Mormon church or church administration." Nothing in the purpose or operation of Deseret gym suggests that it was intended to spread the beliefs, doctrine, or sacred ritual of the Mormon Church, either; the gym was indistinguishable from any other health club operated for profit. Nor did the church contend that religious tenets required it to discriminate in employment. (Note that in the companion case, *Amos II*, which was dropped before the Supreme Court reviewed it, Mormon enterprises were shown to enforce religious-based personnel policies erratically, or not at all.[24] The implication is that practical considerations rather than exigencies of faith guided employment practices.)

Nonetheless, Congress's intent with Section 702 was to exempt all activities, religious or not, from Title VII regulations. So the court took up the question of the constitutionality of the law under the Establishment Clause, applying the three-part *Lemon* test.[25]

The legislation had a valid secular purpose: to make good on the liberal democratic commitment to religious free exercise. The court acknowledged "the goal of assuring that the government remains neutral and does not meddle in religious affairs by interfering with the decision-making process in religions."[26] The exemption also passed the "entanglement" prong of the test, which constrains government from involvement in a religious association's daily business.[27] The proviso against "entanglement" is not concerned with the direct effect of a particular regulation on associational life. Rather, it gives independent weight to the entangling accompaniments of regulation—investigation, monitoring, routine auditing, etc. However, Title VII is not triggered until an individual brings a complaint; the law does not involve day-to-day regulation or surveillance.

The decisive consideration for the lower court arose under *Lemon*'s third prong: the law has as a primary effect advancing religion. The limitations of this test for establishment emerge clearly as we try to follow the court's reasoning.

Clearly, Section 702 singles out religious associations for preferential treatment. As the district court observed: if a religious group "should own and operate a trucking firm, a chain of motels, a race track, a telephone company, a railroad, a fried chicken franchise, or a professional football team," it could limit employment to members of the sect, whereas the same enterprises owned and operated by a nonreligious organization could not.

> It is not mandated under the Constitution that Congress prohibit discrimination on grounds of religion in private sector employment. However, having elected to do so . . . the Congress is under a constitutional obligation to do so in a way that neither favors nor disfavors secular, private sector enterprises that may be conducted by religious association."[28]

The district court concluded that government should not favor religious groups "when they themselves choose to be submerged, for profit or power, in the 'all-embracing secularism' of the corporate economy."[29]

The court did not oppose all accommodations as unconstitutional preferences for religion. Some accommodations do not discriminate between religious and nonreligious groups. *Walz v. Tax Commission*, for example, involved the constitutionality of tax exemptions to religious associations. For constitutional separationists keenly sensitive to establishment, a tax exemption amounts to state subsidy of religion and a de facto financial exaction from unbelievers; money that would otherwise be paid as taxes can be used to advance the faith. Nevertheless, this exemption was upheld because the broad class of exempted groups includes all nonprofit institutions that provide charitable services, among them antireligious groups, the exemption avoids any appearance of selectivity or favoritism.[30] (Indeed, tax-exempt status was seen as the true separation because it *restricts* fiscal relations between church and state; taxation requires government evaluation of church property, tax liens and foreclosures, and so on.)

It is not hard to see that *Amos* involves a new kind of accommodation—a discretionary exemption exclusively for religious associations. Nor is it hard to see that the *Lemon* test for whether an exemption amounts to an unconstitutional establishment of religion is unsuited to discretionary accommodation. The core of the test is neutrality and separationism—no entanglements. Title VII grants a preferential exemption that clearly goes beyond "a benevolent neutrality which will permit religious exercise to exist without sponsorship and without interference."[31] What determines whether a preferential exemption is impermissible? According to the court's application of the *Lemon* test, when it has the primary effect of advancing religion. The district court specifically asks whether this exception grants the association "exclusive authorization to engage in conduct which can directly and immediately advance religious tenets and practices," and answers that it does.[32] In connection with the church's demand that employees satisfy the Mormon worthiness requirement, workers had to respond to inquiries regarding their sexual activities, moral cleanliness and purity, income and contributions to the church, and obedience and allegiance to Mormon leaders. The church is able to subject employees to the discipline of religious authority, including exaction of a portion of their wages as tithes, in return for continued employment. For "those religious sects having the wealth and inclination to buy up pieces of the secular economy," the district court reasoned, the potential to further its beliefs is enhanced by the fact that "peoples' opportunity to earn a living is at stake."[33] The court ruled the amended Title VII a violation of the Establishment Clause.

The Supreme Court overturned this decision in 1987. Briefly, the justices diverged from the lower court on the key point: the law does not have the principal effect of advancing religion. Justice White's argument is perfunctory: "A law is not unconstitutional simply because it allows churches to advance religion, which is their very purpose. For a law to have forbidden "effects" under *Lemon*, it must be fair to say that government itself has advanced religion through its own influence and activities."[34]

Justice O'Connor takes exception to the majority's application of the "effect" part of the test. It is disingenuous to say that the statute simply allows religion to advance itself; that reasoning could justify any government preference or benefit to religion. Judicial deference to legislation that simply purports to facilitate the free exercise of religion is liable to completely vitiate the constraints of the Establishment Clause. The majority uses the wrong baseline when it says that the church rather than government penalizes the janitor's refusal to adhere to doctrine. "The Church had the power to put Mayson to a choice of qualifying for a temple recommend or losing his job because the Government had lifted. . .the general regulatory burden imposed by 702." [35]

Nevertheless, O'Connor concurs in the result, proposing an alternative test for establishment. Her "endorsement" test turns on the message the government action sends to an objective observer. She argues that this exemption does not convey a message of state endorsement because the gym was not a profit-making enterprise. The nonprofit character of the enterprise was also salient for Justice Brennan. It adds to the plausibility that these activities are infused with a religious purpose and "makes inappropriate a case-by-case determination whether its nature is religious or secular.[36] Both opinions leave open the possibility that the exception to Title VII would be unconstitutional as applied to religiously owned businesses for profit.

It is fair to say that Section 702 is not a clear-cut establishment of religion; there is reasonable disagreement on this score. What is clear is that the exemption is not constitutionally required. Neither the district court nor the Supreme Court uncovered a religious basis for the church's exclusionary employment practices. Moreover, since *Smith*, constitutionally mandated exemptions have been diminished; burdens on religion need not be justified by a compelling state interest (and antidiscrimination law would likely qualify as compelling in any case). *Smith* turned the matter of accommodation over to democratic decision-makers: "values that are protected against government interference through enshrinement in the Bill of Rights are not thereby banished from the political process."[37] The critical question for liberal democratic theory has become what nonconstitutional considerations should guide the political branches? What could justify democratic deference to religious autonomy here?

Autonomy and Self-Definition

One way legislatures justify accommodating religion beyond what is constitutionally mandated is by showing that an important secular purpose is served by lifting a public obligation. But the legislative record of Section 702 is unilluminating. Debate focused almost entirely on hiring in parochial schools; there was no discussion of the implications of exempting all the activities of religious groups. The Supreme Court had to construct its own account of the statute's public purpose. It did not attribute to Congress the view that employment by a religious association is always a religious exercise or that churches must have the undivided commitment of all employees, their subordination to religious authority.[38] Instead, it said that the purpose of the exemption was to alleviate government interference with a religious organization's ability to define and carry out its mission. The striking element of the *Amos* decision is the Court's explanation of why enforcing Title VII would have inhibited this aspect of religious autonomy.

We can agree with the Court that "determining that certain activities are in furtherance of an organization's mission, and that only those committed to that mission should conduct them, is thus a means by which a religious community defines itself."[39] We can agree further that "employment practices that are religiously based are an exercise of religion, regardless of the employee's activities within the religious community."[40] Yet it would have been perfectly consistent to require associations *to demonstrate* that discriminatory employment practices are religiously based, when challenged. But the Court went on to say that the exemption was designed to avoid requiring religious associations to *predict* which of its activities judges would consider regulable and which exempt. The presumptive legislative purpose was to ward off the unanticipated effect not of regulation per se but of having to justify a claim of exemption (which may turn out to be warranted). Associations are insulated from the potential effects of the *fear* of litigation. Borrowing from free speech doctrine, Justice White insisted for the majority that fear of potential liability could "chill" associational life. Justice Brennan expanded on this theme:

> [I]deally, religious organizations should be able to discriminate only with respect to religious activities, [but] while a church may regard the conduct of certain functions as integral to its mission, a court may disagree. A religious organization therefore would have an incentive to characterize as religious only those activities about which there likely would be no dispute. . . . As a result, the community's *process of self-definition* would be shaped in part by the prospects of litigation.[41]

A bright line test, allowing religious discrimination in employment for all the activities of a religious association, serves this purpose.

The "conditionals" peppering Brennan's formulation indicate that *any* risk that having to demonstrate the religious nature or basis of an activity would effect the group's ongoing "self-definition" is too much risk. The "chill" would inhibit the association all the way down. This is the mirror image of arguments made by opponents of constitutionally required accommodation like Justice Scalia who fear that the unpredictable, cumulative effect of religious exceptions would cripple the normal administration of public life. Contrast this speculative burden on religious self-government—"fear of litigation might chill religious self-definition"—with the burden lifted by those rare exemptions the Court has constitutionally mandated. It does not approach the danger government regulation would pose to religious autonomy if courts were to intervene to settle internal disputes over who is the rightful church authority or who controls church property, for example. It does not impinge on church authority requiring collective bargaining under the

National Labor Relations Act, say. It does not impose financial costs on the association.

Nor is there reason to assume that if the exemption were restricted to religious activities courts would chill the group's self-definition by imposing a narrow view of "religious." Nothing dictates that inquiries into the religious basis of discriminatory employment practices must be guided solely by scripture or officially promulgated doctrine, which would require judges to become immersed in canon law and tenets of faith. Granted, there is always a danger that in using substantiality, centrality, or importance to decide whether to grant or withhold an exemption courts will impose legalistic criteria that are not part of the church's self-understanding. There is a danger that courts will fail to give due consideration to the association's own account (that is, authoritative spokespersons' account) of the religious foundation of practices. The district court may have erred in this direction when it found that nothing in Mormon tenets requires all employees in secular activities to be temple-worthy; it should have been open to other explanations of the religious basis for discrimination besides formal doctrine.[42] Similarly, the district court took a narrow view of regulatory burdens when it asserted categorically that the relevant question "is not the impact of the statute upon the institution, but the impact of the statute upon the institution's exercise of its sincerely held religious beliefs."[43] Substantial burdens on church polity and self-government are perfectly valid grounds for accommodation.

The point is, these cautions do not militate against requiring religious associations to demonstrate their grounds for discrimination against nonmembers in questionable instances. Courts are institutionally competent to assess these arguments, and Congress implicitly conceded as much. After all, Congress did not exempt associations from having to demonstrate the religious basis of race or sex discrimination. But when it comes to discrimination in favor of coreligionists, Congress and the Supreme Court were deferential. They disavowed judgment out of fear that "the community's self-definition would be shaped in part" by the prospect of legal challenge. The Court echoed the sweeping claim of one proponent's view that "government-induced changes in religion are too unpredictable to be avoided on a case-by-case basis. They can be minimized only by a strong rule of church autonomy."[44]

This reasoning defends against nothing less than uncertainty. It is alarmist, based on doubtful assumptions about the fragility of religious community. Perhaps unwittingly, it lends credence to the political strategy of representing religion in the United States as vulnerable and under siege. Most important, it does not acknowledge the difference between change and threats to a group's viability.

Fragility and Viability

The standard of viability had been used before to assess whether the burden of a general obligation should be lifted from a religious associations. In a remarkable opinion I referred to earlier in *Brown v. Dade Christian Schools*, a majority of the circuit court ruled that the church's request for an exemption from desegregation law lacked a religious basis, judging it a "policy decision" designed to evade the law. Justice Goldberg concurred in the conclusion though not in the reasoning. He conceded that for this group racial separatism was a sincere expression of faith. He also found that according to church tenets, violating the command to segregate is disobedience to God. From that reasonable starting point, Goldberg went on to invent his own theology. He called segregation a "minor tenet" of faith. He argued that disobedience would not endanger salvation. And he concluded that so long as salvation is not imperiled, membership in the church will not be affected by legally enforced integration: "the rights of blacks to participate in our society on equal terms must have ascendancy over a religious practice that *can be subordinated without impairing the religion's viability.*"[45]

Viability is an elastic notion. To see just how elastic, it helps to contrast *Amos* with *Wisconsin v. Yoder* where the Court had the bottom of the presumptively slippery slope—the group's survival—in view. In *Yoder*, the Supreme Court ruled that exempting the Old Order Amish from Wisconsin's requirement that children attend school until the age of sixteen was constitutionally mandated by the Free Exercise Clause. The community had not claimed that religious tenets forbid public secondary education or compel strict separatism. The argument was that their faith and way of life were interdependent and that the community could maintain its hold over Amish youth only by sheltering them from the worldly seductions they would encounter in high school "during the crucial and formative adolescent period of life":

> During this period, the children must acquire Amish attitudes favoring manual work and self-reliance and the specific skills needed to perform the adult role of an Amish farmer or housewife. . . . The Amish child must also grow in his faith and his relationship to the Amish community if he is to be prepared to accept the heavy obligations imposed by adult baptism.

Without accommodation, Chief Justice Burger concluded, the Amish could reasonably fear for the survival of their community: "they must either abandon their belief and be assimilated into society at large or be forced to migrate to some other and more tolerant region."[46]

In *Yoder* the threat to viability had concrete content: attrition through the loss of willing members and failure to attract new ones. Viability was a matter of the critical number of believers necessary for carrying on a particular way of life. Burger has been commended for his "holistic or 'ecological' understanding of what was at stake in the case."[47] Plainly, a community's way of life depends on commitment by future generations. Plainly, too, certain groups—"internal exiles" like the Amish with a history of communal separatism—are more vulnerable than others to external forces drawing members away. Burger's opinion was explicitly targeted to this group; the decision turned on the rare, perhaps unique, character of the Amish community—separatist, self-sufficient, and law-abiding.

Even so, the relation between communal self-definition and changes in both doctrine and nondoctrinal practices is more complex than Burger's analysis suggests. Religious associations, like every other, are plagued by internal differences, contests among clerical authorities and factions of the faithful. Associations continually alter interpretations of doctrine and rules of conduct. Religious associations face critical precipices, brought on by an amalgam of outside political and cultural forces as well as their own group dynamics. Members are divided over the defining characteristics of the community, hence over what changes threaten its viability. These divisions challenge authority and test members' commitments. They give rise to formal divisions within the faith, to divergent traditions, and sometimes to schism. (The Amish order, recall, originated in schism with the Mennonites.) Precisely because religious associations are living communities, courts have decisively rejected the "departure from doctrine" test for adjudicating intrachurch disputes; that is, they refuse to award authority or property to the party faithful to the church's founding statement of corporate purpose.

In *Yoder*, Amish faith and associational life were identified with the preservation of the Amish community as it exists in Wisconsin. "Traditionalists," that is, complainants' views of what was necessary to preserve parental and communal authority (to insure that Amish boys would settle into farming and Amish girls would become housewives), were taken as authoritative on the question of viability. Is this a tenable way to approach the viability of religious association? How many defections would threaten the community's ability to carry on? What sort of internal changes might some or most Amish tolerate in order to keep members? I agree with the Court's ruling in *Yoder*, though on different grounds.[48] Simply, it is not necessary to accept the standard of viability, or to concede Burger's histrionic assertion that the only alternatives for the Amish were migration or being forced to abandon their belief and be assimilated into society at large.

Taken literally, the standard of viability is too stringent a standard for accommodation. It directs government to lift burdens from religious associations at the point where survival is in doubt. Autonomy is contingent on crisis. As discussed in *Amos*, on the other hand, the standard of viability is impossibly lax. When it comes to the church's participation in the secular economy and social life, Mormon assimilation was accomplished some time ago (what could be more in step with popular culture than a gym?). The institutional survival of the Mormon church and community was not at stake in the exemption from antidiscrimination law, only the risk of chilling the association's self-definition. And "self-definition" gets its force from its abstraction from any particular aspect of self-government. It smacks of some elusive group "identity" or "integrity" rather than the specifics of authority, discipline, doctrine, or management. Justice Brennan seemed to make the possibility that the Mormon community's self-definition "might be shaped in part by the prospect of litigation" the equivalent of a coerced change of identity. The fragility of association self-definition is simply asserted. As one approving commentator put it: "these matters are so highly reactive when placed in contact with public authority that religious liberty requires any appreciable risk of involvement be avoided."[49] There are no parameters to "highly reactive," no standards of "appreciable risk." In *Amos*, self-definition/viability/survival are fused.

The sound core of the Court's concern is clear: it is a legitimate state purpose to avoid requiring courts and religious groups to authoritatively identify and settle the defining characteristics of faith and community that warrant protection. But the majority errs in replacing essentialism with ineffable "self-definition." It errs in employing the elastic standard of viability to justify a statutory exemption that *eliminates* precisely the sort of concrete analysis of particular cases it undertook in *Yoder*.

I want to take a step back from this case and consider alternative approaches to religious autonomy in contemporary democratic theory.

Separationism vs. Structural Pluralism

In *Amos*, the aim of protecting religious associations' presumably fragile self-definition is rooted in familiar voluntarist and separationist premises. There is nothing alien to liberal democratic theory about the idea that "free exercise has associational and institutional as well as individual dimensions."[50] At the same time that Justice Brennan characterized a religious community as "an organic entity not reducible to a mere aggregation of individuals," he pointed out that solicitude for communal self-definition "reflects the idea that the furtherance of the autonomy of religious organizations often furthers individual religious freedom as well."[51] *Amos* also reflects the classic liberal separationist view of Religion Clause doctrine. The justices saw Congress' purpose as defending religious self-government against government, though in this case the check is not constitutionally mandated by the Free Exercise Clause but the product of democratic self-restraint.

Today, influential political and legal theorists reject the orthodox liberal democratic justification for religious autonomy—separationist, antimajoritarian, taking its bearings from concern for individual conscience, minority faiths, and vulnerable communities. The temper and reasoning of the approach to democracy and religion that I will refer to as "structural pluralist"is positive and assertive rather than self-defensive. It sees religion as a preferred value, not only in general terms of human needs and capabilities but for democracy specifically. It posits a public commitment to the flourishing of religious groups (a view shared by those Supreme Court justices who do not see "endorsement" of religion as a violation of the Establishment Clause).[52] From this perspective, there is no need to aver the fragility of religious associations or to direct protection toward weak and unpopular groups "relegated to the margins."[53] The Bill of Rights "is not only a catalog of negative individual liberties, but a charter of 'positive protection,'" Mary Ann Glendon and Raul Yanes insist.[54] Michael McConnell explains, "[T]he concern of the Religion clauses is with the preservation of the autonomy of religious life, not (just) with the process value of ensuring that government does not act on the basis of religious bias."[55] Structural pluralism is marked by approval for "liberty-enhancing governmental accommodation," a "unified, across-the-board deferential approach in church-state matters," and rejection of key elements of separationism.[56] Readers will recognize it as a version of "integralism" I spoke of in the introduction to this book.

I will turn to the constitutional implications of this position in a moment. First, it is significant for democratic theory that structural pluralists arrive at this common ground in defense of religious autonomy from different premises. For McConnell, the intrinsic importance of religious community represents a legitimate challenge to the supremacy of the state and dictates democratic deference to religious self-government. Religious associations cannot provide meaning if their lives are cramped or development impeded, so it is imperative to acknowledge and support associations' autonomous sense of what is necessary for them to thrive. Since "judgments about the dictates of the higher power can be made only by individuals and communities of believers, and not by the state," McConnell argues, "the First Amendment. . .undermines any claim by the state to ultimate normative authority."[57]

Except for the fact that he is exclusively concerned with religious associations and disregards other communities of meaning, the affinity between McConnell's position and the British pluralist tradition of Maitland, Figgis, and Laski is clear. For the British pluralists, an association "is no fiction, no symbol, no piece of the State's machinery, no collective name for individuals, but a living organism and a real person, with a body and members and a will of its own."[58] The political corollary is that the state must share sovereignty with all the self-governing sources of law within it. In Figgis's terms, the state is a "community of communities." Or, as Laski puts it, its parts are "as real, as primary, and as self-sufficing as the whole."[59] The resonance is plain in McConnell's observation that "believers inevitably face two sets of loyalties and two sets of obligations. In this respect, they resemble resident aliens, or at best, persons with dual citizenship."[60] Religious pluralism, he concedes, "dilutes the concept of 'citizen.'"[61] But "citizenship ambiguity" is not fatal to political cohesion if democracy is properly understood. It is a framework for subcommunities, a regime committed to promoting the conditions of flourishing religious pluralism, whose principal value and purpose is to protect and support these independent sources of meaning.

For Glendon and Yanes, by contrast, the justification for religious autonomy stems less from the intrinsic value of religious community than from democratic ideology and the public interest. Along with community militia and juries, the U.S. Constitution assigns religious associations special status. These institutions are singled out "in part to promote self-government by fostering participation in public life, protecting the seedbeds of civic virtue, and educating citizens about their rights and obligations."[62] At work here is a conception of democracy as a distinctive moral regime rather than a framework for pluralist associations. The assumption is that so long as government respects and supports the "structural balance," that is, so long as public policy is geared to the fact that "for vast numbers of American men and women, religion is . . . inseparable from the rest of social life," religious associations will undergird rather than dilute citizenship.[63]

From these different starting points, structural pluralists share categorical support for religious autonomy, and with it an interpretation of the Constitution's religion clauses according to which *both* clauses aim at maximizing free exercise. They argue for what Amy Gutmann calls "one-way protection." Specifically, they argue for a general right to exemption from public obligations. (They would return to a pre-*Smith* standard for interpreting the Free Exercise Clause: only a compelling state interest allows government to require compliance with public obligations that interfere with the exercise of faith.) They encourage the political branches to provide discretionary accommodation (accommodations are "sometimes required and, within rigorous limitations . . . are always permitted"[64]). They argue that the Establishment Clause ensures protection for religion from government, not protection for government against religion systematically using public institutions and funds for sectarian purposes. The Establishment Clause prohibits government from coercing belief and discriminating among faiths (McConnell's test for impermissible establishment is whether a government action has the purpose or probable effect of increasing religious *uniformity*). It is no constitutional barrier to government endorsement or aid to religion.[65]

In short, structural pluralists reject both separationism and the egalitarian-neutral alternative, which treats religious associations on a par with other voluntary associations when it comes to regulation and the distribution of public goods. Instead, the moral and constitutional status of religious associations dictates that they be treated equally in regard to public benefits—tax exemptions, grants, and so on—but not neutrally, since among the benefits they claim are self-government, exemption from general obligations, and direct endorsement and aid.[66] From this pluralist perspective there is no Establishment Clause obstacle to democratic decisions to provide preferential public support to religion:

> [W]hen legislatures adjust the benefits and burdens of economic life among the citizens, they regularly impose more than a de minimis burden for the purpose of protecting important interests of the beneficiary class. The legislature should have as much latitude to protect the exercise of religion as it has to protect other important values in life.[67]

Not surprisingly, structural pluralists advocate affirmative public measures to enable mainstream faiths to thrive. They encourage religious associations to enter democratic arenas to actively seek material and symbolic aid—both promoting public policies that facilitate privatization (home schooling, for example) and church-state partnerships in which the church party is not subordinate (public funding for religious schools). They do not seem to fear that religious associations, whose autonomy is precious precisely because they are distinctive sources of meaning and seedbeds of virtue, may be deformed as a result of political, even partisan, involvement.

Nor do they fear trespassing across what voluntarist-separationist liberal democratic theory sees as the threshold for impermissible establishment of religion. The baseline separationist position is defined by Isaac Kramnick and R. Laurence Moore: "If the Establishment Clause . . . does anything, it bars government aid to religious proseletyzing, no matter what general social benefits may follow or be attributed to that proseletyzing."[68] Structural pluralists reject this constraint outright and would reverse the policy of conditioning government support for the activities of religious associations on the secular purpose of these projects and the functional equivalence of religious and nonreligious groups. The distinctive pluralist justification for accommodation is that religious associations are *not* counterparts of the general array of secular groups but incommensurate, uniquely valuable, and constitutionally recognized as preferred structures. This marks the fundamental divide between structural pluralists and civil libertarian liberals like myself who are sympathetic to religious autonomy but unwilling to eviscerate separationism.

The term "structural" indicates that communities of faith are the basis of this pluralist account. From this perspective, *Amos* referees a clash between associational autonomy and the state rather than a clash between free exercise claims: the Mormon Church versus the janitor's conscience. Indeed, neither the Supreme Court nor structural pluralists acknowledge the tension between religious self-government and a wider regime of free exercise. This consideration is integral to any liberal democratic account of religious autonomy, though. It lay behind the district court's observation that *abolition* of the expansive Title VII exemption would enhance religious liberty. A voluntarist concern with individual free exercise is one of two crucial elements missing from both the Court's reasoning and structural pluralist arguments; the other is a deeper understanding of the moral uses of pluralism. These justify limits on democratic accommodation; specifically, they argue against blanket exemption from antidiscrimination law in employment.

Costs of Accommodation #1:
Free Exercise

In *Amos*, church autonomy comes at the expense of the janitor's free exercise rights. Employees' liberty (which includes the right not to believe or to profess belief) was clearly restricted by the church's exemption from federal law, as was the religious liberty of other non-Mormons, potential employees. Some shifting of burdens among citizens is inevitable. Exempting religious groups from taxation and making contributions tax deductible adds to the financial burden on nonbelievers. But these costs are diffuse and impersonal. By lifting the requirement of nondiscrimination in hiring, Congress and the Court gave the Mormon Church power to put the janitor to a choice of qualifying for a "temple recommend" or losing his job.

There is no sharper deviation from liberal democratic practices than conditioning vital secular goods on declarations of faith. The gym is not a government agency, of course, and this is not a case of "unconstitutional conditions" along the lines of *Sherbert v. Verner*. But one reason for disallowing religious opt-outs from protective legislation involving employment opportunities, wages, and benefits is to defend believers against religious authorities who use religious discipline to coerce and exploit their economically dependent member-employees.[69] Recall that the district court ruled the Title VII amendment unconstitutional because it enhanced the ability of religious associations to further their beliefs in situations where "peoples' opportunity to earn a living is at stake."[70] Justices Brennan and O'Connor acknowledged that the broad Title VII exemption gives religious groups the advantage of economic leverage in the secular realm, where Mormon Church activities are firmly and successfully planted.[71] Whether or not we classify this as economic coercion, the statute does change incentives. Michael McConnell and Richard Posner have observed that "religious believers . . . are not insensitive to considerations of cost. So if the state, whether through pecuniary or nonpecuniary exactions, makes it more costly to adhere to one creed than to another. . .this may cause a shift in religious affiliations."[72] In this case, the "substitution effect" is not away from religion toward secular activity (from parochial to public schooling, for example), but toward a particular faith for the purpose of getting and keeping jobs. The Court explicitly assumed that the church was fragile—its self-definition easily "chilled"; presumably it was more tenuous than the janitor's religious liberty since associational autonomy overrides it.

What weight should economic leverage have in the democratic decision to grant a discretionary exemption, and what assumptions were actually at work? In cases involving internal conflicts over religious doctrine, authority, or property, deference to religious autonomy is justified by the voluntarism of membership. The assumption is that when a religious association is felt to be either unfair according to public standards or unfaithful to the group's own tenets—whether the standard is the association's rules or members' changing expectations—believers are free to leave and to join or form some other association, or none. The result is internal dissent, splitting, and joining or creating rival institutions. In a wide range of cases, courts echo political theorists in posing the possibility of exit and the existence of pluralist alternatives as conditions for associational autonomy.

Defenders of the broad Title VII exemption cast employment in these voluntarist terms. The janitor could conform to temple requirements or find other work. The state has no interest sufficient to protect church member/workers against "merely" arbitrary or unfair treatment: "the remedy for that is to resign or renegotiate the terms of employment."[73] (In this context, they deviate from their usual objection to conceiving religious association in terms of consent and to liberal solicitude for personal autonomy.) Were assumptions of economic opportunity at work in *Amos?* The justices may have assumed that alternative employment existed for the fired janitor and other potential employees, though they did not inquire into the facts. They may have assumed that workers are able and should be willing to move from the local community to earn their livings elsewhere. Or they may have reasoned that employees fired under these circumstances could fall back on unemployment benefits or public welfare; perhaps the thought was that government would compensate for the consequences of religious freedom to discriminate. In fact, neither the background condition of economic opportunity nor the impact of the church's economic leverage appear to have figured in legislative or judicial reasoning.

Contrast the *Amos* decision with the ruling the same year in *Roberts v. Jaycees*, where the Supreme Court decided that insuring equality of economic opportunity for women was a sufficiently compelling state interest to justify legally requiring the all-male group to admit women members. Nondiscriminatory economic opportunity outweighed the Jaycees' First Amendment right of association.[74] Strong advocates of antidiscrimination law would apply it to religious associations, with no exceptions. Equal opportunity absolutists do not differentiate religious associations from secular enterprises or "public accommodations." Nor do they distinguish the religious from the secular activities of religious groups. They insist that Title VII should be uniformly enforced. Even exclusion from a ministry on the basis of race or sex is impermissible because it denies women and minorities access to powerful institutions and resources.[75] This absolutist position, which declines to weigh the public interest in antidiscrimination against free exercise claims, is morally and constitutionally indefensible. Economic opportunity ought to be an independent consideration in assessing whether accommodation is warranted, but it is not decisive.

The stronger justification for limiting accommodation is the balance of free exercise claims, and the use of economic power to compel adherence to religious practices. As we have seen, consideration of the consequences of a broad Title VII exemption for free exercise generally is missing from both Congress's deliberations and the Court's opinions. It is an empirical question when hiring on the basis of religious belief measurably redistributes employment opportunities from the population generally to the faithful of particular groups, becoming a significant constraint on the free exercise of nonmembers. As a practical matter, the public interest in setting limits to this accommodation may be minimal if only a few religious groups seek exemptions for a narrow range of employees. In 1996, religious organizations employed 894,000 people. This figure covers only churches and temples, religious-affiliated schools, missionary organizations, and so on (which were adequately protected by the narrow, unamended Title VII exemption).[76] It does *not* include employees in religious-owned enterprises, for- and not-for-profit, which is where plausible doubts about the religious bases for discriminatory employment practices arise. The numbers are significant, and growing.

Ecclesiastical entrepreneurship is not unusual; leaders of religious organizations in the United States typically agree that "profit-making enterprise is a legitimate and necessary way of sustaining a nonprofit organization." The axiom that "religion does not belong in commerce," for example, along with the acerbic rule that there should be no relationship between "praying on one's knees on Sunday [and] preying on other persons in the marketplace on Monday" has been eclipsed.[77] It is not only ministers of "megachurches" who learn from business, though the senior pastor of Willow Community Church may be the only one with a Peter Drucker poster on his office wall. Among its commercial assets, the Mormon Church owns the top beef ranch in the world, the largest producer of nuts in America, the country's fourteenth-largest radio chain, and the Beneficial Life Insurance Company, with assets of $1.6 billion. "If the Church were a corporation, its estimated $5.9 billion in annual gross income would place it midway through the Fortune 500."[78]

At some point, a religious association, especially when it is a dominant establishment and economic force in a region, may wield practically inescapable economic power over members and nonmembers. Or the general proliferation of religious-owned enterprises, large and small, in every area of social and economic life, can have a significant impact on the distribution of jobs overall.

Employees' free exercise rights and the independent value of employment opportunity are not the only considerations passed over in thinking about whether the amended Title VII exemption is justifiable, however. Even if workers were indifferent to religion and willing to obey temple rules as a condition of employment, and even if alternative economic opportunities were available, there is another rationale for democratic limits on religious autonomy in this area. Discrimination on the basis of faith has implications for the cultivation of liberal democratic practices and dispositions. When it comes to shaping certain moral dispositions, workplaces are crucial. A notion of religious autonomy and "sacred space" that swallows up the domain of employment where public principles of justice are supposed to reign can be imperial. *Amos* opens out to this larger question of democratic education and the moral uses of pluralism.

Costs of Accommodation #2: Subverting the Moral Uses of Pluralism

We know that workplaces are sites for cultivating skills, exhibiting excellences, and garnering self-respect. Beyond that, they are one of the few quasi- private/quasi- public settings normally governed by a number of liberal democratic norms to which most men and women are regularly exposed and where they are expected to conform. When employers and workers abide by or assert rights under state and federal antidiscrimination law, employment practices introduce them to at least minimal requirements of impartiality. Workplaces can foster expectations that habits of due process and the disposition to nondiscrimination will be exhibited (and subject to scrutiny) at least in the limited area of hiring, promotion, and firing. By imposing general public obligations on businesses, "public accommodations," and many voluntary associations government assigns them a part in cultivating liberal democratic dispositions. Or, more realistically, government limits the areas in which associations have a free hand to *inhibit* these practices and dispositions. Exemptions withdraw these groups from the domain of indirect public education.

Of course, hiring only faithful Mormons may not reflect illiberal intolerance or a generally discriminatory attitude toward outsiders, and we have no reason to think that the bishops with authority over the gym were disinclined to respect the religious liberty of non-Mormons in other settings. (Mormon practices like strenuous proseletyzing and even conversion of the dead are not coercive, though they have been characterized as disrespectful.)[79] In any case, liberal democracy does not subject religious groups to the Lockean requirement that they preach toleration—as either a religious duty or civic obligation—as a condition of their own liberty.

I want to consider briefly the appropriate parameters of government attempts to direct the moral uses of pluralism by restricting religious autonomy. This much is certain: there should be few if any limits on democratic government when it comes to democratic education in its capacity as educator, patron, or participant in the marketplace. But in its capacity as sovereign, government attempts to enforce conformity with public principles should stop far short of the censorious position that looks on associations, including religious groups, as private boot camps for citizenship. This stern pedagogical perspective dictates that the internal lives of associations be made to conform to public norms. The logic of congruence is inexorable.

For example, Stephen Macedo represents liberal democracy as a pervasively educative public order: "modern liberal democracy needs the right sort of civic culture, and religious communities *of the right sort* are an important part of this culture." Government is justified in exercising direct and indirect influence on these groups, he insists, and he denies a general right to constitutionally mandated exemptions and religious self-government. He would accommodate religion only when government imposes burdens for trivial public purposes (the opposite of the compelling interest test). He would also allow a particular accommodation when it actually "helps draw them [religious groups] into the public moral order." His severe instrumental test of accommodation is whether it contributes to "the right sort of liberal partisanships in all spheres of life." Macedo's "transformative constitutionalism" is guided by "the supreme political importance of constituting diversity for liberal ends."[80] This strenuous policy of congruence goes well beyond what Gary Jacobsohn characterizes as American constitutionalism's "assimilative" aim in an essay in this volume.[81]

The moral uses of pluralism in democracy should also stop far short of treating employers and employees instrumentally, as agents of public policy. This flawed approach is evident in *EEOC v. Pacific Press*, the gender discrimination case referred to earlier. The court weighed the employee's right to nondiscrimination under Title VII against the Adventists' claim that doctrine prohibits members from bringing suit against religious authorities. The problem with the ruling in favor of the employee is, first, that the judges discounted the religious basis for the church's conduct toward the employee, and then that they weighted the other side of the balance by representing the employee as an agent of public policy. When an employee initiates an action "[he] not only redresses his own injury but also vindicates important congressional policy against discriminatory employment."[82] This line of reasoning gives unjustified paramountcy to civic roles and administrative goals.

What is wrong with a congruence approach to religious autonomy, and with an intrusive regime of civic education? It is insufficiently solicitous of personal and associational liberty. The congruence thesis is also flawed on its own terms because it disregards the actual dynamic and scope of the moral uses of pluralism in liberal democracy. The catalogue of ways in which liberal democracy is the beneficiary of the broad moral education provided by religious membership is beyond the compass of this essay. Suffice to say that religious associations (and other voluntary associations as well) have moral effects on members' dispositions and habits besides cultivating specifically liberal democratic virtues. These faces of associational life may be subverted by attempts to transform them into schools of citizenship. Of course, religious associations are not always benign. That is why a key element of my theory of associational freedom is the recognition that sometimes even reprehensible associations serve democratic public life by containing irrepressible vices. They serve as a safety valves for illiberal and undemocratic dispositions. My main point, however, is that shifting involvements among often *incongruent* groups provides opportunities for cultivating a range of vital moral dispositions only some of which are civic virtues, for correcting a range of moral failings, and for compensating for individual experiences that inhibit the capacity for any sort of association.[83] The logic of congruence eclipses all this.

From the standpoint of the moral uses of pluralism, what is the appropriate relation between democracy and religious autonomy? I would afford wide latitude for religious self-government including accommodation in the area of employment where religious associations are able to demonstrate a religious basis for their practices. This sets a low threshold for accommodation. I have also argued that neither the defensive standard of viability nor the structural pluralist view that democracy is responsible for positively promoting religious flourishing justify allowing religious associations to define for themselves what falls within the scope of activity that is *conceivably* part of their self-definition. This degree of deference undercuts government's real but limited responsibility, which is not to ensure congruence to public principles of justice or to enforce them all the way down. Rather, it is to check broad discretionary accommodation by legislative majorities and to assign to courts the case-by-case scrutiny of challenges to the religious basis of claims for exemption.[84] There is no warrant for legislatures or courts to disavow their own judgment, or to relieve religious associations of having to exercise judgment in deciding whether to claim an exemption or defend against a charge of discrimination rather than adjust their employment practices.

The inescapability of judgment links my objections to Congress's expansive Title VII exemption and the Supreme Court's *Amos* decision to an important facet of the moral uses of pluralism. Particularly for individuals whose other affiliations may be incongruent with liberal democracy, workplaces provide the principal experience in the discipline of liberal democratic culture. This is not to say that work experiences necessarily compensate for or offset the moral effects of other, incongruent settings, so that character as a whole is transformed and civic virtues predominate. Simply, employment practices requiring an element of due process and nondiscrimination demand that we differentiate among social contexts and the conduct and dispositions they countenance. They call up the capacity to adjust dispositions as we shift involvements. The *Amos* court was keen to avoid the messy business of sorting out work that is by its nature religious from work that is not. It refused to require the Mormon Church to demonstrate that discrimination in hiring at its gym was a matter of faith or effected religious life in terms of doctrine, ritual, or authority. But decisions analogous to these are inescapable for ordinary men and women, personally. As a daily matter we have to discriminate among groups and social spheres, and muster the moral habits appropriate to each. Quite apart from cultivating specific virtues, workplaces are where most people get experience in negotiating the complex moral demands of liberal democracy and pluralist society. Which is why *Amos* concedes too much.

Notes

I want to thank Joshua Cohen, Stuart White, and participants in the MIT Philosophy and Political Science Colloquium, colleagues at the Taubman Center for Public Policy at Brown University, Kent Greenawalt, and Gary Jacobsohn for helpful comments on this chapter.

   1. 483 US 327 (1987).
   2. *City of Boerne v P.F. Flores*, Archbishop of San Antonio et al., 117 S.Ct. 2157 (1997). As a practical matter, employment litigation is the fastest growing area of civil litigation in the federal system; the number of religious groups as employers is increasing, too: cf. "Developments in the Law: Employment Discrimination," 109 *Harvard Law Review* 1568 (1996) at 1571.
   3. For a full discussion see Nancy L. Rosenblum, *Membership and Morals: The Personal Uses of Pluralism in America* (Princeton, N.J.: Princeton University Press, 1998).
   4. Alexis de Tocqueville, *Democracy in America*, ed. J. P. Mayer (New York: Harper and Row, 1969), p. 448.
   5. Michael McConnell, "Accommodation of Religion: An Update and a Response to the Critics," 60 *George Washington, Law Review* (March 1992) 685 at 739.
   6. Douglas Laycock, "Towards a General Theory of the Religion Clauses: The Case of Church Labor Relations and the Right to Church Autonomy," 81 *Columbia Law Review* 1373 (November 1981) at 1413.
   7. Frederick M. Gedicks, "Toward a Constitutional Jurisprudence of Religious Group Rights," *Wisconsin Law Review* 99 (1989) at 158, 162.
   8. Richard Epstein argues that free exercise and establishment conflicts (as well as conflicts between the clauses) would be minimized if the 1937 revolution that extended federal control and permitted redistributions of all kinds were reversed. "The dominant question is how to parcel out the turf of the religious

institution between two radically disjointed constitutional regimes, one that looks with favor on any government regulation of employment and labor matters, and one that respects the autonomy of religious organizations. The conflict is inescapable so long as religious liberty stands on firmer footing than ordinary economic liberties." "The Bill of Rights at 200 Years: Bicentennial Perspective: Religious Liberty in the Welfare State," 31 *William and Mary Law Review* 375 (1990) at 391; 382.

9. Richard J. Neuhaus, *A New Order of Religious Freedom*, cited in Mary Ann Glendon and Raul F. Yanes, "Structural Free Exercise," 90 *Michigan Law Review* 477 (1991) at 486. Lupu catalogues the "hostile" tendencies of the Court: to deny the presence of a burden and so avoid balancing free exercise claims against state interests, to elevate the state interest in uniform laws to a compelling one, to characterize exemptions as impermissible establishment favoritism toward religion, or at best to rule that while statutory exemptions are not constitutionally required federal or state legislatures may grant them if they like. Ira Lupu, "Where Rights Begin: The Problem of Burdens on the Free Exercise of Religion," 102 *Harvard Law Review* 933 (1989) at 936. On the other side, accommodation and exemption can be seen as preference for religious over nonreligious beliefs and associations: they "bestow a credibility and legitimacy upon the religious belief in question simply by its being judicially recognized as constitutionally sacrosanct." This was Justice Harlan's position vis-à-vis conscientious objection—either all objectors should be exempt whether or not their grounds are religious, or none. Cited in Lupu, "Where Rights Begin," at 947. See too William P. Marshall, "In Defense of *Smith* and Free Exercise Revisionism," 59 *University of Chicago Law Review* 308 (1991) at 322.

10. "It is no business of courts to say that what is a religious practice or activity for one group is not religion under the protection of the First Amendment." *U.S. v Seeger*, 380 US 163 (1965). See too John Davison Hunter, "Religious Freedom and the Challenge of Modern Pluralism," in *Articles of Faith, Articles of Peace*, ed. John Davison Hunter and O. Guinness (Washington, D.C.: Brookings Institution, 1990), pp. 54–74.

11. Cited in Laycock, "General Theory," at 1375, discussing *EEOC v Southwestern Baptist Theological Seminary*.

12. We recognize inquiry into whether the motives of a religious group are secular in disguise as the flip side of efforts to determine whether a legislature's motives are actually religious in secular disguise. Publicly acceptable reasons may be offered in bad faith, to give secular color to sectarian purposes, and pretexts have occasionally been uncovered and laws struck down. *Larson v Valente*, 456 US 228 (1982) .

13. Bruce N. Bagni proposes less dichotomous categories: concentric circles around an epicenter of religious activity, in "Discrimination in the Name of the Lord: A Critical Evaluation of Discrimination by Religious Organizations," 79 *Columbia Law Review* 1514 (1979).

14. *EEOC v Pacific Press Publishing*, 676 F2d 1272 (1982).

15. Shelley Saxer, "When Religion Becomes a Nuisance: Balancing Land Use and Religions Freedom When Activities of Religious Institutions Bring Outsiders into the Neighborhood," 84 *Kentucky Law Journal* 507 (1995–96).

16. Because Title VII exemptions apply only to religious *corporations*, courts have consistently upheld employee complaints over these private employers' free exercise claims. Steven D. Jamar, "Accommodating Religion at Work: A Principled Approach to Title VII and Religious Freedom," 40 *New York Law School Law Review* 719 (1996).

17. 42 U.S. Code 2000e-1. Emphasis added.

18. Bagni, "Discrimination," at 1535.

19. Laycock, "General Theory," at 1377 re *Walker v First Orthodox Presbyterian Church.*

20. *EEOC v Pacific Press Publishing*, 676 F2d 1272 (1982) [10].

21. "It is apparent that the proposed change in section 702 that the Committee sent to the Senate had nothing to do with the exemption of religous organizations; it focused entirely on narrowing the exemption for educational institutions." *Amos v Corporation of the Presiding Bishop* U.S. District Court for the District of Utah, Central Division 651 (1984).

22. 118 *Cong. Rec.* 4503 (1972); 118 *Cong. Rec.* 4813 (1972).

23. *Amos v Corporation of the Presiding Bishop* U.S. District Court for the District of Utah, Central Division 594 F.Supp. 791 (1984).

24. Beehive Enterprises employed non-Mormons and excommunicants, and in plants abroad only the managers were Mormon. 618 F.Supp. 1013 (1985).

25. *Lemon v Kurzman* (referred to deprecatingly as "the aptly named Lemon test"), 403 US 607 (1971).

26. 594 F.Supp. at 812.

27. Entanglement was first announced as part of a three-prong test for establishment in Lemon. When the NLRB was denied jurisdiction over unionization of lay teachers in parochial schools, for example, the issue was not the Catholic Church's doctrinal objection to unions but the fact that official resolution of charges of unfair labor practices would require intrusive investigation, since "nearly everything that goes on in the schools affects teachers and is therefore arguably 'a condition of employment.'" *National Labor Relations Board v Catholic Bishop of Chicago* 440 US 490 at 501; 503; 496. Entanglement doctrine wards off government intervention, but it can also work against awarding benefits to religious associations, which may have to choose between independence and aid—described as "Caesar's revenge."

28. At 821 n.54; 812 n.36.

29. At 825.

30. 397 US 664. As a policy matter, there is no good way to assess the charitable status of religious groups that operate exclusively to benefit their own, and that may be contrary to the public interest; see Lord Justice Balcombe, "The Attitude of the Law to Religion in Secular Society" (Oxford Centre for Postgraduate Hebrew Studies and the Institute for Advanced Legal Studies, 1989), pp. 13–15.

31. At 813.

32. At 825.

33. At 826.

34. At 337.

35. At 348.

36. In fact, the district court had left open whether Deseret Gym was a profit-making enterprise; its beauty shop and women's massage salon were profit-making private concessions within the gymnasium building, at 345 and 341. For an attempt to identify "zones" of commercial/noncommercial activities for accommodation purposes see David B. Cruz, "Piety and Prujudice: Free Exercise Exemption from laws Prohibiting Sexual Orientation Discrimination" 69 *New York University Law Review* 1176 (1994).

37. *Employment Division of Oregon v Smith*, 494 US 872 (1990) at 1605.

38. Laycock, "General Theory," insists that associations are even more dependent on their employees than on their "marginal members" at 1408–9.

39. *Amos* at 345.

40. Treaver Hodson, "Comment: The Religious Employer Exemption under Title VII: Should a Church Define its Own Activities?" 3 *Brigham Young University Law Review* 571 (1994) at 586.

41. *Amos* at 343. Emphasis added.

42. That ruling has been faulted for failing to acknowledge that "the church's intuition of religious propriety" is as much a matter of collective history as written doctrine. If the court had considered the place of tithing in the Mormon founding and the group's history of persecution and personal sacrifice, it would have appreciated that salaries are paid in part from contributions, which should be used to support only committed church members, Gedicks, "Constitutional Jurisprudence," at 113–14. However, when important state interests are at issue in an Establishment case, it matters that the conection to faith eludes outsiders.

43. 594 F.Supp. 791 (1984), at 818.

44. Laycock, "General Theory," at 1392.

45. 566 F2d 310 at 321; 314. Emphasis added.

46. 406 US 20 (1972) at 211–12; 218.

47. Glendon and Yanes, "Structural Free Exercise," at 506.

48. The *Yoder* ruling was correct, but not because free exercise was mandated by the threat to the community's viability. In balancing the free exercise claim against the state interest, the association should win because the public interest in two additional years of schooling was not compelling. Justice Burger stated that the state's educational purposes were satisfied by the education provided by the Amish parents and community.

49. Carl H. Esbeck, "Establishment Clause Limits on Governmental Interference with Religious Organizations," 41 *Washington and Lee Law Review* 347 (1984) at 381.

50. Glendon and Yanes, "Structural Free Exercise," at 501.

51. *Amos* at 343.

52. *County of Allegheny v ACLU* 492 US 573 (1989): Kennedy, Rehnquist, White, and Scalia dissenting, discussed in Kathleen Sullivan, "Religion and Liberal Democracy," in *The Bill of Rights in the Modern State*, ed. Geoffrey Stone, Richard Epstein, and Cass Sunstein (Chicago: University of Chicago Press, 1992), pp. 195–203, p. 203.

53. Sanford Levinson, "Religious Language and the Public Square (Review of Michael Perry: *Love and Power: The Role of Religion and Morality in American Politics*," 105 *Harvard Law Review* 2061 (1992) at 2076–7.

54. Glendon and Yanes, "Structural Free Exercise," at 543. "Structural pluralism" is their term.

55. McConnell, "Accommodation of Religion," at 690, 739.

56. Glendon and Yanes, "Structural Free Exercise," at 523, 530, and note 259.

57. McConnell, "Accommodation of Religion," at 690, 739.

58. Ernest Barker and F. W. Maitland, cited in Sheldon Leader, *Freedom of Association: A Study in Labor Law and Political Theory* (New Haven, Conn.: Yale University Press, 1992), p. 56.

59. John Neville Figgis, "Churches in the Modern State," in *The Pluralist Theory of the State*, ed. Paul Q. Hirst (London: Routledge, 1989), p. 121; Harold J. Laski, "Personality of Associations," 29 *Harvard Law Review* 404 (1916) at 425.

60. McConnell, "Believers as Equal Citizens," chapter 3 of this volume.

61. Ibid.

62. Glendon and Yanes, "Structural Free Exercise," at 543, 544.

63. Ibid. at 516.

64. McConnell, "Accommodation of Religion" at 715; 687.

65. From the orthodox liberal democratic standpoint—voluntarist and separationist—these positions are in tension. It would seem that in rejecting separationism, structural pluralists attenuate their case for mandatory free exercise exemptions and for the Supreme Court as protector. After all, as Kathleen Sullivan observes, constitutional "exit" is critical precisely insofar as religious groups are not participants in the politics of distribution. The usual corollary of free exercise opting out is the privatization of religious life. "God as a Lobby," 61 *University of Chicago Law Review* 1655 (1994).

66. McConnell "Accommodation of Religion."

67. Ibid. at 703.

68. Isaac Kramnick and R. Laurence Moore, "Can Churches save the Cities? Faith-based services and the Constitution," *American Prospect*, no. 35 (November/December 1997): 47–53.

69. An important case requires a religious group to conform to minimum wage and hour laws for its member-employees: *Tony and Susan Alamo Foundation v Secretary of Labor*, 471 US 290 (1985). For an extended discussion see Rosenblum, *Membership and Morals*, chapter 3.

70. 594 F.Supp. 791 (1984) at 818.

71. *Amos* at 345.

72. Richard Posner and Michael McConnell, "An Economic Approach to Issues of Religious Freedom," 56 *University of Chicago Law Review* 1 (1989) at 5.

73. Laycock, "General Theory," at 1406–9; 1409.

74. *Roberts v Jaycees*, 468 US 609 (1984). 468 U.S. 609 (1984). For a critical discussion see Rosenblum, *Membership and Morals*, chapter 5, and Rosenblum, "Compelled Association: Public Standing, Self-Respect, and the Dynamic

of Exclusion" in *Freedom of Association*, ed. Amy Gutmann (Princeton, N.J.: Princeton University Press, 1998).

75. The wholly inapt analogy is to *Roberts v. Jaycees*, where the Court (erroneously in my view) required restricted all-male membership groups to admit women. Jane Rutherford, "Equality as the Primary Constitutional Value: The Case for Applying Employment Discrimination Laws to Religion," 81 *Cornell Law Review* 1049 (1996) at 1095. This position is also taken by Ira Lupu, "Free Exercise Exemptions and Religious Institutions: The Case of Employment Discrimination," 67 *Brigham Young University Law Review* 391 (1987).

76. *The Current Population Survey*, 1996 Annual Average Tabulations on Detailed Occupations and Industries, Table 2 (Department of Labor, Bureau of Labor Statistics, Washington, D.C.).

77. *Sports and Health Club, Inc.* 370 NW2d cited in Jamar, "Accommodating Religion at Work," at 813.

78. David Van Biema, "The Empire of the Mormons," *Time*, August 4, 1997, 51–57 at 53; 52.

79. Mormons agreed to end their posthumous baptism of Nazi Holocaust victims (and to remove the 380,000 names of those who had already been baptized from its Genealogical Index) in deference to complaints by Jewish groups. Gustav Niebuhr, "Mormons to End Holocaust Victim Baptism," *New York Times*, April 29, 1995, p. A 9.

80. Stephen Macedo, "Transformative Constitutionalism and the Case of Religion: Defending the Moderate Hegemony of Liberalism," *Political Theory* 26, no. 1 (February 1998): 56–80 at 73.

81. On assimilative, transformative or "ameliorative" constitutionalism see Gary Jacobsohn, " 'By the Light of Reason': Corruption, Religious Speech, and Constitutional Essentials," chapter 10 in this volume.

82. *EEOC v Pacific Press* 676 F.2d 1272 (1982).

83. This is the argument of Rosenblum, *Membership and Morals*.

84. I would apply the same logic to employment practices of political groups; the Democratic Party, for example, should be able to discriminate on partisan grounds in hiring if it can show a relation between the job and the associations' political activities. The party could not fire a janitor who changed party allegiances. This was the test employed in patronage cases *Elrod v Burns*, 427 US 347 (1976), and *Rutan v Republican Party of Illinois*, 497 US 62 (1990).

7

FIVE QUESTIONS ABOUT RELIGION
JUDGES ARE AFRAID TO ASK

Kent Greenawalt

APARADOX lies at the heart of the religion clauses of the First Amendment. Government may not prohibit the free exercise of religion, or make a law respecting an establishment of a religion. These guarantees seem to demand that someone identify what counts as religion. If people's claims do not concern religion or are blatantly fraudulent, their free exercise of religion is not at stake. And government support of an organization or activity does not establish religion, if religion is not involved. Yet, if officials decide what counts as religious and assess the honesty of people who make religious claims, they may favor some religions over others. From the perspectives of the values the religion clauses embody, determinations of sincerity and of what constitutes religion carry costs.[1] Judges understandably hesitate to address and answer these questions, but sometimes they must determine whether religion is present and review whether claimed conviction is genuine.

This essay is mainly about these subjects and the related topic of what is important to a religion or constitutes a substantial burden on its exercise. The deep problems these inquiries introduce are reasons for avoiding the inquiries or for casting them in some particular form. But any acceptable constitutional regime makes such inquiries necessary on some of the occasions when courts deal with constitutional and statutory rights.

My discussion concerns itself more with nuances of difference in alternative legal approaches than do most of the other contributions to this book. I hope that this concentration conveys some of the difficulties that are involved in giving practical application to appealing general principles. In particular, I show that the acceptability of courts and other officials answering questions about religion can depend partly on subtle variations in the way the questions are formulated. The texture of this essay is more "legal" than its companions, but, like the others, it is designed to give readers a broad sense of how law may deal with our society's religious life.

Before I consider in turn sincerity, definition, and importance, I briefly discuss two other questions courts do not want to address: Are religious views true? Are they faithful to a tradition? As to these questions, the law has developed in a way that allows courts to "stay out." This law is strongly justified in its major aspects, but some wrinkles are controversial, and some doctrines should be altered.

Religious Truth

The core idea that the government may not make determinations of religious truth is firmly entrenched. The government cannot treat the doctrine of a particular religion as being true, as it might be said that England has formally treated the doctrines of the Anglican Church as true. But controversy remains over the application of the Establishment Clause to the states and over the principle that governments should not promote religion in general. I defend those approaches, and then acknowledge that one kind of indirect approval of some religious positions over others is inevitable and perfectly acceptable.

The original Bill of Rights applied only against the federal government. Under the language of the Establishment Clause, Congress could neither establish a national religion nor interfere with existing state establishments.

"Incorporation" of the Establishment Clause against the states, via the Due Process Clause of the Fourteenth Amendment, raises two difficulties of justification.[2] The first is this: so long as religious liberty is respected, as say in modern England and the Scandinavian countries, how does an established church take life, liberty, or property without due process of law?[3] The second difficulty is related: since the Establishment Clause required Congress not to undermine state churches, how does that provision now forbid state forms of establishment? One answer to the first difficulty is that a principle of "no establishment" promotes and enhances the *liberty* of the free exercise of religion.[4] Another answer is that the use of state money to support religion constitutes a deprivation of *property* (in taxation) without due process. Finally, the Fourteenth Amendment's requirement that states not deny people the equal protection of the laws may bar favoring some or all religions. The linguistic barrier to incorporating the Establishment Clause is, thus, not hard to surmount.

The worry about historical ambition is more troubling, yet one can understand the Establishment Clause as reflecting choices to create principles of nonestablishment for federal domains and to leave most decisions about religion to the states.[5] In any event, since the issue for incorporation is what the Fourteenth Amendment did, the views that are crucial are those at the time that amendment was adopted. By the end of the Civil War, no state had an established church. The First Amendment clause probably was then understood mainly as directed against established religion. Extending the "no establishment" principle to the states does not violate any historical understanding about established religion.[6]

Whatever the merits of applying the Establishment Clause to prohibit state support of religion, constitutional law for half a century has included that principle in its fabric, and not a single Supreme Court justice has proposed its retraction. Entirely apart from how judges construe the federal constitution, the vast majority of states have antiestablishment language in their own constitutions. Although the language of these documents varies greatly,[7] many state courts interpreting their own language find themselves following approaches that various United States Supreme Court Justices have suggested for the federal constitution.

In the United States, no one proposes that government designate a particular religion, such as Roman Catholicism or Presbyterianism, as true; but many people do object to the prevailing doctrine that government may not promote religion in general. They believe that favoring a broad range of religions is all right.

On examination, the distinction between favoring some religions and favoring all religions is murky.[8] Since variant religions maintain sharply divergent beliefs about the significance of the universe and the nature of human beings, no one can coherently claim that religion in general is true. Most crucially perhaps, not all religions suppose that a Supreme Being exists. Were a state to endorse belief in a Supreme Being, it would favor familiar American religions over religions such as Buddhism that lack such a belief. Someone who was primarily interested in doctrinal truth, and wished to defend the position that the state may favor religion in general, would need to say something like this: "The state can endorse beliefs that have been reflected in the major religions within the United States, beliefs such as (1) a Supreme Being exists; (2) that Supreme Being cares about all human beings; (3) human life has ultimate significance; (4) human beings should care for each other." A candid and informed adherent of this position would acknowledge that it does favor some religions over others, and that, given the country's present immigration standards, which keep drawing more residents from East Asia than in earlier stages of our history, the percentage of the citizenry who are religious but do not subscribe to the "endorsed" religious view will continue to grow. The need to protect minority religions itself provides a powerful reason why government should not promote claims of religious truth.

Although government cannot coherently endorse all religious doc-trines, it might recommend religious practice as broadly desirable. While recognizing that religions embrace some mutually incompatible ideas, offlcials might nevertheless encourage citizens to practice religion, which beneficially draws individuals out of themselves and teaches con-cern for others.[9] Thus, government might endorse the practice of reli-gion in general without favoring some religions over others.

Present constitutional doctrine forbids supporting or endorsing reli-gion over nonreligion in most contexts. The government may not broadly promote the truth or value of religion. This basic principle ap-plies both to government speech and to government assistance of pri-vate groups. As I have explained, the principle of nonsupport is sound as it applies to religious truth. I believe the principle is also sound as it applies to religious practice. Recommendations of religious practice veer too close to endorsement of dominant beliefs, and their vacuousness makes them offensive to many deeply religious people. Most crucial, given serious disagreement in the society about the value of much reli-gious activity, the government should not line up on one side of that debate.

I have not yet spoken of measures that governments adopt that fit some religious views and are at odds with others. A court orders a state to desegregate its schools, the country goes to war, educational funds are made available equally to men and women. The government has implicitly rejected religious notions that (1) God wishes rigid racial sep-aration, (2) all killing in war violates God's commandments, (3) all women should occupy themselves with domestic tasks. A vast array of laws and policies similarly imply the incorrectness of particular religious views.[10]

I emphasize rejection, because such government action need not im-plicitly endorse any religious view as correct. Why is that? The desegre-gation order, for example, could be supported by a secular view that all human beings are inherently equal or by a religious view that in God's eyes all people are equal. The state's action, by itself, does not assert the correctness of the religious reason. Nevertheless, it definitely does take a position on issues that divide religious understandings and implicitly treats some positions as mistaken.[11] Since this implicit rejection of reli-gious views is inevitable, it cannot be unconstitutional. Thus, any sug-gestion that the government should do nothing that *reflects* a view about religious truth is ill conceived. Further, when government action implic-itly rejects certain religious views, such action will have some influence on the religious groups that people join. A government policy against racial segregation may diminish the attraction of religious groups that assert that such segregation is divinely ordained.[12]

Faithfulness to Religious Tradition and Practice

Parties fighting over the property of a religious organization may claim that they have been more faithful to the doctrines and practices of the group than their opponents. Such questions may arise because of express trusts or contracts, or because of a principle that charitable property should not be diverted from its purposes. Although, in theory, a court might decide if people are following the standards of a religion without determining whether those standards are true or good, in practice judges will be hard put to resolve genuinely debatable disputes apart from their own views about sound religion and about desirable evolution in religious doctrines and practices.

The Supreme Court, as I discuss elsewhere,[13] has sensibly taken the stance in modern times that civil courts cannot resolve debatable matters of doctrine and practice: courts must either defer to the decisions of authoritative religious tribunals or employ so-called neutral principles of law that do not require religious judgments. No approach gets courts totally out of the business of resolving issues of religious practice and governance, but the basic idea is to limit this as far as possible. The related rationales are that civil judges are incompetent in such matters, that they should not inject their own ideas of sound religion into civil decisions, and that they should not entangle themselves in religious affairs. My own overall assessment is that prevailing doctrines withdraw the civil courts too far. Judges should resolve straightforward matters of church practice and government when these are relevant to civil decision, much as they would resolve similar matters for other associations. But I shall leave this topic here with the observation that courts, in general, do not, and should not, resolve debatable matters of faithfulness, i.e., whether one side or another has better followed the doctrines, practices, and principles of governance of a religious organization.

Sincerity

Should courts or juries assess the sincerity of religious claimants? Such judgments are troubling, but, as we shall see, some assessment of this kind is unavoidable if religious claimants receive special privileges. The basic problem is set well by a confusing fifty-year-old case in which the Supreme Court said more about sincerity than it has before or since.

In *United States v. Ballard*,[14] leaders of the I Am movement were prosecuted for mail fraud. According to the indictment, the Ballards claimed that Guy Ballard had been visited by Jesus and by Saint Germain and had been designated as a divine messenger; they also claimed Guy and his wife and son had the ability to cure diseases and injuries and had cured hundreds of people.[15] The indictment charged that the Ballards knew that these representations were false. The Ballards argued that it would not be constitutionally appropriate for a jury to decide either whether their religious representations were true or whether they sincerely believed them. Were that position accepted, it would follow that people could not be guilty of mail fraud for religious representations.

The trial court allowed the jury to pass on the sincerity of the Ballards, but not on the truth of what they believed. It advised the jury, "The issue is: Did these defendants honestly and in good faith believe those things? If they did, they should be acquitted."[16] The Court of Appeals decided that, under the indictment, the government had to prove that some representations were actually false; therefore, the jury's decision should not have been restricted to the question of good faith.

No one suggested before the Supreme Court that juries should decide directly whether essentially spiritual events had actually taken place. The principle that government should not say what is true in matters of religion precludes judges and jurors assessing the underlying truth of spiritual claims. If prosecution for mail fraud required that, prosecution would be unconstitutional and the Ballards would have escaped conviction.

One can imagine an argument that juries should be able to pass on the truth of some kinds of spiritual claims. If someone does not believe in a personal spiritual experience that he asserts happened, the experience almost certainly did not happen. If a woman claims that Jesus (the historical figure) spoke to her and she has no belief that he did, it is very unlikely that Jesus spoke to her. Perhaps if a jury finds insincerity about the assertion of such experiences, it should be able to infer falseness as well. This is a subtle argument. Ordinarily, truth is distinguishable from belief. I may claim that Thomas is a thief without any belief that he is; but Thomas may turn out to be a thief. The special wrinkle about the kinds of spiritual occurrences the Ballards claimed is that they involved direct perceptions by the Ballards.[17] If people lie about extranatural events that they alone claimed to have witnessed, it is highly improbable the events have transpired.[18] But it would be inconvenient for courts to develop a special doctrine that untruth can be inferred from insincerity for certain kinds of spiritual claims.[19]

A different argument for preserving mail fraud prosecutions concedes that the truth of religious claims cannot be determined. It concentrates instead on people's states of mind. When I say an event has occurred, I implicitly assert that I believe it occurred. If I say Jesus visited me, I assert belief in his visit. If I am insincere, I falsely represent my state of mind. Why cannot that false representation be the basis for prosecution?

Someone might respond that "consumers" do not care about my state of mind, only the truth of whether Jesus has visited me. That would be an artificial view, however. Others do not pay attention to such spiritual claims if they think the speaker is lying. If a recipient of some mailing by the Ballards supposed they were lying, she would not seriously consider the possible truth of what they claimed. Thus, an implicit misrepresentation of one's state of mind is a very important misrepresentation. If juries appropriately determine sincerity about claimed spiritual experiences, insincerity should be sufficient to convict for fraud. (One nettlesome aspect of the *Ballard* case for this approach is that the indictment apparently required proof of falseness, not just insincerity.)

The government pressed yet a different argument most strongly before the Supreme Court. Although the district court had told the jury not to assess the truth of representations of religious ideas, the government urged that the jury had found some claims to be false: namely, that the Ballards had cured hundreds of persons, that they had had particular religious experiences, and that phonograph records would contribute to salvation.[20] These determinations were, the government urged, adequate to sustain the conviction. We can quickly see that a claim that a woman has cured people is not quite like a claim that a spiritual being has addressed her. Someone who has cured hundreds of people should have supporting evidence—if not medical testimony, at least the witness of some of the cured individuals. The Supreme Court did not accept the government's effort to distinguish among the Ballards' representations, finding that the trial judge had withdrawn the issue of falsity for all their claims.

Justice Douglas's opinion for the Court expressed uncertainty whether the court of appeals had believed the indictment could be construed only as charging fraud by misrepresentation of religious doctrines or beliefs, or had concluded that the withdrawal of the truth of representations "resulted in a substantial change in the character of the crime charged." Whatever the particular indictment might demand, "the First Amendment precludes determination of the truth or verity of respondents' religious doctrines or beliefs." The opinion continued, "Heresy trials are foreign to our Constitution. Men may believe what they cannot prove. They may not be put to the proof of their religious doctrines or beliefs. . . . The Fathers of the Constitution . . . fashioned a charter of government which envisaged the widest possible toleration of conflicting views. Man's relation to his God was made no concern of the State."[21] The district court had properly withheld all questions about the truth of religious beliefs from the jury.[22]

The Court's opinion has a mystifying quality. It implies, as the district court had supposed, that a fraud conviction can be based on insincerity, but it does not explicitly say so. Nor does it explicitly resolve whether the Ballard indictment, or the mail fraud statute more generally, permits conviction based on insincerity about spiritual claims. If the Supreme Court agreed with the district court that such convictions are all right, the Douglas opinion is less than straightforward. It eloquently evokes a tradition of religious liberty reaching the most unorthodox views, but formally gives the unorthodox less protection than had the court of appeals. The Supreme Court apparently allows conviction on a finding of insincerity; the court of appeals had required the government to establish both insincerity and falsity. Why was the Supreme Court not more precise about its view of the district court's disposition? Possibly Justice Douglas had to cobble together an opinion that would satisfy the five Justices necessary to make a majority, and these Justices may have had distinctly different outlooks on crucial questions.

The two dissenting opinions occupied opposite ends of the spectrum. Chief Justice Stone, joined by two other Justices, would have reinstated the district court's judgment. He urged that the indictment had charged that the Ballards' representations were both false and insincere, that the parties had agreed with the judge's decision to submit to the jury "only the issue of . . . good faith belief in the representations of religious experiences,"[23] and that misrepresentations of one's state of mind can underlie a mail fraud prosecution.

Justice Jackson took a very different view. He argued that one could not separate the issue of truth from the issue of sincerity. "The most convincing proof that one believes his statements is to show that they have been true in his experience. Likewise, that one knowingly falsified is best proved by showing that what he said happened never did happen. . . . If we try religious sincerity severed from religious verity, we isolate the dispute from the very considerations which in common experience provide its most reliable answer."[24] He went on to say that juries could not "separate fancied religious experiences from real ones, dreams from happenings, and hallucinations from true clairvoyance. . . . When one comes to trial which turns on any aspect of religious belief or representation, unbelievers among his judges are likely not to understand and are almost certain not to believe him."[25]

Drawing from William James, Jackson made the more subtle point that faith often involves a degree of disbelief and that religious symbolism may be used with mental reservation. To take a familiar example the Justice does not employ, the Apostles' Creed, one of the most basic formulations of Christian faith, includes affirmations that Jesus "was born of the Virgin Mary" and that on the third day after he was crucified "he rose." To most worshipers, those phrases mean literally that Jesus was not conceived by ordinary sexual intercourse and that his physical body came to life again after it was buried. Many Christian ministers do not believe these propositions. If they repeat the Apostles' Creed Sunday after Sunday without explaining that their belief in the phrases is other than literal, are they misrepresenting their beliefs to their congregations? Jackson's observation raises this delicate question.

Jackson concludes that prosecution for fraud about religious claims "easily could degenerate into religious persecution."[26] He would have allowed prosecutions for fraud only "for false representations on matters other than faith or experience," as when someone claims that funds actually being spent for personal use are being employed to build a church. Jackson does not say how claims about physical cures would fit in this dichotomy, but he seems to suppose they typically fall on the side of unprosecutable claims of faith and experience. Justice Jackson would have dismissed the indictment.

For crimes of fraudulent misrepresentation, Justice Jackson's position is very attractive. Jurors reviewing the sincerity of spiritual claims will draw on their own sense of what beliefs are plausible. If the state does not involve itself in prosecutions for spiritual fraud, people will have notice they must rely on themselves for protection. Almost certainly, most recipients of spiritual literature now do suppose that. They do not reflect: "As sellers of food fear prosecution if they make bogus claims for their products, I assume people are deterred from making outrageous spiritual claims." A clear legal rule against enforcement for fraud would reinforce most people's assumption that they must rely on their own judgment about religious claims. Although any rule of this sort requires courts to distinguish essentially spiritual claims from more ordinary ones, the law should not touch false representations in the spiritual realm.[27]

Unfortunately, this position cannot resolve all the circumstances in which religious claims arise. For at least some circumstances, an inquiry about sincerity is necessary. The exact inquiry may vary. It will not always be whether an individual claimant is probably sincere about the legal claim at issue. Judges may adjust the standard of probability or the exact issue to be assessed, or both. The occasions to assess sincerity could be reduced by abolishing all legal distinctions based on religion, but they could not be eliminated.

The law of conscientious objection illustrates each of these truths. This law has had primary importance during military drafts, exempting young men from conscription, but the law continues to have significance for a volunteer army. Volunteers sign on for a period of service during which they cannot resign. However, if they become conscientious objectors during that period, they are allowed to leave the military.

Barring a considerable change in controlling legal rules, someone must evaluate the sincerity of those who claim conscientious objector status.[28] Suppose units of a volunteer army are sent to an extremely dangerous war zone, or the government reintroduces conscription during wartime. If everyone who asserts that his religious convictions make him a conscientious objector is relieved from service, all those willing to lie about that will be excused. This consequence will be dispiriting, to say the least, for those who also want to avoid serving but not at the price of lying. Some test of sincerity is needed, unless all those subject to service are given a choice between military duty and some alternative, with the conditions of the alternative being onerous enough so most people will choose military duty.[29]

As I shall explain in the section on "defining religion," the precise status of religious conviction in the qualifications to be a conscientious objector is complicated. Congress aimed to restrict the exemption to those with religious convictions; a plurality of the Supreme Court responded by interpreting "religious" to cover all objections to military service that are genuinely conscientious. Thus, someone without traditional religious belief may acquire conscientious objector status. But this does not mean draft boards or military tribunals can avoid passing on the sincerity of religious beliefs. Most men and women who seek to be classified as conscientious objectors assert some traditionally religious belief in God. Liars will be especially likely to do this, since a liar will want to make his beliefs as appealing as possible. Someone has to assess a claimant's honesty, giving due regard to the uncertainty that is often a part of religious conviction and to the possibility of a kind of cognitive dissonance that allows people to embrace propositions that are in severe tension with each other.

The inquiry into sincerity need not be whether the claimant has probably told the truth. The law on judicial review of these matters changed drastically during the Vietnam War, in a way that profoundly affected draft boards. Congress had provided that courts should sustain draft board decisions if they had "a basis in fact."[30] This standard was conceived as providing very limited judicial review of administrative action. If draft board members concluded that an applicant was lying, because they found his personal presentation unconvincing, they denied the exemption; and courts let the determination stand. But as the law evolved, courts construed "a basis in fact" to mean an objective basis in fact, something other than mere disbelief of a claimant.[31] Once that became the law of judicial review, a wise draft board did not deny relief without objective evidence that a claimant was lying, e.g., actual contradictions or false claims of church membership. Such objective proof was not common. Draft boards upheld some claims they disbelieved, or they were overturned by judges unable to discern any objective basis to deny the exemption. Neither draft boards nor courts were deciding exactly whether a claimant was probably lying.

For Amish claims to withdraw children from school after the eighth grade,[32] courts have not had to focus carefully on the sincerity issue, but probably the definitive question does not concern a parent's exact views about further school education. No one doubts that some groups of Amish, in general, sincerely believe that their children should not receive ordinary education beyond the eighth grade. Individual parents should succeed in a claim to withdraw their child once they show they are practicing members of an Amish community that educates children within the community after that grade. The parents' status in a religious group whose members feel compelled to engage in this group practice should be sufficient, even if the particular parents happen to doubt the wisdom of withdrawing children from school at exactly that stage. If all practicing Amish are expected to participate in Amish community education beyond a certain age, individual Amish children should be able to do so even if their parents personally could accept further ordinary education.[33] The Amish claim is more closely related to corporate religious practice, is less individual, than the claim to be a conscientious objector, and this affects the precise inquiry about sincerity.[34]

I have said enough to indicate that often some inquiry into sincerity is essential but that the precise inquiry can shift according to the subject. Both the best inquiry and the range of constitutionally permissible inquiries will vary.

I want to make one final point. In any context, inquiries into sincerity of religious belief are troubling, for just the reasons Justice Jackson offered. Alternative approaches are preferable if they are otherwise feasible. This is why I support an approach to required military service that allows anyone to opt out by undertaking alternative service that most people would consider more onerous. The undesirability of inquiries into sincerity, and especially the risk of discriminatory disbelief of the unorthodox, have constitutional relevance. It counts against a scheme of legal regulation that officials must evaluate sincerity, but not all schemes in which officials assess sincerity are invalid. Sometimes tests of sincerity are a necessary price to attain objectives that the Constitution requires or permits.

"Defining" Religion

Another inquiry that courts occasionally face is whether a claim or practice is religious. The simplest context is when someone seeks a privilege available only to those with religious grounds. For example, the Religious Freedom Restoration Act protected individuals against substantial burdens on their "exercise of religion."[35] Someone who wished to succeed under the statute had to persuade officials that his claim of liberty concerned religion.[36] The issue whether something is religious can also arise when opponents try to stop an arrangement they assert establishes religion. For example, when parents and taxpayers objected to a course in transcendental meditation in the New Jersey schools, courts had to decide if transcendental meditation was religious. Finally, courts may have to decide if a classification is religious when religious classifications are less acceptable than other classifications.[37]

The subject of "definition" and religion is complex. I describe what the major cases have said, explore various alternatives, and suggest an approach that best fits what the decisions have done and the standards for a sound approach. Seven preliminary points help focus the discussion. (1) Any judicial test of what counts as "religious" and what does not is worrisome. Courts find it hard to say just what is religious, and the danger that they will favor the familiar over the unorthodox is ever present. (2) Some test of what counts as religious is unavoidable for some cases. Everyone seems to agree that religious discrimination is unacceptable.[38] Officials and courts enforcing such a ban must be able to say whether lines of division, or motivations, are religious. (3) How often the law calls on courts to say whether something is religious or not will depend on substantive principles of constitutional and statutory law. For example, *Employment Division v. Smith*,[39] a case involving use of peyote in worship services, announced that people with religious reasons to violate criminal laws fare no better under the Free Exercise Clause than other violators. This decision eliminated a need to decide whether some claims are religious that the preexisting constitutional standard required. Congress responded to *Smith* with the Religious Freedom Restoration Act, which reintroduced the need to determine what is religious for many circumstances. The Court then declared in *City of Boerne v. Flores*[40] that Congress lacked power under the Fourteenth Amendment to create such an exemption from state and local laws. That decision drastically reduced the occasions when courts will entertain free exercise claims and need to determine if they are really religious.[41] (4) Some approaches to the question of definition generate greater problems than others. If an approach is simple and minimizes dangers that courts will disregard the values underlying the religion clauses, that argues in its favor. (5) Any overall evaluation requires attention to definitional approaches and substantive rights and prohibitions. An approach to definition should fit well with existing or desirable substantive standards, and a substantive standard should be able to accommodate a sensible approach to definition. (6) Of all cases involving claims about religion, only a very small percentage raise the problem of "definition."

Usually, a claim or practice is indisputably religious, and the courts need decide only what constitutional or statutory consequence follows. (7) The practical infrequency of the definitional problem[42] affects its bearing on the overall law of church and state. A threshold test for religion is more tolerable if its application is usually simple. Whether the manner in which a test applies is debatable in 50 percent or in 1 percent of cases matters greatly.

Given the intricacies of defining a concept as complex as religion, the Supreme Court understandably has remained relatively silent. It did offer a constitutional definition of religion in 1890, speaking of "one's views of his relations to his Creator, and to the obligations they impose of reverence for his being and character, and of obedience to his will."[43] In a 1931 dissent, Chief Justice Hughes similarly referred to "belief in a relation to God involving duties superior to those arising from any human relation."[44] The Court adopted a much more inclusive concept of religion in 1961 in *Torcaso v. Watkins.*[45] Reviewing a state law that required officeholders to declare a belief in God, Justice Black's opinion for the Court indicated that Buddhism, Taoism, Ethical Culture, and Secular Humanism (at least in the organized form of the Fellowship of Humanity) were religions, and the Court held that the state's preference for theistic religions over nontheistic ones violated the Establishment Clause. The Court later made clear that an individual's belief can be religious even if it does not correspond with the standard doctrines of the faith to which he belongs.[46]

In conscientious objector cases during the Vietnam War, the Supreme Court gave its fullest exposition of religion, and managed to turn the language of the controlling statute upside down. Section 6(j) of the Universal Military Training and Service Act required that conscientious objection be based on "religious training and belief." Congress provided a further definition that drew from the language of Chief Justice Hughes; religious belief was "an individual's belief in a relation to a Supreme Being involving duties superior to those arising from any human relation, but [not including] essentially political, sociological, or philosophical views or a merely personal moral code."[47] Despite the statute's evident endorsement of a traditional theistic idea of religion, the Supreme Court interpreted it more broadly, to cover applicants like Daniel Seeger, who rejected dependence on a Creator for a guide to morality and had a "belief in and devotion to goodness and virtue for their own sakes, and a religious faith in a purely ethical creed."[48] After considering modern conceptions of religion, the Court concluded that "[a] sincere and meaningful belief which occupies in the life of its possessor a place parallel to that filled by the God of those admittedly qualifying for the exemption comes within the statutory definition."

A plurality of four Justices went even further in *Welsh v. United States*.[49] Welsh, who had struck the word "religious" from his application, based his objection to military service on his perception of world politics and the wastefulness of devoting human resources to military endeavors. According to Justice Black and his three colleagues, since Welsh's beliefs "play the role of a religion and function as a religion in [his] life," he was religious. The exemption covered "those whose consciences, spurred by deeply held moral, ethical, or religious beliefs, would give them no rest or peace if they allowed themselves to become part of an instrument of war."

Since *Seeger* and *Welsh* were impossible to square with the ordinary sense of Congress's language, commentators believed that the Court's interpretation was based on constitutional doubts about the line Congress had tried to draw. Justice Harlan, who also voted to exempt Welsh, said that Congress had differentiated between religious conscientious objectors and nonreligious objectors who possessed the same intensity of moral conviction; he concluded that the distinction was an unconstitutional establishment.[50]

The Supreme Court's broad statutory construction of religion, as well as its decision in *Torcaso*, has led other courts and scholars to assume that the constitutional definition of religion is now very broad.

Applications by the Washington Ethical Society and a California Fellowship of Humanity for tax exemptions available to churches yielded important opinions about the boundaries of religion. In the former case the United States Court of Appeals for the District of Columbia held that the Ethical Society, although it propounded no theist beliefs, was a religious corporation or society within the meaning of the District's tax code.[51] Traditional religious practices and aims strongly resembled those of the Society. The Society focused on spiritual values and guidance and the need for inward peace; it held Sunday services with bible readings, sermons, singing and meditation, as well as Sunday school classes; and it used "Leaders," trained graduates of established theological institutions who preached and ministered and conducted services for naming, marrying and burying. The court's opinion, by the future Chief Justice Burger, emphasized the broad purposes of the tax exemption statute; it adopted a wide notion of religion without attempting a definition.

A California court of appeal took a similar approach to the nontheist Fellowship of Humanity.[52] It also considered an expansive view of religion apt for the tax exemption, and commented that a narrow construction of the term "religious worship" might impermissibly discriminate among types of religious belief.[53] It said that religion includes "(1) a belief, not necessarily referring to supernatural powers; (2) a cult, involving a gregarious association openly expressing the belief; (3) a system of moral practice directly resulting from an adherence to the belief; and (4) an organization within the cult designed to observe the tenets of belief."[54]

Various courts have considered whether Scientology and its practices are religious. In one case, decided by the United States Court of Appeals for the District of Columbia, the government had proceeded against Hubbard "E-meters" on grounds of misleading labeling.[55] The crucial question was whether claims about the physical benefits of a process using the "E-meters" were essentially spiritual or nonreligious. Since the movement's leader had developed a theory of mind similar to the ideas of some eastern religions, and ministers performed functions like those of traditional ministers, Scientology was a religion. The process of auditing with "E-meters," which was designed to enable people to work clear of "engrams" that cause mental disorder, was substantially religious; many claims on its behalf were essentially spiritual and could not be challenged on any ordinary theory of misleading labeling.

Courts divided over the character of the Church of the New Song, a sect seeking religious rights within prisons. Stating that "a succinct and comprehensive definition of [religion] . . . would appear to be a judicial impossibility," one district court held in the group's favor, noting its belief in a supreme force called Eclat, the existence of an Eclatarian bible, and claimed therapeutic value for participants.[56] Another district court dismissed the group's doctrines as political and nonreligious— doctrines that encouraged a "do-as-you-please" philosophy disruptive of discipline—and said that the services were nothing more than "gripe sessions."[57] The Court of Appeals for the Fifth Circuit responded that the district court's finding of fact had no basis.[58]

Two opinions by Judge Arlin Adams of the Third Circuit are the most careful and sophisticated about the concept of religion. In *Malnak v. Yogi*,[59] his court reviewed a challenge to a course in Creative Intelligence-Transcendental Meditation offered as an option in the New Jersey public schools. The teachers claimed that the course was nonreligious. The court disagreed, largely because students received individual mantras at a puja where the student heard teachers chant and make offerings to a deified "Guru Dev." Concurring, Judge Adams concluded that cases had established a "new definition" which could be described as one by analogy.[60] In determining the criteria from which courts should draw analogically, Judge Adams emphasized that religions concern themselves with "fundamental problems of human existence"[61] and lay claim to a "comprehensive 'truth.'"[62] A third element was the presence of formal or surface signs similar to those of accepted religions. Adams was clear that external signs need not always be present, but he seemed to suggest that the other two criteria embody necessary conditions of religion. Yet, he subsequently cautioned that the three indicia "should not be thought of as a final 'test' for religion."[63] Adams regarded the challenged course as religious, partly because its teachers were associated with an organization devoted to the Science of Creative Intelligence, whose doctrines concerned a pervasive and fundamental life force.[64]

In *Africa v. Commonwealth*[65] Judge Adams, now for a unanimous panel, employed the same basic approach to determine whether a state prisoner was entitled to a "religious" diet of raw food based on his membership in MOVE, a "'revolutionary' organization absolutely opposed to all that is wrong."[66] Africa's wish to eat raw food was related to organizational tenets about peace, nonviolence, purity, and harmony with the natural; but the court determined that MOVE lacked the structural characteristics of religion and had an ideology that was not sufficiently comprehensive and focused on fundamental questions to be religious.[67]

A modest review of possibilities reveals a number of ways in which courts might decide whether something is religious or not. For certain borderline instances of religion, different approaches will yield different conclusions. Courts have not always said how they decide what counts as religious, but they must implicitly use some approach, whether they explicate it or not.[68] Since courts generally should indicate reasons for conclusions, I assume they should explain how they determine what is religious; but even if judicial silence in the face of this complex problem is a part of wisdom,[69] courts need to have some approach to use.

In addressing possible approaches to "defining" religion, we need to remember that courts must make such decisions for a wide variety of cases. An approach that is appealing for one kind of case may not be for another. A defensible approach must cover the variety of situations.

The simplest way to define religion is according to some single factor. This feature is taken as crucial to religion, and a court inquires whether it is present.

One might define religion in terms of belief in a Supreme Being. The main objection to this approach is that it restrains the legal concept of religion artificially. If Free Exercise protections extend only to those who believe in a single Lord of the universe, traditional western religions would be strongly favored. That approach might be defended on the basis of "framers' intent," the idea that those who adopted the First and Fourteenth Amendments conceived of religion in relation to a Supreme Being. However, given familiarity with Greek and Roman religious ideas at the country's founding, the argument that religion could thus be limited to believers in a Supreme Being is implausible. The Supreme Court clearly rejected that approach for constitutional purposes in *Torcaso* v.

Watkins,[70] in *United States v. Seeger*, it interpreted the statutory reference to belief in a Supreme Being not to mean what it said.

Jesse Choper, a leading expert on the religion clauses, has urged that an appropriate constitutional test of a religious claim is belief in extra-temporal consequences.[71] He has defended this limited conception of religion on the ground that people have distinctively strong feelings about performing acts when they believe extratemporal consequences are involved: "[I]ntuition and experience affirm that the degree of internal trauma on earth for those who have put their souls in jeopardy for eternity can be expected to be markedly greater than for those who have only violated a moral scruple."[72] This passage indicates that a person who asserts a free exercise right to perform an act must, to be successful, believe that extratemporal consequences would flow from his failing to perform that particular act.

This test is very restrictive. Traditional Christians may believe use of wine for communion is highly important, without supposing damnation, or something similar, will follow if the practice is abandoned. Under Choper's test, they would have no claim to use wine during this central moment of worship services.

Reflection on the varieties of belief practicing Christians have about extratemporal consequences reveals deeper difficulties of Choper's standard. Many Christians believe that God forgives the sins of the contrite, thus removing potential extratemporal consequences for those who repent. Many suppose that sins bring definite negative consequences, such as time in purgatory, but these consequences need not be eternal. Other persons who believe in extratemporal consequences do not suppose that they follow from particular sinful acts. Some believe in divine love and an afterlife, but not in extratemporal divine punishment. Others are uncertain what happens after death, while retaining faith in the continuing power of God's love. Many Christians are deeply unsure about the precise relation of sins in this life to the nature of existence in a possible afterlife. This wide range of views among Christians who believe in some life beyond this one renders it doubtful whether persons with such faith generally suffer more torment from violating conscience than persons who think they have done a terrible wrong in the only life they have to live.

Choper's position does not provide a viable approach to a free exercise of religion. Were claimants required to believe in a tight connection between nonperformance of an act and severe extratemporal consequences, protection for religious practices would be much too narrow. Moreover, courts would have to investigate specific beliefs about life after death with great care; and the uncertainty many people feel about the precise nature of extratemporal consequences would severely complicate issues of sincerity. Under a broader construction, virtually any belief in extratemporal consequences might suffice; but then many claims might be protected that lack the underlying rationale of special psychological pain that supports Choper's proposal.

The inaptness of Choper's test for Establishment Clause cases is obvious. States cannot teach in public schools the truth of religions that do not refer to extratemporal consequences, nor may they financially support activities of prayer and worship by persons who do not believe in life after death.[73]

The idea that the central feature of a religious claim is "ultimate concern" gained currency after *United States v. Seeger*,[74] in which the Supreme Court drew from Paul Tillich's writings the suggestion that an individual's ultimate concern is his God.[75] In *Welsh v. United States*,[76] a plurality interpreted the statutory exemption requiring "religious training and belief" to cover avowedly nonreligious persons. Courts using "ultimate concern" as their standard of religion could avoid parochial and narrow understandings of religion. But ultimate concern is not sustainable as a single criterion for religiousness.[77]

As a phrase, "ultimate concern" is seriously ambiguous and vague. The standard focuses on what matters in someone's life, not just the grandness of questions answered by a system of belief; but beyond this solid ground, one faces perplexing choices. One question is whether a person's cognitive beliefs or her psychological attitudes are central. The intensity with which people care about things often does not fit their intellectual beliefs. A man believes that salvation matters more than earthly happiness and also believes that remarriage will forfeit his hope of salvation, yet he remarries. His intellectual priorities are reversed in his feelings. The plurality opinion in *Welsh* resolved an issue left open in *Seeger* and adopted a psychological approach that concentrates on what individuals really care about.

If we think abstractly about "ultimate concern," we are likely to equate absolute mandates of conscience with people's most powerful concerns, but these do not always match. People addicted to drugs may center their lives around drug use; they may be willing to do almost anything rather than be deprived of their drug. Yet their obsession does not concern their conscience. On the other hand, people suppose they have absolute duties, such as never worshiping an idol, to which they rarely give thought. The response to the example of idol worship may be that beliefs about that flow from an ultimate concern of living according to God's will. This is a reasonable construction of ultimate concern, but it has sweeping implications. For people devoted to doing God's will, any judgment about right and wrong may connect to their ultimate concern. This would include such nonabsolute judgments as "it is preferable to use wine rather than grape juice for communion unless members of the congregation who are alcoholics suffer too much." Once "ultimate concern" is opened up in this way, it no longer demarcates strong claims deserving protection from weaker ones. If someone's ultimate concern was the welfare of her children, then any honest assertion relating to their welfare, say to have a particular third-grade teacher, would become religious.

Any apparent simplicity of "ultimate concern" is dispelled further when one recognizes that many people care a great deal about a number of things—their own happiness, the welfare of their family, their country, their religion—without any clear ordering among these *and* without any single ordering principle for clashes between them.[78] Unless one says that such people lack any ultimate concerns, one must understand these concerns as amalgams of the things about which they care deeply and the ad hoc resolutions they make among them.

If "ultimate concern" were to be used as the free exercise test of religion, it should be understood as requiring a claimant to be moved by a very powerful claim of conscience.[79] Conscience, in this sense, would include a very powerful feeling that performance of an act or ritual, such as use of peyote in worship, represents the best way to act.[80] However, such an approach to religion would be misconceived; some claims should count as religious even though they do not satisfy a standard of ultimate concern or overarching conscience. Although most modern religions answer major questions about human existence and offer a comprehensive focus for people's lives, some belief systems, commonly regarded as religious, have not made such claims. Worship has been to placate the gods and enlist their help for one's own projects. People with these views should have rights to religious exercise, yet their religious activities (in the ordinary sense) would not involve ultimate concern. If the test demands a close connection between particular claims and overarching feelings of claimants, it would also unduly restrict rights of members of more traditional religions. For example, members of Protestant churches might have no religious claim to use wine during communion if they believed wine to be preferable to grape juice, but not required. Another drawback of a restrictive ultimate concern test would be the inquiry into sincerity it would require. In order to decide whether claims were religious, courts would have to assess whether people accurately described their intensity of commitment and unwillingness to compromise.

An ultimate concern standard is plainly inadequate for establishment cases. Consider again people who enlist the help of gods but do not develop ultimate concerns in response to them. Despite the absence of ultimate concern, the state could not give such a group a direct grant to carry out its activities of prayer and sacrifice, nor could it teach the group's doctrines as true in the public schools. Yet the state may promote ethical principles, such as caring for fellow human beings, that may represent the ultimate concerns of some persons. Ultimate concern is not, finally, a defensible approach for either free exercise or establishment problems.

The most plausible single-factor approach to religion is "higher reality," in some suitably broad sense. Under this approach, the essential feature of religion is faith in something beyond the mundane observable world—faith in some higher or deeper reality than exists on the surface of everyday life or can be established by scientific inquiry. The phrase "higher reality" includes both belief in a "transcendent" reality, and belief that the deepest truths are "immanent," found within oneself once layers of illusion are peeled away. Stanley Ingber, for example, refers to Emile Durkheim's view of religion as a "unified system of beliefs and practices relative to sacred things" and urges that it "is the role played by the sacred or divine that separates religions from other belief systems . . . for legal purposes."[81] Since the edges of natural and social science, and of rational philosophy, are hardly sharp, and some overarching perspectives about life make claims to scientific support that outsiders view as ill founded, the proper application of a "higher reality" approach is not always evident; but its main outlines are clear. It treats as religions the vast majority of groups, practices, and beliefs now thought of as such. It does not treat as religious the activities or groups, such as Ethical Culture, that engage in practices closely resembling those of traditional religions but do not assert a realm of meaning inaccessible to ordinary observation.[82] The exclusion of such groups is, indeed, the main difficulty with this approach. It downgrades the significance of forms of social practice that replicate those of undoubted religions.

Our survey of single-factor approaches suggests tentatively that none is acceptable. Before I turn to more promising approaches that are not restricted to single factors, I shall look briefly at two strategies to avoid or sharply limit inquiries about the boundaries of religion.

One enduring worry about courts "defining" religion is that they will inevitably favor some religious views over others. This worry is a basis for proposals that the First Amendment should always be read to forbid government action favoring (or disfavoring) particular religions or religion in general. Were strict neutrality adopted, there would be no constitutional free exercise accommodation to religious exercise;[83] indeed, there would be no permitted legislative accommodation to religious exercise.[84] The strict neutrality approach would greatly reduce the occasions when courts must decide what is religious, but it would not eliminate them. Courts would need to determine when classifications and legislative purposes fall along forbidden religious lines.

Another way courts could minimize their involvement would be to accept an individual's own determination whether a practice is religious or not. If a person honestly thought his or her claim was religious, a court would treat it as such. An individual's judgment might be completely dispositive. But protection of religious exercise should not depend on idiosyncratic views of what constitutes religion. Suppose two members of a group that uses a forbidden drug share opinions about ultimate reality and the place of drugs in human life, but because they have taken different college courses about religion, they disagree about whether their use of drugs is religious. This disagreement about the concept of religion should not entail a difference in legal protection.

A more moderate reliance on self-definition would require that some minimum objective requisites of religion be met *and* that the individual regard his claim as religious.[85] The moderate version would avoid making highly unusual opinions about religion controlling, but it suffers from the same basic problem as its more extreme sibling. The Free Exercise Clause (and relevant statutes) protect religious beliefs and practices, however hard these may be to categorize; protections should not depend on an individual's notions about the edges of the concept of religion.

Self-definition is even more obviously ill suited for establishment cases, since for these the perspectives of most outsiders are typically important. Whether a government can provide financial support to an organization, for example, should not depend exclusively on whether its members conceive of their activities as religious. Nor should classification depend only on the views of the particular persons who sue to challenge support. Rather, the opinions of others in society should count as much as those of members and challengers.

It is time to pause over what we have learned. Courts cannot avoid determining what amounts to religion in some cases. Some approaches to the substantive law of the religion clauses, most particularly the strict neutrality approach, could greatly reduce the occasions when determinations of religion would be necessary. Given the drawbacks of courts determining what is religion, such a reduction counts in favor of an approach. But the overall value of any substantive approach depends on its ability to serve the purposes of the religion clauses. Very briefly, the strict neutrality approach restricts too severely both constitutional privileges for the exercise of religion and the range of statutory accommodations to religion. It would also allow some assistance to religious groups that should be impermissible.

In light of our conclusions that single-factor approaches to religion and self-definition are too crude in their application to the range of phenomena that should count as religious for legal purposes, we should look to see if a multi-factor approach may work better. Three points of difference highlight varieties among these approaches. (1) Courts might require that each factor be present to some degree; or they might allow satisfaction of some factors to make up for a failure to satisfy others (or they might make one (or more) factor(s) necessary, while leaving others as relevant but not necessary). (2) For any important factor, courts might insist that it be satisfied to a particular degree (if it is to count at all); or they might allow strength in respect to one factor to compensate for weakness in another. (As a college might require that applicants have high school grades of at least B and test scores of at least 600, or instead evaluate applicants by grades and test scores, with high performance in one making up for weak performance in the other.) (3) Courts might say that what is religious for one purpose is religious for another; or they might say that what counts as religious should be somewhat sensitive to the legal issue involved. If what counts as religious varies somewhat, the difference might be between free exercise "religion" and establishment "religion," or differences might depend on more subtle nuances among particular legal issues.

In the approach I defend, no factor is essential, strength in some factors can make up for weakness in others, and what counts as religion may vary with legal issues but not along the lines of a simple free exercise-establishment split. In the rest of this part of the article, I defend this approach against other alternatives.

The most straightforward multifactor approach posits a number of necessary conditions which together are sufficient to constitute religion. In the case granting a tax exemption to the nontheist Fellowship of Humanity, the California Court of Appeal said that religion includes "(1) a belief, not necessarily referring to supernatural powers; (2) a cult, involving a gregarious association openly expressing the belief; (3) a system of moral practice directly resulting from an adherence to the belief; and (4) an organization within the cult designed to observe the tenets of belief."[86] The opinion implies that each standard must be satisfied. This particular specification is both underinclusive and overinclusive. An exemption should not be denied to a theistic group with otherwise traditional religious practices that takes no position on moral questions. Yet the third criterion makes such a group nonreligious. By contrast, some fraternal orders and professional associations that should not count as religious are covered by the criteria. They have some belief, gregarious association, moral practice, and organization. Of course, one court's failure to elaborate generally adequate criteria does not show that another effort will not succeed, but it should make us cautious about whether this is the right way to proceed.

The approach that Judge Adams takes in his opinions on Transcendental Meditation in public schools[87] and on whether a member of MOVE is entitled to a special prison diet[88] is more flexible. He cautiously avoids a rigid commitment to the status of his three fundamental criteria, but they clearly will have overarching importance for evaluation.[89] A court applying his approach looks to see how closely the practice at issue resembles what is undoubtedly religious; if a practice exhibits some "religion-making" characteristics with great strength, that can make up for weakness in respect to some other characteristics.

An approach that lies close to that of Judge Adams but is somewhat more open ended is to inquire how closely the practice in question resembles undoubted religious practices, without prejudging that some conditions are absolutely necessary or usually crucial. This approach assumes that religion is a highly complex concept and that all that may connect some examples of religion may be what Wittgenstein calls "family resemblance." The reason why agreement on defining religion has proved so elusive may be that any definition by "necessary and sufficient conditions" is inadequate.

A better approach to what constitutes religion is to see when the concept of religion indisputably applies, and ask how close doubtful instances are analogous to the indisputable instances. What is distinctive about this "definition by analogy" is not the reasoning by analogy. Commonly, when people apply concepts to borderline instances, they consider how closely those instances resemble instances clearly within the concept; that is, they reason by analogy. To do so, they must develop some sense of what aspects of the clear instances are relevant. "Definition by analogy" *shares* with most reasoning about the application of concepts use of analogy in light of important criteria. It does not dispense with criteria of religion, but it declines to say that any are essential. Indeed, one special feature of this approach is that it may yield applications of a concept to instances that share no common feature. If skepticism about a search for essential conditions of religion is warranted, analogical reasoning has a kind of exclusivity here that it lacks when people use it to discern the presence of necessary and sufficient conditions.

To determine the boundaries of religion, one begins with what is indisputably religious. Agreement about clear instances of religion do not require a consensus either about all the concept of religion signifies or the classification of borderline cases. No one in our society doubts that Roman Catholicism, Greek Orthodoxy, Lutheranism, Orthodox Judaism, and Islam are religions. We identify what is indisputably religious largely by reference to their beliefs, practices, and organizations. These (usually) include: a belief in God; belief in a spiritual domain that transcends everyday life; a comprehensive view of the world and human purposes; a belief in some form of afterlife; communication with God through ritual acts or worship and through corporate and individual prayer; a particular perspective on moral obligations derived from a moral code or from a conception of God's nature; practices involving repentance and forgiveness of sins; "religious" feelings of awe, guilt, and adoration; the use of sacred texts; and organization to facilitate the corporate aspects of religious practice and to promote and perpetuate beliefs and practices.[90] One could alter this list, but the critical point is that a number of elements join in religions familiar in this society.

If it were a matter of concern that beginning with religions familiar in the United States might slant conclusions undesirably, the starting point could be major world religions instead. (As more Hindus and Buddhists come to the United States, the difference between these two beginning points lessens.)

The next step is to see how closely the disputed beliefs and practices resemble the clear instances. Whether one begins with American religions or world religions, the absence of a single element does not render a group or practice nonreligious. A set of practices could be religious if participants were not theists, or if they saw no connection between transcendental reality and moral practices. No single feature is indispensable for religion, and two things might be religious without sharing any common features.[91]

Someone might resist the claim that no feature of religion is indispensable with the assertion that a deep characteristic such as "faith" or the "transcending of ordinary experience" unites all instances of religion. Were a feature cast at a high enough degree of generality and vagueness, it might unite all instances of religion, but such a feature would be too amorphous to greatly assist someone classifying beliefs and practices as religious.[92] Judges in legal cases need features specific enough to employ usefully. With this understanding, we can conclude that no feature is indispensable for religion.

Whether any feature by itself is sufficient to make a practice religious is more complicated. Many features common to religious practices and organizations are also found in nonreligious settings. Professional organizations have nonreligious rituals and ethical codes. Marxism has a comprehensive view about human existence, but is not (usually) considered religious. Ordinary nonreligious psychotherapy helps people assuage their feelings of guilt. Belief in God may always be religious, but a simple requirement that all members have that belief would not, alone, make an organization religious, nor does a starting prayer make a meeting religious. One categorizes an organization or set of practices in light of its combination of characteristics and how these compare with paradigm instances of religion.

Although no single feature makes an organization or set of practices religious, a single feature could nonetheless make a claim to perform a certain act religious. Suppose a person says honestly, "God has ordered me to refuse jury service." Assuming that her sense of "God" is not highly unusual, her claim is religious. For some kinds of assertions, a single feature, thus, could be sufficient to make them religious; but usually more is needed.

Judges could apply an analogical method in a relatively context-free or context-sensitive way. Under a context-free approach they would inquire whether a practice or organization is religious in general, independent of the specific legal controversy that has arisen. Their inquiry would be context-sensitive if they considered "definition" in light of the particular legal issue. Under that approach, what would be religious for one purpose might not be for all others. Given the wide range of issues under the religion clauses, we should not assume that the borderlines of religions will be exactly the same for every purpose. Inquiry should be sensitive to context.[93]

Some suggestions about line drawing in this regard mark a basic distinction between free exercise and establishment cases. Lawrence Tribe, for example, once proposed that everything "arguably religious" should count as religious for free exercise purposes, and everything "arguably nonreligious" should count as nonreligious for establishment purposes.[94] He supported this dual standard in terms of promoting voluntarism, which can be achieved by broad free exercise and narrow establishment concepts of religion. Yet no neat separation of free exercise from establishment issues supports his position.

The "arguably" standards are highly amorphous, and the unclear boundaries of religion make many practices arguably religious and arguably nonreligious. Not every "arguably religious" practice should be treated as religious for free exercise. Perhaps any use of psychedelic drugs is "arguably religious," but not every use should count as religious. Not every "arguably nonreligious" practice should be treated as not religious for establishment purposes. Transcendental Meditation may be arguably nonreligious, but the Third Circuit rightly concluded that it should not be taught in public schools. The standards of arguably religious and arguably nonreligious yield a crucial intermediate category that is too large for wise interpretation of the religion clauses.[95]

An illustration helps show why this approach is inapt and why any bright line distinction between free exercise and establishment issues is likely to be misguided. An arguably religious–arguably nonreligious organization sponsors arguably religious–arguably nonreligious meditation for both members of the general public and students in the public schools. Under Tribe's approach, the organization would have a free exercise right to be treated by taxing authorities like religious groups, but it could overcome the establishment argument that its school activities involve forbidden state sponsorship of religion. The organization would be more favored than explicitly religious and plainly nonreligious organizations. The free exercise issue is not different enough from the establishment issue to warrant this paradoxical result. What counts as religious should be sensitive to context; but no rigid categorization of free exercise and establishment issues makes sense.

Competing approaches to "defining" religion have different strengths and weaknesses. One way to examine these is to elaborate criteria for a sound approach and examine how well various approaches satisfy them. Six relevant criteria are comprehensiveness, correspondence to concepts of religion in ordinary language, unity of approach, fit with Supreme Court jurisprudence, ability to produce sound results, and compatibility with adequate tests of sincerity. The best approach overall might not satisfy each standard well, but satisfying a standard counts in favor of an approach. I shall not review each approach systematically against the six criteria; rather, I shall comment on how the analogical approach does, drawing occasional comparisons to its competitors.

An adequate approach has to work whenever courts must decide whether something is religious. This point is obvious, but it forces attention to two truths.[96] One is that an approach that looks good for one problem may not work for others. As we have seen, some proposals fail precisely because they do not relate well enough to a wide range of religious claims. The second, corollary, truth is that one must attend not only to issues presently resolved under the religion clauses, but also to those that arise under statutes and other constitutional provisions, such as the Equal Protection Clause.[97]

The analogical approach as I have outlined it works well for all sorts of situations. It applies smoothly to relevant constitutional provisions and related statutory protections.

Since the term "religion" is one of natural language that refers to a deep and important social phenomenon, it would be unfortunate if the law's idea of religion differed greatly from other ideas. Although legal applications of a concept may not correspond precisely with how people use the concept in other contexts, it counts in favor of an approach to legal definition of a basic constitutional concept that it ties to more general understandings. An analogical approach to defining religion fits our culture's ideas of what counts as religious better than approaches depending on necessary and sufficient conditions. It possesses the further advantage of remaining open to changing ideas of what constitutes religion.

One possible argument that a legal approach need not correspond to modern ideas about religion rests in a "framer's intent" position about constitutional interpretation. According to this argument, what the adopters of the First and Fourteenth Amendments had in mind is what counts.[98] They certainly conceived of religion mainly as theistic, though some of them understood nontheistic eastern religions at least vaguely. This article is not the place to challenge a general "framer's intent" approach to interpretation, or to examine exactly how it would apply to religion. Were this approach applied to statutes as well, what counted as religion in modern statutes would be discerned according to notions of modern legislators. The result might be that the statutory range of religion would differ significantly from religion according to constitutional law. I have adopted an assumption of virtually all modern courts and commentators: that courts have a scope for interpretation that at least encompasses changing concepts of religion.

The First Amendment proscribes any law "respecting an establishment of religion, or prohibiting the free exercise thereof." The single appearance of the word "religion" and the place of the word "thereof" strongly point toward a concept of religion that applies to both clauses. Although this implication of the language of the religion clauses might be overcome by powerful reasons to use different concepts of religion for the two clauses, a "unitary" approach is more natural. As I have explained, the analogical approach should not be unitary in the sense that whatever amounts to religion in one context automatically amounts to religion in another. But the approach is unitary in the more subtle sense that courts employ a uniform strategy to make determinations about religion. This strategy allows the sensitivity to context that has led scholars to propose different ideas of religion for free exercise and establishment cases, but without the awkwardness that a dual approach involves.

If an approach to religion is to be applicable by courts here and now, it must fit reasonably well with what the Supreme Court has said about "defining" religion and with the substantive principles the Court has employed to decide cases involving religion. The analogical approach fits well with the cases that deal with definition. It is flexible enough to correspond with a variety of substantive approaches to free exercise and establishment rights, including the changing principles the Supreme Court has used for free exercise and establishment cases during the last five decades.

When combined with appropriate substantive principles, an approach to the concept of religion should have the capacity to yield sound results when claims involving religion are made. One requisite is that an approach be workable; another is that it fit existing or desirable substantive principles.

A major challenge to a flexible analogical approach is that its application is uncertain. This is a serious worry. The worry is reduced, but not eliminated, by recognition that usually the presence of religion is not in doubt. The problems with definition arise infrequently. Nevertheless, when they do arise, courts need an approach that works.

The fundamental answer to the worry about uncertainty is that the analogical approach is not much less determinate than other plausible positions. Even apparently hard-edged standards like "extratemporal consequences" or "ultimate concern" are seriously vague in their actual application. A "higher reality" standard is still more vague. Indeed, since an analogical approach focuses partly on manifested practices and institutions, it has more solid reference points than "higher reality." Focus on a handful of crucial factors, as Judge Adams has done in his insightful opinions, reduces the vagueness of the analogical approach *somewhat*. But insisting that satisfaction of any particular factor is always required would be a mistake. Such an insistence might yield a slight gain in determinacy, but it would sacrifice the greater sensitivity to the values of the religion clauses that a more flexible approach allows.

The connection between an analogical approach and existing and desirable substantive standards of decision is a crucial inquiry. Here I settle for a few general observations. An unduly restrictive approach to threshold definition may foreclose appropriate relief; an unduly generous approach may compel legal relief that is unwarranted.[99]

If applied with relative generosity, the analogical approach will not foreclose consideration under the religion clauses and important statutes of all that should matter. The approach does not artificially restrict what counts as religion and, thus, prematurely bar examination of a legal claim.

What of the potential difficulty that designation of something as religious may propel a court to apply a doctrine derived form the religion clauses when the outcome dictated by the doctrine is inapt? The Supreme Court's treatment of Establishment Clause problems has avoided this difficulty.[100] Even when activities or organizations receiving some form of aid are identified as religious, invalidity has not followed when effects of aiding religion are remote, indirect, and slight. Thus, categorization of things as religious does not push courts to invalidate when that would be inappropriate.

The compelling interest test for free exercise claims may seem more troublesome. Although the Supreme Court no longer uses that test for many constitutional claims of free exercise, and has held invalid Congress's attempt to reintroduce that standard across the board, Congress remains free to adopt that standard for the federal government, and state legislatures have a similar latitude.[101] In other domains, the Supreme Court has said that to satisfy the compelling-interest test, the government must convincingly establish that restricting the otherwise protected activity is required to satisfy some interest of major importance. On that understanding, the government would face a very heavy burden whenever a forbidden activity was labeled religious. However, courts have hesitated to impose such a heavy burden on the government whenever a genuinely religious claim appears. So long as courts recognize that they need not employ a highly stringent compelling-interest test for free exercise claims, the analogical approach to definition does not raise any serious difficulty for it.

For a broad range of free exercise cases, a court or jury has to determine whether a claimant, or members of the claimant's group, sincerely believe the ideas that are espoused. An approach to the concept of religion must adequately fit with an appropriate test of sincerity. The analogical approach does so.

Importance or Substantial Burden

Even when people make sincere claims that government action interferes with their religious practice, an issue may arise whether they suffer a serious burden or whether the practice is important to their religion. The basic idea is that the government should not have to demonstrate a significant public need if its actions interfere only slightly with religious practice. One basis for the decision in *Employment Division v. Smith* that religious claims do not receive special consideration under the Free Exercise Clause was that courts should not be in the business of deciding what matters are central to religions. Congress responded to *Smith* with the Religious Freedom Restoration Act, which required that courts determine if there has been a "substantial burden" on the exercise of religion. The Supreme Court's invalidation of the act's coverage of state and local laws leaves that standard as possible one for federal laws, and a similar inquiry is necessary when state legislatures afford a like protection, or state courts interpret their own constitutions as more generous toward free exercise than is *Smith*.[102] An inquiry about the importance of a practice or degree of burden on religion is even more disturbing than inquiries into sincerity or religiousness, but some such assessment is needed for statutory or constitutional tests that appropriately strike a balance between public need and religious freedom.

The Supreme Court case most starkly raising this issue was *Lyng* v. *Northwest Indian Cemetery Protective Association*.[103] Native Americans argued that timber harvesting and a proposed road on federal land would interfere gravely with worship at sacred sites. The Court disposed of the claim on the ground that, since no coercion was involved, the Free Exercise clause was not violated, no matter how much religious practice would be impaired. Justice Brennan, with two other Justices, dissented. Brennan recognized that the government should not be constrained if its activities impacted only marginally on religious exercise. He suggested that claimants must make a showing of "centrality" of practices and beliefs, similar to the Amish demonstration about their objection to compulsory school in *Wisconsin v. Yoder*.[104]

Given the court's opinion in *Lyng*, and more crucially its broad abandonment in *Smith* of free exercise accommodation that is constitutionally required, "centrality" or "importance" is now only rarely (if ever) an aspect of a federal constitutional standard. In *Smith*, the Court did not challenge the line of cases from *Sherbert v. Verner*;[105] under which people unwilling to work on Saturday for religious reasons are entitled to unemployment compensation, which would otherwise be given only to those who are available for Saturday work. A case under *Sherbert* might arise when someone refused Saturday work for reasons in which religion figured tangentially: "My faith tells me family time is important and Saturday is an opportunity to be with my children." A Court might have to decide how substantial was the interference with religious exercise. (The same basic issue could be differently formulated as whether the claim to spend time with children is "really" religious, in which event the issue would become one concerning the borderlines of what counts as religious.)

Despite the Supreme Court's invalidation of most, or all, of the Religious Freedom Restoration Act, it is worth asking whether a "substantial burden" test is essentially the same test as a requirement of "centrality" or "importance" of a belief or practice. A person's exercise of religion overall is not substantially burdened if interference is only with a trivial aspect of his religion (as he understands it); for that situation, the two standards have the same application. Similarly, if a central practice is forbidden, that would constitute a substantial burden. But one could have a "substantial burden" if a frustrated practice is "moderately significant" but not "central." And a slight impairment of a central practice could impose a burden that is less than substantial. For example, for members of a particular church communion might be central and hymn singing less than central. But a ban on all singing might constitute a substantial burden, whereas a ban on the use of wine in communion might not, if the members regarded grape juice as nearly as effective. Focus on the importance of an affected practice is not exactly the same as focus on a substantial burden, but one should not slice these distinctions too finely. In *Lyng*, Justice Brennan said at one point that those challenging a proposed use of federal land should have to show that the use "poses a substantial and realistic threat of frustrating their religious practice."[106] This inquiry sounds like one about substantial burden. Moreover, a number of courts applying the "substantial burden" language of the federal act have considered it critical whether interference is with central tenets or practices. For example, Chief Judge Posner, whose court was reviewing a claim by Muslim prisoners to have conditions suitable for observance of Ramadan, has written, "We hold . . . that a substantial burden . . . is one that forces adherents of a religion to refrain from religiously motivated conduct, inhibits or constrains conduct or expression that manifests a central tenet of a person's religious beliefs, or compels conduct or expression that is contrary to these beliefs."[107] Whatever the exact phraseology, a test of "substantial burden" calls for investigating of the importance of what is burdened and the extent to which that is burdened.[108]

How can the substantiality of a burden to religious practice possibly be determined?[109] We can start with the basic premise that civil courts cannot decide what is really important religiously. It cannot tell Roman Catholics that, after all, grape juice is just fine for communion. Second, in line with the general treatment of controversies involving disputes over requirements of religious traditions, courts cannot decide that according to some correct understanding of a religious tradition, interference with one practice is important and interference with another is not.

When they have decided cases under the Religious Freedom Restoration Act, federal courts have struggled with the question of substantial burden. Although abstract formulations may have varied more than results of cases, such formulations help direct judicial inquiries. The two vital aspects of any formulation are whose perspective is to count and how stringent is the legal test to be. Courts sometimes seem to suppose that focus on "the religion", as contrasted with focus on the individual's perspective, goes naturally with a stringent standard—what does the religion require?—but that need not be the case.[110] If the claim is one to wear religious jewelry, a court might ask whether that is regarded by the religion as one appropriate form of devotion. For status as a conscientious objector, the focus of perspective is on the individual, but the test is stringent—does he feel religiously compelled not to participate in war? Perspective and stringency are separate issues, and there is no obvious linkage of one perspective with any particular degree of stringency.

In principle, the appropriate perspective to adopt is usually that of individual claimants. How do they understand their own religious beliefs and practices? The individuals are the ones seeking to act in certain ways, for example, to wear crosses or to have a special diet. One aspect of a focus on the individual's perspective is recognition that doctrinal belief figures more importantly for some people than others. For some religious persons, liturgies and other practices loom larger then propositional beliefs.

Can it be objected that focusing on individuals somehow favors more Protestant views of religion over those in which corporate institutions are more dominant? I do not believe so. If someone belongs to a religious group in which members have closely similar understandings that follow those of a powerful leadership, the free exercise rights of all members will depend on these shared understandings. The law is not taking a stand for or against hierarchical authority. Even were it true that focusing on individual claimants has some slight effect of encouraging individuality in religion, the law has little choice. Free exercise rights are mainly individual; legal rules should not insist that members see things according to prevailing views within a denomination.

Existing law strongly supports a focus on individual perspectives. That is the undoubted lesson of Supreme Court cases on conscientious objection[111] and unemployment compensation. In *Thomas v. Review Bd.*,[112] a Jehovah's Witness said he could not engage in the production of materials to make arms; the Supreme Court held that as long as his views were sincere, it did not matter whether other Witnesses agreed, or even whether Thomas's views were comprehensible. When individuals seek to vindicate free exercise rights, the focus should be on their beliefs, feelings, and practices.

This conclusion requires modest qualification. Suppose claimants ask for an action that would be reasonable only if it affects a larger group. For example, one would not expect the government to forgo road building or logging over a large area if one individual regarded the area as a sacred site and honestly claimed that his worship would be severely disturbed. The claim in *Lyng*[113] was appealing because it represented the religious sentiments of a large number of Native Americans. In cases of this sort, a court must investigate the views of a larger group, though such a group need not necessarily be the authoritative representative of a tradition.

A similarly broad inquiry is necessary for most Establishment Clause issues that depend on perceptions. If, for example, a court asks if the government has endorsed a religion, the perceptions that count are not those of particular individuals. As the endorsement test has developed, Justice O'Connor has emphasized that the test involves a reasonable observer, not any actual persons.[114] But judges who ask how a reasonable (informed) observer would react must have some sense of how most actual people would react if they were suitably informed.

The following argument might be made for a test that focuses on religious entities rather than individuals. "Whatever may be true about boards passing on conscientious objectors, most administrators have neither the talent nor time to scrutinize individual religious sentiments. The best they can do is to apply conclusions about the prevailing views among groups." This argument has some force, but not enough to override the powerful reasons against official versions of various religious faiths and in favor of focus on the individual. Perhaps a regard for standard doctrines or practices may help officials understand individual claims or test their sincerity, but the claimants' own perceptions should usually be the final determinant.

How stringent should the requirement of a substantial burden be? In this context, I take a more stringent requirement as one that is more difficult for the claimant to satisfy. We can mark out three rough possibilities. Courts might demand that a claimant feel that a legally forbidden act is religiously compelled or that a legally required act is religiously forbidden. I shall call that a standard of absolute conflict. Courts might find that any act (or refusal to act) motivated by a sincere religious conviction satisfies a substantial burden test. I shall call that a sincere motivation standard. Courts might use some intermediate test; such a test might or might not refer to centrality of belief or practice. Finally, courts might adopt somewhat variant standards depending on the sort of claim involved.

Chief Judge Posner's language in *Mack v. O'Leary* reads as if it is a combination test of this sort. He says, to repeat, that a substantial burden "forces adherents to refrain from religiously motivated conduct, inhibits or constrains conduct or expression that manifests a central tenet of a person's religious beliefs, or compels conduct or expression that is contrary to those beliefs."[115] The language does not demand "centrality" if adherents are forced to refrain from religiously motivated conduct (or compelled to engage in conduct that offends religious convictions).[116] Whatever the exact distinction that is drawn, saying that a more important practice or belief has to be involved if behavior is only discouraged rather than forbidden outright makes sense.[117]

Apart from possible difficulties of administration, some intermediate approach is preferable to each of the other major alternatives. Although a few courts of appeals spoke as if an absolute conflict was necessary to establish a substantial burden,[118] that approach was unfaithful to the Religious Freedom Restoration Act and would be unfaithful to similar future laws. The two major supreme Court cases sustaining claims of free exercise are *Sherbert v. Verner* and *Wisconsin v. Yoder*. *Sherbert* clearly did not involve an absolute conflict; Mrs. Sherbert's refusal to work on Saturday entailed (only) losing unemployment compensation. Even in *Yoder*, it was doubtful whether the Amish involved felt compelled to remove children from ordinary school after the eighth grade.[119] In its actual language and in its endorsement of the approach of those cases, the Religious Freedom Restoration Act was more generous to claimants than a requirement of absolute conflict.[120] For states that similarly seek to protect free exercise, a requirement of absolute conflict would be too strict.

The difficulty with a simple religious motivation standard is that it protects too much. Not every interference with a sincere religious motivation constitutes a substantial burden.[121]

Someone might argue that a sincere motivation approach will work fine because no one will sue over peripheral religious concerns. One difficulty with this argument is that people care a great deal about some matters, such as spending time with family on Saturday, even when they think the religious implications of the behavior are minor. A second difficulty is that executive officials, not courts, are often the first recipients of claims of free exercise. Were it once established that every sincere religious motivation was sufficient, that is the standard that would guide careful administrators. Perhaps few people will bother to litigate when they do not care very much; many more will be ready to make requests or demands of prison authorities or other officials.

We could expect some offsetting developments if sincere religious motivation became the basic standard of substantial burden. When the religious component of a claimant's motivation was not too important, as perhaps in the family time illustration, a court would be likely to say the motivation was nonreligious. Courts would also be likely to say that certain categories of claims do not qualify as concerning the free exercise of religion. Failing to discover coercion, the Court in *Lyng* took this approach, despite the possibility that the effect of the government's activities on the exercise of religion might be devastating. Finally, courts would be likely to decide that government interests were compelling when they judged the religious claims to be trivial. Although "substantial burden" and "compelling interest" (with its component of least restrictive means) stand as separate, successive, inquiries, in reality courts tend to decide whether the government has a strong enough reason to engage in a particular interference with religion. When a judge regards a "substantial burden" as slight, he will treat a less than compelling interest as compelling.

What is called for is an intermediate test, something less demanding than absolute conflict and more demanding than sincere motivation alone. The only reasonable ground for preferring something other than an intermediate approach is doubt that judges are capable of formulating a standard that can allow sensitivity to individual perspectives and nonarbitrary decision of cases. The underlying problem for courts is to try to develop such a standard, or at least to develop a standard that does reasonably well in light of these two objectives.

A crucial question about any intermediate standard is whether it should include a requirement concerning a central belief or practice. If "centrality" is taken seriously and limited to a handful of beliefs and practices, and if there must be a tight connection between what is central and the behavior in the claimant seeks to engage, the requirement would be too strict. A prisoner might not regard wearing a cross to be central practice or to follow closely from a central belief, and yet he could regard wearing the cross as an important symbol of witness and commitment, and a great aid to devotion. Such a person should definitely get over the "substantial burden" threshold. If central aspects of the religion were understood expansively *or* the connection between the behavior at issue and what is central were weakened, the centrality test might preclude few claims. For example, wearing a cross, or indeed the abstract fish design associated with Christian belief, represents something central about Christian beliefs. That representation would exist for someone who attaches only slight religious significance to wearing religious jewelry. (One thinks here of Christians who have earrings of various designs and occasionally choose to wear ones with Christian design.) If such a person were forbidden to wear jewelry, that would not constitute a substantial burden on his religious exercise. Perhaps in some inexact way, centrality of practice or belief helps courts to be realistic about magnitude, but I am inclined to think that the assistance is more illusive than actual.

A cleaner, more coherent approach would be to rely more exclusively on the language of "substantial burden," recognizing that other, more complicated, formulations do not aid very much in resolving the crucial question about the weight of interference. The magnitude of interference depends on the importance of a practice and the extent to which it is constrained. Once judges reasonably understand someone's religious belief and practices, they will be able to identify some interferences as very great and others as trivial. The difficulties arise "in between." Any vague standard of magnitude is troublesome to apply, as Justice Scalia has been at pains to emphasize.[122] Inconsistent treatments are a serious risk, a risk that is heightened because judges may not understand the religious lives they evaluate.[123] Yet a standard with this drawback is preferable to one that fails to do justice to what is at stake.[124]

Chief Judge Posner's opinion in *Mack v. O'Leary* suggests, interestingly, that courts can better administer a test that asks about religious motivation and centrality of religious belief than they can determine absolute conflicts.[125] His point is that courts cannot easily determine whether, according to the religion to which the claimant belongs, a direct conflict is created; further such determinations are inappropriate. I do not think we can reach any such straightforward conclusion about comparative administrability, once we focus on the individual. In cases where it is reasonably arguable that a direct conflict may exist, some intermediate standard will be easier to apply, because it will almost certainly be satisfied. For less pressing claims, an intermediate standard will be less certain, because a claimant would lose under a direct conflict requirement. Judge Posner's remarks about the relative administrability of an intermediate standard give only modest reassurance. Nevertheless, a somewhat amorphous intermediate standard is preferable to any of the possible alternatives: no protection (the Supreme Court's present Free Exercise approach), absolute conflict, or sincere religious motivation.

The principle that courts should adopt the claimants' perspectives and use a standard that measures magnitude of burden needs to be understood in a fairly precise way. A court (or jury) may say that a claim is not sincere. It might conceivably conclude that a claimant honestly asserts that the state is interfering with a religious practice, but is not sincere about the importance of a practice or the magnitude of the burden on it. (However, anyone would be hard put to make such a refined judgment about sincerity without impermissibly invoking his own view of comparative importance.)

Ultimate categorization is the court's responsibility. A court must accept sincere claims about the structure of religious practices, attachments to aspects of religious exercise, and feelings about impairments. Courts cannot say that wine does not really matter for communion if Catholics sincerely assert that wine matters a great deal. But the final labeling of a burden as substantial is for judges. A conclusory allegation on this score is not dispositive. Suppose, for example, a minister representing a congregation in the United Church of Christ said, "We decide whether to use wine or grape juice by a congregational vote. Either substance is acceptable for the fundamental purpose of commemorating the last supper and Christ's life and death, but various people think that one or the other substance is preferable. We recently decided to use wine by a vote of 100–93. Therefore, using wine is important, even central to us, and any interference substantially burdens our religious exercise." If it became relevant whether an interference with use of wine for this church constituted a substantial burden, a court might decide that the minister's comments indicate the burden is less than substantial, despite her own contrary conclusory label (which may have been responsive to some lawyer's encouragement). Courts must accept the account of religious understanding that claimants provide, but they themselves must determine what interferences satisfy the prevailing legal standard.[126]

It is worth pausing finally to ask whether difficult judgments about substantial burden could be avoided. One constitutional argument against the Religious Freedom Restoration Act, not (yet) relied upon by the Supreme Court, has been that these judgments are *so difficult* that courts cannot be required to make them consistent with the Establishment Clause and with separation of powers.[127] I shall briefly consider three strategies of avoidance. One such strategy, of course, is for courts to provide no free exercise rights against the application of general, valid, statutes—the approach of *Employment Division v. Smith*—and for legislatures to limit their grants of free exercise rights to very specific terms. If, for example, a state legislature provides that members of particular Native American religious groups can use peyote during worship services, courts need not determine how greatly a prohibition of the use of peyote burdens those religions. The problem with such an approach is that it allows too great a frustration of religious liberty.

A second possible way to avoid difficult judgments about substantial burden is to categorize in terms of different kinds of government acts, as the majority of the Court did in *Lyng* and in the earlier case of *Bowen v. Roy*.[128] In *Bowen v. Roy*, the Court refused to entertain a religious complaint about the government's internal use of social security numbers; in *Lyng* it said that since development of government lands did not coerce anyone to forgo religious practices, there was no prohibition under the Free Exercise Clause.[129] This strategy, standing alone, has two serious drawbacks. The first is that if religious practice suffers as much as was claimed in *Lyng*, those affected should obtain relief. Unless the government acts that were held not to raise free exercise issues were very narrowly defined, deserving claimants would lose. The second drawback is that this strategy could hardly solve the entire problem of determining importance. Among the government acts that would be of the kind to generate free exercise claims, some would have effects too slight to require the government to show a compelling interest.

A third strategy would be to determine the importance of a practice in light of general characteristics of religious believers and religious institutions.[130] Thus, for example, a burden on corporate worship would be more substantial than a burden on providing social services to nonmembers. Courts would be required to make some judgments under this approach, but the judgments would be about general categories and their applications, not about importance to particular claimants. In reducing difficulty of assessment and in curbing judicial discretion, this approach has something to recommend it; but it is much too insensitive to the needs of particular groups and individuals. For example, the Salvation Army and its members should not be treated like a typical church if they say that serving the poor is the center of their mission. Further, this "sociological approach" to importance reinforces to some degree the outlook of dominant religions. Perhaps in otherwise doubtful cases courts appropriately look to religious practices in general, but these should not be an exclusive guide to the degree of burden.

Although I have suggested that categorization of kinds of government acts cannot eliminate delicate judgments about substantial burdens, some specific inquiries can help courts resolve cases. Ira Lupu has suggested that courts inquire whether an action by a private party similar to what the government has done would violate a common law right.[131] Michael Dorf has proposed that courts consider what alternatives may be available to religious claimants and whether they suffer more from a challenged regulation than others who are affected.[132] All these inquiries can assist courts, but neither singly nor in combination should they eliminate all matters of judgment about degree of burden.

I should enter a final caveat here. Because of the subject matter of the article, I have talked only in passing about the government's interest in restriction, and more particularly the compelling interest test, with its least-restrictive-means component, or some alternative formulation.[133] As I have mentioned, realism counsels that substantiality of burden and strength of government interest are not viewed in isolation, that one is assessed with an eye toward the other. To be more precise, a burden is likely to be judged less substantial if the government's reason to restrict is seen as strong.

Conclusion

We have reviewed five questions about religion courts prefer not to ask: truth, faithfulness, sincerity, definition, substantial burden (and importance). For courts to address each of these questions is troubling, given values that lie behind the religion clauses. Civil courts should assiduously avoid assessments of religious truth, and with few exceptions, they should refrain from passing on faithfulness. This is, indeed, what constitutional law now provides.

For some domains, such as mail fraud, courts may also escape assessing sincerity about religious claims; but if religious exercise is to receive special protection under federal or state constitutions and statutes, some inquiry about sincerity is unavoidable. Even when a nonreligious grounding for a claim *would* suffice, officials or juries may have to determine the honesty of religious claims when these are presented. (One may be a conscientious objector without belief in God, but if a claimant says he thinks God forbids fighting and there is powerful evidence he has no such belief, an exemption may be denied.) The inquiry about sincerity will not always be whether the individual claimant *probably* believes in the religious need to act as he wishes, but some test of sincerity is typically needed.

Deciding whether a practice, belief, claim, or purpose is religious is necessary when the status of something as religious or not matters. Usually the inquiry is simple, but difficult borderline cases arise. The most fruitful approach to "definition" is decision by analogy to the indisputably religious.

When some inhibition of religious practice is shown for free exercise claims, courts may need to assess whether the burden is substantial and the practice is important. In this regard, courts must accept honest representations of religious understandings. Sometimes the understandings will be those of individual claimants; sometimes the understandings of most of a group's members will control. In any event, the final assessment of importance or degree of burden remains the court's.

Notes

1. This paradox may lead us to empathize with the plight of a prominent scholar who proposed some years ago that the government must make special accommodations to exercises of religion. He went on to say that judicial evaluation of the sincerity of claims of religious conscience could itself interfere with the free exercise of religion and, further, that even for courts to "define" religion was constitutionally inappropriate, because that would be likely to favor traditional faiths over novel forms of religion and would inject the state into making religious judgments. Despite the attraction of each of these positions standing alone, in combination they are incoherent. Milton Konvitz, *Religious Liberty and Conscience: A Constitutional Inquiry* (New York: Viking Press, 1968), reviewed in K. Greenawalt, 70 *Columbia Law Review* 1133 (1970).

2. According to standard modern constitutional doctrine, the first section of the Fourteenth Amendment, and in particular the rule that no state shall "deprive any person of life, liberty, or property without due process of law," makes most of the Bill of Rights applicable against the states. Many scholars, including myself, have thought that other language—"No state shall make or enforce any law which shall abridge the privilege or immunities of citizens of the United States"—is at least as relevant, though early decisions virtually read this clause out of existence.

3. If focus is on the privileges and immunities clause, a similar difficulty arises as to how anyone's privileges or immunities are violated.

4. *School Dist. of Abington Township v Schempp*, 374 U.S. 203, 230 (1963) (Brennan, J., concurring).

5. This is a complicated point. One crucial aspect of the inquiry (if one casts it in terms of framers' intent rather than how a reasonable reader would take the language) is what was intended for the territories that were fully under the control of the federal government. If the Establishment Clause was exclusively about states' rights, it would have constituted no bar to established religion within federal territories.

6. I do not discuss general arguments against incorporation of the Bill of Rights. I address only arguments that suggest specific difficulties about incorporating the Establishment Clause that do not apply to the Free Exercise and Free Speech clauses or, for example, the privilege against self-incrimination.

7. See generally Linda S. Wendtland, "Note, Beyond the Establishment Clause: Enforcing Separation of Church and State through State Constitutional Provisions," 71 *Virginia Law Review* 625 (1995); G. Alan Tarr, "Church and State in the States," 64 *Washington Law Review* 73 (1989).

8. See *Lee v Weisman*, 506 U.S. 577, 609 (1992) (Souter, J., concurring).

9. The incompatibility problem may arise at another level. Some religious practices are so idiosyncratic that they must be bad if most religious practices are good; thus, one cannot recommend practicing religion without qualification. Nevertheless, government officials might deem the harmful religious practices to be rare, and might also recognize that officials should not be in the business of determining what practices are harmful (absent direct physical injury or risk to individuals). Thus, officials might recommend the practice of religion in general, accepting the consequence that they will provide some encouragement for a small number of bad religious practices.

10. John H. Mansfield, "The Religion Clauses of the First Amendment and the Philosophy of the Constitution," 72 *California Law Review* 847 (1984).

11. I will briefly mention an ingenious way to try to avoid these conclusions. Suppose we start from the premise that government action should never be based on anyone's religious convictions, that those formulating laws and policies should put their religious views and the religious views of constituents wholly to one side. Were this exercise successful, one could say that desegregation is what seems right if one puts religion aside, but it reflects no view about whether correct religious principles call for total separation of the races. Therefore, it should not influence people's religious views on racial segregation (even if it has some slight psychological effect of that sort).

The problem with this ingenious division of labor between state business and true religion is not hard to find. No society is going to institute state practices that most of its citizens regard as gravely contrary to God's will for human beings. If people are fervent racial separationists about the organization of society in their religious convictions, they will not blithely adopt desegregation measures while they "put religion aside." The division of religion and policy will never come close to being as absolute as this model proposes. Therefore, when the government strongly adopts policies, it does implicitly accept the view that religious beliefs that call for radically opposed policies are untrue to that extent.

12. A group may "stick to its guns" and suffer declining membership or shift

its doctrines over time. Of course, if the government action is highly unpopular, it may strengthen groups with opposed doctrines. A very controversial war may draw people to "peace" churches and churches with strong just war traditions.

13. See Kent Greenawalt, "'Hands Off'!: Religious Property and Civil Courts," 98 *Columbia Law Review* 1843 (1998).

14. 322 U.S. 78 (1944).

15. By the time the Supreme Court decided the case, Guy had died.

16. 322 U.S. at 81 (1944).

17. I pass over the further complexity that if Edna Ballard believed that Guy Ballard had the experience Guy insincerely claimed, Edna would not be guilty of fraud although Guy had lied and the spiritual event had not occurred.

18. People frequently do believe that claims of spiritual events are sincerely made by others but are nonetheless false.

19. A further difficulty of this approach as applied to the *Ballard* case is that it does not cover all of the claims involved. The Ballards might successfully have cured some people of illness even though they did not believe that they had done so, attributing apparent successes to confusion and deception. As to such matters, falsity would need to be independently established.

20. Ibid. at 83–84. If one were to distinguish religious concepts and beliefs from other claims, it is arguable on which side the "experience" and "phonograph record" claims should fall.

21. Ibid. at 86–87.

22. The Court did not pass on other grounds for reversal that the Ballards had asserted, rather remanding the case to the Court of Appeals to deal with those.

23. 322 U.S. at 91.

24. Ibid. at 92–93.

25. Ibid. at 93.

26. Ibid. at 95.

27. In an illuminating paper, Paul Horwitz, "Scientology in Court: A Comparative Analysis and Some Thoughts on Selected Issues in Law and Religion" (forthcoming), argues for a very limited range of prosecutions for religious fraud when individuals fraudulently invent and benefit from a religion (or insincerely deviate from church doctrine to their benefit) and their insincerity is evidenced by their own admissions, the commission of secular fraud, or activity attempting to cover up fraud.

28. The standards and procedures for claiming conscientious objector status are in 32 CFR 75.1–75.11. When military personnel claim they are conscientious objectors, initial hearings and evaluations are made by officers not in the chain of command of the applicants. Final decision is by the headquarters of the military service concerned. 32 CFR 75.6. Although administrative discharge is discretionary, and conscientious objectors are not provided an absolute right to discharge (or relief from combat duty, if one is willing to serve as a noncombatant), the relevant provision indicates that relief should ordinarily be given. 32 CFR 75.3.

29. For example, were there a draft, young men (and young women, if they were subject to the draft) might choose between two years of military service

and three years of alternative civilian service at lower pay. See K. Greenawalt, *Conflicts of Law and Morality* (New York: Clarendon Press, 1987), 327–28. See "German Military Today: Job Grows, More Say No," *New York Times*, July 5, 1996, p. A10, on how such a system works in Germany.

30. 50 U.S.C. App. 460(b)(3).

31. See *United States v Owen*, 415 F.2d 383, 389 (8th Cir. 1969); K. Greenawalt, "All or Nothing at All: The Defeat of Selective Conscientious Objection," 1971 *Supreme Court Review* 31, 45–46 (1972).

32. See *Wisconsin v Yoder*, 406 U.S. 25 (1972).

33. The situation would be different in a community in which the Amish were divided on this issue and many Amish children attended ordinary school beyond the age in question.

34. Membership in a pacifist group is not enough alone to qualify as a conscientious objector; one needs to have the pacifist beliefs oneself.

35. 107 Stat. 144 (codified principally at 42 U.S.C. 2000bb (Supp. V 1993)). In June, 1997, the Supreme Court declared the act invalid, at least as it applies to state and local laws. *City of Boerne v Flores*, 117 S.Ct. 2157 (1997).

36. In some instances that definitely involve a religious group, the question will be whether a particular practice or claim counts as religious. If a religious organization sold food and claimed (falsely) that it contained specific vitamins, that claim would not be religious. In *Founding Church of Scientology v United States*, 409 F.2d 1146 (D.C. 1964), the court held that claims by The Church of Scientology about the health benefits of using E-meters are religious.

37. Even if a classification itself were not regarded as religious, some impermissible religious objective might underlie it.

38. Some people believe that religious discrimination in the private sector should not be illegal, as it is under civil rights statutes. Most of these critics object to interference with private employment choices; they do not claim that for nonreligious organizations religious discrimination is more proper than other kinds of discrimination that are made illegal.

39. 494 U.S. 872 (1990).

40. 117 S.Ct. 2157 (1997).

41. In *Flores*, the Court seems to speak as if the Religious Freedom Restoration Act is invalid as it applies to federal statutes; but its reasoning reaches only state and local laws. (I am unable to tell whether the Court assumes that it is holding the act invalid in toto, including its federal applications. See Greenawalt, "Why Now Is Not the Time for Constitutional Amendment: The Limited Reach of *City of Boerne v. Flores*," 39 *William and Mary Law Review* 689 (1998). My equivocations in this chapter reflect this uncertainty.) Given what the Court has said thus far, Congress may enact a statute like RFRA that applies only to the federal government, state legislatures may adopt similar laws for their own states, and state courts may establish such free exercise privileges under their state constitutions There are challenges to laws like RFRA that would bar such laws, but these challenges have not been embraced by courts. Thus, there still remains considerable room for broad religious exemptions.

42. If individual claims counted as religious only when individual claimants reflected the dominant view in their group, the definitional problem would arise

more frequently. The Supreme Court rightly dismissed such an approach in *Thomas v Review Bd.*, 450 U.S. 707 (1981), a case in which the state supreme court had called Thomas's objection to working on tank turrets "nonreligious," apparently because the objection was idiosyncratic and uncertain.

43. *Davis v Beason*, 133 U.S. 333, 342 (1890).

44. *United States v McIntosh*, 283 U.S. 605, 633–34 (1931).

45. 367 U.S. 488 (1961).

46. *Thomas v Review Bd.*, 450 U.S. 707 (1981).

47. Congress had adopted this definition after a dispute among the courts of appeals over how broadly religion should be understood.

48. *United States v Seeger*, 380 U.S. 163 (1965).

49. 398 U.S. 333 (1970).

50. Ibid. at 344–67.

51. *Washington Ethical Soc'y v District of Columbia*, 249 F.2d 127 (D.C. Cir. 1957).

52. *Fellowship of Humanity v County of Alameda*, 153 Cal. App. 2d. 673, 315 P.2d 394 (1957).

53. 153 Cal. App. 2d, at 691–92, 315 P.2d at 405–06.

54. Id. at 693, 315 P.2d at 406.

55. *Founding Church of Scientology v United States*, 409 F.2d 1146 (D.C. 1964). Subsequently, however, the district court determined that some claims made were scientific and could be distinguished from religious propositions. It restricted assertions that could be made on behalf of E-meters in order to ensure that their use was only in religious counseling. *United States v Article or Device*, 333 F.Supp. 357 (D.D.C. 1971).

56. *Remmers v Brewer*, 361 F.Supp. 537, 540 (S.D. Iowa 1973).

57. *Theriault v Silber*, 391 F.Supp. 578, 582 (W.D. Tex. 1975).

58. 547 F.2d 1279 (5th Cir. 1977).

59. 592 F.2d 197 (3d Cir. 1979).

60. Id. at 207 (Adams, J., concurring). In a case sustaining a claimed exemption from payroll taxes for the Church of Scientology, the opinions of the High Court of Australia discussed the American cases and Judge Adams's *Malnak* opinion at some length. *Church of the New Faith v Commissioner of Pay-roll Tax*, (Vict.) 154 *CLR* 120 (1983). Justice Murphy wrote, "There is no single acceptable criterion, no essence of religion," and the opinion of Justices Wilson and Deane also evidenced sympathy with the analogical approach. Justices Mason and Brennan proposed a twofold standard of religion for legal purposes: belief in something supernatural and acceptance of canons of conduct to give effect to that belief. Their assumption is that any religion must display both characteristics, though the degree of emphasis might vary.

61. 592 F.2d at 208.

62. Id. at 209.

63. Id. at 210.

64. Id. at 213–14. The organization possessed only some of the surface aspects of traditional religious groups.

65. 662 F.2d 1025 (3d Cir. 1981).

66. Id. at 1026.

67. The opinion bears the signs of some agonizing, for it concedes that whether MOVE deals with ultimate ideas is "not wholly free from doubt." Id. at 1033, and that the conclusion about comprehensiveness "is not unassailable." Id. at 1035. Furthermore, the court acknowledges that other members of MOVE might be able to establish free exercise rights. Id. at 1036 n. 22, and it strongly intimates that prison officials should exercise their discretion to give Africa his diet of raw food. Id. at 1037.

68. A court might (implicitly at least) decide that something would be religious under any plausible approach, and thereby avoid determining which of the plausible approaches is most sound. The court could explain that this is what it is doing, or simply reach the conclusion without outlining the plausible approaches.

69. One might think that most judges would have a good sense of what is religious and what is not but would become tangled in any attempt at explanation.

70. 367 U.S. 488, 495 (1961).

71. Jesse H. Choper, "Defining 'Religion' in the First Amendment," 1982 *University of Illinois Law Review* 579. More recently, Dean Choper has maintained his position against criticisms, including my own. Jesse H. Choper, *Securing Religious Liberty: Principles for Judicial Interpretation of the Religion Clauses* (Chicago: University of Chicago Press, 1995), 77. Paul Horwitz gives a broad reading of Choper's standard in "The Sources and Limits of Freedom of Religion in a Liberal Democracy: Section 2(a) and Beyond," 54 *University of Toronto Faculty of Law Review* 1, 11 (1996).

72. 1982 *University of Illinois Law Review* at 598.

73. Choper is able to employ his approach for establishment cases only by giving a very broad reading of the free speech clause. See Choper, "Defining 'Religion,' " at 610–12.

74. 380 U.S. 163, 187 (1965).

75. Id. at 187.

76. 398 U.S. 333 (1970).

77. "Ultimate concern" receives careful articulation and a spirited defense in "Note, Toward a Constitutional Definition of Religion," 91 *Harvard Law Review* 1056 (1978), written by John Sexton, now dean of the New York University Law School. In Greenawalt, "Religion as a Concept in Constitutional Law," 72 *California Law Review* 753, 806–811 (1984), my discussion of ultimate concern focuses on that Note.

78. Most people with traditional religious beliefs accept intellectually that religious concerns are ultimate, but their feelings and behavior often do not accord with that premise.

79. Such an understanding falls very close to a proposal that religious claims not be favored over nonreligious ones, that equally powerful feelings of conscience be treated equally whether or not they arise from traditionally religious sources. One doctrinal approach that embodies such a principle is to treat the free exercise clause as providing protection to claims of conscience. This principle has been powerfully defended by David Richards, *Toleration and the Constitution* (New York: Oxford University Press, 1986), 103–31, and Laura Underkuffler-Freund, "The Separation of the Religious and the Secular: A

Foundational Challenge to First Amendment Theory," *William and Mary Law Review* 837 (1995). Under this approach, decision whether a claim is sufficiently conscientious functions as a kind of definition of religion for free exercise purposes.

An alternative doctrinal approach that can yield similar results is to say that the Free Exercise Clause protects some claims based on religion, more narrowly defined, and allows some legislative accommodation to religion, more narrowly defined; but then, when constitutional or legislative protection obtains, an independent principle of equal categorization (drawn from the Establishment Clause, the Equal Protection Clause, the Free Speech Clause, the Free Exercise Clause, or some combination) may require equal treatment of analogous nonreligious claims, as Justice Harlan suggested in *Welsh*. I prefer this latter alternative; it fits the text of the religion clauses better and allows a more nuanced appraisal of whether grounds that rest on religion, in some ordinary sense, may be treated differently from other claims of conscience. I discuss this problem at greater length in "Diverse Perspectives and the Religion Clauses: An Examination of Justifications and Qualifying Beliefs," 74 *Notre Dame Law Review* (1999).

80. That is, one would not *necessarily* need to think one was committing a moral wrong if one refrained from the act.

81. Ingber, "Religion or Ideology: A Needed Clarification of the Religion Clauses," 41 *Stanford Law Review* 233, 285 (1989). Ingber's discussion, especially at 286 n. 326, makes clear that he sees his proposal as one specification of what I term a "higher reality" approach. Paul Horwitz suggests a criterion of "a belief that is spiritual, supernatural or transcendent in nature." Horwitz, "Sources and Limits," at 10. (Horwitz has two other criteria, but these concern what he regards as necessary for a claim in Canada to fall under the constitutional guarantee of freedom of religion; they are not requisites of religion itself.)

82. Ingber, "Religion or Ideology," at 286 n. 326, is explicit that he so understands his proposed standard. Criticizing my a priori assumption of the accuracy of decisions such as that awarding the Ethical Society a tax exemption available to churches or religious societies, he says his "position is that these cases were decided wrongly."

83. However, one might combine a constitutional principle that religion must or may receive an accommodation with a constitutional principle that all otherwise similar nonreligious claims must be treated similarly.

84. If legislative accommodation is allowed but not required, courts infrequently have to decide what is religious for constitutional free exercise purposes. This is the present posture of federal constitutional law under *Employment Division v Smith*, 494 U.S. 872 (1990).

85. See Gail Merel, "The Protection of Individual Choice: A Consistent Understanding of Religion Under the First Amendment," 45 University of Chicago Law Review 805 (1978).

86. *Fellowship of Humanity v County of Alameda*, 153 Cal. App. 2d 673, 693, 315 P.2d 394, 406.

87. 592 F.2d 197, (3rd Cir 1979) (Adams, J., concurring).

88. *Africa v Commonwealth of Pennsylvania*, 662 F.2d 1025 (3rd Cir. 1981).

89. See the discussion earlier in this chapter.

90. See Alston, "Religion," in *Encyclopedia of Philosophy*, ed. P. Edwards (New York: Macmillan, 1967), 140.

91. See Greenawalt, "Religion as a Concept," at 768.

92. If the phrasing of the deep characteristic were to be broad enough to embrace groups like the Ethical Culture Society, it would have to cover sets of beliefs that do not include a "higher reality" or "deeper reality" in the usual senses of those terms.

93. As I indicate in "Diverse Perspectives and the Religion Clauses," I disagree with Douglas Laycock's suggestion that atheism and agnosticism count as religious under the Free Exercise Clause. Laycock, "Religious Liberty as Liberty," 7 *Journal of Contemporary Legal Issues* 313, 326–37 (1996). Insofar as Laycock's proposal is based on concerns about unequal treatment of convictions that should be treated similarly, my response is that these concerns can be met by direct reliance on constitutional doctrines of equality.

94. L. Tribe, *American Constitutional Law* (1978); 828. He abandoned this proposal in his second edition. *American Constitutional Law* at 1186 n. 53 (Mineola, N.Y.: Foundation Press, 1988).

95. In *Malnak v Yogi*, 592 F.2d 197, 212–13 (3d Cir. 1979) (Adams, J., concurring), Judge Adams makes a similar criticism.

96. Of course, an overall approach might consist of different approaches to different kinds of issues. Such an approach would meet the criteria of covering all cases if the overall approach contained standards for when each of the more particular approaches would be used.

97. Courts must decide what makes a classification religious under that clause; that determination involves a judgment deeply informed by the values underlying the Religion Clauses.

98. Alternatively, one might emphasize what people generally thought at those times.

99. In ordinary establishment cases, a generous approach to what counts as religion favors those challenging the practice, not the practitioners, but for both free exercise and establishment claims a generous definition favors those who seek legal redress.

100. I discuss the Supreme Court's present approaches to the religion clauses and uncertainties about the future in "Quo Vadis: The Status and Prospects of 'Tests' under the Religion Clauses," 1995 *Supreme Court Rev.* 323 (1996).

101. I discuss the uncertain implications of *City of Boerne v Flores* in note 41, supra.

102. See Angela Carmella, "State Constitutional Protection of Religious Exercise: An Emerging Post-Smith Jurisprudence," 1993 *Brigham Young University Law Review* 275; Ira Lupu, *Employment Division v. Smith* and the Decline of Supreme Court Centrism, 1993 *Brigham Young University Law Review* 259; Tracey Levy, "Rediscovering Rights: State Courts Reconsider the Free Exercise Clauses of Their Own Constitutions in the Wake of *Employment Division v. Smith*," 67 *Temple Law Review* 1017 (1994).

103. 485 U.S. 439 (1988).

104. 406 U.S. 205 (1972).

105. 374 U.S. 398 (1963). The *Smith* Court said that *Wisconsin v. Yoder* was also justified, because it was based on two different constitutional claims. With many others, I doubt that this "hybrid" category will prove significant, see Greenawalt, "Quo Vadis, at 335. Insofar as the hybrid category will yield successful free exercise claims, issues of burden could arise there as well.

106. 485 U.S. at 475 (1988).

107. *Mack v O'Leary*, 80 F.3d 1175 (7th Cir. 1996); see, e.g., *Bryant v Gomez*, 46 F.3d. 948 (9th Cir. 1995) (per curiam); *Werner v McCotter*, 49 F.3d 1476 (10th Cir. 1995).

108. For example a curfew during all hours of darkness would constitute a complete impairment of night time worship services; the scheduling of a public fireworks display on July 4 (a Sunday that year) at 9:00 p.m. (the usual hour of church services) on a lot next to a church would constitute only a modest interference with nighttime services. For some churches, any nighttime services might not be a matter of importance, for others it would be very important.

As this example also illustrates, different ways of phrasing what is essentially the same issue will affect perceptions of importance and extent of burden. If one asks about *worship services*, in general, the practice is immensely important, but a curfew's preclusion of nighttime services may or may not be a large burden on those. If one asks about nighttime worship, the extent of the burden of a general curfew on that is severe, but the importance of having nighttime services may not be great.

109. The difficulties of such an endeavor are emphasized in a case in which debtors in bankruptcy claimed a religious obligation to donate one hundred dollars monthly to their church. *In re Tessier*, 190 Bankr. Rptr. 396, 403–4 (D. Mont. 1995). In another case, in which a trustee in bankruptcy sought to recover money given as tithing to a church while debtors were insolvent, the Court of Appeals for the Eighth Circuit ruled that the bankruptcy code, under which the trustee would have succeeded, imposed a substantial burden on the exercise of religion and that the government lacked a compelling interest in recovering the money. In re: *Bruce Young*, 82 F.3d 1407 (1996), vacated and remanded, 17 S.Ct. 2502 (1997), earlier judgment reinstated, 141 F.3d 854 (1998).

110. See, e.g., *Sasnett v Sullivan*, 908 F. Supp. 1429, 1440 (W.D. Wis.), affirmed, 91 F.3d 1018 (1996). As this opinion reflects, one reason for the linkage is that the government argues for a stringent test focusing on "the religion," whereas claimants argue for a relaxed test focusing on the individuals.

111. *United States v Seeger*, 380 U.S. 163 (1965); *Welsh v United States*, 398 U.S. 333 (1970).

112. 450 U.S. 707 (1981).

113. *Lyng v Northwest Indian Protective Association*, 485 U.S. 439 (1988).

114. I discuss this issue in Greenawalt, "Quo Vadis," at 370–75.

115. 80 F.3d 1175, 1179 (1996).

116. An initial reading of the opinion's language might suggest that when conduct is compelled, the claimant can succeed only if the religious belief that

forbids the legally compelled conduct is central. But "those beliefs" in Posner's formulation do not include the element of centrality explicitly, and it would be illogical to treat compelled behavior differently from forbidden behavior (as to which centrality is not required).

117. In *Sasnett v Sullivan*, 91 F.3d 1018, 1022 (1996), involving a prohibition on wearing jewelry, Posner referred to religious motivation without mentioning centrality.

118. *Goodall v Stafford County School Bd.*, 60 F.3d 168, 172–73 (4th Cir. 1995); *Cheffer v. Reno*, 55 F. 3d 1517, 1522 (11th Cir. 1995); *Bryant v Gomez*, 46 F.3d 998 (9th Cir. 1995) (per curiam).

119. See Ira C. Lupu, "Of Time and the RFRA: A Lawyer's Guide to the Religious Freedom Restoration Act," 56 *Montana Law Review* 171, 203 (1995).

120. On relevant legislative history, see *Sasnett v Sullivan*, 908 F.Supp. 1429, 1441–44, affd, 91 F.3d 1018 (1996).

121. Greenawalt, "Judicial Resolution of Issues About Religious Conviction," 81 *Marquette Law Review* 461, 467–69 (1998).

122. See, e.g., *Employment Division v Smith*, 494 U.S. 872 (1990).

123. Winifred Fallers Sullivan, "Judging Religion," 81 *Marquette Law Review* 441 (1998). It may be that there are serious limits on our capability to understand the religious lives of others, and even our own religious lives. Here I refer mainly to avoidable failures to understand.

124. On why people should have constitutional protection against indirect burdens on rights, see Michael Dorf, "Incidental Burdens on Fundamental Rights," 109 *Harvard Law Review* 1176 (1996); on burdens on free exercise, see Ira C. Lupu, "Where Rights Begin: The Problem of Burdens on the Free Exercise of Religion," 102 *Harvard Law Review* 933 (1989).

125. 91 F.3d at 1179. See also *In re Bruce Young*, 83 F.3d 1407 (8th Cir. 1996), vacated and remanded, 17 S.Ct. 2502 (1997), earlier judgment reinstated, 141 F.3d 854 (1998).

126. See, e.g., *Thiry v Carlson*, 78 F.3d 1491 (10th Cir. 1996) (holding that parents would not suffer substantial burden if land condemning gravesite of stillborn child was condemned and gravesite relocated).

127. I address this position in Greenawalt, "Quo Vadis," at 340–42.

128. 476 U.S. 693 (1986). See also In re *Tessier*, 190 *Bankruptcy Rptr.* 390 (DMont. 1995).

129. The reports leading to the Religious Freedom Restoration Act contain limited support for the view that a burden on free exercise must be an external impact, and therefore that *Lyng* is not affected by the act. See Greenawalt, "Quo Vadis," at 354. I conclude that the act should not be understood to leave situations like that presented in *Lyng* unaffected.

130. See Marc Galanter, "Religious Freedoms in the United States: A Turning Point," 1966 *Wisconsin Law Review* 217.

131. Lupu, "Where Rights Begin," at 966–77. Lupu supplements this approach by attention to entitlements, ibid. at 977–82, and he assumes that a burden resulting from discrimination is unconstitutional, ibid., at 982–87.

132. Dorf, "Incidental Burdens," at 1217–18.

133. RFRA explicitly includes a least-restrictive-means component. Some of the constitutional cases before *Smith* did not do so. But if the question is seen (as it should be) as whether the government has a compelling interest in applying the law or regulation against the claimant and people like him, the government will lack a compelling interest of this kind if it has a less restrictive means available to achieve its purpose. Thus, it should not matter greatly whether the formulation of a compelling interest test includes explicit reference to the least restrictive means.

8

THE FULLNESS OF TIME

Aviam Soifer

By superficial and purposive interpretations of the past,
the Court has dishonored the arts of the historian and
degraded the talents of the lawyer.[1]

THUS DID Mark DeWolfe Howe—generally renowned for his graciousness—begin his famous series of lectures reviewing the United States Supreme Court's treatment of the social and intellectual history of church and state. The Court's decisions since the 1965 publication of *The Garden and the Wilderness* make Howe's critique seem understated.

Despite a flood of illuminating and directly relevant scholarship about religion in the last decade,[2] the Supreme Court has inserted significant new ahistorical "synthetic strands into the tapestry of American history."[3] The interplay of *Employment Division, Department of Human Resources v. Smith*[4] and *City of Boerne v. Flores*,[5] for example, suggests a current Court majority that disregards history not only in general but also in particulars, as well as the Court's own precedents and the usual demands of internal consistency.

After a majority of the Justices relegated religious freedom claims to the majoritarian political process in *Smith*, the Court in *Boerne* invalidated one of the clear products of that process—the Religious Freedom Restoration Act, passed after extensive hearings by a nearly unanimous Congress. The Court acted in the name of extremely abstract versions of the separation of powers and federalism. As in other recent opinions about religion, the Court in *Smith* and *Boerne* relied on tub-thumping about its responsibility in guarding constitutional turf, a key component within the Court's proclaimed role as guarantor of neutral laws of general application. Instead of close consideration of particular disputes in the context of living communities, the Court has adopted a breathtakingly broad New Formalism. With a few possible exceptions,[6] the fundamental premise of the *Smith/Boerne* approach is that religious matters may be left to majoritarian political processes, but only at the state level.

Critical to this New Formalism maneuver is concern with jurisdiction, an abstract legal construct that is used and abused most comfortably by those with legal training. Decisions couched as questions of jurisdiction allow judges to claim that they are the exclusive gatekeepers, patrolling essential binary choices between the states and the federal government and among the separate branches of the federal government. Neither the lower federal courts nor Congress may continue to require that state and local authorities justify general intrusions on religious freedom, so long as any such limitations are unintended or not aimed specifically at religious belief and conduct.

In the name of the basics of constitutionalism, judges now purport to maintain a different kind of wall of separation, a Great Wall upon which judges may perch high above the messy intricacies of daily life. Our marble cake of federalism[7]—a mishmash of intersecting federal, state, and local powers and the intricate crisscrossing by private individuals with multiple memberships, loyalties, and moral commitment—can hardly be discerned from the judicial watch post high atop the Great Wall. This Great Wall actually may separate nothing lasting, and it may become the functional legal equivalent of a tourist attraction. For the moment, however, the new Great Wall casts a giant shadow in constitutional law.

To be sure, the very complexity of contemporary life underscores how important it is for there to be some legal order amid the chaos, and for what at least appear to be final decisions about vexing conflicts.[8] Moreover, any formal legal system—and for that matter any regimen of norms, customs, and usages whether formal or not—must rely upon jurisdictional assumptions at or near its foundation.[9] Just as most modern lives involve shifting, negotiated boundaries of loyalty, membership, and kinship, however, most legal disputes occur in the shadow of several different normative sources.

We have traveled a great distance from vigilance concerning "a gap in the hedge or wall of separation between the garden of the church and the wilderness of the world."[10] Indeed, there have been numerous recent attacks upon the very metaphor of a wall of separation, now generally attributed to Thomas Jefferson without acknowledgment of its earlier appearance in the radical religious thought of Roger Williams. It has become almost a standard trope to pin Jefferson to the "wall of separation" and then to proclaim, for example: "It is impossible to build sound constitutional doctrine upon a mistaken understanding of constitutional history, but unfortunately the Establishment Clause has been expressly freighted with Jefferson's misleading metaphor for nearly 40 years."[11]

Tending One's Garden:
"Full and Equal Rights of Conscience"

The Court's lack of concern for the fragility of both hedges and walls protecting full freedom of conscience suggests a pressing commitment to assert the Court's own homogenizing authority. At such a time, Candide's famous advice to withdraw and to tend one's own garden is enticing, but also dangerous.[12] Instead of quiet acceptance of the New Formalism, at least for the time being, it is worth pondering Mark DeWolfe Howe's clear warning: "[T]he importance of the Court's work lies not merely in the results of its deliberations but in the processes by which it reaches them. The complexities of history deserve our respect."[13]

What is most striking about the New Formalism is how rigidly statist the current Court turns out to be. The Court is statist in a double sense: in its willingness to defer to government decision makers generally over claims anchored in religious beliefs,[14] and in its enthusiastic embrace of the power of states qua states to regulate and even to penalize religious action and belief. What is even more startling, however, is how often the Court's recent decisions seek to chop through the Gordian knots of free exercise and establishment clause interpretation. Sweeping initial premises and simplified binary choices now dominate. These decisions are hardly true to text or precedent, history, or even logic, but the demands of the perceived metes and bounds of formal neutrality rule the day.

This essay does not claim that we are firmly bound by the Framers' original intent, even were we able to discern it. This is so whether or not those present at the creation—whenever that was and whoever they were—intended to bind the future with their words or intentions.[15] Instead, by briefly examining a largely overlooked strand of intellectual and social history concerning a guarantee of full rights that directly connects texts surrounding the First Amendment to texts surrounding the Fourteenth Amendment, I seek to illustrate how the formal neutrality desperately sought by the current Court begins to seem much more the problem than part of the solution to legal controversies about religious freedom. Attention to historical nuances emphasizes the importance of multiple perspectives and the need for sensitivity to different contexts within the realm of freedom of conscience. The approach taken in this essay is quite different from the current fad for pronunciamentos—in the name of neutrality, detachment, and objectivity—that now dominate judicial discourse. Stories of origins have great significance in any society and, for that matter, for individuals and families, too.[16] Rather than ignoring such elemental accounts, I suggest that we should attend to them and their histories with care. This different historical vector contrasts sharply with the current Court's freeze-dried version of Framers' intent.

If we were to grapple with early commitments to "freely and fullye have and enjoy his and their owne judgments and consciences, in matters of religious concernment,"[17] for example, or if Madison's proposed guarantee of "full and equal rights of conscience"[18] were to be taken seriously, it would be much more difficult to propagate the New Formalism's intransigent commitment to statism. Instead, we might have to consider specific cases in context while heeding the perspectives of those whose beliefs and actions are protected by the Free Exercise Clause particularly because, in the words of Justice Jackson, "freedom to differ is not limited to things that do not matter much. That would be a mere shadow of freedom. The test of its substance is the right to differ as to things that touch the heart of the existing order."[19] Let me explain.

Burdens and History:
"The Dung heape of this Earth"[20]

Origins

Roger Williams was extraordinary. A generation ago, Williams's role as the founder of Rhode Island who led the little colony to unprecedented toleration for religious dissent seemed quite significant, and Howe, Perry Miller, and Edmund S. Morgan provided considerable accessible detail about Williams's ideas and actions. Yet today hardly anyone seems to know or care that Williams actually forged toleration out of his deep religiosity and his unyielding belief in predestination.

Massachusetts Bay Colony, populated largely by Puritan dissenters, actually went further than had any other government in the western world in separating church and state, yet Roger Williams's brand of separatism proved too radical for Massachusetts. Williams was banished and headed south in the dead of winter, 1635–36.[21]

It was indeed radical for Williams to assert that the link between church and state had been improper from the start and was a grave disservice to Christ. When Constantine adopted Christianity, Williams argued, "then began the great Mysterie of the Churches sleepe, the Gardens of Christs Churches turned into the Wildernesse of Nationall Religion, and the World (under Constantines Dominion) to the most unchristian Christendome."[22] To Williams, God's true religion could and would take care of itself. It should not be defended with anything but spiritual weapons.

"By accepting the alleged help of the temporal sword," Williams believed, "a church proclaimed itself false."[23] In following his radical ideas about the role of Christ to their logical conclusions, Williams severed not only the connection between God and the established Church but also the nexus between God and secular government. The theory of the divine right of kings that James I developed during Williams's lifetime partially as a bulwark against Roman Catholic hierarchical claims was but a logical extension of the overlapping authority of church and state that permeated English life. Williams liked to cite his own banishment from Massachusetts to emphasize the wrongheadedness of any such use of secular power for sectarian ends.

Given Williams's own experiences, together with the developing role of Rhode Island as a haven for dissenters, it is hardly surprising that when the colony finally procured a royal charter from Charles II, protection for both "free" and "full" enjoyment of judgment and conscience—individual and collective—had become a central concern. The 1663 Charter, which had been obtained primarily through the efforts of the Baptist Dr. John Clarke, to assure "full liberty, in religious concernments," even trumped contrary law, custom, or usage, at least to the point that the exercise of free and full liberty of conscience might interfere with public peace or cause civil injury or disturbance to others.[24] The Charter thus formalized Williams's evocation of a long-standing Christian tradition that differentiated between two tables of the Decalogue: the first four Commandments were taken to refer to duties to God, the fifth through tenth to duties owed to fellow human beings. The first table was religious; only the second table was properly subject to legitimate civil coercion. From his own firm religious position, therefore, Roger Williams developed the crucial importance of a sharp separation between the commands of church and state.

Though sorely pressed at times (particularly by the troublesome radical views and actions of Quakers), Rhode Island thus began a tradition of religious tolerance for which the colony soon became notorious. A leading originalist legal scholar recently claimed, "It is unlikely that the Rhode Island provisions had much direct influence on subsequent developments of the free exercise principle."[25] Yet the very words of the Rhode Island Charter—particularly its guarantee of protection for manifestations of free and full conscience, including actions as well as beliefs—began to recur in other texts. Moreover, toleration proved difficult to contain within a new world full of relative diversity, generally anxious for more settlers, and affording numerous avenues of escape.[26]

Echoes: Jefferson and Madison

Extensive recent scholarship has been devoted to the history and meaning of the Free Exercise Clause, tracing in particular its roots in the vehement, even revolutionary, controversies surrounding religious freedom and the disestablishment of the Church of England and its successors in Virginia.[27] Indeed, we have been treated to an unusually direct clash within the Court over who or what constitutes the relevant history for the First Amendment's religion clauses.[28] Even the Library of Congress recently has been pulled into the fray.[29]

This is surely not the place to respond systematically to the sustained assault on the "wall of separation" metaphor launched by "conservative" Justices and commentators,[30] though some refutation beyond Justice Souter's careful and quite gentle response seems in order. Perhaps the most striking recent revisionist effort has been the attempt to drive apart the thought of Jefferson and Madison and thereby to lower or poke holes in what is alleged to be Jefferson's more insistent "wall of separation" by emphasizing Madison as more prominent for constitutional purposes and more inclined to favor religion.[31] This purported division between Jefferson and Madison seems dubious at best.[32]

It is helpful first to take a step back. As Thomas Jefferson grudgingly awaited his first and perhaps most noteworthy brush with greatness in Philadelphia in the late spring and summer of 1776, he could hardly contain his frustration at being obliged to be away from Virginia while a new Virginia Constitution was in the works. Failing in his effort to be recalled, Jefferson prepared and sent three drafts of a Constitution to the Convention, but it remains unclear when his drafts actually arrived. It is clear that Jefferson's third draft, sent via George Wythe and Richard Henry Lee, did reach the delegates before they had formally finished their work, and parts of it were added as a preamble to the Virginia Constitution, albeit not enough to quell Jefferson's serious doubts about the Constitution as it was enacted.

For our purposes, however, it is striking that Jefferson's draft echoed Rhode Island and Pennsylvania when it provided: "All persons shall have *full and free liberty* of religious opinion; nor shall any be compelled to frequent or maintain any religious institution." The similarity is hardly surprising. Lawyers tend to look to what others have done in similar situations, and Jefferson was exceptional for many things, including his dogged willingness to do extensive historical research and to take pains about his writing, often invoking phrases he had heard or read elsewhere.[33]

If anything, however, James Madison sought to go further, though his language was quite similar to what Jefferson proposed. As Madison overcame his shyness in his fight to amend George Mason's proposed language for the Virginia Constitution, Madison suggested the following:

> That Religion or the duty which we owe to our Creator, and the manner of discharging it, being under the direction of reason and conviction only, not of violence or compulsion, all men are *equally entitled to the full and free*

exercise of it, according to the dictates of Conscience; and therefore that no man or class of men, ought, on account of religion to be invested with peculiar emoluments or privileges, nor subjected to any penalties or disabilities, unless under colour of religion, the preservation of equal liberty and the existence of the State be manifestly endangered.[34] (Emphasis added)

Like Jefferson, his trusted ally in the long campaign for religious freedom in Virginia, Madison thus invoked the old Rhode Island "full and free" formula. Madison went further in that he attached the "full and free" guarantee to the exercise of one's reason and conviction—explicitly covering more than did Jefferson's connection of the "full and free" guarantee only to "opinion."[35] Madison also sought to link the new guarantee directly to the demands of equal entitlement. Moreover, for Madison, religion could not be the basis either for favorable emoluments or privileges, or for any penalties or disabilities. The only limitation upon this sweeping Madisonian principle, in fact, was when it was necessary to preserve equal liberty *and* if the existence of the state were "manifestly endangered."[36]

It is well known that Madison got his start as a vocal proponent of religious freedom when, as a twenty-two-year-old, he was shocked to discover five or six "well meaning" Baptists in close confinement in the jail in a neighboring Virginia county. In his famous letter to his Princeton friend William Bradford, Madison revealed "unaccustomed fervor" as he wrote concerning "[t]hat diabolical Hell conceived principle of persecution rages among some and to their eternal Infamy the Clergy can furnish their quota of Imps for such business."[37] Madison early in life thus experienced and viscerally identified with those persecuted for their religious beliefs. Madison's strong reaction—"This vexes me the most of any thing whatsoever"[38]—apparently anchored his lifelong fervor in favor of religious freedom. There may have been political advantages, to be sure, but it is striking that Madison repeatedly demonstrated an unusual ability to understand the demands of various points of view about religion, even when they differed markedly from his own perspective. Empathy with dissenters, for example, helps explain Madison's insistence that government could not incorporate the Episcopal Church, give land to a Baptist Church, or even run the risk of being seduced by the "laudable" motive of supporting the chaplaincy in the armed forces and Congress.[39]

Despite all the recent revisionism, there seems little disagreement as to the central constitutional role played by James Madison. After all, he was the initial proponent of language that, following redrafting, became the text of the First Amendment. Yet there has been little notice of some of the most suggestive wording of the constitutional guarantee as James Madison first proposed it in the First Congress in June 1789.[40] Madison moved to amend the Constitution as follows: "The civil rights of none shall be abridged on account of religious belief or worship; nor shall any national religion be established, nor shall the full and equal rights of conscience be in any manner, or on any pretext, infringed."[41]

Most revealing for our purposes is Madison's proposed guarantee of "*full and equal* rights of conscience." The guarantee reads as absolute. It disallows any pretext or any manner of infringement. This is note-worthy in itself, particularly because this guarantee was not redundant but was an addition to the proposal's initial protection against infringe-ment of civil rights on account of religious belief or worship. More sig-nificantly, however, Madison's very phrase "full and equal" encapsulates an approach to freedom that, in its very terms, appears to extend beyond formal equal treatment.

Madison's draft was altered significantly, of course, in the process of becoming the First Amendment we know. Yet it is likely that, as Profes-sor McConnell put it, "the deletion of 'full' by the [Select] Committee was no more than stylistic and that the word 'equal' was deleted so as not to create a negative inference."[42] It may be sensible, in fact, to dis-cern elements of Madison's guarantee of "full" rights of conscience in the Free Exercise Clause, and to see some of his "equal rights" concern in the guarantee against the establishment of religion. Such an approach would not resolve all the tension between the two clauses, to be sure, but it would bolster a unitary, structural approach to the Religion Clauses.[43] Such an approach wisely echoes Madison's proposal, made as early as 1776, providing that a feared breach of the peace would not provide adequate justification for governmental intrusion on beliefs or actions embedded within the freedom of conscience of an individual or a dissenting religious group.[44]

At the very least, Madison's initial proposal on religious freedom pro-vides relatively clear evidence of this crucial constitutional actor's con-ception of an appropriate guarantee of religious freedom. It is also con-sistent with the major innovation at the Constitutional Convention that eliminated religious qualifications for federal office holders.[45] Madison promised Baptist leaders in Virginia that, if elected to the First Con-gress, he would do his best for "the most satisfactory provisions for all essential rights, particularly the rights of Conscience in the fullest lati-tude."[46] Far from being the reluctant dragon portrayed by Justice Rehn-quist, Madison became a veritable nag in that Congress due to his efforts to amend the Constitution.[47]

As Jefferson and Madison discussed whether it was necessary or wise to amend the federal constitution, both repeatedly gave freedom of reli-gion pride of place. These two friends, who characteristically studied past precedent carefully and who delighted in their mutual abilities as wordsmiths, repeatedly struggled in various venues to protect fundamental principles of religious freedom. In addition to guaranteeing free and equal treatment, both men also explicitly sought to protect *full* freedom of conscience.

Full and Equal in the Reconstruction Era

As a matter of logic, full protection may be different from equal protection. "Full" implies substantive content—and perhaps some particularized consideration of differences—while "equal" generally is taken to require only evenhanded process.[48] Equal protection doctrine now centers almost entirely on equal treatment. The "protection" element of the equal protection guarantee has virtually disappeared. Indeed, even unequal treatment is not considered constitutionally problematic unless there has been a showing of discriminatory motive.[49] It is as if the Court has decided that equality has been achieved, albeit at an unspecified magic historical moment, and that now only purposeful deviations from this happy norm need be remedied.[50]

This attitude surely was not and hardly could have been the general approach during and immediately following the Civil War and the liberation of millions of slaves. In addition to the Reconstruction amendments, often rightfully called a Second Constitution, Congress passed statute after statute seeking to provide effective federal protection for the civil rights of the newly freed slaves and their allies. Again and again, Congress guaranteed "full and equal" benefits of the laws, rights, and access. The story of this sustained congressional effort to ensure that the war's horrific carnage was not in vain has been told in considerable detail elsewhere and is well beyond the scope of this essay.[51]

For our purposes, it is significant enough that the 39th Congress—the very body that drafted and passed the text that was declared ratified in 1868 as the Fourteenth Amendment we know today—adopted the Civil Rights Act of 1866. Congress based this statute on its new enforcement power as provided by Section 2 of the Thirteenth Amendment. Indeed, the issue of Congress's authority was clearly joined when President Andrew Johnson vetoed the bill and Congress overrode a presidential veto on a major piece of legislation for the first time in its history.

The 1866 Civil Rights Act directly rejected the *Dred Scott* decision even more forcefully than the Religious Freedom Restoration Act of 1993 (RFRA) rejected the *Smith* decision. The 1866 Act began: "That all persons born in the United States and not subject to any foreign Power, excluding Indians not taxed, are hereby declared to be citizens of the United States." According to Congress, "such citizens of every race and color" were to be guaranteed a list of enumerated legal rights "without regard to any previous condition of slavery or involuntary servitude." Moreover, these new citizens now were promised the same right "to *full and equal* benefit of all laws and proceedings for the security of person and property, as is enjoyed by white citizens" (emphasis added).[52]

Extensive hearings had emphasized the quotidian horrors under the Black Codes, as well as numerous blatant atrocities and failures to intervene by state and local authorities in the South. The 39th Congress therefore believed it necessary to act on the federal level. In their view, this was hardly a time for great deference to the wisdom of the Supreme Court—the very people who brought the nation *Dred Scott*. Nor did the 39th Congress believe the country could afford to wait for ratification of the new constitutional amendment it was drafting to make constitutionally permanent the guarantees of the 1866 Act, including the reassertion of the enforcement power first constitutionalized in the Thirteenth Amendment.

When the Court struck down RFRA in *Boerne*, it simply ignored this history of congressional power to remedy the deprivation of rights against a background of judicial failure to do so. Congress's bold rejection of *Dred Scott* in the 1866 Civil Rights Act simply cannot be reconciled with *Boerne*'s proclamation of the Court's exclusive authority.[53] Under *Boerne* and its insistently formalistic view of the separation of powers, only the Court could determine that the time was ripe to overrule *Dred Scott*. As a formal matter, in fact, the Supreme Court has never overruled its own tragic blunder in that decision.[54]

Boerne's Striking Ahistoricism

The *Boerne* Court's crabbed view of Congress's Enforcement Clause power under the Fourteenth Amendment paid no heed whatsoever to historical context. Instead, Justice Kennedy declared for the majority somewhat testily: "When the political branches of the Government act against the background of a judicial interpretation of the Constitution already issued, it must be understood that in later cases and controversies the Court will treat its precedents with the respect due them under settled principles, including *stare decisis*, and contrary expectations must be disappointed."[55]

Purportedly concerned about "vital principles necessary to maintain separation of powers and the federal balance,"[56] *Boerne* forbade Congress to alter the difficult burden of proof required in free exercise cases that the Court established in *Smith*.[57] Defining and categorizing this "burden" has been a long-standing and key gatekeeping device in religion cases.[58] In the Religious Freedom Restoration Act, Congress sought to alter the burden of proof and the standard employed by judges so that Free Exercise rights could be protected beyond overt discrimination or indifference. Appearing quite defensive about its recent *Smith* ruling, however, the *Boerne* majority boldly swept away RFRA, apparently a good deal more of Congress's power to enforce other constitutional rights, and certainly a critical element of the nation's historical commitment to the protection of minority rights.

Strong arguments have been made for and against both the wisdom and the constitutionality of RFRA.[59] In the factual context of the *Boerne* case, for example, RFRA raised significant Establishment Clause problems that only Justice Stevens worried about directly. Moreover, RFRA's very breadth—and the fact that the claim made by Archbishop Flores to renovate and expand a church building had substantial implications for zoning power generally—undoubtedly contributed to the *Boerne* result. Finally, the realities of lobbying by religious groups and the obvious political danger that lurked beneath nearly unanimous support for a bill proclaiming itself to restore religious freedom might well produce judicial skepticism.

If it was puffing somewhat for Congress to lay claim to the restoration of religious freedom through RFRA, however, the aggressive sweep of Justice Scalia's *Smith* opinion did make it seem that the rare victories for Free Exercise over the previous decades were to be obliterated entirely. Ironically, it is likely that Archbishop Flores would and should have lost his case had his property dispute gone to trial both before RFRA took effect and even under RFRA. Prior to *Smith*, the nettlesome legal question revolved around determining if some government action imposed a substantial burden on religious activity; then, if the rarity of a substantial burden were found, a judge had to determine if some compelling state interest, narrowly drawn, might nevertheless prevail.

The degree of deference thus generally afforded government interests within the pre-*Smith* universe might not have fit comfortably within the "full and free" guarantees of conscience propounded by Madison and Jefferson. But the *Smith/Boerne* Court's brusque unwillingness to take acts of conscience into account at all—whether or not such acts are religiously based—seems to mark a substantial departure from the bold experimental hopes of the founders' generation. Cloaked in the abstract garb of separation of powers and federalism, the New Formalism rejects much of the painful progress we have made as a nation, at least in part through a kind of constitutional common law construing Free Exercise. The Supreme Court now seeks to preclude any such progressive approach. The Court's new precedents are sure to constrain, at least somewhat, the countless decisions made by individuals and groups throughout the United States who pursue freedom of conscience to some degree aware that they operate within the shadow of our law.

Boerne's Three Jurisdictional Levels

It is useful to recognize how the *Boerne* majority opinion operated simultaneously on three separate, significant jurisdictional levels. First, as already discussed briefly, in defense of the *Smith* decision the Court felt obliged to rebuff emphatically what the Justices perceived to be Congress's intrusion onto turf the Court had staked out exclusively for itself. Second, in the name of the "federal balance," the Court emphasized its enthusiasm in *Smith* for leaving matters of religious accommodation to local and state political processes. Third, *Boerne* also firmly rejected a more personal claim: that religious belief might trump some general laws of neutral application, even when those laws were not "passed because of religious bigotry."[60] A brief separate discussion of each of the three may prove illuminating.

"Substantive in Operation and Effect"[61]

To limit Congressional power, *Boerne* promulgated a new constitutional standard of "proportionality and congruence," to be used as the general measure of Congress's power under the Fourteenth Amendment's enforcement clause.[62] As a legal standard, "proportionality and congruence" necessarily requires judges to make discretionary judgments. No benchmark is set in advance, and the inquiry required to adjudicate proportionality and congruence pushes judges into doubly subjective decision making about policy and politics, apparently unwilling to be aided by the views of Congress. This is hardly judicial restraint. Nor does it begin to resonate with the historical context of the Fourteenth Amendment.

The *Boerne* Court never mentioned the 1866 Civil Rights Act in the course of its dip into Fourteenth Amendment history. The majority invoked "[s]cholars of successive generations" but relied on nothing published later than 1966. Taken at face value, *Boerne*'s obsession with exclusive judicial authority not only would have made *Dred Scott* the law of the land until at least 1868, but it would also apparently invalidate the 1866 Civil Rights Act's broad array of federal protections for enumerated civil rights.[63]

That this comparison with 1866 is not simply a provocative extrapolation became chillingly clear when the Court invoked the *Civil Rights Cases* as a primary source for its constitutional views. Infamously, the

Court's decision to invalidate the guarantee made in the 1875 Civil Rights Act of "full and equal enjoyment" of a broad range of public accommodations did a good deal to legitimate the rise of Jim Crow.[64] In *Boerne*, the Court declared that the reasoning of the *Civil Rights Cases* about Congress's Section 5 power "has not been questioned."[65]

This remarkable assertion poses an important further question: not questioned by whom? Does questioning by anyone other than the Justices of the Court qualify? In their defensiveness about *Smith* and their haste to establish judicial exclusivity, the Justices apparently simply missed broad societal refutation of the *Civil Rights Cases* through statutes as well as in more general ways. Many Americans have had and still do have serious questions about what the Court said and did when it failed to allow Congress to reach "unjust discrimination" in the *Civil Rights Cases*:

> If the laws themselves make any unjust discrimination, amenable to the prohibitions of the 14th Amendment, Congress has full power to afford a remedy under that amendment and in accordance with it. When a man has emerged from slavery, and by the aid of beneficent legislation has shaken off the inseparable concomitants of that state, there must be some stage in the process of his elevation when he takes the rank of mere citizen, and ceases to be a special favorite of the laws.[66]

According to the *Civil Rights Cases*, the time for formal equality had already arrived eighteen years after the end of slavery. By 1883, the time had come for former slaves to stop looking for federal protection. "It would be running the slavery argument into the ground," said the Court, to allow Congress's constitutional enforcement power to apply to the denial of access to places of public accommodation on the basis of race.[67]

To be sure, the question of what the limits ought to be when Congress invokes its enforcement power has long been nettlesome. But the *Boerne* Court's egregious use of the *Civil Rights Cases* as its key precedent, and the insistent exclusivity of its proclamation about constitutional wisdom—and constitutional jurisdiction, for that matter—are striking attempts to knock most of the pieces off the board. The holding in *Boerne* seems to go much further than the case actually before the Court and to extend well beyond issues of religious freedom. Instead of recognizing the Court's own complicity in aiding Jim Crow by eviscerating a broad range of protections that Congress sought to provide in the decade after the Civil War, the *Boerne* Court may have struck at least a comparable blow against the protection of rights by severely constricting Congress' protective power, granted explicitly by the Enforcement Clauses of the three Reconstruction Amendments.[68]

"The States' Traditional Prerogatives"[69]

In the name of states' rights within the interminable federalism debate, the current Court has cut back vigorously on the power of Congress and other federal sources to limit state authority. That campaign advanced significantly in several decisions handed down the same week as *Boerne.*[70] Indeed, it is clear that a major element of the Court's objection to RFRA was the Justices' sense of too much intrusion by Congress into matters best left to state authorities. They reasoned, for example, that [t]he substantial costs RFRA exacts, both in practical terms of imposing a heavy litigation burden on the States and in terms of curtailing their traditional general regulatory power, far exceed any pattern or practice of unconstitutional conduct under the Free Exercise Clause as interpreted in *Smith.*"[71]

This quasi-legislative judicial balancing is surprising in itself. It seems even more surprisingly subjective if one recognizes that the absence of a pattern or practice under the Free Exercise Clause as interpreted in *Smith* must be based on a very small sample indeed, given the very brief time between *Smith*'s radical doctrinal departure and the passage of RFRA. Moreover, the Court's lack of concern for those who suffer from unconstitutional conduct that affects their religious practices, combined with the solicitude it expresses for state and local regulatory interests such as zoning, contrasts starkly with the Court's recent substantial constitutional concern for even *de minimis* intrusions on property rights through zoning and other forms of state and local regulation.[72] Finally, the *Boerne* Court was so eager to repel "a congressional intrusion into the States' traditional prerogatives and general authority to regulate for the health and welfare of their citizens" that it gave no indication at all as to whether RFRA's coverage of federal governmental entities was valid or not.[73]

The Court's federalism claims almost surely would have greatly surprised supporters of the 1866 Civil Rights Act and the Fourteenth Amendment. Deference to the states was hardly the lesson drawn by the Radical Republicans, and the Moderates allied with them by President Johnson's blunders, from a gruesome war fought in large measure to defeat states' rights claims.[74] Nonetheless, whether there is much precision possible in the *Boerne* concept of "traditional general regulatory power" of the states, or in the more basic idea of federalism as a constitutional standard proclaimed by the current Court is deeply problematic today.

Yet by focusing briefly on the issue of perspective in a small sampling of recent Religion Clause cases, we can discern the crucial, vexing issues of judicial role and suitable detachment. Justice O'Connor has led the way in recent years in directly discussing the importance of perspective within the larger problem of religious and secular coexistence in our society. "Because of this coexistence," she stated in one of her first opinions construing the Religion Clauses, "it is inevitable that the secular interests of government and the religious interests of various sects and their adherents will frequently intersect, conflict, and combine."[75]

Through her emphasis on the importance of social context, O'Connor has developed an approach that would "preclude government from conveying or attempting to convey a message that religion or a particular religious belief is favored or preferred."[76] In part, this approach incorporates a very important recognition of what effect apparent state endorsement may have on those who are dissenters, skeptics, or simply losers in the many political battles that are interlarded with religious issues.[77]

For Justice Scalia, by contrast, there should be little—if any—judicial second-guessing of how matters affecting religion are resolved by *state or local* authorities. (Scalia actually may believe that the opposite is true regarding the judgments of elected *federal* officials). According to Scalia, the issue is "quite simply, whether the people, through their elected representatives, or rather this Court, shall control the outcome of these concrete cases." With vigor, Scalia asserts that *Smith* has answered already: "It shall be the people."[78]

There is no template, of course, to fit over the multitude of complex disputes about federalism, particularly when they are commingled with sorting out basic Religion Clause tensions in the "crucible of litigation." This is the case even if one were still to agree that "the Court has unambiguously concluded that the individual freedom of conscience protected by the First Amendment embraces the right to select any religious faith or none at all."[79] But the question of whom, if anyone, will comprehend and fully protect the rights of minority religions, fringe beliefs, and doubters has become much more pressing after *Smith* and *Boerne*.

In earlier cases, it often seemed possible to map the votes of the Justices by concentrating on whose perspective they adopted or found worthy of empathy. Justice Stevens for the majority in *Wallace v. Jaffree*, for example, expressed concern for the views of nonbelievers and those who feel silently coerced, while Justice O'Connor was drawn to the role of "objective observer." On the other hand, Chief Justice Burger wholeheartedly identified with the Alabama authorities and embraced their argument that the statute under review "affirmatively furthers the values of religious freedom and tolerance that the Establishment Clause was designed to protect," while his fellow dissenter, Justice Rehnquist, argued primarily from a critical history of the "wall of separation" metaphor that he took to be obvious to "any detached observer."[80]

The significance of perspective is particularly acute in the context of legal scrutiny of religious matters. Chief Justice Burger may have been blustering a bit, but he had a point. A position of neutrality concerning religion is indeed hard to establish and hard to maintain either legally or personally.[81] We all make our own arrangements regarding religion, volitional or not.[82] Moreover, because religious issues are exceptionally sensitive, multilayered, and elusive to outside observers, the paradigmatic judicial role of objectivity and/or detachment becomes particularly difficult to identify or to maintain.[83]

Perhaps because issues of law and religion are so complicated, and so personally charged, the current Court seeks to establish some lower common denominators. *Boerne* makes it seem clear that a majority of the Justices believe that formal voting equality within state and local political processes affords sufficient protection for free consciences. If, but only if, the popular will is so blatantly biased as to adopt a "religious gerrymander"[84]—as the city of Hialeah was held to have done in *Lukumi*—will the Court allow federal judicial intervention. Absent overt gerrymandering based on religion, state politics as usual must prevail. In the name of deference to the proper authority of the states, therefore, there ought to be no special constitutional solicitude, no particular concern to shield dissenters, no obligation to protect the politically vulnerable from "intolerance of the disbeliever and the uncertain."[85] There seems great haste to get the job done, to have at last "paved paradise & put up a parking lot."[86]

"The Essential Autonomy of Religious Life"[87]

By contrast to the ebb and flow of the jurisdictional aspects of federalism, the autonomy of religious bodies in ecclesiastical matters has been well established as a federal matter for over a century. Faced with one of the multitude of disputes that arose in the era of the Civil War over who controlled a particular church, the United States Supreme Court held as early as 1871 that "whenever the questions of discipline, or of faith, or ecclesiastical rule, custom, or law have been decided by the highest of these church judicatories to which the matter has been carried, the legal tribunals must accept such decisions as final, and binding on them, in their application to the case before them."[88]

In *Watson v. Jones*, the Court recognized the far-reaching importance and practical impact of conceding such exclusive and final authority to church bodies. Indeed, Justice Miller, writing for the majority, somewhat wistfully noted that the dispute involved a jurisdictional issue, but he then added, "There is, perhaps, no word in legal terminology so frequently used as the word jurisdiction, so capable of use in a general and vague sense, and which is used so often by men learned in the law without a due regard to precision in its application." Nonetheless, the Court held that deference to religious authority was inescapable because "In this country the *full and free* right to entertain any religious belief, to practice any religious principle, and to teach any religious doctrine which does not violate the laws of morality and property, and which does not infringe personal rights, is conceded to all" (emphasis added).[89]

The *Watson* Court's statement of broad deference to the jurisdiction of religious groups was fenced round with caveats, to be sure, ranging from the limits anchored in what judges might discern as problems of morality, property, and personal rights to ultimate judicial control over what constitutes an ecclesiastical matter, properly understood.[90] It is in the nature of jurisdictional disputes, in fact, to be partly about power, partly about relative autonomy—but nearly always about the interpretation of authority on a continuum. This problem of overlapping jurisdictions seems to frustrate the current Court, particularly as a majority seems to be committed to the discovery of settled, easily discerned either/or principles.

The current Court's discomfort with the jurisdictional tension at the heart of the Religion Clauses has led a majority to stir Free Exercise claims into a pabulum of unexamined general, neutral rules. This discomfort may help explain why the Justices appear so inclined to castigate those who litigate at the crossroads of law and religion. Paradoxically, some of the same Justices who declare themselves anxious to reduce what they take to be the excessive separation of church and state simultaneously reject Free Exercise arguments by maintaining that these religious claims conflict with the special needs of the military, for example, or the strictly internal affairs of the social security bureaucracy.[91]

Nancy Rosenblum has pointed out substantial dangers looming within the potential imperialism of "sacred space."[92] On the other hand, secular authority has a strong "jurispathic" tendency, as Robert Cover explained, which continuously challenges our nation's "breathtaking acknowledgment of the privilege of insular autonomy for all sorts of groups and associations."[93] Jurisdictional tension enlivens some of the best recent scholarship about groups, particularly the developing focus on the wonderfully diverse capacity to create meaning. Such creativity often is accomplished by individuals and groups who operate in realms quite apart from the state.[94]

Conclusion: Alternative Histories

The core problem in the constitutional jurisprudence of law and religion may be that in the United States there is not now, nor has there ever been, a clear way to identify or to cabin neatly the essential autonomy of religious life. It is uncommonly easy in the realm of religion, in fact, to identify exceptions and limitations—thus the tendency to argue from extreme examples of one slippery slope or another.[95] Perhaps for this very reason, it would be wise to heed the nuances of historical context, rather than seeking some simple originalist key to unlock definitively some purported Framers' intent.

It should matter, for example, that Roger Williams believed strongly that "The Christian magistrate could best advance the cause of his own religion by doing it no favors."[96] But we should also be aware that for all his pathbreaking commitment to tolerance, Williams saw nothing wrong in disarming Catholics and making them wear distinctive clothes or in suppressing the "incivilities" of the Quakers, whom he detested— though he would not allow suppressing their modes of worship.[97] Moreover, it is fitting that we attend to the kinetic quality of the relationship of law and religion across time, to say nothing of the dramatic flux in religious identities within our nation.

Arguments from history do not compel outcomes. In fact, it is striking to see how the same decision makers can feel comfortable in gliding back and forth between levels of generality and the kinds of history they find compelling. For example, in the span of five years, the Supreme Court held both that it was unconstitutional for Tennessee to exclude ministers from holding public office and that it was constitutional for Nebraska's unicameral legislature to begin each session with "a prayer in the Judeo-Christian tradition" offered for sixteen straight years by a Presbyterian chaplain paid by the state. In both cases, Chief Justice Burger wrote the lead opinions, and he relied in both on America's historical experience. That experience, according to Burger, meant that Tennessee's position as the lone state to retain the once commonplace prohibition had to give way to the tide of the lessons of time.[98] In the Nebraska decision, by contrast, Burger argued that it was crucial to recognize: "The opening of sessions of legislative and other deliberative public bodies with prayer is deeply embedded in the history and tradition of this country."[99] In an important sense, the use of history in these two decisions underscores the Court's tendency to embrace "winners' history" as if it were definitive.

What this approach misses, however, is the need for judges to hear and to understand the perspective of skeptics and dissenters who invoke the courts' jurisdiction as they seek to resist the majoritarian tide. From at least the time of Roger Williams, the history we celebrate has included refuge for those unable or unwilling to go along with the majority because of beliefs and practices anchored in their religious views, or even their lack of religious beliefs altogether.

We aspire to treat like cases alike. Simultaneously, however, Americans like to emphasize that every person is different from every other person. This helps to explain why the protection of full rights of conscience so often seems to be in direct tension with the protection of equal rights. To treat everyone the same is to miss the critical contextual differences. These differences tend to matter a great deal when religion and freedom of conscience are directly at issue.

Despite the current Court's considerable enthusiasm to settle these difficult matters by flattening them into general rules or by stuffing them into jurisdictional cubbyholes, one may take comfort from the very complexity and resilience of the matters in dispute. Chief Justice Rehnquist was correct when he paraphrased Mark DeWolfe Howe and insisted that "stare decisis may bind courts as to matters of law, but it cannot bind them as to matters of history."[100]

Fortunately—one might even say blessedly—our history seems to include enhanced general acceptance of a core belief: "One's right to life, liberty, and property, to free speech, a free press, freedom of worship and assembly, and other fundamental rights may not be submitted to vote; they depend on the outcome of no elections."[101] Such rights still must be taken largely on faith and attended to outside the courtroom. But they remain key elements of an ongoing quest to make real a broad promise: "If there is any fixed star in our constitutional constellation, it is that no official, high or petty, can prescribe what shall be orthodox in politics, nationalism, religion or other matters of opinion or force citizens to confess by word or act their faith therein."[102]

If those who dare to differ today reflect a constellation of values from the past, we seem barely able to perceive why it is so important for the law to protect what currently seems unorthodox. Certainly we have yet to guarantee the "full and equal rights of conscience."[103]

Notes

I would like to express my great thanks to my good friends Milner Ball, Mary Bilder, Lash LaRue, Martha Minow, Saul Touster, and Carol Weisbrod, all of whom read an earlier draft and offered wonderful suggestions, some of which I had the wisdom to heed. I am particularly grateful for the excellent research assistance afforded by Meredith Geller and George Linge, and for Nancy Rosenblum's remarkable combination of generosity, good sense, and a keen editorial eye. Once again, my greatest thanks are for Marlene Booth, who was there through it all.

1. Mark DeWolfe Howe, *The Garden and the Wilderness: Religion and Government in American Constitutional History* (Chicago: University of Chicago Press, 1965), 4.

2. See, e.g., Nancy Rosenblum, *Membership and Morals: The Personal Uses of Pluralism in America* (Princeton, N.J.: Princeton University Press, 1998); Bette

Novit Evans, *Interpreting the Free Exercise of Religion: The Constitution and American Pluralism* (Chapel Hill: University of North Carolina Press, 1997); John H. Garvey, *What Are Freedoms For?* (Cambridge: Harvard University Press, 1997). Arlin M. Adams and Charles J. Emmerich, *A Nation Dedicated to Religious Liberty: The Constitutional Heritage of the Religion Clauses* (Philadelphia: University of Pennsylvania Press, 1990); Merrill D. Peterson and C. Robert Vaughan, eds., *The Virginia Statute for Religious Freedom* (Cambridge, U.K.: Cambridge University Press, 1988); Kurt T. Lash, "The Second Adoption of the Free Exercise Clause: Religious Exemptions Under the Fourteenth Amendment," 88 Nw. U.L. Rev. 1106 (1994); Philip Hamburger, "A Constitutional Right of Religious Exemption: An Historical Perspective," 60 Geo. Wash. L. Rev. 915 (1992); Philip Hamburger, "Equality and Diversity: The Eighteenth-Century Debate About Equal Protection and Equal Civil Rights," 1992 *S.Ct. Rev.* 295 (1992); Mary Ann Glendon and Raul F. Yanes, "Structural Free Exercise," 90 *Mich. L. Rev.* 477 (1991); David C. Williams and Susan H. Williams "Volitionism and Religious Liberty," 76 *Cornell L. Rev.* 769 (1991); Michael McConnell, "The Origins and Historical Understanding of Free Exercise of Religion," 103 *Harv. L. Rev.* 1409 (1990); Douglas Laycock, "Formal, Substantive, and Disaggregated Neutrality Toward Religion," 39 *DePaul L. Rev.* 993 (1990); Ira C. Lupu, "Where Rights Begin: the Problem of Burden on the Free Exercise of Religion," 102 *Harv. L. Rev.* 933 (1988).

3. Howe, *The Garden and the Wilderness*, at 4.

4. 494 U.S. 872 (1990) (Oregon need not demonstrate compelling state interest to deny unemployment benefits to members of Native American Church for use of peyote in religious ceremony). I should mention that I coauthored an amicus curiae brief for the American Civil Liberties Union before the Supreme Court in this case.

5. 117 S.Ct. 2157 (1997) (invalidating Religious Freedom Restoration Act of 1991, in which Congress attempted to return to pre-Smith requirement that government demonstrate compelling state interest and narrowly tailored regulation to overcome legitimate Free Exercise Clause claim).

6. *Church of the Lukumi Babalu Aye, Inc. v City of Hialeah*, 508 U.S. 520 (1993) (invalidating local "religious gerrymander" banning ritual animal sacrifice as violation of "fundamental nonpersecution principle" of First Amendment). To meet the test announced in Lukumi, however, there must be convincing proof of an overt governmental effort to "infringe upon or restrict practices because of their religious motivation." The *Smith* decision leaves a further possible future opening for governmental intrusions impinging upon what the Court might consider "hybrid" constitutional rights, i.e., rights that combine, for example, freedom of expression with free exercise. If this judicial innovation is unduly complicated and formalistic, it is also not at all convincing as a way to distinguish key precedents such as *West Virginia State Board of Education v Barnette*, 319 U.S. 624 (1943), and *Wisconsin v Yoder*, 406 U.S. 205 (1972) from *Smith*. Ironically, the Court's sweeping proclamations in *Boerne* seem, in turn, to be anchored largely on defensiveness about the brave new constitutional world proclaimed in *Smith*.

7. Morton Grodzins apparently first offered the image of American federal-

ism as a "chaotic marble cake" in response to cleaner, less realistic "layer cake" metaphors, Morton Grodzins, "Centralization and Decentralization in the American System," in *A Nation of States: Essays on the American Federal System*, ed. R. Goldwin (Chicago: Rand McNally, 1963), 1, 4.

8. This helps explain what was particularly noteworthy about the Court's innovative use of Federal Rule of Civil Procedure 60 (b)(5) in *Agostini v Felton*, 117 S.Ct. 1997 (1997) as it overruled several Establishment Clause decisions about aid to sectarian schools for remedial programs. The *Agostini* majority held that under that Rule, which is couched in terms of relief from a decision "no longer equitable," parties challenging a Supreme Court precedent were entitled to relief from a District Court injunction on the grounds that the precedent might be and should be overruled.

9. The biblical command "You shall not displace your neighbor's boundary-marks which your forerunners have set up" nicely illustrates the concern, for example, as well as some of the basic conservatism of customary legal systems. Deut. 19:14. As the Hellenist commentator Philo explained, "For customs are unwritten laws, the decisions approved by men of old, not inscribed on monuments nor on leaves of paper which the moth destroys, but on the souls of those who are partners in the same citizenship." Quoted in James L. Kugel, *The Bible As It Was* (Cambridge: Harvard University Press, 1997), 512.

10. Roger Williams, "Mr. Cotton's Letter Lately Printed, Examined and Answered, 1644," quoted in Perry Miller, *Roger Williams: His Contribution to the American Tradition* (Indianapolis: Bobbs-Merrill, 1953; reprint, New York: Atheneum, 1970), 89, 98.

11. Rehnquist, J., dissenting in *Wallace v Jaffree*, 472 U.S. 38, 91–92 (1985). Then-Justice Rehnquist's choice of a forty-year timeframe is somewhat curious. Clearly, however, he very much dislikes the results of decisions during these forty years, particularly given that his opening quote of the "wall of separation" metaphor is from *Reynolds v United States*, 98 U.S. 145, 164 (1879), a case more than a century old. To Rehnquist, Jefferson "would seem to any detached observer as a less than ideal source of contemporary history as to the meaning of the Religion Clauses of the First Amendment." Ibid. We will return to the role of Jefferson and James Madison, and the issue of detached observers shortly.

12. Voltaire, *Candide*, trans. Lowell Bair (New York: Bantam Books, 1959), 120.

13. Howe, *The Garden in the Wilderness*, at 174, 176.

14. The Court emphasized and relied upon what it termed "internal government matters" in *Lyng v Northwest Indian Cemetery Ass'n* 485 U.S. 439, 448 (1988), and *Bowen v Roy*, 476 U.S. 693, 699–700 (1986). For a powerful critique, *see* Williams and Williams, "Volitionism and Religious Liberty."

15. See, e.g., Jack Rakove, *Original Meanings: Politics and Ideas in the Making of the Constitution* (New York: Alfred A. Knopf, 1996), 3–34, 339–68; H. Jefferson Powell, "The Original Understanding of Original Intent," 98 *Harv. L. Rev.* 885 (1984). It may be relevant that, at the time of the American Revolution, church membership and even church attendance in the United States was remarkably low, Tom Paine was a runaway best-selling author—

despite or perhaps in part because of his scathing attacks on religion; and the population of non-Protestants was infinitesimal—25,000 Roman Catholics and 2,000 Jews—within a white population beginning to approach 3 million people. James MacGregor Burns, *The Vineyard of Liberty* (New York: Alfred A. Knopf, 1982), 7. As Burns put it, "From the start the colonies had been alive with religious controversies, doctrinal disputes, sectarian splits and secessions, revivalism and evangelism, the importation of new creeds and dogmas from Europe, along with their carriers—alive also with rationalist, deist, and atheistic counterattacks on religion." Ibid., 8. Much changed, of course, by the end of the Civil War, yet our filiopietistic approach to "the Framers" has all but blinded us to fundamental changes not only in the structure and relationships within the constitutional document, but within society. See generally Charles Miller, *The Supreme Court and the Uses of History* (New York: Simon and Schuster, 1969; reprint, New York: Simon and Schuster, 1972); Charles L. Black, Jr., *A New Birth of Freedom* (New York: Grosset/Putnam, 1997).

16. Such stories are "how one generation tells another how the future shapes the present out of the past." Milner Ball, *Leading Stories* (Durham, N.C.: Duke University Press, 2000). (forthcoming).

17. Office of the Rhode Island Secretary of State, *Rhode Island Charter of 1663*, republished Providence, R.I., 1996.

18. Madison's proposal for what became the First Amendment, *Annals of Congress*, 1st Cong., 1st Sess., 1789, 434. There are two printings of the first two volumes of the *Annals of Congress*. This article cites to the 1834 "Gales & Seaton" edition.

19. *West Virginia State Board of Education v Barnette*, 319 U.S. 624, 642 (1943).

20. In New England in the mid-1630s, when John Winthrop urged Roger Williams to consider whether everyone else could be wrong but him as he pursued the logic of his separatist beliefs, Williams in reply urged Winthrop to join him in splendid isolation: "Abstract yourself with a holy violence from the Dung heape of this earth." Quoted in Edmund S. Morgan, *The Puritan Dilemma* (Boston: Little Brown, 1958), 130. Williams's views on the need for purity in the Church had become quite extreme. It was at this point that Williams "having, a little before, refused communion with all, save his own wife," according to Winthrop, decided that "now he would preach to and pray with all comers." Ibid., 131.

21. Edmund S. Morgan offers an admirably clear and succinct account of the complicated series of confrontations between Massachusetts Bay governmental and religious authorities. Ibid., 115–33.

22. Roger Williams, quoted in Edmund S. Morgan, *Roger Williams: The Church and the State* (New York: Harcourt Brace & World, 1967), 96.

23. Ibid., 98. Thus Williams anticipated Kathleen Sullivan's position that on current church-state issues "We should have more faith in faith," Kathleen M. Sullivan, "Religion and Liberal Democracy," 59 *U. Chi. L. Rev.* 195, 223 (1992).

24. "[T]hat noe person within the colonie, at any time hereafter shall be in any wise molested, punished, disquieted or called in question for any differences

in opinions in matters of religion . . . but may from time to time, and at all times here after, freelye and fullye have and engage in his and their own judgments and consciences, in matters of religious concernments . . . not useing this libertie to licentiousnesse and profanenesse, nor to the civil injurye or outward disturbance of others." Charles M. Andrews, *The Colonial Period of American History* (New Haven, Conn.: Yale University Press, 1936), 2:46. After quoting this portion of the Rhode Island Charter in her dissent in *City of Boerne v Flores*, 117 S.Ct. 2157, 2179–80, Justice O'Connor made the point that other colonies "similarly guaranteed religious freedom, using language that paralleled that of the Rhode Island Charter of 1663." Concurring, Justice Scalia countered by emphasizing the "'provisos' that significantly qualify the affirmative protections" granted in the early "'free exercise' enactments." Scalia relied primarily on Hamburger, "A Constitutional Right of Religious Exemption," 915 and on Ellis West, "The Case Against a Right to Religion-Based Exemptions," 4 *Notre Dame J. of Law, Ethics & Public Policy* 591, 624 (1990). Neither of these scholars dealt with the issues presented by the "full" guarantee.

25. McConnell, "Origins and Historical Understanding," at 1427. McConnell relies primarily on William Gerald McLoughlin, *New England Dissent: The Baptists and the Separation of Church and State, 1630–1833* (Cambridge: Harvard University Press, 1971). McConnell adds, however, that the language of the Rhode Island Charter "had a second and third life elsewhere in the colonies," and that "the substance of these early provisions later re-emerged as the most common pattern in the constitutions adopted by the states after the Revolution." It is difficult to prove or disprove "direct influence," of course; and the standard McConnell invokes—"subsequent developments of the free exercise principle"—defies easy calibration. Moreover, leaders in the Great Awakening of the 1740s and then within the successful activism of Baptists in the Revolutionary era rediscovered Williams and celebrated the experiments in religious freedom in Rhode Island and Pennsylvania. Isaac Backus, for example, "utilized also the long-forgotten arguments of Roger Williams to defend the doctrines of separation," and these were arguments which Backus "knew thoroughly," according to his biographer, who claimed in his Preface that Backus merits comparison with Williams. William Gerald McLoughlin, *Isaac Backus and the American Pietistic Tradition* (Boston: Little, Brown, 1967) 124, 191, xii.

Some experts have emphasized the broad familiarity of those at the Constitutional Convention with the religious freedom guarantees of Rhode Island and Pennsylvania, see, e.g., A. P. Stokes, *Church and State in the United States* (New York: Harper, 1950), 1:231; Leo Pfeffer, *Church, State, and Freedom* (Boston: Beacon Press, 1953), 88. Other scholars have emphasized a direct link between a long-standing Christian tradition and Williams's radical ideas as to how to make freedom of conscience real in a new world literally surrounded by the wilderness. According to a religious studies expert, for example, the Jefferson-Madison "one-two punch on behalf of religious freedom in the 1780s" had its "strongest connection . . . to the 'free church' strand of the tradition, represented most characteristically by Roger Williams." David Little, "Religion and Civil Virtue in America: Jefferson's Statute Reconsidered," in *The Virginia Statute*, ed. Peterson and Vaughan 237, 249. Even Perry Miller, who asserted in the early 1950s that Williams "exerted little or no direct influence on theorists of the Revolution and the Constitution," went on to explain that "as a figure and a reputation he was always there to remind Americans that no other conclusion than absolute religious freedom was feasible in this society. . . . As a symbol, Williams has become an integral element in the meaning of American democracy, along with Jefferson and Lincoln." Miller, *Roger Williams*, 254–55.

26. For example, as William Penn set about to create a haven for Quakers in the New World, who at the time were still being banished, whipped, and occasionally hung in Massachusetts, the initial laws of Pennsylvania unsurprisingly emphasized freedom of conscience. Yet in 1705, the General Assembly adopted a new Law concerning Liberty of Conscience guaranteeing that, in addition to not being molested or prejudiced for conscientious persuasion, the populace could henceforth "Freely and fully enjoy his or her Christian liberty in all respects, without molestation or interruption." John D. Cushing, ed., *The Earliest Printed Laws of Pennsylvania, 1681–1713* (Wilmington, Del.: M. Glazier, 1978), 36.

27. The best recent account of the history of the free exercise clause is McConnell, "Origins and Historical Understanding." For a careful critique of McConnell, see Hamburger, "Origins and Understanding," and for McConnell's reply see Michael McConnell, "Accommodation of Religion: An Update and a Response to the Critics," 60 *Geo. Wash. U. L. Rev.* 685 (1992). These and other scholars have not much heeded earlier important work such as that by Leo Pfeffer and Mark DeWolfe Howe. The numerous gems concerning the antecedents, context, and conflicts over ideas of religious freedom in the late eighteenth century within a fine series of essays published for the bicentennial of the Virginia Statute for Religious Freedom, written by Thomas Jefferson in 1777 and pushed through the thickets of Virginia politics by James Madison in 1785. Peterson and Vaughan, eds., *The Virginia Statute*.

28. Compare then-Justice Rehnquist's dissent in *Wallace v Jaffree* 472 U.S. 38, 91 (1985) with Justice Souter's concurrence in *Lee v Weisman* 505 U.S. 577, 609 (1992). See also the competing opinions of Justices Thomas, concurring, and Justice Souter dissenting—joined by Justices Stevens, Ginsburg, and Breyer—in *Rosenberger v Rector and Visitors of University of Virginia*, 515 U.S. 819 (1995).

29. Diego Ribadeneira, "New debate flares over Jefferson's view of church and state," 1 August 1998, *Boston Globe*, 1 August 1998, sec. B2; Laurie Goldstein, "Fresh debate on 1802 Jefferson Letter," *New York Time*, 10 September 1998, sec. A20 (reporting letter from two dozen historians criticizing paper by James Huston, chief of the Library's manuscript division, about Thomas Jefferson's 1802 Letter to the Danbury Baptist Association that contains famous "wall of separation" metaphor).

30. See, e.g., Rehnquist, J., dissenting in *Wallace*, 472 U.S. 38, 91 (building upon an argument made in a brief filed on behalf of Douglas T. Smith and other intervenors in the *Wallace* case); Thomas, J, concurring in *Rosenberger*, 515 U.S. 819, 852. But see, e.g., Justice Souter's reply ibid. at 868–74 This campaign is said to contrast to that of "ideological plaintiffs," who insist on a strict separation approach to school funding issues. For a particularly irascible

example of the argument, see Richard E. Morgan, *Disabling America: The "Rights Industry" in Our Time* (New York: Basic Books, 1984), 22–45. See also Glendon and Yanes, "Structural Free Exercise," at 482.

31. Michael McConnell, for example, insists on the importance of "the contrasting positions of Jefferson and Madison regarding the religion issue," McConnell, "Origins and Understanding," 1449. He associates Jefferson with Locke, and with an "Enlightenment-deist-rationalist stance toward religious freedom." Ibid., 1452. McConnell claims that, by contrast, Madison had a "more affirmative stance toward religion" and a "more generous vision of religious liberty" that "more faithfully reflected the popular understanding of the free exercise provision that was to emerge both in state constitutions and the Bill of Rights." Ibid., 1453, 1455.

32. See, e.g., Jack Rakove, *James Madison and the Creation of the American Republic* (New York: Harper Collins, 1990), 14; Dumas Malone, "The Madison-Jefferson Friendship," in *James Madison on Religious Liberty*, ed. Robert S. Alley (Buffalo, N.Y.: Prometheus Books, 1985), 303, 304 ("The two men may not have been entirely consistent about other forms of freedom, although they were powerful advocates of them, but on religious freedom they were absolutely consistent"); Adrienne Koch, *The Great Collaboration* (London: Oxford University Press, 1950), 30, 40. While those who would divide the two Virginians stress that Jefferson derived his ideas from John Locke, other experts note that John Locke "was not merely a religious man. He was a master theologian with his own view of revelation and its exposition, with his own very clear, very moderate, very persuasive vision of the essentials of Christianity free from the dogma and the controversies, the elaborations, and, as he thought, the quibbles that had marred that exposition up to his time. That he constantly appeals to reason and makes reasonableness his criterion should lead no one to suppose that he is a rationalist in the sense of a critic of Christianity superior to its influences." John T. Noonan, *The Believer and the Powers That Are* (New York: Macmillan, 1987), 76. Moreover, in an earlier attack on the "wall of separation" approach, Madison was also criticized precisely because of the closeness of his thought to that of John Locke. See, e.g., John Courtney Murray, "Law or Prepossessions?" 14 *Law and Contemporary Problems* 23, 29 (1949). For the initial disagreement between Jefferson and Madison about clergy serving in public offices, see *McDaniel v Paty*, 435 U.S. 618, 624 (1978). Madison eventually convinced Jefferson that clergymen should not be banned on grounds both of protecting free exercise of religion and because "it violate[s] another article of the plan which exempts religion from the cognizance of Civil power." Robert A. Rutland and Charles F. Hobson, eds., *Papers of James Madison* (Charlottesville: University Press of Virginia, 1977), 11:288. (I often have supplied full citations to the Madison Papers, because the series had different editors and places of publication since it began in 1962.)

33. See generally, Pauline Maier, *American Scripture: Making the Declaration of Independence* (New York: Knopf, 1997); Thomas E. Buckley, S. J., "The Political Theology of Thomas Jefferson," in Peterson and Vaughan, eds., *Virginia Statute for Religious Freedom* at 85. Jefferson had no doubt that "[i]f is *unalienable right* . . . is religious," (emphasis in original), as he put the point in

his cryptic debate notes for a speech in the Virginia House of Delegates in the Fall of 1776. Julian P. Boyd, ed., *The Papers of Thomas Jefferson* (Princeton, N.J.: Princeton University Press, 1950), 1:537. In "Equality and Diversity," Philip Hamburger provides a careful, illuminating study of the role of natural rights claims for religious freedom in the context of an ongoing dispute between advocates of equal protection and equal civil rights. However, Hamburger does not discuss the contemporaneous attention given to the vindication of "full" and "complete" religious freedom.

34. William T. Hutchinson and William M. E. Rachal, eds., *The Papers of James Madison* (Chicago: University of Chicago Press, 1962), 1:177. Madison went out of his way to annotate in his own hand a printed version of the 1776 enactment, and to claim it emphatically as his own. The editors of the Madison Papers assume that Madison penned what they call this "remarkable footnote" many years later, and that his memory was not entirely accurate. See ibid., 174–79. There is a similar problem, of course, in the frequent reliance on Madison's notes of the Constitutional Convention—the best source we have—which he edited and did not make available until many decades later. In any event, the version quoted (which the editors consider "a largely meaningless whole") reflects Madison's mature reflection as to what at least he wished he had done as a young man. As illustrated in quotations *infra* in text at notes 35–36, Madison did recall accurately the parts of his contemporaneous 1776 amendments that are directly relevant.

35. Ibid., 174. The quotation is from Madison's first proposed amendment, dated between May 29 and June 12, 1776.

36. Madison's second proposed amendment, which also dates from between May 29-June 12, 1776, would protect "the free exercise of religion, according to the dictates of conscience, unpunished and unrestrained by the magistrate, Unless the preservation of equal liberty and the existence of the State are manifestly endangered." *Ibid.*, 174–75. It thus somewhat anticipates the "compelling state interest" test, the standard of review generally used in free exercise cases until that standard was rejected in *Smith*. Though much has been written in recent years about the breach of the peace limitation on religious freedom, see, e.g., Hamburger, "Constitutional Right," Madison's own explicit rejection of that standard as early as 1776 has received little notice.

37. Hutchinson and Rachal, eds., *The Papers of James Madison*, at 1:106.

38. Ibid.

39. J. D. Richardson, ed., *Messages and Papers of the Presidents* (New York: Bureau of National Literature, 1900), 1:489–90. See generally Elizabeth Fleet, "Madison's 'Detached Memoranda,'" 3 *William and Mary Quarterly*, 3d ser. (1946): 559.

40. Those who seek to undermine or to breach the "wall of separation" approach to the Establishment Clause emphasize the fact that once, during the War of 1812, Madison invoked God in a presidential proclamation. It seems more telling that otherwise Madison several times refused such proclamations on grounds of his fear of religious establishment and later expressed his great regret that he had abandoned his principles under political pressure during wartime. *Lee v Weisman*, 505 U.S. 577, 609. Madison's 1813 Thanksgiving Procla-

mation hardly counteracts his long campaign against religious establishment throughout his adult life, just as a stipend to support a religious chaplain to an Indian tribe does not outweigh Jefferson's manifold objections to religious establishment. Such arguments tend to isolate each historical figure at a particular moment and to extrapolate very liberally from some specific deed, rather than to attend to the substantial efforts and great pride these two men invested throughout the rest of their lives in the pursuit of freedom of religion.

Those who doubt Madison's rigorous opposition to the establishment of religion, for example, have to explain away his eloquence in his "Memorial and Remonstrance." Where Madison invoked the proofs of history in the "American Theatre" that had demonstrated already how much the "equal and compleat liberty" of religion could successfully counter the "malignant influence on the health and prosperity of the state, which was discoverable throughout history whenever the secular arm sought to 'intermeddle with Religion.' Noonan, *The Powers that Are*, at 110. They also must overlook Madison's successful joint venture with Jefferson during which they advocated vigorously on many fronts and persuaded Virginia to adopt its pioneering Statute for Religious Freedom. Ironically, one does not find those who would case asunder Jefferson and Madison, purport to be bound by original intent, and who tend to favor states' rights and even at times to question the application of the First Amendment to the states through the Fourteenth Amendment, mentioning that, on the eve of the Constitutional Convention, Madison favored an approach that allowed "a due supremacy of the national authority, and leave in force the local authorities so far as they can be subordinately useful." Letter to Edmund Randolph, *Papers of James Madison*, ed. Rutland and Rachal (Chicago: University of Chicago Press, 1975) 9:368. Unlike James Madison, who as author of the Virginia Resolutions protested the Alien and Sedition Acts of 1798, James Madison in Philadelphia in 1787 fought for a congressional veto over state laws and advocated power in Congress to legislate in all cases when Congress deemed the states incompetent to act. And the James Madison who proposed the religion clauses in the First Congress that became the first part of the First Amendment "conceived this to be the most valuable amendment in the whole list. If there was any reason to restrain the Government of the United States from infringing upon these essential rights, it was equally necessary that they should be secured against State Governments. He thought that if they provided against the one, it was as necessary to provide against the other." *Annals of Congress*, 1st Cong., 1st Sess., 1789, 755.

41. Madison's proposal and the subsequent cryptic debate and redrafting process are set out usefully in Noonan, *The Powers That Are*, at 119–26. These materials, as well as state and other sources, are carefully analyzed in McConnell, "Origins and Understanding."

42. McConnell, "Origins and Understanding," at 1482. Moreover, for those anxious to recapture Madison's thought as accurately as possible about what became the First Amendment, it should be significant that he did not seek to limit only the power of the national government, but rather that he would have guaranteed that "[n]o state shall violate the equal rights of conscience, or the freedom of the press, or trial by jury in criminal cases." Robert A. Rutland and

Charles F. Hobson, eds. *Papers of James Madison* (Charlottesville: University Press of Virginia, 1979): 12:202. See generally Irving Brant, "Madison: On the Separation of Church and State," 3 *William and Mary Quarterly*, 3d ser. (1950): 3.

43. Justice Brennan, concurring in the decision invalidating Bible reading in the public schools, proclaimed, "[T]he role of the Establishment Clause as co-guarantor, with the Free Exercise Clause, of religious liberty. The Framers did not entrust the liberty of religious beliefs to either clause alone." *Abington School District v Schempp*, 374 U.S. 203, 256 (1963). For surprising overlapping support for such an integrated approach, compare, e.g., Pfeffer, *Church, State, and Freedom*, at 121–24; with Glendon and Yanes, "Structural Free Exercise." Perhaps like misery and politics, law and religion make strange bedfellows. A unified approach—though it is not without internal tension, can easily be overly abstract, and does entail considerable unpredictability—seems to echo Madison's concerns in his 1785 "Memorial and Remonstrance." Madison repeatedly warned that the majority would tend to trespass on the rights of the minority. Thus, for example, he asked rhetorically, "Who does not see that the same authority which can establish Christianity, in exclusion of all other Religions, may establish with the same ease any particular sect of Christians, in exclusion of all other Sects?" Noonan, *The Powers That Are*, at 108. To Madison, it was obvious that "equality . . . ought to be the basis of every law," and he proclaimed that "Above all are [all men] to be considered as retaining an '*equal* title to the free exercise of religion according to the dictates of Conscience.'" Robert A. Rutland and William M. E. Rachal, eds., *The Papers of James Madison* (Chicago: University of Chicago Press, 1973), 8:300, quoting Article XVI of the Virginia Declaration of Rights (emphasis in original).

44. It is a commonplace that in the early years of the Republic, one state after another embraced Madison's position, disestablished churches, and began to accommodate the free exercise of religion by dissenters. Thus, Isaac Backus spotted a trend and could proclaim in 1805: "The liberty that [Roger Williams] was for, civil and religious, is now enjoyed in thirteen of the seventeen of the United States of America. No tax for any religious minister is imposed by authority in any of the said thirteen States, and their power is much weakened in the other four." Quoted in McLoughlin, *Backus*, at 209. The remarkably kinetic quality of such legal change within American history is seldom acknowledged by lawyers and judges who seek simplistic abstract rules—purportedly established with clarity in the past—at a particular frozen moment in order to resolve complex contemporary questions.

45. Morton Borden, *Jews, Turks, and Infidels* (Chapel Hill: University of North Carolina Press, 1984). Those who like to emphasize the presence of chaplains in Congress tend not to discuss their absence in the Constitutional Convention. When Benjamin Franklin proposed that each session begin with a prayer, his motion was given the silent treatment and defeated by a motion to adjourn. Max Farrand, ed., *Records of the Federal Convention of 1787* (New Haven, Conn.: Yale University Press, 1937), 1:450–52.

46. Letter from James Madison to the Rev. George Eve (January 2, 1789), in *The Papers of James Madison*, ed. Rutland and Hobson (Charlottesville, Va.:

University Press of Virginia, 1977), 11:404. Madison needed the support of the Baptists to defeat his friendly rival, James Monroe, for a seat in the House.

47. In his argument from history within his dissent in *Wallace v Jaffree*, then-Justice Rehnquist perceived Madison as "less. . .a dedicated advocate of the wisdom of such measures than. . .a prudent statesman seeking the enactment of measures sought by a number of his fellow citizens which could surely do no harm and might do a great deal of good." 472 U.S. at 93–94. Rehnquist conceded that Madison was "undoubtedly the most important architect among the Members of the House of the Amendments which became the Bill of Rights," but he insisted without citations that "it was James Madison speaking as an advocate of sensible legislative compromise, not as an advocate of incorporating the Virginia Statute of Religious Liberty into the United States Constitution." Ibid, 97–98. But see e.g., Douglass Adair, *Fame and the Founding Fathers* (New York: W.W. Norton, 1974); Rakove, *Original Meanings*. Madison tried for nearly a month to get the House to consider his proposed amendments, and finally on July 21, 1789, he successfully "begged the House to indulge him in the further consideration of amendments to the Constitution" during what seemed "a moment of leisure." *Annals of Congress*, 1st Cong., 1st Sess., 1789, 660. See generally Neil Cogan, ed., *The Complete Bill of Rights: The Drafts, Debates, Sources, and Origins* (New York: Oxford University Press, 1997).

48. Martha Minow, *Making All the Difference: Inclusion, Exclusion, and American Law* (Ithaca: Cornell University Press, 1990). Peter Westen, "The Empty Idea of Equality," 95 *Harv. L. Rev.* 537 (1982). For critical responses to Westen, see, e.g., Anthony D'Amato, "Comment: Is Equality a Totally Empty Idea?" 81 *Mich. L. Rev.* 600 (1983); R. Kent Greenawalt, "How Empty is the Idea of Equality?" 83 *Colum. L. Rev.* 1167 (1983); Kenneth Simons, "Equality as a Comparative Right," 65 *B.U.L. Rev.* 387 (1985). Westen responded to his critics in several articles, and then published Peter Westen, *Speaking of Equality: An Analysis of the Rhetorical Force of Equality in Moral and Legal Discourse* (Princeton: Princeton University Press, 1990). *See also* Hamburger, "Equality and Diversity."

49. *Washington v Davis* 426 U.S. 229 (1976); *Personnel Administrator of Mass. v Feeney* 442 U.S. 256 (1979).

50. For a clear description and cogent critique of this approach in the realm of public policy discourse, *see* Deborah Stone, *Policy Paradox: The Art of Political Decision Making* (New York: W.W. Norton, 1997). I tried to put the Court's sanguine doctrinal approach into a larger historical and constitutional context in the chapter, "Involuntary Groups and the Role of History in American Law," in Aviam Soifer, *Law and the Company We Keep* (Cambridge: Harvard University Press, 1995): 127–49.

51. See, e.g., James M. McPherson, *Abraham Lincoln and the Second American Revolution* (New York: Oxford University Press, 1990); Eric Foner, *Reconstruction: America's Unfinished Revolution* (New York: Harper and Row, 1988); William E. Nelson, *The Fourteenth Amendment: from Political Principle to Judicial Doctrine* (Cambridge: Harvard University Press, 1988); Harold M. Hyman and William M. Wiecek, *Equal Justice Under Law: Constitutional Development, 1835–1875* (New York: Harper and Row, 1982); Leon F. Litwack,

Been in the Storm So Long: The Aftermath of Slavery (New York: Alfred A. Knopf, 1979). My efforts include Soifer, "Status, Contract, and Promises Unkept," 96 *Yale L. J.* 1916 (1987), and Soifer, "Protecting Civil Rights: A Critique of Raoul Berger's History," 54 *N.Y.U. L. Rev.* 651 (1979). See also, e.g., Steven J. Heyman, "The First Duty of Government: Protection, Liberty and the Fourteenth Amendment," 41 *Duke L. J.* 507 (1991); Earl M. Maltz, "The Concept of Equal Protection of the Laws—A Historical Inquiry," 22 *San Diego L. Rev.* 499 (1985).

52. Civil Rights Act of 1866, Ch. 31, Sec. 1, 14 Stat. 27 (1866) (current version at 42 U.S.C. Secs. 1981 (1991) and 1982 (1978), see *Cong. Globe*, 39th Cong., 1st Sess. 1857 (1866).

53. In *Planned Parenthood of Southeastern Pennsylvania v Casey*, 505 U.S. 833, 998 (1992), Justice Scalia, joined by Chief Justice Rehnquist and Justices White and Thomas, excoriated his colleagues for their refusal to overturn *Roe v Wade*, 410 U.S. 113 (1973). He wrote: "In my history book, the Court was covered with dishonor and deprived of legitimacy by Dred Scott v. Sandford, an erroneous (and widely opposed) opinion that it did not abandon, rather than by West Coast Hotel, which produced the famous 'switch in time' from the Court's erroneous (and widely opposed) constitutional opposition to the social measures of the New Deal."

54. In his classic work, Don Fehrenbacher quoted dictum from *Downes v Bidwell*, 182 U.S. 244, 273–74 (1901), to the effect that the Civil War "produced such changes in judicial, as well as public sentiment, as to seriously impair the authority of [Dred Scott]." Fehrenbacher then observed, "This was perhaps as close as the Supreme Court ever came to declaring the Dred Scott decision totally overruled." Don E. Fehrenbacher, *The Dred Scott Case* (New York: Oxford University Press, 1978), 585–86. While it generally has been assumed that the post-Civil War constitutional amendments rejected *Dred Scott*, as a formal matter no Supreme Court opinion has purported to overrule it.

The *Boerne* logic, moreover, does not fit the context in which the 39th Congress passed the 1866 Civil Rights Act and drafted what became the Fourteenth Amendment. The early Reconstruction period was hardly a time of great respect for, or deference to, the United States Supreme Court. As the English historian W. R. Brock observed: "If one prong of the drive for legislative supremacy was directed against the Executive, the other was necessarily directed against the Supreme Court. The prestige of the Court, with the odium of Dred Scott still hanging about it, did not stand high, and the whole question of its political function was brought to a head by the famous case of ex parte Milligan." W. R. Brock, *An American Crisis* (London: MacMillan, 1963), 262. Indeed, it was largely fear of the Supreme Court that led the men of the 39th Congress to try to "constitutionalize" through the Fourteenth Amendment the federal guarantee they had provided in the 1866 Civil Rights Act, based on the Thirteenth Amendment. For a detailed discussion of this point and its context, see Soifer, "Protecting Civil Rights."

55. 117 S.Ct. 2157, 2172 (1997).

56. Ibid.

57. Indeed the Court criticized the legislative record behind the Religious

Freedom Restoration Act of 1993 (RFRA) because it "lacks examples of modern instances of generally applicable laws passed because of religious bigotry." Ibid., 2169. This might seem a careless overreading of *Smith*, which never mentioned "bigotry" as necessary to meet the constitutional standard. Yet the *Boerne* Court also criticized the legislative hearings: "It is difficult to maintain that they ["anecdotal evidence" introduced in the hearings] are examples of legislation enacted or enforced due to animus or hostility to the burdened religious practices or that they indicate some widespread pattern of religious discrimination in this country." Ibid. This second-guessing of the legislative process is revealing, particularly because the Court recognized that "As a general matter, it is for Congress to determine the method by which it will reach a decision." 117 S.Ct. at 2170. Protesting much too much in this way suggests considerable defensiveness about the *Smith* decision's departures from settled law. It also indicates how difficult actual proof of a violation of religious freedom will be after *Smith*, notwithstanding *Lukumi*, discussed in note 6.

58. Lupu, "Where Rights Begin." Indeed, "[s]ome shifting of burdens is inevitable wherever there is religious liberty," Rosenblum, *Membership and Morals*, at 92.

59. See, e.g., Christopher L. Eisgruber and Laurence G. Sager "Why the Religious Freedom Restoration Act is Unconstitutional," 69 *N.Y.U. L. Rev.* 437 (1994); William P. Marshall, "The Religious Freedom Restoration Act: Establishment, Equal Protection and Free Speech Concerns," 56 *Mont. L. Rev.* 227 (1995); Ira C. Lupu, "Of Time and the RFRA: A Lawyer's Guide to the Religious Freedom Restoration Act," 56 *Mont. L. Rev.* 171 (1995), and other articles in this Montana Law Review Symposium on RFRA.

60. *City of Boerne v Flores*, 117 S.Ct. 2157, 2169 (1997).

61. Ibid., 2164. Conceding that the line "is not easy to discern," the Court drew a constitutional boundary line between "measures that remedy or prevent unconstitutional actions," which are within Congress's broad power under Section 5 of the Fourteenth Amendment, and "measures that make a substantive change in the governing law," which Congress may not enact.

62. It probably is hard to find reasonable people in the United States today who are opposed to proportionality and congruence, though the Court seems thus to characterize the vast congressional majorities who approved the Religious Freedom restoration Act of 1993. But cf. "Extremism in the pursuit of liberty is no vice," Sen. Barry Goldwater (R-Ariz.), during 1964 presidential campaign.

63. The constitutional basis for the 1866 Civil Rights Act was the Enforcement Clause of the Thirteenth Amendment, whose words were repeated as Enforcement Clauses in the Fourteenth and Fifteenth Amendments. The Court has upheld numerous federal civil rights statutes based entirely on these post-Civil War constitutional grants of power to Congress, even in the face of federalism attacks, see, e.g., *Fitzpatrick v Bitzer*, 427 U.S. 445 (1976) (holding, in a unanimous opinion written by then-Justice Rehnquist, that Fourteenth Amendment enforcement power allowed Congress to abrogate state's Eleventh Amendment immunity and to permit state to be sued directly for retrospective damages); *City of Rome v United States*, 446 U.S. 156 (1980) (upholding amendments of

Voting Rights Act of 1965, based on Fifteenth Amendment enforcement power, that required federal preclearance of electoral changes that need not violate the Constitution). Even the decision in the *Civil Rights Cases* acknowledged more congressional power than *Boerne* appears to recognize.

64. 1875 Civil Rights Act (March 1, 1875): 18 Stat. 335: "That all persons within the jurisdiction of the United States shall be entitled to the *full and equal* enjoyment of the accommodations, advantages, facilities, and privileges of inns, public conveyances on land or water, theaters, and other places of public amusement; subject only to the conditions and limitations established by law, and applicable alike to citizens of every race and color, regardless of any previous condition of servitude" (emphasis added).

65. 117 S.Ct. at 2166.

66. 109 U.S. 3, 25 (1883). For the 8–1 majority, Justice Bradley went on to argue that before the abolition of slavery, "no one, at that time, thought" that the denial of "all the privileges enjoyed by white citizens" or being "subjected to discriminations in the enjoyment of accommodations in inns, public conveyances, and places of amusement" might be "any invasion of their personal status as freemen." Ibid., 31–32. That the majority was wrong as a matter of the law is demonstrated in Joseph Singer, "No Right to Exclude: Public Accommodations and Private Property," 90 *Nw. U.L. Rev.* 1283 (1996). But a careful reading of the *Civil Rights Cases* in its entirety reveals how chilling it is that the *Boerne* Court borrowed from the *Civil Rights Cases* and invoked the "not questioned" trope about that decision. In doing so, the Court performs its own utterance—it directly echoes the *Civil Rights Cases* decision and blatantly ignores what has been widely regarded as societal progress in the realm of racial discrimination since 1883, including the guarantee against racial discrimination in access to places of public accommodations in the 1964 Civil Rights Act, 42 U.S.C.A. § 2000a. Indeed, the 1964 Civil Rights Act itself—and the need to stretch to find a Commerce Clause basis because of the *Civil Rights Cases* precedent—itself might properly be viewed as some serious questioning of the *Civil Rights Cases* reasoning and holding, if one is willing to look up even briefly from the pages of the U.S. Reports.

67. 109 U.S. at 24.

68. The *Boerne* majority acknowledged that "the specific holdings of these early cases [several decisions between 1875 and 1903 that narrowed or invalidated civil rights guarantees] might have been superseded or modified," yet Justice Kennedy insisted that "their treatment of Congress' Sec. 5 power as corrective or preventive, not definitional, has not been questioned." *City of Boerne v Flores*, 117 S.Ct. 2157, 2166. It remains solely the Court's own murky business, of course, to define what is in fact an unconstitutional definitional power, as compared to constitutionally more tolerable corrective or preventive congressional efforts.

69. Ibid., 2171.

70. *Printz v United States*, 117 S.Ct. 2365 (1997) (invalidating provisions of Brady Handgun Violence Prevention Act as unconstitutional commandeering of state officials by requiring them to perform background checks of prospective handgun purchasers); *Idaho v Coeur d'Alene Tribe of Idaho*, 117 S.Ct. 2028

(1997) (distinguishing *Ex parte Young* doctrine, 209 U.S. 1234 (1908) and holding Eleventh Amendment implicitly barred declaratory and injunctive action by tribe alleging ownership of state lands.)

71. *City of Boerne v Flores*, 117 S.Ct. 2157, 2171 (1997).

72. See, e.g., *Phillips v Washington Legal Foundation*, 118 S.Ct. 1925 (1998); *Dolan v City of Tigard*, 512 U.S. 374 (1994); *Lucas v South Carolina Coastal Council*, 505 U.S. 1003 (1992); *Nolan v California Coastal Commission*, 483 U.S. 825 (1987).

73. 117 S.Ct. at 2171. This omission may be simple sloppiness, or it may be an effort implicitly to leave the federal reach of RFRA in place. It is peculiar that the Court did not even drop a footnote to explain whether or not the majority meant to imply anything about the issue. See Michael McConnell, "Institutions and Interpretation: A Critique of City of Boerne v Flores," 111 *Harv. L. Rev.* 153 (1997).

74. "The first constitutional problem encountered by Reconstruction had been the need to give the national government as a whole powers which had been exercised by the States; the second was to assert the right of the legislative branch within the national government." Brock, *An American Crisis*, at 254.

75. *Wallace v Jaffree*, 472 U.S. 38, 69 (1985) (O'Connor, J., concurring in the judgment).

76. Ibid., 70. Justice O'Connor argued that courts are obliged to examine whether "government's purpose is to endorse religion and whether the statute actually conveys a message of endorsement." Ibid., 69. The bitter debate within the Court about both the purpose and the effect of Alabama's moment of silence and voluntary prayer statutes, however, suggests how difficult the role of "objective observer." Ibid., 76, may be in context of the coexistence and conflict of secular and religious interests at the state level.

77. There are numerous examples of intense conflict, and litigation, about prayer in the schools in the nineteenth century: Donald E. Boles, *The Bible, Religion, and the Public Schools* (Ames: Iowa State University Press, 1965); See, e.g., Charles Fairman, *The Oliver Wendell Holmes Devise: History of the Supreme Court of the United States*, vol. 6, part 1, *Reconstruction and Reunion 1864–88* (New York: Macmillan, 1971), 1310–16; Charles Morris, *American Catholic* (New York: Times Books, 1997). Cf. *Jackson v Benson*, 578 N.W.2d 602 (Wis. 1998), cert. denied, 119 S.Ct. 466 (1998) (upholding Milwaukee tuition voucher plan).

78. *City of Boerne v Flores*, 117 S.Ct. 2157, 2176 (1997) (Scalia, J., with Stevens, J., concurring in part).

79. *Wallace v. Jaffree*, 472 U.S. 38 (1985) (Stevens, J., for the majority).

80. Ibid., 53–54; 76, 83; 89; 92. Thus for Justice O'Connor, "The solution to the conflict between Religion Clauses lies not in 'neutrality,' but rather in identifying workable limits to the government's license to promote the free exercise of religion," ibid., 83, whereas for Chief Justice Burger, "If the government may not accommodate religious needs when it does so in a wholly neutral and noncoercive manner, the 'benevolent neutrality' that we have long considered the correct constitutional standard will quickly translate into the 'callous indifference' that the Court has consistently held the Establishment Clause does

not require," ibid., 90. Justice Powell concurred separately, primarily to urge retention of the *Lemon v Kurtzman* test, and Justice White dissented separately, primarily to repeat his call for basic reconsideration of the Court's precedents dealing with the Religion Clauses.

81. Laycock, "Disaggregated Neutrality."

82. Williams and Williams, "Volitionism."

83. Shortly before he was murdered in El Salvador along with five other Jesuits and their housekeeper and her daughter in 1989, Father Ignacio Martin-Baro explained: "Objectivity is not the same as impartiality with regard to the processes that necessarily affect all of us. Thus, for an objective psychosocial analysis it is more useful to become conscious of one's own involvements and interests than to deny them and try to place oneself on a fictitious higher plane 'beyond good and evil.'" Ignacio Martín-Baró, "Religion as an Instrument of Psychological Warfare" in *Writings for a Liberation Psychology*, ed. Adrianne Aron and Shawn Corne (Cambridge: Harvard University Press, 1994), 149–50. See also Soifer, *Law and the Company We Keep*, at 150–81.

84. *Church of the Lukumi Babalu Aye v City of Hialeah*, 508 U.S. 520, 535, discussed in note 6 of this chapter.

85. *Wallace v Jaffree*, 472 U.S. 38, 54 (1995).

86. Joni Mitchell, "Big Yellow Taxi" in *Rise Up Singing*, ed. Peter Blood and Annie Patterson (Bethlehem, Pa.: Sing Out, 1992).

87. *Marsh v Chambers*, 463 U.S. 783, 796 (1983) (Brennan, J., dissenting).

88. *Watson v Jones*, 80 U.S. (13 Wall.) 679, 726 (1871) (rejecting implied trust judicial review and instead deferring to General Assembly of Presbyterian Church that had awarded Walnut Street Church in Louisville, Kentucky to antislavery faction). The *Watson* decision was not based on constitutional law, but rather was within the Court's common law review power at the time. *Watson* was followed and transformed into a federal constitutional rule in subsequent decisions. See, e.g., *Jones v Wolf*, 443 U.S. 595 (1979); *Serbian Eastern Orthodox Diocese of America and Canada v Milivojevich*, 426 U.S. 696 (1976); *Presbyterian Church in the United States v Mary Elizabeth Blue Hull Memorial Presbyterian Church*, 393 U.S. 440 (1969); *Kedroff v Saint Nicholas Cathedral*, 344 U.S. 94 (1952). State courts had established the principle of deference to ecclesiastical jurisdiction earlier, though not without great struggles, for example as they faced bitter disputes over church control and property between Congregationalists and Unitarians—all of which helped to induce the gradual disestablishment of religion under state law, which in 1833 finally reached even Massachusetts. See, e.g., "The Unitarian Controversy," in Leonard Levy, *The Law of the Commonwealth and Chief Justice Shaw* (Cambridge: Harvard University Press, 1957), 29–42.

89. 80 U.S. at 732, 728.

90. All these possible limits, in fact, help explain how the elementary and dear *Watson* principle has found an apparently secure home in American jurisprudence.

91. See, e.g., then-Justice Rehnquist for the Court in *Goldman v Weinberger*, 475 U.S. 503, 507 (1986) (proclaiming great deference to the military's professional judgment regarding military interest "within military community"); Chief

Justice Burger for the Court in *Bowen v Roy*, 476 U.S. 693, 712 (1986) (emphasizing need to leave "sufficient operating latitude" to government entities).

92. Rosenblum, *Membership and Morals*, at 93, discussing *Corporation of the Presiding Bishop of the Church of Jesus Christ of Latter-Day Saints v Amos*, 483 U.S. 327 (1987) as a prime example.

93. Robert Cover, "Supreme Court, 1982 Term—Foreword: Nomos and Narrative," 97 *Harv. L. Rev.* 4, 60–62 (1983).

94. See, e.g., Rosenblum, *Membership and Morals*; Evans, *Free Exercise*.

95. A good recent example may be found in Justice Scalia's opinion for the Court in *Smith*: "Any society adopting such a system would be courting anarchy, but the danger increases in direct proportion to the society's diversity of religious beliefs, and its determination to coerce or suppress none of them." 494 U.S. 872, (1990) 888. As Professor Lupu pointed out, however: "Behind every free exercise claim is a spectral march; grant this one, a voice whispers to each judge, and you will be confronted with an endless chain of exemption demands from religious deviants of every stripe," Ira Lupu, "Where Rights Begin," at 947.

96. Morgan, *Roger Williams*, at 140.

97. Ibid., 134.

98. *McDaniel v Paty*, 435 U.S. 618, 625 (1978). The Court was unanimous (Justice Blackmun did not participate), but for very different doctrinal reasons. Writing for the plurality, Burger relied on historical change rather than being bound by the fact that a majority of the states had enacted prohibitions parallel to Tennessee's at the time of the Constitution and throughout most of the nation's early history.

99. *Marsh v Chambers*, 463 U.S. 783, 786 (1983).

100. *Wallace v Jaffree*, 472 U.S. at 99 (Rehnquist, J., dissenting).

101. *West Virginia State Board of Education v Barnette*, 319 U.S. 624, 638 (1943) (invalidating mandatory stiff-arm flag salute in public schools).

102. Ibid., 642. Even if there are no fixed stars, and the starlight we currently see is really from very long ago, there is still something noble about those who dare to reach for the stars. This is also so of the effort to secure constitutional protection for dissenters, including those bold enough to exercise freedom of conscience and religion "fully and freely," unless and until they "manifestly endanger" very substantial governmental interests.

103. James Madison's proposed amendment to the U.S. Constitution in the First Congress in 1789, quoted and discussed in notes 41–47 of this chapter and accompanying text.

9

LET THEM EAT INCIDENTALS:

RFRA, THE REHNQUIST COURT, AND

FREEDOM OF RELIGION

H. N. Hirsch

N O SUBJECT in constitutional law has caused more consterna-
tion during the second half of the twentieth century than religion. This was again made abundantly clear at the conclusion
of the Court's 1996–97 term, when it declared unconstitutional the Religious Freedom Restoration Act (RFRA), amidst enormous amounts of
public notice and commentary.[1] RFRA itself was a Congressional response to another Supreme Court decision, *Oregon v. Smith*, handed
down in 1990.[2]

These two cases are worth examining in depth, for they reveal a great
deal of what is most essential, and interesting, about the process of constitutional interpretation, the nature of American constitutionalism,
and, indeed, American social reality. Together, these two cases demonstrate the centrality of the Court's construction of what can be called
"social facts" to the decisions it makes. It is the Court's refusal to recognize and weigh appropriately the relevant social facts that leads it to
make a surprising and dubious decision in *Smith*. In response, Congress
passes RFRA, which poses a direct threat to the Supreme Court's authority as the final arbiter of the Constitution. The Court declares RFRA
unconstitutional, as it must,[3] but in so doing it again presents a construction of social facts that is morally troubling. At stake is not just the
power to interpret the Constitution, but the degree to which American
society and law will honor its commitment to respect the rights of vulnerable minorities.[4]

In the RFRA case, the Catholic archbishop of San Antonio, Texas,
wanted a building permit to enlarge a church in nearby Boerne, Texas.
The church, built in 1923, seated 230; the congregation was growing,
and 40 to 60 worshippers could not be seated at some Sunday masses.[5]
Local zoning officials denied the permit under a local ordinance gov-

erning historic preservation. The archbishop filed suit, arguing that the zoning decision violated RFRA.

RFRA, enacted by Congress in 1993, prohibited government at any level from "substantially burdening" an individual's free exercise of religion, even if the burden resulted from a general law, unless the government could demonstrate that the burden was necessary to further a compelling government interest, and the law in question was the least restrictive means of furthering that interest.[6] This sweeping law was enacted by Congress "in direct response"[7] to the Court's decision in 1990 in the case of *Oregon v. Smith*.

In *Smith*, the Court had considered the First Amendment rights of members of the Native American Church who had been denied unemployment benefits; they had lost their jobs for using peyote, a controlled substance considered a sacrament by their Church. The Court, rather surprisingly, denied their free exercise claim under the First Amendment, and instead used the case to announce a sweeping rule: that the First Amendment could not be used to shield individual behavior from the "incidental effect" of "a generally applicable and otherwise valid provision."[8]

Justice Scalia's opinion in *Smith*, like many of his opinions, stresses the importance of judicial restraint in the face of democratically enacted laws. "Values that are protected against government interference through enshrinement in the Bill of Rights," he states boldly, "are not thereby banished from the political process."[9] To the standard argument that this view of the Court's role "will place at a relative disadvantage those religious practices that are not widely engaged in," Scalia replies that this is an "unavoidable consequence of democratic government."[10] Scalia goes so far as to cite and quote Justice Frankfurter's 1940 opinion in *Minersville School District v. Gobitis*, the original case concerning a required flag salute opposed by Jehovah's Witnesses;[11] the overturning of *Gobitis* within a few short years—and the rejection by the majority of the Court of Frankfurter's austere version of judicial self-restraint—is widely regarded as the beginning of the contemporary era in Supreme Court history—an era in which the Court is attentive to, and protective of, the rights of minorities, and in particular religious minorities.[12] This seems not to phase Justice Scalia in the least; he blithely cites Frankfurter's overturned opinion.

The protection of religious minorities, endorsed by the majority of the Court in the early 1940s, produces numerous precedents over the years with which Scalia must contend in *Smith*. For example, in *Sherbert v. Verner*, decided in 1963, the Court overturned South Carolina's denial of unemployment benefits to an individual who refused to work on

Saturday for religious reasons.[13] The Court found the denial of benefits to be a "substantial burden" on the free exercise of her religion, a burden that could not be justified absent a compelling government interest. Subsequent cases strengthened the *Sherbert* precedent.[14] And in *Wisconsin v. Yoder*, decided in 1972, the Court exempted Amish parents from the requirement that they send their children to school past the eighth grade, finding that Wisconsin's compulsory school attendance law unconstitutionally burdened the parents' right to freely exercise their religion.[15]

Scalia attempts to distinguish the *Sherbert* line of cases by saying simply that "the conduct at issue in those cases was not prohibited by law."[16] Although Oregon would be free to exempt the religious use of peyote, it has not done so, and, Scalia says, is not obligated to do so. Scalia claims that the only decisions in which the Court has held that the First Amendment prohibits the application of a neutral, generally applicable law to religiously motivated action are cases that involve "not the Free Exercise Clause alone, but the Free Exercise Clause in conjunction with other constitutional protections," such as the right of a parent to direct the upbringing of her child in *Yoder*, or the freedom of speech.[17] The peyote case, Scalia says, involves a free exercise claim "unconnected with any communicative activity or parental right."[18]

As Justice O'Connor points out in her separate opinion in *Smith*, Scalia's interpretation of *Yoder* is wide of the mark. In *Yoder*, the Court explicitly relied on the Free Exercise Clause, and it rejected the interpretation of that clause Scalia is here promoting; in *Yoder*, the Court correctly states that its decisions

> have rejected the idea that religiously grounded conduct is always outside the protection of the Free Exercise Clause. . . . To agree that religiously grounded conduct must often be subjected to the broad police power of the State is not to deny that there are areas of conduct protected by the Free Exercise Clause. . .even under regulations of general applicability. . . . A regulation neutral on its face may, in its application, nonetheless offend the constitutional requirement for government neutrality if it unduly burdens the free exercise of religion.[19]

As for the argument that the behavior in *Smith*—ingesting peyote—is criminal while the behavior in *Sherbert*—refusing to work on a Saturday—is not, Justice Blackmun correctly points out in his dissent that there is no evidence that the religious use of peyote has ever harmed anyone; nor is there any evidence that the religious use of peyote has led to trafficking in peyote. Blackmun also points out that Oregon has not even attempted to enforce its law against those who use peyote as a sacrament.[20] By paying attention to these highly relevant facts, Blackmun is able to conclude that "the State's asserted interest. . .amounts only to the symbolic preservation of an unenforced prohibition."[21] He then cites another case in which the Court made clear that a government interest in symbolism, "even symbolism for so worthy a cause as the abolition of unlawful drugs, cannot suffice to abrogate the constitutional rights of individuals."[22]

As the separate opinion of Justice O'Connor[23] and the dissenting opinion of Justice Blackmun make clear, *Smith* represented a major departure in the Court's treatment of religious minorities and its interpretation of "free exercise." RFRA was the direct Congressional response. Indeed, Congress in passing RFRA announced that

> (1) The framers of the Constitution, recognizing free exercise of religion as an unalienable right, secured its protection in the First Amendment to the Constitution; (2) laws "neutral" toward religion may burden religious exercise as surely as laws intended to interfere with religious exercise; (3) governments should not substantially burden religious exercise without compelling justification; (4) in [*Smith*], the Supreme Court virtually eliminated the requirement that the government justify burdens on religious exercise imposed by laws neutral toward religion; and (5) the compelling interest test as set forth in prior Federal court rulings is a workable test for striking sensible balances between religious liberty and competing prior governmental interests.[24]

Congress, in other words, passed RFRA to overturn *Smith* and reestablish the strict scrutiny required by *Sherbert* and other cases. Congress attempted to justify its bold action by saying it was authorized by Section 5 of the Fourteenth Amendment, which gives Congress the power "to enforce" through "appropriate legislation" fundamental rights and liberties—at least those protected by the Fourteenth Amendment, which, by previous Court rulings, includes the free exercise of religion.

It is here, in a direct confrontation with the Court over the power to interpret the Constitution, that Congress goes too far, at least according to the majority of the Rehnquist court. Indeed, the Court cites both *Marbury v. Madison* and *McCulloch v. Maryland*—the two major nineteenth-century cases establishing the Supreme Court's authority—thus clearly signaling that it regards RFRA as a direct threat to its own power.[25] The Court reasonably says that Congressional power under Section 5 of the Fourteenth Amendment is "remedial" and "preventive" but not "substantive."[26] And the Court finds that "RFRA is so out of proportion to a supposed remedial or preventive object that it cannot be understood as responsive to, or designed to prevent, unconstitutional behavior." RFRA "appears, instead, to attempt a substantive change in constitutional protections." Preventive measures would pass muster "when there is reason to believe that many of the laws affected by the congressional enactment have a significant likelihood of being unconstitutional," but RFRA "is not so confined." RFRA provides "sweeping coverage," which "ensures its intrusion at every level of government, displacing laws and prohibiting official actions of almost every description and regardless of subject matter."[27]

To make its point that RFRA is too sweeping to be considered "preventive" or "remedial" under Section 5, the Court contrasts RFRA with various voting rights statutes passed by Congress, which did pass constitutional muster. Voting rights statutes were confined "to those regions of the country where voting discrimination had been most flagrant" and were applied to a "discrete class" of state laws. The voting rights statutes also contained sunset provisions. Moreover, the state laws restricting voting by members of racial minority groups, such as literacy tests, were "notorious."[28]

In contrast, the "stringent" test RFRA demands of state laws "reflects a lack of proportionality or congruence between the means adopted and the legitimate end to be achieved." The costs of RFRA "far exceed any pattern or practice of unconstitutional conduct."[29] How does the Court know this? It considers the kinds of violation of religious liberty targeted by RFRA and finds that "in most cases, the state laws to which RFRA applies are not ones which will have been motivated by religious bigotry." The burdens imposed by such laws will in most cases be "incidental." Congress had only "anecdotal" evidence of "incidental" burdens on religion, such as "evidence of autopsies performed on Jewish individuals and Hmong immigrants in violation of their religious beliefs," and "zoning regulations and historic preservation laws" like the one at issue in *Boerne*, "which as an incident of their normal operation have [had] adverse effects on churches and synagogues." It is "difficult" to argue, the Court concludes, that these "anecdotal" and "incidental" effects are due to "animus or hostility to the burdened religious practices or that they indicate some widespread pattern of religious discrimination in this country." All of this contrasts with the "notorious" violations of equal protection in the voting rights cases, and the clear racial hostility motivating the laws in question.[30]

The Court here is thus making a series of judgments about social facts. They begin with the judgment that people burdened by the law such as the one in *Boerne*—the parishioners who cannot attend their own church service because the town in which they live will not allow their church to expand—are not experiencing religious hostility, or discrimination, but rather are experiencing the "incidental" effects of a general law, whereas people protected by voting rights legislation who were not allowed to vote because (for example) they could not pass a literacy test were, in contrast, experiencing a "notorious" example of racial hostility.

But the Court here is conflating two separate things: the source of the violation, and its importance to the individual involved. The Court is undoubtedly right that the Catholic parishioners in Boerne, Texas, are not being subjected to precisely the same kind of prejudice experienced by African Americans in the South—but does that mean their personal experience is really so fundamentally different?

Congress, in considering RFRA, heard testimony about autopsies performed on Jews, in violation of their religious law, and the Court labels such evidence "anecdotal" and the effect of this kind of state action "incidental." Here I must interject a personal experience, a profound one touching on the heart of the matter at hand. When my father died—we are Jewish, and he was quite observant—it was in a hospital, away from home, a few days after suffering a heart attack. The hospital had told us he was recovering and that they did not know precisely what happened to cause his death. In accordance with California law, and without consulting us, the hospital performed an autopsy.

Nothing could have made the experience of his death worse to his survivors than this autopsy. If the hospital had conspired to make his death even more of an emotional cataclysm than it already was, it couldn't possibly have picked a better way to do it. Knowing that our father would have recoiled in horror from such a direct violation of his religion, this was not an "incidental" event. And it was not an "anecdote." It was profoundly important, and hurtful.

Now I have no doubt that the hospital and state in question were not motivated by anti-Semitism in this particular episode. But I also have no doubt that if autopsies were a violation of Christian law, the hospital's procedure and the state law would be different: and therein lies the most troubling aspect of the Court's holding in *Boerne*, despite the fact that the Court may well be correct in its argument that what Congress has done here cannot be justified by Section 5 of the Fourteenth Amendment. Violations of religious liberty aren't "incidental" if they happen to you. If you cannot attend mass on Sunday because your town will not allow your church to expand, the effect on your religious life may well be profound, not incidental. There is no question but that your free exercise is being abridged. Whether the source of the violation is direct prejudice—as in race cases—or merely indifference and carelessness, really won't matter all that much to you. You are still a member of a minority group, and you are receiving at the hands of the state a very real slap in the face. If you were a member of the majority religion, then what was happening to you probably would not be happening. America is a deeply and overwhelmingly Protestant country, and an incident such as an autopsy performed on a relative in violation of your religious law will remind you of that in no uncertain terms.

The Court is thus making two errors in *Boerne*: it is glossing over and mischaracterizing the incidents that RFRA was designed to correct, and, perhaps more fundamentally, it is ignoring the fact that its most important mandate is to protect minorities—and that there are times when minorities must be protected not merely from the hostility of the majority, but also from its indifference and carelessness.

Moreover, the manner in which the Court makes this decision—contrasting "notorious" violations of voting rights with "incidental" effects on religious liberty—makes clear a profound truth about the process of constitutional interpretation—that it requires subjective judgments about social facts, and thus cannot be based solely on an interpretation of the text of the Constitution.[31]

Perhaps the Court's error in *Boerne*—again, we are talking about an error in a subjective judgment about social facts—is in drawing a dichotomy—"incidental" versus "notorious" effects on fundamental rights—when in fact reality is not so neat; perhaps the idea of a continuum would better reflect complex social and political realities. Some examples of prejudice are clearly notorious—and the myriad barriers put up in the South to prevent African Americans from voting—literacy tests, grandfather clauses, fees to vote—are a good example. These actions were "notorious" because they were part of a long, concerted, transparent effort to deny fundamental rights on the basis of race. But this does not mean that any other action in violation of the rights of a different minority group are merely "incidental." After all, there is a long history of anti-Semitic, anti-Catholic, and anti-immigrant sentiment in this country; perhaps examples of actions violating the religious rights of these groups are not as innocent as the Court seems to believe. If nothing else, perhaps such examples reflect a carelessness on the part of the country's religious majority; and, as I have tried to argue, the results may be devastating to individuals. A single "incident" can reveal much about a nation's underlying ideology; we need only think of the furor surrounding John F. Kennedy's election to the presidency in 1960 to recognize the depth of anti-Catholic sentiment a mere generation ago.

What should the Court have done in *Boerne*? As several members of the minority argued, it should have reconsidered the decision in *Smith*.[32] The startling decision in *Smith*—that there is never a First Amendment right to claim an exemption from an otherwise valid law—is clearly too sweeping. It ignores the fact that a state's reason for abridging someone's religious liberty could be a very good reason, or a reason that is not very important at all. Consider the case of my father's autopsy. If he had been the victim of a murder, and the autopsy had therefore been necessary to help identify the murder weapon and the murderer, then the state's reasons would be "compelling" under the *Sherbert* test, and an autopsy would be justified. His survivors would still have felt a sense of violation, but to a far lesser degree, and that sense of violation would no doubt have been tempered by our thirst for revenge, and an acceptance of the need to gain vital information about the murder.

On the other hand, consider the following case, decided by a lower court in the wake of *Smith*. Minnesota law requires vehicles such as horse carriages to display an orange triangle, but an Amish farmer objects to the triangle on religious grounds. He is willing to display some other kind of material to alert drivers to his slow-moving carriage, but not the orange triangle The lower court, however, rejects his claim on the basis of the Supreme Court's holding in *Smith*.[33]

There is a world of difference between a murder investigation and that orange triangle. One is clearly more important, more "necessary," than the other. The insistence that the state have its way with the orange triangle seems both arbitrary and cruel. Why *not* accommodate the Amish farmer by allowing him some other form of safety display, one not at odds with his religion?

What these two examples demonstrate is that the reasons behind the state's need to violate the free exercise rights of an individual can show an enormous amount of variability, a variability that the *Sherbert* test— the need for a compelling government interest—is well designed to measure. Moreover, the *Sherbert* test is appropriate because the Constitution's most fundamental commitment is a commitment to liberty, liberty that can only be abridged for agreed, and limited, reasons.[34]

What of the peyote in *Smith*—is the state's interest in that case compelling? Recall that the petitioners in *Smith* were challenging the denial of unemployment benefits for work-related misconduct—they had not been charged with the criminal possession of a controlled substance. Given that unemployment benefits are granted or denied on the basis of an individualized bureaucratic decision, this becomes a relatively easy case; what is really at stake, as Justice Blackmun points out in his dissent, is the state's narrow interest in refusing to make an exception, not its broad interest in the war on drugs.[35] Given the complete absence of evidence that the religious use of peyote has ever led to harm of any kind,[36] the state's interest does not seem compelling enough to override the free exercise claims. If alcohol were again suddenly illegal, would we not expect the state to make an exception for the sacramental use of wine? Of course we would—and, if any state refused to do so, we would expect the Court to do so on the basis of the First Amendment. At a minimum, we would certainly expect that those who did use wine as a sacrament would not be denied unemployment benefits because of it.

What of the church that wants to expand in *Boerne*? Again, the state's interest in preserving historic architecture, while important, does not seem to rise to the level of a compelling state interest—for surely the church could add to its existing building in a manner consistent with its original architecture.

But what of the state's interest in educating the children of Amish parents in *Yoder*? That is not so easy a case.

The Amish parents in *Yoder*—whose Free Exercise rights are being litigated—are willing to allow their children to attend public school through the eighth grade, but not beyond; Wisconsin demands education to the age of sixteen, which would involve for most students the first two years of high school. As detailed in the opinion of the Court by Chief Justice Burger, the Amish parents object to the exposure of their children to "wordly" influences. High school "tends to emphasize intellectual and scientific accomplishment, self-distinction, competitiveness, wordly success, and social life with other students," in contrast to the simple, communal, agrarian life of the Amish. The parents object to taking their children away from the community during "the crucial and formative adolescent period of life," a time when "the children must acquire Amish attitudes."[37]

The Court makes it clear that it would not carve an exemption to Wisconsin's compulsory school attendance laws for parents or children whose action was not directly grounded in religious belief. Contrasting the Amish with Thoreau, the Court points out that Thoreau's choice to live a separate, simple existence "was philosophical and personal rather than religious, and such belief does not rise to the demands of the Religion Clauses."[38] But in the case of the Amish, the record "abundantly supports" the conclusion that "the Amish religious faith and their mode of life are, as they claim, inseparable and interdependent." The Court cites the "unchallenged testimony of acknowledged experts" in support of that conclusion, as well as the evidence of "almost 300 years of consistent practice." It is the "separated agrarian community" that is the "keystone" of the Amish faith.[39]

The most crucial fact about the case, however, is that the children in question were not party to the litigation; it is solely the Free Exercise claims of their parents that is being litigated. The question thus becomes this—although the Court refuses to formulate it in this way: Does Wisconsin have a compelling interest in the education of Amish children who may choose to leave their community? And is that compelling interest sufficient to outweigh the admittedly vital free exercise rights of their parents?

These are agonizing questions. But, as Justice Douglas points out in his partial dissent, there is no getting around the fact that an Amish child "may want to be a pianist or an astronaut or an oceanographer"[40]—or, we can add, that she might develop those ambitions if allowed to attend the first two years of high school. If the paramount value of the American constitution is *individual* liberty—and, as Justice Douglas argues, if religious liberty itself must be understood as an individual experience—then it is difficult to deny the compelling nature of the state's interest in protecting those Amish children who might wish to leave. Amish children must be treated as individuals, not merely as instruments of their parents' religious will, no matter how strong and deserving of protection, or admiration, that religious will may be.

A case decided by the Rehnquist court in 1994 raises issues quite similar to the issues in *Yoder*, although the Court decides in this case, *Kiryas Joel v. Grumet*, against the parents who are members of a religious minority.[41]

The village of Kiryas Joel in New York was settled by a group of Hasidic Jews, members of a sect called the Satmars. Members of the group dress and behave in a particular manner, making them somewhat analogous to the Amish. All of their children attend religious schools sanctioned by the state, except those children who are handicapped.

Until 1985, handicapped Satmar children attended special classes at these religious schools; these special classes were funded by the state of New York. In 1985, however, the Supreme Court ruled (in a case not involving this group) that publicly funded classes on religious school premises violated the Establishment Clause.[42] As a result, handicapped Satmar children were required to attend schools outside the village.

The experience was not a happy one. Already handicapped, these children were thought by their peers to be exceptionally strange, given their manner of dress and deportment. The result, according to their parents, was severe emotional trauma. In response to this problem, the state of New York created a separate school district for the village of Kiryas Joel.

The Supreme Court rules this creation of a separate school district for the Satmars unconstitutional, for it violates religious "neutrality." The state's "unusual act" in creating the school district "is tantamount to an allocation of political power on a religious criterion," Justice Souter explains for the Court. The State is delegating its authority over public schools to a group defined by its character as a religious community, and this the state cannot do without running afoul of the Establishment Clause, which requires government "neutrality" toward religious groups. The Constitution allows states to accommodate religious needs "by alleviating special burdens," but "accommodation is not a principle without limits."[43]

In his concurrence, Justice Stevens argues that the state here is helping "to shield children from contact with others," thereby providing
"official support to cement the attachment of young adherents to a
particular faith."[44] This the state cannot do—although, of course, that
is precisely what the Supreme Court itself does in *Yoder*. Stevens, who
was not a member of the Court at the time of *Yoder*, does not explain
this discrepancy—nor could he if he wanted to, for it is a blatant contradiction. Indeed, one could argue that the Satmar are asking for, or
getting, far less than the Amish, for they are getting their own public schools, whereas the Amish are keeping their children out of school
altogether.

Thus in *Kiryas Joel* it is a state, not the Court, that is accommodating
a tiny religious minority, a group with cultural customs different from
the norm. As Justice Scalia points out in his dissent, one could say in this
case that the New York legislature was motivated by its desire to help
students who "suffer the additional handicap of cultural distinctiveness," rather than judging its motivation to have been a desire to help a
particular religion.[45] And, Scalia rightly points out, "the history of the
populating of North America is in no small measure the story of groups
of people sharing a common religion and cultural heritage striking out
to form their own communities."[46] Nor, he could have added, is the
coincidence of religious groups and political boundaries new; one need
only think of the Utah to see that this is the case.

Is the state of New York in this case "accommodating" students with
special problems and special needs, students who are members of a minority religious group, or is it unconstitutionally "establishing" a particular religious minority, ceding to it too much political power? There is
no answer to this question in the text of the Constitution; the case turns,
once again, on how we define given social facts. As Justice O'Connor
argues in her separate opinion, the question is a close one.[47] But one
thing is clear: it is hard to imagine a more vulnerable group of people
than handicapped, underage members of a tiny religious minority, a
group with customs, dress, and deportment different from the norm.
Anyone who has ever attended a public school would have no doubt
that these children would have inflicted upon them serious abuse. On
that basis, perhaps—remembering and correctly construing what the
case is really about—the more humane answer, the answer more in keeping with the paramount value of individual dignity—would be to allow
the state of New York to make this particular accommodation. Indeed,
given that the Satmars do not wish to keep their children out of school
altogether, this particular accommodation of their needs seems far less
troubling than the accommodation the Court itself makes in *Yoder*.

At a minimum, then, we can say that the Rehnquist Court does not quite have its act together on the subject of religion. Legislative acts such as the New York law in *Kiryas Joel*, or RFRA, are passed to correct what are understandably seen as failures by the Court, failures to consider adequately the rights and needs of members of minority religions. The result is a constitutional hodgepodge, one that at times does not do justice to some of the nation's most vulnerable groups, nor to the Constitution's most fundamental commitment—to uphold individual liberty against the hostility, or indifference, of society's majority.

Notes

1. *City of Boerne v. Flores*, 117 S.Ct. 2157 (1997).

2. 494 U.S. 872 (1990).

3. For a different analysis of the questions of institutional power presented by the case, see Michael W. McConnell, "Institutions and Interpretation: A Critique of *City of Boerne v. Flores*," 111 *Harvard Law Review* 153 (1997). McConnell argues that Congress, as a representative institution, is free to adopt bolder, and more expansive, definitions of civil liberties than the Supreme Court. Although this argument has surface plausibility, especially under the current Court, it ignores the long history of congressional actions *against* minority interests. Civil liberties issues usually present themselves in cases involving a minority group, and there are good reasons for distrusting the ability of Congress, over the long haul, to protect vulnerable minorities, as the constitutional framers clearly understood.

4. For an elaboration of my arguments about social facts and the centrality of the rights of minorities to American constitutional ideology, see H. N. Hirsch, *A Theory of Liberty: The Constitution and Minorities* (New York: Routledge, 1992).

5. 117 S.Ct. at 2160.

6. Id. at 2162.

7. Id. at 2160.

8. 494 U.S. at 878.

9. Id. at 890.

10. Id.

11. Id. at 879, citing *Minersville School District v Gobitis*, 310 U.S. 586 (1940).

12. *Gobitis* was overturned by *West Virginia v Barnett*, 319 U.S. 624 (1943).

13. 374 U.S. 398 (1963).

14. See *Hobbie v Florida*, 480 U.S. 136 (1987), *Hernandez v Commissioner*, 490 U.S. 680 (1989), *United States v Lee*, 455 U.S. 252 (1982), and *Thomas v Indiana*, 450 U.S. 707 (1981).

15. 406 U.S. 205 (1972).

292   H. N. HIRSCH

16. 494 U.S. at 876.

17. Scalia cites *Cantwell v Connecticut*, 310 U.S. 296 (1940), *Murdock v Pennsylvania*, 319 U.S. 105 (1943), *Follett v McCormick*, 321 U.S. 573 (1944), and *Pierce v Society of Sisters*, 268 U.S. 510 (1925).

18. 494 U.S. at 882.

19. Id. at 895, citing *Wisconsin v Yoder*, 406 U.S. at 219–20.

20. Id. at 911–16.

21. Id. at 911.

22. Id, quoting *Treasury Employees v Von Raab*, 489 U.S. 656 (1989); internal quotation marks omitted.

23. O'Connor concurs in the judgment of the Court in *Smith* but does not accept Scalia's rule concerning laws of general applicability. Instead, she endorses the *Sherbert* test and believes that, under that test, Oregon's interest in "preventing physical harm" is a compelling one.

24. 117 S.Ct. at 2161–62, citing 42 U.S.C. sec. 2000bb(a) and (b).

25. Id. at 2162, citing *McCulloch v Maryland*, 4 Wheat. 316 (1819), and *Marbury v Madison*, 1 Cranch 137 (1803).

26. Id. at 2164.

27. Id. at 2169–70.

28. Id. at 2170–71.

29. Id. at 2171.

30. Id. at 2170, quoting *South Carolina v. Katzenbach*, 383 U.S. 301 (1966).

31. See Hirsch, *A Theory of Liberty*, esp. chapters 4 and 5.

32. Justices O'Connor and Breyer state that *Smith* was "wrongly decided," 117 S.Ct. at 2176, while Justice Souter states that he has "serious doubts" about it, id. at 2186.

33. *State v Hershberger*, 462 N.W. 2d 393 (Minn. 1990).

34. I demonstrate that this is the understanding of liberty embedded in the American Constitution in Hirsch, *A Theory of Liberty*.

35. 494 U.S. at 910–17.

36. Id.

37. 406 U.S. at 211.

38. Id. at 216.

39. Id. at 219, 222.

40. Id. at 244–45.

41. 114 S.Ct. 2481 (1994).

42. *Aguilar v Felton*, 473 U.S. 402 (1985). Justice Brennan ruled for the Court that such classes involved the "excessive entanglement" of church and state, "owing to the nature of the interaction of church and state in the administration" of the classes; "detailed monitoring and close administrative contact" would be required. Id. at 3236, 3238. This case represents a recent entry in a long line of cases in which the Court has struggled with the question of various forms of state aid to religious schools. For a discussion of the general issue, see Leonard W. Levy, *The Establishment Clause: Religion and the First Amendment* (New York: Macmillan, 1986). See also *Agostini v Felton*, 117 S.Ct. 1997 (1997), which overrules *Aguilar*.

43. 114 S.Ct. at 2484, 2492.
44. Id. at 2495.
45. Id. at 2509.
46. Id. at 2507.
47. Id. at 2498.

10

"BY THE LIGHT OF REASON":

CORRUPTION, RELIGIOUS SPEECH, AND

CONSTITUTIONAL ESSENTIALS

Gary Jeffrey Jacobsohn

S EVERAL YEARS AGO, the governor of Mississippi made what many people thought was an outrageous observation when he asserted that America was a "Christian nation." For the outraged, few statements could have matched the governor's in what it revealed about a political leader's fundamental disregard for the essentials of American democracy. The governor, however, had no need to fear political retribution; after all, the intensity of the outrage precipitated by his statement correlated strongly with the distance one traveled from his state. Nor had he any need to fear any serious legal repercussions, it being quickly evident that a principled defense of his right to utter silly and offensive things was most likely to be found among those harboring the gravest misgivings about his questionable characterization. Moreover, he would no doubt have enjoyed the same immunity had he gone on to suggest that voters withhold their support from any candidate for public office whose faith was other than that of the favored Christian majority.

American social norms explain why the governor could feel politically secure in his job, just as American constitutional norms explain why there is no mystery in the governor's presumed confidence regarding possible legal liability. Thus we expect controversial speech to be sheltered by the speech clause of the First Amendment, and we assume further that the religious liberty guarantees of that Amendment would, in the case of the governor's remarks, augment this already considerable constitutional protection.[1] Justification for these expectations is well grounded in American constitutional jurisprudence. At the same time, skepticism about the normative standing of religiously inspired speech has become a subject of some controversy among contemporary theorists of liberal democracy.

What I want to do in this essay is place the issue of religious speech in the public forum, or at least one facet of it, within a comparative constitutional framework, giving specific attention to the example of India. Comparing across nations gives a richer context for understanding the political interface of spiritual and temporal concerns as it relates to the vexing problem of religious involvement in the affairs of State. Thus in India a politician who, while campaigning for office, voiced analogous sentiments to those expressed by the governor would be vulnerable to serious legal challenge. The possibility that such a challenge would be upheld by the courts provides an opportunity to reconsider the argument for public reason, which, as it has been advanced by John Rawls and others, appeals to certain constitutional essentials of a liberal polity to derive guidelines for the appropriate discourse of democratic politics.

The Indian case suggests that the way in which we conceptualize the relationship between religious argumentation and democratic deliberation must take stock of the diversity of experience in secular constitutionalism. The commitment to secular democratic institutions may express itself in different ways, which means that the attempt to frame norms of public reason with reference to *the* constitutional essentials of a liberal polity will fail to explain why in some places these norms require the sanction of law, while in others such sanctions would rightfully be judged illiberal and unconstitutional. I will argue that in India, where certain kinds of religious rhetoric are proscribed as "corrupt practices," the justification for legally seeking to minimize the occasions in which elected officials exercise their powers on religious grounds needs to be premised on the particularities of the *Indian* experience in secular constitutionalism, rather than on general principles deducible from a liberal democratic polity. I will argue further that the "corrupt practices" approach of Indian law echoes a recurrent theme in political philosophy, in which the corruption of the State is linked to systemic structural inequalities, such that the civic virtue necessary to sustain a just and stable political order is seriously and dangerously compromised.[2] As these structural inequalities are in India directly and profoundly implicated in religious belief and practice, they can only be addressed through policies that limit religious freedom—possibly including speech—in ways that would not pass constitutional scrutiny in a polity such as the United States, where religion is much less of a factor in configuring the shape of the temporal world.

In the first section I discuss a Supreme Court case from India that, in highlighting a distinctive approach to the challenge of religious advocacy in the public forum, tends to undermine our confidence in any univocal principle that should govern the practices of liberal secular polities.

The Court's invocation of Rawlsian reasoning to defend a law that in the United States would be found constitutionally infirm points to the inadequacies of abstract moralizing in addressing the problem of religious advocacy. In the second section I present an alternative non-Rawlsian account for limiting "corrupt" speech in India that draws specifically upon the constitutional essentials peculiar to that polity. Here we see that the best rationale for speech restrictions lies in the threat posed by religion to the achievement of substantive constitutional aspirations for equality, more so than in the political commitment to the *process* of democratic deliberation. Finally, in the third section I turn to the "corrupt practice" of campaign financing in the United States to show that the constitutional logic behind the Supreme Court's treatment of that issue reveals the alternative assumptions distinguishing Indian and American liberalism, and the implications that follow for religious speech in the public arena.

What Is Political Corruption?

On December 11, 1995, a three-judge panel of the Indian Supreme Court announced a set of related judgments that had potentially far-reaching implications for Indian politics. They all concerned the interpretation and application of a 1951 electoral law, the Representation of the People Act (RPA). Section 123 of the law detailed a number of activities that were designated as "corrupt practices," the commission of which subjected the transgressor to serious legal consequence, including the reversal of an electoral victory. The Court found this section to be constitutional, interpreting and applying its two subsections in a way that produced mixed results in the specific cases under consideration.

To what activity did the language of "corrupt practice" apply? For Americans, whose recent elections have dramatically increased the level of public awareness of ethical abuses in politics, the statutory invocation of the term "corruption" in the regulatory context of campaign behavior has only one meaning, the improper use of money to secure electoral advantage. In India the term has broader application; it includes not only money and political irregularities but also covers the inappropriate use of speech to advance one's electoral prospects. Accordingly, in RPA a "corrupt practice" may be either of two things: (1) "The appeal by a candidate or his agent. . .to vote or refrain from voting for any person on the ground of his religion, race, caste, community or language or the use of, or appeal to, religious symbols. . .for the furtherance of the prospects of the election of that candidate or for prejudicially affecting the election of any candidate." (2) "The promotion of, or attempt to promote, feelings of enmity or hatred between classes of citizens of India on grounds of religion, race, caste, community, or language, by a candidate or his agent. . .for the furtherance of the prospects of the election of that candidate or for prejudicially affecting the election of any candidate."

In its rulings, the Court held that Balasaheb K. Thackeray, the leader of an extreme Hindu nationalist party (Shiv Sena), could be barred from electoral competition on the basis of intemperate campaign rhetoric, including a reference to Muslims as "snakes." His remarks were found to be in clear violation of RPA's second "corrupt practice" category. But in companion cases the Court reversed findings against two other Hindu nationalist politicians, one involving a campaign pledge to turn Maharashtra into India's "first Hindu state" and the second concerning appeals to voters on the basis of the candidate's support of "Hindutva," a term widely held to signify the religious faith of Hindus, but which the Court chose to interpret as referring to the culture and ethos of the people of India.[3] A lengthy rumination on the essence of Hinduism led the judges, ironically as we shall see, to conclude that "no meaning in the abstract can confine it to the narrow limits of religion alone, excluding the content of Indian culture and heritage."[4] So "the term 'Hindutva' is related more to the way of life of the people in the subcontinent."[5] In short, by effectively blurring the distinction between religion and culture, the Court was left with insufficient evidence to substantiate the charge of corruption.

But why should the kind of speech detailed in RPA—especially that of the category 1 variety—be construed as a form of corruption? Until we have an answer to that question, the irony in the Court's reflections on Hinduism will go unappreciated, and the comparative and theoretical significance of the Indian approach to religious speech in the public arena (one upheld by the Court as both constitutional and wise) will not be apparent. In pursuing the question, however, we should not be constrained by the narrow understanding of corruption most evident in common usage (including the social science literature), namely the betrayal of the public trust for private (generally financial) benefit. Instead it will be useful to embrace an older view, one with a respectable lineage in the tradition of political philosophy, and perhaps best expressed in Montesquieu's observation that "The corruption of every government generally begins with that of its principles."[6] Accordingly, a "corrupt practice" should be understood in the light of regime principles, those constitutive commitments that establish a polity's constitutional identity. Critical here is the concept of *integrity*, as applied both to our modern intuition about corruption as the abuse of a public trust and to its conceptualization here, where it speaks to a lack of fit between a given practice and the animating precepts of the surrounding constitutional order.[7] How helpful, then, is the Court's defense of the Representation of the People Act?

The defense begins reasonably with an approving account of statutory intent. "Obviously the purpose of enacting the provision [in RPA] is to ensure that no candidate at an election gets votes only because of his religion and no candidate is denied any votes on the ground of his religion. This is in keeping with the secular character of the Indian polity."[8] But the meaning of this legitimation, as clear as it may on first inspection seem, ultimately must rest upon a matter of inflection left unresolved by the Court's imprimatur. Is the law in keeping with the *secular* character of the Indian polity, or rather with the secular character of the *Indian* polity? We know, of course, that the secular character of other polities (including the American) has not led to the regulation of campaign rhetoric featuring sectarian religious appeals. So either these other polities have not done what they should in order adequately to support their commitments to secularism, or there is something special about the secular character of the Indian polity that in this case at least justifies restrictions on religious speech as an appropriate response to "corrupt practices." In the next section I will argue that the latter understanding best comports with what is distinctive about Indian constitutionalism. But we need first to see how the Court's discussion assumes an idealized model of liberal democratic politics more than it does the particularities of the Indian experience.

In emphasizing the sustaining features of a secular polity (i.e., where "the State has no religion and the State practices the policy of neutrality in the matter of religion"),[9] the Court appealed to language from an earlier decision. "No democratic political and social order, in which the conditions of freedom and their progressive expansion for all make some regulation of all activities imperative, could endure without an agreement on the basic essentials which could unite and hold citizens together despite all the differences of religion, race, caste, community, culture, creed, and language."[10] What these "essentials" are may be gathered from the fact that "In order that the democratic process should thrive and succeed, it is of utmost importance that our elections to Parliament and the different legislative bodies must be free from the unhealthy influence of appeals to religion, race, caste, community, or language."[11] Thus the success of the democratic project is predicated on the exclusion of certain forms of argumentation from the electoral arena, specifically those that appeal to voters on the basis of ascriptive affiliation. But what precisely is it that is "unhealthy" in such appeals? The Court said, "[O]ur *democracy can only survive if those who aspire to become people's representatives and leaders understand the spirit of secular democracy*. That spirit was characterized by Montesquieu long ago as one of 'virtue.' . . . *For such a spirit to prevail, candidates at elections have to try to persuade electors by showing them the light of reason and not by inflaming their blind and disruptive passions.*"[12]

The Court's understanding of a "corrupt practice" relies on a normative view of politics in which the presence of procedurally correct reasoned deliberation becomes the measure of viable secular democratic institutions. Those activities that depart from this defining norm are therefore corrupt in the sense adverted to earlier; that is, they tend to undermine the essential principles of secular democratic governance. In this regard, the specific invocation of Montesquieu reminds us that the "spirit of the laws" is not self-sustaining; rather it requires the support of law, in this case the statutory prohibition against certain kinds of campaign rhetoric. The intent behind the section 123 prohibition may not have been to guarantee that elected officials would exercise their powers on a nonreligious basis, but, as one analysis of some early RPA decisions suggests, probably it was to minimize that possibility.[13] In clearly endorsing this interpretation, the Court's argument bears a striking resemblance to formulations advanced in contemporary liberal political theory which, as Ronald Thiemann aptly puts it, "grant[s] virtual axiomatic status to the belief that religious convictions must be limited solely to the realm of the private."[14] This segmentation is essential for a "liberalism of reasoned respect," the goal of which is a structured society that places a premium on the virtue of civility.[15]

The derivation of these limitations in contemporary liberal theory mirrors the structure of the Court's arguments, in which democracy's survival is placed in jeopardy by the presence of irreconcilable group-based differences (or comprehensive views), only to be maintained and preserved by a shared commitment to basic essentials, including a process for reaching public decisions by the light of reason. For example, in *Political Liberalism*, Rawls tackles the pluralist conundrum of "How [it is] possible for there to exist over time a just and stable society of free and equal citizens, who remain profoundly divided by reasonable religious, philosophical, and moral doctrines[.]"[16] While Rawls rightly assumes that all societies with aspirations to political justice confront this vexing dilemma, it is of course a question with special significance for India, arguably the most diverse society in the world.[17] For this reason the Indian Court had a very easy time upholding the constitutionality of that section of the RPA under which the Shiv Sena leader, Mr. Thackeray, had been prosecuted. Thus political rhetoric that promotes enmity and hatred among different classes of citizens must be appraised in India against that country's sad history of religiously and ethnically inspired violence. Appropriately, the constitutional guarantee in Article 19 of freedom of speech and expression includes a public order exception, in accordance with which restrictions on group-directed assaultive speech, especially in the highly charged setting of an electoral contest, could be (and was) comfortably accommodated.[18]

The Constitution also includes a "decency and morality" exception, which is the provision the judges appealed to in order to uphold RPA's other prohibition on religiously inspired speech. This affirmance could not be obtained as straightforwardly as was the hate speech proscription, and so it became necessary for the Court to rely on interpretive ingenuity, which in this instance meant abjuring the narrow, if more obvious, sexually oriented intention behind the exception, in favor of a meaning more consonant with liberal norms of political propriety. "Thus, seeking votes at an election on the ground of the candidate's religion in a secular State, is against the norms of decency and propriety of the society."[19] What is here given constitutional mooring is presented in Rawls as a morally desirable, but not legally enforceable, standard for liberal polities as they confront the critical pluralist challenge. "[I]t is normally desirable that the comprehensive philosophic and moral views we are wont to use in debating fundamental political issues should give way in public life."[20] The Indian Court's "norm of decency and propriety" is in essence a corollary of Rawls' ideal of public reason, a norm deducible from the fundamentals of the liberal democratic polity. While the norm, as incorporated in RPA, is intended to cover only the specific kind of political appeal delineated in the statute (and thus not to religiously articulated perspectives on public issues in general), its underlying logic is fundamentally consonant with the Rawlsian aspiration.[21] "[T]he ideal of public reason. . .hold[s] for citizens when they engage in political advocacy in the public forum, and thus for. . .candidates in their campaigns and for other groups who support them. It holds equally for how citizens are to vote in elections when constitutional essentials and matters of basic justice are at stake."[22] Although there is no citation of Rawls in the Court's judgment, the author of the opinion, Justice Verma, was familiar with the argument of *Political Liberalism*, having cited it two years earlier in the majority opinion of one of the Supreme Court's most eagerly awaited cases, the so-called *Ayodhya Reference Case*.[23]

Rawls's ideal has been the subject of withering critique and flattering emulation. Its detractors have found it intolerant of illiberal views whose very divisiveness should be present in public debate;[24] mistaken in its assumption that shared premises are the prerequisite for public deliberation among contestants holding widely disparate views;[25] illusory in its presumption of having transcended religious-like dogma;[26] impractical in its rendering of liberalism inaccessible to those most in need of its principles;[27] and opposed to a life of integrity in its insistence on refashioning arguments to make them conform to the dictates of reason.[28] On the other hand, theorists of note have borrowed from and refined the Rawlsian ideal, as they have developed reciprocity-based exclusions of religion from the jurisdiction of political action;[29] formulated a "principle of secular rationale" to govern advocacy in the public forum;[30] and established limiting principles for the intervention of religious convictions in the making of political choices.[31]

In reflecting on the Indian Court's consideration of political corruption, these perspectives can be deployed in supportive or critical ways. My argument, however, does not require taking a position on the merits of these claims, except to observe in regard to both sides of the debate that their focus, like that of Rawls, is on the criteria appropriate for secular democracies in general. The Court's constitutional evaluation of RPA proceeds in similar fashion, as it develops an understanding of corrupt practices on the basis of theoretically driven liberal aspirations to a just political order. In so doing, however, it fails to provide an adequately textured account of political corruption, one that conveys a fuller sense of why it is that an appeal to voters to exercise their democratic freedom on the basis of religious considerations threatens the core principles of *this* secular regime; and how the *legal* proscription of such appeals may possess a logic consistent with secular democratic expectations. In the next section I will try to show what such an account might look like.

Religion, Equality, and Constitutional Essentials

The ideal of public reason in Rawls is meant to apply to the discussion of constitutional essentials and matters of basic justice. Constitutional essentials are of two kinds: (1) fundamental principles specifying the general structure of government and the political process; and (2) equal basic rights of citizenship, including rights connected to voting and political participation, conscience, thought and association, and the rule of law.[32] Specifically excluded by Rawls from this enumeration are principles regulating basic matters of fair opportunity and social and economic inequalities.[33] These latter are of course important, but they are more contestable than the essentials dealing with basic freedoms; also there is less urgency in settling them than is the case for the basics.

Upon first glance the Indian Constitution displays textual consistency with Rawls's decision about constitutional essentials. Part III of the document contains a detailed enumeration of the sort of fundamental rights mentioned by Rawls in (2), followed in Part IV with a listing of the Directive Principles of State Policy. Included in this latter section are directives to the State concerning the achievement of social justice. "The

State shall strive to promote the welfare of the people by securing and protecting as effectively as it may a social order in which justice, social, economic and political, shall inform all the institutions of the national life" (Article 38). But as the preceding Article states, this section, unlike Part III, is not enforceable by any court; while important, it is essentially hortatory in nature. Thus one might suppose that the principles contained therein are both more contestable and less urgent than those specified in Part III.

Such a supposition, however, is unwarranted. If under the rubric of constitutional essentials in India are not to be found principles regulating basic matters of social and economic inequality, then much of the history of the Indian Constitution will need to be rewritten. And more directly to the point of this essay, the regulation of these matters is deeply enmeshed in constitutional policy concerning religious freedom, so much so that to imagine one without the other is radically to misconstrue the essence of Indian constitutionalism. Thus the nonjusticiable aspirations of the directive principles are in fact manifest in the explicit limitations attached to constitutionally guaranteed rights. For example, Article 25 provides that "Subject to public order, morality and health . . . all persons are equally entitled to freedom of conscience and the right freely to profess, practise and propagate religion." The second section of the Article then goes on to say: "Nothing in this article shall affect the operation of any existing law or prevent the State from making any law—(a) regulating or restricting any economic, financial, political or other secular activity which may be associated with religious practice; (b) providing for social welfare and reform, or the throwing open of Hindu religious institutions of a public character to all classes and sections of Hindus." Thus with admirable clarity the document guarantees all Indians a broad right to religious freedom, only to declare that this right is subject to substantial possible limitation.[34] The application of the term "corrupt practice" to religiously framed campaign rhetoric is consistent with the underlying logic of these limitations. The constitutional essentials of the Indian polity were forged out of the tension between religion and equality. To the extent that political corruption represents an erosion of the core commitments of a given polity, then the most compelling interpretation of RPA is that it seeks to reinforce the special character of *Indian* secular constitutionalism.

In this connection I have elsewhere developed a typology for understanding alternative secular constitutional possibilities that is built around two critical dimensions, one involving the explanatory power of religion in apprehending the structural configuration of a given society and the other concerning the extent to which the State is decisively identified with any particular religious group.[35] The first dimension is captured by the anthropological concept of a cultural "way of life," in which a (religious) system of beliefs, symbols, and values becomes engrained in the basic structure of society and ultimately sets the parameters within which vital societal relations occur. In this holistic conception, the distinction between the secular and the religious largely disappears. It is a disappearance that, in the case of India, renders problematic (as we shall see) the application of Rawlsian public reasoning, which, predicated on the existence of a distinct secular realm, insists on separating what may be indivisible.[36] Thus the religious presence in a society may be conceptualized as *thick* or *thin* (demanding or modest), the latter referring to a situation where religion bears only tangentially upon the life experiences (in a sociopolitical rather than personal sense) of most people. The second dimension refers to the official cognizance of religion, more specifically, how closely the State adheres to a commitment to neutrality in its relations with religious groups. This dimension is a familiar staple of American constitutional law; simply put, the official favoring (or not) of one religion over others for special benefits.

The resulting analysis yields three secular models—*ameliorative, assimilative,* and *visionary*—that are meant to be suggestive of orientations toward the secular constitution as well as expressive of salient aspects of national identity. They highlight contrasting emphases, rather than set forth mutually exclusive approaches to the constitutive problem of religion and politics.[37] In the case of India, the constitutional promise of State neutrality toward religious groups is a corollary of the transformational agenda of Indian nationalism, a principal objective of which is the democratization of a social order inhabited by a thickly constituted religious presence that is in severe tension with liberal political aspirations. The *ameliorative* model embraces the social reform impulse of Indian nationalism without ignoring countervailing impulses within the entrenched religious diversity of Indian society.[38]

Consider in this regard Alexis de Tocqueville's famous insight that Americans possessed the distinct advantage of having "arrived at a state of democracy without having to endure a democratic revolution." While no longer as uncontroversial as it once was, it still offers a useful clarifying lens through which to obtain comparative perspective on many things, including secular constitutional development. If Tocqueville and his latter-day intellectual disciples, most notably Louis Hartz, exaggerated the differences between the United States and Europe, their emphasis on the absence of a feudal tradition in the United States (the South excepted) was not misplaced. The Americans' fortunate circumstance of having been "born equal, instead of becoming so" meant that their social and political development could proceed largely in the absence of the bitterly divisive ideological battles that prevailed in most

other places. As for their secular constitutional development, what is interesting is not simply the founding commitment to a secular polity, but
that in order to achieve that goal they did not have to break the chains
(again with some local exceptions) of a dominant religion. By contrast,
in having to overcome a feudal religious order, Indian constitutionalists
understandably moved in the direction of a more transformative constitution, in which the commitment to secularism was directly related to
the goal of social reconstruction.[39]

This brings us back to the irony of the Court's rumination on the
dominant religion of India. Correctly construing Hinduism as much
more than theology, as a social and cultural presence that requires treatment as "a way of life," it then went on to reverse holdings against politicians who had promised to establish a Hindu state and commit it to
the essentials of *Hindutva*. But it is precisely the fact that religion in
India *is* so pervasive and all-encompassing, with consequences deeply
problematic for the egalitarian objectives of the Constitution, that provides RPA's campaign restrictions with a measure of coherence and principled consistency.[40] Thus, the very blurring of the distinction between
religion and culture that the Court then proceeded to find exculpatory
as applied to the charge of political corruption, is what provides a compelling policy rationale for RPA. Moreover, it is a rationale that fits comfortably within the secular logic and commitments of the Constitution,
the latter aptly characterized by an observation from an earlier opinion
cited by the Court, but not fully appreciated by the judges for the implications it contains. "The concept of secularism is one facet of the right
to equality woven as the central golden thread in the fabric depicting the
pattern of the scheme in our Constitution."[41] One does not have to embrace wholeheartedly the late nineteenth-century Indian social reformer
K. T. Telang's indictment of Hinduism for "preach[ing] not the equality of men but their inequality," and for being in a state of "war against
the principles of democracy," to grasp the significance in India of religion's challenge to the secular State and its reconstructive aspirations.[42]

That challenge, of course, is most evident in the resurgence of Hindu
nationalism, a movement that should never be viewed as representing
Hindus generally (an impossibility given the radically heterodox nature
of the religion), but one that voices a sociocultural agenda that historically qualifies as the foil of Indian nationalism. The democratization of
a rigidly hierarchical social order that is correlated strongly with a thickly
constituted religious presence had always been an animating principle of
the Indian independence movement, one that continued to give meaning to postcolonial constitutional politics. Hence it must be observed
with more than just passing interest that historically the spirit of Hindu
nationalism has been nurtured by high-caste Hindus who have been no-

table in their insensitivity to India's downtrodden. As Christophe Jaffrelot has pointed out, "Hindu nationalism . . . largely reflects the Brah-
minical view of the high caste reformers who shaped its ideology."[43] Indeed, it has been the pervasiveness of this ethic in both ideology and
practice that explains why it has had only minimal success in attracting
support from low caste Hindus.[44] Even the efforts to reshape the movement's appeal to disadvantaged Hindus by capitalizing on resentments
against Muslims have been notably unproductive as exercises in mass
mobilization. In this respect Hindu nationalism, if not unique, is distinguishable from most contemporary religious nationalist movements in
not being a populist based movement directed against the entrenched
economic power of established interests. The threat in all of this to the
ameliorative constitution, which is to say secular constitutionalism in
India, is clear.[45]

What, then, is wrong with this bit of nasty campaign rhetoric from
Mr. Thackeray? "We are fighting this election for the protection of Hinduism. Therefore, we do not care for the votes of the Muslims. This
country belongs to Hindus and will remain so."[46] The Court found this
sentiment in violation of RPA's proscription against speech that promotes enmity and hatred against classes of citizens, which it most as-
suredly does. But it might also be seen as a verbal assault on secular democracy in India, because indirectly it serves to perpetuate an unjust
status quo structured around a radically skewed distribution of wealth,
status, and influence. Votes gained as a result of an attack on the Muslim
minority are votes that surely will, if sufficient in number, translate into
policies adverse to the interests of lower-class Hindus (as well as Muslims and others), and so may be seen as violating the spirit of secular
democracy as outlined in the Constitution. What qualifies this speech as
a "corrupt practice" is only partially revealed by its explicit attack on
Indian national unity; a complete account must also clarify the meaning
of its implicit attack on ameliorative secularism.

Indeed, this attack is evident in some of the journalistic reactions to
the Supreme Court decisions by Hindu nationalist writers. "It is unfortunate," says one, "that fault is being found with a clear, rational, fair,
incisive and sound enunciation of law, constitution and culture of India
by the apex court."[47] This approval provides an opportunity to claim
vindication for longstanding political positions. Thus another writer
points out, "A major sin of the judgment for the secularists arose from
the fact the Court accepted, indeed adopted in toto the definition of
Hindu, of Hindutva which the RSS and the BJP have been maintaining
is what they have meant whenever they have used these expressions."[48]
The author then revealingly moves from approval to advice, expressing
the hope that one day the Court will examine, as part of its interpretive

role in relation to the illegalities of corrupt practices, the solicitation of votes on the basis of class antagonism. "How come that, while it is an offense under our laws to spread hatred or solicit votes on the basis of religion, caste, etc., it is perfectly all right to spread hatred and enmity, and to solicit votes on the basis of class?"[49] To which the secularist disturbed by the Court's obliviousness to the ameliorative logic of RPA might respond with wry admiration—as well as contempt—for his opponents' clever effort to steer the Court towards the embrace of an opposing logic.

We now have a plausible non-Rawlsian answer to the question of why section 123 seeks to minimize the occasions for elected officials to exercise their powers on religious grounds. Or at least it is an answer that illustrates that the norms of public reason must be framed in such a way that culturally specific iterations are given their due. Indian restrictions on religious speech can be justified according to content-neutral principles that conform to contemporary conceptualizations of the liberal State; but those principles do not readily conform to the non-neutrality of the Indian State as delineated in the nation's Constitution. It is only when political liberalism is identified with neutrality that the alternative rationale for these restrictions—one that finds in the substance of religious belief and practice a reason for action—will be deemed illiberal. And as I take up in the next section, notions of corrupt practices engrained in legal precedent reinforce the noninterventionist constitutional requirement of contemporary liberalism, while providing a sympathetic, if ultimately unsuccessful, hearing for the Rawlsian case for public reason.

Corruption: Process and Substance

Section 298 of the Indian Penal Code makes punishable whoever "with the deliberate intention of wounding the religious feelings of any person, utters any word or makes any sound in the hearing of that person." It is the sort of regulation that may remind Americans of some campus speech codes, most of which are widely seen, since the Supreme Court's decision in *R. A. V. v. St. Paul*, as unconstitutional viewpoint based violations of the First Amendment. *R. A. V.* was the case cited by the Court in *Rosenberger* v. *University of Virginia*, where it held that a public university could not withhold funding for a Christian publication while providing support to other student publications. In his majority opinion, Justice Anthony Kennedy wrote, "The government must abstain from regulating speech when the specific motivating ideology or the opinion or perspective of the speaker is the rationale for the restriction."[50] There was much in Justice Kennedy's opinion that the minority contested, including the application of this principle to the case at hand; but as to the correctness of the underlying doctrine, there was general assent.

Viewpoint neutrality has become the axiomatic precept of First Amendment jurisprudence, as well as the *grundnorm* of the "procedural republic." That it should apply to religious speech as it does to other types of expression is unproblematic, since in a liberal polity a religious point of view is in principle no different from any other perspective one chooses to embrace. This follows from what Michael Sandel refers to as "the voluntarist justification of neutrality," the requirement that "[g]overnment should be neutral toward religion in order to respect persons as free and independent selves, capable of choosing their religious convictions for themselves."[51] Sandel of course is critical of this ascendant view. "Protecting religion as a life-style, as one among the values that an independent self may have, may miss the role that religion plays in the lives of those for whom the observance of religious duties is a constitutive end, essential to their good and indispensable to their identity."[52] In the American context this argument leads to deference and accommodation in the face of religious obligations that compete with State policies. In India just the opposite is true; where it more readily may serve to legitimate an unjust status quo, such accommodation is a much costlier indulgence.

As we think about restrictions on religious speech in Indian penal and electoral law, the case for their reasonability turns on the sociopolitical implications of deeply encumbered selves. The Constitution's various exceptions to "First Amendment" freedoms are an implicit rejection of the American neutrality axiom, since religion as a lived experience is, for most people in India, much more than a constellation of views and beliefs that one chooses to adopt. Hence State indifference to the substance of ideas can not so easily be justified as it can in the United States. Interestingly, Justice Kennedy's opinion in *Rosenberger* acknowledges that the doctrine of viewpoint neutrality possesses a certain awkwardness when applied to religious speech. "It is, in a sense, something of an understatement to speak of religious thought and discussion as just a viewpoint, as distinct from a comprehensive body of thought. The nature of our origins and destiny and their dependence on the existence of a divine being have been subjects of philosophic inquiry throughout human history."[53] But there is nothing in this acknowledgment to the effect that religious expression, though comprehensive, is anything more than "a vast area of inquiry,"[54] that it might constitute, in the phrase of an Indian Supreme Court Justice, "a way of life and nothing more."[55] It is this characteristically American separation between comprehensiveness and consequence that makes a principled commitment to judicial agnosticism relatively uncontroversial.

Viewpoint neutrality has a connection as well to political corruption. In the United States, the constitutional debate over corrupt practices centers on statutory restrictions on campaign financing. Nothing in this debate bears directly on questions of religion; nevertheless American judicial scrutiny of these restrictions shows why the notion of *corruption* is important to a comparative analysis of religious speech in the public arena. The same principle that protects candidates and politicians who publicly proclaim the Christian content of American identity also protects the unlimited expenditures of those who support their political ambitions.

Consider in this regard Justice Antonin Scalia's criticism of a majority opinion upholding a Michigan limitation on corporate campaign expenditures. "Under [the Court's] mode of analysis virtually anything the Court deems politically undesirable can be turned into political corruption—by simply describing its effects as politically 'corrosive,' which is close enough to 'corruptive to qualify."[56] Scalia was objecting to the Court's discovery of a "New Corruption," found to exist in the distortive effect of massive infusions of corporate wealth into the political process. According to the Court, there was no correlation between immense aggregations of corporate wealth and the public's support for the corporation's ideas, a lack of association that constitutionally justified the State's representation-reinforcing restriction. Scalia's critique parallels Martin Shapiro's argument that "By calling various inequalities corruption we can ignore the risks to freedom that are endemic in the pursuit of equality."[57] Underlying the criticisms of both Scalia and Shapiro is the latter's further observation: "Americans enjoy an ambivalent relationship with freedom of speech. They believe in it for the good guys but not the bad guys. There was a time when the bad guys were on the left and the hated danger was 'subversion.' Today the bad guys are on the right and the danger is 'corruption.'"[58]

From this perspective the judicial abuse of the term "corruption" represents a departure from the constitutional requirement of viewpoint neutrality. It is a perspective perhaps reflective of what has been called "the liberal transvaluation of corruption," a development traceable to Hobbes, in which "[t]o call a regime corrupt is to say something about the speaker's preferences, not about the regime itself."[59] Just as "subversion" was a term used in the past to delegitimate ideas on the left, "corruption" has assumed a similar role today in attacking the system opposed by the left. In both instances the terms should be applied narrowly by judges only to specific acts of malfeasance, for example, a conspiracy to overthrow the government or a bribe offered to a public official. Scalia's sharply worded dissent in *Austin* seeks to restore to the law of campaign finance restrictions the logic behind the Court's landmark decision in *Buckley v. Valeo*, in which the meaning of corruption was to be limited to *quid pro quo* arrangements (or the appearance thereof) connected to large contributions. Or as Chief Justice William Rehnquist wrote in *Federal Election Commission v. NCPAC*: "Corruption is a subversion of the political process. Elected officials are influenced to act contrary to their obligations of office by the prospect of financial gain to themselves or infusions of money into their campaigns. The hallmark of corruption is the financial *quid pro quo*: dollars for political favors."[60] This *quid pro quo* emphasis had led the Court in *Buckley* to strike down limitations on independent expenditures, since the implicit meaning of corruption contained in such limitations was a broader political one having to do with the best way to organize a society. "[T]he concept that government may restrict the speech of some elements of our society in order to enhance the relative voice of others is wholly foreign to the First Amendment, which was designed. . .'to assure unfettered exchange of ideas for the bringing about of political and social changes desired by the people.'"[61]

What, under this account, can we say of the Indian use of the term "corrupt practice" to refer to certain kinds of religiously inspired speech in electoral campaigns? Following the argument in the previous section, we might conclude that the validity of the usage hinges on the fact that the Constitution itself is a principal agent of social change, not just the people as suggested in *Buckley* about the American scheme. Moreover, in the spirit of ameliorative secularism, it is a specific kind of social change that is constitutionally prescribed, so that corruption—the departure from the politics of first principles and collective self-understanding—need not be subject to the American-like limitations of viewpoint neutrality. Where, in the United States, "[p]olitical corruption violates and undermines the norms of the system of public order which is deemed indispensable for the maintenance of political democracy[,]"[62] in India a more ambitious democratic agenda serves to broaden the scope of corrupt practices to cover, as we have seen, campaign speech that advances the prospects that governmental policy will be based on religious considerations.

To be sure, the Court in *Austin* ignored Justice Scalia's concerns about the New Corruption and extended the mantle of corrupt practices beyond the narrow *quid pro quo* focus of *Buckley*. But the Court's extension stays well within the procedural boundaries of representative government. The infirmity of massive corporate expenditures to advance particular policy objectives is found in the disjunction between political speech and the amount of public support for the funded positions. This introduces a distortion into the political process that may be legislatively corrected consistent with constitutionally mandated First Amendment requirements, including viewpoint neutrality. As Dennis Thompson notes, "The idea that corruption involves bypassing the democratic process is not partial toward any particular view about democracy."[63] Removing the distortion opens the way to a fuller realization of what Rawls refers to as "a political conception of justice for the main institutions of political and social life."[64] Indeed, as one commentator points out, "[W]e can best explain *Austin's* redefinition of political corruption by returning to some basic legal and political theory," namely Rawls's principle of an equal right to participation, a principle of course included among the constitutional essentials for a liberal and just polity.[65]

Another finds in *Austin* support for Thompson's deliberative theory of liberal democratic governance, in which Rawlsian public reason considerations are much in evidence. "[I]f representation involves deliberation about the public good, then contributions that influence representatives are a corruption of the democratic process."[66] Genuine deliberation will not occur if representatives are, by virtue of their obligations to contributors, essentially unreachable through reasoned argument. What Thompson refers to as "the improper use of public office" can mean both the pursuit of private gain through official misconduct, and the subversion of the democratic process through the construction of obstacles in the way of reasoned deliberation. It is this second invocation of the language of impropriety that links campaign financing and religious speech, since the excesses of both have in common the tendency to undercut the liberal polity's ideal of public reason. "A belief in the importance of public deliberation is essential for a reasonable constitutional regime, and specific institutions and arrangements need to be laid down to support and encourage it."[67] Acting on this belief might cause one to favor limitations on activities that lead to the making of public decisions on the basis of "nonpublic reasons"—as arguably would be the case for the legislative recipient of large amounts of money and for the exponent of a comprehensive religious doctrine.[68]

Of course, despite this connecting logic, it is extremely doubtful that an American court would ever use the "new corruption" as a constitutional impetus for upholding restrictions on religious speech in the public arena. Were the judges all political liberals in the Rawlsian sense they very likely would still value untrammeled speech rights over public reason inspired legal limits on expression; but they would undoubtedly see the restrictions as having some principled foundation. Yet if they were so inclined, they could view their efforts as responsive to corrupt practices, as a judicial defense of the constitutive commitments of a liberal polity. That indeed is what the Indian Court appears to have done in upholding the constitutionality of RPA's regulation of religious speech in campaigns. The fact that the Court then proceeded to overturn the convictions of Hindu nationalist politicians prosecuted under the statute suggests very strongly that the principled underpinnings of the constitutional ruling were more in line with Rawlsian assumptions about liberal constitutionalism than with the logic of ameliorative secularism.[69] But the Court never made clear why the need to govern "by the light of reason" required legally enforceable sanctions, why unlike other secular democratic polities such as the United States, reliance on other mechanisms would not be sufficient. Indeed, Rawls himself does not advocate the legal codification of his ideal of public reason. The most telling criticism of the Court's rulings—that together they constituted a "watering down" of the provisions of RPA and "a very severe blow to the principle of secular democracy"—derives whatever force it may have from the special needs of *this* secular democracy and not from the constitutional essentials of political liberalism.[70]

Conclusion

Suppose a familiarity with Indian law persuaded American lawmakers of the wisdom of enacting a RPA in the United States. Let us assume further that after its enactment into law it is quickly applied to the governor of Mississippi, who has persisted in pushing his Christian nation claim. For example, in campaigning for one of his followers who is running for Congress he is quoted as saying: "Joe deserves your support because he understands the meaning of America, that it is and has always been in essence a Christian nation. I can promise you that in all that Joe will do as your representative, he will be guided by the precepts of his Christian identity." Joe then gets elected but is deprived of his victory for having permitted his campaign to run afoul of the new law.

How might the U.S. Supreme Court respond to this result? Consider three possibilities. (1) The finding against Joe is reversed, and the statute under which his election was denied to him is held unconstitutional. The law violates both the Freedom of Speech and Free Exercise clauses of the First Amendment. (2) The finding against Joe is reversed, but the statute under which the election was denied to him is held constitutional. Joe has done nothing wrong since his Christian identity is a cultural affiliation, not a religious calling. The law, however, is consistent with the spirit of the Constitution, specifically its secular commitment to reasoned deliberation in the public arena. (3) The finding against Joe is upheld, and the statute under which his election was denied to him is constitutional. The First Amendment is not an absolute, and the rights guaranteed under it are bounded by important public welfare considerations, among which is the discouragement of religious motivations in the making of public policy.

Option (1) is the obvious candidate for selection for reasons that should be quite evident. It fits all of the expectations we bring to the case based on prevailing precedent and doctrine. But it is worth considering why (2) and (3) appear on their face to be implausible choices; doing so will highlight the major point of this essay, which is that the effort to derive guidelines and principles for the regulation of religious discourse in the public sphere cannot proceed only from an exercise in abstract moral reasoning but must confront as well the diversity of experience in secular constitutional arrangements.

Option (2) represents the approach taken by the Indian Supreme Court in the RPA cases. It involved a decision by the Court to understate the religious significance of Hinduism in favor of a cultural understanding, thereby freeing the defendant Hindu nationalists of legal liability in the face of a statute that legitimately seeks to structure campaign debate according to a constitutional norm of reasoned deliberation. In the American context this norm (deduced from the essentials of a liberal polity) must, unlike in India, confront the categorical language of the First Amendment without the support of any exception clauses that might be viewed textually as a convenient constitutional location for asserting the relevant ideal. An additional (and more interesting, if debatable) obstacle resides in the greater difficulty one would have in making a cultural claim on behalf of Christian identity, which much more than its Hindu counterpart is something one experiences as a matter of faith rather than (at least in most instances) as a way of life. So an American court would have even less success than an Indian one in eliding the religious significance of a candidate's promise to pursue a sectarian agenda grounded in religious tradition.

Option (3) looks like a coherent and perhaps sensible solution for India, but makes very little sense for the United States. Not only is there much less warrant for perceiving the majority religion in the United States as a way of life, but to the limited extent that it can be so viewed, its role in structuring social institutions and relations hardly compares in magnitude with the role in that regard of the majority religion in India. Therefore, the legally sanctioned discouragement of religiously motivated public policy has minimal constitutional standing when, as in the United States, it is not necessary for the attainment of public welfare objectives that are at once urgent and constitutionally directed. To be sure, the secularization of political discourse can always be asserted to have policy consequences. And occasionally, as, say, in the case of legislation affecting people's sexual behavior, religious arguments may play a critical role in explaining, for better or worse, the evolution of policies. But to imagine something comparable to the Indian situation would require viewing the historic systematic subordination of a class of people in the United States as having been the result largely of religious beliefs and practices that are now illegal by dint of constitutional mandate.

It is quite revealing that when public welfare considerations *are* introduced in the United States as an occasion for limiting religious freedom it occurs in response to someone's claim for an exemption on religious grounds from an otherwise unexceptionable law. Since the Supreme Court's controversial decision in *Employment Division v. Smith*, and its subsequent invalidation of the Religious Freedom Restoration Act, upholding the public welfare, defined neutrally as the need to reinforce civil authority, does not require the demonstration of a compelling state interest. The Indian Constitution, on the other hand, defines with unmistakable certainty what *constitutes* a compelling State interest. So clear is its incorporation of the egalitarian ideal into the text of the document that the meaning of corruption as having something to do with the direct (or as in the case of RPA, indirect) frustration of that aspiration is not a fanciful notion. This suggests that the appeal of public reason as an ideal for liberal polities is more variable than any abstract account of its virtues might lead one to presume. Indeed, it turns out that the case for limiting certain kinds of religious speech in democratic deliberation is strongest when it is identified with the defense of constitutional essentials that are not recognized as such in the articulated premises of political liberalism.

Notes

1. The key case is *Cantwell v Connecticut*, 310 US 296 (1940). In reversing the conviction of someone who employed offensive and abusive speech in denouncing the Roman Catholic Church, the Court concluded that "[T]he people of this nation have ordained in the light of history, that, in spite of the probability of excesses and abuses, these [First Amendment] liberties are, in the long view, essential to enlightened opinion and right conduct on the part of the citizens of a democracy." *Cantwell v Connecticut*, at 310.

2. On this point see J. Patrick Dobel, "The Corruption of a State," 72 *American Political Science Review* 958 (1978). Dobel appeals to Plato, Aristotle, Macchiavelli, and Rousseau for the view that "the source of systematic corruption lies in certain patterns of inequality." (961)

3. The latter two decisions were extremely controversial. While they were applauded in Hindu nationalist circles, they were seen by others as a watering down of the provisions of the Representation of the People Act. For example, one commentator wrote: "Would the normal electorate in India understand that

what is meant by Hindutva is the culture of all the people of India including those of non-Hindu faiths? Obviously, by Hindutva most of the voters would understand the culture of Hindus including their religious faith, and not the faith and culture of non-Hindus." He concluded: "These decisions of the Supreme Court Bench are thus highly derogatory to the principle of secular democracy and the letter and spirit of Section 123(3) of the Representation of the People Act, 1951." V. M. Tarkunde, "Hindutva and the Supreme Court," *Hindustan Times*, January 10, 1996, 13. Said another scathing review: "The judgment is yet another instance of a widespread confusion in the discourse on secularism, pluralism, and humanism." Anil Nauriya, "The Hindutva Judgments: A Warning Signal," 31 *Economic and Political Weekly*, no. 1, January 6, 1996. Criticism of the Court for its interpretations of RPA extends to judgments in earlier years as well. See, for example, V. S. Rekhi, "Religion, Politics and Law in Contemporary India: Judicial Doctrine in Critical Perspective," in *Religion and Law in Independent India*, ed. Robert D. Baird (New Delhi: Manohar, 1993).

4. *Prabhoo v Kunte*, 1 S.Ct. 130 (1996), at 159.

5. Ibid., at 159.

6. Montesquieu, *The Spirit of the Laws* (New York: Hafner, 1966) , 109. For an interesting discussion of corruption as it has been understood in political philosophy, see Dobel, "The Corruption of a State." See also J. Peter Euben, "Corruption," in *Political Innovation and Conceptual Change*, ed. Terence Ball, James Farr, and Russell L. Hanson (Cambridge: Cambridge University Press, 1989).

7. Integrity as a virtue in liberal political theory has been most fully developed by Ronald Dworkin. "Integrity becomes a political ideal when we make the same demand of the state or community taken to be a moral agent, when we insist that the state act on a single, coherent set of principles even when its citizens are divided about what the right principles of justice and fairness really are." Ronald Dworkin, *Law's Empire* (Cambridge, Mass.: Harvard University Press, 1986), 166. Corruption, in short, represents the loss of integrity. J. Peter Euben's discussion of corruption in Aristotle's thought also captures this sense of integrity. "When a constitution systematically falls short of the paradigms of action, character, and justice which give it unity and definition, it is corrupt." Euben, "Corruption," 227.

8. *Prabhoo v Kunte*, at 145. For the history of the RPA see, Hans Raj Jhingta, *Corrupt Practices in Elections: A Study under the Representation of the People Act, 1951* (New Delhi: Deep and Deep Publications, 1996). Most of the RPA is modeled after a similar English law, but the section on religious appeals appears only in the Indian law. See also Keshari Tripathi, *The Representation of the People Act, 1951* (Allahabad: Dardeval Publishing House, 1974). "Section 123(3) is a provision which is in consonance with the policy of the framers of the Constitution to make India a secular State, a State which has no religion of its own and which refrains from discrimination on grounds of religion." Ibid., at 499. As in most discussions of the electoral law, only a superficial consideration of the Indian secular State is provided, leaving unresolved an explanation for the comparative uniqueness of the statute.

9. Ibid., at 147.

10. Ibid., at 149. Obviously the reference to caste speaks directly to the Indian experience, but for present purposes its connection to religion is so intimate that the general argument in which it appears may still be viewed as derivative from the nature of a secular polity and not just the Indian case.

11. Ibid., at 160.

12. Ibid., at 150. Emphasis in the original.

13. John H. Mansfield, "Religious Speech under Indian Law," in *Comparative Constitutional Law*, ed. Mahendra P. Singh (Lucknow, India: Eastern Book Co., 1989), 223. Mansfield, however, does not investigate the reasons for this policy objective, something I take up in the next section.

14. Ronald F. Thiemann, *Religion in Public Life: A Dilemma for Democracy* (Washington, D.C.: Georgetown University Press, 1996), 89.

15. Paul J. Weithman, "Religion and the Liberalism of Reasoned Respect," in *Religion and Contemporary Liberalism*, ed. Paul J. Weithman (Notre Dame, Ind.: University of Notre Dame Press, 1997), 4. Weithman argues that the liberalism of reasoned respect is addressed to advanced democracies, one manifestation of which is that reasoned discourse rather than the prevention of civil strife is the animating concern driving its proponents. Ibid., 33. This of course raises the obvious question as to the appropriateness of the principled application of the scheme to a place such as India.

16. John Rawls, *Political Liberalism* (New York: Columbia University Press, 1993), 4.

17. Rawls's philosophic method is occasionally insufficiently sensitive to questions of degree as they relate to societal division. He says, for example, that "Liberty of conscience and freedom of association, and the political rights of freedom of speech, voting, and running for office are characterized in more or less the same manner in all free regimes." Ibid., 228. Much depends on the meaning of "more or less," but as the differences between India and the United States on the issue of religious expression illustrates, free regimes can differ rather significantly on constitutional essentials in light of their alternative pluralist experiences. I pursue these differences in detail in *Apple of Gold: Constitutionalism in Israel and the United States* (Princeton, N.J.: Princeton University Press, 1993), chapter 6.

18. There are, in addition, many cases concerning provisions of the Penal Code in which restrictions on religious speech have been upheld under the Article 19 exception. However, as John Mansfield points out, "[T]he struggle between conflicting values—freedom of speech in matters of religion on the one hand and the protection of public order, religious sensibilities and religious identities on the other—has continued at the level of statutory interpretation." Mansfield, "Religious Speech under Indian Law," 211.

19. *Prabhoo v Kunte*, at 153.

20. Rawls, *Political Liberalism*, 10. "[T]he ideal of citizenship imposes a moral, not a legal, duty—the duty of civility—to be able to explain to to one another on those fundamental questions how the principles and policies they advocate and vote for can be supported by the political values of public reason." Ibid., 217.

21. "[A] democratic constitution," Rawls writes, "is a principled expression in higher law of the political ideal of a people to govern itself in a certain way. The aim of public reason is to articulate this ideal." Ibid., 232.

22. Ibid., 215.

23. The case, actually several combined cases, concerned the controversy stemming from the destruction of the Babri Masjid Mosque by Hindu nationalists on December 6, 1992. While the Court sidestepped the immediate issue of ownership of the property on which the mosque stood, it delivered important commentary on the nature of secularism in India. Justice Verma's opinion quotes a speech of a judicial colleague, in which the latter said: "In a pluralist, secular polity law is perhaps the greatest integrating force. A cultivated respect for law and its institutions and symbols; a pride in the country's heritage and achievements; faith that people live under the protection of an adequate legal system are indispensable for sustaining unity in pluralist diversity. Rawlsian pragmatism of 'justice as fairness' to serve as an 'over-lapping consensus' and deep seated agreements on fundamental questions of basic structure of society for deeper social unity is a political conception of justice rather than a comprehensive moral conception." *The Ayodhya Reference: The Supreme Court Judgement and Commentaries* (New Delhi: Voice of India, 1995), 36.

24. Michael Perry, *Religion In Politics: Constitutional and Moral Perspectives* (Oxford: Oxford University Press, 1997).

25. Jeremy Waldron, "Religious Contributions in Public Deliberation," 30 *San Diego Law Review* 817 (1993).

26. Miriam Galston, "Rawlsian Dualism and the Autonomy of Political Thought," 94 *Columbia Law Review* 1842 (1994).

27. Heidi Hurd, "The Levitation of Liberalism," 105 *Yale Law Journal* 795 (1995).

28. Elizabeth H. Wolgast, "The Demands of Public Reason," 94 *Columbia Law Review* 1936 (1994).

29. Amy Gutmann and Dennis Thompson, *Democracy and Disagreement* (Cambridge, Mass.: Harvard University Press, 1996).

30. Robert Audi, "The Separation of Church and State and the Obligations of Citizenship," 18 *Philosophy & Public Affairs* 259 (1989).

31. Kent Greenawalt, *Religious Convictions and Political Choice* (Oxford: Oxford University Press, 1988).

32. Rawls, *Political Liberalism*, 227.

33. Ibid., 228.

34. Indeed, the leading authority on law and religion in India, J. Duncan M. Derrett, notes that the Article is "subject to so many qualifications and restrictions that the reader wonders whether the so-called 'fundamental right' was worth asserting in the first place." Derrett, *Religion, Law and the State in India* (New York: Free Press, 1968), 451. The reference to "fundamental right" refers to the fact that Article 25 appears in Part III of the Constitution, labeled "Fundamental Rights." There are additional rights present in this section that relate to religion, such as the freedom of religious institutions to manage their own affairs, and the freedom to avoid being taxed for the promotion or maintenance of any particular religion or religious denomination.

35. Gary Jeffrey Jacobsohn, "Three Models of Secular Constitutional Development: India, Israel, and the United States," 10 *Studies in American Political Development* 1 (1996).

36. For an insightful analysis of Rawlsian theory and the anthropological view, see Nomi Maya Stolzenberg, "A Tale of Two Villages (Or, Legal Realism Comes to Town)," in *Ethnicity and Group Rights*, ed. Ian Shapiro and Will Kymlicka (New York: New York University Press, 1997). Stolzenberg focuses on the Satmar Hasidim of Kiryas Joel, where, she argues, "The conventional distinction between the religious and the secular realms is not a part of the Hasidic vocabulary." Ibid., 309.

37. Israel exemplifies the *visionary* model, and the United States the *assimilative*. Thus for Israel, Zionist aspirations for a homeland for the Jewish people frame the debate over church/state relations, but the predominantly secular orientation of most Israeli Jews tends to dampen whatever theocratic impulse might reside in the founding commitment to ascriptively driven nationalism. A *visionary* model seeks to accommodate the particularistic aspirations of Jewish nationalism within a constitutional framework of liberal democracy. For the United States, where the Constitution is the paradigmatic case of a governing charter that is central to its people's sense of nationhood, the relative thinness of religion in the United States, conjoined with a constitutional requirement of nonestablishment, encourages the assimilation of a diverse population into a constitutive culture of ideas. An *assimilative* model manifests the ultimately decisive role of political principles in the development of the American nation.

38. Some accounts attach much greater emphases to these countervailing impulses, seeing the commitment to group autonomy as more prominent than egalitarian justice. See, for example, Gurpreet Mahajan, *Identities and Rights: Aspects of Liberal Democracy in India* (New Delhi: Oxford University Press, 1998). Consistent with this view, Mahajan's interpretation of the Hindutva cases differs from mine. She understands the rulings to be an affirmation of the constitutional value of group autonomy. "The interpretation of the Supreme Court has. . .affirmed the autonomy of the religious domain, including its right to participate in the political domain. . . . By refusing to restrict the use of religion in politics, the Supreme Court has ensured that religious denominations and institutions are not excluded from or disadvantaged in the public realm." Ibid., at 67–68.

39. This is evident from the debates surrounding the framing of the Indian Constitution. Typical of the statements made at the time was delegate K. M. Panikar's comment that "If the State considers that certain religious practices require modification by the will of the people, then there must be power for the State to do it." Government of India Press, *The Framing of India's Constitution: Select Documents* (New Delhi: Indian Institute of Public Administration, 1967), 2:265. With this, scholarly opinion agrees. Granville Austin describes the Constitution as "first and foremost a social document." *The Indian Constitution* (Oxford: Oxford University Press, 1966), 50. Mark Galanter calls it "a charter for the reform of Hinduism." *Law and Society in Modern India* (Delhi: Oxford University Press, 1989), 247.

40. V. S. Rekhi's criticism of earlier rulings on RPA is predicated on the

recognition of this all-encompassing religious presence. "No opinion of the Court shows an awareness of the relation of religion to social structure either in general or in particular relation to elections." "Religion, Politics and Law in Contemporary India," 200. In particular, Rekhi is dismayed by the Court's failure to appreciate that religion may be the only way for the have-nots in India to organize politically in pursuit of their interests. While perceptive in its critique of the Court's failures, his analysis is insufficiently attentive to the ways in which religious practices and discourse serve to limit the socio-economic progress of the disadvantaged, and thus the reasons why a consistent application of RPA may reasonably be seen as serving these people's long term interests.

41. *Prabhoo v Kunte*, at 148.

42. Quoted in Charles H. Heimsath, *Indian Nationalism and Hindu Social Reform* (Princeton, N.J.: Princeton University Press, 1964), 326. The entrenched character of Hinduism in the social fabric of Indian society is a description widely accepted in a variety of literatures. Social theorists: Charles Y. Glock and Rodney Stark, *Religion and Society in Tension* (Chicago: Rand McNally, 1965), 34; S. N. Eisenstadt, ed., *The Protestant Ethic and Modernization: A Comparative View* (New York: Basic Books, 1968), 34; Charles P. Loomis and Zona K. Loomis, eds., *Socio-Economic Change and the Religious Factor in India: An Indian Symposium on Max Weber* (New Delhi: Affiliated East-West Press, 1969), 79. India specialists: Nirad C. Chaudhri, *Hinduism: A Religion to Live By* (New Delhi: Oxford University Press, 1998), 10–11; Myron Weiner, "The Politics of South Asia," in Gabriel A. Almond and James S. Coleman, eds., *The Politics of the Developing Areas* (Princeton, N.J.: Princeton University Press, 1960), 178; Robert Stern, *Changing India: Bourgeois Revolution on the Subcontinent* (Cambridge: Cambridge University Press, 1993), 24. And legal scholars: Derrett, *Religion, Law and the State in India*, 57; Dhirendva K. Srivastava, *Religious Freedom in India: A Historical and Constitutional Study* (New Delhi: Deep and Deep Publications, 1992), 103; C. H. Alexandrowicz, "The Secular State in India and the U.S.," 2 *Journal of the Indian Law Institute*, 283 (1960). All of these perspectives generally share a consensus in highlighting the profound extent to which the religions of India—in particular, Hinduism—are solidly embedded in the existent social structure.

43. Christophe Jaffrelot, *The Hindu Nationalist Movement in India* (New York: Columbia University Press, 1996), 13. See also Sumit Sarkar, "Indian Nationalism and the Politics of Hindutva," in *Contesting the Nation: Religion, Community, and the Politics of Democracy in India*. ed. David Ludden (Philadelphia: University of Pennsylvania Press, 1996), 277. "The votaries of Hindutva have tended to come in the main from high castes quite self-conscious about their status privileges." And Arun Patnaik and K. S. R. V. S. Chalam point out that the discourse of Hindutva "aims at a reaffirmation of the Hindu caste order." To the extent that "[I]ndian history is a history of unfinished tasks set by the critics of Brahminism," the Hindu nationalists can rightly be viewed as historically retrograde. Arun Patnaik and K. S. R. V. S. Chalam, "The Ideology and Politics of Hindutva," in *Region, Religion, Caste, Gender and Culture in Contemporary India*, ed. T.V. Sathyamurthy (Delhi: Oxford University Press, 1966), 3:268, 263.

44. Jaffrelot, *The Hindu Nationalist Movement in India*, 47.

45. As Sumit Sarkar points out, "A construction of Hindu unity that evaded rather than sought to reform or even significantly ameliorate hierarchy needs for its sustenance the notion of the Muslim as an ever-present, existential threat, actualized and renewed, furthermore, in recurrent communal riots." Sarkar, "Indian Nationalism and the Politics of Hindutva," 289.

46. Quoted in *Prabhoo v Kunte*, at 139.

47. Jagmohan, "Hinduism and Hindutva: What the Supreme Court Says," *Hindustan Times*, January 8, 1996.

48. Arun Shourie, "The Hindutva Judgments: The Distance That Remains," *BJP Web Page*, April 24, 1996. But this vindication provided only partial satisfaction. "The Court's formulation is also evidence of our state—namely that the only way in which references to Hinduism in election speeches can be defended is by defining Hinduism out of existence. . . . It can be small satisfaction that a formulation that came to be put out as a defensive reaction is now to be the official definition of the faith, that is, by which it is not a faith at all." The author then shrewdly employs the logic of the Court's obfuscation of the distinction between religion and culture to defend the nationalist position against the Court's criticism of its campaign rhetoric. "As the word Hindu is not to be understood in terms of narrow-minded religion, as Hindutva, . . . how come it became despicable to say that Maharashtra shall be the first Hindu state, by what reasoning did the expression merit the disdain of the Court?"

49. Ibid.

50. *Rosenberger v University of Virginia*, 515 US 819 (1995), at 829.

51. Michael J. Sandel, *Democracy's Discontent: America in Search of a Public Philosophy* (Cambridge, Mass.: Harvard University Press, 1996), 63.

52. Ibid., 67.

53. *Rosenberger v University of Virginia*, at 831.

54. Ibid., at 831.

55. Justice Gajandragadkar in *Yagnapurushdasji v Muldas*, S. Ct. J. 502 (1966), at 513. Or as another justice said while sitting as a delegate in the Constituent Assembly that framed the Constitution, "[Y]ou can never separate social life from religious life." *Select Documents*, 2:266.

56. *Austin v Michigan Chamber of Commerce*, 494 US 652 (1989), at 684.

57. Martin Shapiro, "Corruption, Freedom and Equality in Campaign Financing," 18 *Hofstra Law Review* 385 (1989), 393.

58. Ibid., 393.

59. Euben, "Corruption," 230.

60. *Federal Election Commission v NCPAC*, 470 US 480 (1985), at 497.

61. *Buckley v Valeo*, 424 US 1 (1976), at 48.

62. Larry L. Berg, Harlan Hahn, and John R. Schmidhauser, *Corruption in the American Political System* (Morristown, N.J.: General Learning Press, 1976), 3. This is fairly typical of the definitions found in the literature of political corruption in the United States.

63. Dennis F. Thompson, *Ethics in Congress: From Individual to Institutional Corruption* (Washington, D.C.: Brookings Institution, 1995), 29. Thompson focuses on what he calls "the modern conception of corruption,"

which he suggests is more limited in scope than the traditional conception in its emphasis on the pursuit of private purposes rather than on broader social and economic forces. The distinction, however, could be misleading if it deflects attention away from critical differences engrained in the constitutive choices of different constitutional polities. As the Indian example suggests, the relevant distinction has less to do with contrasting *conceptions* of corruption than with the fact that alternative conceptions of *democracy* produce contrasting understandings of what constitutes a corrupt act. In both cases, though, corruption involves an attack on regime principles.

64. Rawls, *Political Liberalism*, 175.

65. Paul S. Edwards, "Defining Political Corruption: The Supreme Court's Role," 10 *BYU Journal of Public Law* 1 (1996), 20.

66. Thomas F. Burke, "The Concept of Corruption in Campaign Finance Law," 14 *Constitutional Commentary* 127 (1997), 148.

67. Rawls, *Political Liberalism*, lix.

68. Or as Gutmann and Thompson write, "Deliberative democracy asks citizens and officials to justify public policy by giving reasons that can be accepted by those who are bound by it. This disposition to seek mutually justifiable reasons expresses the core of the process of deliberation." *Democracy and Disagreement*, 52.

69. I take no position in this essay on the question of whether Justice J. S. Verma, the author of the opinion, was fully committed to these liberal principles, or whether he was using them to advance the Hindu nationalist cause. My focus here is on *what* he wrote, not on why he wrote it. I am pursuing the latter question in a larger study of secularism in India.

70. The criticism is taken from V. M. Tarkunde, "Hindutva and the Supreme Court." The weakness of Tarkunde's argument is precisely that it does not explain *why* "an appeal for the creation of a Hindu State is obviously contrary to the principle of secular democracy and is a corrupt practice." Clearly, the creation of such a state, just as the creation of a Christian state, would conflict with secular democracy; but why the speech itself is a corrupt practice requires an argument that connects the expression to the specific aims of secular democracy in India. One version of such an argument may be found in Martha Nussbaum's essay, "Religion and Women's Human Rights," in *Religion and Contemporary Liberalism*, ed. Weithman. Focusing on India, she argues that all religious discourse that encourages the denial of equality to women should be viewed as unacceptable within a constitutional democracy.

11

REMEMBER AMALEK:

RELIGIOUS HATE SPEECH

Yael Tamir

RELIGIOUS SPEECH, or speech delivered within religious institutions, by religious leaders, making reference to religious texts, enjoys dual protection. It is sheltered under the umbrella of two basic liberties: freedom of speech and freedom of religion. There is no need to elaborate here on either the theoretical grounds for freedom of speech or its contribution to a free and stable democratic regime. Nor is it necessary to explain the importance of freedom of religion. Religious freedom and religious tolerance would seem an unlikely source of controversy. Surely if anything is settled in modern liberal democracies, Stephen Macedo argues, "it is the broad principle of tolerance for religious diversity."[1]

While this chapter accepts and endorses the importance of both liberties, it claims that religious speech has a potential for being far more dangerous than many other kinds of speech, and consequently that we should not hesitate to supervise and restrict it when necessary.

The lenient attitude of modern liberalism toward religion has been motivated by the assumption that since the Reformation, religious life has undergone profound changes. During the wars of religion, Rawls argues, "people were not in doubt about the nature of the highest good, or the basis of moral obligation in divine law. These things they thought they knew with the certainty of faith, as here their moral theology gave them complete guidance."[2] Modern religions, Rawls believes, have lost their authoritative, salvationist, and expantionalist dimensions. And though they retain a transcendent element not admitting of compromise, they acknowledge that "this element forces either moral conflict moderated only by circumstance and exhaustion, or equal liberty of conscious and freedom of thought."[3] Being rational, they opt for the latter.

Rawls's analysis of religion fits well into de Tocqueville's description of religion in America. According to de Tocqueville, religious beliefs impose no burden on democracy, and can actually be useful and desirable. In a chapter titled "Religion and Democratic Instincts," he writes:

> The great usefulness of religion is even more apparent among egalitarian people than elsewhere. . . .[4] Equality lays the soul open to an inordinate love of material pleasure. Religion's greatest advantage is to inspire diametrically opposed urges. Every religion places the object of man's desire outside and beyond worldly goods and naturally lifts the soul into regions far above the realm of the senses. Every religion also imposes individual obligations on mankind—to be performed in common with the rest of mankind—so drawing him away, from time to time, from thinking about himself. That is true even of the most false and dangerous religions.[5]

A religion like Islam or Judaism that has a political dimension and therefore poses a threat to the separation of church and state, de Tocqueville believed, "will not be able to hold its power long in an age of enlightenment and democracy. . . . A religion that becomes more detailed, more inflexible, and more burdened with petty observances at a time when people were becoming more equal would soon find itself reduced to a band of fanatic zealots in the midst of a skeptical multitude."[6]

As we now know, de Tocqueville's liberal democratic optimism was unfounded. While he was right to predict that encounters with modern, skeptical modes of thought would engender religions that are practice oriented and embody a detailed political agenda, he was too quick to conclude that such religions will lose their audience. From the Enlightenment framework in which he observed the American experience, de Tocquville was bound to misapprehend the attraction of such religion to ever-growing audiences. This misapprehension masked the danger inherent in religious life and set the ground for the benevolent attitude toward religion and the firm commitment to protect its freedom. If all that religion cares for is the redemption of the soul and the spreading of otherworldly, universal commitments, then there is no reason for the state to monitor its actions. But what if it does not? What if religious teachings have unsettling, even dangerous, social and political outcomes?

This question has escaped the attention of the courts and the academic community writing within the Anglo-American tradition, as most of the religious groups they encounter are of a moderate nature. The docile nature of such groups is reflected in Macedo's description of religious extremism. "Few zealots and dogmatists refuse to make their peace with the modern world," he writes. "In the United States, some Protestant fundamentalists charge that public schooling promotes secularism. They seek to revise textbooks or to require that equal time be given to the teaching of 'creation science' alongside the theory of evolution."[7] If this is the main example of religious zealotry in the United

States, then it clearly should be tolerated. But what about other, more extreme types of religious practices and speech? Should these be protected just because they are delivered under religious auspices?

Before answering these questions, let me state that this chapter does not dismiss religion; on the contrary, it emphasizes religion's immense importance and weight in the life of many individuals. The dangers embodied in religion, it argues, are a direct consequence of the eminent role it plays in the life of its adherents.

It concludes by arguing that a more realistic assessment of the role religion plays in private and public life is needed, a more accurate evaluation of the benefits and harms embodied in religious practices in general and in religious speech in particular. The former task exceeds the scope of this chapter; I shall therefore concentrate on the latter, examining cases of what I define as *religious hate speech*. This speech is *religious* in a dual sense: (a) it is delivered by religious leaders who make repeated references to religious texts; (b) it is delivered in religious institutions and in other religious spaces. It is *hate speech* as it "inflicts injury or tends to incite immediate violence."[8] Should hate speech be restricted? Are there special reasons to treat religious speech more leniently than other types of hate speech? In what follows I would claim that hate speech should be restricted and offer reasons to restrict religious hate speech by the same, or possibly more stringent measures, than those used to restrict other kinds of hate speech.

Religious Hate Speech

One sunny winter day, Rabbi Meir* Kahane and his followers arrived at one of the biggest Palestinian villages in Israel, Um el-Pachem. They squatted in the village's square, where Rabbi Kahane read aloud the following passage from Deuteronomy:

> Remember what Amalek did to thee on the way, when you were coming out of Egypt; how he met thee on the way, and smote the hindmost of thee, all that were feeble in thy rear, when thou wast faint and weary; and he feared not God. Therefore it shall be, when the Lord thy God has given you thee rest from all thy enemies round about, in the land which the Lord

---

* Meir Kahane was a leader of an extreme right-wing political party whose political platform was considered by many, including the Israeli Supreme Court, to reflect racist views. Kahane served in the Israeli parliament for one term. In 1988 the Court ruled that his party, Kach, could not stand for election as its platform contradicted the democratic nature of the State of Israel. Kahane was assassinated by a Palestinian at a public meeting held in New York. His followers are still active in Israel.

thy God gives thee for an inheritance to possess it, that thou shalt blot out
the remembrance of Amalek from under heaven; thou shalt not forget.
(Deut. 25)

If not for the intervention of the Israeli police, blood would have been
shed that day. Should Rabbi Kahane's speech be qualified as hate speech
and therefore be banned? After all, all Kahane did was to read outloud
a passage from the Bible, a most respectable source. How can this count
as either hate speech or an incitement to violence?

This is a particularly poignant question when we consider that the
Amaleks no longer exist. How could God's words against a people long
extinct be seen as an affront to anyone? Who could be offended or
harmed by their mention? Why would Palestinians take offense, or see
these words as a threat?

The answer is obviously subtextual. "Amalek" has turned into a ge-
neric name for all Israel's enemies, in both ancient and modern times.
From King Nebuchadnezzar, who destroyed the Second Temple and
sent the people of Israel to a long and tormented diasporic life, to Hitler
and Arafat, all were identified at some point as "Amalek." The reference
to the Palestinians is, however, particularly clear. Amalek is mentioned
in Deuteronomy in the context of God's warning against assimilation
into the nations that inhabited the land of Israel. Throughout these
chapters, a worry is expressed that the people of Israel will not find
within them the power to resist the pull of idolatry which was practiced
by these nations and will thus betray their God. In order to prevent this
danger, God doesn't fortify their heart or teach them to resist temptation. Rather, he commands them to annihilate all the idol worshippers
and icons. The eradication must be complete.

> When the Lord thy God has cut off the nations, whose land the Lord thy
> God give thee, and thou hast driven them out, and dost dwell in their
> cities, and in their houses. . . . You shall utterly destroy all the places, in
> which the nations whom you are to dispossess serve their gods, upon the
> highest mountains, and upon the hills and under every leafy tree: and thou
> shall overthrow their alters, and break their pillars, and burn their asherim
> with fire: and thou shall hew down the carving of their gods, and destroy
> the name of them out of the place. (Deut. chapters 11 and 19)

According to Rabbi Kahane, the Palestinians like the ancient nations,
were not merely political enemies—they were, first and foremost, religious enemies, threatening the religious and sexual purity of the people
of Israel. Taking these facts into account, it becomes clear why the reading of the previously cited biblical text in the midst of a Palestinian village is so intimidating. Does reference to a religious source grant the
speaker special protection? Should one censor the Bible?

These questions could be raised in relation to a wide range of religious texts that are part and parcel of all the major religions. Judaism is not the only religion whose texts and convictions could be used to incite hatred. In her stimulating book *The Origins of Satan*, Elaine Pagels investigates the social implications of the figure of Satan in early Christian scripts and demonstrates how this figure has been used to characterize one's enemies and interpret social conflict. What may be new in Western Christian tradition, Pagels argues, is how the use of Satan to represent one's enemies leads to a particularly poignant interpretation of moral and religious conflicts according to which "we" are God's people while "they" are God's enemies, and ours as well. Each of the Gospels, she argues, frames its narrative at the beginning and the end with episodes depicting the clash of supernatural forces that the Gospels see played out in Jesus's life and death. They explained the cleavage between human beings by distinguishing between the holy ones who are still faithful to God and those seduced and deceived by the evil one.

This unearthly interpretation of human conflicts, Pagels argues, has proven extraordinarily effective throughout Western history in consolidating the identity of Christian groups; But it had disastrous consequences as it justified "hatred, even mass slaughter."[9]

This hatred has a particular target. The New Testament Gospels virtually never identify Satan with the Romans but consistently tend to associate him with Jesus's Jewish enemies. For nearly two thousand years, Pagels writes, "[M]any Christians have taken for granted that Jews killed Jesus and the Romans were merely their reluctant agents, and that implicates not only the perpetrators but (as Matthew insists) all their progeny in evil."[10] The figure of Pontious Pilate, the Roman governor,

> grows increasingly benign with each successive Gospel; the Jewish enemy is formed in ever more hostile rhetoric. While historical testimonies of the time, from Philo and Josephus, describe Pilate's cruelty in detail, recounting that he would routinely round up Jews suspected of anti-Roman activity, he becomes in the Gospels a nearly sympathetic character, the better to depict the Jews as the satanic agents of Jesus' execution. The social result of this interpretation in the Gospels is that, as the Christian movement becomes more Gentile, its followers could find canonical justification for the hatred of Jews.[11]

How should we treat these texts? Should we restrict the public reading of the Gospels? Should we disallow the public display of the Easter Play?

Support for hatred and violence can also be found in Islam. As I wrote these words, another member of the Battalions of Martyrs, Izz ad-Din al-Qassam, blew himself up in a Tel Aviv coffeeshop, leaving the shards of death and misery in his wake. This act is seen by Hamas followers as a mission done for the sake of God and His pleasure. The martyr walks on the path of God. He must therefore "prepare for his death lovingly . . . think of it in terms of happiness, as in the Islamic slogan, 'I will die smiling in order that my religion will live.'"[12] The tradition of Jihad, a holy war against the infidels, plays an important role in Islam. Consider the following lines chanted by the Hamas Cubs youth groups:

> O mother, my religion has called me to Jihad
> and self-sacrifice.
> O mother, I am marching toward immortality;
> I will never retreat.

When a young man dies in a suicide attack, his fellows are thought to accept his death with envy and happiness. "We greet the spirit of martyrdom in the souls of our Muslim *shabab* and those who submit themselves to the Word of God, Mighty and Majestic. 'Let those who would barter the life of this world for the hereafter fight on the path of God. And we will give the one who fights on the path of God, be he killed or victorious, a mighty reward'" (Qur'an 4:47)[13] Jews are not the only target of Jihad. The Phattwa against Iranian author and activist Salman Rushdie offers another example of how Islamic texts are used to inspire violence and consign an author to hell. How should we treat religious leaders calling for Jihad? Should we protect those who celebrate acts of martyrdom? Should we ban reading passages from the Qur'an? How should we treat a Palestinian who shouts in a public space the words of the Muslim prayer, "Allah whu Akbar!," now synonymous with an impending attack on the infidels?

There is no doubt in my mind that the preceding examples are indeed religious speech, but they also fall under the rubric of "hate speech." The umbrella of freedom of speech and freedom of religions should therefore offer them, at the most, limited protection. In what follows, moreover, religious hate speech should be regarded as even more harmful than hate speech delivered in secular contexts and should therefore be supervised more closely.

Restricting Hate Speech

The ideas that underlie justifications of freedom of speech derive from the most fundamental premises of liberal democracy. Some of the defenses of freedom of speech are "consequential, looking for the positive effects of liberty; others are non-consequential, claiming that independent of consequences, restrictions deny a right or constitute an injustice."[14] Kent Greenawalt enumerates some of the benefits associated with freedom of speech; it can contribute to the accommodation of interests; teach a tolerance of differences; help achieve social stability; and, most importantly, promote individual autonomy. The kind of religious speech I am discussing here lacks all these qualities. It often intensifies conflict, spreads intolerance, fosters social instability, and defies personal autonomy.

There is obviously nothing new in claiming that there are reasons for restricting speech:

> There are certain well-defined and narrowly limited classes of speech, the prevention and punishment of which have never been thought to raise any Constitutional problem. These include the lewd or obscene, the profane, the libelous, and the insulting or "fighting words"—those which by their very utterance inflict injury or tend to incite an immediate breach of the peace. . . . [S]uch utterances are no essential part of any exposition of ideas, and are of such slight social value as a step to truth that any benefit that may be derived from them is clearly outweighed by the social interest in order and morality.[15]

The preceding passage is an excerpt from the U.S. Supreme Court decision in the case of *Chaplinsky v. New Hampshire*. Chaplinsky, a Jehovah's Witness, cursed and insulted a federal marshal who warned him to "go slow" and refrain from annoying people by proselytizing. Chaplinsky was convicted, and the Supreme Court later upheld his conviction. Yet how would the Court rule if Chaplinsky, in order to insult the marshal, had used passages from the Bible, the utterance of which, at least in the eyes of some, are of immense social value, if not an expression of Truth?

What is special, then, about religious hate speech is that, unlike racist speech or pornography, it is grounded in texts, practices, and beliefs that are commonly cherished and respected. Religious hate speech thus raises a set of poignant questions: Should we forbid the usage of otherwise valuable texts for immoral purposes? Can the words of a religious text be defined as "fighting words"? These words are neither lewd, obscene, profane, libelous, nor directly insulting; they were not originally designed to hurt or humiliate. And yet they do hurt and humiliate—and worse still, incite hatred and violence. Should such words be suppressed? Should their expression be restricted?

The main four reasons for suppressing speech, Greenawalt claims, are:

1. The danger of immediate violence
2. Psychological hurt for persons who are the object of abuse
3. General offense that such language is used

4. Destructive long-term effects from attitudes reinforced by abusive remarks.[16]

He then adds a fifth reason: states have some authority to legislate in favor of political equality, even when that legislation directly restricts private activities, since "hate speech can seriously interfere with equality, restriction of it . . . implements a constitutional value."[17] All five reasons apply to religious hate speech.

In the case of three appeals the Israeli Supreme Court has considered the question whether reasons that pertain to hate speech could be applied to religious speech. The first appeal followed a decision to forbid Rabbi Kahane's list, the Kach Party, to run for election. In the appeal Kahane argued that the Kach Party adopted Jewish law—including the Pentateuch, the Mishna, and latter Jewish sources—as its platform. It is inconceivable, he argued, that those who adopt these Jewish sources will be accused of racist incitement or of negating the democratic nature of the state of Israel.

The Court rejected Kahane's claims, arguing that "the fact that a party relies on the Bible and other Jewish sources as its operative platform cannot refute the conclusion that its activities contradict clause 7a of the election law (determining that no party can stand for elections if it denies either the Jewish or the democratic nature of the state of Israel)." The Court cited a previous decision according to which a publication of a citation from a religious book or a book of prayers will not be seen as an offense according to clause 144b (which forbids the publication of racist texts or any text that incites racism unless it has been done with *the intention* of inciting racism. Yet it stated that in the case of the Kach Party such intention was demonstrated. The Court thus concluded that there were sufficient legal grounds on which to bar the party from standing for election.

The introduction of the notion of intention draws a rift between the text and its various applications. The responsibility, it suggests, lies with the user. In the spirit of this judgment, in the case of a second appeal raised by Kahana-Chai ("chai" in Hebrew means "alive"; the group sprang out of Kahane's ideology after his assassination and was also barred from standing for elections), the court made no attempt to evaluate the accuracy of the group's interpretation of religious sources. The question before us, the court argued, "is not whether the views of the plaintiff accord with the Hallachic interpretation, but whether their ends and acts accord with clause 7a."[18] This phrasing implies that if the acceptable religious interpretation of the Halachic texts does stand in contradiction to clause 7a, its dissemination could be restricted.

The third appeal was brought up by Rabbi Elba. Elba is a teacher and a Halachic guide in a yeshiva near the Burial Cave of the Four Fathers in

Hebron, which is sacred to both Jews and Muslims. A few months after Baruch Goldstein massacred twenty-four Palestinians and wounded dozens of others as they knelt in prayer in the cave, Elba published a booklet titled *Analysis of the Laws Regarding the Killing of Gentiles*. The abstract stated that the text was written after consultation with one of the greatest teachers of the generation. It is also emphasized that the text does not constitute a ruling and is no more than learned reflections to be discussed by scholars.

The booklet offers a collection of Jewish sources on the issue discussed and ends with the following conclusions:

> (1) The prohibition "thou shall not kill," as well as the prohibition against shedding human blood do not apply to Gentiles;
> (2) There is a direct command to kill all those Gentiles who follow religions teachings that reject Judaism and the eternity of the Torah, and take upon themselves an evangelical task, such as missionaries and Muslims who believe in Jihad;
> (3) In times of war there is a command to kill every member of the rival nation including women and children who do not constitute an immediate threat and that when it is known that the Gentile are likely to harm Jews there is a command to kill them even on a Shabbat.[19]

Rabbi Elba's defense lawyer claimed that these conclusions follow closely the Jewish sources cited and that the text was not a purposeful incitement and did not justify the conviction of the author. "The booklet," the lawyer claimed, "is no more than the publication of a citation from religious text and books of prayer."[20]

The Court voted three to two to convict Elba. It is interesting to note that none of the judges was ready to claim that the religious text itself was carrying a hateful massage. Those who convicted Elba and saw the booklet as falling under the description of hateful incitement placed the blame on Elba's interpretation of the religious text. Those who claimed that Elba's work fell within the Jewish interpretive tradition found no fault with either Elba's intensions or the text he had written, and voted to acquit.[21]

The Court, it was agreed, should not involve itself in either an evaluation of the accuracy of the interpretation or the nature of the text itself but should rule on one ground only: whether the act of publication was contrary to state laws. And yet the Court's decision implied that the teachings of a religious text by a religious leader could be seen as an incitement to hatred or violence.

In light of this ruling, I will put aside, for now, the question whether a religious text can itself be banned and ask whether the speech of religious leaders using religious texts can be banned.

Dangerous Encounters

Once we conclude that religious speech and practices should not be exempt a priori from state supervision, we must estimate the dangers embedded in them. In this section I would like to suggest that religious speech is more likely to bring about harm than other kinds of hate speech for the following four reasons:

First, religious communities are often relatively small, close, and authoritarian; in such communities the leaders' words carry much more weight than in open egalitarian ones. The social pressure to abide by the leader's rulings and the community's laws, norms or traditions is hard to ignore.

Second, as the ideas and rulings expressed by religious teachers are supported by both the community's tradition and the leader's own religious status they are seen not merely as an expression of opinions but as commands that must be obeyed.

In many religious communities, the norm is that one ought to follow the religious commands unquestioningly. In such communities, the act of passing a ruling that a certain person should be killed is far closer to commanding "Ready, aim, fire!" to a firing squad than to expressing a political view.

Under such conditions, religious words become, in themselves, violent acts. Words, Catharine MacKinnon writes, "are presumed 'speech' in the protected sense. . . . But social life is full of words that are legally treated as the acts they constitute."[22]

Third, MacKinnon adds, speech is often seen as a form of communication that must be conceived in terms of "what it says, which is imagined more or less effective or harmful as someone then acts on it, rather than in terms of what it does. Fundamentally, in this view, a form of communication cannot, as such, do anything bad except offend. Offense is in the head."[23]

But in a religious setting words not only command, but also create, a new reality. To define something or someone as sacred or profane, pure or impure, is to make that person sacred or profane, pure or impure. Declaring someone a "moser," is to make that person's blood permitted. The notion "moser" [giver] refers to someone who betrays one's own people. It is permitted to execute a "moser." After the Oslo agreements in which Rabin agreed, on principle, to exchange land for territories, some rabbis belonging to the extreme right ruled that Rabin was a "moser." This ruling may have been interpreted by Igal Amir, who assassinated Rabin, as a religious authorization of the assassination. To say the ritual words of excommunication is to excommunicate a person.

In all these cases, words neither stand for nor substitute for reality; they create it. Such speech clearly falls under Greenawalt's definition of communication, which is "*situation altering*"; it is much more of an "action" than an "expression."[24]

Fourth, the other-worldly aspect of religion—praised often by de Tocqueville—allows religious leaders to offer their followers benefits and punishments of a magnitude no other type of leader can afford. Religious leaders can promise eternal bliss or eternal suffering as "faith treats of eternal life and eternal suffering, prospects in comparison of which earthly laws and earthly sanctions pale into insignificance. A church invests the most mundane objects and actions with immense importance, at once furnishing our culture with the richest symbolism and laying it out as the most deadly minefield of offenses and misunderstanding."[25]

The power of the other-worldly promises is exemplified in Oliver and Steinberg's analysis of the training of the Hamas suicide attackers. With the first drop of his blood,

> [T]he martyr is said to go straight to Paradise, his sins wiped clean from the Book of Life. He is buried in the clothes in which he died, the blood-stains of his wounds serving as witnesses of postmortem decay and disintegration. He is exempt from "the torment of the tomb," the interrogation of the dead by the angels Munkar and Nakir. . . . He will waken not on Earth but rather in the Garden of Delight, where he will be surrounded by all good things . . . rivers of holy wine, rivers of milk, rivers of honey, from which he will drink to his heart's content. He will recline on luxurious couches beneath trees without thorns. He will suffer neither heat nor cold. He will know no pain, for, as we are told in The Giants, "God derives away his grief." He will enjoy forever the company of maidens whom "neither man nor jihn has deflowered before." (Qur'an 55:74)[26]

No human punishment or reward can compete with these promises.

For all the above reasons, religious speech has the potential to be more dangerous than other kinds of speech. It can bless or curse as no other speech can. When it is used to do the latter, it must be stopped.

Slaughtering a Holy Cow

What is freedom of expression, Salman Rushdie asks: "Without the freedom to offend, it ceases to exist. Without the freedom to challenge, even to satirize all orthodoxies, including religious orthodoxies, it ceases to exist."[27] Should we then protect a Nazi who mocks Jews, a follower of Rabbi Kahane who expresses disrespect to Islam and its believers, Tatiana Suskin who draws a picture of a pig Muhammad reading the

Koran? All these acts can be seen as satire, but they are meant not to amuse or to offer a criticism but to hurt and offend.

Rushdie, Biku Parekh argues, "reduces speech, a publicly oriented and interpersonal act, to expression, a subjectivist and personal act, and shifts the focus from a shared public realm to the individual's right or need to express himself. He says, further, that *he* is free to offend others and satirize deeply held beliefs but does not explain why *they* should put up with the offense."[28] Freedom of speech, Parekh argues, "has to be balanced against the rights of others to their individual and collective self-respect."[29] Insult and humiliation, he concludes are good enough reasons to restrict speech.

And yet, as Waldron rightly argues, "[I]t is fatuous to think there is a way of running a multicultural society without disturbance or offence."[30] This is because some "hold their beliefs so devoutly that even the most sober and respectful criticism would count as a moral insult to their personality."[31] Sensitivity, he concludes, "is not trump in this game; the stakes are already too high for that."[32] This analysis leads Waldron to offer a "three dimensional tolerance. Persons and peoples must leave one another free to address the deep questions of religion and philosophy the best way they can, with all the resources they have at their disposal."[33] According to this view, religious speech could be used to mock, or insult others, but it cannot be used to incite either hatred or physical harm. When used for these purposes, it must be restricted.

An unqualified defense of religious freedom may have devastating consequences. One unhappy example is the policies implemented by Israel in the occupied territories. While Israel allowed itself to restrict the workings of those Palestinian political organizations that were suspected of subversive political activities, it was reluctant to restrict activities carried out within religious institutions. The government of Israel feared that restricting religious freedom would provoke international condemnation and criticism.

The ironic result of such policies was that while the moderate, political branch of the Palestine Liberation Organization was exposed to close supervision and severe limitations, the activities of the Hamas were almost uninterrupted. Hamas supporters gathered in mosques, held classes for children of all ages, spread a religious call for a Jihad, distributed material, and planted the seeds of the cruelest and most devastating terrorist activities. All these activities were done under the auspices of religious freedom. The painful results of this policy are still with us today. Similar toleration toward Jewish religious groups bred the kind of extremism that led to the assassination of Prime Minister Rabin. So maybe it is time to call for a tighter supervision of religious speech. Maybe the idea that religious speech should enjoy special protection is one holy cow that should be slaughtered.

The concept of *a holy cow* is not wholly metaphorical in the context of the present discussion. In the spring of 1996, a small red calf was born in a barn in the religious youth village of Kffar Hasidim ("The Village of the Pious"). Its birth caused great excitement within religious circles, as it could change the course of Jewish history. As yet, Jews are not allowed to enter the Temple Mount, because they are "impure." Their only way to redeem their impurity is through a purifying ritual, described in Deuteronomy, which involves the ashes of a red cow. In Jewish history, there have been only nine red cows, the first of which was sacrificed by Moses. Its ashes lasted until the Babylonian Diaspora. The second was sacrificed by Ezra, and the other seven by the high priests during the days of the Temples. In modern Jewish history there is no record of a birth of such a calf until now.

When, in two years, the calf comes of age and can be burned, religious Jews may see themselves as qualified to enter the Temple Mount where the Al-Alqsa Mosque now stands. The consequences might be a religious war that will sweep the Middle East.

In a newspaper interview, following the birth of the calf, Rabbi Menachem Ha'Cohen argued that the Chief Rabbis ought to ban discussions about the implications of the renewal of the practice of the red cow. The issue of a red cow, he says, "is tremendously complicated. We know very little about it and its implications, just as we still don't know the identity of the Amaleks. Remember that our sages, God bless their memory, warned that there is no way for us, today, to know the Amaleks and I would extend this attitude also to the question of a red cow, lest a religious war come into sight."[34]

Fortunately, when the calf turned two, a few white hairs were discovered on his back, disqualifying it from being used for ritualistic purposes. But the debate over the ability to renew the ritual of a red cow as well as other practices used during the days of the Temple still continues.

In view of the disastrous outcomes of such a debate, should not the state follow it closely and intervene if it will turn from an abstract teleological debate into a practical political one? Surely no state can be aloof from the danger such debates embody, nor should it be. Freedom of speech, even if the speech is a religious one, must have its limits.

Notes

1. S. Macedo, "Toleration and fundamentalism," in R. E. Goodin and P. Pettit, *A Companion to Contemporary Political Philosophy* (Blackwell, 1993), p. 622.

2. J. Rawls, *Political Liberalism* (Columbia University Press, 1995), p. xxiv.

3. Ibid., p. xxvi.

4. A. de Tocqueville, *Democracy in America* (HarperPerennial, 1969), p. 444.

5. Ibid., p. 445.

6. Ibid.

7. Macedo, "Toleration," p. 622.

8. Kent Greenawalt, *Fighting Words: Individuals, Communities, and Liberties of Speech* (Princeton University Press, 1995), p. 56.

9. E. Pagels, *The Origins of Satan* (Random House, 1995), p. xix.

10. Ibid., p. xx.

11. D. Remnick, "The Devil Problem," *New Yorker*, April 3, 1995, p. 64.

12. A. M. Oliver and P. Steinberg, "Embodied Imperative: The Command of Death in the Underground Media of the Intifada" (unpublished paper), p. 3.

13. Ibid.

14. Greenawalt, *Fighting Words*, p. 3.

15. Cited in ibid., p. 51.

16. Ibid., p. 50.

17. Ibid., p. 61.

18. *Supreme Court Review* 63 (1992): 473.

19. *Supreme Court Review* 96 (1996): 99.

20. *Supreme Court Review* 96, no. 3 (1996): 117.

21. Ibid., 119, 165.

22. C. MacKinnon, *Only Words* (Harvard University Press, 1993), p. 12.

23. Ibid., p. 11.

24. Greenawalt, *Fighting Words*, p. 6.

25. J. Waldron, "Rushdie and Religion," in *Liberal Rights* (Cambridge University Press, 1993), p. 137.

26. Oliver and Steinberg, "Embodied Imperative," p. 8.

27. Quoted in B. Parekh, "The Rushdie Affair: Research Agenda for Political Philosophy," *Political Studies* 37 (1990): 706.

28. Ibid., 707.

29. Ibid.

30. Waldron, "Rushdie and Religion," 139.

31. Ibid.

32. Ibid.

33. Ibid.

34. Rabbi Menachem Ha'Cohen, in *Ha' Aretz*, March 24, 1997.

12

RELIGION AND WOMEN'S EQUALITY:
THE CASE OF INDIA

Martha C. Nussbaum

What is left of the Law of the kings? From of old, we have
heard, they do *not* bring law-minded women into their hall.
This ancient eternal law is lost among the Kauravas. . . . For this
foul man, disgrace of the Kauravas, is molesting me, and I
cannot bear it any longer.
*(Queen Draupadi, as the men of Duryodhana's entourage
attempt to undress and molest her.* The Mahabharata, *II.62)*[1]

Although all religions were initially founded with the aim of
purifying men and women and helping them to lead ethical lives
through prayer, it was found in some instances that blind traditions,
customs and superstition often resulted in—not the cathartic
effects of religion—but the spread of communalism, fanaticism,
fundamentalism and discrimination.
(Heera Nawaz, law student, Bangalore College of Law, 1993)[2]

Religious Liberty and Sex Equality: A Dilemma

MODERN LIBERAL democracies typically hold that religious
liberty is an extremely important value and that its protection
is among the most important functions of government. These
democracies also typically defend as central a wide range of other human
interests, liberties, and opportunities. Among these are the freedom of
movement, the right to seek employment outside the home, the right to
assemble, the right to bodily integrity, the right to education, and the
right to hold and to inherit property. Sometimes, however, the religions
do not support these other liberties. Sometimes, indeed, they deny such
liberties to classes of people in accordance with a morally irrelevant characteristic, such as race or caste or sex. Such denials may not mean much
in nations where the religions do not wield much legal power. But in

nations such as India, where religions run large parts of the legal system, they are fundamental determinants of many lives.

In this way, a dilemma is created for the liberal state. On the one hand, to interfere with the freedom of religious expression is to strike a blow against citizens in an area of intimate self-definition and basic liberty. Not to interfere, however, permits other abridgments of self-definition and liberty. It is not surprising that modern democracies should find themselves torn in this area—particularly a democracy like India, which has committed itself to the equality of the sexes and non-discrimination on the basis of sex in the list of Fundamental Rights enumerated in its Constitution—alongside commitments to religious liberty and nondiscrimination on the basis of religion.[3]

The normative argument I shall make is universalistic: it makes a set of recommendations that should be applicable to nations of many different kinds. I focus on India because that has been the focus on my own work on women's development issues, and also because its structure, as a constitutional democracy with an explicit commitment to women's equality, makes the dilemma with which I am concerned especially easy to study.

Consider these three cases, all involving conflicts between claims of religious free exercise and women's claims to other important rights under the Indian Constitution:

1. In 1983, Mary Roy, a Syrian Christian woman, daughter of wealthy parents, went to court to challenge the Travancore Christian Act, under which daughters inherit only one fourth the share of sons, subject to a maximum of Rs. 5000. The Indian Supreme Court declared that the relevant law superseding the Travancore Christian Act was the Indian Succession Act of 1925, which gives equal rights to daughters and sons.[4] (By ruling in this narrowly technical way, the Court avoided confronting the question whether the Act violates Constitutional guarantees of sex equality.) The Court also declared the change retroactive to 1951, thus bringing the property of many Christian males into dispute. Protest greeted the judgment. A Christian MP from Kerala (representing a district including many wealthy Christian landlords) introduced a private members' bill in Congress seeking to block the retroactive effect of the law. Meanwhile, the Christian churches of Kerala vociferously protested the Court's interference with the free exercise of religion. It was argued that the judgment would "open up a floodgate of litigation and destroy the traditional harmony and goodwill that exists in Christian families."[5] The Synod of Christian Churches took an official position against the ruling and actively mobilized protests against it.[6] Priests belonging to the Roman Catholic, Jacobite, Church of South India, and Kananya Christian Churches all criticized the judgment from

the pulpit. One reason for the strength of opposition may be that a portion of the traditional daughter's inheritance automatically went to the Church; this would not be the case under the Indian Succession Act.[7]

2. In 1947, at the time of Independence, the Hindu Law Committee submitted a list of recommendations for reform in the system of Hindu personal law. These were presented to Parliament in the form of the Hindu Code Bill. Backed by Nehru's law minister, B. R. Ambedkar, the Bill proposed to grant women a right to divorce, remove the option of polygamous marriage for men, abolish child marriage for young women,[8] and grant women more nearly equal property rights. A storm of protest from Hindu MPs (led by conservative Pandits or Hindu religious authorities) greeted the proposed legislation. Debate focused on the new laws' alleged violations of the free exercise of religion, as guaranteed in the new constitution. Pandit Mukul Behrilal Bhargava held that equal property rights for women represented a forcible intrusion of Muslim ideas into the Hindu tradition. (Muslim women in India had had somewhat more equal inheritance rights since 1937, when the Shariat was substituted for customary law.[9]) Others objected to the fact that monogamy would be required for Hindus but not for Muslims. Still others objected to the whole idea of state-initiated reform of the Hindu code: "Hindu law is intimately connected with Hindu religion and no Hindu can tolerate a non-Hindu being an authority on Hindu law." Traditional Hindu MP's attacked female MP's for violating Hindu tradition, speaking of "the tyranny of modern women. . . . [T]he days of their persecution are gone, it is nowadays men who are being persecuted."

Shortly after the new Constitution took effect, in the summer of 1951, a tumultuous session of Parliament formally debated the bill; conservative Pandit Govind Malviya spoke for two hours against the Bill, which he called "wrong in principle, atrocious in detail and uncalled for in expediency." Despite Ambedkar's passionate support, the bill seemed bound for defeat, and even Nehru withdrew his support for the time being. In consequence, Dr. Ambedkar resigned his ministerial position, saying: "To leave untouched the inequality between class and class, between sex and sex, and to go on passing legislation relating to economic problems is to make a farce of our Constitution and so build a palace on a dung-heap." The bill lapsed. Its provisions were eventually adopted in 1954, 1955, and 1956.

Fifty years after the initial proposal, these provisions continue to arouse controversy. The new laws are weakly enforced. Child marriage, for example, remains common in some regions, and is vigorously defended in both religious and cultural terms.[10] With the rise of Hindu fundamentalism, charges of violation of free exercise and discrimination in favor of Muslims are increasing, especially over the issue of polygamy. Substantial numbers of Hindu men continue to make bigamous marriages; others have converted to Islam in order to escape the polygamy prohibition.[11] To make things more complex still, Hindu courts have recently adopted an extremely stringent definition of a valid marriage, with the result that a large number of existing Hindu marriages, if challenged in court, would not withstand scrutiny, and the male would be acquitted of charges of bigamy attendant on a second marriage. [12]

3. In Madhya Pradesh in 1978, an elderly Muslim woman named Shah Bano was thrown out of her home by her husband, a prosperous lawyer, after forty-four years of marriage. (The occasion seems to have been a quarrel over inheritance between the children of Shah Bano and the children of the husband's other wife.) As required by Islamic personal law, he returned to her the *mehr*, or marriage settlement, that she had originally brought into the marriage—Rs. 3,000 (less than $100 by today's exchange rates). Like many Muslim women facing divorce without sufficient maintenance, she sued for regular maintenance payments under Section 125 of the uniform Criminal Procedure Code, which forbids a man "of adequate means" to permit various close relatives, including (by special amendment in 1973) an ex-wife,[13] to remain in a state of "destitution and vagrancy." This remedy had long been recognized as a solution to the inadequate maintenance granted by Islamic personal law, and many women had won similar cases. What was different about Shah Bano's case was that the Chief Justice of the Supreme Court of India, awarding her maintenance of Rs. $180 per month, remarked in his lengthy opinion[14] that the Islamic system was very unfair to women, and that it was high time that the nation should indeed secure a Uniform Civil Code, as the Constitution had long ago directed it to do. The Chief Justice wrote, "Undoubtedly, the Muslim husband enjoys the privilege of being able to discard his wife whenever he chooses to do so, for reason good, bad, or indifferent. Indeed, for no reason at all." Although of Hindu origin, the Chief Justice also undertook to interpret various Islamic sacred texts and to argue that there was no textual barrier in Islam to providing a much more adequate maintenance for women.

A storm of public protest greeted the opinion. Although some liberal Muslims backed Chief Justice Chandrachud, he had made their task difficult by his zealous incursion into the interpretation of sacred Islamic texts. The Islamic clergy and the Muslim Personal Law Board organized widespread protest against the ruling, claiming that it violated their free exercise of religion. In response to the widespread outcry, the government of Rajiv Gandhi introduced the Muslim Women's (Protection after Divorce) Act of 1986, which deprived all and only Muslim women of the right of maintenance guaranteed under the Criminal Procedure Code. Women's groups tried to get this law declared unconstitutional on grounds of both religious discrimination and sex equality, but the Supreme Court (in rapid retreat from charges of religious intolerance and excessive activism) refused to hear their claim. Hindu activists, meanwhile, complained that the 1986 law discriminates against Hindus, giving Muslim men "special privileges."[15]

Here are three examples of our dilemma, no different in kind from dilemmas that arise in the United States and Europe, but different in degree, since the religions in India control so much of the legal system. On the one side is the claim of religious free exercise; on the other, women's claims to various fundamental rights. In the first case, women won a clear victory—interestingly, in the case involving a small and politically powerless religion. In the second case, women made some strides, but the provisions are weakly enforced, and the current climate of Hindu fundamentalism and conservatism makes the future very unclear. In the third case, women suffered a particularly painful and prominent defeat. Free exercise and sex equality appear, at least sometimes, to be on a collision course.

Secular Humanists and Traditionalists

Feminists have taken a range of positions on this dilemma. Here are two extremes, both prominent in the international debate. The first position, which I shall call the position of *secular humanist feminism*, treats the dilemma as, basically, a nondilemma.[16] The values of women's equality and dignity, and of the basic human rights and capabilities more generally, so outweigh any religious claim that might conflict with them that the conflict should not be seen as a serious conflict, except in practical political terms. Indeed, the secular feminist tends to view religion itself as irredeemably patriarchal, and a powerful ally of women's oppression throughout the ages. She is not unhappy to muzzle it, and does not see it as doing a whole lot of good in anyone's life.[17]

Many secular humanist feminists are Marxists; if they follow Marx on religion, they are bound to take a negative view of religion's social role and are unlikely even to give the free exercise of religion a high degree of respect. But some liberal feminists also take a secular humanist line. These feminists—usually comprehensive rather than political liberals—will be committed to preserving the liberty of conscience, but only within limits firmly set by a secular moral understanding of basic human rights and capabilities: religion, as Kant would have it, "within the limits of reason alone." This is in effect the position of J. S. Mill in *On Liberty*, where he excoriates Calvinism as an "insidious . . . theory of life" that creates a "pinched and hidebound type of human character." Mill holds that it is perfectly proper for public policy to be based on the view that by teaching obedience as a good, Calvinism undermines "the desirable condition of human nature." He thus advocates liberalism as a comprehensive doctrine of life, rather than (in political-liberal fashion) as simply the basis for core political principles.[18] Some secular humanists in this comprehensive liberal tradition have, like Marxists, a general hostility to religion; Bertrand Russell is just one obvious example of a widely held view among liberal intellectuals. Others are not hostile to religion as such but simply insist that it fall into line with a rational secular understanding of value; Joseph Raz and Susan Okin would seem to be in this group.

The second approach, which I shall call that of *traditionalist feminism*, also sees the dilemma as basically a nondilemma. The understandings of each community, both religious and traditional, are our best, perhaps our only, guides in charting women's course for the future. All moral claims not rooted in a particular community's understanding of the good are suspect from the start, but those that challenge the roots of traditional religious practices are more than usually suspect, since they threaten sources of value that have over the ages been enormously important to women and men, forming the very core of their search for the meaning of existence.[19] Although such a position will frequently converge with mere traditionalism and antifeminism, I think it can be a genuine type of feminism, in the sense that its proponents are committed to defining feminism in terms of what has deep importance to real women, and in sheltering those deep values from the assault of other feminists.

Some traditionalist feminists are cultural relativists, who hold that as a matter of theory it is impossible to justify any crosscultural moral norms. Some, on the other hand, are worried more about normative moral substance than about justification: they just think local sources of value are more likely to be good for people than are international human rights norms, more in tune with and beneficial to the real lives they lead. In Indian terms, traditionalist feminists typically make common cause with other "nativist" defenders of tradition, opponents of secularization and modernization, who hold that the essence of Indian national identity resides in Hindu traditions[20] and that traditional female roles lie at the core of a Hindu identity. Analogous claims are made on the Muslim side. Nativists often support their attack on human rights norms by holding that Indian values are radically different from Western values.

Secular humanism is deeply appealing for feminists, since there is no doubt that the world's major religions, in their real-life historical form, have been unjust to women both theoretically and practically. In contemporary politics, religious groups have frequently had a pernicious influence on women's lives, as our three cases from India suggest. It is indeed very tempting to say, fine, let religion exist, but let it clean up its act like anything else, bringing its own norms and conduct into line with a basic set of international moral standards, without receiving any special protections from the state.[21] When religion is clearly doing wrong, this position seems sensible. This was, it seems, the position of Chief Justice Chandrachud in the Shah Bano case, when he called for an end to state protection for religious courts.[22]

There are deep pragmatic difficulties with secular humanism, as the Shah Bano case shows us. It is rash and usually counterproductive to approach religious people with a set of apparently external moral demands, telling them that you know that these norms are better than the norms of their religion. In the Indian situation it was bad enough when the demands were made by Hindus to Hindus; but when similar demands were made by Hindus to Muslims, they were read, to some extent correctly, as both insulting and threatening, showing a lack of respect for the autonomy of a minority cultural and religious tradition. Today, such demands are all the more clearly threatening, since the call for reform of Muslim personal law has been taken up as a rallying cry of Hindu nationalist forces, eager to portray Hinduism as enlightened toward women, Islam as backward and oppressive. Although the goal of a uniform code continues to be backed by many feminist and otherwise progressive thinkers, in practice it is so prominent a part of the goals of Hindu fundamentalism that it is difficult to dissociate it from the idea of Hindu supremacy and a relegation of Muslim citizens to second-class status.

A related pragmatic error of the secular humanist is to fail to pursue alliances with feminist forces within each religious tradition. Religious traditions have indeed been powerful sources of oppression for women, but they have also been powerful sources of protection for human rights, of commitment to justice, and of energy for social change. For example, they have been primary sources of U.S. abolitionism and of the more recent civil rights movement, and they are primary sources of the Gandhian anticolonialism and of the contemporary Gandhian SEWA movement.[23] Muslim feminists like Heera Nawaz find ideas of justice in their religion important sources of empowerment. By announcing that she wants nothing to do with religion, or even (in the milder cases) by announcing that religion will be respected only insofar as it lives up to a comprehensive liberal view of life, the secular humanist dooms herself to a lonely and less than promising struggle and insults many people who would otherwise be her allies. In the Indian context especially, secularist grass-roots politics has had a hard time capturing people's imaginations. By ceding religion's moral authority and all its energy of symbol and metaphor to the side of patriarchy, or even (in the milder cases) by insisting that religions be feminist or liberal in all respects, the secularist further compromises her own political goals. Finally, she abandons the terrain of argument on which she is strongest, namely sex equality, and wades into contentious metaphysical issues. Why do this, when she doesn't need to?

But the difficulties with secular humanism are not merely pragmatic and political. Three arguments cast doubt on it at a deeper level. First is an argument from the *intrinsic value of religious capabilities*. The liberty of religious belief, membership, and activity is among the central human capabilities.[24] To be able to search for an understanding of the ultimate meaning of life in one's own way is among the most important aspects of a life that is truly human. One of the ways in which this has most frequently been done in human history is through religious belief and practice; to burden these practices is thus to inhibit many people's search for the ultimate good. Religion has also been intimately and fruitfully bound up with other human capabilities, such as the capabilities of artistic, ethical, and intellectual expression. It has been a central locus of the moral education of the young, both in the family and in the larger community. Finally, it has typically been a central vehicle of cultural continuity, hence an invaluable support for other forms of human affiliation and interaction. To strike at religion is thus to risk eviscerating people's moral, cultural, and artistic, as well as spiritual, lives. Even if substitute forms of expression and activity are available in and through the secular state, a state that deprives citizens of the option to pursue religion in these important areas has done them a grave wrong.

For political purposes, the capabilities approach aims at religious capability or opportunity, rather than religious functioning, in order to leave to citizens the choice of whether to pursue the pertinent human functions at all and whether to pursue them through religion or through secular activity. For political purposes, then, the liberal state, as I envisage it, takes the position that citizens may reasonably pursue both religious and nonreligious conceptions of the good—or no definite conception. But the very defense of religious capability as central involves the recognition that religious functioning has in many cases had high intrinsic value: religious conceptions of value are among the reasonable ones that we want to make room for, as expressions of human powers.

Because religion is so important to people, such a major source of identity, there is also a strong argument from *respect for persons* that supplements these considerations of intrinsic value. When we tell people that they cannot define the ultimate meaning of life in their own way— even if we are sure we are right and that their way is not a very good way—we do not show full respect for them as persons. In that sense, the secular humanist view is at bottom quite illiberal. It is precisely this consideration that leads me to prefer *political liberalism* to *comprehensive liberalism*; the secular humanist view is a form of comprehensive liberalism. Obviously no state can allow all citizens to search for the ultimate meaning of life in all ways, especially where these ways involve harm to others. But secular humanism frequently errs in the opposite direction, taking a dismissive and disrespectful stance to religion even when no question of harm has arisen. Even were such a position correct, even if a certain group of religious beliefs (or even all beliefs) were nothing more than retrograde superstition, we would not be respecting the autonomy of our fellow citizens if we did not allow them these avenues of inquiry and self-determination. As Roman Catholic thinker Jacques Maritain expressed the point:

> There is real and genuine tolerance only when a man is firmly and absolutely convinced of a truth, or of what he holds to be a truth, and when he at the same time recognizes the right of those who deny this truth to exist, and to contradict him, and to speak their own mind, not because they are free from truth but because they seek truth in their own way, and because he respects in them human nature and human dignity and those very resources and living springs of the intellect and of conscience which make them potentially capable of attaining the truth he loves, if someday they happen to see it.[25]

Frequently, I sense that my fellow feminists, when they treat religion dismissively as a mere "opiate of the masses," do not sufficiently respect the "springs of conscience" in religious women (and men).

Finally, there is an argument from the *internal diversity of the religions*. Secular humanists who marginalize religion tend to treat religion as an enemy of women's progress. In so doing, they make a most unfortunate concession to their traditionalist opponents: they agree in defining religion as equivalent to certain reactionary, often highly patriarchal, voices.[26] This, as I have already said, is a pragmatic error: the humanist feminist thus alienates people who could be some of her most influential allies, by indicating that she thinks their whole enterprise of effecting change (or a return to better earlier norms) within their religious traditions a silly waste of time. Sometimes she even reveals ignorance of the very existence of such contesting voices.[27] But her error is also a theoretical error about what a religious tradition is. It is simply mistaken to treat cultures as homogeneous, neglecting internal diversity and conflict. The same point can be made at least as emphatically about religious traditions. No religious tradition consists simply of authority and sheeplike subservience. All contain argument, diversity of belief and practice, and a plurality of voices—including the voices of women, which have not always been clearly heard. All, further, are dynamic: because they involve a committed search for ultimate meaning, they shift in at least some ways in response to participants' changing views of meaning; and because they are forms of communal organization, they shift in response to their members' judgments about the sort of community in which they want to live.[28] What counts as Jewish, or Muslim, or Christian is not in any simple way read off from the past: although traditions vary in the degree and nature of their dynamism, they are defined in at least some ways by where their members want to go.

Thus any account of Judaism that fails to include the fact that Reform and Reconstructionist congregations address God as "you" rather than "he" and acknowledge the (four) mothers alongside the (three) fathers is a false account of what the Jewish tradition is.[29] By this argument, secular-humanist feminists are giving a false account of Judaism when they call it inherently patriarchal; equally false is the account given by political forces in Israel that would refuse recognition to non-Orthodox branches of Judaism.[30] Any account of the Roman Catholic tradition that treats it as in principle anti-Semitic neglects a recent evolution in doctrine prompted by statements and actions of the current Pope. Jews may have good historical reasons for doubting whether the leopard can change his spots, but they also should not be blind to what is going on. A similar evolution may eventually take place with regard to women's role in the priesthood; many Catholics support such a change. Such changes, of course, have already been made in most major Protestant denominations.[31] Any account of the Hindu tradition that holds that Rama is the one central divinity, or that Hinduism is in principle inseparable from the tradition of misogyny exemplified in the *Laws of Manu*, is again a false account, one that neglects the tremendous regional, temporal, and ideological diversity that has always obtained within Hinduism, including the deep religious commitments of campaigners for sex equality such as Rammohun Roy in the eighteenth century, Rabindranath Tagore in the early twentieth, and Ela Bhatt in our generation, all of whom understand themselves to be representing an authentic Hinduism, freed from historical and cultural distortions.[32] Any account of Islam that holds it to be essentially and irredeemably misogynistic once again confuses fundamentalist voices (which frequently purvey their own highly synthetic accounts of tradition) with the whole of a tradition and displays considerable ignorance about the texts (for example, about the fact that equal inheritance for women was secured by a return to the Quran from less authoritative interpretations, and that both Quran and Hadith regard men and women as sharing a single essential nature).[33] Such ignorance is offensive to fellow citizens and is objectionable for that reason alone, but it is also simply bad to be wrong!

If secular humanism has these practical and theoretical problems, how does traditionalist feminism fare? Interestingly enough, it suffers from very similar problems. In practical terms, as we shall soon see in more detail, it is highly divisive to neglect critical and dissenting voices within a religious tradition, equating it with its most patriarchal elements,[34] and failing to acknowledge each tradition's dynamic character. Such ways of thinking about both Islam and Hinduism are implicated in the current bad state of group relations in India; narrow and static representations of tradition by the members of the traditions themselves are at least as much to blame for this as are ignorant representations by outsiders. Similarly, traditionalists about women's role have also made the pragmatic political error of dividing where they could fruitfully pursue alliances, since feminists of all stripes share certain common goals in the areas of material well-being.

In the theoretical domain too, similar problems can be identified. The traditionalist feminist seems to slight the intrinsic value of women's religious capabilities just as much as does the secular humanist, if she refuses to acknowledge the many ways people search for religious meanings outside the most patriarchal element of a tradition.[35] The ultra-Orthodox in Israel slight the intrinsic value of religious capabilities when they deny Conservative and Reform Jews the free exercise of their religion in areas such as marriage, divorce, and conversion; in similar ways, traditionalist Hindu, Islamic, and Christian authorities slight the value of dissident types of functioning in their own traditions, defining their way as the only legitimate way. This error is not only an assault on intrinsic value, it is also very much an assault on one's fellow citizens, who ought to be respected when they search for the good in their own way, even if one should hold, as fundamentalists typically do, that critical ways are erroneous departures from the correct way. Finally, it is evident that these traditionalists are frequently engaged in massive simplifications and rewritings of their own traditions, which distort and deform tradition and history by denying both diversity and dynamism, just as surely as do secularist feminists' misreadings.

The traditionalist view has one further difficulty that does not appear to be present in the secular humanist view. Namely, at least in some of its political forms, it rides roughshod over other human capabilities, giving religion (tendentiously interpreted) broad latitude to determine a woman's quality of life, even when it threatens not only dignity and equality, but also health, the wherewithal to live, and bodily integrity.[36] The secular humanist is at least motivated by an admirable goal: to guarantee to women the full range of rights and capabilities, including both those already on the agenda for men and those that involve women's freedom from gender-specific abuses. I have argued that in the process she slights a very important range of concerns related to religious capabilities and respect for persons, but she does so without fully recognizing this fact, and with an eye to promoting women's equal citizenship. I don't think there is anything so positive to be said about the motives lying behind traditionalism, where women are concerned. It is rare to find a serious argument to the effect that a certain type of harm or inequality toward women is required, as such, by the spiritual or moral values inherent in a religious tradition. It was not argued that unequal inheritance rights for Mary Roy were a noble goal, essential to Christian worship; that polygamy and child marriage were of the essence of Hindu spiritual values; or that the failure to pay a monthly maintenance to Shah Bano was a high moment in Islam. Usually, instead, even the overt arguments of traditionalists allude to the value of preserving the power of traditional religious courts of law and traditional religious authorities—a value far more dubious in moral terms than the value of the basic human capabilities.[37] And frequently their arguments have the paradoxical result of allowing women to suffer discrimination in property rights, or maintenance, or whatever, just because they happen to be members of that particular religion—surely a dubious way of showing respect for the moral values inherent in that tradition. Insofar as there is a moral argument of substance, it is likely to be an indirect one, alleging that the power of traditional authorities or courts is necessary for the maintenance of other valuable aspects of tradition. But such claims are empirical, and they should be tested.

Two Orienting Principles

Any adequate approach to the dilemma must, then, begin by treating it as a real dilemma, acknowledging the weight of the values on both sides. I have argued that it must respect the intrinsic value of religious capabilities and it must respect religious women and men as choosers of a way of life (a basic commitment of political liberalism), while at the same time taking just as seriously the importance of the full range of the human capabilities that are sometimes at risk for women in traditional religious cultures. Finally, it must understand and respect the plurality and diversity of voices in each religious tradition, both traditional and critical, both female and male. This entails being skeptical from the start of any account that fails to recognize the complexity both of religion and of women's interests.

Two further principles now orient my approach. The first guiding principle has been with us from the start of this project: it is the *principle of each person as end*, which, thinking of the capabilities approach, we may also call a *principle of each person's capability*. Like all the central capabilities, religious capabilities are capabilities of individual people, not, in the first instance, of groups. It is the person whose freedom of conscience and freedom of religious practice we should most fundamentally consider. Although religious functioning is usually relational and interactive (like political functioning and functioning in the family), and although it often involves shared goals and ends, the capabilities involved are important *for each*, and it is *each person* who should not be prevented from having access to these capabilities. As with politics and the family, so here: an organic good for the group as group is unacceptable if it does not do good for the members taken one by one. In liberal democracies we standardly hold that not just some but *all* citizens should enjoy the political rights and liberties. The religious analogue is the idea that *all* (in the sense of *each and every one*)[38] should enjoy the liberty of conscience and religious exercise (and the other human capabilities). Thus, any solution that appears good for a religious group will have to be tested to see whether it does indeed promote religious capabilities (and other capabilities) in the group's members, taken one by one. To subordinate the capabilities of some to the organic purposes of the whole is to violate people with respect to a capability that may lie at the core of their lives.

I am emphatically not saying that all religious functioning, to be acceptable, must be individualistic, in the sense that the individual regards herself as an independent and self-willed member of the religious group. Such an account of religious functioning and capability would obviously leave out many of the ways in which people search for the good by subordinating themselves to authority or hierarchy, or by joining up with the purposes of a corporate body. What is ruled out by the type of focus on the person for which I have argued is any approach that seeks a good for Hinduism or Judaism, let us say, by denying the liberty of conscience of individual Hindus or Jews. Israel's failure to give legal recognition to Reform and Conservative Judaism, for example, violates this principle, for it says, for the sake of a strong Judaism let us forbid individual Jews to worship in their own way where marriage, conversion, and divorce are concerned. Whether this is indeed conducive to a strong Judaism may be doubted, but it certainly falls afoul of my principle. So does the refusal of Muslims in India to permit individual Muslims to adopt children, a practice that is controversial within Islam and accepted in many Islamic nations.[39] So does the failure of the Indian system generally to allow individuals free egress from one religious tradition into another, given the impossibility of extricating ancestral property from the system of personal law into which one is born.

A good way of thinking of the type of focus on the individual person in religious matters that I am proposing is to think of the twin U.S. constitutional principles of nonestablishment and free exercise. The motivation behind the Establishment Clause is to prevent citizens from being violated in conscience and practice by the pressures of a dominant religious group with political and legal power behind it; the motivation behind the Free Exercise Clause is to prevent belief and worship from being impeded or burdened by public action. The history of these clauses is notoriously difficult and tortuous. At times they have appeared to be on a collision course with one another; at other times it is difficult to separate the strands of argument that the two clauses suggest. But in the most abstract terms we can say that together they aim at a regime in which each citizen's liberty of conscience is preserved inviolate, despite the pressures that corporate bodies of various types, whether religious or secular, may bring to bear. As we shall see, this tradition has been cognizant of the fact that one way of denying individuals the free exercise of their religion would be to destroy a group or tradition of which that person is a member; so group values do enter into the equation.[40] But they are not considered to be ends in their own right, and certainly they are not permitted to trump the value of the individual person's conscience.

My second orienting principle is one that I shall call *the principle of moral constraint*. Religion is given a high degree of deference and protection in many constitutional conceptions, as it will be in mine. One reason for this deference is surely that religion is extremely important to religious people, as a way of searching for the ultimate good. But another important part of this deference surely involves the role religions play in transmitting and fostering moral views of the conduct of life. As Heera Nawaz says, the major religions are all, at their heart, concerned with the conduct of life, and all the major traditions can plausibly be seen as attempts to reform or improve the conduct of life. Furthermore, it would not be too bold to add that all the major religions embody an idea of compassion for human suffering and an idea that it is wrong for innocent suffering to occur. All, finally, embody some kind of notion of justice. This doesn't mean that religions do not concern many other things, such as faith and ritual practice and celebration and pleasure and contemplation, but at least a part of what they are is moral.

When we give deference to religion in politics, we do not do so simply because of the moral role of the religion; nor need the political liberal assert that this moral role is the central object of the state's interest. To say such things would involve an unacceptably paternalistic stance toward religious traditions and what is central in them. We may and do, however, judge that any cult or so-called religion that does not contain this conduct-improving element does not deserve the honorific name of religion. Thus U.S. law has persistently refused to give religion status to Satanist cults and other related groups. Controversies over Scientology have a similar character: insofar as states judge that it is really a money-making scheme, they refuse to give it the honorific status of religion. Comprehensive ethical or political views do not suffice for religion under U.S. law; I shall express my own unease about this situation later in this essay. But systematic views of the conduct of life that are non-traditional, and in the end rather hard to distinguish from comprehensive ethical views, have been termed religion in two draft board cases.[41] It has been explicitly stated that belief in a deity is not required: otherwise Buddhism and Taoism would not get protection, as they clearly do. A moral constraint is applied, then, to the definition of what counts as religion when we protect religion. And further—what interests me here—such a constraint is also applied to more finely tuned distinctions involving state protection of religion. Even when a group clearly counts as religion, we may judge that it forfeits its claim to state deference when it goes outside certain moral understandings, especially those that are protected in the core of the basic constitutional conception. Thus, U.S. constitutional law has consistently denied that expressions of racial segregation or hierarchy are legitimate prerogatives of religion as such, when the state gives religion special tax benefits.[42] The Indian Constitution made a similar move when it offered religion protection similar to that given it under the U.S. Constitution and yet made untouchability illegal: Hinduism gets protection only within moral constraints supplied by the core constitutional understanding of the equal worth of citizens. Laws against *sati* express a similar idea.

In keeping with the idea of political principles that I develop in a larger project of which this essay is a part, I understand the moral constraints in terms of my list of central capabilities (see Appendix), in the following way. We should refuse to give deference to religion when its practices harm people in the areas covered by the major capabilities. Obviously problematic will be practices involving harm to nonmembers of the religion (e.g., a refusal by Hindus of a certain caste to allow any woman to go outside because their own caste norms forbid that); practices involving harms to coreligionists will also be problematic where they significantly infringe a central capability (particularly where there is reason to doubt the voluntariness of the practice), especially when it is not established that individual members have the opportunity of exiting from the religion should they disapprove of it.[43] Thus refusals by Hindus to allow Hindu women to go outside to work will also get critical scrutiny, especially when we feel that women are under duress and threat in this matter, and also when we have doubts about their opportunity to define themselves as non-Hindu should they wish to.

Formally and in the core of the political conception, the *principle of moral constraint* says nothing about matters internal to the religion itself. Political liberalism prevents this: the public political conception should take no stand on disputed issues of the good outside the core of the constitutional principles. But the principle of moral constraint has an informal social corollary, which members of the religion may use in discourse with one another, and which may also be used across religious lines in informal social deliberation. One of our greatest problems, in talking about the prerogatives of religious actors and groups, is to decide when there is a legitimate religious issue on the table and when the issue is, instead, cultural or political. Religions are intertwined in complex ways with politics and culture. Even when a religion is based on a set of authoritative texts, culture and politics enter into the interpretation of texts and the institutionalized form of traditional practice. Jews differ about where to draw the line between what is genuinely religious in the tradition and what is the work of specific contextual and historical shaping. Similar debates arise in Christianity and Islam. In all cases, many interpreters are inclined to regard at least a part of tradition or even text as a historical or cultural artifact, expressive of human ideas of the good at a particular time, but not binding without translation for our time.[44] Where Hinduism is concerned, the absence of scriptural authority makes it all the more difficult, if not virtually impossible, to identify a necessary religious core distinct from layers of history and culture, all powerfully infused with imperfect people's desire for political power.

When we are thinking, then, of curtailing some activity highly desired by some religious actor or actors speaking in the name of religion, it is useful to determine whether they are *really* speaking religiously, accurately understanding the core of that religion, or just going all out for political power. But it is not just difficult to discover this; sometimes there may be no determinate answer to be discovered. Judges are not well qualified to judge in such matters, and in general they are rightly deferential to the claims of religious actors about what a legitimate claim of free exercise in their religion is.[45] They should stick to a strictly limited political use of the *principle of moral constraint*. But in more informal social discourse it is sometimes important to take a stand. Do the Christians have a case that Mary Roy's inheritance claim jeopardizes

Christian worship, or is this simply a ploy on the part of church leaders to keep tax revenue? Do Nehru's and Ambedkar's opponents have superior insight into the essence of Hinduism, or are they just trying to shore up power for religious courts?

The social version of the principle allows us to go further in commenting on these questions. It suggests that when we assess such debates we should be skeptical of any element that seems prima facie cruel or unjust—again, especially in the areas of the central capabilities. But now, in addition to saying that we may not give such elements state deference, we press the question whether that is really a core element in the religion. You say that your religion is dedicated to the good, we argue. But this is so patently bad that it seems dubious that it can really be a part of the religion, as we understand its central purposes.

This social principle would strike me as a valuable one even if major religions had not endorsed it. But it clearly has deep roots in Indian religious history, as well as in the West. When the emperor Ashoka (a convert to Buddhism, in the third century B.C.) saw acts of religious intolerance being carried out in the name of religion, he invoked the principle of the moral core in order to conclude that damage to other religions is simply not a way of expressing or exalting one's own:

> the sects of other people all deserve reverence for one reason or another. By thus acting, a man exalts his own sect, and at the same time does service to the sects of other people. By acting contrariwise, a man hurts his own sect, and does disservice to the sects of other people. For he who does reverence to his own sect while disparaging the sects of others wholly from attachment to his own, with intent to enhance the splendour of his own sect, in reality by such conduct inflicts the severest injury on his own sect.[46]

In other words, no matter what religious actors say about their conduct, we may conclude that they are in error about what religion requires: acts of intolerant harm damage and do not express or glorify one's own religion, Hindu or Buddhist. Had he been a state actor in a political-liberal state, Ashoka would have been well advised to speak in a more restrained way, simply saying that when people behave this way they forfeit a claim to state protection. But his informal social use of the stronger social version of the principle is highly effective.

A similar appeal to the principle of moral constraint was made by Abraham Lincoln, in his second inaugural address, delivered at the end of the Civil War. Speaking of the fact that both (former) slaveholders and abolitionists think of themselves as Christian and their cause as a Christian cause, he commented, "Both read the same Bible, and pray to the same God; and each invokes His aid against the other. It may seem strange that any men should dare to ask a just God's assistance in wringing their bread from the sweat of other men's faces; but let us judge not that we be not judged."[47]

Lincoln, like Ashoka, says in effect: whatever they think about the religious character of their acts, if the acts are unjust we must be highly skeptical. The idea that God is just lies behind and constrains more specific ideas of what God does and does not endorse. That God is really a backer of slavery is simply implausible.[48] Again, U.S. courts speak more agnostically, simply saying that segregationists lose a claim to state protection in tax matters; but Lincoln's use of the stronger form of the principle is valuable, when religion is being invoked to back evil. For a Christian leader to say that slavery is anti-Christian does not seem to exceed the boundaries of public reason.

Moral-constraint arguments naturally arise in the context of women's livelihood. A young wife in Bangladesh, told by local mullahs that religion forbade her to work in the fields alongside men, said that if Allah really was requiring them to stay hungry, then "Allah has sinned." She meant, of course, to express skepticism about the mullah's interpretation. Her view of her religion was that a just and good god would not permit women to starve simply on the ground that it seems to some men improper for a woman to go out of the house. A just god, presumably, would let her gain her livelihood and ask men to conduct themselves modestly toward her (as the Quran, in any case, explicitly requires).[49] Since Allah, by definition, does not sin, then any statement that implies that he does sin must be false. In general, this is the style of argument feminists in all religions have typically used to bring about change: if we're agreed that God is just and good, and if we can show you that a certain form of conduct is egregiously bad, then it follows that this conduct does not lie at the heart of religion and must instead be a form of human error, which can be remedied while leaving religion itself intact. Again, it was a bad idea for the Chief Justice to say something like this; in his judicial role, especially as a Hindu, he should have confined himself to the more restricted political version of the principle. But these women, speaking socially and within their own religion, make a powerful use of its stronger social version.

Such arguments are common in both the Hindu and Muslim traditions in India, where women's issues are concerned. Nineteenth-century Bengali reformers Rammohun Roy and Iswarchandra Vidyasagar, campaigning against *sati*, child marriage, and polygamy, based their campaign on recalling Hindu tradition to its moral core. Similar moral arguments about Muslim conceptions of modesty were made by reformers such as Rokeya Sakhawat Hossain, who challenged the seclusion of women from within religious orthodoxy by pointing to its morally objectionable consequences, as well as its nonnecessity for truly moral conduct.[50] The Indian Constitution uses the more restricted political version of the principle, as seems appropriate for basic constitutional matters in a pluralistic democracy. It makes no pronouncements about what Hinduism is or is not, it simply makes untouchability illegal. But moral-constraint arguments do valuable work socially, in connection with such constitutional reforms.

To invoke the principle of moral constraint, we need not deny that a given form of immorality may at one time have been absolutely central to the beliefs and practices of the religion. It would be foolish, for example, to deny that the subordination of women was central in many religions at many times, that the caste system was a core feature of Hinduism, that racial hierarchy was a prominent feature of the Church of Jesus Christ of Latter-day Saints, and so forth.[51] What we are saying is that what makes religion worthy of a special place in human life (and of special political and legal treatment) is something having to do with ideals and aspirations, something that remains alive even when formerly core understandings shift in the light of moral debate, and indeed, something that guides that evolution. In the following section I shall focus on the narrower political use of the principle. But we shall later see that the informal social version of the principle does valuable work in guiding debate in a time of religious upheaval.

Central Capabilities as Compelling State Interests

Let me recapitulate. We have two constraints that limit interference with religion: respect for the intrinsic value of religious capabilities, and respect for religious people as citizens. Next, we have a constraint that pushes the other way, toward at least some scrutiny of religion and religious actors: respect for the other central human capabilities. Next, we have two orienting principles: the principle of each person's capability, and the principle of moral constraint, which we now interpret in terms of the central capabilities. And, finally, we have a fact that both secular humanists and traditionalists generally neglect, the internal diversity and plurality of the religions themselves. I shall now describe the approach that I would favor, arguing that it does not violate the constraints and is a good way of following the guidance of the orienting principles. I shall then show how it would handle each of the three problem cases.

This proposal is conceived of as a good idea, not necessarily as the best reading of any particular constitutional tradition. It draws on ideas in U.S. law, and it is very easy to adapt to the Indian constitutional tradition, which in most cases draws heavily on U.S. constitutional jurisprudence for precedents involving the interpretation of fundamental rights.

But, obviously, interpreting a particular constitutional tradition involves asking questions other than whether something is a good idea, questions about precedent, text, history, and institutional competence. I have not attempted that larger task here.

My approach is modeled on the United States Religious Freedom Restoration Act of 1993. This act prohibits any agency, department, or official of the United States, or any state, from "substantially burden[ing] a person's exercise of religion even if the burden results from a rule of general applicability," unless the government can demonstrate that this burden "(1) is in furtherance of a compelling government interest; and (2) is the least restrictive means of furthering that compelling governmental interest."

We now need some background on the origin and current fate of this law, in order to see how it grew out of a concern for the protection of minority religion, a central concern in my own argument. For some years there had been an issue in First Amendment jurisprudence about how far laws "of general applicability" might be upheld against a religious group or religious individuals, when those individuals claimed that the law imposes a "substantial burden" on their exercise of their religion. For quite a few years, the legal situation was, theoretically at least, more or less as RFRA later reestablished it: the Supreme Court consistently held that laws of general applicability might impose a substantial burden on an individual's free exercise of religion only if the law furthered a compelling state interest, and in the least burdensome manner possible. The governing case was *Sherbert v. Verner* (1963).[52] A South Carolina woman refused to work on Saturday because her Seventh-Day Adventist beliefs forbade it. Fired, she was also refused state unemployment benefits on the grounds that she had refused suitable employment. She claimed that the state had violated her religious free exercise; the U.S. Supreme Court agreed. The Court held that to attach to a benefit a condition that required violation of a religious duty did impose a substantial burden on her free exercise of her religion; the problem was compounded, the Court held, by the discriminatory impact of the benefits laws on workers who celebrate the Sabbath on Saturday. Under the regime established by *Sherbert*, other laws of general applicability were also found to violate religious free exercise: notable in this regard is the case of compulsory public education of Amish children in *Wisconsin v. Yoder*, which I shall be discussing later.[53]

In 1990, however, the Supreme Court changed course with its decision in *Employment Division v. Smith*.[54] Significantly, this case involved an unpopular minority religion and the scary topic of legalized drug use.[55] The case concerned native American tribes in the state of Oregon, who claimed that it was essential to their religion to use peyote in a particular ceremony and thus claimed exemption (not generally, but in this one ceremonial instance) from the drug laws of the State of Oregon.[56] The sincerity of their religious claim was not disputed, nor the centrality of the peyote ceremony to their religion. [57] In a lengthy opinion by Justice Scalia, the Court held that the free exercise clause did not protect the plaintiffs, since "[w]e have never held that an individual's religious beliefs excuse him from compliance with an otherwise valid law prohibiting conduct that the State is free to regulate." The Court explicitly rejected the "compelling government interest" requirement, as making the lawmaker's job far too difficult.[58] The dissenters, however, emphasized the danger of disfavoring minority religions[59] and invoked the Founders' interest in securing "the widest possible toleration of conflicting views." Justice O'Connor, who joined this part of the dissenting opinion, concluded: "The compelling interest test reflects the First Amendment's mandate of preserving religious liberty to the fullest extent possible in a pluralistic society. For the Court to deem this command a 'luxury,' is to denigrate '[t]he very purpose of a Bill of Rights." This is an important moment for my approach, because the need to protect minority religion is my central motivation in favoring the ample protection of RFRA to the regime inaugurated by *Smith*.

The decision generated public outrage.[60] RFRA was passed in 1993 by an overwhelming bipartisan majority in both houses, and signed into law by President Clinton.[61] It was declared unconstitutional in June 1997 on grounds relating to the scope of Congress's powers under the Fourteenth Amendment.[62] The principle involved in RFRA continues to enjoy strong support, including, it would appear, the support of a vast majority of the American people. The unresolved issue is how to translate this support into law, and, in particular, how to resolve the thorny issues of institutional competence raised by the clash between the legislative and the judicial branches. Since I believe that each nation must resolve those particular issues on its own, in the light of its own traditions and constitution, I make no suggestion on that aspect of the issue here.

My own RFRA-based proposal has two parts. The first part is that the principle of RFRA be accepted as the guiding principle in dealing with the religious dilemma. The state and its agents may interfere with religion only when it can show a compelling interest. *But*, second, protection of the central capabilities of citizens should always be understood to ground a compelling state interest: this is the way we interpret the principle of moral constraint. In legal terms, I have suggested that the central capabilities are like a list of fundamental rights that might be embodied in constitutional guarantees. Many of them are already so embodied in the Indian Constitution and other constitutions around the world;

others are embodied in human rights instruments that most of the nations under discussion have endorsed; still others are embodied in legal precedents through which Indian constitutional law has incorporated considerations of bodily integrity into its jurisprudence. So my proposal is meant as a set of moral guidelines that could in many respects be legally implemented under existing law.[63] I do not suggest that capabilities are the only state interests that could ever be compelling; there might be other independent political interests, for example in stability, that could also ground such a claim.

On my principle, *Smith* ought to come out the other way. No compelling government interest was established in the case as argued, nor would thinking about the central capabilities help us to make a stronger argument than was in fact made. One might point to the parallel Indian case of the legalization of marijuana use during Holi, the Hindu spring festival: it seems just right to say that there is no compelling government interest in forbidding this festival use and that forbidding it would impose a substantial burden on Hindu religion. (It is obvious, indeed, that Holi raises a far more serious issue of public order than the Native American ceremony, to put it mildly, for when a majority of the population is getting stoned, that can and does lead to rioting and looting. Nonetheless, the Indian government is correct, in my view, to tolerate this exception and to focus on controlling disorder.) Other areas in which this principle would support an exemption would include the wearing of yarmulkes in the military,[64] the wearing of religious jewelry in prisons,[65] and reasonable accommodations to the religious dietary needs of prisoners.[66] On the other hand, a case like *Bob Jones*[67] would come out as it did: the government's interest in eradicating humiliating and stigmatizing racial discrimination would count as a compelling interest in connection with the account of the central capabilities. After I have discussed my Indian cases of sex discrimination, I shall say more about what latitude a religion might have for engaging in forms of sex discrimination internal to that religion, but *Bob Jones* already gives us one paradigm to employ: the government must not give favorable treatment to practices that humiliate and stigmatize individuals on account of their sex, especially where the voluntariness of the individuals' participation in those practices is far from certain.[68] Such forms of discrimination are straightforward cases of capability failure, in that they compromise the social bases of dignity and non-humiliation.

I do not at all neglect the difficulty of appropriately specifying the level of each capability, but I think that this difficulty obtains in any constitutional tradition where we are going to hammer out the best account of basic rights and liberties and say when a substantial burden has been applied to one of them. The best way to fix the boundaries more precisely is an incremental way, relying on cases to enlarge our understanding of what we want to say. I remain agnostic about the proper role of the legislature and the judiciary in this evolution; the resolution of such institutional questions depends on contextual features about the nature of democratic traditions in each nation.

This two-part approach seems to do well by the guidelines I have set out. It respects religious citizens and the intrinsic value of religious capabilities by imposing a taxing standard on the state in any case of state action that would substantially burden religious free exercise. It also respects the claim of the other human capabilities, giving them a central place in the account of potential limits on religious freedom. It respects the principle of each person's capability by framing the question as that of when government may legitimately burden citizens' free exercise of their religion; it remains to be seen precisely how interference with religious leaders and the authority of religious courts may be related to such burdens. Finally, it obeys the principle of moral constraint by saying that when a religion does violate a central human capability (whether religious or nonreligious), that is an instance where we will not give religion the deference that is usually due to it.

The most powerful objection to my approach will come from the side of Justice Scalia and the *Smith* opinion. Scalia's claim is that we give too much latitude to religion when we allow it to be a ground for the violation of otherwise valid laws of general applicability, even in the absence of a "compelling state interest." A public law that is neutral (that applies similarly to all the religions and to the nonreligious) and that has a rational basis should be obeyed by all citizens, no matter what their religious convictions. Otherwise, Scalia argues, we will face a flood of claims for exemption to the law, and it will be beyond the capacity of judges to sort these out in a way compatible with public consistency and order. Insofar as Scalia's argument rests purely on an issue of institutional competence (he does not, for example, object to the granting of exemptions by individual state legislatures), I have no general disagreement with it; I have said that questions of institutional division of labor must be settled by each separate constitutional tradition as it evolves. Insofar as the argument rests on more general concerns about arbitrariness of judgment and on a general view that laws of general applicability should be exceptionless, I believe that it is insufficiently protective of religion, especially minority religion. But his argument raises important concerns that must be faced by any proposal in this area. By offering a clear account of "compelling government interest," my capability-based account of what supplies a "compelling state interest" goes some way, I think, toward reducing the dangers about which he worries. If, however, we can show that even my very generous account of the role of religion still renders unacceptable many actions taken by the religions in the context of sex equality, we will also have shown, *a fortiori*, that they are unacceptable by the more stringent Scalia test.

We now face an important issue: does the approach require equality in basic capabilities, or only a basic minimum threshold? In other words, does sex discrimination with respect to the basic capabilities trigger a claim of compelling state interest, or only discrimination that pushes women into a situation of destitution or extreme capability failure? Let us try to get at this by looking at things in the other direction. Typically, the state has been held to impose a substantial burden on religion when it treats members of one religious group unequally to others. The plaintiff in *Sherbert v. Verner* was losing a benefit that the state might not have offered at all, but the holding was that, so long as it does offer such benefits, to condition them on a practice that violates some people's religious freedom is to impose a substantial burden on the free exercise of religion. Forcing Sherbert to choose between the exercise of her religion and forfeiting benefits was said to be equivalent to fining someone for Saturday worship—a practice that would be unacceptable no matter how small the fine and no matter how great the individual's ability to pay. The inequality of treatment is itself a violation; to make X jump through hoops that Y is not forced to jump through, on account of X's religion, is ipso facto to burden the exercise of that religion. (It may also involve an Establishment Clause issue, although that was not the way *Sherbert* was argued.) So too, I think we should say, with the capabilities on the other side. The very singling out of women for differential treatment in a central area of human functioning is itself unacceptable and gives rise to a compelling state interest in eradicating that discrimination, even if women are not by this means pushed into a basement level of functioning. Here we have the Indian constitution on our side, since, unlike the U.S. Constitution, it contains an explicit provision of nondiscrimination on the basis of sex, listing this among the fundamental rights of citizens. Moreover, as with race, any discrimination that stigmatizes and humiliates is ipso facto a case of capability failure: so even outside the domain of the other capabilities there will be little scope for permissible discrimination, although some choices internal to the religion should still be protected.

Finally, we face two very difficult questions. First, should religion be singled out for specially protective treatment, or should the same protections apply to all other expressive or ultimate-truth-pursuing activities? In framing and commenting on my list of the central capabilities, I have already suggested that religion is one of the ways in which people use thought and imagination in pursuit of an understanding of what is most important in life; it is also among the ways in which people pursue community and affiliation. But there are other ways, some involving comprehensive ethical views, some involving less systematic forms of personal search, some involving poetry, music, and the other arts. It seems difficult to distinguish religious belief systems from nonreligious beliefs and practices in any principled and systematic way. The features that make religion worthy of deference are frequently found in non-religious belief systems or practices. Moreover, even if one were to argue that religion is to be preferred not because of its role in people's search for meaning and community but because it involves loyalty to a tran-scendent source of authority,[69] an argument I would not favor, this still would not yield a principled way of dividing what is conventionally called religion from what is conventionally called nonreligion: not all religions are theistic, Buddhism and Taoism being only two examples. One attractive feature of the *Smith* decision, for some of its supporters, is its fairness to nonreligious belief systems.[70] To accommodate religion and to reject a similar accommodation for Thoreau's philosophy[71] seems arbitrary and unfair.

U.S. constitutional law has handled this question in a very complex and sometimes quite murky manner, through the twin principles of non-establishment and free exercise. With respect to free exercise claims, reli-gion is given special deference. But any privileging of religion over non-religion can potentially trigger an Establishment Clause issue, and with respect to Establishment issues, religion is in some respects more cur-tailed than nonreligion. Thus a public display honoring Thoreau would present no problem; such a display honoring Moses or Jesus would po-tentially raise an Establishment issue. Government endorsement of envi-ronmentalism is appropriate; government endorsement of Christianity is not. The two clauses to some extent balance one another; thus, it has recently been argued that any free exercise exemption to laws of general applicability "offends Establishment Clause principles" and "connotes sponsorship and endorsement."[72] Sticking to the free exercise side of the issue, however, we may still feel uneasy when a religious capability is supported and another highly similar human capability is impeded.

We have two distinct issues, a theoretical/moral issue and a practical issue. On the side of theory, there seems little to be said in favor of priv-ileging religion over nonreligious beliefs and practices. A political-liberal political conception based on an idea of human capability should not play favorites among the comprehensive conceptions of the good citi-zens may reasonably hold; my approach reflects this by making religion one of the permissible ways of pursuing a wide variety of human capabil-ities, rather than a separate capability all its own.

On the practical side, however, there are enormous difficulties involved in treating religious and nonreligious conceptions equally.

Religion is usually organized and involves some publicly accepted body of doctrine and/or practice. It is not open to any and every believer to state ad hoc that a given law offends against his religion; however difficult such an inquiry may be, and however problematic an exercise of judicial faculties it may involve, such an inquiry must and frequently does take place. The Court in *Yoder* satisfied itself of the centrality of work in the Amish understanding of community; the Court in *Smith* granted the centrality of the peyote ceremony in Native American religious ceremonies. With nonreligion, such inquiries become absurdly taxing, and frequently they will yield no definite answer. If the belief system is comprehensive and textually based (as, for example, in the Thoreau case), things may not be too bad; but in many other perfectly legitimate cases the task of assessing the claim will be absurdly difficult, beyond the competence of any court or legislative body. If X says that his personal search for the meaning of life requires him to get stoned and listen to Mahler, he may be entirely sincere, and he may well have just as good a case morally as those who use drugs in a religious context, but ascertaining the centrality of this practice to his search for meaning will be virtually impossible, and granting exemptions in this way would quickly make a mockery of the drug laws, of mandatory military service, and many other laws of general applicability.

For some, these difficulties provide a strong reason to prefer *Smith*. Given that I continue to prefer to give religion a larger measure of deference, how do I propose to handle them? Tentatively, I believe that they can be handled in the following way. First, we confine the explicit area of potential exemptions to religion; but we allow religion to have a somewhat broad definition, including nontheistic belief systems such as the one that won Seeger his draft exemption.[73] It remains essential, however, to determine that the exercise of freedom of conscience is religionlike in having a systematic and nonarbitrary character; thus my Mahler fan, however sincere his practice, would still be excluded.

The disadvantage that would thereby be incurred by the nonreligious can to at least some extent be remedied by adopting strong protections for expressive speech and conduct. Thus, although the Mahler fan will not get an exemption from the drug laws, he can at least count on the protection of his right to listen to the music of his choice, to read the books of his choice, and so forth. By recognizing that the expressive interests involved in artistic and philosophical speech may be very religionlike, involving people's search for meaning and understanding, we give some account of why they should not be peripheral to the concerns of free speech jurisprudence.[74] But these subtleties take us rather far from our topic, since all of our Indian cases involve claims made by paradigmatic cases of organized religion to exemptions from generally applicable laws involving sex equality.

Our second difficult question is, however, directly pertinent to the case of India. It is the question of religious establishment. I have presented my approach so far in terms of the concept of free exercise alone; I have argued that the central concern in the area of religion is that of religious capabilities, set over against the other capabilities of citizens. But I also said that in the U.S. case the *combination* of the Free Exercise Clause with the establishment clause offered us a good way of thinking about what it would be to protect religious capabilities: "The motivation behind the Establishment Clause is to prevent citizens from being violated in conscience and practice by the pressures of a dominant religious group with political and legal power behind it; the motivation behind the free exercise clause is to prevent belief and worship from being impeded or burdened by public action." Why, then, have I been silent up until now about religious establishment? The answer emerges from the way I interpreted the function of the Establishment Clause in the U.S. setting: it was to protect the capabilities of citizens. In other words, I understand nonestablishment as, at bottom, another way of shoring up free exercise, together with other capabilities of citizens. This approach suggests to me that it should be a contingent contextual question whether that protecting is best done through a regime of nonestablishment or through a regime of limited establishment with sufficient safeguards for citizen equality and free exercise. Given our specific history of intolerance toward minority religion, it seems wise for the United States to support a strong form of nonestablishment; only this regime, in the social context, guarantees the equal worth of religious liberty for all citizens. In the Scandinavian states, however, it seems plausible that the established Lutheran churches actually protect religious pluralism more effectively than would a purely secular regime: they have been staunch defenders of religious pluralism in education, for example, and of other measures favorable to minorities. This is absolutely crucial to the case of India, because the existing regime of secularism in India involves a type of limited plural establishment: certain religions are entitled to maintain their own systems of civil law, and others (those too small or new to have a codified system of personal law) use the secular system. In the next section I shall give this system a highly qualified type of support; given the history of Muslims in India, it seems that any abolition of the system of Islamic law would be a grave threat to religious liberty and a statement that Muslims are not fully equal as citizens, and that even a total nonestablishment would be de facto a type of Hindu establishment.

One might argue that any type of establishment puts minorities in a situation of indignity: in the public square a declaration is made that some believers are more privileged than others, even if the rights of others are duly protected. This is a grave point, which should not be dismissed. But I am inclined to think that this argument, too, must be assessed contextually. It is probably true of Britain, given Britain's history of antisemitism and xenophobia. But in India it would be disestablishment that would constitute a statement that Muslims were not fully equal citizens, absent a time of mutual respect and civic harmony, which may not come about in the foreseeable future. In the mean time, it seems to me that the totally nonestablished religions (Judaism, Buddhism) are not in any difficulty through their nonestablished status: in many ways they have an easier time than the others, since they simply go straight to the secular system, avoiding many difficult conflicts of law issues.

In short: if the core issues underlying nonestablishment are really issues about both free exercise and full equality as citizens, it is plausible to suppose that, although non-establishment is usually the best way of promoting those goals, this may not always be the case.

Applying the Approach: The Three Cases

How does my approach work, in our three cases? We must begin by asking how it applies to the whole question of having distinct religion-operated systems of personal law. There is a large asymmetry between the United States and India, since the United States has never permitted the religions to take charge of lawmaking. India, by contrast, since the time of the British Raj, has permitted large areas of civil law to be the province of each of the religions. The areas covered by these systems of "personal law" include family law (marital consent, conjugal rights, divorce, adoption), property law, and related areas of personal contract (inheritance, above all). By contrast, personal law does not cover commercial law or criminal law, since the British early on saw that these were spheres they needed to control and render uniform. Their retention of the personal laws thus had something of the character of a compromise, but it also reflected a genuine recognition of cultural pluralism.[75]

The systems themselves have a variety of origins. Islamic law was established in India at least by the thirteenth century under the Moghul Empire. (The Moghuls left Hindus to be governed by their own customary laws except in criminal matters.) Under the Raj, Islamic law was modified, notably by the Shariat Act of 1937, which substituted the Shariah for customary laws that prevailed in various regions. By contrast, the whole enterprise of codifying the previously informal and regionally various systems of Hindu law was a British enterprise, and Hindu law bears many marks of the English law (including ecclesiastical law), on the model of which the British legal thinkers of that era conceived it. In 1864 the Parsis won the right to be governed by their own separate system of personal law. Christians came to be governed by a plurality of distinct systems of Christian personal law, which reflect the heterogeneity of national origins of Christians in India. (For example, until recently Catholic Christians in Goa were still governed by the Portuguese Civil Code.) Jews never had a codified system of personal law; in matters of succession they were governed by the Indian Succession Act of 1865 and are currently governed by its post-Independence successor.[76]

At the time of Independence there was some support for a uniform civil code, but the abolition of Muslim personal laws proved too sensitive an issue, given the overriding importance of reassuring Muslims that India was a truly pluralistic nation and not a Hindu nation. The ideal of Indian secularism was always that of state neutrality among the religions, not that of the separation of church and state; therefore it seemed in principle possible to combine a commitment to secularism with the maintenance, for the time being, of the separate systems of religious law. In consequence, the goal of a uniform civil code was included in the Constitution among the unenforceable "Directives of State Policy," as something that the state "shall endeavour to secure" in the future—the idea being that when things had calmed down and people were ready for it, this next step would be taken. It never has been taken, and by now it is further away than it was fifty years ago.[77]

The way the system operates is labyrinthine and uneven, and it is not easy to get two legal experts to agree on a description of what the system is.[78] But, to give a reasonable general description: at birth, a child must be classified into some religious group. Usually it is that of both or one of the parents, and usually some religion is chosen, although it is possible not to mention a religion at all. Children who are enrolled as members of some religion are henceforth governed by that system of personal law. Since the passage of the Special Marriage Act in 1954 (itself much opposed by various religious leaders as an infringement of their power), they may elect secular marriage and secular divorce (although secular laws are quite similar to the reformed Hindu laws). This is usually taken to mean that they will also be governed by secular inheritance law, but in 1975 the relevant law was amended under pressure from Hindu leaders so that two Hindus who elect a secular marriage will still be governed by the Hindu law of inheritance. Religious conversion typically results in a change of legal system, although there are cases in which Hindus who convert to Islam in order to contract polygamous marriage are still charged with bigamy in Hindu courts, and it remains quite unclear which system finally governs.[79] Conversions into Hinduism are extremely rare—in large part because it would be unclear what the caste of such a convert would be.[80] What makes mobility among systems especially difficult is the arrangement for hereditary property, which typically involves complex family consortia (called the "coparcenary" in the Hindu system), in which individuals have rights that are not transferrable should one individual within the family decide to switch to another system. This discourages conversion, secular marriage and divorce, and the declaration of a secular identity for a newborn child.

What should my two-pronged approach say about this system in general? On the one hand, this brand of secularism is extraordinarily generous to the religious traditions, giving them a type of latitude shown in no European or North American democracy. Given, especially, Muslims' legitimate fears that they would be slighted and unfairly treated in a largely Hindu state—given, indeed, the hostility toward Muslims evident in some Hindu quarters during the constitutional founding—this approach may have been preferable on religious-liberty grounds to the establishment of a uniform civil code. On the other hand, it has large difficulties, which are now evident. First is the sheer practical difficulty of achieving any predictability in a nation governed by so bewilderingly many codes and variants of codes. Second, and more important for my approach, is the likelihood of inequality between the religions (and between religion and nonreligion) in the approach to basic human capabilities. It seems virtually inevitable, in such circumstances that citizens will end up being unequally treated on the basis of religion one way or another—getting better inheritance deals or divorce settlements or whatever on account of being a Hindu or a Muslim—and that the national state will refrain from rectifying the situation for fear of infringing the prerogatives of some religion. So a huge free exercise dilemma is created: an individual incurs a substantial burden by, let us say, being born Hindu rather than Muslim, but the reason the state can't fix this is that the religions say this fixing itself imposes a substantial burden.

Third, the system makes it very difficult to exit from one system to another, or to prefer nonreligion to religion. This itself is a major free exercise problem. One is so wrapped up in religion in relation to one's entire livelihood that one's free exercise is thoroughly compromised, in the sense that liberty of conscience can't by itself settle the question of religious membership. A Muslim wife who doesn't like Islamic divorce law is stuck with it regardless; so is a Hindu child who might wish to inherit under the secular system.

Fourth, and most central for our purposes, other inequalities in basic capability, most prominent of which is the inequality between sex and sex, will be much more difficult to rectify in this plural decentralized system. Change of all systems at once is a virtual impossibility. But if one religion changes first, many of its members, as we have by now seen, are sure to claim that they are being discriminated against by being made to pay more maintenance, or being denied polygamy, and that other non-changed groups are being given "special rights." On the other hand, efforts to do away with those so-called "special rights," bringing the less equal group into line with equality norms, are seen as sinister attempts to impose a Hindu standard on Muslims, or whatever. Interestingly this has not been the case with the Parsi system, which has amended its inheritance law several times in the direction of gender equality, and since 1991 has a fully gender-equal law. Regional reforms have also taken place within the Hindu and Muslim systems.[81] But in the current climate of Hindu-Muslim mistrust, full equality in the nation as a whole is unlikely to be achieved by such internal reforms. What frequently emerges instead is a furious race to the bottom, each group striving to show its power by resisting all change. Such a legal regime makes it difficult to achieve capability equality for women.

On the other hand, nothing in my approach militates against separate systems of personal law, so long as these problems are solved: so long as (a) there are guarantees of sex equality in each, where central capabilities are concerned, and these are enforced; (b) there is adequate provision for individuals who wish to define themselves as nonreligious or to change religion; and (c) there is a continual effort to ensure parity among the religious systems so that individuals do not lose out in basic matters because of the accidents of their religious membership. It is surely difficult to solve these problems. But in today's India the most productive approach may well be to keep the separate codes and try to solve them through a vigilant set of legislative and judicial constraints.[82] An alternative, sure to be vigorously resisted, would be to secularize all property law under a uniform code, and to leave the regulation of family law to the separate systems, with the provisos mentioned. This would go a long way to easing the burden placed on individuals who wish to exit from a religious system and would also thereby give the religious systems new incentives to retain their members by promoting their interests.

One valuable strategy in solving these problems would to promote more public dialogue over norms of sex equality inside the religious codes. This can probably best be done at present by relying on the international human rights documents that India has ratified, together with a provision in the Indian constitution that India is bound by all the contents of international treaties it has ratified. In the area of sexual harassment, the Supreme Court has ordered parliament to come up with suitable legislation in conformity with the principles outlined in the Convention on the Elimination of All Forms of Discrimination Against Women (CEDAW).[83] Similarly, the religious legal systems might be invited to submit their plans for reform, showing how they would bring their legal systems into conformity with the Indian Constitution and with international treaty norms. (The capabilities approach itself could be used in this connection.) The tricky issue is who should do this inviting: not the current government, given its religious bias, and probably not the Supreme Court, given the history of the Shah Bano case. Perhaps concerned nongovernmental organizations and women's groups, in alliance with political parties that favor pluralism, could succeed in promoting such a dialogue.

Now let us turn to the concrete cases.

The case of Mary Roy is straightforward. The claim that is being made by the Christian church is simply not a claim about the religious capabilities of individuals. Although judges are not well equipped to determine what is central to a religion and what is not, one thing that they can say with confidence is that the ability to rake in larger amounts of tax revenue, while highly desirable from the point of view of a religious institution, is not itself a religious capability. However difficult it is to say what the core of Christianity is, we ought to be able to agree that the ability of an institutionalized church to enrich itself does not lie within that core. No citizen's Christian worship is being burdened by the drop in church revenue that would be occasioned by the new inheritance structure. Even if the drop meant that some local churches would close their doors, we should say that the church's entitlement to this money in the first place is highly questionable. If the Christian church were being denied a tax benefit that other churches enjoy, there would indeed be a free exercise issue, as in the denial by the United States of tax-exempt status to a racially discriminatory religious college.[84] But that is not the situation here: Christian inheritance structure was simply being brought into line with the structure that already prevailed in secular law, in Hindu law, and in Islamic law. In fact, the issue of burden is far more the other way round: before the Supreme Court decision, Christian women were being fined, in effect, for being Christian—just the situation that the U.S. Supreme Court viewed as a paradigm violation of free exercise in *Sherbert v. Verner*.

On the other side, the capability of women to control property is among the central capabilities, and as such would supply a compelling state interest even were there a *prima facie* legitimate claim on the other side. Mary Roy was herself very poor, so in her personal case it was clear that the capability threshold was at issue. Unequal property rights can be shown to be ubiquitous causes of women's general poverty and misery in much of India—certainly before the reforms of Hindu and Muslim personal law, and still in those systems today on account of rigidity in the rules governing control of the "coparcenary" and of jointly owned family land.[85] But I have argued that even in cases where an individual's control of property would in any case be above the threshold, discrimination on the basis of sex with respect to a basic capability is itself a case of capability failure. So it would have been right to declare the inheritance laws unconstitutional in general, not only as applied to women who would otherwise be destitute. It is somewhat unfortunate that the Supreme Court decided the case on a narrowly technical basis, concerning what law applies, rather than addressing the issue of sex equality head on. Nonetheless, the result for Christian women was a good one.

The reform of Hindu personal law poses far more difficult problems. Hinduism is a diverse set of traditional practices, with no easily identifiable core. But there is no doubt that some of the proposed reforms touched on very central matters: the substantial uprooting of the caste system, the denial of polygamous marriage, the ban on marriage contracts with women still in childhood, women's right to divorce on a basis of equality with men,[86] the right of women to seek employment outside the home and to participate fully in political life whether or not they are married and without the permission of any male. (Even property rights for daughters were argued to lie within core religious areas, since, as was argued in parliamentary debates, more economic autonomy for women would make prohibited cross-cousin marriages possible and thus upset the structure of the Hindu family.) Although it was much stressed, and accurately, that one recognized system of Hindu law already mandated monogamy and gave women divorce rights, so that one could say that in some areas the government was simply substituting that system for the more prevalent system, nonetheless it was not surprising that the proposed reforms provoked protest from many Hindu leaders.[87] They protested both the proposed changes per se and the fact that they were imposed on Hindus and not on others.[88]

In at least some of these cases, unlike that of Mary Roy, we should grant that a substantial burden is being imposed by the state on the free exercise of religion. (The abolition of polygamy and caste, along with subsequent laws making dowry giving illegal, are the clearest such cases, since in all of these cases adults are prevented from performing religious acts they wish to perform. Child marriage is a dubious case of burden, since the child is too young to give meaningful consent, and we should not grant that marrying off a young daughter is a legitimate parental religious prerogative. Divorce rights for women clearly do not impose a substantial burden, since free exercise has never been interpreted to give one person the right to impose his religious will on another.) Moreover, the burden affects the capabilities of individuals, not just of religious institutions or authorities. This burden is all the more invidious because it is imposed selectively and not neutrally, restricting Hindu tradition in a way that other traditions are not restricted. On the other hand, we can see clearly that central human capabilities are at issue on the other side, just as they were in the contemporaneous abolition of caste. Control over property, the right to control the integrity of one's person (at risk in violence associated with dowry), rights to mobility, assembly, and political participation, the right to marital consent and to divorce on an equal basis, all these clearly provide the state with a compelling interest in the proposed reforms. Polygamy seems to do so as well, given its historical connection with unequal control over the integrity of one's person, unequal economic rights, and unequal dignity; but that issue, I think, raises special problems and I shall discuss it separately later in this essay. Where the caste system is concerned, fundamental capabilities are once again at issue: equal political rights, rights to the free choice of employment, rights to education and property, and, finally, to equal dignity and self-respect. As *The Hindustan Times* commented: "The Hindu Code Bill is the counterpart on the social side of the new Constitution in which is embodied the political ideal of liberty, equality and fraternity."[89]

My approach suggests that in less central matters the state should allow Hindus broad latitude to act in accordance with their traditions. (I have argued, for example, that marijuana use during Holi is one such matter.) But on these matters of fundamental civic dignity and equality, Ambedkar (himself a member of one of the scheduled castes) was correct when he said that the state could not wait for Hinduism to undertake voluntary internal reform: "[W]hatever else Hindu society may adopt it will never give up its social structure—the enslavement of the Shudra and the enslavement of women. It is for this reason that law must come to the rescue in order that society may move on."[90] This decision should not have been, and was not, taken lightly, since it concerned extremely important religious matters. (Ambedkar did not simply adopt a secular humanist stance, for he continued to support ample constitutional protections for religion, which were clearly necessary in the context in order to protect the status of Muslims as equal citizens.) And, although one can understand the political pressures and the legitimate concern for minority rights that led to an uneven implementation of these changes, in principle the reforms should not have been made in a discriminatory fashion. On the other hand, not to make the reforms would have involved the government in other forms of discrimination on the basis of religion: against the lower castes, who would have unequal rights because of being Hindu, and against Hindu women, who would do less well, even at that time, than Parsi and Christian and Muslim women, in at least some of the areas covered by the Code. In effect, the reforms upheld the intrinsic value of religious capabilities within limits imposed by the principle of the moral core—a religious claim should not have the same weight if it involves harms.

Here we should consider the internal diversity of traditions and the social principle of the moral core. When a step is taken against the core of a tradition in pursuit of a compelling state interest, it is a great help to recall that the tradition itself has contained powerful voices calling for exactly these changes in the name of religion itself, interpreting the core of the religion in accordance with the contraints of a moral understanding. Thus Mahatma Gandhi defined the essence of Hinduism as "the pursuit of truth by non-violent means," using this account of the core to launch his famous attack on the caste hierarchy. Other reformers, such as Rammohan Roy and Rabindranath Tagore, also called into question many of the religion's hierarchical practices, including child marriage and the seclusion of women. Like Gandhi, they argued that these practices were not part of the core of Hinduism but rather expressions of imperfect historical ideas. At the time of reform, it was also pointed out that the very practice of reform and modification was in accordance with traditional precedent, and prominent Hindus were obviously on both sides of the measures. This internal debate helps show that the burden imposed on the tradition as a result of the state's interest in equality need not be considered a fatal burden; indeed, in some religious quarters it might be considered no burden at all. Thus the social principle helps support the formal political principle.

Subsequent developments in Hindu law have continued to address the religious dilemma in very much the terms my approach recommends. A case in point is the debate over the remedy of "restitution of conjugal rights" in the reformed Hindu Marriage Act of 1955. In retaining this remedy, the new laws failed to protect women's bodily integrity: a woman who had left the marital home could be forcibly returned to it. The remedy originated in British ecclesiastical law (indeed it was abolished in Britain only in 1970), and it had long been a feature of some Hindu systems, but the new codes actually made the remedy more uniformly available. Thus a woman who had suffered from domestic abuse could be forced to return to the scene of her suffering; a woman who no longer wanted to bear a child with the man she lived with could be forced to bear a child. Women could pay a fine to avoid forcible return, but women leaving abusive marriages were not generally in a position to meet that requirement. In 1983, in *T. Sareetha v.*

T. Venkata Subbaiah, Judge Choudary of the Andhra Pradesh High Court declared this remedy unconstitutional, on the ground that it violates a women's autonomy interest in controlling the integrity of her body and her childbearing capacities:

> A decree for restitution of conjugal rights constitutes the grossest form of violation of an individual's right to privacy. It denies the woman her free choice whether, when and how her body is to become the vehicle for the procreation of another human being. [It] deprives a woman of control over her choice as to when and by whom the various parts of her body should be allowed to be sensed. The woman loses her control over her most intimate decisions.[91]

In a supplementary argument, Judge Choudary pointed out that the law violates the constitution's equality provisions as well. Although formally neutral, given "our social reality," the remedy "works in practice only as an oppression to be operated by the husband for the benefit of the husband against the wife."

As for the religious issue, the judge was careful to point out that the forcible return of a spouse was nowhere mandated in Hindu traditions: the law went beyond tradition by enforcing legally what religion considers to be a moral duty. Indeed, he insisted on the British origin of the remedy. But there was no doubt that his primary concern throughout was the compelling nature of the state's interest in protecting a woman's rights over her body, and that this interest was held to trump the interest of Hindu religion in the maintenance of a (by now) traditional feature of Hindu law. The Supreme Court disagreed, overruling the lower court with the argument that the remedy "serves a social purpose as an aid to the prevention of break-up of marriage." In related decisions, the Court opined that a Hindu woman's duty is to live with her husband in the matrimonial home.

Obviously, my approach supports Judge Choudary's reasoning, and his constitutional reasoning shows that the Indian constitution contains all the materials necessary to implement this approach. (A similar case in Bangladesh came out this way at the Supreme Court level, so the remedy has now been eliminated from Bangladeshi law).[92]

The *Shah Bano* case raises difficult issues, since it concerns the rights of a minority religion, the issue that has motivated my approach from the beginning. While it seemed clear that a recognizable core of Hinduism would surely survive the reorganization of Hindu personal law, there were legitimate reasons to fear that Islam in India would suffer greatly were the system of Muslim personal law to be gravely curtailed in its power. Chief Justice Chandrachud was probably correct in his argument that the order of maintenance under the Criminal Procedure Code was in no way inconsistent with traditional Islamic law, but the very fact that he undertook to say what Islamic law was and was not was itself alarming, raising the specter of Hindu domination. He was entitled to invoke the principle of moral constraint, refusing to defer to Islamic law in the matter of basic maintenance, but his attempt to use a strong social moral-constraint argument was incendiary and highly unwise in a case dealing with constitutional fundamentals and matters of basic justice. Typical of the reaction was that of Z. R. Ansari, a Muslim government minister, who made a speech in Parliament condemning the Court for exceeding its authority by presuming to interpret sacred Islamic scripture: "If you have a *tamboli* (tobacco vendor) doing the work of a *teli* (oil-seller), things are bound to go wrong." The Muslim *ulema* condemned the judgment as an assault on the authority of the Shariat. This clerical reaction, accompanied by widespread street demonstrations, set the scene for an intractable political debate. Moral-core arguments were also used by Islamic feminists, and it would have been better to have left to them the role of making such informal social arguments, resting official state policy only on the interpretation of core political principles.

In theoretical terms, there seems little doubt that the issue of maintenance after divorce is a serious issue, affecting central capabilities. This is all the more obvious when we consider the subset of maintenance cases that can be appealed under the Criminal Procedure Code. To win an award of maintenance, the female plaintiff has to show that she would otherwise be without means to support herself, that she has suffered cruelty or neglect that makes it impossible for her to live with her husband, that she did not leave him of her own accord, and that her husband does have adequate means. The refusal to order maintenance in cases like these creates a most dramatic and urgent case of capability failure. Subsequent cases in which maintenance has been denied show the burden that the Muslim Women's Bill has put on Muslim women. Maitrayee Mukhopadhyay's study of West Bengal in the post-1986 period shows women facing grave disadvantages and being forced to depend on relatives for even a meager living. (These women are most often illiterate and untrained for any work; frequently they are of advanced age—Shah Bano was seventy-four when her husband threw her out of the house.) Worse still, the destitution of these women (many of whom are much younger than Shah Bano) has had the practical effect of crippling their children's education, as children who would otherwise be in school are put to work supporting their mothers.[93]

In addition to the infringement of capabilities, Muslim women can also point to serious problems of free exercise on their side, and of discrimination on the basis of religion. The free exercise issue arises from the fact that, although they may not be especially thrilled about their

Muslim identity and may have no interest in being or remaining Muslims, they are classified under the Muslim legal system by the sheer fact of family membership. Once marriage and divorce are under a particular system, the issue of maintenance must be handled by that system. Shah Bano is thus effectively deprived of her opportunity to define herself as secular, as Hindu, or as whatever she might like to be.

This leads directly to the issue of discrimination on the basis of religion. Only Muslim women are denied maintenance under the Criminal Procedure Code. As Muslim scholar Zoya Hasan argues, there is "little reason to doubt that the denial of rights to Muslim women, which are available to women of other faiths, is a violation of the constitutional provision that the State shall not discriminate against any citizen on grounds of religion."[94] Muslim women's activist Shahjahan (also known as Apa) put the matter more bluntly in a speech in front of the House of Parliament the day the 1986 law was passed: "If by making separate laws for Muslim women, you are trying to say that we are not citizens of this country, then why don't you tell us clearly and unequivocally that we should establish another country—not Hindustan or Pakistan but Auratstan (women's land)."[95] Muslim leaders seem to have been so worried about the impact of the Criminal Procedure Code on the power of Muslim leaders that they simply forgot about the serious religious issues that pointed the other way. In effect, they were indeed treating Muslim women as noncitizens. They violated both the principle of individual capabilities, neglecting the free exercise and nondiscrimination claims of Muslim women, and also the principle of the moral core, inflicting harm on a group in order to shore up their own power. As I have mentioned, women's groups repeatedly challenged the Act by petition in the Supreme Court as being in violation of constitutional provisions against religious discrimination,[96] although the Supreme Court, having suffered sufficient public abuse in the aftermath of the *Shah Bano* decision, has not responded to any of these petitions.

To summarize: the religious issues themselves do not point in a single direction; indeed, the weightier free exercise claims seem to be on the side of Muslim women. And the capabilities issue is squarely on their side. The result was therefore a very unfortunate one, both for women and for religion.

The case came out this way because the government of Rajiv Gandhi persistently ignored the diversity of the Indian Islamic tradition, listening only to the voices of powerful conservative clerics. Throughout the debate, many Islamic thinkers, among them politicians, intellectuals, and Islamic women's organizations, opposed the retrograde Muslim Women's Bill. They made compelling moral-constraint arguments, claiming that compassionate moral concerns central to Islam made more adequate maintenance for destitute women mandatory even in religious terms. Thus they demonstrated very convincingly that there was not really a gap between core constitutional principles and the core of Islamic tradition. But the government totally disregarded their views, according legitimacy to a small group of established patriarchal clerics as the true representatives of the community—even though one Muslim minister resigned from the government in protest against this sidelining of Muslim opinion in favor of sex equality. (There are good reasons to believe that Rajiv Gandhi behaved this way because he had struck a deal with leading Islamic conservatives, trading a concession to them on women's maintenance for concessions to Hindus concerning the reopening of the disputed shrine at Ayodhya). As one of the leading liberal Muslim intellectuals summarizes the matter:

> Liberal and progressive opinion within the community was ignored, allowing the ulema to appropriate the task of defining the overarching concerns and interests of Muslims. Admittedly, the objective of the Muslim divines was to defend the Shariat and resist legislation that would, in their perception, lead to a change in divinely ordained laws. But the government should have known better. Interpretations by the ulema were neither final nor irrevocable; there were other trends of thought, other interpretations which the government chose to ignore, partly because the government itself shared the underlying assumption that Muslims are a religious community, that the theologians are its sole spokesmen, and that there exists a clear equation between religious law and community identity.[97]

In effect, the government made the error of my traditionalist opponent at the start of this lecture, equating a religious tradition with its most patriarchal and politically entrenched voices. He would have done better to acknowledge the moral-constraint arguments being made within Islam, which supported a change in women's status in the name of religion itself.

This error, though perhaps inspired by serious concern for religious pluralism, has actually left pluralism a great deal worse off, since now Hindu fundamentalists point to the Muslim Women's Bill as a sign that Hinduism is morally superior to Islam. The typical Muslim male, as portrayed in Hindu nationalist discourse, is a polygamous oppressor of women, very likely also a rapist, whereas the Hindu male is represented as both moderate and enlightened, incapable of treating women as mere sex objects. These stereotypes contribute to discrimination against Muslims, including legal discrimination. One magistrate, interviewed under condition of anonymity, stated: "[W]hen a Muslim comes to our court we are already biased . . . their 3–4 marriages are repugnant to us." The subdivisional judicial magistrate of Alipore criminal court stated openly to his (Hindu) female interviewer, expecting approval: "For them mar-riage is nothing. They get married, have a few children and then they leave their wives . . . Muslim women are worse off than the household dog."[98] This can hardly be a desirable result for a religion whose basic tenets are in some crucial respects very supportive of sex equality, pro-claiming male and female equal in nature and capacity. The actions of the Muslim clerics were thus counterproductive as well as unjust.

In all three cases, in different ways, my approach backs laws of general applicability against religious practices. I have said that this would not always be the case, but when would it not be the case, one might ask, with a practice involving the inequality of women? This is a difficult question to answer, since most areas of traditional women's inequality under personal laws do involve central capabilities. There are, however, areas of religious practice in which the government probably does not have compelling interest in forcing change, at least so long as the free-dom of individuals to change their religion is also firmly established. Such areas would prominently include the assignment of religious func-tions. I have argued elsewhere that public norms of sex equality should not force the Roman Catholic Church to hire female priests, although it probably should force them to hire female janitors on a basis of equality with men.[99] This is so, however, only so long as women are completely free not to be Catholics if they don't want to be—which is not the case in India, given the system as I have described it. Were such freedom secure, analogous religious practices in all the religions are probably protected by my principle. Orthodox Jews, for example, will be permit-ted to retain sex-segregated places of worship—although the case for this exemption is surely undercut by government policies that deny equal recognition to non-Orthodox Jews, thus denying women an effec-tive right of choice. Similarly protected would be sex-divided norms of dress and decoration, where these run afoul of some law of general ap-plicability. For example, on this principle the French government would be required to permit girls to attend school in Muslim scarves, even if there is a general sense that the wearing of the scarf is a symbol of sex hierarchy. The schools may and should teach the equality of the sexes, preparing the girls for an independent choice in this matter, and they should back up the girls if they want to take off the scarves. But they should not forbid the practice.

A difficult group of cases involves educational institutions controlled by religious bodies. Racial discrimination lost Bob Jones University its tax-exempt status, but the fact that the president of the University of Notre Dame is required to be a priest, ergo male, has not lost that uni-versity its tax-exempt status. This is a case where, as in *Bob Jones*, the government might appropriately judge that a compelling state interest in sex equality mandates a withdrawal of the exemption. It is characteristic of many modern debates that racial discrimination is taken to be an impermissible expression of religious tradition, while sex discrimination is taken to be just the way things have always been; with regard to a function that is administrative and educational, rather than at the core of worship, we should judge that granting a tax exemption involves the federal government in an unacceptable endorsement of sex inequality. India's universities are mostly public and thus controlled directly by public norms regarding sex-equality, but it has large numbers of Christian schools, some of which may be appropriate targets of scrutiny under this requirement.

One of the most difficult cases under my principle will be polygamy, typically seen as inextricable from a history of sex discrimination, and yet religiously central in some traditions. Should Muslims or Hindus, or Mormons, receive exemptions to laws of general applicability on this account? I believe that no answer can be given to this question in the abstract. There is nothing in polygamy in the abstract that is oppressive of women, especially if the practice is available to both sexes. Women in Kerala, for example have been able to contract multiple marriages since the eleventh century, and this liberty is a major source of women's high status in that region.[100] What is objectionable about polygamy is that it is often available only to males, and that it is connected with a legal and traditional regime under which women have unequal property rights and rights of mobility, association, and self-determination. But it is also the case that the reasons for opposing polygamy have often been very bad reasons, connected with fear and ignorance about a group whose practices are different. Thus, I believe that Mormon polygamy should have been permitted so long as the legal equality of women, and their freedom to exit from the community should they wish to, were securely established and protected, and so long as the law extended similar opportunities to women who for some genuine religious reason wished, themselves, to contract polygamous marriages.

In India, the situation today is inseparable from specific aspects of Hindu-Muslim conflict. Muslim polygamy was first perceived, and to some extent is still perceived, as an enviable liberty, which Hindus struggled to retain for themselves. More recently, it has increasingly been defined by the Hindu right as a practice oppressive of women, hence an opportunity for Hindus to look down on Muslims.[101] I believe that it was right, in practical terms, to eliminate polygamy for Hindus and to retain it for Muslims, despite the inequality involved, given the vulnerability of the Muslim minority at the time of Independence (and given, too, that polygamy is somewhat more central to Muslim than to Hindu practice). Over time, given that polygamy in this context probably cannot be separated from sex hierarchy, it would be good to move toward a general ban—after all, polygamy is practiced by a small minority of Muslims,[102] is not religiously required, and is nowhere near as religiously central as it is for Mormons—but in a climate of respect and support for the Muslim community as a whole. That this climate does not now exist can hardly be doubted. Polygamy should probably therefore be retained, while an effort is made to promote liberal Muslim viewpoints and to encourage internal reform of the system of personal law.

Children and Parents

I have focused so far on how my approach will protect the capabilities of adult women as fully equal citizens. But the upbringing of children is equally important and still more complex. In one way, the state has an especially strong interest in protecting the capabilities of children, for they are its future citizens and are not voluntary members of the family unit. But in another way, the state should acknowledge at least some limits to its power to intervene in children's lives, given its interest in the maintenance of the family. Parents have an extremely strong interest in bringing up children in their own religion and continuing traditions to which they are attached. The state should acknowledge this interest, and it must treat children somewhat differently from adult women—both because their parents have at least some legitimate rights over them and because it is difficult to ascertain the child's own choice, given parental power and the child's economic dependency.

Numerous conflicts have arisen between parents' religious education of their children and the state's interest in its future citizens. Many of the most interesting cases involve compulsory education and child labor. India has laws mandating compulsory education, usually up to age fourteen, but the nation is in no position to enforce either these laws or laws against child labor at this time; the constitutional tradition has therefore not yet articulated clear boundaries in this area. I shall therefore turn again to U.S. constitutional law, discussing three cases that give at least a general idea of what my approach would recommend.

In *Pierce v. Society of Sisters*[103] the Court invalidated an Oregon law that required parents to send their children to the public school system, and it forbade them to elect a religious school. The Court argues that parents have a fundamental liberty interest in directing the education of their children "by selecting reputable teachers and places." The law was held to be an unreasonable interference with that liberty interest: the state cannot "standardize its children by forcing them to accept instruction from public teachers only."[104] The Court was careful to limit the latitude given to parents:

> No question is raised concerning the power of the State reasonably to regulate all schools, to inspect, supervise and examine them, their teachers and pupils; to require that all children of proper age attend some school, that teachers shall be of good moral character and patriotic disposition, that certain studies plainly essential to good citizenship must be taught, and that nothing be taught which is manifestly inimical to the public welfare.

Nonetheless, the opinion is a fundamental affirmation of the right of parents to choose religious schooling for their children.

My approach strongly favors this solution, including the reservation that the state may require certain studies deemed necessary to citizenship. (I have problems with the idea that the state can require teachers to be "patriotic" and can rule out some studies as "inimical to the public welfare," but these are not the issues on which I want to focus here.) The compelling interest the state has in the appropriate education of its future citizens can be satisfied by such appropriate regulation and does not justify interfering with parents' liberty to the extent represented by the Oregon law. States need to consider carefully what studies are essential to citizenship. It seems to me that Israel has made some grave errors here, by not only certifying, but even funding, ultra-Orthodox schools that offer no instruction in history or current affairs. John Rawls's suggested requirement that all students be taught the rudiments of civic affairs and of the existing public constitutional order seems a bare minimum, and this teaching would include, in India as in the United States, the teaching that women, under the public constitutional order, are fully equal citizens with equal rights and responsibilities.[105] This teaching about the public political conception is fully consistent with the religion's teaching, as well, its own comprehensive view. Given that the religion has agreed to sign on to a constitution of a certain type, it will figure out how to square this "overlapping consensus" on public political matters of basic justice with the rest of what it teaches.[106] Within these constraints, religious schooling should be a protected (though not, I believe, a publicly funded) option.

Sometimes compulsory education appears to interfere with religious requirements. In these cases, the balancing approach I favor comes into play, as we must ask whether a substantial burden has been imposed on religious free exercise, and whether, if so, the state has a compelling interest in the education in question. In *Wisconsin v. Yoder*, [107] members of the Old Order Amish religion sought exemption from Wisconsin's compulsory school law, which would have required them to send their children to public or private school until age sixteen. They declined to send their children after age fourteen, arguing that the continuation of their religious tradition required them to withdraw their children from the secular world at that point, teaching them skills of farming and domestic labor and imparting to them "attitudes favoring manual work and self-reliance." The Court agreed that the law in question imposed a substantial burden on their free exercise of their religion; it also judged that the state had failed to show a compelling interest in these last two years of education for this particular group of children. The state does indeed, in general, have a "compelling interest" in preparing "citizens to participate effectively and intelligently in our open political system . . . [and] to be self-reliant and self-sufficient participants in society." But the evidence is, they said, that the Amish are quite effective and self-reliant citizens and do not "place burdens on society through their educational shortcomings."

This is a truly hard case for my approach; indeed, it shows exactly where the line drawn by my approach falls. On the one hand, the state does have a compelling interest in the capabilities of its future citizens; on the other hand, it is not so clear that these particular two years are the crucial determinant of capability, and to require them clearly does impose a substantial burden on religious free exercise. A further complication is that the case has a serious sex-equality aspect, ignored in the opinions and rarely mentioned in discussions. Male Amish children learn farming and carpentry, skills that are highly marketable in the outside world, while females learn domestic skills that would be less easy to market should they choose to leave the community. Thus the state's interest in education is connected with an interest in the equality of its citizens, and this might support the view that, after all, the interest is a compelling interest.[108]

That is what I am inclined to believe; but it is a truly difficult case, where the two parts of my proposal most clearly conflict. Finally, we arrive at the issue of child labor. *Prince v. Massachusetts*[109] involves a Massachusetts child labor law, applied to a nine-year-old girl whose aunt, her guardian, had taken her with her to distribute Jehovah's Witness pamphlets on the street, as required by that religion. Despite the fact that the child herself plainly wanted to accompany her aunt and believed that she would be doomed "to everlasting destruction at Armageddon" for failure to do so, the Court held that the state's interest in protecting children's welfare was compelling, trumping both the guardian's and the child's free exercise rights:

> To make accommodation between these freedoms and an exercise of state authority always is delicate. . . . On one side is the obviously earnest claim for freedom of conscience and religious practice. With it is allied the par-

ent's claim to authority in her own household and in the rearing of her children. . . . Against these sacred private interests, basic in a democracy, stand the interests of society to protect the welfare of children. . . . A democratic society rests, for its continuance, upon the healthy, well-rounded growth of young people into full maturity as citizens, with all that implies. It may secure this against impeding restraints and dangers within a broad range of selection. Among evils most appropriate for such action are the crippling effects of child employment, more especially in public places, and the possible harms arising from other activities subject to all the diverse influences of the street.

The state's interest triumphed—although the Court was careful to say that this should not be taken as a warrant for further state intervention into religious upbringing.

I think this is another hard case, but that it was probably wrongly decided. The child was in school; the "labor" in question was neither physically dangerous nor exhausting. Indeed, it is hard to know whether it is "labor" at all, just on the grounds that people paid five cents for the pamphlets.[110] It seems likely that Jehovah's Witnesses are getting unfair treatment because they are an unpopular religion and because they do their preaching on the street. Like most American children who have a religious upbringing, I spent many hours selling things at church bazaars and fairs and never encountered the slightest police problem, nor did any child I knew. Could this be because the police don't bother wealthy Episcopalians inside their well-appointed parish halls? Yet selling cookies at the parish bake sale is far from the core of even Anglican religion, whereas selling *Watchtower* was very much at the core of Betty Prince's religion. (Indeed, the police don't even bother children who sell things at their *school* fairs, even though no First Amendment claim prevents them.) It seems to me that the complainants were right to speak of religious discrimination and that the case, properly understood, does not contain any ills the state has a compelling interest in preventing. However, this case is so far from the Indian situation—where child labor is pervasive, deeply woven into the economy, and ineradicable with existing resources—that it seems almost a mockery of the grave disabilities suffered by Indian children to dwell on cases involving such refined balancing.

To summarize: my balancing test suggests slightly different outcomes for children, since parents have legitimate interests in the religious education of their own children. These interests suggest at least some limitations to the state's interest in education. That interest, however, is on balance and in general a compelling interest, and this gives the state broad power to ensure that all types of schooling prepare children for equal citizenship.

Capabilities and Loss

What is lost if we follow my approach? Do these proposals involve a tragic aspect? The principle of the moral core informs us that nothing of value is lost when we tell people that they cannot lord it over other people in immoral and harmful ways. By using the central capabilities as our guide, we allow considerable latitude for the preservation of tradition in cases that do not involve grave harms to others. And yet one should nonetheless acknowledge that some valuable ways of life will become difficult to sustain for oneself in a climate of choice. Although an emphasis on the capabilities does not in any way preclude the choice to live a traditional hierarchical life, and indeed is intended to protect that opportunity, although we carefully create spaces within which such forms of life may continue and be supported, and although we stress that religion has always been a diverse and changing set of practices and therefore won't be killed off by being nudged in the direction of support for the capabilities—despite all this, we should acknowledge that at least some price will be paid for the sheer emphasis on choice and capability. There are some ways of life that people find deeply satisfying and that probably do not involve unacceptable levels of indignity or capability inequality, which are likely to cease to exist in a regime of choice, simply through social pressure and the availability of alternative choices. Veiling is available in a regime that does not make veiling mandatory, and it seems quite wrong of a regime to impose veiling by force on women who do not choose it. Yet the motivation for this move can at least be comprehended when we recognize a woman who may wish to remain veiled has an extremely difficult time doing so in a fast-moving capitalist society in which her husband is likely to be working for a multinational corporation many of whose members view veiling as primitive.

One such story was told to anthropologist Hannah Papanek by an elderly Indian Muslim woman, Hamida Khala.[111] It helps us see where the tragedy potentially lies in a regime of choice and also helps us understand how human ingenuity and the dynamic nature of religious practices can surmount tragedy.

Brought up in an educated family in north India, Hamida Khala had a fine education under her father's supervision and longed to wear the *burqua* as a sign of maturity. At the age of thirteen she was betrothed to a much older widower in the civil service, a man reputed to be of "modern" views. Hamida consented to the marriage on the condition that if he asked her to stop observing purdah she would return to her family. She began living with her husband at the age of fifteen, and he took her to Calcutta, far away from her family. As a civil servant, he worked with

British, Hindu, and Muslim colleagues, and social life was organized around couples who typically attended dinners and tea parties together. Her husband began to resent her seclusion, which was cramping his own social life and his professional advancement. Although some colleagues arranged dinner parties at which women sat in a separate room, many refused to do so. And at last one host played a trick.

One night the women were seated at a table with empty seats at every other place. Suddenly a group of men came in and sat in the vacant seats. Hamida recalls this event with tremendous pain: "What I experienced, I just can't tell you. There was darkness all around me. I couldn't see anything. I had tears in my eyes. . . . What I ate I don't remember. . . . All my attempts, my endeavours to keep my purdah were over. I felt I was without faith, I had sinned. I had gone in front of so many men, all these friends of my husband. They've seen me. My purdah was broken, my purdah that was my faith." Her husband insisted that he had not been aware of the plan and apologized profoundly to her. Nonetheless, she recognized that her life would have to change if she were to stay with him. She wrote to her father, asking his advice. He told her that if her marriage might be endangered she would have to leave purdah, adding that her extreme type of purdah does not represent an ancient Islamic tradition; she could behave with reticence and modesty even after leaving it. After reading sacred texts on her own, she came to the conclusion that there was a way of living as a devout Muslim outside strict purdah. She worked out her own rules of modest dress and demeanor—long-sleeved blouses, downcast eyes, no makeup or jewelry—and followed them the rest of her life, while going outside and learning how to conduct daily business and social affairs. Her husband supported her and showed respect for her religion.

Hamida reports some good aspects of the change. She developed greater physical agility and strength by walking outside. She learned how to manage accounts, which came in handy when her husband died prematurely of a heart attack. Coming to the conclusion that "the real purdah is modesty," she refused to lend her support to a political campaign to bring back widespread purdah in Pakistan when a conservative leader asked her for help. She feels that she has been able to define successfully a Muslim identity that included the central precepts of her religion—and yet she acknowledges that there has been a real cost. "It was a big sacrifice for me to leave purdah." If that is so even in this very favorable case, where, because of Hamida's personal strength and her husband's respect, she was able to construct a viable religious alternative, we can easily imagine that other women might experience the sacrifice without discovering a viable alternative. Hard though it is for Western feminists to imagine a life in which physical movement, practical command, and a variety of associative ties are not central, we can see that Hamida's old life contained genuine religious values and did not strike her, even in retrospect, as humiliating or as unacceptably subordinating. She does judge that women should focus more on exercise and should learn to manage things in case they need to: in these respects she faults the earlier regime. Papanek adds evidence that women in purdah were and are frequently cheated by middlemen, when they are unable to deal with managers and employers directly.[112] But she appears to think that the old regime was not as such unacceptable, and might have accommodated these changes.

This case shows, I believe, that a capability-based approach to religious liberty does involve the potential for tragedy. Nonetheless, it also shows how resourceful deeply religious women and men can be in adapting the religion's moral core to a changing reality. It is especially significant that Hamida Khala strongly opposed mandatory purdah. Her final judgment was that she and her husband "learned a lot from each other." Indeed, her response to the conservative leader—which she reported, Papanek says, with great delight—showed that she thinks the problem of modesty can be well solved by women without purdah, if only men will cooperate. "Let a thousand women come out at once, not just a few," she reported herself as saying. "Then you will see how quickly men get used to seeing women and think nothing of it." She had kept her modesty while coming out of purdah, she added to the leader, and that is what really matters.

Through religion, people search for the transcendent. But religious groups and practices are human phenomena. The humanity of religion means that its practices are fallible and need continual scrutiny in the light of the important human interests that it is the state's business to protect. On the other hand, religion is itself among the important human interests, both in itself and because it represents a central exercise of human choice. For these reasons, any solution to the dilemmas created when religion and sex equality clash must be complex, relying on the ability of judges and other political actors to balance multiple factors with discernment. One thing they should not do, however, is to abandon a commitment to equal justice, in the face of political intimidation.

On November 2, 1985, Shah Bano, in the presence of four male witnesses, signed with her thumbprint an open letter to all Muslims, stating that Islamic leaders had explained to her the commands concerning divorce and maintenance, in the light of Quran and Hadith. Using legal language that she is extremely unlikely to have chosen or perhaps even understood, she renounces her claim to maintenance and demands that the Indian government withdraw the Supreme Court decision. She further states that "Article 44 of the Indian Constitution, in which there is a directive for enacting a uniform civil code for all, is quite contrary to the Quran and the hadith." She asks that the government renounce the goal of uniformity and resolve that "no interference would be ever attempted in future" with the operation of the Islamic courts. "In the end," she concludes, "I thank Maulana Habib Yar Khan and Haji Abdul Ghaffar Saheb of Indore who showed me the straight path and helped me follow the Truth and thus saved me in this world and in the hereafter." [113]

It is extremely difficult to avoid the conclusion that the faith of a devout and penniless woman is being exploited for political purposes. And, to paraphrase Lincoln, it seems extremely strange that a just God would indeed require a destitute aged woman to renounce her claim to a minimal livelihood. Respecting the freedom of religion does not mean giving a small number of religious leaders limitless license to perpetuate human misery, to inhibit the religious freedom of individuals, and to push the law around. It is not an assault on religious freedom, but a deeper defense of its basic principle, to say that in such cases, the law indeed must "come to the rescue" in order that "society should move on."

Appendix: The Central Human Capabilities

1. Life. Being able to live to the end of a human life of normal length; not dying prematurely, or before one's life is so reduced as to be not worth living.

2. Bodily Health. Being able to have good health, including reproductive health; to be adequately nourished; to have adequate shelter.

3. Bodily Integrity. Being able to move freely from place to place; to be secure against violent assault, including sexual assault and domestic violence; having opportunities for sexual satisfaction and for choice in matters of reproduction.

4. Senses, Imagination, and Thought. Being able to use the senses, to imagine, think, and reason—and to do these things in a "truly human" way, a way informed and cultivated by an adequate education, including, but by no means limited to, literacy and basic mathematical and scientific training. Being able to use imagination and thought in connection with experiencing and producing works and events of one's own choice, religious, literary, musical, and so forth. Being able to use one's mind in ways protected by guarantees of freedom of expression with respect to both political and artistic speech, and freedom of religious exercise. Being able to have pleasurable experiences and to avoid non-beneficial pain.

5. Emotions. Being able to have attachments to things and people outside ourselves; to love those who love and care for us, to grieve at their absence; in general, to love, to grieve, to experience longing, gratitude, and justified anger. Not having one's emotional development blighted by fear and anxiety. (Supporting this capability means supporting forms of human association that can be shown to be crucial in their development.)

6. Practical Reason. Being able to form a conception of the good and to engage in critical reflection about the planning of one's life. (This entails protection for the liberty of conscience and religious observance.)

7. Affiliation.

A. Being able to live with and toward others, to recognize and show concern for other human beings, to engage in various forms of social interaction; to be able to imagine the situation of another. (Protecting this capability means protecting institutions that constitute and nourish such forms of affiliation, and also protecting the freedom of assembly and political speech.)

B. Having the social bases of self-respect and nonhumiliation; being able to be treated as a dignified being whose worth is equal to that of others. This entails provisions of nondiscrimination on the basis of race, sex. ethnicity, caste, religion, and national origin.

8. Other Species. Being able to live with concern for and in relation to animals, plants, and the world of nature.

9. Play. Being able to laugh, to play, to enjoy recreational activities.

10. Control over One's Environment.

A. Political. Being able to participate effectively in political choices that govern one's life; having the right of political participation, protections of free speech and association.

B. Material. Being able to hold property (both land and movable goods) and having property rights on an equal basis with others; having the right to seek employment on an equal basis with others; having the freedom from unwarranted search and seizure. In work, being able to work as a human being, exercising practical reason and entering into meaningful relationships of mutual recognition with other workers.

Notes

This paper is chapter 3 of my *Women and Human Development: The Capabilities Approach,* forthcoming from Cambridge University Press, 2000. The chapters were originally delivered as Seeley Lectures at Cambridge University and as Thalheimer Lectures at Johns Hopkins University; chapters 1 and 3 were delivered as Hesburgh Lectures at the University of Notre Dame. In addition, I have presented this chapter at Creighton University, UCLA, the University of Chicago, Northwestern University, the University of Oregon, the University of Pennsylvania, and Stanford University. I owe thanks to many people who commented on these occasions and who gave me comments on drafts of my manuscript, and also to people who helped me learn about personal laws and other aspects of the situation of women in India: Bina Agarwal, Jasodhara Bagchi, Mary Ann Case, Joshua Cohen, Juan Cole, Thomas D'Andrea, Samuel Freeman, Barbara Herman, Zoya Hasan, Indira Jaising, Frances Kamm, Andrew Koppelman, Susan Moller Okin, Eric Posner, Richard Posner, Amartya Sen, Seana Shiffrin, Quentin Skinner, David Strauss, Cass Sunstein, Patricia Uberoi, and Paul Weithman. Sonia Katyal provided invaluable research assistance. Because I refer often to the list of central human capabilities, I present that list in the appendix, above.

1. *The Mahabharata*, trans. J. A. B. van Buitenen (Chicago: University of Chicago Press, 1975), 2:148. Draupadi is wagered, along with many material objects, by her dice-obsessed husband Yudhisthira, and one of the unresolved questions of the episode is whether he had any right so to wager her. (The dice game was reluctantly authorized by King Dhrtarastra at the request of his son Duryodhana.) Vidura, a wise uncle of both contending groups, argues that Yudhisthira was no longer of sound mind when he made the wager. The aged Bhisma, uncle of Pandu and Dhrtarastra (thus great-uncle to the contending groups), maintains that wives belong to their husbands (60); nonetheless, a person without property cannot wager another person's property, and Yudhisthira has already lost all his property, while Draupadi belongs to all five Pandava brothers. So he says there is no clear legal solution. Draupadi, unsurprisingly, is not satisfied by this reply, and Bhima, her second-oldest husband, protests vigorously, noting that even prostitutes are not used as commodities in gambling (61). He takes the view that Yudhisthira had no right at all to wager Draupadi, not because of his own property-interest in her, but because of sympathy for the plight of Draupadi herself. He threatens to assault his brother, until Arjuna restrains him. Nowhere, however, is the view that a wife is property explicitly repudiated.

2. From Nawaz, "Towards Uniformity" (a defense of a uniform civil code), in *Justice for Women: Personal Laws, Women's Rights and Law Reform*, ed. Indira Jaising (Mapusa, Goa: The Other India Press, 1996).

3. Article 14 guarantees the equal protection of the laws to all persons; Article 15 prohibits discrimination on the grounds of religion, race, caste, sex, or place of birth; Article 16 guarantees all citizens equality in matters relating to employment, and prohibits employment discrimination on the basis of religion, race, caste, sex, descent, place of birth, and residence; Article 17 abolishes untouchability: "its practice in any form is forbidden." Article 19 guarantees all citizens rights of free speech and expression, assembly, association, free movement, choice of residence, choice of occupation; Article 21 (the basis for privacy jurisprudence in cases involving marital rape and restitution of conjugal rights) says that "no citizen shall be deprived of his life or personal liberty" without due process of law; Article 25 states that all citizens are "equally entitled to freedom

of conscience and the right freely to profess, practice and propagate religion," although there is an explicit qualification stating that this does not prevent government from abolishing the caste system and "throwing open . . . Hindu religious institutions of a public nature to all classes and sections of Hindus"; Article 26 gives religious denominations the right to manage their own affairs and to acquire property, "subject to public order, morality, and health"; Article 28 guarantees freedom to attend religious schools, states that no religious instruction shall be provided in institutions wholly funded by the State, and also states that where a school is aided by state funds students may not be compelled to perform religious observances. Finally, Article 13 renders invalid all "laws in force" that conflict with any of these Fundamental Rights and forbids the State to make any new laws that take away or abridge a Fundamental Right. (A subsequent judicial decision, however, declared that "laws in force does not include the religious systems of personal law: see *State of Bombay v Narasu Appa Mali*, 1952.) For related constitutional discussion, see my "Religion and Women's Human Rights," in *Religion and Contemporary Liberalism*, ed. Paul Weithman (Notre Dame, Ind.: University of Notre Dame Press, 1997), 93–137, and, in a revised form, in Nussbaum, *Sex and Social Justice* (New York: Oxford University Press, 1999).

4. *Mrs. Mary Roy v State of Kerala and Others, All India Reports* (hereafter cited as AIR) 1986 SC 1011. (Mary Roy is the mother of Booker Prize–winning novelist Arundhati Roy.) For discussion of this case, see Bina Agarwal, *A Field of One's Own: Gender and Land Rights in South Asia* (Cambridge: Cambridge University Press, 1994), 224–26, and Archana Parashar, *Women and Family Law Reform in India: Uniform Civil Code and Gender Equality* (Delhi: Sage, 1992), 190–92. For a general description of the system of personal laws, see the text above.

5. P. J. Kurien, author of the Private Members' Bill, in a public statement.

6. See *Indian Express*, June 20, 1986.

7. See E. D. Devadasan *Christian Law in India* (Delhi: DSI Publications, 1974).

8. For discussion of the debates, with many references, see Shahida Lateef, "Defining Women Through Legislation," in *Forging Identities: Gender, Communities, and the State in India*, ed. Zoya Hasan (Boulder, Colo.: Westview, 1994), 38–58. This issue had already been dealt with in the Child Marriage Restraint Act of 1929, the first occasion in which the Indian women's movement achieved a big legislative success. It was now included in a more comprehensive package of reforms for the new republic.

9. 1937 saw the passage of the Shariat Act, which stopped the common custom of leaving all property to male heirs and returned the Muslim community from customary law to the prescriptions of the Shariat (where, however, women do not have fully equal shares). The bill was supported by Jinnah on grounds of sex equality: he stated that "the economic position of woman is the foundation of her being recognized as the equal of man and shar[ing] the life of man to the fullest extent." Nonetheless, the bill explicitly exempted agricultural land; thus many inequalities remained unaddressed. See Parashar, *Women and Family Law*, 145–50; Agarwal, *A Field of One's Own: Gender and Land Rights in South*

Asia (Cambridge: Cambridge University Press, 1994), 98–99, 227–37; Agarwal, "Women and Legal Rights in Agricultural Land," *Economic and Political Weekly*, March 25, 1995.

10. See "Children are still married off in Indian State," Agence-France Press, May 26, 1997, describing mass ceremonies in Rajasthan involving girls as young as seven, and supported by overwhelming community sentiment. Also John F. Burns, "Though Illegal, Child Marriage is Popular in Part of India," *New York Times*, May 1998, A1, 8. Police say that if nobody makes a complaint they cannot arrest anyone. Child marriage does not necessarily imply sexual consummation, which is usually delayed until after puberty. Nonetheless, the child bride leaves her natal home and is transferred to the power of the husband's home; usually her schooling ends at this point.

11. See Indira Jaising, "Towards an Egalitarian Civil Code," in Jaising, *Justice*, 24, describing a conversion and remarriage in Bombay high society; six months later, however, the Supreme Court declared the new marriage invalid and stated that the husband was liable to be prosecuted for bigamy.

12. The requirement is now that all steps of the traditional Brahminic religious ceremony must have been performed. Many couples omit one or more steps—in some cases in order to indicate opposition to women's subordination. Others use distinct regional forms, or simply marry before a registar; in all these cases marriages have been declared invalid. See discussion of cases in Saumya, "Bigamous Marriages by Hindu Men: Myths and Realities," in Jaising, *Justice*, 27–33. Sometimes the first marriage is shown to be invalid, sometimes the second. The risk of invalidation deters prosecution by first wives, and also makes the task of gathering the requisite evidence of bigamy far more difficult.

13. The recognition of ex-wives as included relations under Section 125 was itself controversial in 1973. When the amendment was discussed in the Lok Sabha, members of the Muslim League objected, claiming violations of free exercise. Initially the government denied that there was any religious issue: the purpose of the amendment was simply humanitarian. Later, however, the government changed its stand, adding yet a further amendment to exclude divorced Muslim women from the purview of the new amendment. Nonetheless, Muslim women continued to bring petitions to the courts, and the Supreme Court explicitly pronounced, in two prominent judgments, that they were entitled to do so: the purpose of the law was to help destitute women, and the text had to be interpreted in accordance with this social purpose. See *Bai Tahira v Ali Hussain*, 1979 2 *Supreme Court Reporter* (hereafter cited as *SCR*) 75, and AIR 1980 Supreme Court 1930. Thus the conflict between the Supreme Court and the Muslim leadership was of long standing.

14. The opinion opens as follows:

This appeal does not involve any questions of constitutional importance but, that is not to say that it does not involve any question of importance. Some questions which arise under the ordinary civil and criminal law are of a far-reaching significance to large segments of society which have been traditionally subjected to unjust treatment. Women are one such segment. *Na*

388   MARTHA C. NUSSBAUM

stree swatantramarhati said Manu, the Law-Giver: The woman does not deserve independence. And, it is alleged that the "fatal point in Islam is the degradation of woman." [Footnote reference is made to a British commentary on the Quran by Edward Lane.] To the Prophet is ascribed the statement, hopefully wrongly, that "Woman was made from a crooked rib, and if you try to bend it straight, it will break; therefore treat your wives kindly."

This appeal, arising out of an application filed by a divorced Muslim woman for maintenance under section 125 of the Code of Criminal Procedure, raises a straightforward issue which is of common interest not only to Muslim women, not only to women generally, but, to all those who, aspiring to create an equal society of men and women, lure themselves into the belief that mankind has achieved a remarkable degree of progress in that direction.

From these words alone, one can get a sense of the strange combination of progressive courage with political obtuseness (referring to a *British* critic of Islam!) that characterize the opinion throughout.

15. *Mohammed Ahmed Khan v Shah Bano Begum & Others*, SCR (1985). This famous case has been discussed in many places. The central documents are assembled in *The Shah Bano Controversy*, ed. Asghar Ali Engineer (Delhi: Ajanta Publishers, 1987). See also Veena Das, *Critical Events* (Delhi: Oxford University Press, 1992), chapter 4; Kavita R. Khory, "The Shah Bano Case: Some Political Implications," in *Religion and Law in Independent India*, ed. Robert Baird (Delhi: Manohar, 1993),121–37; Amartya Sen, "Secularism and Its Discontents," in *Unravelling the Nation*, ed. Kaushik Basu and Sanjay Subrahmanyam, 1995; Parashar, *Women and Family Law*, 173–89 (an unusually comprehensive account of different attitudes within the Islamic community); Zoya Hasan, "Minority Identity, State Policy and the Political Process," in Hasan, *Forging*, 59–73; Danial Latifi, "After Shah Bano," in Jaising, *Justice*, 213–15, and "Women, Family Law, and Social Changes," 216–22 (criticizing Muslims who opposed the Supreme Court decision). On general issues about the Indian legal system and its history, see also John H. Mansfield, "The Personal Laws or a Uniform Civil Code?" in Baird, *Religion and Law*; Tahir Mahmood, *Muslim Personal Law, Role of the State in the Indian Subcontinent*, 2nd ed. (Nagpur: All India Reporter, Ltd., 1983).

16. Secular humanist feminist is a very common position among feminists; in American philosophy, it is perhaps the most common position. But today's secular philosophers rarely follow the example of Bertrand Russell, attacking religion explicitly. Instead, they tend to ignore it, and thus secular humanists in philosophy rarely write about religion. Many major works of feminist political philosophy include no discussion of religion at all: to cite just two examples I mention Alison Jaggar *Feminist Politics and Human Nature* (Totowa, N.J.: Rowman and Littlefield, 1988), and Catharine MacKinnon, *Toward a Feminist Theory of the State* (Cambridge, Mass.: Harvard University Press, 1989). The two best recent anthologies of feminist social-political thought devote no space to religion, although they discuss many topics only contingently linked to feminism, such as environmentalism and vegetarianism: Jaggar, *Living with Contradic-*

tions: Controversies in Feminist Social Ethics (Boulder, Colo.: Westview, 1994), and Diana Meyer, *Feminist Social Thought: A Reader* (New York: Routledge, 1997). In law, feminists more frequently take on religion, because it is a part of their material; thus, one striking representative of the secular humanist position I have in mind here is Mary Becker's fine article "The Politics of Women's Wrongs and the Bill of 'Rights': A Bicentennial Perspective," *University of Chicago Law Review* 59 (1992): 453–517. I shall use this article as a central example of the position criticized, in part because I admire it. It is not a perfect example, because the article ends by proposing less radical change in current policies than its argument would suggest, largely, but not wholly, for practical political reasons.

A perspective closely related to Becker's is developed by Susan Okin in "Is Multiculturalism Bad for Women?" first published in *The Boston Review* October/November 1997, 25–28, and forthcoming in *Is Multiculturalism Bad for Women?* ed. J. Cohen, M. Howard, and M. Nussbaum (Princeton, N.J.: Princeton University Press, 1999); See my response, "A Plea for Difficulty," in the same volume. Okin's position is more nuanced than Becker's; insofar as she focuses on cases of genuinely egregious violation of woman's capabilities, our practical conclusions are not very dissimilar.

17. Becker does note that "all people need sources of authority outside government" (486), and considers this a reason not to muzzle religion too much. But all her other general statements about religion are strongly negative: "religion perpetuates and reinforces women's subordination, and religious freedom impedes reform" (459); "[r]eligions ... contribute to women's subordinate status, not only within religious communities' hierarchies, but also in the broader culture" (460); "[a]ll mainstream religious traditions in the United States replace the wonder of women's reproductive power with stories of creation by a male god" (461); "[r]eligion encourages women to live with the status quo rather than destabilizing it by insisting on equality." Okin has a more subtle position, contrasting "progressive, reformed versions" of various major religions with their "more orthodox or fundamentalist versions", but even this begs many questions. Reform Jews typically understand the core of Judaism as a set of timeless moral ideas that are imperfectly captured in biblical and legal texts: thus they do not concede that their version is less "orthodox" than that of the people who call themselves "orthodox", and they understand the term "reform" to mean not that they advocate a religion "reformed" from the original Judaism, but rather that they advocate a reform of defective historical practices in the direction of a full realization of Judaism. Nor, of course, do Roman Catholics and mainstream Protestants concede that "fundamentalist" versions are more original or authentic and that theirs are "reformed."

18. The comprehensive liberalism of Joseph Raz in *The Morality of Freedom* (Oxford: Clarendon Press, 1986) appears to have similar consequences: religious liberty within limits set by a shared comprehensive public view of autonomy. Unlike Mill, Raz discusses religion only briefly (251–2), and only to advocate religious liberty. Although Okin has not to my knowledge taken a position on the contrast between comprehensive and political liberalism, her views appear to be of the Mill-Raz sort.

19. Examples of this position include Stephen A. and Frédérique Marglin, eds., *Dominating Knowledge: Development, Culture, and Resistance* (Oxford: Clarendon Press, 1988), esp. essays by the Marglins and A. Nandy; in the American context, Christina Sommers, *Who Stole Feminism?* (New York: Simon and Schuster, 1994).

20. Such as the Marglins and Ashis Nandy. This group is known for its nostalgic glorification of child temple prostitution: see F. Marglin, *Wives of the God-King: The Rituals of the Devadasis of Puri* (Delhi: Oxford University Press, 1985), and for ambiguous statements about the positive value of *sati*: see Ashis Nandy, "*Sati*: A Nineteenth Century Tale of Women, Violence, and Protests," in his *At the Edge of Psychology: Essays in Politics and Culture* (Delhi: Oxford University Press, 1980). For a different view of *devadasis*, see Gail Omvedt, "*Devadasi* Custom and the Fight Against It," *Manushi* 4 (November–December 1983): 16–19. For critique of Nandy's position on *sati*, see Sanjukta Gupta and Richard Gombrich, "Another View of Widow-Burning and Womanliness in Indian Public Culture," *Journal of Commonwealth and Comparative Politics* 22 (1984), 262–74, and Imrana Qadeer and Zoya Hasan, "Deadly Politics of the State and Its Apologists," *Economic and Political Weekly* 22 (1987), 1946–49. For further discussion of laws forbidding the glorification of *sati*, see my "Religion and Women's Human Rights" (above n. 3).

21. This is in essence the position of Judith C. Miles, "Beyond *Bob Jones*: Toward the Elimination of Governmental Subsidy of Discrimination by Religious Institutions," *Harvard Women's Law Journal* 8 (1985): 31–58, who, on sex-equality grounds, favors ending all tax benefits and other related benefits (postage, etc.) to religious institutions, not only those that have discriminatory practices. Becker sympathizes with this approach, but in the end does not favor it: she would ban tax exemptions and postal subsidies only for those religions that close leadership positions to women.

22. The Chief Justice was not a total secular humanist, however: although he advocated getting rid of religious courts of law, he did not advocate abolishing special constitutional protections for religion.

23. See, for example, Kalima Rose, *Where Women Are Leaders: The SEWA Movement in India* (London: Zed Books, 1992), 83–4, where the story of Draupadi's prayer to Krishna is used to illustrate an episode of Ela Bhatt's life. Bhatt told me in conversation that at the death of her father, a prominent Brahmin judge, her family (in a step unusual for her caste) granted her wish to perform the religious death ceremonies, which are traditionally assigned to a male.

24. Because the religious capabilities have multiple aspects, I have included them among the valuable capabilities of the senses, imagination, and thought, and also in the category of affiliation. This reflects my view that religion is one extremely important way of pursuing these general capability goals, though not the only one. I shall comment further later in the text on the implications of this view for the political treatment of religion.

25. Jacques Maritain, "Truth and Human Fellowship," in *On the Uses of Philosophy: Three Essays* (Princeton, N.J.: Princeton University Press, 1961), 24.

26. Becker states that "Jewish marriage and divorce law do not treat women and men as equals" and that "for purposes of the minyan . . . , [a woman] does

not count at all"—ignoring the fact that both of these features have been challenged since the early nineteenth century, and a vast majority of American congregations have rejected such practices. Similarly, Becker ascribes to Judaism as a whole the prayer in which a man thanks God that he was not born a woman: this again was rejected by many early in the nineteenth century and is relatively rare by now. Okin stresses internal diversity, though (see n. 27) she understands the more egalitarian versions of Judaism to be "reformed" versions of the tradition rather than its authentic form, a highly controversial (and to my mind mistaken) claim.

27. See the remarks in n. 26 on Becker's treatment of Judaism. One might also focus on her claim that "the Jewish faith relegates women to serving others, rather than recognizing them as creatures with important spiritual lives" (464)—inaccurate concerning a tradition three out of whose four major branches in the United States treat women as full equals in all liturgical and political as well as spiritual matters; the fourth (Orthodox) certainly would also reject this characterization, holding that women have very important spiritual lives, only in a different style from that of males. (Becker's presentation is sometimes hard to follow because she alternates between claims about what "Orthodox" women do and claims about "Judaism" and "the Jewish faith," making no distinction.) Similarly one-sided is Becker's claim that "the Christian valuation of suffering encourages women to accept abuse" (465), and that the Christian view of women's sexuality is consistently negative (466–7). Okin is generally less polemical, but she simply asserts that god in Christian, Jewish, and Islamic traditions is male; again, this claim would be rejected by large numbers of believers in all these traditions (and not only the most evidently liberal), who would insist that a transcendent being is correctly understood to be entirely beyond gender, and that mythic personifications of god as male are not at the core of the religious conception.

28. This is true even of small communities relatively separate from mainstream culture, which have often been portrayed, nostalgically, as zones of homogeneity and harmony. For a fascinating account of internal diversity and conflict in one such religious tradition, see Fred Kniss, *Disquiet in the Land: Cultural Conflict in American Mennonite Communities* (New Brunswick, N.J.: Rutgers University Press, 1997).

29. See my "Judaism and the Love of Reason," forthcoming in *Among Sophia's Daughters: Reflections on Philosophy, Feminism, and Faith*, ed. Marya Bower and Ruth Groenhout (Indiana University Press).

30. One might reply that Orthodox Jews really do not accept the non-Orthodox as Jews, so in calling their view false I am simply taking one side in this debate. Here I can make two replies. First, it is simply dishonest to refuse to recognize the historical reality of the evolution of Judaism *in some way*, whether by treating the other branches as separate religions, analogous to Christianity, or by recognizing them as Jews. What is objectionable about the Israeli situation is that neither course has been taken, and thus Christians have far more rights than Reform and Conservative Jews. Second, it simply is not true that Orthodox Jews do not and cannot recognize Reform and Conservative Jews as Jews. Very few Orthodox Jews, and even Orthodox rabbis, make such a judgment. I was

converted by an Orthodox rabbi, who knew that my practice would not be Orthodox. He gave me some reasons why I should consider Orthodox practice, but he also listened respectfully to my reasons against it; in the end, we agreed to share a core group of commitments, while differing about others. He performed the conversion ceremony, and he maintained vigorously to my fiancé's grandmother that this conversion did in fact make me a Jew. This is a common position. Respect for the Jewishness of other Jews is perfectly compatible with a personal commitment to the idea that Orthodoxy is the only fully correct way of being a Jew: indeed, a common position in the United States resembles the sort of political consensus that members of different comprehensive views are imagined as forming within Rawlsian political liberalism. Thus, for example, the director of the University of Chicago Hillel, David Rosenberg, is an Orthodox rabbi; qua rabbi, he believes that his type of Jewish practice is best; nonetheless, as he has prominently stated, qua director of Hillel, he is committed to recognizing, respecting, and working with Jewish individuals and groups of all types *as Jews*, including the gay and lesbian Jewish students and many others. He has made a point of this political stance, which clearly involves more than a mere modus vivendi. For valuable discussions of feminism in the Jewish tradition, see Rachel Adler, *Engendering Judaism* (Philadelphia and Jerusalem: The Jewish Publication Society 1998); Judith Plaskow, *Standing Again at Sinai: Judaism from a Feminist Perspective* (San Francisco: Harper San Francisco, 1990).

31. For one clear, balanced, and well-argued treatment of Christian feminism, see Lisa Cahill, *Sex, Gender, and Christian Ethics* (Cambridge: Cambridge University Press, 1996).

An excellent illustration of the point about dynamism can be found in the recent election of Frank Tracy Griswold, Bishop of Chicago, to the office of Presiding Bishop of the Episcopal Church of the United States of America. Griswold (who was a strong defender of women's role in the Church long before it was fashionable, when he was a young assistant minister at the Church of the Redeemer in Bryn Mawr, Pennsylvania, which I attended as a girl) campaigned for office on a long record of support for women in the priesthood, as well as a more cautiously expressed support for the ordination of openly gay priests. His opponent, an African American, took more conservative stands on both issues. Griswold won: the voting body decided that this was where they wanted the Church to go. His opponents currently speak of him as a "heretic"—see "The Bishop Moves Up a Rank," *Chicago Tribune*, December 30, 1997, section 5, 1, 10; but history will likely judge that theirs are the outlier views (as is currently the case with Roman Catholics who refuse the vernacular Mass and other changes introduced by Vatican II).

32. Here the historical falsity is even more patent, since Hinduism has no conception of heresy, and has always been a loosely organized set of practices exhibiting much regional variation. This was also true of the Hindu legal system—until the British decided to systematize it for the nation as a whole! Contemporary Hindu fundamentalism is a recent social construct that no more represents Hinduism as a whole than the views of Pat Robertson represent Christianity as a whole.

33. A valuable general exposition of Islamic positions on interpretation and

change (criticizing Okin's treatment of Islam) is in Azizah Y. al-Hibri, "Is West-ern Patriarchal Feminism Bad for Third World/Minority Women?" forthcom-ing in J. Cohen and M. Nussbaum, *Multiculturalism and Women*. For the role of ideas of equal nature in the Muslim women's movement, see Barbara Metcalf, "Reading and Writing about Muslim Women in British India," in Hasan, *Forg-ing*, 1–21. On the construction of "synthetic traditions" that represent them-selves as having great antiquity but do not accurately represent a tradition in all its complexity, see Hannah Papanek, "Afterword: Caging the Lion, a Fable for Our Time" in Rokeya Sakhwat Hossain, *Sultana's Dream*, ed. Roushan Janan (New York: The Feminist Press at the City University of New York, 1988), 58–85, at 61, discussing the wide range of Muslim practices regarding *purdah*. On the creative role of powerful women in the formation of Shi'ite Islam in India, see Juan R. I. Cole, "Shi'ite Noblewomen and Religious Innovation in Awadh," in *Lucknow: Memories of a City*, ed. Violette Graf (Delhi: Oxford University Press, 1997), 83–90. Cole shows that women were so successful in inscribing women's reproductive role into the idea of religious leadership that male leaders had to adopt a female gender model in order to create new rituals. One example from the 1820s, the son of the creative female religious leader Badshah Begum: "On the day of the birth of the Imams he would behave like a woman in child-bed and pretended that he was suffering from the pains of childbirth. . . . The selected attendants prepared dishes used by women in childbed and served them to the king."

34. These may, of course, not be at all the same. In quite a few religions, including Judaism, Hinduism, Islam, and Christianity, there is evidence that earlier practices were much less patriarchal than later: Draupadi enjoys a status unknown the laws of Manu, Deborah plays a prophetic role unknown again among Jewish women until recently, and early Christian communities seem to have been more egalitarian than post-Pauline communities. Similarly, many Is-lamic feminists believe that many, if not most, oppressive patriarchal elements were introduced by the interpretive tradition and have no solid basis in Quran and Hadith.

35. Again, one should not say "oldest" or even "most orthodox," because this begs all kinds of questions about what the tradition really is. The version of Hinduism espoused by the BJP (Bharatija Janata Party), for example, is quite new. Moreover, many liberal religious thinkers deny that the oldest stratum of the religion is the most important or essential.

36. Thus F. Marglin (*Wives of the God-King*) seems little interested in the constraints brought to bear on young girls who enter the *devadasi* way of life, or on the material conditions of their lives. The book focuses on traditions of dance, on symbolism, and on ritual, in quite a nostalgic manner, without asking about issues such as bodily integrity and health. Marglin was led to the study of *devadasis*, she says, by her own training in classical Indian dance; and through-out she tends to regard the life of temple prostitutes as an aesthetic activity, and to criticize the critique of this form of prostitution as inspired by Western values. Nonetheless, devadasis are in fact strongly opposed by the indigenous women's movements in India: the federal government's Mahila Samakhya program, for example, both discovers and further supports poor rural women's resistance to

the pressure to sell daughters into this life, in part by providing free residential schooling to girls who are thought to be at risk (personal communication, Yedla Padmavathi of the Andhra Pradesh office of Mahila Samakhya); other similar programs are numerous throughout the country. In an extremely poor rural desert area of Andhra Pradesh that I visted in March 1997, illiterate women, asked to draw what they wanted, drew a little girl dressed as a devadasi, with a big red X across the picture.

37. At some point, of course, we should stop calling such forms of tradition-alism feminist at all, and that point is surely reached when not even a show is made of defending the traditional values as in women's interests.

38. Aristotle already makes the distinction between a corporate sense of "all" and a distributive sense at *Politics* 1261b16–27, saying that in Plato's ideal city it may possibly be true that "all" the city, taken as a whole, will use the terms "mine" and "not mine" in the same way, but not in the sense that "each one of them" will use these terms of the same objects.

39. See details in my "Religion and Women's Human Rights," cited in n. 3.

40. *Wisconsin v Yoder.*

41. *United States v Seeger*, 3800 U.S. 163 (1965) and *Thomas v Review Board*, 450 U.S. 707, 713 (1981), 73.

42. In *Bob Jones University v United States*, 461 U.S. 574, 103 S.Ct. 2017 (1983), the Court upheld the Internal Revenue Service's denial of tax-exempt status to a religiously grounded institution that had a racially discriminatory ad-missions policy. Although not affiliated with any specific denomination, the school's stated purpose is "to conduct an institution of learning. . ., giving spe-cial emphasis to the Christian religion and the ethics revealed in the Holy Scrip-tures" (2922). The primary focus of the institution was on preventing interracial dating. Until 1973, the institution completely refused to admit black students; from 1971 to 1975 it admitted only black students "married within their race," giving a few exceptions to long-term members of the university staff. After 1975, unmarried black students were permitted to enroll, but a disciplinary rule forbade interracial dating and marriage, stating that violators would be expelled. The Court argued that the government's fundamental, overriding interest in eradicating racial discrimination in education substantially outweighs whatever burden denial of tax benefits places on petitioners' exercise of their religious beliefs. "Petitioners' asserted interests cannot be accommodated with that com-pelling governmental interest, and no less restrictive means are available to achieve the governmental interest." The opinion concludes that a racially dis-criminatory institution is not a "charitable institution" within the meaning of established Internal Revenue standards. The opinion did not deny that the re-fusal of tax-exempt status imposed a burden on religiously based conduct (so it did not exactly express the principle of the moral core in my sense), but it did hold that the compelling state interest in eradicating racial discrimination justi-fied the burden. McConnell ("Free Exercise Revisionism and the *Smith* Deci-sion," *University of Chicago Law Review* 57 (1990) 1109–53) argues that this is a case where government should make an accommodation: if harm is inflicted on non-coreligionists, it is only through the offensive speech of the institution, and this speech is protected by the Free Speech Clause of the First Amendment. The

"direct effects" of the prohibition "are purely internal to the religious group." One difficulty in assessing this argument is that there is no determinate "religious group" in question, since the school is non-denominational; a second difficulty is occasioned by the fact that many of the parties affected would be minors, who may not choose to attend *Bob Jones* and who cannot easily extricate themselves from the situation if they don't like the practices. (Presumably black parents would choose such a school for a variety of economic and geographical reasons, prominently including the fact that they were themselves employees of the institution; their children might have little say in the matter if they wished to continue their education.) McConnell argues that the harm these practices may impose on outsiders, if the tax exemption were to be granted, would be a form of speech protected by the Free Speech clause of the First Amendment. This is highly dubious. It is not the institution's speech that is in question—obviously there was never any question of making their expressive conduct illegal—it is, rather, the act of the government in giving that institution a favored status. For the federal government to favor a discriminatory institution by granting it a tax exemption would involve the federal government in supporting or at least countenancing racial discrimination.

43. Thus *sati* would always be suspect, even when practiced entirely within a religious tradition, because its voluntariness is generally suspect. Even a fully consensual case could be made illegal, because the state has reason to prevent citizens from forfeiting life and (in certain ways) health, except in special circumstances. Similarly problematic too would refusals to permit women to go out to look for work, where women are not choosing modesty as a norm but are being forced into this practice by economic dependence, intimidation, and so forth. For an interesting development of the distinction between harms to co-religionists and harms to others, see McConnell, "Free Exercise Revisionism," at 1145, urging that governmental interests do not extend to protecting the members of a religious community "from the consequences of their religious choices." Thus he defends an exemption to minimum wage/maximum hours laws for a sect that urged members to work without wages for the glory of God (*Alamo Foundation v Secretary of Labor*, 471 U.S. 290 (1985)). That this practice involves no harm to nonmembers may surely be questioned: on this, see William P. Marshall, "In Defense of *Smith* and Free Exercise Revisionism," *University of Chicago Law Review* 58 (1991): 308–28, at 314, arguing that business competitors are unfairly disadvantaged by the Foundation's reduced labor costs. But we should also ask some questions about the voluntariness of the practice: are members of the Foundation, including its dependent and female members, coerced into working without wages? How free are they to leave? I am inclined to think that the potential for exploitation of the powerless is so great that such an exemption should never be granted. McConnell's other central example of an intrareligious practice that should be accommodated is the *Bob Jones* case, which I discuss in n. 42. Once again, I shall disagree with his conclusion.

44. For Islam, see Abdullahi An-Na'im, who distinguishes between two Quranic periods: see his *Toward an Islamic Reformation: Civil Liberties, Human Rights and International Law* (Syracuse, N.Y.: Syracuse University Press, 1990); others who distinguish between Quran and Shari'a; Azizah

Al'Hibri, who distinguishes between the Quran, which must, she holds, remain uncriticized, and later schools of interpretation. For a valuable discussion of the Koranic sources for *purdah*—where an adjacent verse, rarely mentioned, mandates a symmetrical norm of purity and modesty for men—see Huma Ahmed-Gosh, "Preserving Identity: A Case Study of Palitpur," in Hasan, *Forging*, 169–87; the relevant verses are cited in n. 49 of this chapter.

45. See Kent Greenawalt, "Five Questions about Religion Judges Are Afraid to Ask," chapter 7 of this volume, for examples of this, and also examples of when judgments have to be made. See also Michael McConnell, "Free Exercise Revisionism," 1144.

46. Edict XII.

47. Abraham Lincoln, in *The Portable Abraham Lincoln*, ed. Andrew Delbanco (New York: Viking, 1992), 321.

48. "Judge not that we be not judged" is the utterance, I think, of mercy rather than exculpation. Lincoln does not mean "don't say that this was wrong," but "withhold the punitive and vindictive attitude that could all too easily animate people at this time." This reading is borne out by the famous conclusion of the speech ("With malice toward none, with charity toward all"), which renounces malice while remaining firm in the right. Lincoln's point is that "firmness in the right" should not lead us into a vindictive attitude that would impair our ability to join together to "bind up the nation's wounds."

49. Often quoted in defense of the veiling of women is Quran 24.31, "And say to the believing women that they should lower their gaze and guard their modesty; that they should not display their beauty and ornaments except what must ordinarily appear thereof." But immediately preceding is 24.30: "Say to the believing men that they should lower their gaze and guard their modesty; that will make for greater purity for them. And God is well acquainted with all that they do." See Ahmed-Gosh, "Preserving Identity."

50. See Rokeya Sakhawat Hossain, *Sultana's Dream and Selections from "The Secluded Ones,"* ed. Roushan Jahan (New York: Feminist Press of the City University of New York, 1988). Especially in *The Secluded Ones*, Rokehya focuses on the moral harms of purdah, pointing to damages to women's health and even life caused by the extremes to which tradition pushed the norm that they should not be seen by men.

51. The Church of the Latter-day Saints has a doctrine of "continuing revelation"—God's purposes are revealed to us gradually in the course of history—that was invoked on June 9, 1978, to justify admitting males of African descent to the priesthood.

52. 374 U.S. 398 (1963).

53. Both opponents and critics of the *Smith* decision agree, however, that "in practice the Court sided only rarely with the free exercise claimant, despite some very powerful claims" (McConnell, "Free Exercise Revisionism," 1110), usually finding either that the free exercise right was not burdened or that the government interest was compelling (see ibid., 1110, 1127–8, Marshall, "In Defense of *Smith*," 310–11). In effect, the test in practice was weaker than the usual understanding of "compelling interest," which would have allowed government to override a religious claim only in unusual circumstances; some type

of heightened scrutiny was applied, but the relevant standard was never very clearly articulated. It is also clear that claimants from religions that seem closely related to the culture's predominant religious traditions fared better than claimants from religions that seem bizarre. "Thus," as William Marshall puts it, "Mrs. Sherbert's claim that she is forbidden to work on Saturday is likely to be accepted as legitimate; Mr. Hodges's claim that he must dress like a chicken when going to court is not" (311, citing *State v Hodges*, 695 S.W. 2d 171 (Tenn. 1985), in which the defendant, held in contempt of court, maintained that dressing like a chicken when in court was "his spiritual attire and his religious belief"). On the weakness of pre-RFRA protections of religion, see also C. Eisgruber and L. Sager, "Why the Religious Freedom Restoration Act is Unconstitutional," *N.Y.U. Law Review* 69 (1994): 437–52.

54. 110 S.Ct. 1595 (1990).

55. This helps to explain the otherwise somewhat surprising political lineup of the Court, as Justice Scalia and other usually religion-sympathetic conservatives supported a striking departure from settled precedent (though not practice: see above) in the direction of narrowing the sphere of religious liberty, while three liberals—Justices Marshall, Brennan, and Blackmun—backed the more traditional religious libertarian course. (Centrist O'Connor agreed with the dissenters to the extent of deploring the sharp theoretical departure from traditional Free Exercise jurisprudence, though she concurred in the judgment in the particular case.) Scalia's argument is less surprising, however, if one focuses on the issue of institutional competence and the limiting of judicial discretion, which is one of the prominent themes of his jurisprudence.

56. For a detailed description of the litigation, see McConnell, "Free Exercise Revisionism," 1111–4. The plaintiffs were Native American employees of a drug rehabilitation clinic who applied for unemployment compensation after being fired for ingesting peyote sacramentally during a ceremony of the Native American Church. The Oregon Supreme Court repeatedly held that the illegality of the sacramental use of peyote was irrelevant to the determination of unemployment compensation: if religiously motivated, the conduct could not be treated as work-related "misconduct" under the First Amendment. Thus it was somewhat surprising that the question of the law's constitutionality came before the Supreme Court in the first place.

57. Twenty-three states, moreover, specifically exempt the religious use of peyote from their drug laws; the federal government not only exempts peyote but licenses its production and importation, and Oregon itself does not enforce its law.

58. Scalia wrote that such a requirement would produce "a private right to ignore generally applicable laws," thus creating "a constitutional anomaly." The three liberal Justices dissented, arguing that no convincing reason had been given to depart from settled First Amendment jurisprudence. The discussion of precedent in the majority opinion is entirely unconvincing, and has received heavy criticism from all sides. McConnell calls it "troubling, bordering on the shocking" ("Free Exercise Revisionism," 1120, and detailed analysis at 1120–7); Marshall says that the majority's "use of precedent borders on fiction" ("In Defense of *Smith*," 309).

59. The majority opinion acknowledged this danger: it speaks of "plac[ing] at a relative disadvantage those religious practices that are not widely engaged in."

60. For documentation, see McConnell, "Institutions and Interpretation: A Critique of *City of Boerne v. Flores*," *Harvard Law Review* 111 (1997): 153–95, at 159.

61. There has been considerable analysis of the debate preceding the passage of RFRA, discussing whether it was genuinely deliberative or merely the jockeying of interest groups; I pass over this question, since it is not relevant to my proposal.

62. *City of Boerne v Flores*, 117 S.Ct. 2157 (1997). The vote was 6–3, and the majority opinion was written by Justice Kennedy. The case concerned a conflict between a Catholic church that wanted to enlarge its building to allow the entire congregation to celebrate Mass at the same time and the historic landmark preservation laws, which forbade alterations to the church's building, whose facade was located in a historic district. (The church's plan was to build out from the back wall, leaving the old Spanish-style structure virtually intact, but the city refused to approve any plan of expansion that would require demolition of any part of the church building, whether inside or outside the historic district.) In August 1997, the church and the city came to an agreement that the church may build a new 850-seat sanctuary behind, and partly hidden by, the original building, most of which will be repaired and preserved at church expense; thus the church accomplished its primary objective, though at much greater expense.

63. I do not say that nothing other than the central capabilities can ever provide such a compelling interest; I leave that to be hammered out by each legal tradition as it evolves. In the United States, an account of these interests was evolving, before the demise of RFRA. See, for example, *Mack v O'Leary*, 80 F. 3d 1175 (1996), offering a generous definition of "substantial burden," but holding that the maintenance of order in federal prisons was a compelling state interest; and *Sasnett v Sullivan*, 91 F. 3d 1018 (1996), holding that restrictions on the wearing of religious jewelry in prisons are not justified by any compelling state interest and are in violation of RFRA.

64. Contrast *Goldman v Weinberger*, 475 U.S. 503 (1986).

65. *Sasnett v Sullivan*.

66. See *Hunafa v Murphy*, 907 F. 2d 67 (7th Cir. 1990) (upholding Muslim prisoner's right to receive food uncontaminated by pork and remanded for factfinding on government interest; the court noted that the intervening *Smith* decision may be raised on remand and may change the outcome. For discussion of other relevant pre-Smith cases, see McConnell, "Free Exercise Revisionism," 1142 n. 143.

67. For discussion of the case and McConnell's argument for an accommodation, see n. 42.

68. See Becker, "Women's Wrongs," 484–6, arguing that a *Bob Jones* approach to religion (denying state benefits) is probably constitutionally compelled (not merely permissible) in the case of race and might also be viewed as compelled in the case of sex. Becker supports banning tax exemptions and postal

subsidies and the award of government contracts to religious organizations that close leadership positions to women. She would not favor altogether ending those subsidies or requiring state regulation of religion to eliminate sexism. I support Becker's position where educational institutions are concerned, but not with regard to the assignment of religious functions.

69. This is the argument McConnell makes in "Free Exercise Revisionism."

70. See Marshall, "In Defense of *Smith*"; Marshall does not defend the argument in *Smith*, only the result.

71. *Thomas v Review Board*, see n. 41.

72. Marshall, 320. McConnell, while not accepting that particular argument, also draws attention to the balancing effect of the two clauses, arguing that favoring religion in the context of free exercise is not unfair, since religion is disfavored in the context of establishment: see his "A Response to Professor Marshall," *University of Chicago Law Review* 58 (1991): 329–32. McConnell has in some areas sought to mitigage the unequal treatment of religion under the Establishment Clause: see his brief in *Rosenberger v Rector and Visitors of the University of Virginia*, 115 S.Ct. 2510 (1995).

73. *United States v Seeger*, see n. 41. The Court explicitly distinguished "religious training and belief" from "essentially political, sociological, or philosophical views." The test proposed was "whether a given belief that is sincere and meaningful occupies a place in the life of its possessor parallel to that filled by the orthodox belief in God of one who clearly qualifies for the exemption." In ascertaining that Seeger's beliefs did indeed play such a role, the Court drew attention to Seeger's "'belief in and devotion to goodness and virtue for their own sakes, and a religious faith in a purely ethical creed.'" Attention was drawn to the systematic nature of his beliefs (and to Seeger's own references to Plato, Aristotle, and Spinoza); to the similarity of his nontheistic ethical creed to aspects of Hinduism, Buddhism, and the Christian theology of Paul Tillich. The Court concluded that if the proposed test is passed by a system of beliefs, it follows that it is not a "merely personal moral code" in the sense already rejected as a legitimate basis for conscientious objection. See also *Thomas v Review Board*, 450 U.S. 707 (1981): "Courts should not undertake to dissect religious beliefs because the believer admits that he is 'struggling' with his position or because his beliefs are not articulated with the clarity and precision that a more sophisticated person might employ."

74. For a position on "expressive interests" and free speech jurisprudence with which I largely agree, see Joshua Cohen, "Freedom of Expression," *Philosophy and Public Affairs* 22 (1993).

75. A comprehensive account of this history, and of later changes in the systems of law, is in Archana Parashar *Women and Family Law Reform*; see also Barbara D. Metcalf, "Reading and Writing about Muslim Women in British India," in Hasan, *Forging*, 1–21; Kirti Singh, "The Constitution and Muslim Personal Law," in Hasan, *Forging*, 96–107; Maitrayee Mukhopadhyay, "Between Community and State: The Question of Women's Rights and Personal Laws," in Hasan, *Forging*, 108–129; Jaising, *Justice*.

76. India once had a large Jewish population, especially in the princely states of Cochin and Travancore; most of that population has now emigrated to Israel,

and an entire synagogue from Cochin now rests in the Israel Museum in Jerusalem. See Orpa Slapak, ed., *The Jews of India* (Jerusalem: Israel Museum Publications, 1995).

77. For a forceful Muslim argument in favor of a uniform code—in the period prior to the Shah Bano case and the rise of Hindu fundamentalism—see Mohammed A. Qureshi, *Marriage and Matrimonial Remedies: A Uniform Civil Code for India* (Delhi: Concept Publishing Company, 1978).

78. The best account of the contemporary systems, with comprehensive detail and many discussions of legal challenges, is in Jaising, *Justice.*

79. See ibid., 24–26.

80. Converts out of Hinduism lose all caste, something that has large legal relevance, given the affirmative action programs established for "scheduled castes." See Marc Galanter, *Law and Society in Modern India* (Oxford: Oxford University Press, 1989), part 4, for a discussion of legal cases involving converts from Hinduism to Buddhism who still tried to claim these benefits. For a comprehensive account of the affirmative action programs, see Galanter, *Competing Equalities: Law and the Backward Castes in India* (Delhi: Oxford University Press, 1984; paperback ed., 1991).

81. Kerala abolished joint family property in 1976. Karnataka, Tamil Nadu, Andhra Pradesh, and Maharashtra have all amended the Hindu Succession Act to include daughters as coparceners in joint family property on a par with sons. In most of South India, the Muslim Shariat Act of 1937 has been amended to include agricultural land in its domain. (I owe these data to Bina Agarwal.)

82. One plausible reason cited by Muslims for keeping the separate systems is that the secular courts are extremely slow and inefficient: see Danial Latifi, "Women, Family Law and Social Changes," in Jaising, *Justice,* 216–22.

83. See Nussbaum, "The Modesty of Mrs. Bajaj: India's Problematic Route to Sexual Harassment Law," forthcoming in volume edited by R. Siegel and C. MacKinnon, Yale University Press.

84. *Bob Jones v U.S.,* see n. 42.

85. See Bina Agarwal, *A Field of One's Own: Gender and Land Rights in South Asia* (Cambridge: Cambridge University Press, 1994).

86. I see no reason why a religious system, to be acceptable, has to permit divorce, so long as exit from the system is readily available, but if it permits divorce for men, it must do so for women: see my discussion of equality above, p. 365.

87. See publication of All India Women's Conference, 1944–5, and discussion in Shahida Lateef, "Defining Women Through Legislation," in Hasan, *Forging,* 49, and Parashar, *Women and Family Law Reform,* chapter 3.

88. A further issue was the extremely broad definition of "Hindu," which included Jains, Buddhists, and Sikhs, without much input from them; these minorities plausibly felt discriminated against by the tough reforms, which did not apply to other minorities such as Muslims, Christians, Parsis, and Jews.

89. September 22, 1951.

90. *The Statesman,* September 21, 1951.

91. AIR (1983) A.P. 356. I discuss Sareetha's case further in Nussbaum, *Sex*

and Social Justice, introduction and chapter 3. Sareetha had become a well-known movie actress after leaving her husband, and the husband's motives were clearly financial. Under the law, a woman is able to avoid forcible return on payment of a fine, so Sareetha was not in physical jeopardy, although she eventually lost her case. Poor women remained vulnerable to the actual restitution.

92. *Nelly Zaman v Ghiyasuddin*, 34 D.L.R. 221 (1982). See discussion and citation from the opinion in "Religion and Women's Human Rights," in *Sex and Social Justice*, chapter 3.

93. See case studies in Mukhopadhyay, "Between Community and State," in Hasan, *Forging*.

94. Hasan, *Forging*, 62.

95. Cited by Amrita Chhachhi in "Identity Politics, Secularism, and Women: A South Asian Perspective," in Hasan, *Forging*, p. 74. (She in turn cites a tape recording of the speech.)

96. For example, see *Susheela Gopalan and Others v Union of India*, Writ Petition No. 1055 of 1986.

97. Hasan, "Minority Identity, State Policy, and the Political Process," in Hasan, *Forging*, 68. See also Danial Latifi, "After Shah Bano," in Jaising, *Justice*, 213–5, and Latifi, "Women, Family Law and Social Changes," in *ibid.*, 216–22, criticizing the reasoning of conservative Islamic legal scholars.

98. Both interviews by Maitrayee Mukhopadhyay, in "Between Community and State: The Question of Women's Rights and Personal Laws," in Hasan, *Forging*, 108–29. Mukhopadhyay notes that in fact the incidence of polygamy is about the same for Muslim men (5.7 percent) as for Hindu men (5.8 percent), although it is not legal for Hindus.

99. See my "Religion and Women's Human Rights," in *Sex and Social Justice*.

100. Personal communication, Sardamoni (a leading historian of Kerala), Trivandrum, March 1997.

101. See p. 374 above for examples.

102. See statistics in n. 98.

103. 268 U.S. 510 (1925).

104. The Court's argument is somewhat opaque and invalidates the law on Fourteenth Amendment Due Process grounds, rather than First Amendment Free Exercise grounds. Nonetheless, its basic principle was invoked in subsequent First Amendment cases.

105. See John Rawls, *Political Liberalism* (New York: Columbia University Press, expanded paperback ed., 1996), 199.

106. Thus, for example, a religion may teach that the political conception holds men and women to be equal because they really are in some deeper metaphysical sense equal; or it may teach that, although in some metaphysical sense men and women are ultimately unequal, we agree to count them as equal for certain political purposes. It is not clear whether any of the major religions would actually hold that men and women are "unequal," and in what sense, although many deny women certain privileges and opportunities that they grant to men.

107. 406 U.S. 205 (1972).

108. For a related argument see Richard Arneson and Ian Shapiro, "Democratic Autonomy and Religious Freedom: A Critique of *Wisconsin v. Yoder*," in Ian Shapiro, *Democracy's Place* (Ithaca, N.Y.: Cornell University Press, 1996), 137–74, arguing that the last two years of required public schooling are crucial in developing abilities of citizenship, especially the ability to question authority.

109. 321 U.S. 158 (1944).

110. The Court noted that this question had been resolved against Sarah Prince by the state court's definition of labor and was no longer in their power to reconsider.

111. Hannah Papanek, in "Afterword," in Hossain, *Sultana's Dream*, 72–6; Papanek had known Hamida Khala for a long time, and the telling of the story of her life, in the late 1970s, took many days.

112. Papanek, "Afterword," 77, describing Muslim home workers who send their children as intermediaries to deal with the middlemen who sell their products. See also Cornelia Sorabji, *India Calling* (London: Nisbet, 1934), describing her struggle as India's first female lawyer (and the first woman to be allowed to take a law degree at Oxford), helping women in purdah who were being cheated by male relatives and were forbidden before her arrival on the scene to see a lawyer, all lawyers being male. The many attempts on Sorabji's life are evidence of the magnitude of the problem.

113. "Shah Bano's Open Letter to Muslims," published in *Inquilab*, November 3, 1985, and translated into English by A. Karim Shaikh. Reprinted in Engineer, *Shah Bano*, 211–2. Shah Bano died in Indore in 1992 at the age of eighty-nine.

13

WOMEN AND INTERNATIONAL
HUMAN RIGHTS: SOME ISSUES
UNDER THE BRIDGE

Carol Weisbrod

Law may be viewed as a system of tensions or a bridge linking
a concept of reality to an imagined alternative.
(Robert Cover, "Nomos and Narrative," Harvard Law Review *[1983])*

The completed work, when constructed in accordance with my
designs, will not only be the greatest bridge in existence, but it
will be the great engineering work of the continent and of the age.
(John Roebling, on his proposal for the Brooklyn Bridge)

THE CURRENT discussion of women and international human
rights is marked by a lack of agreement on a number of points,
only some of which directly involve the status of women.[1] Dis-
cussants may differ as to issues of religion, the state, and groups, as well,
of course, as to ideas of the good life and the truth and authority of
revealed religion. Most importantly, underneath the debate over women
and international human rights is an issue concerning not only international law[2]—whether it is law and, if so, what kind—but the nature,
power and range of law itself.

This chapter attempts to outline some broad differences that often
exist on these questions and to indicate the relevance of these issues to
considerations of the question of women and international human
rights.[3]

The first two parts of the chapter ("Law" and "Groups") describe but
do not literally offer a script for a dialogue between two kinds
of lawgivers; one, conventionally, would be named Rex,[4] the other,
following a suggestion by Simmel,[5] would be named Pontifex, the
bridge builder.[6] The third and fourth sections ("Church and State"
and "Bridges") attempt a treatment of some structural questions that

political regimes must somehow resolve, whatever the lack of agreement in the dialogue.

I have suggested elsewhere that the concern for pluralism is less a rule than a stance, or preoccupation.[7] The most general effort here has been to impose some of that preoccupation on the subject of women in traditional religious communities and human rights.

Law

Rex and Pontifex could be seen as participants in a humanist dialogue of another age, or we might imagine them as real, historical figures, authors of some lost correspondence on Roman law. Certainly they are not simple antagonists. They might, indeed, be the same official or scholar in different moods, or at different times.

Rex assumes, following the idea of law laid down for example in Cicero's *De Legibus*, that law is something about universals, a mandate good for all times and places. Law, Cicero wrote, "is the highest reason, implanted in nature, which commands what ought to be done and forbids the opposite."[8] The issue for Rex is to determine what the appropriate universal is and what the law therefore should be and to use such force as is necessary to put that law into effect. State power to enforce is assumed to exist and to be sufficient. Rex might say that law was a bridge, but that bridge could easily represent the bridge between the main culture and the subordinate one, a bridge transmitting the proper values.[9]

Pontifex sees a different world, one filled with normative communities all of which have and apply ideas in legal categories, all of which have at their disposal certain sanctions. For Pontifex, the issue is how those different communities can survive together. An overstatement of the differences would go something like this: Where Rex's thinking is dominated by certain views of natural law and reason, Pontifex is obsessed by history. For Pontifex, a leading truth of particularity is, as Harold Isaacs put it, that "with all the beauty goes all the blood."[10] In part because of this, Pontifex is interested less in a universal correct answer than in a variety of possible coexisting answers.[11]

We can begin with a statement of the specific problem.

First, the oppression of women is a major wrong in the world. This oppression exists against the background of an international commitment to universal humanistic values—human rights.

Second, traditional religion has over many centuries contributed a great deal to the creation and support of women's situation, both in its original teachings and in its current responses to demands for change, whether these demands come from inside or outside the religious or cultural group. As the legal historian Julius Goebel remarked on the general issue, among the conservative influences in relation to the family "have been the factors, chiefly religious, that fostered a pessimistic opinion of the capacity of women."[12]

Third, in many parts of the world, women's situation is—at least from the perspective of the Western world—so downgraded that we can legitimately wonder about women's ability to choose in any context. We see a world in which traditional societies deny women what would be taken, at least in the West, to be ordinary human rights. For example, the right to drive a car or to contract a marriage is based on consent. This may be true even in a society in which formal political rights exist.

Rex has urged that the equality guarantee for women is of such importance that it must come ahead of other values and, moreover, must be enforced over the objections of, for example, some women who support the inequality. Pontifex has found more to think about in the fact that sometimes women support the inequality. In the role of bridge builder, Pontifex has been committed to the idea of diversity, including tolerance of behavior that he/she does not like, though even a bridge builder's commitment to diversity is, of course, not unlimited.

It is clear to both Rex and Pontifex that religion can not be used to justify everything. One issue is what is a serious threat to an individual. Another is what is a serious threat to a religious tradition.[13]

The general problem is well known. Thus, in a recent discussion of international human rights, Dr. Natan Lerner notes that "[e]quality of women in today's society is affected by the fact that some religions, including major ones, do not respect, even today, the principle of full equality among men and women."[14] Dr. Lerner adds that the 1979 Convention on the Elimination of All Forms of Discrimination Against Women had to take notice of the fact that 'the most comprehensive challenges mounted by states to the international norms guaranteeing women's rights, and their application, have been couched as defenses of religious liberty.' The issue is "especially complicated," he said, "in those states which adopt religious law for the governance of family relations and personal status."

Material on this question is filled with stories of individual women attempting in very difficult circumstances to free themselves of some particularly oppressive religious and political systems, often exerting their force through the family and particularly the extended family.[15]

Strategies are available to Western observers which minimize some quite serious questions. For example, one can define religion[16] and religious liberty narrowly, so that the focus is on worship and ritual and the inner religious life—freedom to believe—while one excludes the more social or collective aspects of the religious tradition. A protection of religious liberty is limited, then, to rituals and belief itself. One can describe the problem in terms of "religion," which oppresses some people. Here, "women" will be the victims of religion. Even if adherents of the faith and supporters of the practice are not seen as victims of the religious practice, they still may not "choose" it, or if they do, their choice is seen as coerced directly or indirectly, so that their preferences do not matter and need not be taken seriously.[17] One can assume that "law" means only secular law, and that religious law, when enforced by the state, raises a problem all by itself.[18] One can assume that the religious basis for the practice is a kind of fraud or camouflage, covering quite different and often political or mysogynist or pecuniary motivations. Again, on this view, the religious liberty claim is seen as at best secondary to the equality claim. Finally, one can stress that the tradition itself contains many strands, some of which will be more sympathetic to equality than others and support the interpretation one likes.[19]

By way of comment on these strategies, we may note initially that on a pluralistic view, it is only a kind of convention or even prejudice that leads us to reserve the word "law" for the state rules.[20] Religions have rules. There may be courts. There may be decision makers. There may be processes for dispute resolution. Religious legal systems are legal systems parallel to those of the state and often much older. At this moment in time, when the triumph of the nation-state seems complete, the issue is as Marc Galanter sees it: "The [official] law must face the question of the mode in which it should recognize and/or supervise [other normative traditions]. The alternatives emerge vividly in the law-religion relationship because religions are systems of control with complex learned traditions, expounded by their own specialists and even with their own doctrines concerning their relationship to law."[21]

What does seem to be the case is that, for each of the powerful systems, the religious systems and the state system, there is an attempt, at least in theory, to claim a monopoly of the lawmaking power. The state says only the state makes law, though of course we acknowledge that religious "law" has some place. But state law is, as Robert Cover said, "[j]urispathic."[22] Religions say they are the highest law. Religions, on their side, may say that the state has its place and one must render unto Caesar etc., but still the mission of the religion is independent and primary. Pontifex, who tries to emphasize this understanding by religious groups, might use the exposition of John Courtney Murray to represent the general position: Murray offered his comments as the "reflections of a citizen who considers it his duty to be able to answer the fundamental question: "What are the truths we hold?" His are "the reflections of a Catholic who, in seeking his answer to the civil question, knows that the principles of Catholic faith and morality stand superior to, and in control of, the whole order of civil life."

> The question is sometimes raised, whether Catholicism is compatible with American democracy. The question is invalid as well as impertinent; for the manner of its position inverts the order of values. It must, of course, be turned round to read, whether American democracy is compatible with Catholicism. The question, thus turned, is part of the civil question, as put to me. An affirmative answer to it, given under something better than curbstone definition of "democracy," is one of the truths I hold.[23]

Pontifex at his most intense rejects the idea that sovereignty is only in the state. As a simple observer of the world, he may simply note that each side claims to be the highest law player, while he or she simultaneously acknowledges the presence and real power of the alternative view. Pontifex thinks that much of what we see in the world is an attempt to try to avoid reaching situations of crisis on this point.[24] Occasionally, of course, situations of conflict cannot be avoided. The well-known American polygamy case was one such case. (One, incidentally, that was certainly understood in its time to relate to questions of women's rights, since the Supreme Court when it handed down the *Reynolds* case thought that it was defending innocent women and children from something along the lines of the horrors of the harem.)[25]

Rex may acknowledge some description but emphasizes that from the point of view of the state, certain things cannot be tolerated. As noted, this is a point that Pontifex accepts in theory. Both urge that even when allowing autonomy to religious groups, we do not allow religious groups to execute their own members, and that we allow corporal discipline even in the family only in a very limited way.[26] The difference between them is that Rex tends to define the things that cannot be accepted in terms of legal violations, where Pontiflex stresses a difference between mandatory and "yielding" regulations,[27] or important and merely conventional norms.

Pontifex notes, finally, that positivist state-centered definitions of "law" and the assumptions of state power that go along with that definition are not universal in some of the countries under discussion in the women's rights debates. Thus, a 1950s survey made in response to the British leaving India was abandoned when it developed that many native villagers interviewed did not know that the British had come to India.[28] Marc Galanter noted that "law" in highly heterogeneous society represents "law" for those elites who use it. For large parts of the country, existing law would be local and tribal. Thus, in India, to find "the law" we must look beyond the records of the legislatures and the higher courts to the working of lawyers and the police and, beyond that, to informal tribunals and to "popular notions of legality."[29] Peter Berger applied the general point to the international area: "I find law is a very peculiar institution. In different societies it relates to the society as a whole in different ways. The previous speaker said that different nations accepted the human rights conventions. This is a surrealistic statement that could only be made by a lawyer. These laws were not adopted by nations but by a small clique of lawyers, bureaucrats and intellectuals who are highly westernized and most of whom have absolutely nothing to do with the cultures in which most of their fellow nationals live."[30]

As to the specific issue of what is a human "right," there are additional questions. Writing some years ago, Richard Bilder said[31] that a list of human rights might purport to represent:

1. an international consensus of moral aspirations regarding the conditions to be found in some Utopian future;

2. an international consensus as to the fundamental rules for the treatment of man in society which are accepted as inherent in philosophical or religious concepts or deductively derived from the biosocial facts of human existence;

3. an international consensus of practical judgments as to the most rational and enlightened relation of man and authority under the actual conditions and values of most present societies;

4. a compilation of those claims of individuals and groups respecting their relation to authority and society which most contemporary societies perceive as basic and which the claimants assert with particular energy;

5. those claims of individuals and groups respecting their relation to authority and society which the international community, through its organized institutions, is prepared to formally recognize as having a high order of legitimacy.

Professor Bilder concluded: "We seem never to have agreed which of these possibilities human rights represent."[32]

Rex, when speaking from the background of Western feminism, might assume that an equality norm is more than aspirational. Perhaps it is even "fundamental." Rex might worry that the right would be compromised by the emphasis on actual conditions, or rejected (inappropriately) by a statistical approach. But the central difference between Rex and Pontifex is that Rex, who limits the word "law" to those rules emanating from the state,[33] has very little to say about groups in general, and little regard for what might be thought of as a group claim to be a lawmaker. Indeed, when speaking as a feminist, Rex may sign on to the position of the Women's Declaration, which sees the international standard as controlling both public and private agencies, rejecting the public/private distinction because of its role in creating a shield for discrimination and oppression in the sphere designated "private." Pontifex, in the role of liberal feminist, sees some of this differently. First, as noted, Pontifex sees all groups as making law of some kind. The super group that we call the state, of course, makes law, but so in a way does every club, or family, or church. The case at its strongest is that law is, from this point of view, that which anybody accepts as law.[34] Acknowledging the fact that the "private" category has often operated to leave individuals to the power of other stronger individuals, Pontifex might also see the public/private distinction as a protection from the state, an entity as to which the twentieth-century example, alive in our conscious, has left a good deal of doubt.[35]

Groups

As Rex sees the problem of groups, it is the state that decides what a group is, who is in it, what it can or can't do, and what its "essence" is or might be correctly understood to be. Rex notes that, in the modern situation, religious affiliations, like many other affiliations and identities, are voluntary, so that religions are only another form of voluntary association.[36] Of course, this might not be true from the point of view of the group.

The range of groups we have to consider would be voluntary groups, involuntary groups, voluntary associations as groups, religions as groups, biological or ethnic characteristics as creating group characteristics, and nationhood linked to land as creating groups.[37] For all, we would have to be clear about whose point of view we are using in asking the questions. A membership that the state calls voluntary might, from the point of view of the group, be a matter of birth, and thus involuntary. "What is a group?" "Who are its members?" As the next section of this chapter will discuss further, in countries that use systems of personal law these are threshold questions. For now it is enough to say that for Rex, using the universal optic, the question tends to have a single answer, while for Pontifex the definitional question may have many answers.

Pontifex stresses that groups and subgroups may involve not only "membership" but also identities and priorities which shift over time. Women under "women's law,"[38] for example, may involve as much an imposition of identity as Muslims under Muslim law. If "women" are as much a group as the "tribe," as some feminists have argued, it is also true and very widely recognized that women as a group are divided into many subgroups. And women's stories include many different narratives, stories of the mother-in-law as well as the young bride in the dowry deaths. These are presumably not the same story, though they can both be fit into an account focused on male domination.

Pontifex agrees that to some extent group characteristics or group definitions are imposed by the outside or by physical facts. In that sense, "women as a group" surely exists. That is, biology is a basis for classification as a group. But it is equally true that women, like all other individuals, belong to many many different groups, which overlap and have different importance at different times. As a matter of individual psychology, group identification is often fluid. The examples that are typically used assume something static. One particular group identification—*religion*—is used as the index or the point of entry for the entire discussion of rights and after that, we use a further group, here "women," as a subgroup.

Rex, adopting a modern liberal position, often sees group life as a vague background of local loyalties and commitments, all of which should be subordinated to a global human allegiance.[39] In saying this, Rex takes a position consistent with liberal theory, which, as noted, has very little to say about groups, focusing its attention on the individual and the state. Rex is willing to say that groups can be seen as formed initially by the choices of individuals and that certain things often described as group rights can be viewed as individual rights, exercised by individuals in association.

This individualistic understanding of groups, in which groups are formed by the exercise of individual rights, makes it possible to minimize what we might call the self- perception of groups. This is what Rex tends to do, often, for example, describing groups largely in terms of their responses to questions important to the larger society rather than in terms of their own ideologies and narratives.[40] Pontifex urges that we have at the very least an association formed by the choices of individuals. What these individuals want is to live in a community that recognizes a set of values that may or may not be held by the majority. What they do not want is to live in a community with those who do not hold these values.

Rex, because of a commitment to universals, tends to think that the small communities must be run on the same principles as the state and in fact that the largest justification for the communities would be a role in training citizens for the democratic state. Pontifex tends to think that this approach would, finally, destroy the idea of normative pluralism, understood, within limits, as a positive value. Both speakers are opposed to a theocratic state that imposes the same religiously founded law on everyone, at great cost to the rights of dissenters. A more difficult problem is that in a democratic pluralist state, there may be considerable opportunity for self-definition of small internal communities, including the right to expel and otherwise sanction dissidents. This idea does not have an obvious resonance with Rex's view that international human rights imperatives on equality mean that equality must be an invariable and nonwaivable right imposed as value universally across the public/private line.

The idea that normative pluralism might turn out in fact to be minimal or nonexistent would not seem such a cost to Rex, who sees the dark side of religion with particular intensity,[41] and who may make the assumption that, since proper information and education will lead right thinking people to the same answer, groups can really not exist which are deeply different. Like some utopians, universalists sometimes seem to think more of variety than of pluralism.[42] An account in *For Love of Country* of the trees honoring the righteous gentiles at Yad Vashem in Israel suggests the point. In that discussion, Martha Nussbaum attributes the good works of the Righteous Gentiles to their commitment to universal humanistic values that are seen as higher than tribal or religious values. Yet surely it is just as possible to say that the efforts of these Gentiles on behalf of Jews were exactly a working out of their religious commitments, just as in the United States individuals have worked for the civil rights movement because of religious commitment.[43]

If the discussion of small-group identification in the life of individuals seems thin in some of the Rex discussions, the sense of religion as powerful and threatening to some people is clear. As noted, what is not as clear is that these religious groups rest on a power base that includes women. Some work engages the issue of pluralism and choice (and particularly choices other than those that the wise legislator might make) by stressing that certain things are preconditions of choice. Pontifex assumes that this is true but wants more debate over what these things are. Pontifex thinks that if the preconditions are seen as large enough, this move may, in effect, create a capacity question geared to well being, before any choice can be exercised at all.[44] This has, Pontifex notes, happened in various contexts not all that long ago. Thus: if a woman's preference is to be given "little weight" when it is expressed in, for example, a public opinion poll (desire-based poll) on literacy, are we to say that suffrage itself must wait on conditions leading to healthy preferences?[45] That women's votes must be withheld or count less? And what, particularly, of the choice to join or remain in a religious group? And if women in "almost all" parts of the world have no conception of possibilities and do not choose their lives (or even significant parts of their lives),[46] how do we explain either exit or change?[47]

It seems that both Rex and Pontifex think that the right of exit is the significant right. The question then becomes the role of the state in preserving the possibility of exit. Education is clearly a critical component here, and Rex and Pontifex agree that children must be exposed to ideas that present them with options as to their own futures. They must particularly know that the outside world exists and will receive them. The American approach to the monitoring of private and home education is at least in part consistent with this goal.[48] It is an aspect of state policy relating to the importance of education.

Of course, there is a problem of how much the state should do, as Rex often concedes. If the state does too much in the area of education, we may see it as cultural genocide.[49] If it does too little, we may say that it is not adequately protecting its own future citizens.

Rex and Pontifex agree that the future of children is the central issue here, but perhaps they do not share a common description of the facts. Pontifex, for example, thinks that some groups enforce isolation from the social world in a large way. But the total isolation from and ignorance of the modern world Rex sometimes suggested as a consequence of reduced schooling may exist (if at all) in geographically remote parts of the United States, Canada, or the old U.S.S.R. As the Amish are in our world, we are in theirs. "Ignorance" of the modern world is perhaps not the best description of the problem. (Anectodal material indicates that the Amish children in America try to watch drive-in movies. Two young Amish men were recently prosecuted for dealing cocaine.)[50] Total isolation does not seem to be the issue. Rather we are dealing with the rejection by at least some of the group's parents (and even some of its children) of a system many of whose values are known.

Clearly the traditions of many groups are more internally diverse than any single representative of a group is likely to admit. But the idea that the group as a living tradition must sort these differences out by itself, within, of course, the framework of the state law, is a point given more weight by Pontifex than by Rex. Rex thinks more in terms of state sanctions and incentives to change.

In the end, the reflections, ruminations, and debates between such figures as Rex and Pontifex are essentially without end. The differences over ideas may never be resolved, and the reasoning together in political conversation may not reach common conclusions. But the real world goes on, and the political forms of the real world present provisional decisions at least about some of the questions in the perennial debate. The last two parts of the chapter reopen some of these intellectual issues through a focus on two structural questions, first, church and state, and second, the question of official law as a bridge to the future.

Church and State

In systems such as that in Iran or Pakistan, two aspects of a regime are brought together that could be separated and, in the contemporary Western world, following the disestablishment of the churches, typically are to some degree separated. Where these religiously based regimes are committed to tolerance—not, of course, in every case—they are seen to involve "nonliberal toleration," since individual autonomy is not the fundamental value underlying the regime's toleration.

Whether tolerant or not, religiously based regimes tend to use religious law to govern at least those individuals who want to be under religious personal law. Sometimes this approach is applauded. More positive descriptions of structured personal law are available than the ones that understand the issue solely in terms of the oppression of women.[51] Marc Galanter, commenting on his own interest in the Indian caste system, surfaces the origins of his interest in a way that makes plain the possible strengths of such a system: he notes that he saw underneath "the rigidity and domination of the caste system a possibility of melioration in which the system could be turned on its side, so to speak, dehierarchized, drained of coerciveness, infused with voluntarism." India seemed to him to contain "the possibility of a benign compartmentalization which would permit to flourish a variety of less than universal fellowships. This vision of a non-hierarchic pluralistic India also represented a fantasy solution to the Jewish problem of how to maintain continuity and integrity without isolation, how to attain participation and acceptance without assimilation."[52]

Of course this assumes the fact and also the desirability of what Galanter called "less than universal fellowships."

In the United States we do not have religious law as an aspect of the legal system in the way that countries do that use religious personal law as state law.[53] That is, we do not have a system in which people declare themselves—or are declared—members of a religious tradition and then operate under that system's religious law. But we know first that the religions themselves may see the affiliation as resting in birth rather than choice and second that they may indeed reject the idea of exit. The religion may impose law and sanctions on those who insist that they are not members. The liberal state cannot accept the second position and has a somewhat complex relation to the first. It is here that the differences between the situation in the United States (and to a greater or lesser extent other Western democracies) and states whose church/state system is built neither on disestablishment nor on separationist ideas can be brought into focus.

The underlying issue is the same: What is the relation of the state to religious groups that maintain values other than or subversive of liberal values, here "equality" as to gender? But the structural aspect of the issue is controlled now by whether the religious legal system has an official role as part of state law. In some systems it does, so that the religious identification of an individual is a critical first question in dealing with his or her legal status. In other countries, based on disestablishment or separationist propositions, the state does not directly enforce religious law. The state may still, however, enforce religiously based norms, particularly relating to family law and private morals, and at this point we will become very interested in questions of the political participation of religious groups.

Illustrations of these issues often relate to non-Western countries, with a subtext that in the United States these matters are less important or less interesting. But the situation in the United States is not as remote from those concerns as we might like to think. A long view of this question might note, for example, that the American law of annulment and divorce and the law of monogamous marriage itself, which are often assumed to be unproblematic, are, in their origins, pieces of religious law considered as a part of the state's law in a Christian nation.[54]

It is true that major religious groups in the United States do not emphasize a structural inequality between men and women. This is particularly true of those within the Christian tradition that have been called postmillennial and are in some respects very close to the Western secular tradition. It is also true of Reform Judaism, which similarly has its base in postemancipation political values. Other groups, however—whether one wants to call them "influential" or not, they are well known[55]—talk fairly consistently in terms of a difference in roles that can easily be translated into a disparagement of rights. Orthodox Judaism certainly has a clear conception of traditional roles for women and a very clear view of the different rights of men and women in relation to divorce. Traditional Roman Catholicism has also mandated a particular role for women. If groups like the Amish socialize both men and women to reject the modern culture fairly completely, it is also true that a certain degree of rejection marks many traditional societies in the United States, including the more traditional wings of conventional religious groups.[56] But one can overstate the consequence of this rejection for greater issues. It is unclear to me that a system like that of the Amish prejudices women more than men. The Supreme Court in dealing with this issue in *Wisconsin v. Yoder* responded to the question with a variety of background assumptions and a fairly selective approval of the "facts" of Amish life.[57] We may make such assumptions also, as when we think that women may be less likely to exit successfully than men. But women's skills as cooks, child rearers, and even midwives would presumably be marketable.[58] Male carpenters without training in hi-tech carpentry might be at a greater disadvantage. The assumption that nothing marketable can be learned in the home is the opposite of those approaches that suggest that administrative skills developed by mothers in coordinating carpools in a suburban nuclear family might be immediately and profitably transferred to larger economic units. Neither seems quite adequate.

The Amish aside, illustrations of traditional culture in Western cultures (including the United States) can be found in the patterns of new immigrant groups. New immigrants bring with them traditional ideas of paternal authority, including, for example, marriage by capture. They sometimes ask for systems of enforceable personal law. The domestic debates over what is called, in law, the "cultural defense," as well as aspects of litigation under the Free Exercise Clause, implicate practices not very different from the ones with which feminist human rights advocates are concerned.

We might say, regarding the immigrant examples, that they are problems that are essentially transitional, since the communities are on the way to assimilation. But this interpretation may not in fact carry us the whole way. The Amish were once immigrants, as were the communities of the ultra-Orthodox Jews who fled Europe in the middle of the twentieth century. Neither group has assimilated to the degree that might have been expected. And the revival of "muscular Christianity" suggests again that the triumph of liberal thought is not inevitable, even in America.[59]

The question becomes for us very specific: What will this liberal regime in the United States—which is already committed to a rights discourse and to an idea of the free exercise of religion not limited to devotional activity—do with the problem of traditional[60] societies and women?

In the United States, on the basis of individualistic assumptions about rights, we might at this point ask whether people can alienate basic human rights. We say that in a liberal society basic human rights, whatever they turn out to be, are inalienable. Does that mean that they cannot be taken away from us? That we can or cannot decide to abandon them at least for a time? When Zechariah Chafee noted that people who followed the prophet John Alexander Dowie presumably knew what they were getting into, he seems to have thought that it might be possible to relinquish some part of a basic right as an exercise of religion.[61] Perhaps we will say that not all rights can be given up this way. Perhaps we will stress that some religions involve status and not contract, or that the contract argument is most difficult for those born into highly separatist communities. The test of this in the philosophical discussion is the contract of slavery. Could one decide to make oneself irrevocably a slave? Lesser examples might be decisions to adhere to polygamy, to reject education, or to refuse participation in public life by voting.

Sometimes discussions of women's rights and the rights of religion cover cases in which, if women vote, their vote is suspect because of general subordination, as well as cases in which women are assumed to vote freely. The discussion includes cases in which the religious group has co-opted the state (Islamic states particularly)[62] as well as instances in which religions want to make space for their own traditions within secular democratic states. In terms of ideas of exit, this last difference would seem to be important. In the first case, a women has to leave the jurisdiction; in the second, she has only to withdraw from the religious group, conceivably founding a new reformed and revised religious group.[63] If exit is not possible, we have a human rights issue independent of the equality right.

Ultimately, these are the problems raised in the United States by education cases by the groups—or should we say here groups of *parents*?[64]—which do not want their children to read certain texts or who want home schooling.

We assume that the rights bearer is the individual, and we stress that individuals here have rights to choose their own version of life. But, and again it is Pontifex who has often stressed this point, these groups tend to believe that the object of education is not in fact to be able to choose for oneself. Rather the object of education and of good teaching is to teach children to follow The Way. A secular humanist education is understood—with reason—as an attack on that goal.[65]

A universal law for many purposes is an entirely plausible state structure. But it seems that an overriding set of state values ordinarily goes with it. Some aspect of life is a sufficiently great community value that, like the criminal law or monogamy (in some countries), it must be imposed on everyone, above any system of personal laws. As to these issues of overriding importance, individuals say that it is not sufficient to maintain a strict moral standard oneself in a society that is understood as morally lax. One must enforce the rule on everyone. Adoption—controversial in some places—may not seem to us to raise the issue, but the relevance of the point to issues of abortion or contraception is clear.

What we must discuss here essentially is what those values are.

Treating these matters as questions of logic is not the obvious answer here. It is possible to say, looking at the systems of establishment with toleration that are found in, for example, England and Canada, that these should be opposed, because necessarily those who hold minority views will feel unequal.[66] This is, in effect, advocacy of the system of church-state separation found in the United States but almost nowhere else in the world. To that extent alone, one might say that advocacy of this system as a universal goal in the current political climate has little utility. Moreover, certain aspects of our own experiment are still being explored. Applications of the idea of free exercise and establishment are not always obvious. A conventional example of uncertainty of the application of the ideas of the First Amendment is the historical dispute between Jefferson and Madison over the issue of the clergy holding public office.[67]

We are still working out the implications of the possibility that secularism may itself constitute a religion that makes others feel unequal. In a way, it took the decision of conservative Christianity to reenter the political arena after decades of a separatist orientation to open certain questions about, for example, the restriction of public facilities to secular groups—does this discriminate against religious groups?—that had once seemed more obvious. It now seems that "establishment" questions can also be seen as "open access" questions. Moreover, the issue of what the American approach substantively adds to other approaches is still being considered.

The suggestion that we must distinguish, as an either/or question, between truly religious behavior and behavior influenced by the desire for, say, political power seems difficult.[68] This is the case partly because there are things we do not know ("the devil himself does not know the thought of man,")[69] and partly because what we do know is highly complex. Much political work and economic accumulation can be undertaken as part of work which, in the minds of the religiously affiliated, is understood as work "for the greater glory of God."[70] Without eliminating entirely the idea of purely political power masquerading as religion,[71] it seems also true that religions may well have religiously based reasons for wanting strong institutions and even formal establishments. The comments of Justice Brennan in a church property dispute also have some relevance here: "It is the essence of religious faith that ecclesiastical decisions be reached and are to be accepted as matters of faith whether or not rational or measurable by objective criteria. Constitutional concepts of due process, involving secular notions of fundamental fairness or impermissible objectives, are therefore hardly relevant to such matters of ecclesiastical cognizance."[72]

Any decision relating to the imposition of a state norm on religious groups would have to consider fairly difficult and sometimes competing policies.

Donna Sullivan's discussion lists a number of factors to be considered, stressing "the relationship between the specific equality right at issue and the overarching goal of gender equality," "the importance of the religious law or practice to the right of religious freedom upon which it is premised,"[73] "the degree to which each practice infringes the other or the underlying rights and interests," "whether other human rights are implicated," "the effect of multiple restrictions of religious practice on the religion concerned," and finally, "the proportionality of the restriction."[74] Perhaps, then, we should think of these problems not in terms of a perfect match between some absolute standard and a political reality, but rather in terms of an accommodation in which all sides withhold certain demands in the interest of an accommodation, of not pushing things to their limits. John Noonan, considering these questions recently in the American context, offered some ideas about what the balance might look like, stressing proportion and self-consciousness on all sides.[75]

Bridges

The idea that law is a bridge connecting, as Robert Cover said, our concepts of reality with our imagined alternative realities is common in academic conversations about law.[76] The idea operates with particular force in the area of human rights, where our concepts of the imagined alternative are so heavily influenced by the importance of the present problems. Thus, we entirely sympathize with the urgency in the response of Raphael Lemkin, when he was asked how making a crime of mass murder would stop a Hitler or Stalin. His answer was: "Only man has law. Law must be built, do you understand me? You must build the law!"[77]

At the same time, we can see the dangers in a certain kind of utopian bridge building, represented by the second epigraph to this essay, the comment of John Roebling in proposing the Brooklyn Bridge in 1867. Roebling noted that "[a]s a great work of art, and as a successful specimen of advanced bridge engineering, this structure will forever testify to the energy, enterprise and wealth of that community which shall secure its erection."[78]

Robert Cover's image, though physical, is not limited in the sense that Roebling's plan was. The Brooklyn Bridge will presumably not last forever. But the idea of law as a bridge could last. We may then want to think about it some.

One way to refine the metaphor would be to stress that there are different kinds of bridges. Using the example of the city of Venice, we may, then, note the existence of a Bridge of Sighs[79] and a Bridge of Fists.[80] On the Bridge of Sighs, we may deplore practices without insisting on international intervention. On the Bridge of Fists, we consider some more active possibilities.

An agenda for liberals seems to me to require recognition of a point that is rooted in practical politics. That point is that progress is not only slow, it is also reversible. The system of religious law as personal or family law, peculiarly hard on women, can represent, in the modern world, a regression from a quite different position. The case of Iran is well known.[81] A *New York Times* article on the situation in Turkey suggests that some at least see certain possibilities there by way of regression as the Islamic aspects of the regime are discussed by those who do not want another Iran and who note that the westernizing reforms of Kemal Ataturk are relatively recent. It is significant, in terms of the issues of choice and capacity, that the woman's question in Turkey, according to the *New York Times*, is argued in rights terms, the rights of women to, for example, adopt conservative religious dress.[82]

The politics of these issues is as complex as the competing values that are at stake. A *New York Times* discussion of the issue of female genital mutilation illustrates some of the complexities. In Sierra Leone, where the practice is "nearly universal," the "tiny minority of people willing to take a stand against the practice are overwhelmed by militant, if defensive, advocates."[83] Between them stand "millions of women who are, for the most part, willing and sometimes fervent adherents."[84] Sometimes political alignments on these issues seem anomalous. It is reported that Iranian leftists supported the Ayatollah against the Shah to the point of women students adopting traditional female dress.[85]

The religious groups here see themselves in terms of a reform, or formation, and connect themselves with many such efforts over time.[86] At the very least, this would suggest that we are not dealing only with a world in which "modernization" is assumed. We may be facing the rejection of modernization, Westernization, and all associated values, including but not limited to women's equality.

Finally, it is clear, that nonreligious traditions can engage in behavior equally suppressive of women's autonomy. One recalls that in 1936, in Iran, it was the women who wore the veil who suffered harsh penalties.[87] If this is so—if it is a question of power corrupting—isn't it reasonable to think of solutions in terms of balancing of powers, separation of powers, or strengthening of intermediate groups, rather than in terms of a single imposed solution?

In 1958 Eleanor Roosevelt addressed the question of human rights. She asked the question, "Where, after all, do universal human rights begin?" and she answered this way:

> In small places, close to home—so close and so small that they cannot be seen on any map of the world. Yet they *are* the world of the individual person: The neighborhood he lives in; the school or college he attends; the factory, farm or office where he works. Such are the places where every man, woman and child seeks equal justice, equal opportunity, equal dignity without discrimination. Unless these rights have meaning there, they have little meaning anywhere.[88]

Essentially, we have added "home" itself to Eleanor Roosevelt's list. If we are moving cautiously in relation to this issue, that seems only right.

Notes

1. This chapter began as a comment on a paper by Professor Martha Nussbaum on Women and International Human Rights, given at the conference on "Law and Religion: Obligations of Democratic Citizenship and Demands of Faith," held at Brown University in April 1997. The essay was presented in another form at the University of Victoria in January 1998 under the auspices of the Centre for Studies in Religion and Society.

I would like to thank Mark Janis, Carolyn Jones, Richard Kay, and Aviam Soifer for assistance of various kinds.

2. For a general discussion of current approaches, see Harold Koh, "Why Do Nations Obey International Law," 106 *Yale Law Journal* 2599 (1997).

3. This discussion focuses on questions that exist also in domestic systems and are widely debated in Western democracies.

4. "Rex," like "Pontifex," should be taken as either gender-neutral or ironic.

5. Georg Simmel, *Essays on Religion*, ed. and trans. Horst Jurgen Helle (in collaboration with Ludwig Nieder) (New Haven, Conn.: Yale University Press, 1997), indicates that one of the definitions of law is as a mode as coordination (121).

6. The *Oxford English Dictionary* indicates that "bridge builder" is the reputed etymology of "Pontifex."

7. Carol Weisbrod, "Emblems of Federalism," 25 *Michigan Journal of Law Reform* 795 (1992) 836.

8. Cicero, *De Legibus*, trans. Clinton Walker Keyes (Cambridge: Harvard University Press, 1943), 1.18.

9. For a recent symposium using a bridge metaphor, see "Colloquium: Bridging Society, Culture and Law: The Issue of Female Circumcision," 47 *Case Western Reserve Law Review* (1997).

10. Harold Isaacs, *Idols of the Tribe* (Cambridge: Harvard University Press 1975, 1989), 216.

11. Michael Walzer, *On Toleration* (New Haven, Conn.: Yale University Press, 1997), xi. See also Arcot Krishnaswami, *Study of Discrimination in the Matter of Religious Rights and Practices*, UN Doc. E/CN.4/Sub.2/200/Rev.1 United Nations Publication Catalogue No. 60. XIV.2 (1960). On issues of effectiveness in another context see Mark Janis, "Russia and the 'Legality' of Strasbourg Law," 1 *European Journal of International Law* (1997) 93–99; note also the attempts to differentiate major and minor human rights violations.

12. Julius Goebel, *Cases and Materials on the Development of Legal Institutions* (Brattleboro: Vermont Printing Company, 1946), 442.

13. David M. Smolin, "Will International Human Rights Be Used as a Tool of Cultural Genocide? The Interaction of Human Rights Norms, Religion, Culture and Gender," 12 *Journal of Law and Religion* 143 (1995–96). Of course, religion is itself a contributor to the norms of international law. See Mark Janis, ed., *The Influence of Religion on the Development of International Law* (Dordrecht, Netherlands: Nijhoff, 1991).

14. Natan Lerner, "Religious Human Rights under the United Nations," in *Religious Human Rights in Global Perspective: Legal Perspective*, ed. Johan van

der Vyver and John Witte (The Hague: Martinus Nijhoff, 1996), 106. See, recently: Courtney Howland, "The Challenge of Religion Fundamentalism to the Liberty and Equality Rights of Women," 35 *Columbia Journal of Transnational Law* (1997); B. A. Venkatraman, "Islamic States and the UN Convention on the Elimination of All Forms of Discrimination against Women," 44 *American University Law Review* (1995).

15. The current emphasis on the romantic and sexual relationships of the couple makes discussion of the power of the family trivial, focused on psychological and affective relationships. The traditional family was much more powerful than that. A reintroduction of the idea of the power of the family may emerge from looking at certain feminist issues (e.g. violence and the family) or certain psychological issues. On rights in trust, dealing with the problem of the role of the family in creating autonomous adults see Joel Feinberg, "The Child's Right to an Open Future," in *Whose Child? Children's Rights, Parental Authority and State Power*, ed. Willam Aiken and Hugh LaFollette (Totowa, N.J.: Rowman and Littlefield, 1980).

16. Much writing in American constitutional law is devoted to the problems raised by attempts to define religion while also respecting the autonomy (including the capacity for development) of religions. See John C. Murray: "The American Constitution does not presume to define the Church or in any way to supervise her exercise of authority in pursuit of her own distinct ends. The Church is entirely free to define herself and to exercise to the full her spiritual jurisdiction. It is legally recognized that there is an area which lies outside the competence of government. This area coincides with the area of the divine mission of the Church, and within this area the Church is fully independent, immune from interference by political authority." John Courtney Murray, *We Hold These Truths: Catholic Reflections on the American Proposition* (New York: Image Books, 1964).

17. Some of the present discussion echoes a debate of an earlier generation on the question of whether systematic oppression had so distorted the judgment of women that they had to be educated before participating in the political process. See Nussbaum on Christine Sommers's position concerning the antidemocratic implications of some feminist approaches. S. Macedo, ed., *Reassessing the Sixties: Debating the Political and Cultural Legacy* (New York: Norton, 1996), 92ff; see also Tracy Higgins, "Anti-Essentialism, Relativism and Human Rights," 19 *Harvard Women's Law Journal* 89 (1996).

18. Separation of church and state is not, as Donna Sullivan notes, an international human rights norm. Sullivan, "Gender Equality and Religious Freedom," 24 *International Law and Politics* 795, 805 (1992).

19. For a recent treatment of the diversity within groups issue, see Michael Perry, "Are Human Rights Universal?" *Human Rights Quarterly* 19 (1997).

20. See, generally, John Griffiths, "What Is Legal Pluralism," 24 *Journal of Legal Pluralism*. (1986)

21. Marc Galanter, *Law and Society in Modern India* (Delhi: Oxford University Press, 1987), 255.

22. Robert Cover, "The Supreme Court, 1982 Term-Forward: Nomos and Narrative," 97 *Harvard Law Review* 4 (1983).

23. Murray, *We Hold These Truths*, 9.

24. See Carol Weisbrod, "Family, Church and State," 26 *Journal of Family Law* (1987–88) 741, for a discussion of strategies.

25. *Reynolds v United States*, 98 US 145 (1879). The feminist issues seem somewhat different today.

26. Violence in the family is, as between spouses, conceptualized as abuse.

27. This distinction is conventional in the field of commercial law. Some "rules" are only "default" rules, coming into play in the absence of contrary agreements.

28. Manchester, cited in Kukathas, "Cultural Rights Again—A Rejoinder to Kymlicka," 20 *Political Theory* no. 1 (1992), at 680.

29. Galanter, *Law and Society in Modern India*, 4.

30. Peter Berger, quoted in Meron, cited in Smolin, "International Human Rights," 169. Also Mary Ann Glendon on the Beijing conference noting that elites at the women's conference at Beijing were advocating ideas which had not survived, an ordinary political process. Glendon, "What Happened at Beijing," 59 *First Things* (January 1996): 35.

31. Richard Bilder, "Rethinking International Human Rights: Some Basic Questions," *Wisconsin Law Review* 171, 173–74 (1969).

32. Ibid.

33. Following the Austinian positivist approach.

34. Generally, Chester Barnard, *The Functions of the Executive* (Cambridge: Harvard University Press, 1938; reprint, 1968).

35. As Isaiah Berlin has noted, a major lesson of the twentieth century has been our awareness of the fact that given sufficient will and force, tyrants can achieve consequences which would have been previously considered unimaginable. Berlin, *The Sense of Reality: Studies in Ideas and Their History* (New York: Farrar, Straus & Giroux, 1996), 9–11.

36. Pontifex sometimes says this about the state. Zachariah Chafee, "Associations Not for Profit," 43 *Harvard Law Review* 993, 1029 (1930), describing the state as one more kind of association. One issue here is what we take as the unit. See Erwin Strauss, *How to Start Your Own Country*, 2d ed. (Port Townsend, Wash.: Loopanics Unlimited, 1984).

37. See, in general, Aviam Soifer, *Law and the Company We Keep* (Cambridge: Harvard University Press, 1994).

38. The question of what "women's law" might look like is a subject of its own, too large to enter here. See Georg Simmel on *Women, Law and Sexuality*, trans. Guy Oakes (New Haven, Conn.: Yale University Press).

39. See Martha Nussbaum, "Patriotism and Cosmopolitanism" in *For Love of Country: Debating the Limits of Patriotism*, ed. Joshua Cohen (Boston: Beacon Press, 1996), 2–17.

40. Sometimes the refusal to engage the self perceptions of groups results in tragedy. See James Tabor and Eugene Gallagher, *Why Waco? Culture and the Battle for Religious Freedom in America* (Berkeley: University of California Press, 1995).

41. See Hilary Putnam, "Must We Choose between Patriotism and Universal Reason?" in Cohen, *For Love of Country*.

42. On utopias, see Carol Weisbrod, "Towards a History of Essential Federalism: Another Look at Owen in America," 21 *Connecticut Law Review* 979 (1989).

43. See Michael McConnell "Don't Neglect the Little Platoons," in Cohen, *For Love of Country*, 78–84.

44. See Nussbaum, "Aristotelian Social Democracy," in *Liberalism and the Good*, ed. R. Bruce Douglass, Gerald Mara, and Henry Richardson (New York: Routledge, 1990), defining a "thick but vague" conception of the good, and rejecting the tension seen by many between "well being" and "choice," seeing this tension as largely illusory (238).

45. It is noted that "personal status codes continue to be based on Sharia and are in conflict with modern Western style constitutions of Muslim states." Amira el Azherz Sonbol, introduction to *Women, the Family and Divorce Laws in Islamic History*, ed. Amira Sonbol (Syracuse, N.Y.: Syracuse University Press, 1996).

46. A point made in Nussbaum, "Aristotelian Social Democracy," 238.

47. See, for example, the recent case in Pakistan upholding a woman's marriage in the absence of parental consent. "Pakistan Court ok's marriage, parents oppose," *Los Angeles Times*, March 11, 1997, A6. See Shahla Haeri, "Women and Fundamentalism in Iran and Pakistan," in *Fundamentalism and Society*, ed. Martin Marty and R. Scott Appleby (Chicago: University of Chicago Press, 1993). Also, "The Bartered Bride Opts Out of the Bargain," *New York Times*, May 6, 1997, an account of young woman resisting the traditional society as represented by the tribal group and her own family. Also, Barbara Crossette "Uganda tribe fights genital cutting," *New York Times*, July 16, 1998, A8.

48. On the issue of female socialization, some choose home education to preserve traditional gender roles; others to avoid the gender roles found (imposed) in American public schools.

49. Thus we see an Australian Sorry Day, an apology for the forced assimilation of aboriginal children. *New York Times*, May 27, 1998, A4.

50. See "Amish Pair Plead Guilty to Cocaine Conspiracy," *New York Times*, October 6, 1998, A18.

51. See, for example, Peter DeCruz, "Women, Children, Pluralism and the Law," in Andrew Beinham, ed., *The Journal of International Society of Family Law* (1995) 336, on Malaysia. Israel uses some of this system, with the main structure committed not only to Judaism but to Orthodox Judaism. This has resulted in increasing difficulty not only with secular Jews but with Jews who adhere to Conservative or Reform practice.

See "Israeli Melee as Women Pray with Men at the Western Wall," *New York Times*, August 12, 1997, A7. Note that the issue here is not whether women can pray at the Wall (separately) but whether they can pray with men. Where once this might have been seen as an issue on which those who were indifferent, in effect (since they did not say that mixed praying was religiously compulsory) could yield to those with scruples, both sides now see themselves as committed to principled positions.

52. Galanter, *Law and Society*.

53. We do, however, use religious law on some points. It may, for example,

come in as part of a contract or it may be involved in a church property dispute. See also American discussions of religious matching in adoption.

54. Patrick Devlin, *The Enforcement of Morals* (London: Oxford University Press, 1965). On monogamy, we might accept Devlin's point that monogamy got into the law because it was Christian, but stayed there because it was part of the social structure.

55. The Promise Keepers have become a standard example. The National Organization for Women has denounced them formally.

56. Presumably, exit rates for women present an empirical question that could be answered. See also Alfred Kazin, *A Lifetime Burning in Every Moment, from the Journals of Alfred Kazin* (New York: Harper Collins, 1997), quoting Rabi, the Nobel prize–winning physicist, "If I had stayed in Poland, I would have been a tailor" (336).

57. Jeffrey Shaman, "Constitutional Fact: Perception of Reality by the Supreme Court," 35 *Florida Law Review* (1983).

58. See Gertrude Huntington, "Health Care" in *The Amish and the State*, ed. Donald Kraybill (Baltimore: Johns Hopkins University Press, 1993), 163.

59. Mary Douglas noted that the revival of fundamentalism took Western social scientists by surprise. "The Effects of Modernization in Religious Change," *Daedalus* 1 (1982).

60. Or neotraditional.

61. Chafee, "Associations Not for Profit," at 1018.

62. Related issues arise in countries in which the governing coalition requires the support of the orthodox (e.g., Israel).

63. Which may be either more liberal or more conservative than the original group. Dissident groups within the religion may be intensely loyal to their understanding of the tradition as a whole.

64. See Walzer, *On Toleration*, on the head-scarf issue in France (64). Walzer suggests that when students urge that a government position permitting girls to wear head scarves in French public schools—seen first as a desirable compromise recognizing the "right of an immigrant community to a (modestly) multicultural public sphere"—supports patriarchal values then the original compromise would have to be renegotiated. The issue of parental rights seems to be viewed as a term of the "family values" of the minority religion, rather than as the competing right of other individuals.

65. See the description in Stolzenberg, "He Drew a Circle That Shut Me Out: Assimilation Indoctrination and the Paradox of a Liberal Education," *Harvard Law Review* 581 (1993) 106.

66. To avoid this feeling, which may result from demographics as well as establishment, do we conclude that there should be no minority views?

67. See Leo Pfeffer, *Church, State and Freedom*, 2d ed. (Boston: Beacon Press, 1963). Jefferson was originally opposed (138).

68. As questions of religious fraud generally are difficult. See *United States v Ballard* 322 US 78 (1944).

69. Quoted in Arthur Corbin, *Contracts* (St. Paul: West, 1952), 507 n. 42.

70. The motto of the Society of Jesus.

71. See, for example, Justice Jackson in Kedroff, in *St. Nicholas Cathedral of*

the Russian Orthodox Church in North America, 344 US 94 (1952). Jackson refers to a "foreign and unfriendly state masquerading as a spiritual institution."

72. Brennan, in *Serbian Eastern Orthodox Diocese v Milivojevich*, 426 US 696 (1976).

73. Sometimes, it is suggested that tax exemptions should be withdrawn from certain groups. On the tax exemption issue—and whether "exemption" is really the right idea—see Boris Bittker and George Rahdert, "The Exemption of Non-Profit Organizations from Federal Income Taxation," 85 *Yale Law Journal* 301, 304 (1976), urging that nonprofit organizations "are not suitable targets for an income tax."

74. Donna J. Sullivan, "Gender Equality and Religious Freedom: Toward a Framework for Conflict Resolution," 24 *International Law and Politics* 795, 821 ff (1992).

75. John Noonan, "The Tensions and the Ideals," in Witte and van der Vyver, *Religious Human Rights in Global Perspective*. Noonan suggested, "[T]here is no single universal formula for reconciling religious rights and state activity. There are only ways of avoiding bloodshed, blunting the sharpness of the conflict, alleviating the tensions" (600).

76. Robert Cover, "Nomos and Narrative," citing George Steiner, *After Babel*, on alternity.

77. Raphael Lemkin, in Rosenthal, *New York Times*, October 8, 1988, at 31. He particularly wanted to build the genocide convention. See generally Raphael Lemkin, *Axis Rule in Occupied Europe* (Washington: Carnegie Endowment for International Peace, 1944).

78. Roebling, quoted in David McCullough, *The Great Bridge* (New York: Simon and Schuster, l972), 27.

79. Prisoners once crossed the Bridge of Sighs to prison and then execution.

80. A bridge on which Venetian families once fought each other.

81. Described from the point of view of women's interests, Mahnaz Afkhami, "Iran: A Future in the Past," in *Sisterhood Is Global: The International Women's Movement Anthology*, ed. Robin Morgan (New York: Doubleday, 1984), 330–8. See also [Afghanistan] Bob Herbert, "A War on Women," *New York Times*, October 4, 1998, 15.

82. Stephen Kinzer, "A Woman, Her Scarf, and a Storm over Secularism," *New York Times*, March 17, 1998, A4. On this issue in the American setting, see Aminah D. McCloud, "American Muslim Women and U.S. Society," 12 *Journal of Law and Religion* 51 (1995–96).

83. Howard French, "The Ritual: Disfiguring, Hurtful, Wildly Festive," *New York Times*, January 31 1997, A4.

84. Ibid. And what are we to make of the scene in *Absolutely Fabulous* in which Patty and Edina attack a screaming Saffron in her bed, the older women performing a swift surgical removal of the hair above Saffron's upper lip? (Cf. New Thai Tourist Sight: Burmese Giraffe Woman," *New York Times*, October 19, 1996, 4). Do these millions of women become more comprehensible when we note that many Western cultures allow without much controversy ritual circumcision of infant males? Are we to say that that procedure is entirely different or should we denounce it as child abuse?

85. Morgan, *Sisterhood Is Global*, 334.

86. See William H. McNeill's essay in Marty and Appleby, *Fundmentalism and Society*. For science fiction versions, see Margaret Atwood, *The Handmaid's Tale* (New York: Fawcett, 1991), a science fiction Christian version. See also Sheri Tepper, *Gibbon's Decline and Fall* (New York: Bantam Books, 1997).

87. Haeri, "Women and Fundamentalism," 191.

88. Remarks at a ceremony at the United Nations, New York, March 27, 1958, cited in Phillips, *You in Human Rights* 2 (1967), quoted in Richard Bilder, "Rethinking International Human Rights," *Wisconsin Law Review* 171, 178 (1969).

CONTRIBUTORS

KENT GREENAWALT is University Professor at Columbia University. He is the author of *Religious Convictions and Political Choice; Private Consciences and Public Reasons;* and *Fighting Words.*

AMY GUTMANN is Laurance S. Rockefeller University Professor of Politics and the University Center for Human Values at Princeton University. She is the editor, most recently, of *Freedom of Association* and coauthor with Dennis Thompson of *Democracy and Disagreement.*

HARRY N. HIRSCH is Professor of Political Science at the University of California, San Diego. He is the author of, among other works, *A Theory of Liberty: The Constitution and Minorities.*

GARY JEFFREY JACOBSOHN, Third Century Professor of Jurisprudence and Politics, Williams College, is author of many books, most recently *Apple of Gold: Constitutionalism in Israel and the United States,* and coeditor of *Diversity and Citizenship: Rediscovering American Nationhood.* His current project in *Ashoka's Wheel: Indian Secularism in Comparative Constitutional Perspective.*

MICHAEL W. McCONNELL is President Professor at the University of Utah College of Law. He specializes in constitutional law and has written widely on freedom of religion, segregation, unenumerated rights, and constitutional theory. He served as law clerk to Chief Judge J. Skelly Wright on the United States Court of Appeals of the D.C. Circuit and for Associate Justice William J. Brennan, Jr., on the United States Supreme Court, and, among other offices, as assistant to the Solicitor General of the United States. He has argued ten cases in the Supreme Court.

MARTHA C. NUSSBAUM is Ernst Freund Distinguished Service Professor of Law and Ethics at the University of Chicago, with appointments in the Philosophy Department, the Law School, the Divinity School, and the College. She is an associate member of the Classics Department and an affiliate of the Committee on Southern Asian Studies. Her most recent book is *Sex and Social Justice.*

NANCY L. ROSENBLUM is Henry Merritt Wriston Professor and Professor of Political Science at Brown University. She is the editor of *Liberalism and the Moral Life* and author most recently of *Membership and Morals: The Personal Uses of Pluralism in America.*

AVIAM SOIFER is former Dean and currently Professor of Law at Boston College Law School. He specializes in constitutional law and American legal history, and his book, *Law and the Company We Keep*, won the Alpha Sigma Nu National Jesuit Book Award in professional studies.

YAEL TAMIR is Professor of Philosophy at Tel-Aviv University and Deputy Director of the School of Education. She is the author of *Liberal Nationalism* and editor of *Democratic Education in a Multicultural State*. Professor Tamir is a founding member of Peace-Now and chairperson of the Association of Civil Rights in Israel.

RONALD F. THIEMANN is John Lord O'Brian Professor of Divinity at Harvard University. The Founding Director of Harvard's Center for the Study of Values in Public Life, he codirects, along with Mary Jo Bane, the Intellectual Foundations Project on Faith-Based Organizations for Harvard's Kennedy School of Government. Among his publications are *Religion in Public Life: A Dilemma for Democracy* and *Constructing a Public Thology: The Church in a Pluralistic Culture*.

GRAHAM WALKER is Associate Professor of Politics at The Catholic University of America and Visiting Scholar in Religion and Philosophy at the American Enterprise Institute. He is the author of two books: *Moral Foundations of Constitutional Thought* and *The Ethics of F. A. Hayek*. His scholarly interests include classical philosophy, comparative constitutionalism, and theology.

CAROL WEISBROD is Ellen Ash Peters Professor of Law at the University of Connecticut. She is the author of *The Boundaries of Utopia* and coauthor of a casebook on Family Law. She has published law journal articles on political theory, feminist theory, church and state, and legal history. A book of essays on law, narrative, and the family, *Butterfly, the Bride*, is forthcoming from the University of Michigan Press.

ALAN WOLFE is University Professor and Professor of Sociology and Political Science at Boston University and the author of *One Nation, After All*, from which his chapter in this volume is excerpted. He is writing a book about moral freedom.

INDEX

absolutism, religious, 83–84

accommodations for religion, 8–9; increasing claims for, 13–15; integralism, 15–21; voluntarism and separatism, 9–11. *See also* autonomy, religious; Free Exercise Clause; protection of church and state; separation between church and state

Adams, Arlin, 210–11, 218, 223

Africa v. Commonwealth, 211

Agostini v. Felton, 135–37, 141, 265n8

Alexander, James, 46

Allen, James, 170

Almond, Herbert, 61

Amaleks, 324, 333

Ambedkar, B. R., 337, 351, 368

American Civil Liberties Union, 51, 53, 56

American religious belief: acceptance of diversity, 49–51, 56–57; certainty and beliefs of others, 39–44; deliberative democracy and diversity, 51–53; depth of, 36–39; homosexuality, 57–64; individualism, 64–68; issues and background, 32–36; modest virtues, 41–42, 45, 48, 68–69; politicized religion, 45–49; strong believers as victimized minority, 53–56

Amir, Igal, 330

Amish, the: community viability, 177–78; community vs. individual considerations, 287–89; difficulty of case, 377–78; narrow nature of exception in *Yoder*, 146–48, 150–51; separationist quality of, 31n11, 412; sex equality, 414; sincerity of claims, 206

Amos, Corporation of Presiding Bishop of the Church of Jesus Christ of Latter–Day Saints v., 165–66, 171–80, 183, 185, 189–90

Ansari, Z. R., 371

Apa, 372

Aristotle, 394n38

Ashoka, 351–52

Ataturk, Kemal, 419

Audi, Robert, 160n3

Austin, Granville, 317n39

Australia, High Court of, tax exemption for Church of Scientology, 238n60

autonomy, religious, 165–67; *Amos* and exemption to Title VII, 171–74; costs of accommodation, 183–87; democracy and civic education, 187–90; hiring discrimination and Title VII, 167–71; religious accommodation, 174–79, 289–90; structural pluralist position on, 179–83; Supreme Court on, 260–61. *See also* accommodations for religion; protection of church and state

Backus, Isaac, 267n25, 272n44

Bagni, Bruce, 191n13

Bakker, Jim, 46, 48

Ballard, Guy, 200–201

Ballard, United States v., 200–204

Bano, Shah, 338, 341, 346, 370–72, 382–83

Barnette v. Board of Education, 146–47

Bates, Patricia, 43

Becker, Mary, 389n16–17, 390–91n26, 391n27, 398–99n68

Benjamin, Rachel, 52

Berg, Thomas, 134

Berger, Peter, 33, 408

Berlin, Isaiah, 422n35

Bernstein, Richard, 75

Bhargava, Pandit Mukul Behrilal, 337

Bhatt, Ela, 344

Bilder, Richard, 408

Black, Hugo, 80, 208–9

Blackmun, Harry, 282–83, 287

Bob Jones University v. United States, 356, 374, 394n42

Boerne, City of v. Flores: ahistoricism of Supreme Court, 245, 254–60; construction of social facts, 284–86; federalism and religious exemption, 207; overturning of Religious Freedom Restoration Act, 6, 81, 153, 398n62

Bonaparte, Napoléon, 107

Bowen v. Roy, 232

Bradford, William, 251

Bradley, Joseph, 276n66